TEMPLAR FAMILIES

Founded in *c.* 1120, in the aftermath of the First Crusade in Jerusalem, the Order of the Temple was a Christian brotherhood dedicated to the military protection of pilgrims and the Holy Land, attracting followers and supporters throughout Christian Europe. This detailed study explores the close relationship between the Order of the Temple and the landowning families it relied upon for support. Focusing on the regions of Burgundy, Champagne and Languedoc, Jochen Schenk investigates the religious expectations that guided noble and knightly families to found and support Templar communities in the European provinces, and examines the social dynamics and mechanisms that tied these families to each other. The book illustrates the close connection between the presence of Cistercians and the incidence of crusading within Templar family networks, and offers new insights into how collective identities and memory were shaped through ritual and tradition among medieval French-speaking social elites.

JOCHEN SCHENK is Research Fellow (Wissenschaftlicher Mitarbeiter) at The German Historical Institute, London, and a Senior Member of Wolfson College, Cambridge.

Cambridge Studies in Medieval Life and Thought
Fourth Series

The series *Cambridge Studies in Medieval Life and Thought* was inaugurated by G.G. Coulton in 1921; Professor Rosamond McKitterick now acts as General Editor of the Fourth Series, with Professor Christine Carpenter and Dr Jonathan Shepard as Advisory Editors. The series brings together outstanding work by medieval scholars over a wide range of human endeavour extending from political economy to the history of ideas.

A list of titles in the series can be found at:
www.cambridge.org/medievallifeandthought

TEMPLAR FAMILIES

Landowning families and the Order of the Temple in France, c. 1120–1307

JOCHEN SCHENK

CAMBRIDGE
UNIVERSITY PRESS

University Printing House, Cambridge CB2 8BS, United Kingdom

Cambridge University Press is part of the University of Cambridge.

It furthers the University's mission by disseminating knowledge in the pursuit of education, learning and research at the highest international levels of excellence.

www.cambridge.org
Information on this title: www.cambridge.org/9781107530485

First published 2012
First paperback edition 2015

A catalogue record for this publication is available from the British Library

Library of Congress Cataloguing in Publication data
Schenk, Jochen, 1974–
Templar families : landowning families and the Order of the Temple in France, c.1120–1307 / Jochen Schenk.
p. cm. – (Cambridge studies in medieval life and thought ; 4th ser., 79)
Includes bibliographical references.
ISBN 978-1-107-00447-4
1. Templars – France – History. 2. Upper class families – France – History.
3. France – History – 14th century. I. Title.
CR4755.F7S34 2011
944'.025–dc22
2011015546

ISBN 978-1-107-00447-4 Hardback
ISBN 978-1-107-53048-5 Paperback

CONTENTS

MAPS

ACKNOWLEDGEMENTS

Like the Templars it describes, this book has benefited from the support of various bodies, agencies and overlapping kinship and friendship networks.

I am deeply indebted to the Arts and Humanities Research Council, the Master and Fellows of Emmanuel College, the Cambridge European Trust, and the German Institute in Paris for endowing me with generous scholarships and bursaries during (and in the case of the German Historical Institute in Paris also after) my time as a PhD student in Cambridge. Likewise to the President and Fellows of the Pontifical Institute of Mediaeval Studies in Toronto for electing me to an Andrew W. Mellon Research Fellowship in 2006; to the President and Fellows of Wolfson College, Cambridge, for accepting me as a Senior Member to their College in 2007; and to Professor Andreas Gestrich and my wonderful colleagues at the German Historical Institute in London for allowing me to join their team in the same year.

Among the many debts of gratitude to individuals which I have incurred over the years whilst researching and writing first the thesis and then the book the first is due to Jonathan Riley-Smith, my Ph.D. supervisor, who throughout the entire time has been an unfailing source of wisdom and support. Without his diligent guidance and unceasing encouragement this book would not have been seen through to completion. I must also express my profound thanks to Malcolm Barber, Martin Brett, Marcus Bull, Jane Rafferty and Jonathan Shepard, who have read different versions of this study and offered fruitful criticism and helpful suggestions. I am grateful to William Purkis for his friendship, help and encouragement over the years, and to those many friends and colleagues who offered guidance and support at important junctures in the making of this book. I thank Matthieu Rabéchault, Nicolas Ruellet and Nicole Bériou for their hospitality in Paris; Damien Carraz and Simonetta Cerrini for sharing their research and doctoral theses with me; Bernard Hamilton for good counsel over the years; Scott Hiley, Paul Sterzel and

Friederike Sack for their efforts to make sense of old French and Provençal charters; Chris Hobcroft for abandoning a feast to chauffeur me to Douzens; and Nicholas Paul, Ian Russell and Calder Walton for many inspiring conversations on topics within and beyond the realm of medieval history.

I wish to express my gratitude to the staff of the Bibliothèque Nationale in Paris, the Archives Nationales de France in Paris, and the Archives Départementales de la Côte-d'Or in Dijon, whose unceasing efforts to track down and provide documents have allowed me to plough through a great number of sources. Moreover, I would like to thank the editors of the Cambridge Studies in Medieval Life and Thought for accepting my book in this prestigious series, and Michael Watson, Elizabeth Friend-Smith and the production team at Cambridge University Press, first among them Virginia Catmur, my copy-editor, for helping the book develop and seeing it through print.

My greatest debt of gratitude, however, is to my parents, grandparents and siblings, who provided me with strong roots and countered my occasional desperation with love, understanding and good humour, and to my partner Kirsten, who never stopped believing in me. She must be the only person in the world more pleased than I am that the stacks of paper that were drafts of this books have finally gone into the recycling bin.

The transition of my Ph.D. thesis into a book has taken a long time and in the meantime parts of Chapter 1, dealing with lay associations, have already been published separately as an article ('Forms of lay association with the Order of the Temple', in *Journal of Medieval History* 34 (2008), 79–103). These are repeated here with only minor adjustments.

ABBREVIATIONS

AB	*Annales de Bourgogne*
Act Bonne	*Recueil des actes de l'abbaye cistercienne de Bonnefont en Comminges*, ed. Charles Samaran and Charles Higounet (Paris, 1970)
Act Porc	*Les actes de la famille Porcelet d'Arles. Texte (972–1320)*, ed. Martin Aurell, *Collection de documents inédits sur l'histoire de France* (Paris, 2001)
ADCO	Archives Départementales de la Côte-d'Or
AdM	*Annales du Midi*
AN	Archives Nationales de France, Paris
BEC	*Bibliothèque de l'École de Chartes*
BN	Bibliothèque Nationale de France
BuSoScYonne	*Bulletin de la Société des sciences historiques et naturelles de l'Yonne*
CadC	*Cartulaire et archives des communes et l'ancien diocèse et de l'arrondissement administratif de Carcassonne*, ed. Alphonse J. Mahul, 6 vols. (Paris, 1857–71)
Cart An	*Cartulaires des abbayes d'Aniane et de Gellone, vol. II: Cartulaire d'Aniane*, ed. Léon Cassan and Edmond Meynial (Montpellier, 1900–10)
Cart Berd	*Cartulaire de l'abbaye de Berdoues*, ed. Jean-Marie Cazauran (The Hague, 1905)
Cart Béz	*Cartulaire de Béziers (Livre Noir)*, ed. Julien Rouquette (Paris, Montpellier, 1918)
Cart Bonnecombe	*Cartulaire de l'abbaye de Bonnecombe*, ed. Pierre-Aloïs Verlaguet (Rodez, 1918–25)
Cart Boul	*Cartulaire de l'abbaye de Boulancourt: de l'ancien diocèse de Troyes, aujourd'hui du département de la Haute-Marne*, ed. Charles Lalore (Troyes, 1869)

Cart Cast	*El cartulario de la encomienda templaria de Castellote (Teruel), 1184–1283*, ed. Sandra de la Torre Gonzalo (Zaragoza, 2009)
Cart Con	*Cartulaire de l'abbaye de Conques en Rouergue*, ed. Gustave Desjardins (Paris, 1879)
Cart Dax	*Cartulaire de la cathédrale de Dax*. Liber Rubeus *(XIe–XIIe siècles)*, ed. and trans. Georges Pon and Jean Cabanot (Dax, 2004)
Cart Douz	*Cartulaires des templiers de Douzens*, ed. Pierre Gérard and Élisabeth Magnou, *Collection des documents inédits sur l'histoire de France,* III (Paris, 1965)
Cart Gell	*Cartulaires des abbayes d'Aniane et de Gellone, vol. I: Cartulaire de Gellone*, ed. Paul Alaus, Léon Cassan and Edmond Meynial (Montpellier, 1898)
Cart Gim	*Cartulaire de l'abbaye de Gimont*, ed. Adrien Clergeac (Paris, 1905)
Cart Jul	*Cartulaire du prieuré de Jully-les-Nonnains*, ed. Ernest Petit, *BuSoScYonne,* 38 (Auxerre, 1884), 249–301
Cart Lan	*Cartulaire du chapitre cathédral de Langres*, ed. Hubert Flammarion (Turnhout, 2004)
Cart LaS	*Le cartulaire de La Selve. La terre, les hommes et le pouvoir en Rouergue au XIIe siècle*, ed. Paul Ourliac (Paris, 1985)
Cart Léz	*Cartulaire de l'abbaye de Lézat*, ed. Anne-Marie Magnou and Paul Ourliac, 2 vols. (Paris, 1984–7)
Cart Mol	*Cartulaires de l'abbaye de Molesme. Ancien diocèse de Langres 916–1250. Recueil de documents sur le nord de la Bourgogne et le Midi de la Champagne*, ed. Jacques Laurent, 2 vols. (Paris, 1907–11)
Cart Mon	*Cartulaire de Montier-la-Celle*, ed. Charles Lalore, *Collection des principaux cartulaires du diocèse de Troyes,* VI (Paris, Troyes, 1882)
Cart Mont	*Cartulaire des templiers de Montsaunès*, ed. Charles Higounet, *Bulletin philologique et historique du comité des travaux historiques et scientifiques* (1957), 211–94
Cart Montier	*Cartulaire de l'abbaye de Montiéramey*, ed. Charles Lalore, *Collection des principaux cartulaires du diocèse de Troyes,* VII (Paris, Troyes, 1890)
Cart Non	*Cartulaire et documents de l'abbaye de Nonenque*, ed. Camille Couderc and Jean-Louis Rigal, *Archives historiques du Rouergue,* 18 (Rodez, 1950)

Cart Pon	*Le premier cartulaire de l'abbaye cistercienne de Pontigny (XIIe–XIIIe siècles)*, ed. Martine Garrigues (Paris, 1981)
Cart Prov	*Histoire et cartulaire des templiers de Provins. Avec une introduction sur les débuts du Temple en France*, ed. Victor Carrière (Paris, 1919; reprint: Marseille, 1978)
Cart Puy	*Cartulaire des templiers du Puy-en-Velay*, ed. Augustin Chassaing, *Annales de la Société d'agriculture, sciences, arts et commerce de Puy*, 33 (Paris, 1882), 139–263
Cart Rich	*Cartulaire de la commanderie de Richerenches de l'Ordre du Temple (1136–1214)*, ed. Marquis de Ripert-Monclar (Avignon, Paris, 1907; reprint: 1978)
Cart Sil	*Cartulaire de l'abbaye de Silvanès*, ed. Pierre-Aloïs Verlaguet (Rodez, 1910)
Cart S-P	*Cartulaire de Saint-Pierre de Troyes*, ed. Charles Lalore (Paris, Troyes, 1880)
Cart St-L	*Cartulaire de l'abbaye de Saint-Loup de Troyes*, ed. Charles Lalore, *Collection des principaux cartulaires du diocèse de Troyes*, 1 (Paris, Troyes, 1875)
Cart Vab	*Cartulaire de l'abbaye de Vabres au diocèse de Rodez. Essai de reconstruction d'un manuscrit disparu*, ed. Étienne Fournial (Rodez, Saint Étienne, 1989)
Cart Vaour	*Cartulaire des templiers de Vaour (Tarn)*, ed. Charles Portal and Edmond Cabié (Toulouse, Albi, 1894)
CCCM	*Corpus Christianorum, Continuatio Medievalis* (143 vols., Turnhout, 1945–)
CdF	Cahiers de Fanjeaux
CG	*Cartulaire général de l'ordre du Temple*, ed. Alexis Marie Joseph André Marquis d'Albon (Paris, 1913)
CG(Hosp)	*Cartulaire général de l'ordre des hospitaliers de St-Jean de Jérusalem (1100–1310)*, ed. Joseph Delaville Le Roulx, 4 vols. (Paris, 1894–1906)
CG(Yonne)	*Cartulaire général de l'Yonne*, ed. Maximilien Quantin, 2 vols. (Auxerre, 1854–60)
Chart Chem	*Recueil des chartes de l'abbaye de Notre-Dame de Cheminon*, ed. Édouard de Barthélemy (Paris, 1983)
Chart Clairv	*Recueil des chartes de l'abbaye de Clairvaux au XIIe siècle*, ed. Jean Waquet (Paris, 2004)
Chart Font	*Le chartrier de l'abbaye cistercienne de Fontfroide (894–1260)*, ed. Véronique de Becdelièvre, 2 vols. (Paris, 2009)

Chart LanFran — *Chartes en langue française antérieures à 1271 conservées dans le département de la Haute-Marne*, ed. Jean-Gabriel Gigot (Paris, 1974)

Chart Mor — *Chartes de l'abbaye de Mores*, ed. Charles Lalore, *MSA Aube*, 37 (1873), 5–107

Chart Roais — *Chartularium domus Templi Hierosolymitani de Roais dioceses Vasionensis*, ed. Joseph Hyacinthe Albanès and Cyr Ulysse Joseph Chevalier, *Cartulaires des hospitaliers et des templiers en Dauphiné,* III (Vienne, 1975), 61–136

Chart St-Gilles — *Chartes de la maison du Temple de St-Gilles*, in Damien Carraz, *Ordres militaires, croisades et sociétés méridionales. L'ordre du temple dans la basse vallée du Rhône (1124–1312), vol. III: Sources* (Ph.D. thesis, Lyon: Université de Lyon 2, 2003), 477–685

Chart St-Marc/Jully — *Chartes originales provenant de la commanderie des templiers de Saint Marc à Nuits-sur-Amançon et du prieuré de Jully-les-Nonnains*, ed. Ernest Petit, *Bulletin philologique et historique* (1897), 759–89

CHR — *The Catholic Historical Review*

CTGard — *Chartes de la maison du Temple du Gard rhodanien*, in Damien Carraz, *Ordres militaires, croisades et sociétés méridionales. L'ordre du temple dans la basse vallée du Rhône (1124–1312), vol. III: Sources* (Ph.D. thesis, Lyon: Université de Lyon 2, 2003), 408–76

DAEM — *Deutsches Archiv für Erforschung des Mittelalters*

DhT-G — *Documents historiques sur le Tarn-et-Garonne*, ed. François Moulenq, 4 vols. (Montauban, 1879–94)

Doat — Bibliothèque Nationale, Collection Doat

Doc Dur — *Documents sur la maison de Durfort (XIe–XVe siècle)*, ed. Nicole de Peña, 2 vols. (Bordeaux, 1977)

Feud Soc — *Feudal society in medieval France. Documents from the county of Champagne*, trans. Theodore Evergates (Philadelphia, Pa., 1993)

GC — *Gallia christiana in provincias ecclesiasticas distributa*, ed. Paul Piolin, 13 vols. (Paris, 1870–8)

GP(Toulouse) — Antoine du Bourg, *Ordre de Malte. Histoire du grand prieuré de Toulouse et des diverses possessions de l'Ordre de Saint-Jean de Jérusalem dans le sud-ouest de la France* (Toulouse, 1888)

HdB — *Histoire des ducs de Bourgogne de la race capétienne*, ed. Ernest Petit, 9 vols. (Paris, 1885–1905)

HGL	Joseph Vaissète, Claude Devic and Édouard Dulaurier, *Histoire générale de Languedoc*, 16 vols. (Toulouse, 1872–1904)
JMH	*Journal of Medieval History*
La Grasse (I)	*Recueil des chartes de l'abbaye de La Grasse, vol. I: 779–1119*, ed. Élisabeth Magnou-Nortier and Anne-Marie Magnou (Paris, 1996)
La Grasse (II)	*Recueil des chartes de l'abbaye de La Grasse, vol. II: 1117–1279*, ed. Claudine Pailhès (Paris, 2000)
LexMA	*Lexikon des Mittelalters* (9 vols., Munich, 2002)
MGH SS	*Monumenta Germaniae Historica, Scriptores in folio et quarto*, ed. Georg Heinrich Pertz *et al.*, 34 vols. so far (Hanover and Leipzig, 1826–)
MSA Aube	*Mémoires de la Société académique d'agriculture, des sciences, arts et belles-lettres du département de l'Aube*
n.a.l.	Nouvelles acquisitions latines
ObReims	*Obituaire de la commanderie du Temple de Reims*, ed. Édouard de Barthélemy, *Mélanges historiques. Collection des documents inédits,* IV (Paris, 1882), 313–32
OdM	Eugène Mannier, *Ordre de Malte. Les commanderies du Grand-prieuré de France, d'après les documents inédits conservés aux Archives Nationales à Paris*, 2 vols. (Paris, 1872; reprint 1998)
OFWT	*The old French continuation of William of Tyre*, ed. Peter Edbury, *The conquest of Jerusalem and the Third Crusade* (Aldershot, 1998), 11–145
PAC	*Les plus anciennes chartes en langue provençale*, ed. Claude Brunel, 2 vols. (Paris, 1926–52)
PL	*Patrologiae cursus completus, series Latina*, ed. Jacques-Paul Migne, 221 vols. (Paris, 1844–64)
PT	*Le procès des templiers*, ed. Jules Michelet, 2 vols. (Paris, 1841; reprint: 1987)
PTJ I	Hiestand, Rudolf, *Papsturkunden für Templer und Johanniter: Archivberichte und Texte*, Abhandlungen der Akademie der Wissenschaften in Göttingen. Philologisch-Historische Klasse, 77. Vorarbeiten zum Oriens pontificius, I (Göttingen, 1972)
PTJ II	*Papsturkunden für Templer und Johanniter: neue Folge*, Abhandlungen der Akademie der Wissenschaften in Göttingen, Philologisch-Historische Klasse, 3rd series,

	no. 135. Vorarbeiten zum Oriens pontificus, 2 (Göttingen, 1984)
RRH	*Regesta regni Hierosolymitani 1097–1291*, ed. Reinhold Röhricht, 2 vols. (Innsbruck, 1893–1904)
TSS	*The Templars. Selected sources*, trans. Malcolm Barber and Keith Bate (Manchester, New York, 2002)

INTRODUCTION

At the turn of the thirteenth century Bishop Peter of Lérida sent a letter to King James II of Aragon, in which he complained bitterly about the devastation that he, his Church and his people had to endure from the marauding troops of Templar men, who probably belonged to the nearby commandery of Monzón. He asked for intervention; but he was also adamant that he did not want Bernard of Fonollar, who was an important advisor to the infant king, to act as mediator in this affair. He was afraid that Bernard's judgement would be biased in favour of the Templars because it was commonly known that Bernard held the castle of Selma from the Templars and that he had numerous relatives among them.[1]

This book is concerned with Templar establishments in different regions of northern and southern France. The Iberian peninsula rarely features in it; and nothing further will be said about the bishopric of Lérida. But in a nutshell the incident from Aragon encapsulates one important aspect of what I want the book to be all about, and thus serves to show at this early stage that what I will discuss and suggest for the relationship between Templars and society in specific parts of France applies also to other parts of medieval Europe.

The letter was composed some time between 1299, when Peter became bishop of Lérida, and 1307, when the Templars in Spain and elsewhere were arrested on charges of heresy and blasphemy. It implies that through kindred the Order of the Temple maintained close ties with leaders of society and that these relationships were mutually influential. Concentrating on the duchy of Burgundy, the county of Champagne, and mainly the area that is now commonly referred to as Languedoc in southern France, this book investigates how commonplace these ties, contested as they may have been, were in regions where the Order of the Temple demonstrably flourished and what it was that brought about

[1] H. Finke, *Papsttum und Untergang des Templerordens*, 2 vols. (Münster, 1907), II, no. 5, pp. 6–7.

these alliances, which could have very real political implications. The focus of the book is not so much on the Order and the influences of these alliances on its history, as on the families and the reasons which compelled them to gravitate towards this particular hybrid order and, as it turns out, to one another.

HISTORIOGRAPHY

The Order of the Temple was founded in *c.* 1120 by a group of knights under the leadership of Hugh of Payns from Champagne as a religious community associated with the Augustinian chapter of the Holy Sepulchre in Jerusalem, whose members were actively engaged in the protection of pilgrims and the defence and recovery of the holy places in the Levant. In 1129 it received papal recognition and a Rule; ten years later it became an exempt order of the Church, meaning that henceforth its members were no longer subject to episcopal jurisdiction and that, as an institution, it was accountable only to the Pope for its actions.[2] The Templars received their first possessions in France in the early 1120s and over the years brothers with roving commissions picked up endowments in most regions of western Europe.[3] Until the dissolution of the Order of the Temple in 1312 (following the arrest of the Templars first in France and later in other parts of Europe on trumped-up charges including heresy, blasphemy and sodomy and the subsequent Templar trial), France remained the most important country in the growth and development of the Temple. Here the Order was particularly active in Champagne, Burgundy and the south;[4] here, as elsewhere in Europe, landed families provided the brothers with the material and personal means to establish commanderies and granges, some of which developed into major agricultural enterprises. It was with the revenues from their estates and with the knights and non-nobles who flocked to their houses that the Templars were able to organise, finance and maintain a presence in the Latin East for almost two hundred years.

Scholarship on the military orders has produced a number of detailed case studies that illustrate the development of individual Templar houses and the Order's history in individual dioceses and regions, and in them one can see that the interaction between armsbearing families and

[2] The exemption of the Order is discussed in *PTJ II*, pp. 75–95.

[3] J. S. C. Riley-Smith, 'The origin of the commandery in the Temple and the Hospital', in A. Luttrell and L. Pressouyre (eds.), *La commanderie, institution des ordres militaires dans l'Occident médiéval* (Paris, 2002), 12–13.

[4] An overview of the Order's possessions in these regions can be obtained from J.-L. Aubarbier and M. Binet, *Les sites templiers de France* (Rennes, 1997), pp. 14–20, 30–4, 86–148.

Templar communities was often vigorous.[5] In particular, what emerges from these studies is that from very early on the Order attracted followers, from different backgrounds and of both sexes, who associated themselves with local Templar communities. Many of these Templar communities developed into powerful landowners and, as Christina Dondi has demonstrated, it was not uncommon for them to adapt their religious practices to local custom.[6] If one also considers that by the end of the thirteenth century communication between remote western Templar communities and the Order's convent in the East would have been infrequent and that the Order's convent generally tended not to meddle in the internal affairs of Templar commanderies as long as they kept sending *responsiones* (in theory one-third of their income), and if one also considers that until the demise of the Order Templar communities continued to attract recruits and a labour workforce, then it seems reasonable to assume, as Jonathan Riley-Smith has done, that in spite of the Order's international nature, individual Templar communities had their own independence and were deeply rooted in the landscape and society in which they were located.[7]

[5] Of particular interest for this study are R. Vinas, 'Le destin des templiers du Roussillon, 1276–1330', in *Les ordres religieux militaires dans le Midi (XIIe–XIVe siècle)*, CdF, XLI (Toulouse, 2006), 187–210; D. Carraz, 'Présences et dévotions féminines autour des commanderies du Bas-Rhône (XIIe–XIIIe siècle)', in *Les ordres religieux militaires dans le Midi (XIIe–XIVe siècle)*, CdF, XLI (Toulouse, 2006), 71–99; D. Carraz, 'Mémoire lignagère et archives monastiques: les Bourbouton et la commanderie de Richerenches', in M. Aurell (ed.), *Convaincre et persuader: communication et propagande aux XIIe et XIIIe siècles*, Civilisation Médiévale, 17 (Poitiers, 2007), 465–502; D. Carraz, *L'ordre du Temple dans la basse vallée du Rhône (1124–1312). Ordres militaires, croisades et sociétés méridionales* (Lyon, 2005); M. Barber, 'The Templar preceptory of Douzens (Aude) in the twelfth century', in C. Léglu and M. Bull (eds.), *The world of Eleanor of Aquitaine* (Woodbridge, 2005), 37–55; D. Marie, *Les templiers dans le diocèse de Langres. Des moines entrepreneurs aux XIIe et XIIIe siècles* (Langres, 2004); L. Verdon, *La terre et les hommes en Roussillon aux XIIe et XIIIe siècles. Structures seigneuriales, rente et société d'après les sources templières* (Aix-en-Provence, 2001); R. Vinas, *L'ordre du Temple en Roussillon* (Canet, 2001); A. Demurger, 'La constitution d'un patrimoine foncier: les templiers dans le comté d'Auxerre (XIIIe s.)', in I. C. F. Fernandes (ed.), *As ordens militares e as ordens de cavalaria na construção do mundo ocidental – Actas do VI encontro sobre ordens militares* (Lisbon, 2005), 439–50; A. Demurger, 'Les templiers à Auxerre (XIIe–XIIIe siècles)', in P. Boucheron and J. Chiffoleau (eds.), *Religion et société urbaine au moyen âge. Études offertes à Jean-Louis Biget* (Paris, 2000), 301–11; L. Verdon, 'La seigneurie templière à Perpignan au XIIIe siècle', in N. Coulet and O. Guyotjeannin (eds.), *La ville au moyen âge, vol. II: Sociétés et pouvoirs dans la ville* (Paris, 1998), 221–8; L. Verdon, 'Les revenus de la commanderie templière du Mas Déu (Roussillon) d'après le terrier de 1264', *AdM*, 210 (1995), 167–93; A. Demurger, 'L'aristocrazia laica e gli ordini militari in Francia nel duecento: l'esempio della Bassa Borgogna', in E. Coli, M. de Marco and F. Tommasi (eds.), *Militia Sacra. Gli ordini militari tra Europa e Terrasanta* (Perugia, 1994), 55–84.

[6] See C. Dondi, *The liturgy of the canons regular of the Holy Sepulchre of Jerusalem: a study and a catalogue of the manuscript sources* (Turnhout, 2004).

[7] J. S. C. Riley-Smith, 'The structures of the Orders of the Temple and the Hospital in *c.* 1291', in S.J. Ridyard (ed.), *Medieval crusade* (Woodbridge, 2004), 128–9, 139–41. See also J. Burgtorf, *The central convent of Hospitallers and Templars: history, organization, and personnel (1099/1120–1310)* (Leiden, 2008), pp. 56–7; A.J. Forey, *The Templars in the Corona of Aragón* (London, 1973), p. 50.

But who were the individuals and families that provided the Order with the means to establish and maintain a strong presence in certain regions? And what motivated them to lend their support?

So far, historians seem to agree that the families of knights and petty noblemen constituted the backbone of the Order's structure in the West and that members of these families, and non-nobles as well, were inspired to join, or otherwise associate with, the Temple for a number of motives.[8] Piety was one obvious reason why laymen entered the Order, and underlying this piety was the same spirituality that caused many of the Templars' contemporaries to take the cross.[9] Some Templar postulants, however, may have regarded entry as a means of social advancement, and to others the Order may have offered 'a more comfortable existence than the alternatives available in the secular world'.[10] The need for physical protection could also have led to association with the Order,[11] as may, in the individual case, a thirst for adventure and an eagerness to travel to the East for earthly glory.[12]

As I will argue in Chapter 2, what seems to have predisposed some knights and nobles to embrace the Order of the Temple as a new religious institution worthy of association and patronage was the fact that they and their families were already heavily involved in the Order of Cîteaux and were able to reconcile the concept of military religion with reform monasticism. This is one strand of influence that so far has not been given much attention and that this book aims to follow up.

Marcus Bull has stated in a different context that it is impossible to frame a concise statement of the crusaders' motivations that would apply

[8] A.J. Forey, 'Recruitment to the military orders (twelfth to mid-fourteenth centuries)', *Viator*, 17 (1986), 139–73; A. Demurger, *Les templiers. Une chevalerie chrétienne au moyen âge* (Paris, 2005), p. 261; A. Barbero, 'Motivazioni religiosi e motivazioni utilitarie nel reclutamento negli ordini monastico-cavallereschi', in *'Militia Christi' e crociata nei secoli XI–XIII. Atti della undecima settimana internazionale di studio, 28 agosto – 1 settembre*, Miscellanea del Centro di studi medioevali, 13 (Milan, 1992), 717–29; M.L. Bulst-Thiele, 'Die Anfänge des Templer-Ordens. Bernard von Clairvaux. Citeaux', *Zeitschrift für Kirchengeschichte*, 104 (4th series 42) (1993), 319 and M.L. Bulst-Thiele, *Sacrae domus militiae Templi Hierosolymitani magistri. Untersuchungen zur Geschichte des Templerordens 1118/19–1314*, Abhandlungen der Akademie der Wissenschaften in Göttingen. Philologisch-Historische Klasse, 86 (Göttingen, 1974), p. 160. See also *Cart Douz*, p. xxxiii.

[9] These spiritual undercurrents have now become the object of scholarly research. See W.J. Purkis, *Crusading spirituality in the Holy Land and Iberia, c. 1095–c. 1187* (Woodbridge, 2008). For the argument that piety was one reason for entry into the Order of the Temple see Forey, 'Recruitment', 167–8 and M. Barber, *The new knighthood: a history of the Order of the Temple* (Cambridge, 1994), p. 207.

[10] Forey, 'Recruitment', 164.

[11] D. Selwood, *Knights of the cloister. Templars and Hospitallers in central-southern Occitania 1100–1300* (Woodbridge, 1999), p. 17. At least on the Iberian peninsula the Templars seem to have been expected to provide physical protection for the *familiae* of their communities. See Forey, 'Recruitment', 145.

[12] Bulst-Thiele, *Sacrae domus militiae*, p. 160.

accurately to all periods, regions, and social classes.[13] In the end, the same can be argued for Templar recruits and associates. The motives of laymen who joined or gave to the Order in the late thirteenth century would have been different from those of people in the early twelfth, when the Order was still new and unique. Bearing this in mind, however, it is all the more legitimate to ask why some families engaged with the Order continuously over many generations. Individual piety, the longing for security and social advancement or the adventurous spirit of individual knights do not sufficiently explain why large family groups supported particular Templar commanderies along with their friends, vassals and kinsmen sometimes for more than a century.

The Order's local archives, of which more below, support the premise that extended families associating with Templar houses and family relationships between Templars were commonplace.[14] At first sight this seems nothing out of the ordinary. Religious communities had always attracted the loyal support of noble and knightly families. Unlike traditional religious communities, however, the Order of the Temple demanded more of their knightly recruits than submission to the monastic lifestyle. As I will try to show in Chapter 5, the death of Templar brothers drafted to the Holy Land and their dedication to holy war were soon incorporated into the collective memory of medieval society, as were, of course, the deeds and deaths of crusaders. The distinction between 'traditional' religious orders and military orders would therefore have been clear to see. Certainly such a distinction would have informed the decision of laymen whether or not to include a Templar (or other military) community among the institutions worthy of spiritual attention.

As it turned out, alliances with Templar and other military communities were popular. They helped the Order of the Temple to grow. Historians have long testified to the existence of close ties between commanderies and families. Hans Prutz argued that 'personal factors' (*persönliche Momente*), by which he meant kinship and friendship ties between laymen and Templars, had played a part in the rapid development of the Order in France, notably in Champagne.[15] Anthony Luttrell, like Prutz, pointed out that many of the early Templars had in fact been

[13] M. Bull, *Knightly piety and the lay response to the First Crusade: the Limousin and Gascony, c. 970–c. 1130* (Oxford, 1993), p. 282.

[14] J. G. Schenk, 'Aspects of non-noble family involvement in the Order of the Temple', in J. M. Upton-Ward (ed.), *The military orders, vol. IV: On land and by sea* (Aldershot, 2008), 155–62.

[15] H. Prutz, *Die geistlichen Ritterorden, ihre Stellung zur kirchlichen, politischen, gesellschaftlichen und wirtschaftlichen Entwicklung des Mittelalters* (Berlin, 1908), p. 352.

'connected to one another by birth and other ties'.[16] According to Alan Forey, parental and family pressure must have influenced the decisions of Templar postulants. He also believed that in individual cases the parental decision to let a son join the Order was often influenced by existing personal, family, or neighbourhood links with the Order. Very likely, therefore, some recruits did not enter the Order voluntarily or enthusiastically and 'were perhaps only reluctantly persuaded by more determined kinsmen'.[17] Marie Luise Bulst-Thiele has argued that members of the same families – fathers and sons, uncles and nephews – usually joined the same military order, thus implying that family tradition could determine recruitment to the Temple.[18] And drawing on evidence from the Templar depositions, Alessandro Barbero has been able to piece together some of the family networks that existed within the Order at the beginning of the fourteenth century.[19] The 'family element' of Templar communities to which these historians have testified is a barometer demonstrating how deeply particular kin-groups became involved in the Order. How they did so and what motivated their involvement are the two leading questions that I will try to answer in this book.

I have focused my study mainly on the duchy of Burgundy and the adjoining county of Champagne in northern France, and Languedoc in the south. The duchy of Burgundy and the county of Champagne can best be defined by the dioceses which they comprised (at least in part). These were Langres, Chalon-sur-Saône, Mâcon, Autun, Nevers and Auxerre for Burgundy (Map 1), and Sens, Troyes, Châlons-sur-Marne, Reims, Laon, Noyon, Soissons and Meaux for Champagne (Map 2). Languedoc describes the area of southern France in which the Romance language of Oc was spoken. Defined by linguistic rather than political or religious boundaries it thus stretched from the Pyrenees along the coast of the Mediterranean to the Alps. To the north it included much of the Dauphiné, Velay, Auvergne, Périgord and Limousin, to the east Aquitaine, Gascony, Bigorre and Comminges. In modern usage, however, Languedoc usually describes the area of south-central France between the Pyrenees in the south, Albi in the north, the Garonne in the west and the Rhône in the east. It is on this Languedoc that my research on southern France focuses predominantly, although extensive

[16] A. Luttrell, 'The earliest Templars', in M. Balard (ed.), *Autour de la première croisade. Actes du colloque de la Society for the Study of the Crusades and the Latin East, Clermont-Ferrand, 22–25 juin 1995* (Paris, 1995), 199–200.

[17] Forey, 'Recruitment', 164, 170. See also A.J. Forey, 'The military orders, 1120–1312', in J. S. C. Riley-Smith (ed.), *The Oxford illustrated history of the crusades* (London, 1995), 199.

[18] Bulst-Thiele, *Sacrae domus militiae*, p. 171.

[19] Barbero, 'Motivazioni religiosi e motivazioni utilitarie', 721–4.

sorties to adjoining regions, namely Provence, Velay, Auvergne, Gascony and Comminges, will also be made (see Map 3).[20]

My decision to select these regions was guided on the one hand by the well-established fact that the *mentalités* of northern and southern Frenchmen of the twelfth and thirteenth centuries were distinctively different, to the point that they violently clashed in the thirteenth century: how the Order of the Temple grew in both societies is an interesting point of comparison. On the other hand it was guided by the fact that each region possesses rich archives, which have been the subject of intense scholarly scrutiny and which in recent years have formed the basis of a number of high-quality scholarly articles and monographs investigating, and to a large extent explaining, regional religious developments and social and political changes. These include Constance Brittain Bouchard's seminal study of the symbiotic relationships between Church and secular society in Burgundy, Theodore Evergates's prosopographical research into the society of medieval Champagne, which makes use of the county's exceptionally rich comital archives, Laurent Macé's analytical study of political rivalries, alliances and exercise of power in the medieval county of Toulouse, Hélène Débax's examination of the legal implications and social and political consequences of feudal oaths and contracts in the Languedoc of the Trencavels, and Claudie Duhamel-Amado's two-volume genealogical study of medieval Languedoc families.[21] The military orders in general and the Templars in particular are subjected to scrutiny in Dominic Selwood, *Knights of the cloister*, which, despite a number of discrepancies and a few errors, provides valuable examples of how deeply the military orders of St John and the Temple connected with society in southern France and how firmly they placed themselves on the political and religious map of the region.[22] A similar study for Champagne or Burgundy does not exist, but articles by Alain Demurger and a brief study of the Templars in the diocese of Langres by Delphine Marie provide some material on which I could draw in my research for this book.[23]

[20] See Selwood, *Knights of the cloister*, pp. 15–16 and L. M. Paterson, *The world of the troubadours: medieval Occitan society, c. 1100–c. 1300* (Cambridge, 1993), pp. xiii and 1–9.

[21] C. B. Bouchard, *Sword, miter, and cloister: nobility and the Church in Burgundy, 980–1198* (Ithaca, N.Y., 1987), passim; T. Evergates, *The aristocracy in the county of Champagne, 1100–1300* (Philadelphia, Pa., 2007); L. Macé, *Les comtes de Toulouse et leur entourage. Rivalités, alliances et jeux de pouvoir XIIe – XIIIe siècles* (Toulouse, 2003); H. Débax, *La féodalité languedocienne aux XIe–XIIe siècles. Serments, hommages et fiefs dans le Languedoc des Trencavel* (Toulouse, 2003); C. Duhamel-Amado, *Genèse des lignages méridionaux*, 2 vols. (Toulouse, 2001–7). Also helpful are Paterson, *World of the troubadours* and E. Graham-Leigh, *The southern French nobility and the Albigensian crusade* (Woodbridge, 2005).

[22] Selwood, *Knights of the cloister*.

[23] Demurger, 'L'aristocrazia laica e gli ordini militari', passim; Demurger, 'Les templiers à Auxerre', passim; Marie, *Templiers de Langres*.

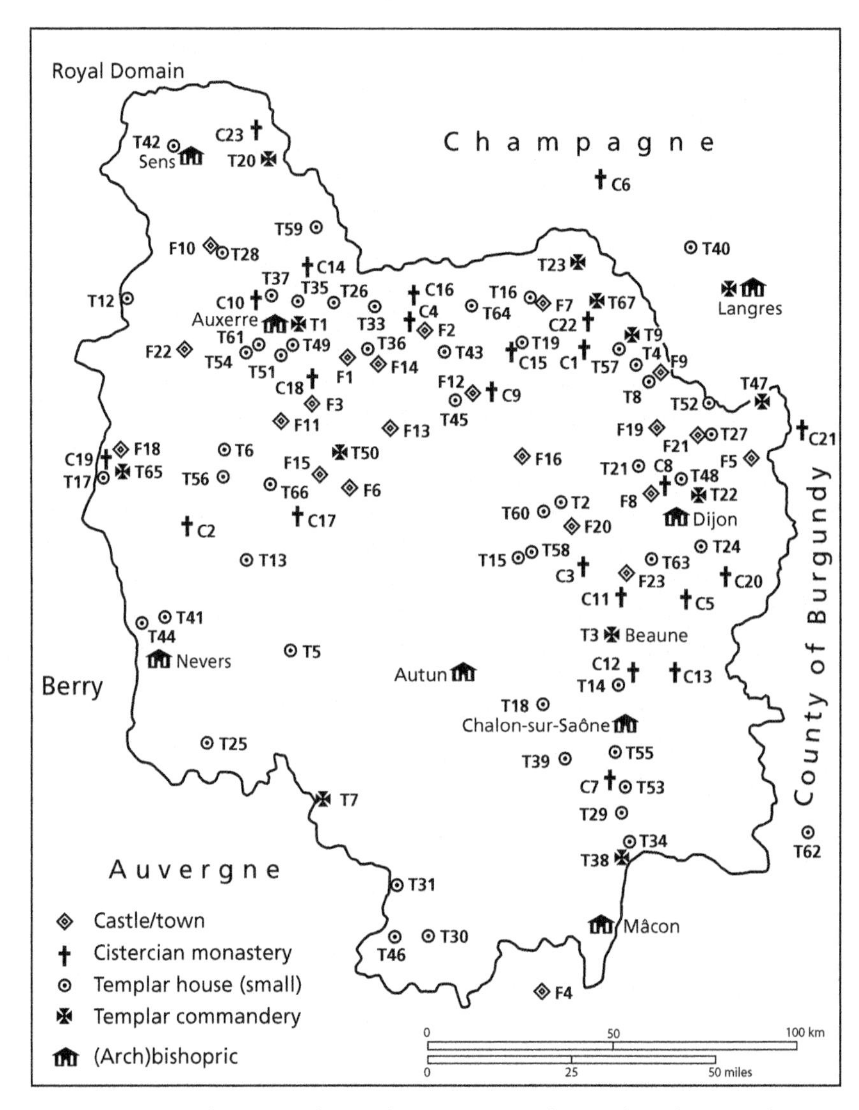

Map 1. Families, Templars and Cistercians in the Duchy of Burgundy

As networks defined by kinship are necessarily amorphous and change shape with each generation, any attempt to put geographical restrictions on them or to confine them to political boundaries is bound to fail. In the duchy of Burgundy and the county of Champagne the families of knights and nobles extended north and south of what was in any case a porous

Templars
T1 Auxerre
T2 Avosnes
T3 Beaune
T4 Beneuvre
T5 Biches
T6 Billy-sur-Oisy
T7 Bourbon-Lancy
T8 Busserotte
T9 Bure
T10 Chagny
T11 Chalon-sur-Saône
T12 Chambeugle
T13 Champallement
T14 La Chapelle
T15 Châtellenot
T16 Châtillon-sur-Seine
T17 Cosne-Cours-sur-Loire
T18 Couches
T19 Coulmier-le-Sec
T20 Coulours
T21 Curtil-St-Seine
T22 Dijon
T23 Épailly
T24 Fauverney
T25 Le Feuilloux
T26 Fonteney-prés-Chablis
T27 Fontenotte
T28 Joigny
T29 Jugy
T30 Launay
T31 Loye
T32 Mâcon
T33 Marsoif (Tonnerre)
T34 Mercey
T35 Merry
T36 Môlay
T37 Monéteau
T38 Montbellet
T39 Les Montots
T40 Mormant
T41 Mougues
T42 Nailly
T43 Nuits (St Marc)
T44 Pougues-les-Eaux
T45 Quincy
T46 Reffey
T47 La Romagne
T48 Ruffey
T49 St Bris le Vineux
T50 La Saulce d'Island
T51 Sauce-sur-Yonne
T52 Selongey
T53 Sennecey-le-Grand
T54 Seraincourt
T55 Sevrey
T56 La Sourcille
T57 Terrefondrée
T58 Thoisy-le-Désert
T59 Turny
T60 Uncey
T61 Vallan
T62 Varessia
T63 Velle-sous-Gevrey
T64 La Vévre (St Marc)
T65 Villemoison
T66 Villiers
T67 Voulaines

Cistercians
C1 Beaulieu
C2 Bourras
C3 La Bussière
C4 La Charité
C5 Cîteaux
C6 Clairvaux
C7 La Ferté
C8 Fontaine
C9 Fontenay
C10 Les Isles (original site)
C11 Lieu-Dieu
C12 Maizières
C13 Molaise
C14 Pontigny
C15 Puits-d'Orbe
C16 Quincy
C17 Réconfort
C18 Reigny
C19 Les Roches
C20 Tart
C21 Theuley
C22 Val des Choues
C23 Vauluisant

Families
F1 Aigremont
F2 Ancy-le-Franc
F3 Arcy-sur-Cure
F4 Beaujeu
F5 Beaumont-sur-Vingeanne
F6 Chastellux
F7 Châtillon-sur-Seine
F8 Fontaine-lès-Dijon
F9 Grancey-le-Château
F10 Joigny
F11 Merry-sur-Yonne
F12 Montbard
F13 Montréal
F14 Noyers
F15 Pierre-Perthuis
F16 La Roche-Vanneau
F17 St-Bris
F18 St-Vérain
F19 Saulx-le-Duc
F20 Sombernon
F21 Tilchâtel
F22 Toucy
F23 Vergy

border. In our modern understanding of counties and duchies we tend to gloss over the fact that in medieval times these were far from being unified political entities and that in reality the knights and noblemen living within them engaged in a wide range of complex feudal arrangements which left them and their lordships vulnerable to outside influences. The counts of Champagne, Auxerre–Nevers and Chalon-sur-Saône, for example,

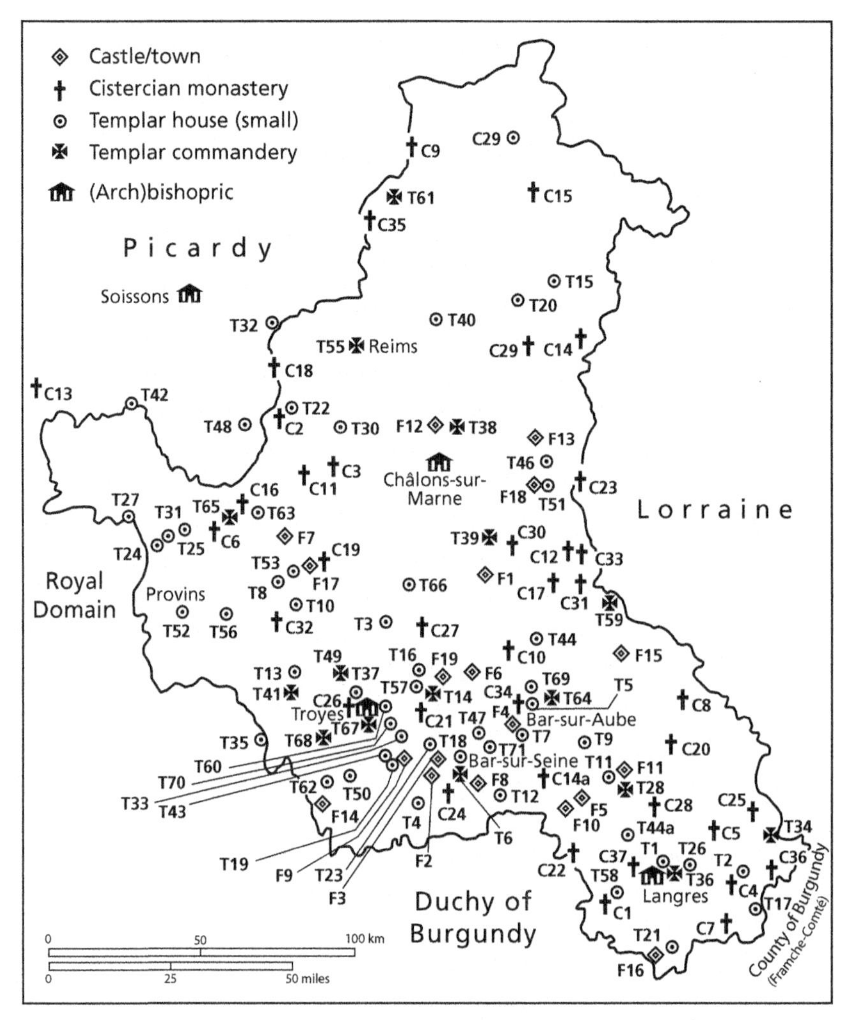

Map 2. Families, Templars and Cistercians in Champagne and Brie

were tied by bonds of vassalage to the dukes of Burgundy for at least a part of their principalities, whereas by the end of the eleventh century the counts of Champagne had successfully extended their influence into the diocese of Langres, which was traditionally considered Burgundian.[24]

[24] J. Richard, 'Les templiers et les hospitaliers en Bourgogne et en Champagne méridionale (XIIe–XIIIe siècles)', in J. Fleckenstein and M. Hellmann (eds.), *Die geistlichen Ritterorden Europas*, Vorträge und Forschungen, 30 (Sigmaringen, 1980), 231.

Templars	
T1	Arbelotte
T2	Arbigny
T3	Arcis-sur-Aube
T4	Arrelles
T5	Arrentières
T6	Avalleur
T7	Bar-sur-Aube
T8	Barbonne
T9	Bas Pré
T10	Baudement
T11	Beauchemin
T12	Beauvoir
T13	Belleville
T14	Bonlieu
T15	Boux
T16	Bouy
T17	Broncourt
T18	Buxières
T19	Cères
T20	La Chambre aux Loups
T21	La Chassagne
T22	Châtillon-sur-Marne
T23	Chauffour-lès-Bailly
T24	Chevru
T25	Choisy-en-Brie
T26	Cordamble
T27	Coulommiers
T28	Corgebin
T29	Damouzy
T30	Épernay
T31	La Ferté-Gaucher
T32	Fismes
T33	Fresnoy-le-Château
T34	Genrupt
T35	Gerbeau
T36	Langres
T37	La Loge
T38	La Malmaison (St-Étienne-au-Temple)
T39	Mancourt
T40	Merlan
T41	Le Mesnil-St-Loup
T42	Moisy
T43	Montceaux
T44	Montier-en-Der
T44a	Mormant
T45	Neuville
T46	Noirlieu
T47	Nuisement
T48	Passy
T49	Payns
T50	Le Perchoy
T51	Possesse
T52	Provins
T53	Queudes
T54	Ramerupt
T55	Reims
T56	Resson
T57	Rosson
T58	Rouelles
T59	Ruetz
T60	Sancey
T61	Seraincourt
T62	Sivrey
T63	Soigny
T64	Thors
T65	Tréfols
T66	Trouans
T67	Troyes
T68	Vallée
T69	Ville-sur-Terre
T70	Villiers
T71	Vitry-le-Croisé
Families	
F1	Arzillières
F2	Avaleur
F3	Bar-sur-Aube
F4	Bar-sur-Seine
F5	Bricon
F6	Brienne
F7	Broyes
F8	Chacenay
F9	Chappes
F10	Châteauvillain
F11	Chaumont
F12	Dampierre(-au-Temple)
F13	Dampierre(-le-Château)
F14	Ervy(-le-Châtel)
F15	Joinville
F16	Occey
F17	Pleurs
F18	Possesse
F19	Villehardouin
Cistercians	
C1	Auberive
C2	L'Amour-Dieu
C3	Argensolle
C4	Beaulieu
C5	Belfays
C6	Belleau
C7	Belmont
C8	Benoîtevaux
C9	Bonnefontaine
C10	Boulancourt
C11	La Charmoye
C12	Cheminon
C13	Chaalis
C14	Chéry
C14a	Clairvaux
C15	Élan
C16	La Grâce-Notre-Dame
C17	Hautefontaine
C18	Igny
C19	Le Jardin
C20	Lacrète
C21	Larrivour
C22	Longué
C23	Monthiers
C24	Mores
C25	Morimond
C26	Notre-Dame-des-Prés
C27	Piété-Dieu
C28	Poulangy
C29	Les Rosiers
C30	St-Jacques
C31	St-Pantaléon
C32	Sellières
C33	Trois-Fontaines
C34	Val-des-Vignes
C35	Valroy
C36	Vaux-la-Douce
C37	Vauxbons

Some of the regions' dominant lords, including the lords of Chacenay, Vignory, Chaumont, Reynel and Vendeuvre, had been drawn into the entourage of the counts, and their collaboration with them rewarded by important offices. Godfrey of Chaumont became the constable of Champagne under Hugh of Troyes. Josbert le Roux, a knight from Châtillon with possessions near La Ferté, also benefited from his collaboration with the counts. He succeeded to the office of seneschal of the Barrois and later, by right of his marriage, took over the office of viscount

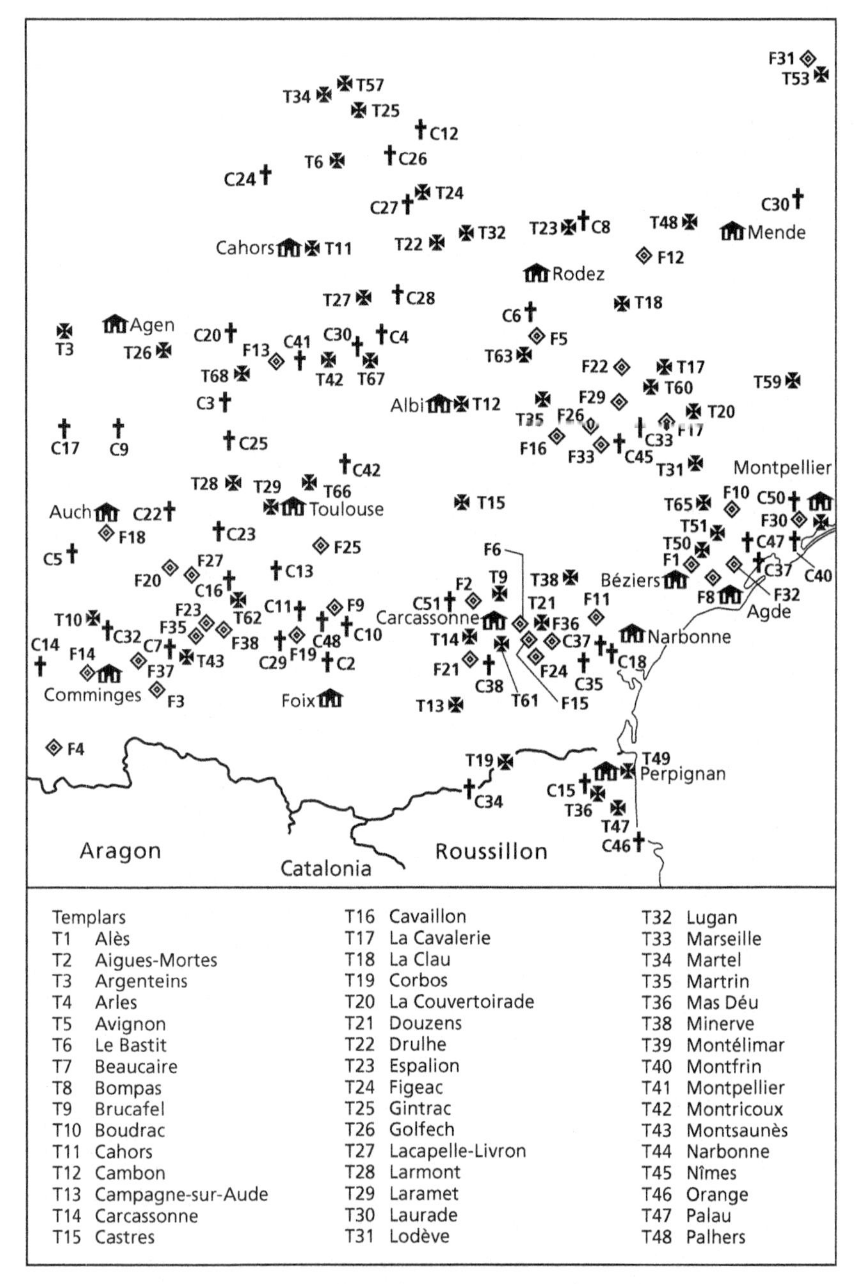

Map 3. Families, Templars and Cistercians in Languedoc and parts of Provence

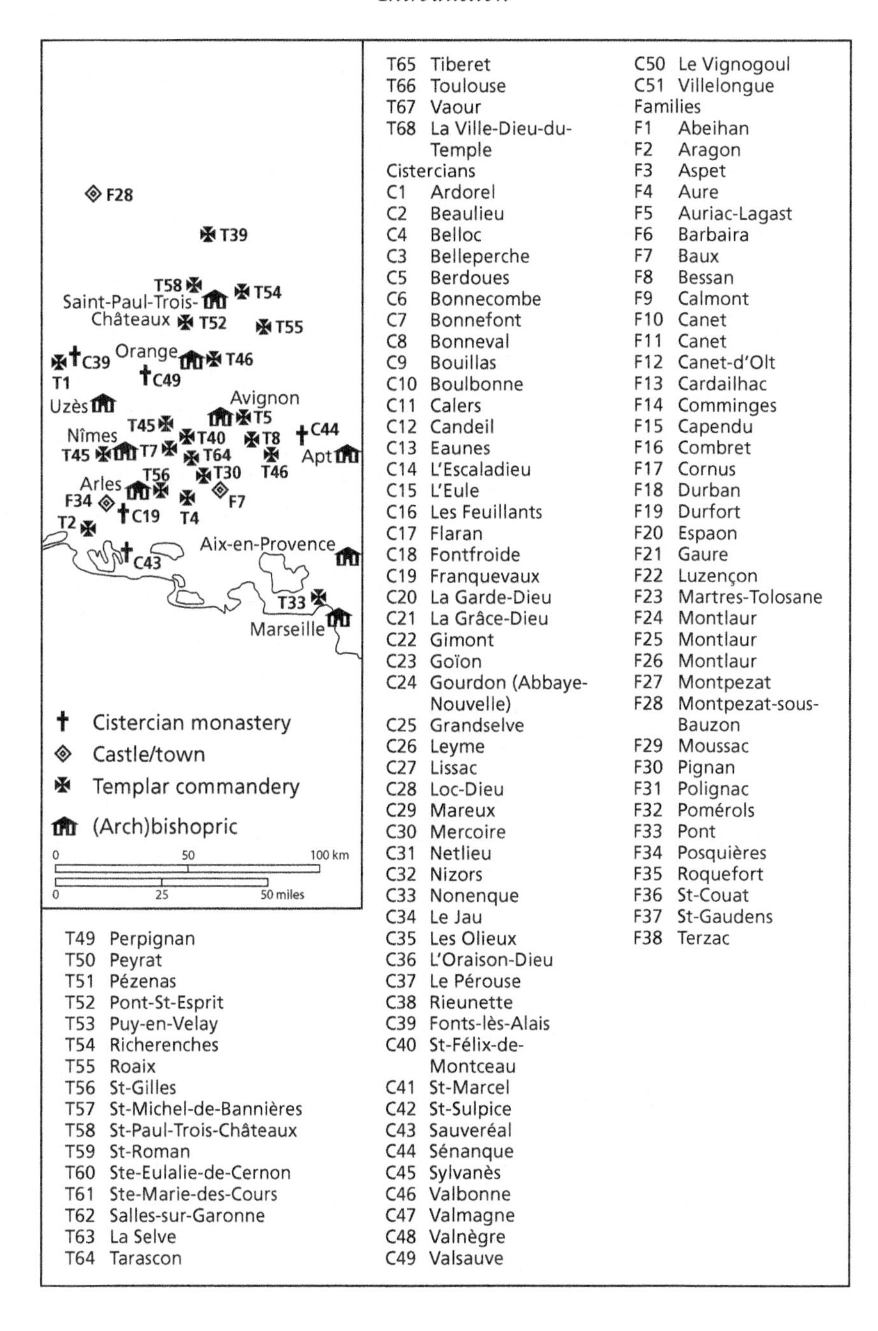
F28
T39
T58
T54
Saint-Paul-Trois-
Châteaux
T52
T55
C39
Orange
T46
T1
C49
Uzès
Avignon
T5
T45
Nîmes
T40
T8
C44
T45
T7
T64
Apt
T56
T30
T46
Arles
F34
F7
T2
C19
T4
Aix-en-Provence
C43
T33
Marseille
Cistercian monastery
Castle/town
Templar commandery
(Arch)bishopric
0
50
100 km
0
25
50 miles
T49 Perpignan
T50 Peyrat
T51 Pézenas
T52 Pont-St-Esprit
T53 Puy-en-Velay
T54 Richerenches
T55 Roaix
T56 St-Gilles
T57 St-Michel-de-Bannières
T58 St-Paul-Trois-Châteaux
T59 St-Roman
T60 Ste-Eulalie-de-Cernon
T61 Ste-Marie-des-Cours
T62 Salles-sur-Garonne
T63 La Selve
T64 Tarascon
T65 Tiberet
T66 Toulouse
T67 Vaour
T68 La Ville-Dieu-du-Temple
Cistercians
C1 Ardorel
C2 Beaulieu
C4 Belloc
C3 Belleperche
C5 Berdoues
C6 Bonnecombe
C7 Bonnefont
C8 Bonneval
C9 Bouillas
C10 Boulbonne
C11 Calers
C12 Candeil
C13 Eaunes
C14 L'Escaladieu
C15 L'Eule
C16 Les Feuillants
C17 Flaran
C18 Fontfroide
C19 Franquevaux
C20 La Garde-Dieu
C21 La Grâce-Dieu
C22 Gimont
C23 Goïon
C24 Gourdon (Abbaye-Nouvelle)
C25 Grandselve
C26 Leyme
C27 Lissac
C28 Loc-Dieu
C29 Mareux
C30 Mercoire
C31 Netlieu
C32 Nizors
C33 Nonenque
C34 Le Jau
C35 Les Olieux
C36 L'Oraison-Dieu
C37 Le Pérouse
C38 Rieunette
C39 Fonts-lès-Alais
C40 St-Félix-de-Montceau
C41 St-Marcel
C42 St-Sulpice
C43 Sauveréal
C44 Sénanque
C45 Sylvanès
C46 Valbonne
C47 Valmagne
C48 Valnègre
C49 Valsauve
C50 Le Vignogoul
C51 Villelongue
Families
F1 Abeihan
F2 Aragon
F3 Aspet
F4 Aure
F5 Auriac-Lagast
F6 Barbaira
F7 Baux
F8 Bessan
F9 Calmont
F10 Canet
F11 Canet
F12 Canet-d'Olt
F13 Cardailhac
F14 Comminges
F15 Capendu
F16 Combret
F17 Cornus
F18 Durban
F19 Durfort
F20 Espaon
F21 Gaure
F22 Luzençon
F23 Martres-Tolosane
F24 Montlaur
F25 Montlaur
F26 Montlaur
F27 Montpezat
F28 Montpezat-sous-Bauzon
F29 Moussac
F30 Pignan
F31 Polignac
F32 Pomérols
F33 Pont
F34 Posquières
F35 Roquefort
F36 St-Couat
F37 St-Gaudens
F38 Terzac

of Dijon.[25] One of his relations was the famous Cistercian abbot Bernard of Clairvaux, who was well known, and liked, by both Hugh of Troyes and Thibaud II.[26]

Since networks created by kinship and marriage ties are at the heart of my investigation it has become necessary for me at times to extend my genealogical and prosopographical research beyond the perceived borders of Burgundy, Champagne and modern-day Languedoc into adjacent regions. Marriage contracts, like feudal contracts, connected landowning families in the duchy of Burgundy and the county of Champagne not only to each other but also to families in, for example, the imperial county of Burgundy, Flanders, and Picardy, and to knights and nobles from what we call Languedoc with families in the marquisat and county of Provence, Gascony, Limousin and Auvergne, and, across the Pyrenees, in the county of Barcelona and the kingdom of Aragon. Material from all these regions has been used, at one point or another, in this book. Equally important for the decision occasionally to look beyond the geographical borders of Burgundy, Champagne and Languedoc was the early realisation that recent research into in particular the rich archival records of Templar and Hospitaller commanderies in Provence, but also into other archival sources pertaining to noble families, provide an exceptionally rich well of material from which additional examples and comparisons can be drawn. In the case of Languedoc, the occasional peek across the borders into Provence carried the additional benefit that it allowed me to draw upon the excellent recent research on noble families, power and the Church in medieval Provence by Florian Mazel and on the development of the Order of the Temple as a religious, economic and political power player in that region by Damien Carraz.[27]

METHODOLOGY

In recent years historians have demonstrated that kinship networks played an important role in creating and maintaining a 'crusading ethos' among European landed families.[28] They have also illustrated the close personal links which tied medieval noble and knightly families to local religious communities and which make it difficult for us to distinguish between knights and ecclesiastics as members of two distinct orders of

[25] M. Bur, 'Le monachisme en Champagne méridionale et dans le nord du diocèse de Langres à l'arrivée de saint Bernard à Clairvaux en 1115', in M. Bur, *La Champagne médiévale* (Langres, 2005), 620–1.

[26] Evergates, *Aristocracy*, p. 12.

[27] F. Mazel, *La noblesse et l'église en Provence, fin* x^e^*–début* xive *siècle. L'exemple des familles d'Agoult-Simiane, de Baux et de Marseille* (Paris, 2002); Carraz, *L'ordre du Temple*.

[28] Bull, *Knightly piety*; J. S. C. Riley-Smith, *The First Crusaders, 1095–1131* (Cambridge, 1997).

society.[29] Familial bonds between knights and monks encouraged mutual influences. Ideas of the world were carried into the monastery and monks incorporated them into their concepts of belief, which they then shared with their armsbearing relatives. What has also become clear is that an investigation of family influences in religious institutions and social movements can enhance and alter our understanding of how medieval institutions functioned and how and from where society received its impulses.

This book examines the involvement of armsbearing families in the Order of the Temple in three regions of France that had from the start demonstrated a keen interest in new forms of religious life and in crusading. On the one hand it attempts to show that in these regions particular families associated themselves with local Templar communities for many generations and provided the Order with much of its material, landed resources and personnel. On the other hand it seeks to illustrate why, how and under what circumstances families turned their attention to the Templars, and how these families were interrelated. Rather than assessing the Order by its structural, organisational and political development, this book therefore emphasises the remarkable achievement of the Templars in gaining and holding the attention and commitment of landed families for almost two centuries.

Any concept with the term 'family' in the label is necessarily loaded with ambiguity, and much of what can be said about Templar families depends on how the term 'family' in general and the term 'Templar family' in particular are defined. By 'families' I mean units within a kin-group, that is: people who were related to one another by blood or marriage, and not the medieval *familia*, which was a product of both kinship and feudal ties. This narrower definition brings its own problems, the two most important ones being that relatives were not necessarily always known to each other and that an individual's social network did not necessarily neatly overlap with the group of people to whom she or he was related by blood.[30] Social historians now seem to agree that the medieval family was an ever-changing construct that included new members and omitted old ones according to the preferences and marriage arrangements of individuals.[31] Its shifting nature was not necessarily determined by patrilineage but more by 'the residential unit formed by

[29] Bull, *Knightly piety*, pp. 115–203; Bouchard, *Sword, miter, and cloister*; C. B. Bouchard, *Strong of body, brave and noble: chivalry and society in medieval France* (Ithaca, N.Y., London, 1998), pp. 145–71. See also J. Dunbabin, 'From clerk to knight: changing orders', in C. Harper-Bill and R. E. Harvey (eds.), *The ideas and practices of medieval knighthood II* (Woodbridge, 1988), 26–39.

[30] Duhamel-Amado, *Genèse*, I, pp. 87–8.

[31] C. B. Bouchard, *Those of my blood: constructing noble families in medieval Francia* (Philadelphia, Pa., 2001), in particular pp. 2–4.

the married couple'.[32] For this reason it is often difficult for the historian to establish who was and was not considered a family member in medieval times. Moreover, what we would today regard as individual family units would in the eleventh or even thirteenth centuries have been regarded as components of much larger entities, which historians today sometimes call clan or simply kinship groups. Although these larger groups were also subject to change over time, they nonetheless 'existed through time and space'.[33] Therefore they allow for a long-term analysis of concepts of belief and conduct that developed and existed among individuals within them.

Examining kinship networks rather than family units in the narrow sense enables us to overcome some of the difficulties generally experienced by medievalists concerned with the social background of religious communities, because it allows consideration of a variety of forms of family relationship. Another way to circumvent problems, in particular those created by a limited source base, is to expand the concept of the 'Templar family' to include families that supported the Order personally and materially over many years but may not have provided it with recruits. All these families could of course be noble or non-noble, but because the deeds and actions of non-nobles are notoriously difficult to trace in the charters, I have mainly restricted myself to the examination of landed families – and thus to those families from whom the Templars recruited most of their knights.

Difficulties with Templar families, and the individuals who constituted them, still abound. Identifying a Templar's or donor's lineage and pedigree is one problem. Although the exact origin of individual Templars cannot always be established, as so many of them were of low noble or non-noble stock, the editors and historians of Templar cartularies tend to agree that the toponyms serving as surnames indicate local recruitment. Of course, onomastic evidence alone does not prove that these Templars were necessarily related to every benefactor and business associate of the Order identified by the same toponym. In fact, Templar charters are full of references to brothers whose surnames, although they suggest a local origin, do not match the names of any known benefactor. Since it was customary for recruits to accompany their entry into the Order with a gift, however, and since many Templars whose family names do not match those of any of the Order's benefactors nonetheless often had fathers, sons, uncles and nephews who witnessed charters or joined the Order, it seems

[32] Evergates, *Aristocracy*, pp. 82–8 (quotation, p. 88).

[33] G. Althoff, *Family, friends and followers: political and social bonds in medieval Europe*, trans. C. Carroll (Cambridge, 2004), pp. 25–6, and Bouchard, *Those of my blood*, p. 2 for the quotation.

that the involvement of families with nearby Templar communities was usually more intense than the scattered sources suggest.

Toponymic surnames do not necessarily imply knightly or noble stock, nor do they necessarily imply that the people bearing them were attached to a castle. Moreover, as has recently been shown, in the twelfth century still only a minority of nobles in Burgundy would have possessed castles and not every castle was held by a nobleman.[34] Within some families members changed toponyms so often that it is hard to keep track of them and connect them with others by name reference alone.[35] Even Templar knights were sometimes referred to by different names. The brother knight Hugh of Chalon, for example, who was identified by this name on a number of occasions during the hearings of the papal commission in 1310, seems to have been identical with the brother knight Hugh of Villiers, who, like him, was recorded as preceptor of Épailly in Burgundy in *c.* 1294.[36] Among medieval scribes, and possibly within the Order itself, it seems to have been common to identify Templar sergeants (and also some knights) by the commanderies into which they had been received or in which they were resident.[37] Because of the great number of communities that existed in France at the end of the thirteenth century it is often difficult to distinguish Templars who came from families which identified themselves by reference to particular villages and *castra* (singular *castrum*, a fortified town or castle) from those of unknown origin, who were, or at one time had been, resident in commanderies located in these places. This, of course, does not exclude the possibility of a kin-relationship between the Templars concerned; but it often makes such a relationship impossible to prove.

Two other difficulties are linked to the fact that castellan and other noble families often shared toponyms with the knights and other members of their household and that popular toponyms, such as Rochefort (*Rocaforte, Rupe Forti*), which was particularly common in southern

[34] H. Mouillebouche, *Les maisons fortes en Bourgogne du nord du XIIIᵉ au XVIᵉ s.* (Dijon, 2002), pp. 251–69.

[35] Bouchard, *Those of my blood*, pp. 6–10. Problems concerning the genealogy of medieval families and the creation of genealogy tables are discussed in the essays collected in G. T. Beech *et al.* (eds.), *Personal name studies of medieval Europe. Social identity and family structures* (Kalamazoo, Mich., 2002), as well as in Duhamel-Amado, *Genèse*, and C. Klapisch-Zuber, *L'ombre des ancêtres: essai sur l'imaginaire médiéval de la parenté* (Paris, 2000).

[36] For Hugh of Chalon as preceptor of Épailly in 1294 see *PT*, 1, p. 628. The fact that he was probably identical with Hugh of Villiers, who was recorded holding the same office from *c.* 1293 until 1301, has already been noted in E.-G. Léonard, *Introduction au cartulaire manuscrit du Temple (1150–1317), constitué par le marquis d'Albon et conservé à la Bibliothèque nationale, suivie d'un Tableau des maisons françaises du Temple et de leurs précepteurs* (Paris, 1930), p. 151.

[37] C. Lavirotte, "Mémoire statistique sur les établissements des templiers et des hospitaliers de Saint-Jean de Jérusalem en Bourgogne', *Congrès archéologique de France*, 19 (1853), 236–7fn.

France, could refer to more than one place. For example, it is difficult to establish whether the Templar brothers Hugh, Itier and John of Rochefort or Roquefort, who were recorded in the charters of the commanderies of Valence (Hugh, 1204–9), Douzens, Marseille, Carcassonne (Itier, 1276–1307) and Carcassonne, Roaix, Toulouse and Laramet (John, 1234–58) respectively, were related to each other.[38] It is equally difficult to tell whether any or all of them came from the family of Roquefort near Ste-Eulalie,[39] or the family of Roquefort near Marseille,[40] or the family of Roquefort near Montsaunès,[41] all of which had produced Templars or Templar benefactors.

Prosopographical and genealogical research always involves some speculation. The responsibility of the historian is to keep this speculation to a minimum and, if necessary, to call it by its name. Combining the study of surnames with the study of first names often helps to narrow down the group of likely relatives, if the investigation is confined to a geographically limited area. The marriage arrangements and lordship ties of families indicate the set of toponyms that family members may have used as names of reference. The religious behaviour of individuals, which is often expressed in their association with particular monasteries or churches, helps identify patterns of beliefs and conduct that were characteristic of particular groups of individuals with matching surnames but alien to others. The geographical location of the religious institutions with which particular individuals associated also helps to distinguish between groups of similar-minded individuals who, if other criteria such as a common name also apply, could have been related to one another.

For some aspects of my investigation into the social background of Templar communities I have relied on the genealogical and prosopographical research of other scholars, notably Bouchard, Duhamel-Amado, Evergates and the contributors to Wilhelm Isenburg's *Stammtafeln*.[42] Most of the information that I have worked into my chapters, however, I have

[38] For Hugh of Rochefort see Léonard, *Introduction*, p. 41; for Itier of Rochefort see K. Schottmüller, *Der Untergang des Templerordens mit urkundlichen und kritischen Beiträgen*, 2 vols. (Berlin, 1887), II, pp. 47–8; Léonard, *Introduction*, p. 57; *CadC*, I, p. 335; for John of Rochefort see Léonard, *Introduction*, pp. 57, 76, 78, 79.

[39] See J. Delmas, 'L'inventaire des biens de la commanderie de Sainte-Eulalie du Larzac en 1308', in A. Luttrell and L. Pressouyre (eds.), *La commanderie, institution des ordres militaires dans l'Occident médiéval* (Paris, 2002), p. 321 (map).

[40] M. Aurell i Cardona, 'Les cisterciennes et leurs protecteurs en Provence rhodanienne', in *Les cisterciens de Languedoc (13e–14e s.)*, CdF, XXI (Toulouse, 1986), 246–50.

[41] C. Higounet, *Le comté de Comminges de ses origines à son annexion à la couronne*, 2 vols. (Toulouse, 1949), I, pp. 265–7.

[42] W.K. Isenburg, F. Freytag von Loringhoven and D. Schwennicke, *Europäische Stammtafeln: Stammtafeln zur Geschichte der europäischen Staaten* (Berlin, Marburg, 1936–78); Bouchard, *Sword, miter, and cloister*, pp. 255–431; Duhamel-Amado, *Genèse*; Evergates, *Aristocracy*.

drawn directly from the charters. And the more charters I consulted the more visible my network of Templar families became. In cases of doubt I have indicated in the text that my interpretation is tentative.

THE SOURCES

Since the central archive of the Temple has disappeared, any assessment of the Order's social history has to rely on the archives of western commanderies, which are scattered throughout Europe. Templar communities, like monasteries, attached importance to the fact that transactions affecting their patrimony were recorded in writing and the records stored, both to keep an inventory of the commandery's possessions and to have evidence that could be used against claimants: *utile est scribi quod non convenit oblivisci*.[43] The charters, if they have survived, tell us about the ways and methods by which Templar communities had obtained certain property (by grant, purchase, pledge or lease) and about the circumstances under which they had done so. They also include information on the individuals and families who had engaged with the Order by means of these transactions and give insight into their motives. Without charters we would know very little about the families on whose help and support the survival and development of the Templar communities in East and West depended.

Charters are stylised documents in which repetitious formulae are employed to convey the legal implications of transactions.[44] They do not provide verbatim accounts of how these transactions were conducted. It is therefore not always possible to establish how much of what was written had actually been said. Some scribes used standard formulae, which could be described as their trademark. 'Peter, monk and priest' (*Petrus monachus et sacerdos*), for example, who recorded Templar charters in Roussillon in the 1130s, habitually ended his charters with the warning that whoever should act against the agreement recorded would be scorned until compensation had been made.[45] As it is very unlikely that donors would ratify a document if they did not approve of its content and language, however, the least that can be said about the motives for donations as described in the charters is that they reflected an interpretation of the event and its underlying intentions that donors could accept.

[43] 'It is useful to write down what is not fitting to forget': AN, S 5038, dossier 101, no. 2 (BN, n.a.l., 51, fols. 9r–10r) (1192×1193).

[44] On this topic see M. Gervers and N. Hamonic, 'Scribes and notaries in twelfth- and thirteenth-century Hospitaller charters from England', in K. Borchardt, N. Jaspert and H. J. Nicholson (eds.), *The Hospitallers, the Mediterranean and Europe. Festschrift for Anthony Luttrell* (Aldershot, 2007), 181–92.

[45] See e.g. *CG*, no. 48, p. 37 (1132), and no. 68, pp. 51–2 (1133).

The silence of the sources poses another problem. The absence of charter evidence for ties between families and Templars is not sufficient proof that such ties did not exist. Donations and sales were selectively recorded. And pledges, if redeemed, are now usually lost. The value of the object that was given or otherwise transferred to the Order played a role in the decision whether or not a transaction was worth recording, as did the likelihood of a later revocation of the act by the donor or his or her heirs. We know from pancartes, which contain abstracts of donations made to particular religious communities over a certain period of time, that among the benefactors of the Temple were also individuals and families of low social standing and with little financial means. Their gifts to the Templars consisted of garments, buckets of wax or candles, rather than seigniorial rights, lands and revenues. But only few individual charters are dedicated to such smaller endowments. The charters, therefore, tell us much about the interrelationship between the Order and families with enough assets to make noteworthy contributions to its wealth and patrimony and little about its relationship with individuals and families without such assets. For every recorded donation there are a multitude of transactions that were never documented or of which the documentation has not survived.

Some Templar communities provided their own scribes and some had the facilities to produce, multiply and store charters. Douzens near Carcassonne, for example, seems to have been in possession of its own scriptorium, in which William of Palacio issued documents and copied them into cartularies for almost thirty years, from 1172 until 1199.[46] William of Palacio never referred to himself as a *frater* of the Temple, however, and seems in fact to have been a hired hand or a lay associate. His position in the Order would not have been unique. It was customary for the Templars to rely on outside help for the task of recording their daily business. Literacy was not a requirement for entry; and within the Order it was not encouraged.[47] Occasionally, the Templars received the help of monks and priests who were trained in letters. I have already referred to 'Peter, monk and priest', who was the scribe of a number of Templar charters from Roussillon in the early 1130s.[48] In particular in southern

[46] *Cart Douz*, pp. xii–xiv; É. Delaruelle, 'Templiers et hospitaliers en Languedoc pendant la croisade des Albigeois', in *Paix de Dieu et guerre sainte en Languedoc au* XIII*e* *siècle*, CdF, IV (Toulouse, 1969), p. 318. See also D. le Blévec and A. Venturini, 'Cartulaires des ordres militaires, XIIe–XIIIe siècles (Provence occidentale – Basse vallée du Rhône)', in O. Guyotjeannin, L. Morelle and M. Parisse (eds.), *Les cartulaires. Actes de la table ronde organisée par l'École nationale des chartes et le G.D.R. 121 du C.N.R.S., Paris, 5–7 décembre 1991*, Mémoires et documents de l'École des Chartes, 39 (Paris, 1993), 453.

[47] See A.J. Forey, 'Novitiate and instruction in the military orders in the twelfth and thirteenth centuries', *Speculum*, 61 (1986), passim.

[48] See fn. 45 above.

France since the mid twelfth century (but to a lesser degree the further north one goes) the Order employed the help and expertise of notaries who at worst 'simply copied routine kinds of documents out of a form book and adapted them to their clients' needs by filling in the appropriate names and dates' or, if they were better qualified, were 'able to prepare original documents that accurately described fairly complex transactions'. The more elite notaries had acquired knowledge of law at a university, but it is unlikely that middling commanderies in rural settings would have hired them.[49] In the thirteenth century notaries who were public officials (the so-called *notarii publici*) took over some of the functions of plain notaries, a move that greatly increased the reliability of the documents.[50] In the late thirteenth century, for example, the Templars of La Selve in Aveyron used as their scribe B. de Vares, who was also the public notary of Marcillac, Cassagnes and Clairvaux–d'Aveyron.[51]

Many archives have fallen victim to fire or war, with the consequence that for some Templar houses, as for many other religious communities, only charter inventories have survived. In spite of these hazards, however, the documentary evidence for the Temple in France, and particularly in Burgundy, Champagne and Languedoc, is rich, with many sources still untapped. But accessibility can be a problem. Only a small percentage of the surviving Templar documents of France has ever been published; the rest are scattered among departmental and municipal archives where they are often interspersed with material pertaining to the Order of the Hospital, which inherited the Templar archives after 1312. Moreover, few charters have survived being copied unscathed. Generations of copyists have weeded out the archives, stripping some title-deeds to the bone and omitting others completely. Some charter collections have been copied or transcribed into user-friendly cartularies and in the process standard formulae have often been abandoned, deeds paraphrased and witness lists abbreviated or summarised.[52]

[49] J. A. Brundage, *The medieval origins of the legal profession: canonists, civilians, and courts* (Chicago, Ill., London, 2008), pp. 394–406; for the quotations see pp. 394–5.

[50] Ibid., pp. 212–13.

[51] See e.g. the testament of William of Combret: 'B. de Vares publicus notarius de Marrilhaco de Cassanens pro illustri domino comite Ruthenae, notariusque publicus de Clarisvallibus, et domus militiae Templi de Silva...', Doat, 41, fols. 59–62 (1286). The Templars of Golfech also used public notaries in the thirteenth century. See *Doc Dur*, I, no. 33, pp. 24–5 (1242) and no. 35, p. 26 (1245).

[52] D. Walker, 'The organisation of material in medieval cartularies', in D. A. Bullough and R. L. Storey (eds.), *The study of medieval records: essays in honour of Kathleen Major* (Oxford, 1971), and p. Chastang, *Lire, écrire, transcrire: le travail des rédacteurs de cartulaires en Bas-Languedoc, XIe–XIIIe siècles* (Paris, 2001), both passim; L. Morelle, 'De l'original à la copie: remarques sur l'évaluation des transcriptions dans les cartularies médiévaux', in O. Guyotjeannin, L. Morelle and M. Parisse (eds.),

Despite these shortcomings, the cartularies are the single most important source for an examination of the Order's social context from a grass-roots perspective, because they constitute a condensed history of the commanderies' economic transactions and their dealings with society. It is therefore unfortunate that only few Templar communities seem to have compiled them, as has been demonstrated for Provence.[53] A number of Templar cartularies and charter collections from Burgundy, Champagne and southern France have been published and are available in printed form. In the course of my research I have consulted most of them. In particular I have made use of the published charters and cartularies (or what is left of them) of Neuville, Le Puy(-en-Velay), Vaour, St-Marc/St-Medard, Richerenches, Provins, Montsaunès, Douzens, Roaix and La Selve.[54] To these must be added the collections of charters, charter transcripts and charter references published by Claude Brunel,[55] Dom Claude Devic and Dom Joseph Vaissette;[56] and Jacques Miquel[57] for Languedoc, and by Ernest Petit for the duchy of Burgundy.[58] It was only after I had completed the draft of this book that I received a copy of the third volume of Carraz's doctoral dissertation containing copies or transcripts of all Templar charters relating to the Templar communities of Arles, Tarascon–Laurade–Lansac, Avignon, Montfrin and Gard rhodanien, and St-Gilles. Owing to the time restrictions to which I was by then subject I have not been able to give these sources the recognition they undoubtedly deserve in this book. Nonetheless, I have been able to include at least some of them.[59]

Most of my material, however, I have taken from rich archives of Champagne that now form part of Series S in the Archives Nationales (AN) in Paris, the Archives départementales de la Côte-d'Or in Dijon, and from the treasure trove for historians of the Order that is the *Cartulaire manuscrit d'Albon* in the Bibliothèque Nationale in Paris. Comprising

Les cartulaires. Actes de la table ronde organisée par l'École nationale des chartes et le G.D.R. 121 du C.N.R.S., Paris, 5–7 décembre 1991, Mémoires et documents de l'École des Chartes, 39 (Paris, 1993), in particular p. 95.

53 Blévec and Venturini, 'Cartulaires', pp. 451–65.

54 *Diocèse ancien de Châlons-sur-Marne, histoire et monuments. Suivi des cartulaires inédits de la commanderie de la Neuville-au-Temple, des abbayes de Toussaints, de Monstiers et du prieuré de Vinetz*, ed. É. de Barthélemy, 2 vols. (Paris, Chaumont, Châlons-sus-Marne, 1861), I, pp. 394–435; *Cart Puy*; *Cart Vaour*; *Chart St-Marc/Jully*; *Cart Rich*; *Cart Prov*; *Cart Mont*; *Cart Douz*; *Chart Roais*; *Cart LaS.*

55 *PAC.* 56 *HGL.*

57 J. Miquel, *État des sources archivistiques et bibliographie des commanderies templières et hospitalières du Rouergue du XIIème au XVIIIème siècle* (Unpublished document available from Conservatoire Larzac Templier et Hospitalier).

58 *HdB*, II–V.

59 D. Carraz, *Ordres militaires, croisades et sociétés méridionales. L'ordre du Temple dans la basse vallée du Rhône (1124–1312)*, 3 vols. (Ph.D. thesis, Lyon: Université de Lyon 2, 2003). I am extremely grateful to Dr Carraz for allowing me to use vol. III of his dissertation.

seventy-one volumes (BN, n.a.l. 1–71), the *Cartulaire*, which supplements Albon's published volume of early Templar charters (*c.* 1119 until 1150), contains thousands of transcripts of Templar charters from all regions of France. The material is arranged geographically. A table of contents, an introduction to the *Cartulaire* and a list of Templar preceptors have been provided by Émile Léonard.[60]

Because the involvement of families in the Temple was often spasmodic, re-creating Templar families only on the basis of the information obtained from Templar charters is a difficult and unrewarding task. Some 'Templar families' have left more traces in the documents of monastic communities than they have in the charters of the Temple. Since they provide evidence of their overall religious activity, I have therefore consulted religious cartularies for supplementary information about the men and women involved with the Temple. I have also used these sources to illustrate the associations of these families with religious communities other than the Temple and their involvement in crusading, which were two factors that seem to have influenced families to turn their attention to the Order in the first place.

STRUCTURE

At the core of this book lies the thesis that the Templars received much of their support from noble and knightly families who were deeply affected by ideas of religious reform, deeply involved in the crusading movement and often closely related to one another. The book is organised into five chapters. The first discusses in general terms the different forms of involvement with the Order to be found among those who were not fully professed. It thus sets the parameters for 'Templar families' by discussing the different incentives behind individual transactions, as well as some of their social meaning and consequences (a topic that is again picked up in Chapter 3). Forms of lay association are of particular interest in this respect and a large part of the chapter is dedicated to explaining them. Determining lay association with the Order of the Temple is not as straightforward as one may hope, for the terminology that scribes used to describe association with the Order is ambiguous at best and at times misleading. The problem that has puzzled scholars the most is the distinction between *(con)fratres* and *donati* (and *(con)sorores* and *donatae*) which some have regarded as simply synonymous but which others have maintained constituted two very distinct forms of lay association, the first being

60 Léonard, *Introduction*.

gradually replaced by the other. I will argue that the two concepts coexisted within the Order from very early on and were complementary rather than exclusive. However, at the turn of the twelfth century the constellation of the Order's confraternities underwent drastic changes that had been instigated by canon lawyers and formulated in the decrees of Lateran III and IV. As a response the donats (i.e. *donati/ae*), as a particular category of *confratres*, established themselves as the most prominent expression of lay association with the Temple . What is more, since the concept of the donat gained prominence when that of the Templar novice was in decline, it can be argued that, for very different reasons, the concept of the Templar donat as well as that of the 'temporary knight' (*miles ad terminum*), which was as old as the Order itself, could eventually have been conceived and employed as two forms of novitiate in disguise, which helped attract the attention of laymen who would have otherwise been reluctant to profess fully into a military order.

The interplay of reformist religious (in particular Cistercian) expansion and increasing family involvement in the Order of the Temple in the twelfth and thirteenth centuries is the subject of my second chapter. Channels of kinship and feudal obligations which become apparent in the charters recording Templar endowments and transactions allowed religious ideas and influences to flow freely across the feudal landscapes of northern and southern France, regardless of political and geographical boundaries, sometimes flooding entire kinship networks with new religious fervour. The Order of the Temple benefited from this situation as much as any other religious order, as is manifested in the large number of houses it was able to establish.[61]

Judging by the number of foundations, the Templars seem to have been particularly popular in the border region between Burgundy and Champagne, which constitutes, roughly, the diocese of Langres.[62] The bishops of Langres were powerful lords both in the county and in the

[61] For the Order's establishments in Burgundy and Champagne see Richard, 'Les templiers et les hospitaliers', passim; M. Mignard, 'Statistique de la milice du Temple en Bourgogne et importance du Grand Prieuré de Champagne qui avait son siège à Voulaine (Côte-d'Or)', *Congrès Archéologique de France*, 19 (1852–3), 205–16; T. Boutiot, 'Les templiers et leurs établissements dans la Champagne méridionale', *Annuaire administrative de l'Aube*, 41 (1866), 27–56; A. Roserot, *Dictionnaire historique de la Champagne méridionale (Aube) des origines à 1790*, 4 vols. (Angers, 1942–8). Templar establishments in Mâcon are included in A. de Charmasse, 'État des possessions des templiers et des hospitaliers en Mâconnais, Charollais, Lyonnais et Forez', *Mémoires de la Société Éduenne* (1879), 105–47.

[62] Marie, *Templiers de Langres*, passim; J. Laurent and F. Claudon (eds.), *Abbayes et prieurés de l'ancienne France, vol. XII: Province ecclésiastique de Lyon, part III: Diocèses de Langres et de Dijon* (Ligugé, 1941); C.-F. Roussel, 'Les templiers dans le diocèse de Langres à l'époque de leur suppression', *Revue de Champagne et de Brie*, 16 (1884), 401–13.

duchy – by 1105 they commanded more than nineteen castles, including Tonnerre, Tilchâtel, Châtillon, Saulx, Grancey, Bar-sur-Aube and Bar-sur-Seine. Their goodwill was therefore instrumental in the Templars' success in the diocese. Expressions of that goodwill were manifold, ranging from generous donations of lands and feudal rights to official confirmations of benefactions made by the bishops' vassals and rear-vassals to Templars in the diocese. One donation, made by the knight Payen of Bure, a rear-vassal of the bishop of Langres, led in 1133 to the foundation of an important Templar commandery at Bure. Substantial donations were also made by other vassals of the bishop, including the counts of Saulx and the lords of Grancey, who became loyal patrons of Templar Bure, and the lords of Tilchâtel.

The first decades of the twelfth century not only witnessed the rise of the Templars in Burgundy and Champagne. It was also the time of rapid Cistercian expansion in the region, an expansion that was largely fed by benefactions and recruitment from the same families that one encounters in Templar charters and that benefited greatly from the support of the bishops of Langres. Sympathy for reformist ideas as expressed by the Cistercians (but also by Carthusians and others) and engagement with the Templars, in other words, seem to have gone hand in hand in many families and were also found in a number of senior ecclesiastics (who often shared the social background of the knights and nobles among whom the Templars recruited most heavily). In the south of France, the situation was different in that the Cistercian Order became a firmly established feature of the religious landscape at a later date than in Burgundy or Champagne and that the chronology of a family's involvement in the orders of the Temple and Cîteaux therefore often put the Temple first. Digging at a deeper level, however, it becomes apparent that families with Templar ties also exhibited a high level of previous attachment to eremitical communities that eventually became absorbed into the Cistercian Order. The situation in southern France was similar to that in Burgundy and Champagne in that here, too, as Carraz has shown for Provence, bishops with a reformist outlook acted as influential patrons of the Order.[63]

Discussing these themes, the second chapter puts family involvement in the Temple into a religious context by juxtaposing it with the activity of the same families with respect to other religious institutions. It investigates in particular the role of relatives of Bernard of Clairvaux in the development of Templar and Cistercian communities in Burgundy and Champagne and the influence of families with links to the eremitical

[63] Carraz, *L'ordre du Temple*, pp. 134–46.

(proto-Cistercian) movement on the early development of the Temple in the south of France.

The third and fourth chapters discuss family networks and some of their social meanings and practical consequences. Medieval men and women were bound by social contracts that informed, determined and restricted their every move and action. This was true even if the individual acted against the contract, in which case it informed and determined the retribution that followed. The ties that these contracts generated are most easily discernible in the names of witnesses, arbitrators, *laudatores* and *confirmatores* recorded in charters.[64] They illustrate clearly the manifold obligations towards lords, 'friends' (a term that needs to be explained), relatives and in-laws (most of whom would have some claim or other on the property in question) that needed to be considered if a donation to a Templar or other religious community were to be made. The transactions in which families engaged with the Templars resulted in the foundation and consolidation of commanderies. These subsequently served the Templars as hubs for widespread networks of dependent houses, including granges and city dwellings, which centred on individual commanderies.[65] Equally important, these transactions, in particular if they included fiscal and seigniorial rights, allowed the Templars to plug into the circuit of feudal agreements between lords and vassals, who in turn were forced by changes to the contracts to meet the Templars on the doorsteps of their commanderies to negotiate their relationship.

Focusing on the feudal and kinship dynamics and how they helped in the establishment and development of new religious foundations like Templar communities – an act that, as one historian stated in a different context, was 'frequently the expression of corporate solidarity within a feudal grouping' – the chapters illustrate how Templar-supporting family networks came into being and what forms they could take.[66] Chapter 3 examines the impulses that caused families to become involved with particular commanderies and discusses in particular the influence of women and the role of marriage ties in these decisions.

Scholarship in the last decades has done much to modify the commonly held view that changes in inheritance patterns and the development of a patrilineal family model in the eleventh and early twelfth centuries reduced the access of noblewomen to property and diminished women's

[64] S.D. White, *Custom, kinship, and gifts to saints: the* laudatio parentum *in western France, 1050–1150* (Chapel Hill, N.C., 1988).

[65] Bure, for example, eventually presided over sixteen dependencies. See Marie, *Templiers de Langres*, pp. 40–1.

[66] For the quotation see C. Harper-Bill, 'The piety of the Anglo-Norman knightly class', *Anglo-Norman Studies*, 2 (1979), 67.

influence within the family.[67] Two decades ago Amy Livingstone argued convincingly that in the region of Blois–Chartres in the early twelfth century at least, women in all stages of life exercised authority over land and resources in various ways and made 'individual and independent' donations;[68] since then other scholars, most recently Evergates in his seminal study of aristocratic families in the county of Champagne in the high middle ages, have reached similar conclusions for other parts of northern France.[69] In the south of France noblewomen in particular seem to have enjoyed greater political and economic power than their northern French counterparts before the twelfth centuries and could still wield considerable power in the twelfth and thirteenth centuries, although in general (and allowing for considerable regional differences) the economic assets at their disposal seem to have declined over time and their position in society to some degree seems to have deteriorated.[70]

As I will show, the evidence from Templar charters in particular from Burgundy and Champagne suggests that wives, daughters and widows played a crucial role in advertising Templar support (that is support for particular Templar communities) among in-law families. Their role in placing the Temple firmly on the mental map of their offspring should not be underestimated, in spite of the fact that the direction of knowledge transfer within networks created by marriage (or otherwise) can seldom be determined with any precision and that, in fact, enthusiasm for the Temple seems to have flared up simultaneously at different ends of the network amongst families unknown to each other.

There are some important caveats to consider if medievalists want to engage in network analysis. One, of course, is that networks can be constructed around pretty much anything and are not necessarily evidence of a collective awareness. In the middle ages (as today) individual actions were largely determined by convenience rather than conviction and then as now these conveniences were often shared by people who otherwise had little in common. Another would be that of course 'all aristocracy belongs to a network of blood and collateral relatives', as George Beech rightly pointed out when discussing Riley-Smith's *First Crusaders*, and that 'the actions and moves of individual members were not necessarily calculated to advocate any collective goals'. Individuals did seek to advance

[67] G. Duby, *Medieval marriage: two models from twelfth-century France*, trans. E. Forster (Baltimore, Md., London, 1978); J. Goody, *The development of the family and marriage in Europe* (Cambridge, New York, 1983); D. Herlihy, *Medieval households* (Cambridge, Mass., 1985). See also the discussion in A. F. Livingstone, 'Noblewomen's control of property in early twelfth-century Blois–Chartres', *Medieval Prosopography*, 18 (1997), 55–71.

[68] Ibid., in particular pp. 56 and 58. [69] Evergates, *Aristocracy*, in particular pp. 101–25.

[70] Paterson, *World of the troubadours*, in particular pp. 220–8.

their personal interests and their individual actions were not always 'part of a collective family strategy'.[71]

Both these caveats have to be considered carefully when embarking on the enterprise of connecting people and families, as I do in Chapter 4. But they do not diminish the value of the exercise. Rather than unmasking a grand strategy of kin-groups to pursue collective ambitions, establishing ties of friendship, kinship or lordship between individuals engaged in similar exercises, and analysing these exercises, allows us to gain a better understanding of the forces and influences that created the canvas on which individual members of these groups painted their goals, fears and ambitions. It allows us, in other words, to capture some of the mental map that guided their decisions.

The fact that all aristocracy belonged to 'networks of blood and relations' must not detract from the fact that some of these networks displayed very clearly their particular religious preferences, that some provided a multitude of crusaders within single generations whereas others did not, and that particular patterns can be observed when eithes was the case. As has recently been shown, for example, the counts of the Perche (the Rotrou family) were involved with the Cistercians and Carthusians and heavily involved in crusading from the late eleventh until the beginning of the thirteenth century. From this melange (enthusiasm for crusading and commitment to reform monasticism), interest in the Temple could blossom: Rotrou II, a veteran of the First Crusade, endowed the Templars with some of his interests in Zaragoza before his death, in Spain, in 1144; Rotrou III made his first benefactions during the siege of Acre in 1191, soon before his death; and his son Stephen gave them certain holdings and woodland before departing on the Fourth Crusade.[72]

The importance of the crusade experience for family patronage of Templar communities is the topic of Chapter 5. What set the Templars and members of other military orders apart from their traditional religious contemporaries was their commitment to crusading and to the Holy Land. The Order of the Temple had been founded, and was organised, for the sole purpose of safeguarding the routes to Jerusalem and guaranteeing the continued defence, or recovery, of the holy places. From letters, chronicles, songs and charters we can today conclude that the efforts of the Templars in the Holy Land were enormous and their death toll often

[71] See George T. Beech's review of Riley-Smith, *First Crusaders*, in *Medieval Prosopography*, 19 (1998), 77–80.

[72] K. H. Thompson, 'Family tradition and the crusading impulse', *Medieval Prosopography*, 19 (1998), 1–13 (p. 1 for quotation).

high.[73] They suffered heavy losses at the siege of Damascus in 1129[74] and again in 1133.[75] If contemporary accounts are to be trusted then 350 brothers died in battle at Ascalon in 1153 and at Cresson and Hattin in 1187.[76] James of Vitry reported the death of 200 Templars, Hospitallers and Teutonic Knights at the siege of Damietta in 1218 and 1219,[77] while between 260 and 300 more Templar knights allegedly lost their lives in the battle of La Forbie in 1244. As many as 280 brothers were killed at Mansourah in 1250, and only a few survived the onslaught on Acre in 1291.[78]

In spite of the criticism that the Templars began to face in Europe in the twelfth century, and which increased during the thirteenth, among the knights and nobles who went on crusade and dealt with the Templars in a crusading context there were always some who praised their discipline, military vigour and religious zeal.[79] Odo of Deuil, who accompanied King Louis VII on the Second Crusade, praised the Order's discipline on the march.[80] Hugh IV of Berzé, who had seen the military orders in action in the Holy Land, commented in *c.* 1220, after the Damietta campaign, that the Templars, like the Hospitallers, 'gave up their bodies in martyrdom and defended the sweet land where the Lord had died and lived'.[81]

[73] For the Templars' military engagement in the Holy Land see Demurger, *Les templiers*, pp. 193–242.

[74] The Templars' participation in the siege of Damascus is recorded in William of Tyre, *Chronique*, ed. R. B. C. Huygens, *CCCM*, 63, 63A (Turnhout, 1986), pp. 620–1; Robert of Thorigny, *Chronique et opuscules religieux*, ed. L. Delisle, 2 vols. (Rouen, 1872–3), I, pp. 175, 178 and Henry of Huntingdon, *Historia Anglorum*, ed. Thomas Arnold (London, 1879), p. 251. See also J. Phillips, 'Hugh of Payns and the 1129 Damascus crusade', in M. Barber (ed.), *The military orders, vol. I: Fighting for the faith and caring for the sick* (Aldershot, 1994), 141–7; Barber, *New knighthood*, p. 35 and Demurger, *Les templiers*, pp. 194–5.

[75] Ibid., p. 195.

[76] William of Tyre, *Chronique*, p. 799 and A. Demurger, *Vie et mort de l'ordre du Temple, 1118–1314* (Paris, 1985), pp. 120–3.

[77] James of Vitry, *Lettres de la cinquième croisade*, ed. R. B. C. Huygens, trans. G. Duchet-Suchaux (Turnhout, 1998), V: 282, VI: 220 and VII: 537.

[78] Barber, *New knighthood*, pp. 147, 149. For the battle of Acre see *Cronaca del Templare di Tiro (1243–1314). La caduta degli stati crociati nel racconto di un testimone oculare*, ed. L. Minervini (Naples, 2000), §§ 253–72 [pp. 206–26] and A. Demurger, *The last Templar. The tragedy of Jacques de Molay, last grand master of the Temple*, trans. A. Nevill (London, 2004), pp. 55–60.

[79] For hostile attitudes towards the Templars see S. Menache, 'The Templar order: a failed idea?', *Catholic Historical Review*, 79 (1993), 1–21.

[80] Odo of Deuil, *De profectione Ludovici VII in Orientem*, ed. and trans. V. G. Berry (New York, 1948), pp. 124–7. See also Demurger, *Les templiers*, pp. 198–202; J. Phillips, 'Odo of Deuil's *De profectione Ludovici VII in Orientem* as a source for the Second Crusade', in M. Bull and N. Housley (eds.), *The experience of crusading, vol. I: Western approaches* (Cambridge, 2003), 90; Barber, *New knighthood*, p. 67; R. C. Smail, *Crusading warfare, 1097–1193* (2nd edn, Cambridge, 1956), p. 96.

[81] *La 'Bible' au seigneur de Berzé*, ed. F. Lecoy (Paris, 1938), lines 261–93, p. 34. See also M. Menache, 'Rewriting the history of the Templars according to Matthew Paris', in M. Goodich, S. Menache and S. Schein (eds.), *Cross cultural convergences in the crusader period. Essays presented to Aryeh Grabois on his sixty-fifth birthday* (New York, 1995), 195.

More than six decades later, in August 1284, Milo VI of Noyers, who counted a Templar brother and crusaders among his relatives, and his wife Mary of Crécy made a donation to the Templar commandery of Hôpital-en-Vermenton, thereby acknowledging the great sacrifices made by the Templars in their daily struggle against the enemies of the faith and to avenge Jesus Christ.[82] And as late as 1310 the Cypriot knight Henry of Byblos testified before the prosecutors of the Order 'that he had seen them (the Templars) fighting at Tripoli for the defence of the Christian faith against the Saracens and enemies of the Christian faith better or at least as well as any of the other good and faithful Christians'.[83]

The chapter offers an analysis of how the Order of the Temple was perceived as a crusading institution by churchmen and laymen at home. It investigates to what extent families associated with, and supported, Templar communities because of the Order's link with the Holy Land and how deeply those who did so were themselves involved in the crusading movement. Taken in conjunction with the results from the previous chapters, this illustrates the predominance of crusading activity in family networks hitherto defined by their communal engagement with the Temple and, in particular, Cîteaux. This in turn allows for wide-ranging conclusions to be drawn regarding the relationship between reform monasticism, crusading, and the military orders.

[82] AN, S 5241, dossier 66, no. 4 (BN, n.a.l., 55, fols. 366r–9r) (1284). See also M. Quantin, 'Les croisés de la Basse-Bourgogne en Terre Sainte', *Mémoires de la société de l'Yonne* (1893), 296, who gives *c.* 1290 as the approximate date.

[83] H. Prutz, *Kulturgeschichte der Kreuzzüge* (Berlin, 1883), App. IV.1, p. 620.

Chapter 1

TEMPLAR FAMILIES

Entry into the Temple was the pinnacle of personal commitment to the Order. In his eulogy *De laude novae militiae* Bernard of Clairvaux portrayed the Templar as the knight who fought piously and died gloriously in battle against Christ's physical enemies. Knights who had abandoned the *malicia* that was their secular life for the *militia* of the Templar brotherhood resembled the Maccabees of old, those fervent warriors before God whose death in battle had been glorious. This was a popular perception of the Templar knight and one that, as I will discuss in more detail elsewhere, was perpetuated in charters and seems to have circulated widely among the brothers.[1] The Templar knight was the embodiment of a new religious *vita activa* that not only condoned violence but made it a spiritually meritorious exercise; but he, like the Order as a whole, could not have survived without other support.

The founders of the Order of the Temple were aware from the outset that the future of their brotherhood rested upon the creation of economic and social networks which could produce men, money, horses and material for the front-line and that the same also applied to the survival of the crusader states at large. As this chapter will show, these networks were created and maintained in various ways and by various means. What is important to state now is that, in the end, the Order was successful in providing the Latin settlements in the Levant with military personnel because it could draw on a network that extended into the most remote regions and smallest villages of Europe. The network was run by Templar brothers and their hired workers and lay associates. It was fuelled by the endowments of individuals and families who provided the commanderies in the cities and in the countryside with money, land and material, while some laymen lent their military expertise to the Templars and fought

[1] Bernard of Clairvaux, *Liber ad milites Templi de laude novae militiae*, ed. J. Leclercq, H.-M. Rochais and C. H. Talbot, *S. Bernardi Opera*, 8 vols. (Rome, 1957–77), III, pp. 205–39.

under the banner of the Order in battle. The lay associates, men and women, had committed themselves to the Order without taking full Templar vows but with the promise to support the Order and its cause to the best of their abilities. It is to these individuals and their relatives that I give the collective title of 'Templar families'. This chapter discusses the various ways in which they engaged with the Order and how they created bonds with Templar communities that could last for many generations.

ENDOWMENTS AND TRANSACTIONS

Donations

Making donations was the easiest and most popular way for lay men and women to express their sympathy for the Order of the Temple, not least because it provided them with the opportunity to voice, and find remedy for, their spiritual concerns. In this respect donors treated the Temple no differently from other religious institutions.[2] Scribes often went to great lengths to report that the purpose of the transactions they were recording was to redeem the sinful status of the donor and his or her relatives. But this sometimes concealed the true nature of a transaction, which could, for example, be a sale described in the terms of a donation in alms. In particular transactions that were rewarded with countergifts are not always easily distinguishable from sales or exchanges; 'inducement', as one historian has proposed, would probably be a more appropriate description for many remunerated donations.[3]

Nevertheless, on parchment at least donations were believed to have intrinsic redemptory value and were usually made to the spiritual benefit of the donor and his or her relatives or 'friends'.[4] Most benefactors gave to the Temple to obtain a remission of their sins and the redemption of their souls and the souls of their kindred. Some donations were made for 'the remission of the sins of all faithful'[5] or to help the donor 'to gain eternal life'.[6] Others were made for a specific purpose, for example to assist in the building of a chapel or oratory, and in expectation of specific rewards in

[2] See generally A. Angenendt *et al.*, 'Counting piety in the early and high middle ages', in B. Jussen (ed.), *Ordering medieval society. Perspectives on intellectual and practical modes of shaping social relations* (Philadelphia, Pa., 2001), in particular pp. 35–8. See also Bull, *Knightly piety*, pp. 157–66.

[3] Barber, 'The Templar preceptory of Douzens', 41. For a discussion of the problem of emunerated donations see also S. Weinberger, 'Donations-ventes ou ventes-donations? Confusion ou système dans la Provence du XIe siècle', *Le moyen âge*, 105 (1999), 667–80.

[4] Bull, *Knightly piety*, pp. 182–3. For friends being included in the deal, see e.g. BN, n.a.l., 7, fol. 13r (1178).

[5] See e.g. *Cart Douz*, A: no. 87, pp. 83–4 (1153), B: no. 73, pp. 245–6 (1172); BN, n.a.l., 15, fols. 382r–90r (1177×1178), fols. 405r-408 (1189).

[6] See e.g. *Cart Douz*, A: no. 60, pp. 66–7 (1147).

return such as prayers. Some were mere token endowments: a few crates of firewood, a candle, or garments. For the relationship between Templars and laymen even these small gifts had great symbolic value, for they demonstrated the donor's concern for, and association with, the Order's material needs, as well as his trust in its spiritual worth.[7] There can be little doubt that laymen regarded donations in alms to the Order as intrinsically valuable, in particular if one considers how many laymen and ecclesiastics had reportedly made endowments to Templar communities for the establishment or maintenance of a chapel or church where votive prayers should be said, or who had given to the Order for the explicit purpose of having the anniversaries of their death or that of a relative commemorated.[8]

Gaining access to the Order's deposit of merit was a powerful incentive for laymen to give to Templar commanderies.[9] But donations also fulfilled more mundane and immediate purposes. As will be shown, prospective crusaders would make endowments to the Order before they embarked on their journeys to gain the benevolence of an institution from which they perhaps expected help and assistance on the journey and overseas. Some made donations after they had returned from crusades or pilgrimages and because they had received help and assistance from the Templars while abroad. Others made endowments and expected the Templars to care for them on their return.[10] Concern for the wellbeing of relatives in the Order could also trigger benefactions. When Andrew of Baudement gave his possessions and revenues in Baudement to the Templars in 1133, he did so 'for his soul and the souls of all his ancestors, but most of all for one of his sons, William, who was then a knight of God and the Temple of Solomon'. The wording of the charter suggests that when this father provided the Order with material support, he had in mind his son, who had professed about four years earlier.[11] In December 1144, in a similar spirit, Ermessendis of Rovira in Catalonia gave 'my entire dowry, which my honourable husband Berenguer, who now, God be thanked, is a brother and knight of the same blessed knighthood, had once given to

[7] For a discussion of the symbolic value of small gifts see D. Postles, 'Small gifts, but big rewards: the symbolism of some gifts to the religious', *JMH*, 27 (2001), 23–42.

[8] See e.g. *ObReims*, 313; *Inventaire de la collection de Chastellux*, ed. C. Porée, *BuSoScYonne*, 57 (1903), no. 60, p. 138; *OdM*, I, p. 347 (1219); AN S 5237, dossier 30, no. 5 (1238); *Act Porc*, no. 324 (1227); J. H. Albanès and C. U. J. Chevalier, *Gallia christiana novissima. Histoire des archevêchés, évêques et abbayes de France d'après les documents authentiques recueillis dans les registres du Vatican et les archives locales, vol. V: Toulon* (Valence, 1911), no. 185 (1243); A. du Roure, *Notice historique sur une branche de la famille de Sabran* (Marseille, 1888), no. 10 (1274).

[9] See e.g. AN S 5241, dossier 75, no. 2 (BN, n.a.l., 55, fols. 496r–7r) (1190).

[10] See e.g. *Cart Douz*, A: no. 138, pp. 126–7 (1155).

[11] *Cart Prov*, p. xli and no. 81, pp. 102–3 (1133).

me' to 'Lord God and the knighthood of the Temple of Solomon in Jerusalem and to the brothers, present and future, who fight there for the highest King'.[12] Another charter, from Douzens in Languedoc, describes how in 1148 the knight Arnold of Gaure and his two sons renounced their rights in a manse in the village of Gaure. They did so 'to gain the love of God and for the salvation of our souls and for the soul of Raymond', who, apart from being Arnold's brother, was already a knight of the Temple.[13] A similar motivation can be assumed for Manasses of Coligny, who made donations to the Templars at Varessia, where his brother had been admitted into the Order,[14] and for Gerard of St-Maurice, who in 1230 donated two manses to the Templars of La Romagne 'for his brother Odo'.[15]

Donations, therefore, may have been intended to facilitate the lives of relatives or friends in the Temple as much as to help the soul of the donors. As spokesmen for the Temple these relatives and other local knights who had joined the Order must have played an important role in persuading family members to direct their charity towards the Temple. When entering the Temple some time before 1143, the uncle of Viscount Raymond Arnold of Dax, Griset, naturally expected to do so with a piece of landed possession as entry gift, and his nephew seems to have welcomed the opportunity to rid himself of the village of La Torte, which had already been the object of a gift to the cathedral chapter of Dax that his great-aunt had denounced, bringing about her excommunication. On the occasion of Griset's entry into the Temple the Order and the chapter were granted joint ownership of La Torte and soon the Templars established a commandery there of which Griset became the first preceptor.[16] In 1134 Pons of Bessan and his wife made endowments in the presence of the Templar knight Hugh of Bessan, who was probably a relative of Pons and almost certainly well acquainted with him.[17] Likewise, Raymond of Gaure, who was a *confrater* of Douzens by 1136 but seems to have taken full Templar vows some time later, was acting on behalf of the Templars when he persuaded his brother Arnold to exchange property with him.[18] In 1153 the brothers Aimeric, William Chabert and Arnold of Barbaira and their

12 *CG*, no. 341, pp. 221–2 (1144).
13 *Cart Douz*, A: no. 187, pp. 164–5 (1148). Raymond of Gaure is recorded among the Templars in ibid., A: no. 23, pp. 35–6 (1139), no. 57, pp. 64–5 (1138), no. 73, pp. 74–5 (1157), no. 83, p. 80 (1141×1150), no. 124, pp. 116–17 (1138), no. 175, pp. 157–8 (1138), no. 186, p. 164 (1136), no. 205, pp. 178–9 (1140), B: no. 1, pp. 185–6 (1136), no. 9, p. 195 (1138), no. 11, pp. 197–8 (1139).
14 Lavirotte, 'Mémoire statistique', 281.
15 ADCO H 1242, La Romagne, liasse St Maurice, no. 32 (BN, n.a.l., 53, fol. 259rv) (1230).
16 *Cart Dax*, no. 9, pp. 102–7 (before 1143), no. 10, pp. 108–10 (before 1143), no. 11, pp. 110–12 (1143×1168).
17 *CG*, no. 81, p. 63 (1134). 18 *Cart Douz*, A: no. 174, pp. 156–7 (1136).

families gave their share in the church of Saint-Jean of Carrières to the Templars of Douzens. One of the Templars who was present on that occasion was another brother of Aimeric, William Chabert and Arnold, by the name of Raymond Ermengau;[19] also present was the Templar knight Pons of Luzençon, who thirteen years earlier had been a witness when his relative Raymond gave to the Order vineyards near the *castrum* of Luzençon and near Craissaguet, and a house and garden near St-Georges in the valley of Cernon.[20] Similarly, when Peter of Capendu agreed on 25 July 1160 to pay the Templars an annual rent in corn and barley for land that he was allowed to keep at Molières, Villefloure and Licairac, he did so after having negotiated the terms with his cousin Isarn of Molières, who, as a *servus militie Templi*, had presumably been acting on the Order's behalf.[21]

Even a skim through the Templar charters leaves the reader with little doubt that families treated Templar communities in the same way as other religious institutions, which means that they engaged with them in similar transactions. Donations were often made *in elemosinam*, meaning that the object of the gift was exempted from all services other than prayer. Most donations involved landed possessions, followed by rights, tithes, rents and revenues. They also included the rights to collect dues, tolls and taxes, which allowed the Templars to exert economic and political influence over people who perhaps would not have engaged with them otherwise.

The influence of the Templars over a place and its inhabitants was of course the greater the more extensive their share in the lordship. Donors could be very generous in this respect. In all three regions under scrutiny in this book landed families endowed the Templars with seigniorial rights and possessions in villages or castles, thus enabling the latter to establish themselves as lords, or at least co-lords, in their lands.[22] These endowments provided the Order with a regular income. More importantly, they also constituted a power base from which it could operate. Considering the network of social contacts that the Templars inherited with each

[19] Ibid.: no. 87, pp. 83–4 (1153). [20] Selwood, *Knights of the cloister*, p. 198.

[21] *Cart Douz*, B: no. 46, p. 225 (1160).

[22] See e.g. *Cart Douz*, A: no. 1, pp. 3–5 (1133), no. 115, pp. 106–8 (1133), D: no. 4, pp. 275–7 (1147); *Cart Prov*, no. 81, pp. 102–3 (1133); *HdB*, II, no. 255, pp. 218–19 (1133); *CG*, no. 138, p. 96 (1137×1138); *HdB*, II, no. 638, pp. 399–400 (1178); BN, n.a.l., 15, fols. 382r–90r (1177×1178); ibid., 52, fols. 48r–9r (1213); E. Petit, *Avallon et l'Avallonnais* (Auxerre, 1867), pp. 49, 471 (1219). And also H. de Faget de Casteljau, 'Les sires de Til-Châtel féaux de Langres aux marches des deux Bourgognes, x–xv siècles', *Cahiers Haut-Marnais*, 143 (1980), 153; Lavirotte, 'Mémoire statistique', 236; V. Alanièce and F. Gilet, *Les templiers et leurs commanderies: l'exemple d'Avaleur en Champagne* (Langres, 1995), p. 60.

castrum and village, it is no surprise that the Templars often founded commanderies in these locations.[23]

Other donations consisted of buildings such as mills, houses, churches, chapels and hospitals. Mills (or fiscal rights in them) were particularly profitable gifts, because they provided the Templars with a steady income in kind or money.[24] Houses could be converted into commanderies or smaller dependencies and sometimes laymen had given them to the Order for exactly that purpose. Churches and chapels, which some donors would have given away only under pressure from religious reformers, became the nuclei of commanderies or continued functioning as parish churches under the protection of the Templars, who collected the tithes and other revenues.[25] The parish priests could be members of the Order, but would in most cases have been secular clergy. Hospitals (which were often hospices) too sometimes developed into Templar communities,[26] but often they were put merely under the protection of the Templars, who treated them as an additional source of income.[27]

[23] Ste-Eulalie, given to the Templars by Raymond Berenguer of Aragon, became a Templar settlement, as did Avaleur, home of the lords of Avaleur; Bure, which was given to the Templars by Payen of Bure; Fontenotte, which was given by Aimo of Tilchâtel; Palau, given by Gerard of Roussillon; Bissey-la-Côte, given by Thibaud of Bissey; and Lansac, which Hugh of Baux had endowed to the Order. See Marie, *Templiers de Langres*, p. 122; Faget de Casteljau, 'Les sires de Til-Châtel', 143 (1980), 153; Alanièce and Gilet, *Avaleur*, pp. 52–3; Vinas, *L'ordre du Temple*, p. 21; Lavirotte, 'Mémoire statistique', 236; A.-J. Durbec, *Templiers et hospitaliers en Provence et dans les Alpes-Maritimes* (Grenoble, 2001), pp. 92–3.

[24] See e.g. *Diocèse ancien de Châlons-sur-Marne*, I, no. 4, p. 396 (1133×1142); *Cart Douz*, A: no. 60, pp. 66–7 (1147); AN S 5244A, dossier 5, no. 1 (*c.* 1190, see also *OdM*, I, p. 336); BN, n.a.l., 32, fol. 12r (1223); ibid., 55, fol. 517r (1219, *vidimus* April 1263); *HdB*, II, no. 622, pp. 393–4 (1178). See also *Diocèse ancien de Châlons-sur-Marne*, I, p. 235. The outlay of medieval mills and their economic significance for the Templars is discussed in Marie, *Templiers de Langres*, pp. 44–8; Barber, 'The Templar preceptory of Douzens', 43–4; L. Macé, 'L'utilisation des ressources hydrauliques par les templiers de la commanderie de Douzens, XIIe siècle (Aude)', *Archéologie du Midi Médiéval*, 12 (1994), 99–113.

[25] Demurger, *Les templiers*, p. 167. For donations consisting of churches, chapels or priories see e.g. *Cart Douz*, A: no. 87, pp. 83–4; no. 88, pp. 84–5 (1153); *HdB*, III, no. 804, p. 289 (1189). Good examples of richly endowed churches that were converted into Templar dependencies are St-Jean of Carrières near Douzens, Ste-Eulalie in Rouergue and La Trinité at Reims. For St-Jean of Carrières see *Cart Douz*, A: no. 74, pp. 75–6 (1168), no. 89, pp. 86–7 (1113×1114), no. 91, pp. 88–9 (1169), no. 93 (1168), pp. 90–1 (1168), no. 96, p. 93 (1135), no. 97, pp. 93–4 (1169), no. 101, p. 96 (1148), no. 102, p. 97 (1136), no. 103, pp. 97–8 (1136). For La Trinité see *ObReims*, passim. For Ste-Eulalie see J. Frizot, *Les grands sites templiers en France* (Rennes, 2005), pp. 24–5. For a comprehensive treatment of the changing attitude towards proprietary churches in the middle ages see S. Wood, *The proprietary church in the medieval West* (Oxford, 2006), in particular pp. 864–82.

[26] See e.g. BN, n.a.l., 51, fols. 115r–16r (1192×1193).

[27] A. J. Forey, 'The charitable activities of the Templars ', *Viator*, 34 (2003), 128. One example is the hospital of St-Nicholas at or near Langres, which was administered by the Templars and to which James, dean of Langres, made endowments in his testament in 1206. See C.-F. Roussel, *Le diocèse de Langres. Histoire et statistique*, 4 vols. (Langres, 1873–9), I, no. 154, pp. 215–16.

Business transactions

The primary incentive for twelfth- and thirteenth-century lay men and women to engage in business transactions with the Templars or any other religious institution was to raise the liquid assets that would allow them to survive and compete in a society that was becoming increasingly fuelled by money. As one historian has observed, after 1180 money 'entered the patrimony like a ferment'.[28] Lords and knights, whose revenues consisted mainly of agricultural products, incurred loans and pledged and sold land and rights to obtain the assets they needed to finance their lifestyle and military campaigns; soon they were borrowing money to redeem their debts.[29] The Templars played a role in fuelling the monetary economy of twelfth- and thirteenth-century rural France. They were able to hand out loans and to guarantee long-distance money transfers, which were important for crusaders to finance their campaigns. The Templars were also used to liquidate pledges which lords had obtained from other laymen.[30]

Sales, pledges, leases and exchanges were the most common forms of business transaction, with sales featuring prominently. Most of them are concerned with landed property, including manses and *casales*, *honores*,[31] fortified dwellings, villages, fiefs and 'lordships', which were sold to the Order wholesale.[32] Other commodities that families frequently traded with the Templars included rents, tithes, rights and privileges,[33] as well as serfs and servile families, houses, mills and victuals.[34] The initiative for a

[28] G. Duby, *Rural economy and country life in the medieval West*, trans. C. Postan (Philadelphia, Pa., 1998), p. 233.

[29] Ibid., pp. 233–5.

[30] See e.g. *Cart Mont*, no. 20, pp. 235–6 (n.d.). The role of the Templars as financiers and bankers has received fresh treatment from I. de la Torre Muñoz de Morales, *Los templarios y el origen de la banca* (Madrid, 2004).

[31] Originally defined as land that came with a particular office, the *honor* was by the twelfth century regarded as hereditary property and an integral part of a noble family's estate.

[32] *Cart Douz*, A: no. 116, pp. 108–9 (1167), no. 117, pp. 109–10 (1153), no. 150, pp. 137–8 (1159); B: no. 72, p. 244 (1170); BN, n.a.l., 15, fols. 57r–60r (1195), 276r–80r (1177×1178), 393r–5r (1187×1188); ibid., 16, fols. 296r–307r (1214); ibid., 17, fols. 312r–15r (1180), fol. 392r (1262, *vidimus*); ibid., 19, fols. 31r–37r (1215); *Doc Dur*, I, no. 62, pp. 45–6 (1269); *Diocèse ancien de Châlons-sur-Marne*, I, no. 151, p. 436 (1306); *PAC*, II, no. 456, pp. 92–3 (1181); AN S 4959, dossier 39, no. 1 (1230×1231); Lavirotte, 'Mémoire statistique', 244 (1230) and 259 (1237). See also e.g. Vinas, *L'ordre du Temple*, pp. 22, 102, 118; Verdon, 'Les revenus', 174.

[33] *PAC*, II, no. 362, p. 11 (1157), no. 453, pp. 88–9 (1181), no. 465, pp. 100–2 (1183); BN, n.a.l., 15, fols. 281r–3r (1177×1178); ibid., 16, fols. 60r–2r (1195), 296r–307r (1214); ibid., 17, fols. 190r–203r (1264, pancarte); ibid., 18, fol. 413r (1176). See also e.g. Verdon, 'Les revenus', 170; A.-R. Carcenac, *Les templiers du Larzac. La commanderie du Temple de Sainte-Eulalie de Larzac* (Nîmes, 1994), p. 91; A. Pételm 'Le Temple de Bonlieu', *MSA Aube*, 74 (1910), 273, 276–7, 281–2.

[34] *Cart Douz*, A: no. 2, pp. 6–8 (1157), no. 68, pp. 71–2 (1167); *Cart Vaour*, no. 112, pp. 100–1 (1199); BN, n.a.l., 20, fols. 88r–9r (1267); Verdon, 'Les revenus', 170, 173; Pétel, 'Bonlieu', 281–2.

sale could come from either of the two parties involved. It is likely that the Templars approached local families with the proposal to buy land and other possessions in areas in which they had a particular interest. At the same time, however, it was possible for families to offer the Templars land near places where they knew the Order had already established a presence. Other charters suggest that families made donations in order to arouse the Templars' interest in adjoining possessions or pieces of property which they then offered to satisfy by putting them up for sale.[35]

Pledges had an important social meaning in that over and above financial rewards they created bonds of friendship and mutual dependence between religious communities and their secular neighbours.[36] They thus played a part in the establishment and maintenance of relationships between families and Templar houses. Laymen pledged property to Templar houses in return for lump sums of money.[37] This was advantageous for both the debtor and the Order because it enabled the former to convert property into cash without having to alienate it permanently from his or her possessions, and the latter to acquire, for a relatively low price, the temporary possession of land or other property that it could use to its advantage provided the property was given as a vifgage (i.e. with the agreement that the fruits of the land should serve to reduce or even repay the debt for which the property was given as security) and not a mortgage (in which case the fruits of the land were regarded as additional interests to the principal debt).

Leases and exchanges enabled the Templars to acquire lands and rights which they did not expect to receive in alms but which they needed and wanted to complement their territorial possessions. They, too, were business transactions. The Templars were granted possession of a particular piece of property in return for an annual rent, which they had to pay to the donor. The rent could entail money or revenues in kind. Its value was individually arranged and it therefore varied, sometimes substantially, from one case to the next.[38] Exchanges, on the other hand, usually entailed no further obligations for either party involved. Most commonly, the Templars asked local families for particular pieces of land for which they offered some of their own property and privileges in

[35] See e.g. ADCO H 1234, dossier Barge, no. 2 (BN, n.a.l., 53, fols. 280r–1v) (1241).

[36] This applies also to other business transactions. See C. B. Bouchard, *Holy entrepreneurs: Cistercians, knights, and economic exchange in twelfth-century Burgundy* (Ithaca, N.Y., 1991), p. 33.

[37] See e.g. *PAC*, II, no. 498, pp. 134–5 (1189).

[38] For example, whereas the Templars rented 120 arpents of wood from the count of Montcuc for 1 *denier* per arpent in 1232, they were asked by Adam of Savignac to pay 17 *deniers* p.a. for 7 arpents of wood, or almost 2.5 per arpent, two years later. See Pétel, 'Bonlieu', 263 and *Cart Prov*, no. 134, pp. 138–9 (1234).

return.[39] Exchanges thus enabled the Templars to take the initiative in developing their territorial possessions to their liking.[40] Sometimes laymen exchanged property for monetary rewards and nothing else. These transactions were *de facto* sales, but the wording of the charters indicates that they were perceived as exchanges.[41] Transactions involving exchanges could also result in lordship arrangements or further business relations if the property that the Templars were to receive through the exchange was of lower value than the property that they were willing to give away. In such cases the Templars agreed to the exchange on condition that the other party would hold its new possession either as a fief of the Order, or as a lease for which the holder would have to make regular payments.[42]

Although the Order received landed possessions throughout its existence, their distribution was irregular, with an emphasis on the twelfth and early thirteenth centuries. It has often been said that in the course of the thirteenth century patrons changed the way in which they engaged with the Order. Generally it was said that laymen grew increasingly reluctant to give landed property to the Temple and in consequence donations to the Templars declined during the second half of the thirteenth century.[43] They were replaced by sales and other business transactions, though these were also decreasing in number.[44] According to one recent estimate 82 per cent of the transactions between laymen and the Templars in the diocese of Langres conducted between 1220 and 1224 had been donations, but by 1244 the number had dropped to 31 per cent. Sales, on the other hand, counted for 69 per cent of the transactions by then.[45]

[39] See e.g. BN, n.a.l., 15, fols. 155r–7r (1286); ibid., 18, fols. 2r–11r (c12th); *Cart Douz*, A: no. 9, pp. 20–1 (1157), no. 18, pp. 30–1 (1166), no. 30, pp. 41–2 (1159), no. 123, p. 116 (1142), no. 127, pp. 119–20 (1156), no. 183, p. 162 (1148), no. 186, p. 164 (1136); *DhT-G*, II, p. 9 (1258).

[40] It was not least by means of exchanges that the Templars of Douzens succeeded in gaining a strong presence in the village of Gaure, outside Carcassonne. See e.g. *Cart Douz*, A: no. 183, p. 162 (1148), no. 186, p. 164 (1136).

[41] Lord Bernard of Fréjus, for example, who gave a piece of land in the tithe area (*decimaria*) of Saint-Jean of Fréjus as 'free allod' (a term used by twelfth-century scribes to specify freehold land) and 'in exchange' to the Templars of Montpellier in 1225, received 30 *sous* in money of Melgueil in return. See BN, n.a.l., 15, fols. 103r–6r (1225).

[42] Such seem to have been the arrangements between Peter Adalbert and the Templars of Douzens. A charter in the Douzens cartulary recalls that in 1157 Peter Adalbert and his wife and children had given their *honor* in one of the Order's vineyards at Brucafel to the Templars of Douzens in exchange for arable land at Combelas, near Brucafel. It was furthermore agreed, however, that they had to pay a quarter of the yield of the land to Douzens. See *Cart Douz*, A: no. 126, pp. 118–19 (1157).

[43] H. J. Nicholson, *Templars, Hospitallers, and Teutonic knights: images of the military orders, 1128–1291* (Leicester, 1993), p. 64.

[44] Forey, 'Military orders', 201.

[45] Marie, *Templiers de Langres*, p. 79. A decrease in charitable donations in the second half of the thirteenth century can also be detected in the Templar cartularies of Provins in Champagne, Huesca in Aragon and Tortosa in Catalonia. See Demurger, *Les templiers*, p. 289.

However, although a general decline in donations in the thirteenth century was likely to have been the case, these estimates do not necessarily help to confirm it; all they seem to imply is that the number of business transactions had increased substantially and that, indeed, business transactions had always been among the methods which individuals and families employed in order to engage with the Temple.[46] From the time when the Templars began to establish their presence in Burgundy, Champagne and southern France, families engaged in business transactions with them.[47] Historians have also established that these business transactions were not evenly distributed over the years. They often constituted only a minor (although still significant) percentage of the transactions recorded in the twelfth and early thirteenth centuries, but outnumbered donations and other spiritually meritorious transactions by the middle of the thirteenth century.[48]

Still, a decline in landed endowments did occur, and it is partly explained by the fact that by the thirteenth century the Templars were quite specific in their requests and partly by the reality that land had become a limited and extremely profitable resource.[49] Local historians in particular have also argued that the decrease in charity in the thirteenth century reflected the changing attitude of society towards the Order. Prospective donors were less willing to support crusading campaigns or the reconquest of Christian lands on the Iberian peninsula than they had been before; consequently, they were also reluctant to give to the

[46] This was certainly the case in the region of Auxerre, where the number of donations remained fairly steady but that of sales changed dramatically between 1180 and 1300. See Demurger, 'La constitution d'un patrimoine foncier', in particular p. 450 (table).

[47] Barber ('The Templar preceptory of Douzens', 41–2) and Verdon (*La terre et les hommes*, p. 30) have demonstrated that most of the charters from Douzens, which date from November 1129 to January 1183, namely 184, are concerned with straightforward gifts or with what Barber called 'gifts with conditions'. The latter included countergifts with their symbolic value as well as 'inducements'. Only twenty-six charters were concerned with exchanges, seventy-one with purchases and six with grants or leases which the Templars gave to or conducted with other parties. This shows on the one hand that the majority of transactions conducted between laymen and the Templars of Douzens in the twelfth century were intended to be at least perceived as donations. It also shows, however, that from very early on the Templars of Douzens were accustomed to pay for the property that was given to them, either in the form of token rewards or indeed in full. In fact, as Barber has shown, straightforward gifts make up only 29% of the transactions collected in the Douzens cartulary. According to Verdon, sales accounted for 32.6%, countergifts for 28.6% and donations in alms for 38.6% of the transactions in the Douzens cartulary. But he seems to have worked from the basis of 331 charters (thus including duplicates *et al.*) whereas Barber based his survey on the 287 charters that were unique and concerned only with transactions between Douzens and outside laymen and institutions.

[48] See e.g. Marie, *Templiers de Langres*, p. 79 and Verdon, *La terre et les hommes*, pp. 29–31.

[49] A.-J. A. Bijsterveld, 'The medieval gift as agent of social bonding and political power: a comparative approach', in E. Cohen and M. B. de Jong (eds.), *Medieval transformations. Texts, power, and gifts in context* (Leiden, Boston, Mass., Cologne, 2001), 148–9.

Templars.[50] Moreover, it has been said that society became increasingly wary about the Order's dwindling success in the Levant and that it grew envious of its apparent wealth. Valérie Alaniėce and François Gilet, for example, in their microhistorical study of the Templars at Avaleur, maintain that by the mid thirteenth century the Order had become too powerful for the liking of the regional ruling classes.[51] Another explanation put forward by scholars has it that in the thirteenth century landed families were hit by poverty and that charitable piety consequently succumbed to the desire for monetary gain.[52]

Some of these arguments are difficult to maintain. By the middle of the thirteenth century the crusades had become institutionalised to such an extent that it was almost impossible for laymen to avoid participation in the preparation of new crusading campaigns. Secular rulers and the Church regularly levied heavy income taxes upon their subjects to finance crusade undertakings; and partial indulgences were granted to those who made additional contributions to the crusader cause.[53] In other words, voluntarily or involuntarily, people in the thirteenth century contributed substantially to the maintenance and sustenance of the Latin East. What is more, they had the opportunity to acquire spiritual rewards by doing so. The fact that the military orders, notably the Temple, received fewer alms and donations in the thirteenth century than in the century before therefore does not necessarily mean that they had become a less attractive channel for contributions to the crusader cause. It merely shows that people distributed – and were forced to distribute – their monetary assets differently. It is true that the military orders were facing criticism in the thirteenth century; and much of what was said against them concerned their conduct and the way they spent their material and monetary assets.[54] As demonstrated by Helen Nicholson, however, judging from the content of pamphlets and polemical writings by religious authors, hostility against the Templars and other military orders diminished notably in the second half of the thirteenth century, and thus at a time when donations to the Temple were reaching a low point.[55]

Moreover, charitable support of the Templars, and of other religious orders, was always spasmodic. Political events like crusades and natural events such as droughts and bad harvests had a great impact on the

[50] See e.g. Vinas, *L'ordre du Temple*, p. 35. [51] See e.g. Alaniėce and Gilet, *Avaleur*, pp. 69–70.

[52] Marie, *Templiers de Langres*, pp. 80–1.

[53] E. Siberry, *Criticism of crusading: 1095–1274* (Oxford, 1985), pp. 110–49; J. A. Powell, *Anatomy of a crusade, 1213–1221* (Philadelphia, Pa., 1986), pp. 92–3; J. S. C. Riley-Smith, *What were the crusades?* (2nd edn, Houndsmills, 1992), pp. 45–9.

[54] Forey, 'Military orders', 211–12.

[55] Nicholson, *Templars, Hospitallers, and Teutonic knights*, pp. 48–9.

quantity and timing of charitable donations. A temporary decline in charitable donations does not therefore necessarily indicate that the Templars were facing increased criticism, nor does it mean that laymen were avoiding the Order altogether; rather that they were often engaging with it in different ways. Although they grew increasingly reluctant to give possessions away for nothing other than prayer, thirteenth-century knights and nobles seem to have had little difficulty in alienating property by means of business transactions. In the commandery of Sauce-sur-Yonne in the county of Auxerre, for example, charters recording sales and exchanges reached an all-time peak between 1250 and 1260.[56] These transactions must have been perceived as being to the benefit of the Order; otherwise it would not have agreed to them.

Charters documenting transactions between the Templars and lay society in the thirteenth century exist in abundance. They are a clear indication that although donations became less frequent and disputes between Templar communities and former donors more commonplace after 1200, many families retained contact and indeed fruitful business relationships with the Order. By the end of the twelfth century the Order of the Temple had developed into an important landholder and an economic force to be reckoned with. The estates and other possessions that it had accumulated over the years were dispersed and needed adaptation in order to remain, or become, manageable. Consequently the Templars' choices of new acquisitions became very selective. What followed, after a period of rapid growth, was a time of adjustment, during which the Order took active measures to organise, and even reduce, its possessions into manageable and productive enclaves. The Templars of the thirteenth century were therefore more specific in their demands and requests for new properties and revenues. New acquisitions had to complement, complete or enhance existing and developing estates.

This being established, it can hardly be disputed that in the thirteenth century landed families were experiencing an economic crisis that made it difficult for many to alienate even more property to religious institutions. As I will discuss in the next chapter, the Temple was seldom the only, and hardly ever the first, religious institution that families supported. In the thirteenth century laymen were determined to put their possessions to the best possible use by distributing them, or whatever they could afford to give, among many, and different, religious communities, hoping that this would increase their chances of spiritual salvation. It was inevitable that charitable gifts reduced the fortunes of these families and left them with a

[56] Demurger, *Les templiers*, p. 289, and AN S 5235, dossier 1, no. 1 for the cartulary.

diminishing number of assets for future endowments. Furthermore, the practice of dividing family property among multiple heirs that was customary in many regions of France gradually led to the impoverishment and demise of once prosperous landed families.[57]

At the same time, society was hit by inflation, which was the consequence of the increasing demand of knights and nobles – but not them alone – for liquid assets. Poverty and the need for cash had always been major incentives for people to sell property to religious institutions; the only thing new was the large scale on which these transactions were now conducted.[58] Throughout the thirteenth century, lords and knights, whose revenues consisted mainly of agricultural products, took up loans and pledged and sold land and land rights to obtain the money they needed to finance their lifestyle and military campaigns and to redeem their debts.[59]

In the light of these circumstances the fact that a number of individuals and families continued making donations to the Templars in the late thirteenth and even early fourteenth centuries is all the more noteworthy. As will become apparent throughout the next chapters, many of these late donors belonged to families with a long history of involvement in the Order. As late as *c.* 1258 and 1300, for example, the Templars of Avaleur in Champagne received substantial charitable endowments from Margaret, daughter and heiress of Milo IV of Avaleur, and from Gaucher of Mutry, who promised that he would defend the Order's claim to the newly acquired possessions against everyone *en jugement et hors jugement* and who, in an unusual move, also subjected himself and his heirs to whatever jurisdiction the Templars would choose, 'that of a court of the Church or that of a lay court'.[60] In 1269, Hugh of Brienne ended his disagreement with the Templars over the house and other buildings which they had erected at Bonlieu and the property and many landed possessions, revenues and privileges that they had acquired there from his vassalas and rear-vassals, among them the knight John of Thil, allowing them to hold these possessions and an additional 78 *jornalia* of arable land in mainmorte, meaning that they were allowed to hold but not sell them.[61] Count

[57] See generally Bijsterveld, 'The medieval gift', and D. Nicholas, *The evolution of the medieval world: society, government and thought in Europe, 312–1500* (London, 1992), p. 255 for a general overview of inheritance practices in medieval France.

[58] See for example the blacksmith Hugh Chaudere and his wife who, in March 1218, sold possessions to the Templars of La Chapelle confirming that *nulla alia de causa hanc venditionem fecerunt nisi sola paupertate cogentes*. See BN, n.a.l., 57, fol. 12r (1218).

[59] Duby, *Rural economy*, pp. 233–5. [60] Alaniëce and Gilet, *Avaleur*, pp. 62–5.

[61] AN S 4958, no. 6 (1269).

John I of Joigny and his wife Mary made extensive endowments to the Templars of Sauce-sur-Yonne, including lands, revenues, serfs and judicial rights in various villages in 1275 and 1276.[62] Milo VI of Noyers endowed them with the entire lordship of Vermenton, near Auxerre, in August 1284, excluding only the fiefs and rear-fiefs held from him there, and made further benefactions involving Vermenton in 1287.[63] In 1299 Hugh of Grancey donated to the Templars of Bure the fiefs that Milo of Occey held from him at Buxières, while Isabel of Grancey made endowments to Bure to secure the celebration of the anniversary of her death and of that of her husband.[64] In 1301 John of Merry endowed the Templars with a house at Merry to show his gratitude for the deeds and courtesies that the Templars had done and shown him in the past.[65] And as late as 1306 Godfrey of Bar, with the consent of the count of Bar, gave his fief of Doncourt-aux-Bois to the Templars.[66]

That these late donations were no isolated cases has been convincingly proven by Carraz, who showed that throughout the late thirteenth century the Templars of Provence continued to receive often substantial donations, which sometimes even accompanied acts of personal association.[67] As I will show in the following chapters, this was also true for other parts of southern France as well as for Burgundy and Champagne.

As I have said before, many of these late donors came from families with long ties to the Templars. They provide evidence that although society as a whole may have grown increasingly reluctant to make charitable donations to local Templar communities, the Order could, almost to the very end, rely on the generosity of influential long-term supporters. What is more, throughout the period of the Order's existence, lay men and women from among the families of Templar benefactors accompanied their endowments to nearby Templar communities with acts of personal commitment. The presence of relatives in the Order was a powerful incentive for families to continue their involvement with local Templar communities. Equally important, however, was the influence of men and women who associated themselves 'body and soul' with the Order but remained in the world.

62 AN S 5236/B, dossier 19, nos. 1, 2 and 3 (1276) (BN, n.a.l., 55, fols. 301r–3r; ibid., fols. 304r–6r).

63 AN, S 5241, dossier 66, no. 4 (1284) (BN, n.a.l., 55, fols. 366r–9r). See also BN, n.a.l., 55, fols. 388r–91r (1287).

64 ADCO, 111 H 1156, Fonds de Bure, no. 3 (1299) (BN, n.a.l., 56, fol. 148r).

65 *OdM*, I, p. 365 (1301).

66 *Catalogue des actes des comtes de Bar, 1022 à 1239*, ed. M. Grosdidier de Matons (Bar-le-Duc, 1922), no. 306, p. 86; Demurger, *Les templiers*, p. 289.

67 Carraz, *L'ordre du Temple*, pp. 407–8.

LAY ASSOCIATION WITH THE TEMPLE

Lay men and women could associate with the Temple in different ways. Apart from making endowments to the Order for which they would be commemorated, laymen could profess themselves fully to the Order if they were of free birth, unmarried (or separated with ecclesiastical approval) and free of debt. Alternatively, they, and women too, could enter the confraternity of a Templar community, in which case they became part of the prayer community of the Order. A third way for a man of knightly stock to associate with the Order was to join its ranks temporarily as a *miles ad terminum*, in which case he would have been expected to fight as part of the Templar contingent on a military campaign. What sounds simple and straightforward was often the result of very complex procedures involving giving gifts, making concessions and swearing oaths. The language of the charters rarely conveys the complexity of the procedures at work, which is partly because the terminology used by medieval scribes to define and describe lay association was often ambiguous.

The wording of an act of donation gives information about the donor's commitment to the Order and about the kind of association the donor hoped to obtain. Simple donations of property could secure the brothers' prayers; the donation of one's body (usually in combination with material concessions) was a request for later burial with the Templars. To give one's soul, on the other hand – which was, again, usually accompanied by another donation of material possessions – indicated the donor's wish to participate, in life and in death, in the spiritual benefits of the commandery to which the donation was made.[68] In order to determine how deeply families identified with the Order it is imperative to understand and accurately evaluate the terminology that medieval scribes applied to describe (or conceal) the relations between the Templars and the laity. This, however, is not an easy task. Many of the terms used in the charters or the Templar Rule, such as *donatus*, *convertus*, *famulus* and even *confrater* and *frater*, are ambiguous and were often used interchangeably. This section aims to provide an overview of how, and for which reasons, laymen could associate with the Order without taking full Templar vows. It examines the meaning and implications of different forms of lay association. In particular it discusses the changes that took place in the constellation of the Order's confraternities at the turn of the twelfth century and how these changes allowed a particular category of *confratres*,

[68] É. Magnou, 'Oblature, classe chevaleresque et servage dans les maisons méridionales du Temple au XIIème siècle', *AdM*, 73 (1961), 377.

the donats, to establish themselves as the most prominent expression of lay association. The importance of the Templar donat and of the *miles ad terminum* for the Templar community will then be assessed in the light of the Order's increasing reluctance to make use of its novitiate. What will become apparent is that throughout its existence the Order of the Temple attracted not only fully professed knights and sergeants to its commanderies, but also a growing number of lay men and women who hoped to associate with the Order without being required to commit fully to it. In the lives of many of these lay associates the Order played a dominant role. Because lay associates were generally allowed to remain in the world – although some submitted to stricter rules of life – their role in communicating the idea and values of the Order to society should not be underestimated.

Confraternity

Confratres and *consorores* were free lay men and women who associated themselves emotionally and spiritually with the Order without fully professing to it. They were not by any means confined to the military orders, although they seem to have been more prominent here than in other institutions.[69] Nor did the *confratres* and *consorores* in the Temple, and elsewhere, constitute a homogeneous group, including as they did men and women who made annual donations in return for prayer, and others who rendered their entire possessions to local Templar communities and lived semi-religious lives within, or near, a Templar compound. *Confratres* and *consorores* were part of the Templar community from very early on. But the former at least are not always easily discernible in the sources. The terminology that was used to describe lay associates and fully professed members of the Order was ambiguous, with the terms *frater* and *confrater* being regularly used to refer to members of both groups. As the editor of the Richerenches cartulary has already noted, the authors of the primitive Templar Rule referred to all lay associates as *fratres*; it was only when the Rule was translated into the French vernacular that the distinction between *frères* and *confrères* was made.[70] Full members of the Order, on

[69] Most of what follows in this chapter is taken directly from J. G. Schenk, 'Forms of lay association with the Order of the Temple', *JMH*, 34 (2008), 79–103. On *confratres* and *familiares* in religious institutions, including the military orders, see C. de Miramon, *Les donnés au moyen âge. Une forme de vie religieuse laïque v.1180–v.1500* (Paris, 1999), pp. 59–96.

[70] *Cart Rich*, pp. cli–clii. The ambiguity of the term *frater* also applies to the Cistercian Order. Here it was employed to label professed monk, lay brother or lay associate alike. In 1275 *frater* officially replaced the term *conversus*, which, in particular in southern France, was associated with heresy. See R. Averkorn, 'Die Cistercienserabteien Berdoues und Gimont in ihren Beziehungen zum

the other hand, were in early Templar charters often referred to as *confratres*. This is curious, but may be explained by the fact that the Order was founded as a confraternity, by knights who rendered their service to the canons of the Holy Sepulchre in Jerusalem. And although there is no evidence that Hugh of Payns and his fellow knights initially referred to themselves and their fraternity as *confratres* and as members of a confraternity of the Holy Sepulchre, for they had taken the three monastic vows of chastity, poverty and obedience and were thus professed, it is possible that for some time outsiders regarded them as such.

To become a *confrater* or *consoror* of the Temple was relatively easy, provided that the candidate was of free birth and had material assets at his or her disposal. According to the bull *Milites Templi* of 1144, an annual rent and a pious disposition were enough to gain a lay man or woman a partial indulgence and burial with the Templars:

> Whoever helps them [the Templars] out from his own resources, accumulated through God, and becomes a member of this most holy brotherhood, granting it benefices annually, strong in the merits of the holy apostles Peter and Paul, we will grant him an indulgence of the seventh part of any penance imposed on him. If he dies and has not been excommunicated, ecclesiastical burial with other Christians will not be denied him.[71]

As the bull indicates, at the beginning of every association with the Temple was a charitable deed. *Confratres*, or 'members of the brotherhood', as they are referred to in the bull, were required to make material contributions to the sustenance of Templar houses, and thus to the sustenance of the Order as a whole. These contributions could take the form of rents, which were paid annually and usually on particular feast days.[72] Sometimes they consisted of single donations which the donors then followed up with less significant annual contributions, as was the case for Hugh of Grancey, who, in 1197, entered the confraternity of Bure, in Burgundy, bringing with him possessions at Neuilly and offering an annual rent of 5 *sous*.[73] On many occasions candidates promised the Templars further donations, which they would bestow upon them at the time of death.[74] If nothing else, then the candidate could always

laikalen Umfeld. Gebetsgedenken, Konversion und Begräbnis', in F. Neiske, D. W. Poeck and M. Sandmann (eds.), *Vinculum societatis. Joachim Wollasch zum 60. Geburtstag* (Sigmaringendorf, 1991), 21.

[71] *PTJ I*, no. 8, pp. 214–15 (1144).

[72] The feast days of Saint Michael, the Virgin Mary and Pentecost were particularly popular with the Order. See e.g. *Cart Douz*, A: no. 53, pp. 61–2 (1167), no. 63, pp. 68–9 (1158), no. 159, p. 143 (1167); BN, n.a.l., 17, fols. 188r–9r (1265).

[73] ADCO, 111 H 1156, no. 5 (1197).

[74] *CG*, no. 68, pp. 51–2 (1133); *PAC*, II, no. 369, p. 16 (*c.* 1160); *Cart Douz*, A: no. 75, p. 76 (1170), B: no. 20, p. 205 (1167); *Inventaire Chastellux*, no. 69, p. 140 (1246).

give him- or herself *ad hominem*, and thus his or her personal labour, to the Order. In this case the candidate did not become a member of the confraternity of the chosen Templar community, but instead joined the group of Templar *familiares*, who, although predominantly of servile status, still enjoyed the Order's protection and, to a limited extent, also had access to its spiritual benefits.

Arms and horses were preferred objects of charity. As gifts their function was twofold. On the one hand they were necessary commodities for a military order.[75] On the other hand they were the instruments of the knight and thus signs of his military prowess and ability to serve. As such their transfer into the possession of the Temple had an important symbolic significance, representing as it did a change of lord and a transfer of service.[76] The transfer of horses and weapons was an integral element of many contracts of confraternity; but it was usually carried out only at the time of the associate's death or when he took full Templar vows – in which case he brought his horse and weapons with him into the Order. When Aimeric of Barbaira and his brother William Chabert became *confratres* of Douzens in 1133, they declared that 'when we will leave this world the above-mentioned knighthood shall have our horses and arms'.[77]

The expression 'leaving this world' is ambiguous, referring, as it does, to the act of dying as well as to a person's spiritual transfer from the secular world to the monastery. The evidence from other charters suggests that most prospective *confratres* expected that the transfer of their horse and weapons would be carried out only after their death. In addition, it seems that horses and weapons were regarded as an adequate means to cover the costs of burial with the Templars. This is suggested by the fact that prospective *confratres* and donats always proposed to pay the Templars a fixed price in cash if they should fail to have a horse in their possession at the time of death. The value of a horse was usually 100 *sous*,[78] but it could also be as little as 50 *sous*[79] or as much as 200[80] or even 300 *sous*.[81] When Dalmas of Valréas joined the confraternity of Richerenches in 1179 he declared that 'at the end of my life I give you my horse and weapons; and if I should not possess a horse, I promise to give you 200 *sous* for it'. Until then, however, his donation of one field and of pasture rights in all his lands had to suffice to secure him a place among the *confratres*.[82] And in his

[75] Selwood, *Knights of the cloister*, p. 176, cites evidence to the effect that cargoes of horses were shipped from southern France to the Levant.

[76] See also Demurger, *Vie et mort*, pp. 72–3, 76–7.

[77] *Cart Douz*, A: no. 1, pp. 3–5 (1133).

[78] See e.g. ibid., no. 1, pp. 3–5 (1133).

[79] *Cart Rich*, no. 129, pp. 123–4 (1156).

[80] Ibid., no. 241, pp. 214–15 (1179).

[81] *CG*, no. 20, pp. 13–15 (1128×1143).

[82] *Cart Rich*, no. 241, pp. 214–15 (1179).

will, which he issued on 11 August 1229, before he embarked on the Majorca crusade, Bernard of Turre made arrangements that in the case of his death on campaign the Templars of Mas Deu should receive his horse and weapons or, alternatively, 1,000 *sous* in good money of Melgueil – a sum that evidently was intended to compensate the Templars for his weapons and horse.[83]

The payment of an annual rent and the donation of one's horse and weapons were acts of charity in their own right. What made them part of a confraternity agreement was the additional donation of the donor's body and soul and the ceremony in which these endowments were embedded. The ceremony by which laymen entered the confraternity of a Templar house is seldom recorded in the charters. In the Order of St John the names of lay associates were written into commemoration books.[84] From the point of view of the Hospitallers an additional reference to the particular relation of the donor to the Order in the charters was therefore deemed unnecessary. There is reason to believe that the Templars too followed this practice. Two long lists of *confratres* have survived for the Templars in Aragon, for example. Under the heading *Hic nominantur confratres Militum Templi* the first lists the names of lay men and women who had entered the confraternity of the Order by making annual endowments and giving their horses and weapons to it.[85] It is from this evidence that one may conclude that of the numerous benefactors who were not explicitly recorded as *confratres*, but who, like R. Sarracenus, gave to individual Templar communities '12 *deniers* and, at the time of his death, 100 *sous* in money of Toulouse', or, like Rorritius, '12 *deniers* and at the time of his death his best horse and his weapons, or, if he has no horse, 300 *sous*', many were in fact entering the confraternity of the Order.[86]

Reasons for becoming a *confrater*

Confraternity held benefits for the Templars and the laity. For laymen, the rewards of joining the confraternity of a religious institution such as the Temple were primarily spiritual.[87] Templar *confratres* and *consorores* could expect to be commemorated in the Order's prayers and to receive burial

[83] Doat, 40, fols. 232–5 (1229).

[84] J. S. C. Riley-Smith, *The Knights of St John in Jerusalem and Cyprus* (London, 1967), p. 244.

[85] For the lists see A. Ubieto Arteta, 'Cofrades aragoneses y navarros de la milicia del temple (siglo XII). Aspectos socio-económicos', *Aragón en la edad media*, 3 (1980), 29–93, and also Miramon, *Les donnés au moyen âge*, p. 90.

[86] The two examples are drawn from a long list of similar donations which the Templars had received from the citizens of Toulouse after they had established their presence in the city. *CG*, no. 20, pp. 13–15 (1128×1143).

[87] A. Vauchez, *The laity in the middle ages: religious beliefs and devotional practices*, trans. M.J. Schneider (Notre Dame, Ind., 1993), p. 110.

in one of the Order's cemeteries.[88] The right to bury *confratres*, *consorores* and other members of the Templar *familia* in their own churches and cemeteries had officially been granted to the Templars in 1139 and been further enhanced in 1144, although there is reason to believe that the bulls containing and enhancing the privilege were merely authorising already existing customs.[89] Burial with the Templars is often cited as the main incentive for association with the Order. The attractiveness of the Templar commandery as a place for burial can be explained with the Order's obvious religious status, but also with its international structure. Because it had dependencies on the way to, and in, Spain and the Holy Land the Order was particularly attractive to prospective pilgrims and crusaders, for people, in other words, who ran a great risk of dying in the absence of relatives and away from their home parishes. Entering the confraternity of the Temple provided these men and women with the opportunity to make arrangements to be buried in one of the Templar churches or cemeteries abroad, if the necessity for this should arise. In his testament R[aymond] Bertrand of Néjan arranged for just that when he entered the confraternity (*dono me pro fratre*) of the Temple at St-Gilles before setting out on his pilgrimage to Compostela. As the scribe recording his transfer recalls, R. Bertrand entered the confraternity of St-Gilles under the condition that should he die, he would be buried in the Templar compound in St-Gilles 'or in any other of the Temple's cemeteries'.[90]

Not only were pilgrims and crusaders attracted to the Templars and sought burial with them. When Rixendis of Abeilhan issued her will in April 1198 and gave her soul to God and her body to Pézenas for burial, for example, she made no allusions to any planned journey, but was clearly expecting to die at home, in her parish.[91]

However, a thorough background check of individuals who associated themselves with the Temple in this way reveals that many in fact had either personal experience in crusading or familial attachments to the Holy Land. William and Johanna Porcelet from Provence, who in 1174 gave their possessions to the Templars of St-Gilles under the condition that they would henceforth be regarded as members of the Order and receive burial with the Templars of St-Gilles,[92] provide a good example

[88] In most cases this would have been the cemetery of the commandery with which the candidate was affiliated, but there were exceptions. See e.g. Selwood, *Knights of the cloister*, pp. 114, 129.

[89] For the bulls in question see *PTJ I*, no. 3, pp. 204–10 (1139) and no. 8, pp. 214–15 (1144). An introduction to and edition of the bull *Omne datum optimum* of 1139 is also provided in *PTJ II*, pp. 67–103.

[90] BN, n.a.l., 5, fol. 63r (1152).

[91] Ibid., 16, fols. 101r–2r and 17, fols. 324r–6r (1198).

[92] H. Prutz, *Entwicklung und Untergang des Tempelherrenordens* (Berlin, 1888), p. 20 and Prutz, *Die geistlichen Ritterorden*, p. 362.

in case. For it is well known that from the early twelfth century the Porcelets had been continuously engaged in the county of Tripoli (in what is today western Syria and northern Lebanon), where they had possessions, and that William, like his father before him, had journeyed to the East frequently.[93] It may well be that they, and many other *confratres* and *consorores*, were attracted by the Order's reputation as a crusading institution. It is in fact very likely, as Charles de Miramon has argued, that in particular during the early decades of the twelfth century, at around the time when the Templars were given the right to have prebends and the patronage of churches, many *confratres* and *consorores* associated themselves with the Templars in an attempt to create a spiritual connection with Jerusalem and the Temple of Solomon.[94] In general, however, the wording of the charters and the very fact that Templar commanderies were considered suitable for burial indicates that laymen regarded Templar communities as religiously sound and association with the Order thus as spiritually rewarding.

The spiritual intercession for Templar *confratres* and *consorores* was regulated for in the Templar statutes, or *retrais*. At the end of every ordinary chapter the brothers were instructed 'to pray especially for peace and for the Church and for the holy kingdom of Jerusalem, and for our house, and for all religious houses, and for all other religious men, and for our *confrères* and *consœurs*, and for all benefactors of our house, living and dead'. Explicitly included in the prayers were also 'all those who have departed this world and who await the mercy of Our Lord, and especially ... those who lie in our cemeteries'.[95] Moreover, every day, at matins, the brothers were required to say 'thirty paternosters for the dead and thirty for the living'. And they were reminded 'not [to] omit to say them except because of an illness of your body, for they are established for our *confrères*, and for our *consœurs*, and for our benefactors, and for our benefactresses, so that Our Lord may lead them to a fine end and give them true forgiveness'.[96]

Spiritual benefits and burial could be extended to the families of associates; and this made association with a Templar community even more attractive for lay men and women with a real concern for the spiritual wellbeing of their next-of-kin.[97] In 1232 Hugh of Moussac

[93] On the Porcelet family's involvement in crusading see M. Aurell i Cardona, *Une famille de la noblesse provençale au Moyen Âge: Les Porcelets* (Aubanel, 1986), pp. 147–54; J. Richard, 'Le comté de Tripoli dans les chartes du fonds des Porcelets', *BEC*, 130 (1972), 339–82; Carraz, *L'ordre du Temple*, pp. 74, 76, 79.

[94] Miramon, *Les donnés au moyen âge*, p. 94.

[95] *La règle du Temple*, ed. H. de Curzon (Paris, 1888), § 541. [96] Ibid., § 683.

[97] E.g. AN S 5009, dossier 40, no. 1 (1190); *Cart LaS*, no. 36, p. 145 (1229), no. 81, p. 175 (1232).

associated with the Templars, hoping that 'they will receive me and my father and my mother in their spiritual benefits'.[98] When in 1264 John of Foulquarans, 'wishing to become a participant in the benefits of the house of the Temple of Solomon', gave himself as *confrater* to Pézenas, he made arrangements that not only he but also his son should be secured a burial in the cemetery of the commandery. For this, as well as for his confraternity, he offered to pay an annual rent of a half pound of wax each year on the day of the Blessed Virgin Mary (15 August) for the rest of his life. Moreover, and presumably to compensate the Templars for the special arrangement concerning the burial place for his son, John also decreed that in the case of his son's death without heirs all his possessions, 'wherever they are', should be given to the Templars.[99]

The Templars, in turn, profited from the *confratres* and *consorores* materially. They received lands, vineyards, customs, rights, weapons, horses and other material and monetary assets. From wealthy *confratres* they sometimes even received villages and lordships, or at least a share in them. Those who could afford less gave sestiers of grain, buckets of wax, garments or clothes. From almost all *confratres* and *consorores* the Templars received annual payments, the monetary value of which, again, depended greatly on the associate's status in life. The earliest surviving charter of the Templars in Toulouse is a list of donations which were made to the newly founded commandery of that city between 1128 and 1132.[100] The charter contains forty-four entries; almost all combine the payment of an annual rent with a one-time donation (usually of weapons and a horse or, instead of the latter, money) at the time of death. Not all of the benefactors were necessarily *confratres* or *consorores* of the Order. But, as I have said earlier, the nature of the donations and concessions suggests that in many cases arrangements for confraternity had been made.

The institution of confraternity also provided the Templars with important secular allies. Friendship and loyalty were essential criteria of any confraternal relationship.[101] What is more, by making *confratres* and *consorores* shareholders in the spiritual merits of the Order, the Templars created a network of associates, among them many powerful lords, whose spiritual salvation was believed to be intrinsically linked to the fate of the Order and who were often bound by oath to act as its advocates, benefactors and defenders.

[98] Ibid., no. 81, p. 175 (1232). [99] BN, n.a.l., 17, fols. 188r–9r (1265).
[100] CG, no. 20, pp. 13–15, where it is dated 1128×1143.
[101] Miramon, *Les donnés au moyen âge*, pp. 65–6.

The ceremony

Ceremonies of profession and affiliation, as Selwood has already pointed out, were seldom recorded in Templar charters.[102] Of the charters which do put donations into the context of such ceremonies, however, some provide a valuable insight into the rituals that were at work. In 1161×1162 Rostaign Carrella and his brother Bertrand granted the Templars pasture rights in all their lands and had their donation confirmed over a book of the Gospels. They then asked for membership in the confraternity of Richerenches. In support of their application they promised to render their arms and horses to the Templars when they died and to be 'good friends and defenders' of Richerenches in the meantime. Upon this, the charter tells us, 'the said brothers of the Temple received us with goodwill into the confraternity'.[103]

Another charter from Richerenches, dating from about 1179, describes how Dalmas of Valréas gave

> myself in the fraternity of the house of the Temple of Solomon, in such a way that I shall not be able to join another religion without their [the Templars'] consent. And at the end of my life I give [the Temple] my horse and weapons. And if I have no horse, I promise them 200 *sous*, which shall be taken from my possessions. Now, in the present moment, I give to [the church of] Holy Mary of Richerenches one of Bosc Raymond's fields and the pasture rights in all my lands. This has been done into the hands of Berenguer of Avignon, in the church of Richerenches, in the presence of Peter Itier, who was the preceptor of the said house ...
>
> And the aforementioned Dalmas swore over the holy Gospel to hold true to all this with good faith, faithfully and firmly. And of the charity of the house he received 50 *sous* ...[104]

Both charters contain evidence that the act of confraternity included a material donation, the candidate's promise to surrender his horse and weapons – or a fixed amount of cash – at the time of death, an oath on the Gospels, and the promise to remain loyal to the Order and to join no other religious institution without the permission of the brethren. These were characteristic elements of lay association with religious communities which had been in place since the early middle ages.[105]

The same characteristics also feature prominently in thirteenth-century contracts of confraternity from Languedoc and Provence, which are often very detailed. These contracts show that in southern France the reception

[102] Selwood, *Knights of the cloister*, p. 123. [103] *Cart Rich*, no. 209, p. 186 (1161×1162).
[104] Ibid., no. 241, pp. 214–15 (*c.* 1179).
[105] J. Orlandis Rovira, '*Traditio corporis et animae*. La *familiaritas* en las iglesias y monasterios españoles de la alta Edad Media', *Anuario de historia del derecho español*, 24 (1954), in particular pp. 152–5, 170–1.

of *confratres* had by the thirteenth-century become standardised and formalised. They demonstrate furthermore that the reception ceremony was a complex procedure during which concessions, counter-concessions, oaths and agreements were made, taken and received. A typical example is the reception of Peter Alazardi into the confraternity of Pézenas, which is recorded in a charter dating from 1237:

I Peter Alazardi, guided by the spirit of God, wishing to participate in the benefits of the house of the Temple of Solomon, give, render and offer myself as a *confrater* in spirit to Lord God and the Blessed Virgin Mary, to the house of the knighthood of Pézenas, and to you, lord brother Peter Ferrier, preceptor of this house, and your successors. I promise that in good faith and to the best of my abilities I will always be faithful and useful to you fully and wholly.

And we, brother Peter Ferrier, witnessing and recognising your, Peter Alazardi's, goodwill and aspiration, with the counsel of our brothers and guided by the love of God and piety, accept you, the said Peter Alazardi, as *confrater*. And we give and concede to you spiritual partnership and complicity in all goods which either have been or will be made to the house of the knighthood of the Temple or to any of its dependencies, on this side or on the other side of the sea.

And I, the aforementioned Peter Alazardi, choose my burial in the cemetery of Our Lady of Pézenas. And, for the love of God and guided by piety and mercy, and for the redemption of my soul and the souls of my wife and my kin, I give to you, lord brother Peter Ferrier, and to all brothers of the house of Pézenas 100 *sous* in money from Melgueil and one piece of land, which I hold from you and of which the lordship is yours, and the *tasque* [a levy imposed on the harvest] that you have there. The 2 *deniers* and the land mentioned above I want you to have at the end of my days, not before. And I, Peter Alazardi, promise never to act against these arrangements; and thus I swear in person on these holy Gospels.[106]

The reception ceremony of *confratres* in Languedoc and Provence, as is discernible from such contracts, resembles that described by Riley-Smith for the Order of St John and can be summarised as follows.[107] Having announced his intention to associate with the Order, the candidate was summoned before the brothers of a nearby Templar convent. In the presence of the local Templar master (who may or may not have been the preceptor of the Templar house in question) the candidate gave his or her body and part of his or her possessions to God, Mary and the community to which he or she would henceforth be aligned. As a demonstration of his or her affection for the Order and its cause the candidate delivered a statement of goodwill,[108] pious

[106] BN, n.a.l., 17, fols. 20r–2r (1237). [107] Riley-Smith, *Knights of St John*, pp. 242–6.

[108] See e.g. *Cart Douz*, A: no. 159, p. 143 (1167), B: no. 20, p. 205 (1167); BN, n.a.l., 16, fols. 65r–73r (1196×1197).

intentions[109] and willingness to provide for the Order's security and future wellbeing.[110] This was followed by a pledge of loyalty to the Order and the candidate's assurance that he or she would not betray his or her bonds with the Temple, nor join any other order without the Templars' permission.[111] Thereupon the candidate was received into the confraternity of the Order. The ceremony ended with the candidate's solemn promise, usually on the book of the Gospels, always to honour his or her arrangements with the Order and to do his or her utmost to prevent others, notably relatives, from breaking them.[112] There is no evidence that the ceremony ended with the Kiss of Peace, as was the custom in the Order of St John,[113] or that the name and the donation of the *confrater* were always entered into a separate book or list. But as both acts were commonly practised in other orders at that time, it is possible that they were also practised in the Temple but not regarded as worth mentioning.

In its simplest form confraternity with the Temple enabled lay men and women to secure for themselves the prayers of a religious community, burial in a Templar cemetery and a link with Jerusalem and the crusades by means of a material investment. The bonds that were thus established did not demand much of the *confrater* or *consoror* in terms of personal commitment. This, however, does not mean that *confratres* and *consorores* were necessarily only loosely associated with the Order. From very early on the Templars received men and, less often, women into their confraternities who regarded association with the Order as a serious commitment to a religious life and the first step towards subsequent full profession. They retained closer ties with the Templars than did most other *confratres* and *consorores*. And over time they became recognised as an independent group of lay associates. It was from among this group with special obligations that the group of Templar donats (Latin *donati/ae*) emerged in the late twelfth century.

[109] See e.g. *CG*, no. 68, pp. 51–2 (1133) and no. 411, pp. 258–9 (1146); *PAC*, I, no. 45, pp. 53–4 (1148); *Cart Douz*, A: no. 75, p. 76 (1170); BN, n.a.l., 15, fols. 54r–6r (1195); ibid., 16, fols. 86r–9r (1197), 101r–2r (1198×1199); ibid., 17, fols. 188r–9r (1265), 324r–6r (1198).

[110] See e.g. *Cart Rich*, no. 209, p. 186 (1161×1162); BN, n.a.l., 15, fols. 54r–6r (1195); *Cart Vaour*, no. 109, pp. 97–8 (1196).

[111] See e.g. *Cart Rich*, no. 241, pp. 214–15 (*c.* 1179); *PAC*, I, no. 201, pp. 188–9 (1182); J. Oberste, *Zwischen Heiligkeit und Häresie. Religiosität und sozialer Aufstieg in der Stadt des hohen Mittelalters, vol. II: Städtische Eliten in Toulouse* (Cologne, Weimar, Vienna, 2003), app., no. 13, p. 332 (1229).

[112] See e.g. *Cart Rich*, no. 209, p. 186 (1161×1162), no. 241, pp. 214–15 (1179); BN, n.a.l., 15, fol. 309r (1182).

[113] Riley-Smith, *Knights of St John*, p. 244.

The confraternities in crisis

The late twelfth and early thirteenth centuries have been described as a time in which the confraternities were in 'crisis'.[114] By that time canon lawyers and Gregorian reformers had embarked on a debate about how to assess the religious merit and status of men and women who had attached themselves to churches without leaving the world and how these men and women could be brought under ecclesiastical control and regulation. Closely interlinked with this discussion, which manifested itself in numerous commentaries, pamphlets and treatises, was the concern with simony in the Church.[115] Attempts were being made to distinguish between men and women who attached themselves temporarily to a church and those who did so perpetually, and then to separate within the latter category the so-called 'true' *conversi*, who had associated with the Order voluntarily, from the 'false' *conversi*, who had been pressurised into conversion. The argument was that only 'true' *conversi* would receive spiritual benefits from their religious association; and only those who associated themselves voluntarily with a religious community could be attributed semi-religious status.[116] Elaborating on these ideas, Vincent of Spain, who was writing between 1212 and 1215, argued that the 'true' *conversi*, who had subjected themselves to a religious life, and therefore had religious merit, needed to be distinguished from the lay men and women who had promised to 'give themselves' to a religious community without ever doing so and who therefore should be called 'friends' of the community and not *conversi*.[117]

The debate on the religious status of lay associates of religious institutions and their expected commitment affected the Templar confraternities to the core. The Third Lateran Council of 1179 and the Fourth Lateran Council of 1215 issued decrees which must have caused many existing and most prospective *confratres* to consider or re-consider the spiritual value of their commitment to the Temple. Canon 9 of the Third Lateran Council contained a harsh response to the increasing efforts of Templars and Hospitallers to have their *confratres* exempt from episcopal jurisdiction.

> Concerning the *confratres* we herewith decree that if they have not rendered themselves completely to the brothers [of the Order], but remain the owners of their own possessions, they must not, for that reason, be in any way exempted from the judicial sentences of bishops.[118]

[114] Miramon, *Les donnés au moyen âge*, p. 111. [115] Ibid., pp. 112–16. [116] Ibid., pp. 114–15.

[117] Ibid., p. 115.

[118] *Conciliorum oecumenicorum decreta*, ed. G. Alberigo (3rd edn, Bologna, 1973), pp. 216–17. See also Miramon, *Les donnés au moyen âge*, pp. 132–3.

What this paragraph tells us is that the confraternities of military orders consisted of two different types of lay associates who were linked by a common terminology. Whereas the *confratres* of the first type continued to live in the world and to hold possessions, *confratres* of the second kind had given up their possessions and had been absorbed into the Templar community. Only they could be exempted from episcopal jurisdiction. The decree was the Council's response to the demand of the Templars and Hospitallers to have one of the most fiercely contested privileges of their orders extended to their lay following.[119] More than that, however, it was also clearly meant to segregate the effectively semi-religious associates from the rest in a confraternity and to privilege them.

The Fourth Lateran Council elaborated on the efforts of its predecessor to transform the confraternities of military and other religious orders into semi-religious bodies under ecclesiastical control. Effectively, it succeeded in reducing *confratres* and *consorores* of the 'classical' type – those who had made regular endowments in return for a share in the spiritual benefits of monasteries and a burial – to second-rate associates whose existence was henceforth outside the confraternities as it understood them.

> *Confratres* we understand, on the one hand, to be they who, while living in the world, have offered themselves to an order by means of abandoning their secular habit; on the other hand we also understand them to be they who have vifgaged their possessions to an order to live off the usufruct as long as they remain in this world. They may be buried in the churches of the regular religious [with whom they are associated], if they [the churches] are not under interdict, or in any other church of their choosing. But we do not count among them those members who buy the fraternity of these last-mentioned [regular religious] for 2 or 3 *deniers*, for this would break up and scorn the discipline of the Church. Instead they will receive a special remission, which has been conceded by the Apostolic See.[120]

By 1215 canon lawyers thus recognised two forms of confraternity: *conversio*, which meant that laymen gave up their worldly possessions and dress and entered the monastery, and economic submission. All those who had hoped to gain access to the spiritual benefits of religious houses by

[119] Riley-Smith, *Knights of St John*, p. 243; Prutz, *Entwicklung und Untergang*, pp. 40–1. In 1229 the Order of St John succeeded in having at least the crusade indulgences granted to its brethren also extended to the secular knights fighting under the Order's banner. See J. Bronstein, 'Caring for the sick or dying for the Cross? The granting of crusader indulgences to the Hospitallers', in K. Borchardt, N. Jaspert and H. J. Nicholson (eds.), *The Hospitallers, the Mediterranean and Europe. Festschrift for Anthony Luttrell* (Aldershot, 2007), 44–5.

[120] *Conciliorum oecumenicorum*, p. 261. See also J. Oberste, 'Donaten zwischen Kloster und Welt. Das Donatenwesen der religiösen Ritterorden in Südfrankreich und die Entwicklung der städtischen Frömmigkeitspraxis im 13. Jahrhundert', *Zeitschrift für Historische Forschung*, 29 (2002), 4 and Miramon, *Les donnés au moyen âge*, pp. 133–4.

making, usually modest, monetary endowments to them were henceforth excluded from the confraternities. They were not banned from making endowments; but the spiritual reward for such mundane commitment was fixed, as opposed to individually negotiable, and subject to the validation of the Pope.

Canon 57 of Lateran IV was aiming at lay association with religious institutions at large. Considering the small sums of money given as examples, it is even likely that the authors had primarily the usually meagre token-payments of the so-called *sainteurs* in mind when they wrote down their verdict.[121] But this cannot detract from the fact that Lateran IV, as Lateran III thirty-six years earlier, had a shattering effect on the composition of Templar confraternities.

The donat

'Donats' first appear in the Templar charters at the end of the twelfth century. By the middle of the thirteenth century they seem to have replaced other forms of confraternity. It is common consensus that Templar donats were semi-religious laymen of noble birth who had given themselves 'body and soul' to a Templar community, often with the intention of taking full Templar vows some time in the future. They swore obedience to the Templar master and frequently subjected themselves to the rules and customs of the Order. They usually made substantial donations to the Temple. Donats who continued to live in the world usually enjoyed the usufruct of their former possessions. Some, however, rendered themselves entirely into the Order's care. The brothers would provide them with meals, clothes and shelter. They also seem to have received a particular habit that distinguished them as affiliates of the Order.[122]

The origin and religious status of the donat are still subjects of scholarly debate. In her essay on oblation in the Temple, Élisabeth Magnou distinguishes between three types of 'autotradition'. The men and women who associated with the Temple out of piety and with the intention of participating in its benefits, but who did not partake in the religious life of the Order or wear a habit, constituted the 'simple donats'. Evidently these 'simple donats' shared the same particulars and

[121] *Sainteurs* were members of religious families who manifested their submission by paying usually small annual rents in money or kind to the monastery or church with which they were affiliated. Duby, *Rural economy*, p. 222.

[122] Oberste, 'Donaten', 2–4. See also Miramon, *Les donnés au moyen âge*, pp. 8–27 for a detailed account of donats in religious orders in general and Riley-Smith, *Knights of St John*, pp. 244–6 for donats in the Hospital.

characteristics that other scholars before and after Magnou have ascribed to the *confrater* – a term that Magnou neither uses nor discusses. The 'simple donats' are juxtaposed with an entirely different category that would be equivalent to the monastic *conversi*. These were men who had either taken vows or who had given their body and possessions to a Templar house and who, clad in a religious habit, were living semi-religiously with or near the brothers of the convent.[123] The *conversi* were identifiable in that they made individual arrangements with the Order which tied them very closely to the communities of their choosing. This aside, however, according to Magnou, the *conversi* were only a sub-category of the group of men and women who gave themselves 'body and soul' – in other words, as *confratres* – to the Order.[124]

Scholars now tend to regard the classification system adopted by Magnou as too rigid,[125] and in recent years authorities on the military orders like Demurger and Nicholson have distanced themselves from their earlier conviction that among the wide variety of Templar lay associates the donat, unlike the *confrater*, had the definite intention of entering the Order.[126] Few would still agree with Selwood that in southern France at least donats and *confratres* were all but the same and that the term *donatus* 'was simply an Occitan word for *confrater*'.[127] According to Demurger's most recent comments on the subject of lay association in the Temple, donats were merely more closely associated with the Order than *confratres* and would often join it.[128] Only recently, Miramon has dedicated a monograph to the development and history of the religious donat in the middle ages. It is the most detailed study on the topic to date and, because of its broad context and its attempt to investigate the donat in terms of his/her relation to other forms of lay association, it is more instructive than Magnou's article. According to Miramon, *confratres* and donats were two fundamentally different forms of lay associates. Whereas the *confrater* defined himself only by his relation to the Order, the donat had a status within it. Miramon dismisses the notion that the *confratres* of the twelfth century were 'proto-donats' with the argument that donats developed first in religious orders that had hitherto shown little or no enthusiasm for attracting *confratres* or *familiares*. Moreover, in other orders (the Order of

[123] Magnou, 'Oblature', 382–3. [124] Ibid., 385–6.

[125] Selwood, *Knights of the cloister*, p. 131; H.J. Nicholson, *The Knights Templar: a new history* (Stroud, 2001), pp. 132–3 (and again confirmed in H.J. Nicholson, *The Knights Templar: a brief history of the warrior order* (updated edn, Philadelphia, Pa., London, 2010), p. 304 fn. 45).

[126] For Nicholson, *The Knights Templar: a new history*, pp. 132–3, see now Nicholson, *The Knights Templar: a brief history*, pp. 144–5. For Demurger, *Vie et mort*, p. 75, see now Demurger, *Les templiers*, p. 126.

[127] Selwood, *Knights of the cloister*, p. 131. [128] Demurger, *Les templiers*, p. 126.

St John is one example), the donats did not replace the *confratres*, but existed independently alongside them.[129] In Miramon's opinion the donats and *confratres* were not the same; but they shared the same origin.

Donats in the early Temple

The fact that the donat as a particular type of lay associate appears in the charters of religious orders only from the end of the twelfth century onwards does not rule out the probability that lay men and women with the mindset of donats had entered the confraternities of religious houses throughout the twelfth century and even before. The confraternity of a religious community was not yet legally defined. It allowed for different forms of association of varying intensity, provided that some basic requirements were met. According to Magnou's definition, which postulates a purely semantic viewpoint on the matter, all lay men and women who rendered themselves *corpus et anima* to Templar communities were donats. One could take this definition a step further by arguing that because all associates were required to give themselves in one form or another to a Templar community, the terms *confrater* and 'donat' should indeed be regarded as synonyms. But this would mean embarking on a semantic discussion, which, ultimately, leads nowhere. The fact of the matter is that from early on the term *confrater* was used as an umbrella term under which could gather Templar lay associates with different degrees of attachment to the Order. And some of them had affiliated themselves with the Order very closely.

The 'transfer of body and soul', which Magnou considered to be the purest form of oblation, evoked a strong spiritual bond between lay men and women and Templar communities that could, in the case of men, result in the candidate's full profession at a later date, and in the case of women in permanent submission under the command of the community's preceptor or chaplain.[130] In 1133, for example, Açalaidis from Roussillon gave her body and soul 'to God the Lord and the holy knighthood of Jerusalem, which is called the Temple of Solomon . . . to work in the service of God under the command of the master'.[131]

In 1143 Peter Bernard, 'for the remission of my sins and for the salvation of my soul', gave his body 'in life and death' to 'God and the knighthood of Jerusalem' and, to the Templars of Mas Deu, 3 *bordas* – or peasant holdings – and one garden which he held as an allodial possession in the village of St-Féliu-d'Amont. It was agreed that Peter would retain the usufruct of two of the *bordas* and the garden for the rest of his life or for as

[129] Miramon, *Les donnés au moyen âge*, p. 60. [130] Magnou, 'Oblature', 382.
[131] CG, no. 68, pp. 51–2 (1133). Translation provided in Barber, *New knighthood*, p. 53.

long as he wished to remain in the secular world. The third *borda* and its revenues went into the immediate possession of the Templars. If he died, Peter Bernard insisted, 'the lords of Mas Deu shall carry my body and bury it and treat me as one of their *confratres*'. If he should ever wish to give up his worldly possessions, however, he insisted that 'the lords of the knighthood shall receive me and give me food and clothing as one of their *confratres*'.[132] When Bernard Sesmon of Bézu rendered himself body and soul to God and the Temple in 1151, he also postulated

that if I will change my life, I will render myself to the blessed knighthood or I will, with the counsel of the brothers of this knighthood, provide for the cure of my soul. And if it should occur that I die while still being occupied with mundane affairs, they will receive me as a brother and carry my body to a place that they consider suitable for my burial; and they will make me a participant in their alms and benefices.

He then gave the Templars 1,000 *sous* for their benefit and for the remedy of his soul and the souls of his parents. In return, Hugh Raymond, the provincial master, received him 'as brother and partaker in the benefices of our houses'. What is more, in what may have been a token of their gratitude but could equally have been the essence of the deal, Hugh Raymond and the Templars who were present appointed Bernard Sesmon the life-long administrator of their *honor* in the village of Espéraza.[133]

Eighteen years after Bernard Sesmon had thus become absorbed into the community and administration of the Templars, a young man with the name of Giles gave himself to Douzens. The charter recording his arrangements with the commandery indicates that he too had the intention of attaching himself closely to the Order and that he was possibly even contemplating joining it. Written in the first person, the charter informs the reader that

I, Giles, in my youth and in good mind and sense, for the love of God and the soul of my mother, and for the remission of my sins and the souls of my kin, and following the counsel of my father Bernard Giles of Canel, give myself, meaning my body and soul, in death and in life, freely and without pressure, but voluntarily and with the will of my father, to Lord God, Blessed Mary and all saints. I give myself and my entire *honor* to the holy knighthood of the Temple of Solomon in Jerusalem, and to you, Peter of St-Jean, master of the honourable knighthood of Carcassès and Razès, and *magister major*, in the presence of John of Silva, preceptor of the house of Douzens, and of the brothers Bernard of Mairac and

[132] *CG*, no. 299, p. 195 (1143).

[133] See e.g. *Cart Douz*, A: no. 199, pp. 171–2 (1151). The case of Bernard Sesmon is also discussed in Barber, *New knighthood*, p. 224 and Magnou, 'Oblature', 387–8.

John of Villerouge, and in the presence of Arnold of Carraira, brother and preceptor of Perpignan . . . This I do under the condition that if I, Giles, because of bad reasoning or because of a bad wish or through the force of my friends or parents, should wish to separate myself from this knighthood, the *honor* which I have mentioned earlier shall remain in the possession of the said knighthood, for all time and without any pledge.[134]

And when in 1170 Peter Fortonus and his brother Pons gave to the Temple themselves and a garden in the territory of Douzens, which they held from the Order, they also promised never to separate from the Temple and always to remain faithful and obedient.[135]

Açalaidis, Peter Bernard, Bernard Sesmon, Giles and Peter and Pons Fortonus gave more to the Order than was necessary to acquire membership in its confraternity. Moreover, all seem to have become personally and deeply involved in the affairs of the Order, and indeed physically attached to it, which in Giles's case can be deduced from the fact that he contemplated the possibility of being forcibly separated from the commandery of Douzens. Similar examples of the expressions *seipsum* and *animae et corporis* are documented for most of the twelfth century.[136] Most of them have in common the fact that the person associating him or herself with the Order made endowments to the Order that were more extensive and more valuable than those made by other *confratres*.

The examples just given suggest that lay associates who could, with hindsight, be described as 'donats', already populated Templar confraternities in the early twelfth century. It was canon lawyers who were to establish the criteria and instruments needed by churchmen to break down the confraternities into categories which assessed their members according to their religious commitment.

Donats in the later Temple

It was at around the time of the Third Lateran Council that the term 'donat' began to appear in the Templar documents.[137] By the time of the Fourth Lateran Council it was already widely used. But donats did not form a category apart from the *confratres*, as some scholars have claimed; they were *confratres* of a particular type who had been brought into prominence in the late twelfth century and were now distinguished from other *confratres* by a new terminology. For the same reason it is

[134] *Cart Douz*, A: no. 7, pp. 16–17 (1169). [135] Ibid.: no. 75, p. 76 (1170).

[136] *CG*, no. 339, pp. 220–1 (1144); *Cart Rich*, no. 67, p. 70 (1151); *PAC*, I, no. 101, p. 100 (1164); *PAC*, II, no. 421, pp. 60–1 (1177), no. 423, pp. 62–3 (1178), no. 201, pp. 188–9 (1182); *Cart Douz*, A: no. 8, pp. 18–19, no. 104, pp. 98–9 (1169); *Cart Vaour*, no. 90, pp. 75–6 (1185).

[137] Oberste, 'Donaten', 1.

wrong to maintain that the donats replaced the *confratres*. Throughout the thirteenth century lay associates are frequently referred to as *confratres* (or *consorores*) *et donati* (or *donatae*) of the Temple, which indicates that the two concepts coexisted and were compatible. In 1234, for example, Grimald of Sales and his wife Aiglina gave notice in a charter that 'both of us, at the same time, have been received ... as *confratres* and donats of the house of the knighthood of the Temple [of La Clau]'.[138]

What distinguishes the concept of the 'donat' – and of the 'donat and *confrater*' – from that of other forms of lay association is the emphasis on spiritual surrender that medieval scribes (and, through them, the donats themselves) attributed to it. In 1264, for example, William Belletus gave notice that 'I ... wishing to participate in the benefits of the house of the knighthood of the Temple of Pézenas, give, surrender and offer myself in spirit as donat and *confrater* to the said house of the Temple.'[139] Three years later the Templar preceptor of Bras in Provence had it recorded in writing that he, with the consent of the convent, considered receiving Agnes Chatella 'as donat and *consoror* of the house of the Temple and in all our spiritual and temporal benefits which have been and will be made'. At Bras, he further announced, Agnes would receive company and partnership 'in all spiritual and temporal possessions of this house as it is customary for one of the donats and *confratres* and according to the customs of the Temple'.[140] In 1276 Peter Bacon from Pézenas, 'wanting to become at once a donat in spirit of the honourable knighthood of the Temple of Pézenas', gave and offered himself 'to Lord God and Holy Mary, His mother, and to you, Lord brother B[ernard] Lavender, who are the prudent and religious preceptor of this house', so that they, 'following the consent and wish of the venerable brethren of this house, may receive me as donat and *confrater* in this house'.[141] The next year, Stephen Anquer from Pomérols approached the preceptor of Pézenas with an almost identical request, stating that 'by divine inspiration, wishing to be a donat in spirit of the venerable knighthood of the Temple at Pézenas ... I give and offer myself to Lord God and Holy Mary, his mother, and to you, Lord brother Bernard Lavender, who is the venerable and religious preceptor of this house'. The charter reveals that he was indeed received *in spiritualem* as a donat and *confrater* of Pézenas.[142]

It is obvious from these examples that at least in Pézenas in the 1260s and 1270s there was some effort made to distinguish lay associates with a strong spiritual commitment to the Order as the 'donats' among the

[138] BN, n.a.l., 20, fols. 149r–50r (1234). See also Carcenac, *Les templiers du Larzac*, p. 30.
[139] BN, n.a.l., 17, fols. 204r–5r (1264). [140] See Durbec, *Templiers et hospitaliers*, p. 195.
[141] BN, n.a.l., 17, fols. 221r–2r (1276). [142] Ibid., fols. 223r–4r (1277).

confratres of the Order. It is also obvious from the terminology that the concept of the 'donat' did not replace the concept of confraternity. It rather became a prominent expression of it. Donats were more closely attached to Templar communities than ordinary *confratres*, who, in turn, may have become degraded to the status of 'friends' (*amici*) of the Order. In 1227 Pons William of St-Couat made arrangements that after his death the Templars of nearby Douzens would receive land at Cabriac. In return for this promise the Templars received him, 'our beloved and friend of the house of the knighthood', as 'our donat and as participant in all our spiritual and temporal goods' (*recipimus dilectum nostrum et amicum domus militie Poncium Guillelmi de Sancto Cucufato in donatum nostrum et participem omnium bonorum spiritualium et temporalium*).[143] The reference to Pons William as *dilectus et amicus domus militie* is interesting because it indicates that, his possible personal friendship with the Templars aside,[144] before he became a donat Pons William was a member of a more amorphous group of people who called themselves the 'friends' of Douzens. His personal friendship with the Templars was certainly influenced by the proximity of Douzens to his home village and by the fact that both the Order and his family had possessions in or near the village of Cabriac. In fact, in March 1165 a certain William of St-Couat, who may have been one of Pons William's ancestors, had acted as witness when Bernard William and his wife Garsendis pledged to Douzens their possessions in the village of Cabriac.[145]

How Pons William became an *amicus* of the house of the Templars, which seems to have been something different from being friends with the Templars themselves, and what this 'friendship' amounted to, however, is difficult to establish. It was certainly an expression of loyalty. As 'friends' of a Templar community the *confratres* would help the brothers in time of need. This, at least, is what can be deduced from arrangements made by Rostaign and Bernard Carrella when they entered the confraternity of Richerenches, which included the promise that they would henceforth act as 'good friends and defenders' of the commandery.[146] With the discourse on the status of lay associates in mind, however, it is also possible to argue that Pons William had risen from amongst *confratres* who had promised to 'give themselves' to the Order but had never actually done so and of whom Vincent of Spain, in a different context, had maintained ten years earlier that they should be called 'friends' and not *conversi*.[147]

[143] Ibid., 19, fols. 46r–8r (1227).

[144] *dilectus* was not necessarily an empty expression but sometimes conveyed real affection and personal bonds: see Macé, *Comtes de Toulouse*, pp. 258–9.

[145] *Cart Douz*, D: no. 9, pp. 280–1 (1165). [146] *Cart Rich*, no. 209, p. 186 (1161×1162).

[147] Miramon, *Les donnés au moyen âge*, p. 115.

The integration of the donat into the Templar community

Donats often made substantial endowments to the Templar communities with which they wanted to associate themselves. Some were granted permission to enjoy the usufruct of their former possessions;[148] others received corrodies. These corrodies could consist of 'bread and water' or 'food and clothing'. Joseph-Antoine Durbec cites a charter in which the Templars promised to provide the prospective donat 'with bread and water and food and clothing as is custom in the house of the Temple for other donats'.[149] Here again we see a parallel between thirteenth-century donats and some of the *confratres* of earlier times. When Peter Bernard had given his body 'in life and death' to the Templars of Mas Deu in 1143, for example, he had stipulated that 'if during my lifetime I wish to relinquish my property, the lords of the knighthood shall receive me and give me food and clothing as one of their *confratres*'.[150] Twenty-four years later Peter of Escau gave himself and his entire *honor* in the village and territory of Cours and in the territory of Layrou to the Templars of Douzens, on condition that they, in return, would 'assign me food and clothing as you would do for one of your brothers'.[151] Peter of Escau is neither described as a donat nor as a *confrater*, but both terms would have been applicable.

Not only did donats often receive corrodies such as food, clothes and shelter from the Templars; they also sometimes took vows of obedience and chastity. Moreover, as I have said earlier, it seems that some wore a habit bearing the Templar cross, which identified them as affiliates.[152] Donats swore loyalty to the Order and promised to choose the Temple over any other order if they should ever decide to leave the world for the cloister. Some decided to live in the community religiously. When William and Johanna Porcelet gave their entire possessions to the Templars of St-Gilles in 1174 to become members of the community of St-Gilles, for example, they were adamant that after the death of one of them the other would live religiously in the commandery of St-Gilles under the tutelage of the chaplain of the house.[153] All this must sometimes have made it quite difficult for outsiders to distinguish male donats from fully professed members of the Order, something that is reflected in the terminology of the charters.

148 See e.g. *Inventaire Chastellux*, no. 69, p. 140 (1246).

149 Durbec, *Templiers et hospitaliers*, p. 230. 150 *CG*, no. 299, p. 195 (1143).

151 *Cart Douz*, B: no. 20, p. 205 (1167).

152 See above, pp. 58–9, and in particular Miramon, *Les donnés au moyen âge*, pp. 26–7; Oberste, 'Donaten', 4.

153 Prutz, *Entwicklung und Untergang*, p. 20.

Two charters dealing with the engagement of Bertrand of Fréjus with the Templars of Montpellier can be taken as examples of how effortlessly medieval scribes, in their writing, sometimes set religious donats on a level with Templar recruits. In 1199×1200 Bertrand, who was then sixteen years old, 'gave, surrendered and delivered' himself as brother (*pro fratre*) to 'Lord God, Blessed Mary and the house of the knighthood of the Temple at Montpellier'. He also gave everything that he possessed at that time to the Templars. In return for this, the provincial master, Fulk of Montpezat, and the preceptor of Montpellier, Peter of Caprespina, received him 'as a brother, to bread and water' into the commandery of Montpellier.[154] It is easy to mistake Bertrand's submission to the Templar commandery of Montpellier for a full profession in disguise. After all, Bertrand gave up his possessions and was received as a brother. What makes the charter of his alleged entry peculiar is the use of a terminology that was usually employed to describe a layman's entry into a religious confraternity. The formula *donare, tradere et reddere seipsum* was customarily employed to express a person's will to enter into close relations with the Order.[155] The preceptor's acceptance of Bertrand as a *frater ad panem et aquam* is also odd. The right to receive bread and water in the Temple was regularly granted to donats who had forfeited their possessions as an act of submission to, and reverence for, the Temple and who were prepared and willing to live semi-religiously under the tutelage of a local Templar convent.[156] Performed literally, or even as a gesture, the act of sharing bread and water with the Templars certainly helped lay associates to bond with the Order. But as a proposal to a prospective Templar brother corrodies such as food seem ill chosen, for this was surely the least that recruits expected from their new brothers. Only a careful reading of the Templar depositions from the early fourteenth century makes clear that by the end of the thirteenth century the request for bread and water (or for company, fraternity, charity and clothing) had in fact, at least in some regions, developed into a standardised formula by which Templar applicants requested full entry into the order.[157] This only strengthens the suspicion that during the final decades of the Order's existence the distinction between donats and men who had hitherto been considered novices had become increasingly blurred. At the very least, the Templar depositions show that by the late thirteenth century some of the outward characteristics of the Templar donat, such as corrodies, also habitually

[154] BN, n.a.l., 15, fols. 75r–7r (1199×1200). [155] Oberste, 'Donaten', 2.

[156] *Cart Puy*, no. 6, pp. 6–7 (1210).

[157] See, for example, *PT*, I, pp. 353, 356, 359, 365, 368, 371, 374–5, 545, 608; Schottmüller, *Untergang*, II, pp. 15, 16–17, 20, 21, 22, 24, 28, 41, 42, 44, 45, 49, 50, 51, 56, 58, 60.

applied to associates who, at one time or other, professed themselves fully into the Order.

Aged sixteen, Bertrand was thus, in accordance with his wishes, received 'as our brother, *ad panem et aquam*' by Peter of Caprespina and the convent of Montpellier. Twenty-five years later, aged forty-one, Bertrand issued another charter, in which he revealed, implicitly, that he had never joined the Order. In the charter, the purpose of which was to raise money from the Templars, Bertrand acknowledged that when he was little more than fourteen years old, he had given all his possessions and rights to Peter of Caprespina and the Templars of Montpellier. He had remained with the Templars for ten consecutive years, during which he had been resident in the commandery of Montpellier. Aged twenty-six, however, Bertrand seems to have left the community. The charter reveals that he and his late mother had become involved in a business transaction with the Templars, the aim of which had been to raise 1,000 *sous* in money of Melgueil as a dowry for Bertrand's sister Alazaicia.[158]

The fact that Bertrand could engage in business transactions with the Templars of Montpellier after having turned his back on ten years of residence in the commandery indicates that he and the Templars had parted on friendly terms, which would certainly not have been the case if Bertrand had broken any vows. There are many possible explanations as to why Bertrand left the Temple, and not all of them entail his abandoning his ambition to join the Order at some point in the future. A family emergency could have necessitated his return to the secular world. What is clear, however, is that for the long period of ten years he had lived as a *frater*, but not as a professed Templar brother, in the house of Montpellier. He had shared 'bread and water' with the Templars and had slept under one roof with them. And even in his mid fifties Bertrand was still regarded, and referred to, as a 'brother donat' (*frater donatus*) of the Templar house of Montpellier.[159]

The example of Bertrand of Fréjus shows how ambiguous the language of the charters often is. It also shows how closely donats could become attached to Templar communities without ever joining them fully. As I have already said, it must sometimes have been difficult for outsiders to distinguish between inhabitants of Templar houses who were professed and those who lived there semi-religiously. The Templars had a habit of employing lay associates as the administrators of their estates; some lay

[158] BN, n.a.l., 15, fols. 99r–102r (1225).

[159] By this time he was married and had two children, Gaucelm and Bertrand. His own brother Gaucelm, on the other hand, had associated himself with the Hospital in Montpellier. See BN, n.a.l., 15, fol. 113r (1238).

associates even functioned as representatives of the Order. Bernard Sesmon, who has been mentioned before, and who effectively became a donat of the Temple in 1151, was put in charge of the Templar possessions in the village of Espéraza.[160] Mary Boverie was recorded as a *soror et donata* of the Templar community of Montpellier in October 1221; as such she seems to have played an important role in the conclusion of a business transaction between the Order and a certain Willelma.[161] In 1243 the donat Arnold functioned as custodian or bailiff (Latin *bajulus*) of the Templar house of Campagne in Languedoc,[162] while the Templar donat William of Servière represented the preceptor of Bras before the archbishop of Aix in 1271.[163]

Donats and the novitiate

The example of Bertrand of Fréjus also shows that not all Templar donats were expected to enter the Order later in life. Other charters confirm this. In 1178 William Arnold of Cornus had already endowed the Templars of Ste-Eulalie with the rights in one of his manses, for which he expected to spend the rest of his life as a donat of the Order. This suggests that the promise to join the Order fully before his death was not considered a prerequisite for William Arnold's admission as a donat.[164] Another example is a charter dating from 1266, in which Raymond of Cardona confirmed that ten years earlier he had given himself, and had been received, as a donat to the Templar house of Bras in Provence. It shows that for a decade he had resisted entering the Order.[165] These examples cannot deflect from the fact, however, that many laymen did give themselves as donats to the Order with the intention of taking full Templar vows later in life.[166] The decline of the novitiate in the Temple in the late twelfth century may have been one reason why many prospective Templar recruits became lay associates of a Templar community before they applied for admittance into a convent of the Order. Donats and novices occupied the same niche in the Order's hierarchical structure. The novice was a member of the Order on probation and the novitiate a period during which Templar recruits accustomed themselves to Templar life and customs, while the members of the convent examined them for their suitability as brothers.

[160] See above, p. 61.

[161] According to the charter evidence the property in question was sold 'to you, Mary Boverie, sister and donat of the house of the knighthood in Montpellier, and to the preceptor Caprespina and to all brothers . . . of this house'. BN, n.a.l., 15, fols. 95r–6r (1221).

[162] Ibid., 19, fols. 107r–25r (1243).

[163] Durbec, *Templiers et hospitaliers*, p. 196.

[164] *PAC*, II, no. 424, pp. 63–4 (1178).

[165] Durbec, *Templiers et hospitaliers*, p. 194.

[166] Oberste, 'Donaten', 8.

For reasons which have never been fully investigated, but which seem to have to do with the Order's growing obligations in the East, the novitiate fell out of practice in the late twelfth century.[167] This was fortunate and unfortunate for the Order at the same time. On the one hand, the demise of the novitiate made Templar recruits immediately available for military duty. On the other hand, the prospect of committing oneself irrevocably to the harsh reality of Templar life without being granted a period of adjustment and consideration certainly did not make profession into the Temple more attractive for potential recruits. To enter the Templar community as a donat must have been a welcome opportunity for laymen with an interest in the Templar profession to become accustomed to the particularities of Templar life without the fear of being drafted to a military campaign straight away.

Because donats were expected to play a more central role in the community life of Templar houses than other *confratres*, their admission was subject to some of the same restrictions and criteria as that of Templar novices. According to a thirteenth-century charter from Auvergne, laymen who became donats of the Temple were freeborn and free from debts and any other restraints and therefore already eligible for full profession.[168] The charters indicate that they expected to be received into the Order without further delay if they felt the desire to abandon the secular life. In 1167 Guilabert gave himself to Douzens on condition that 'if I should ever have the wish to live your life, you shall receive me as a brother, alive or dead, with all my customary rights'. In the meantime, he declared, he would pay the brethren 12 *deniers* every year at Pentecost, as a reminder that 'you shall have possession of me and of what is mine for all time'.[169] A charter that was issued in 1220 at Pézenas recalled how Pons of Magalas, 'having been received into the spiritual and temporal benefits of the house of the knighthood of the Temple that is situated in the *castrum* of Pézenas', offered himself and made numerous material endowments to the Templars of Pézenas, 'hoping that I, by the grace of God and of the brethren of this place, will be received as their brother shortly'.[170]

That the act of becoming a donat of the Temple was regarded by some as the first step towards full admission into the Order is, again, supported by the ambiguity with which the subject was treated in the charters. In 1181, for example, Sicard of la Tour was received as 'donat and as brother'

[167] Forey, 'Novitiate and instruction', 5. [168] *Cart Puy*, no. 6, pp. 6–7 (1210).

[169] *Cart Douz*, A: no. 159, p. 143 (1167).

[170] BN, n.a.l., 16, fols. 367r–70r (1220×1221). See Forey, 'Novitiate and instruction', 8, for more examples.

(*donatus et frater*) into the commandery of Vaour.[171] Seven years later, Raymond Isarn of Cabriac, with the assent of his wife, who gave herself up to a nunnery, donated his body and his son Raymond to the Templars of Douzens, who received them as *fratres*, promising to provide them – *pro nostra consuetudine* – with beds and sufficient garments should they wish to take up the Templar habit.[172] When Berenguer of Canet endowed the Templars of Espalion with six manses in 1277, he also made arrangements that if he and his sons were to enter the Order, the brothers would provide them 'with horses, weapons and everything that is customarily assigned to the knights of this order when they are transferred overseas'. On this the preceptor of Espalion received Berenguer and his sons in the name of the provincial master 'as brothers and donats of this Order', promising, again in the name of the provincial master, 'that we will receive you and your sons as brothers and donats of this Order and that we will confer to you the dress of this Order'.[173]

For the Templars the introduction of the donat as a particular status within the Order had the advantage that they were able to attract the interest, benevolence and support of people who were interested in Templar life but, for the reason just cited, were reluctant to join or were merely interested in the religious aspects of Templar life. Of the donats who used their status to explore and experience Templar life in all its facets some would eventually join the Order; donats with an exclusive interest in the religious aspects of Templar life still provided the Order with valuable contacts in the secular world and helped it to establish a network of lay supporters. Becoming a donat may not have replaced the novitiate; but the number of donats (or *confratres* who, with hindsight, could be described as such) certainly increased when the novitiate was in decline.

Milites ad terminum

By entering the confraternity of a Templar community, be it as simple *confrater* or as donat, lay men and women made a permanent commitment to the Order, the implication being that they could not easily associate themselves with another religious order. Knights had only one other opportunity to benefit spiritually from their affiliation with the Order without associating permanently with it, and this was by consigning themselves temporarily into the service of the Templars as *milites ad terminum*. As I will explain, however, this form of assignment too could lead to a closer and more binding association with the Order than is

171 *Cart Vaour*, no. 56, p. 40 (1181). 172 BN, n.a.l., 18, fols. 486r–8r (1188).
173 Ibid., 20, fols. 227r–32r (1277).

indicated by the terminology. It is obvious from the primitive rule of the Temple, which consisted mainly of customs which the Templars had already been following in Jerusalem, that from very early on the Templars encouraged secular knights to serve in the Order for a limited period of time.[174] As *milites ad terminum* these knights were required to provide their own horses, weapons and provisions. The costs of maintaining a knight, his squire and his horse during the term of his service, on the other hand, were 'given out of fraternal charity according to the means of the house'.[175] The value of the horse which the knight brought with him into the Order was recorded in writing and at the end of his tenure the knight could redeem half of the sum from the Order if he wished to do so. The rest of the money, and thus the horse, remained with the Temple.[176] While he was in the Holy Land the *miles ad terminum* was answerable to the marshal of the Order. If he was in Jerusalem and the marshal was absent, he was under the command, and riding under the banner, of the master of Jerusalem.[177] He was expected to dress as simply as the Templar brothers and to be obedient to the Order's officials.[178] If his horse happened to die while he was in the service of the Temple, the *miles ad terminum* was provided with a replacement if the Order could afford it. Otherwise he was, it seems, required to buy a new horse at his own expense.[179]

How one became a *miles ad terminum* of the Temple is not entirely clear; but it seems to have involved a contract in which the knight committed himself to the Order for a fixed period of time.[180] The Templar Rule stipulated that each associated knight had to serve the Order and Jesus Christ 'out of pity' and 'with a pure heart'. A charitable disposition and not desire for mundane profit was thus the primary motivation for knights to associate themselves with the Order in this way.[181] Godfrey of Arcy-sur-Cure, of whom more later, who in around 1180 asked the Templar master of France to let him participate 'in the knighthood of Christ' as a secular layman, and who embarked for Jerusalem shortly afterwards, was evidently determined to spend his time in the Holy Land in the company – and perhaps in the service – of those 'who battle for Christ', in the hope that it would gain him friends in the afterlife.[182] The main rewards for a

[174] On the role of *milites ad terminum* in the Order of the Temple see generally Magnou, 'Oblature', 378–80, and G. Ligato, 'Fra ordini cavallereschi e crociata: "milites ad terminum" e "confraternitates" armate', in *'Militia Christi' e crociata nei secoli XI–XIII. Atti della undecima Settimana internazionale di studio, 28 agosto – 1 settembre*, Miscellanea del Centro di studi medioevali, 13 (Milan, 1992).

[175] *Die ursprüngliche Templerregel*, ed. G. Schnürer (Freiburg im Breisgau, 1903), § 32.

[176] Ibid.

[177] *La règle*, § 124.

[178] *Templerregel*, §§ 29, 33.

[179] Ibid., § 32. See also Magnou, 'Oblature', 380.

[180] Demurger, *Les templiers*, p. 124.

[181] *Templerregel*, §§ 32, 33; *La règle*, § 65.

[182] AN S 5235, no. 1, fol. 4r–v (*c.* 1180).

temporary commitment to the Order as *miles ad terminum* were spiritual. Godfrey of Arcy-sur-Cure hoped that by associating himself with the Templars he would gain friends who would 'receive me at the eternal tabernacle'. As a *miles ad terminum*, if he indeed became such, he could rest assured that in the event of his death in the service of the Order the Templars would feed one pauper for seven days for the sake of his soul and say thirty paternosters.[183] He could probably also expect to be buried *quasi unus ex fratribus*, as was the case for excommunicated knights who, with the assent of their bishops, had affiliated themselves to the Order.[184]

Many of the knights who dedicated their lives to the Temple for a limited period of time must have done so with a long-term commitment to the Order in mind. At least in the thirteenth century it was not unusual for men who had initially been employed by the Templars to join the Order eventually.[185] But even those who left the Order after a short term of association or employment could still express affection for it in years to come.[186] In the case of Godfrey of Arcy-sur-Cure his commitment to the military cause of the Temple seems to have developed into a bond of confraternity. Other knights may have regarded a temporary association with the Temple as a valuable preparation for a later full profession. If that were the case, then their reasoning would have been diametrically opposed to that of their contemporaries who associated themselves as donats with Templar communities in the West. The status of *miles ad terminum* enabled knights to experience Templar life in its harshest form, for the whole purpose of the temporary knight was to increase the fighting forces of the Order.[187] Yet the distinction between *milites ad terminum*, *confratres* with crusading ambitions and fully professed brothers is not always easily made. In 1156 the southern French nobleman Raymond Ato II of Aspet entered the Templar community of Montsaunès as *frater*. He made what seems like an entry-gift but at the same time retained possessions for himself *in vita autem mea et usque ad mortem meam*, which indicates that he had not, in fact, become a full brother of the Order. Raymond Ato II embarked on a crusade or pilgrimage to Jerusalem shortly after he had associated himself with the Order. This can be

[183] *Templerregel*, § 5. This compares to 100 paternosters and forty days of feeding a pauper for the death of a fully professed brother of the Temple. See *Templerregel*, § 3.

[184] Magnou, 'Oblature', 380.

[185] J. S. C. Riley-Smith, 'Were the Templars guilty?', in S. J. Ridyard (ed.), *Medieval crusade* (Woodbridge, 2004), 118–19.

[186] One such example is Count Fulk V of Anjou, who associated with the Templars in Jerusalem in 1120 and who subsequently endowed them with money. See Orderic Vitalis, *Historia aecclesiastica*, ed. and trans. M. Chibnall, 6 vols. (Oxford, 1969–80), VI, pp. 308–10.

[187] Demurger, *Les templiers*, p. 124.

deduced from a second charter – dated by Brunel to *c.* 1160 – which ratified an agreement between Raymond Ato II's son Roger and the Templars of Montsaunès regarding some of the landed possessions which Raymond Ato II had initially kept for himself but which he allegedly had given to the Order *quan s'en ana en Jherusalem*. He was, therefore, a *frater* of the Order, but not a professed brother. As he embarked on a journey to Jerusalem shortly after his association, it seems likely that the two events were causally linked and that it was Raymond Ato II's ambition to serve the Order during his stay in the East.[188] To experience Templar life in the East could also have been one reason why Stephen Raynald associated himself with the Temple before he departed to Jerusalem. Before he left, Stephen gave all his allods to the Templars, which they were to possess 'as long as I am a brother of this house of the Temple and when I will have been made a brother of this house'.[189] It is obvious that Stephen had made up his mind about joining the Temple eventually. In the prospect of his immediate departure to the East, however, he was content with being an associated layman of the Order only. As a *miles ad terminum*, if that is what he became, Stephen was able to learn more about the Order's tasks overseas and to experience the harsh reality of Templar life on the march and in battle before taking vows to join the Order permanently. These were experiences and insights that he was not guaranteed to gain during his novitiate in one of the local commanderies at home, from where he might or might not have been sent to the East.[190]

Benefactor, business associate, *confrater*, *donatus*, *miles ad terminum* – lay men and women, and in particular those of free birth and knightly or noble stock, could associate with the Order of the Temple in a variety of ways, thus ensuring that the Templars never segregated themselves from society. In fact, the charters suggest that some Templar communities must at times have been buzzing with guests. The least that can be said is that laymen from neighbouring families visited the Templars on numerous occasions. During these visits donations were made, witnessed, confirmed or revoked, business transactions conducted, pledges redeemed, rents and revenues delivered or re-negotiated, contracts of association arranged, entry ceremonies conducted and journeys prepared. As temporary knights in the service of the Order men could follow their crusading ambitions, knowing that in the event of death they would have additional spiritual merit bestowed upon them. As *confratres*, loosely attached to a local

188 *Cart Mont*, no. 40, pp. 247–8 (1156); *PAC*, I, no. 97, p. 94 (*c.* 1160).

189 BN, n.a.l., 15, fols. 287r–9r (1178).

190 According to Matthew Paris (*Chronica majora*, ed. H. R. Luard, Rolls Series, 57 (7 vols., London, 1872–83), IV, p. 416), in 1245 the Templars were also sending novices (*milites neophiti*) to the East.

Templar house, they were free to continue living in the world while resting assured that they had spiritual advocacy and a burial place secured for themselves.

To attach oneself in confraternity to a Templar community may not have required much in terms of material investment (although the endowments that accompanied acts of confraternity were often extensive). In terms of spiritual commitment, however, it was asking a good deal. By associating with a local Templar community, be it as simple *confratres* or *consorores* or as donats, lay men and women made a conscious decision to choose the Temple over every other religious institution. From now on the Templars were chiefly responsible for their spiritual welfare; and it was to them that they were henceforth required to turn first if they wanted to adopt a religious way of life. Entering the Templar confraternity was a once-in-a-lifetime decision that, once taken, could not be revoked. The name and spiritual condition of the lay associate were henceforth intrinsically linked with the name and spiritual condition of the Order. *Confratres* consequently had a personal interest in seeing the Order prosper and the brethren fulfil their religious duties. That lay associates often had a profound interest in the religious aspects of Templar life is illustrated by the fact that many of them submitted themselves to the Order's rules and customs, and even shared the responsibilities of Templar administration and representation. As they were not professed, however, they also maintained close ties to relatives and friends in the outside world, some of whom eventually also gave themselves to the Order.

Chapter 2

THE RELIGIOUS CONTEXT OF TEMPLAR SUPPORT

In February 1299, almost seven years after the fall of Acre and thirteen years before the dissolution of the Order, the nobleman Odo of Grancey from Burgundy confirmed and extended his father's donation of rights, serfs, lands and taxes at Poinson to the commandery of Bure. The charter recalling the donation bears testimony to the troubled mind of a pious man trying to come to terms with the certainty that he will ultimately be held accountable for his deeds and actions.

I, Odo, lord of Grancey-le-Châtel, make known to all who shall see and hear the present letters that we shall all be received, as the apostle says, before the seat of Jerusalem according to what we bear in our hearts, be it good or ill. So it is proper that through works of mercy, under the eyes of the Everlasting, we sow in the earth, keeping firm hope and true faith, if we wish on the day of the last Harvest to gather in Heaven the fruit of eternal life. Not knowing and yet believing that our common lot is death and that nothing is more certain than death and nothing less certain than the hour that the Judge of all creatures will choose for it, and compelled by the ardour of charity and desiring with all my heart to rise up and reach the heavenly realm, I full willingly recognise and affirm that I have granted, quitclaimed and delivered in pure and perpetual alms, to the honour of God Almighty and the blessed Virgin Mary, His mother, and to all sainted men and women of God, to the *commandeur* and brothers of the knighthood of the Temple of the house of Bure, and to their successors – the house that they ... have founded and which I, to benefit my soul and the souls of my ancestors, have under my protection – everything that the late lord of Grancey, William, my dear father, has come to hold, by means of exchange with the brothers of the Temple, in the village and dependencies of Poinson ...[1]

The spiritual sentiments to which Odo of Grancey gave such moving expression, the notion that to give to the Templars constituted a salutary act that could assist redemption, were popular among Templar donors and

[1] ADCO, 111 H 1161/1, dossier Poinson, no. 3 (1299) (BN, n.a.l., 56, fols. 143r–5v).

are repeated in the Order's charters with no preference as to time and place. More than 150 years earlier, the scribe who recorded Lauretta's donation to Douzens gave expression to her inner turmoil when he wrote that she, 'fearing the coming day of judgement when my redeemer, sitting on his throne, will give to everyone according to his deeds', turned to the Templars for the redemption of her soul and the souls of her parents.[2] In Flanders, at around the same time, Count Thierry and his wife gave to the Templars because they too believed that according to Scripture the Lord would repay their gifts many times over.[3] Lord John of Bussy, in Burgundy, was driven by 'fear of God's judgement' – or so the scribe wants us to believe – when he instructed in his will that endowments were to be made to the Templars for the salvation of his and his ancestors' souls,[4] whereas the Burgundian knight Thibaud of La Marche and his wife had apparently been motivated by their great love (*grant amor*) for the Templars to make donations to the commandery of La Romagne.[5]

Formulae such as these were standard repertoire of religious scribes, of course; and as such they were customarily employed to denote the spiritual significance of a gift in alms. But they may still have expressed the donor's concern to secure potent advocates in the afterlife, as could have been the case with the three donors who, as Bishop Bartholomew of Châlons-sur-Marne had to acknowledge, had given to the Templars 'with pious intentions and in expectation of eternal rewards'.[6] Odo of Grancey, as we have seen, expected that he would be judged before the throne of Jesus in Jerusalem. And Godfrey of Arcy-sur-Cure, a nobleman from near St-Bris in Burgundy, whose brother Gerard was the abbot of the prestigious monastery of Vézelay (as the scribe duly noted when recording Godfrey's confraternity agreement with the Templars), expected to see the Templars again at the *eterna tabernacula*.[7] In around 1180, and tormented by the prospect of eternal damnation, he turned to them as his spiritual advocates and with the idea of joining them temporarily.

[2] *Cart Douz*, A: no. 40, pp. 50–1 (1133). [3] *CG*, no. 98 (1134×1147).

[4] BN, n.a.l., 54, fol. 42r (1234).

[5] ADCO, 115 H 1234, dossier 31, no. 12 (*c.* 1277), and Marie, *Templiers de Langres*, pp. 75–6fn. for the dating of the charter.

[6] *Diocèse ancien de Châlons-sur-Marne*, I, no. 9, pp. 397–8 (1150).

[7] On Gerard of Arcy-sur-Cure, abbot of Vézelay (1171–98) see *CG(Yonne)*, II, no. 304, pp. 324–25; *Gesta pontificum Autissiodorensium*, in L.-M. Duru (ed.), *Bibliothèque historique de l'Yonne ou collection de légendes, chroniques et documents divers pour servir à l'histoire des différentes contrées qui forment aujourd'hui ce département*, 2 vols. (Auxerre, 1850–63), I, p. 428; A.-A. Chérest, 'Vézelay. Étude historique', *BuSoScYonne*, 22 (1868), 155.

To the venerable brother A[ndrew], prior of the brothers of the Temple who are in Gaul, and to the convent of brothers. Godfrey of Arcy, brother of the Lord abbot of Vézelay, greetings . . . . Having contemplated the false pleasure that this unstable life holds, and knowing that nothing will come as quickly to an end as this, I have indulged in the thought of how lucky those are who battle for Christ, and how great their profit is. Because while the one for whom the exercise of virtues means bitter labour is dying already, their happiness is endless. This is why I wish to become a participant in the knighthood of Christ. And albeit I have to remain in the secular world, to which mundane occupations tie me, I have thus decided to make mine friends who will receive me at the eternal tabernacle.[8]

To this end he made numerous landed endowments to the Order and erected a house and oratory for use by the Templars (*ad opus fratrum de Templo*), which his wife and children later confirmed.[9] The desires which motivated lay men and women like Odo, Lauretta and Godfrey to seek association with the Templars are not limited in time or place and reflect the sincere belief that the spiritual advocacy of the Templars was worth obtaining. But why did people like Lauretta and Godfrey consider it necessary to seek spiritual protection in the Temple in the first place? Lauretta's in-laws, the lords of Pignan, had close ties to the Order of St John (when it was not yet overtly military), the monastery of Our Lady of Cassan and the traditional Benedictine abbey of Aniane.[10] In 1150, her husband, William of Pignan, founded at Pignan the mixed monastery of Ste-Marie-Magdalene of Vignogoul, which was later converted into a convent for nuns and eventually incorporated into the Cistercian network.[11] Godfrey of Arcy-sur-Cure had close personal ties with Vézelay and was thus linked to a religious community whose spiritual value was beyond doubt. He himself may have founded the priory of Ste-Radegonde near Arcy;[12] he certainly visited the traditional Benedictine abbey of Molesme on several occasions and made donations to the Cistercians of Reigny.[13] At the time when he approached the

8 AN S 5235, no. 1, fol. 4r–v (*c.* 1180, two entries: donation and confirmation).

9 Ibid., fol. 4v (*c.* 1180).

10 *CG(Hosp)*, I, no. 17, pp. 18–19 (1109); *Nécrologe de Sainte-Marie de Cassan*, ed. H. Barthés, *Les documents nécrologiques du diocèse de Béziers. Nécrologes et obituaires du XIe au XVIIe siècles* (St-Geniès-de-Fontedit, 1988), pp. 21, 27 (1109); *Cart Béz*, no. 105, p. 145 (end C11th).

11 P. L'Hermite-Leclercq, 'Reclus et recluses dans le sud-ouest de la France', in *La femme dans la vie religieuse du Languedoc (13e–14e s.)*, CdF, XXIII (Toulouse, 1988), 305.

12 His foundation of the priory of Ste-Radegonde (where an epitaph commemorates his wife Helvis of Bazoches and one of his relatives) is suggested in R. Favreau and J. Michaud (eds.), *Corpus des inscriptions de la France médiévale, vol. XXI: Yonne* (Paris, 2000), no. 83, pp. 87–8 (and no. 84, pp. 88–9 for the epitaph).

13 *Cart Mol*, II.2, no. 158, p. 316 (1163×1164), no. 160, p. 317 (1176×1177); *Inventaire Chastellux*, no. 9, pp. 127–8 (*c.* 1150). The relationship between William of Toucy and Godfrey's brother Gerard of Arcy is illustrated in Bouchard, *Sword, miter, and cloister*, p. 431.

Templars for association he also renounced his rights in a number of tithes in the hands of his blood-relative (*consanguineus*) William of Toucy, bishop of Auxerre, granted possessions at Mailly-le-Château and Mailly-la-Ville to the monks of Vézelay, and made donations to the Cistercian nuns of Crisenon.[14] With his brother holding the abbacy of Vézelay, a cousin occupying the episcopal see of Auxerre and as a patron of Cistercian houses Godfrey of Arcy-sur-Cure was therefore in a good position to assess the spiritual value of his future commitments; this makes his association with the Templars all the more remarkable.

That he chose the Temple for association over, for example, Vézelay may have had to do with the fact that in 1180 he was preparing to journey east, very likely as a Templar *miles ad terminum*. Perhaps his decision was also influenced by the fact that in his youth he had aided the count of Nevers in his battle with the abbot and monks of Vézelay over rights of advocacy and guardianship in the monastery.[15] As his brother was the abbot of Vézelay, however, and as Godfrey obviously felt comfortable about engaging in business transactions with the monks, it seems that the rift between his family and the abbey had been mended by the time when Godfrey wrote his letter to the Templars. That he chose to associate himself with the Temple and that Lauretta turned to the Templars in the hope of salvation therefore indicates that for these two donors the spiritual value of the Templars matched that of the religious communities with which they could otherwise have freely associated.

What still needs to be ascertained is what the spiritual attraction of the Templars actually was and how it was conveyed to laymen who were not members of the Order. This is necessary insofar as the practice of reading out the Templar Rule to a postulant during the reception ceremony but not making it known to the wider public (the receptions were held in private), as well as the fact that the more essential tasks of the Order were accomplished overseas and therefore not visible to anyone who was not involved in crusading, must often have made it difficult for prospective donors or recruits to assess the value of a future commitment to the Temple. In particular during the first decades of the twelfth century the perception of the religious worth of this new order must have been heavily dependent on how it was perceived and promoted by those who had experienced Templar life and conduct in the East or by religious people and institutions with knowledge of the Templars' religious calling.

[14] *CG(Yonne)*, II, no. 293, p. 312 (*c.* 1180), no. 304, pp. 324–5 (1180).

[15] Hugh of Poitiers, *Chronique de l'abbaye de Vézelay*, ed. R. B. C. Huygens, *CCCM*, 42 (Turnhout, 1976), 431, 436. See also J. Richard, 'Vézelay', *LexMA*, VIII, cols. 1609–10.

Although not all prelates had welcomed the Templars with open arms, some, as will be shown, eagerly encouraged their expansion. To some extent, the attitude of churchmen towards the Templars was determined by religious background and vocation. As shall be seen, the Cistercians in particular, who were themselves no strangers to radical ideas, created multiple and personal ties with Templar communities. In general, however, the Templars attracted support (and critique) from every stratum of the ecclesiastical hierarchy, and from every part of the religious spectrum. Positive relations sometimes took on institutional dimensions, but even then a personal relationship between individuals would often be at their core.

TEMPLAR SUPPORT AMONG THE SECULAR CLERGY

It is a commonly held view that since it had become an exempt order of the Church in 1139, the Temple was viewed with apprehension by many of the secular clergy, and in particular by bishops, whose wealth, power and spiritual influence depended to a large degree upon their ability to hold on to ecclesiastical rights and possessions within their dioceses.[16] This was particularly true in urban centres, where, as Carraz has shown for Provence, Templars and Church authorities were frequently at loggerheads over issues concerning ecclesiastical jurisdiction, parish duties or burial rights.[17] A close look at the charters reveals, however, that this state of affairs emerged only after the Templars had been granted the status of exempt order of the Church. Until then, and in many places for a long time afterwards, the Templars would have been ill advised to alienate the secular Church authorities, with whom many of them shared not only social bonds but also their religious values.

As a result of a change in the electoral system of Church leaders and of changes in the social composition of Church chapters – which in turn were the result of wider social and economic changes that enabled hitherto less well-off families to increase endowments to, and thus their influence in, religious houses – bishops in twelfth-century France were no longer drawn predominantly from high noble families. Instead they were chosen from among local candidates of modest or low noble stock whose upbringing reflected that of the cathedral canons who elected them.[18] The

16 Prutz, *Entwicklung und Untergang*, pp. 27, 40–1.

17 D. Carraz, 'Les ordres militaires et la ville (XIIe–début du XIVe siècle): L'exemple des commanderies urbaines de la Basse Vallée du Rhône', *AdM*, 114 (2002), 275–92. See also D. Carraz, 'Les ordres militaires et le fait urbain en France méridionale (XIIe–XIIIe siècle)', CdF, XLIV (Toulouse, 2009), 127–65, for a more general investigation into the military orders' urban commanderies and possessions.

18 See Bouchard, *Sword, miter, and cloister*, pp. 65–86 on the social origins of ecclesiastical leaders in Burgundy, and generally M. Parisse, 'Les évêques et la noblesse: continuité et retournement (XIe–XIIe siècles)', *Chiesa e mondo feudale nei secoli X–XII. Atti della dodicesima Settimana internazionale di studio*

families who thus gained influence in the churches of Burgundy, Champagne and the south of France shared their social background with the majority of the men and women who supported local Templar houses and from whom the Templars recruited their knightly members.

While some bishops from these families tolerated the establishment of Templar communities in their dioceses at first but ultimately came to oppose it, others supported the Order from the outset and for many years. Throughout the twelfth century, and before the Order became exempt, the bishops and cathedral chapters of Langres, Carcassonne and Saint-Paul-Trois-Châteaux, for example, were some of the most prolific benefactors of the Templars in their dioceses, often instigating the foundation of new commanderies with their gifts of landed property, churches and parochial rights.[19] The bishops who occupied these sees at the time were reformers, for example Godfrey of La Roche Vanneau, who had entered Cîteaux in 1113 with his relative the future Abbot Bernard of Clairvaux and had himself been leading the Cistercian community of Fontenay as abbot before his election to the episcopal see of Langres in *c.* 1139.[20] During his episcopate and during those of his successors the Templars in the diocese flourished, with the result that it soon boasted one of the highest densities of Templar foundations.[21]

It is plausible that – as Carraz has argued for Provence – bishops with strong reformist outlooks (a group to which Godfrey of La Roche-Vanneau certainly belonged) used the military orders to complete the network of parishes in their dioceses and to have them instilled with a new spirit of religious fervour and diligence – a strategy that posed many bishops considerable problems when the Templars began to isolate these parishes from episcopal control and elevated their own churches to parish status.[22] Strategic thinking along these lines would explain why as early as 1139 the newly appointed bishop of Périgueux in Dordogne, Godfrey of Cauze,

Mendola, 24–28 agosto 1992, Miscellanea del Centro di studi medioevali, 14 (Milan, 1995), pp. 76–7 and J. Howe, 'The nobility's reform of the medieval Church', *American Historical Review*, 93 (1988), 331. For the increase in non-noble French bishops at the end of the twelfth century see F. Picó, 'Non-aristocratic bishops in the reign of Louis IX', *Medieval Prosopography*, 2 (1981), 41–54. This process of transition did not always go smoothly. See e.g. Mazel, *Noblesse et l'église*, pp. 261–303.

19 For Langres see the charters recorded and transcribed in *HdB*; for Carcassonne see in particular *Cart Douz*; for Trois-Châteaux see *Cart Rich*, in particular no. 128, pp. 121–2 (and also *CG*, no. 120, p. 84) (1136) for Pons of Grillon's donation that instigated the foundation of Templar Richerenches.

20 Bouchard, *Sword, miter, and cloister*, pp. 334–8, 396; M. G. Newman, *The boundaries of charity: Cistercian culture and ecclesiastical reform, 1098–1180* (Stanford, Calif, 1996), pp. 10, 26, 150–1, 173, 249.

21 Godfrey was succeeded by Walter. He also supported the Templars. In 1167, for example, he put the Templars in possession of the church of St-Maurice, which for the time being however they had to share with the current priest. ADCO 115 H 1242, liasse St-Maurice, no. 2 (1163).

22 Carraz, *L'ordre du Temple*, p. 325; J.-M. Allard, 'Le contrôle des paroisses, un enjeu entre les ordres militaries et l'épiscopat: le cas aquitain', in *Les ordres religieux militaries dans le Midi (XIIe–XIVe siècle)*, CdF, LI (Toulouse, 2006), pp. 21–52.

installed the Templars in the old Benedictine convent of Andrivaux to replace the monks who had hitherto 'lived too freely and in notable scandal'. This was a powerful demonstration of the bishop's trust in the Templars' spiritual steadfastness, and it would certainly have registered with laymen and churchmen in his diocese.[23] Other prelates who were supportive of the Templars before 1139 included Bishop Joscelin of Soissons (1126–52), a trusted friend of Bernard of Clairvaux and loyal supporter of the Cistercians; Elbert of Roucy, bishop of Châlons-sur-Marne (1122–7) and his successor Godfrey (1131–42); the archbishop of Auch, William of Andozile (1126–70); and Bishop Humbert of Le Puy (1128–44), whose relatives the counts of Albon would eventually establish a deep and lasting relationship with the Order and become part of a wider web of families tied together by marriage that included powerful Templar allies such as the counts of Forez, the counts of Forcalquier and the lords of Beaujeu.[24]

The benevolence of bishops did not cease after the Order of the Temple had been elevated to the status of exempt order of the Church. The bishop of Vaison, Berenguer of Mornas, for example, who had made substantial endowments to the commandery of Roaix in 1137×1138 and 1141, continued to be involved in Templar affairs at Roaix and Richerenches until at least 1176.[25] On the contrary, episcopal benefactions seem to have been on

[23] *GC*, II, col. 1466. The example is also recorded in Allard, 'Le contrôle des paroisses', p. 36.

[24] For Joscelin, bishop of Soissons see *CG*, no. 59, pp. 42–3 (1131). For Elbert of Châlons-sur-Marne and his successor Godfrey, who acted as key figures in the establishment and sustenance of the Templar commandery of Neuville, see *CG*, no. 46, p. 35 (1132) and *Diocèse ancien de Châlons-sur-Marne*, I, no. 1, pp. 394–5 (1132), no. 2, p. 395 (1134), no. 3, pp. 395–6 (1133×1142), no. 9, pp. 397–8 (1150), no. 10, p. 398 (1147×1151), no. 11, p. 398 (1147×1151), no. 12, pp. 398–9 (1147×1151), no. 13, p. 399 (1151×1153). The earliest donations from the counts of Albon to the Templars date to 1132 (*Cart Douz*, C: no. 3, pp. 266–7); by 1236 another member of the family, Pons of Albon, had joined the Templars and become master of the Order in Francia (Félix Bourquelot, 'Notice sur le cartulaire des templiers de Provins', *BEC* 4th ser., 4 (1858), 171–90, p. 183n.). The counts of Forez supported the Templars in the thirteenth century. See e.g. *Titres de la maison ducale de Bourbon*, ed. A. Lecoy de la Marche and J.-L.-A. Huillard-Bréholles, 2 vols. (Paris, 1867–74), I, no. 239, p. 51 (1244); J.-M. de la Mure, *Histoire des ducs de Bourbon et des comtes de Forez*, I (Paris, 1809), p. 261 (1261). Humbert III of Beaujeu, son-in-law of Amadeus of Savoy and Mathilde of Albon, entered the Order of the Temple for a brief period while on crusade in the Holy Land in 1148×1149; William of Beaujeu joined the Order permanently some time in the mid thirteenth century and was elected its grandmaster in 1273. See *RRH*, I, no. 260, p. 66 (1150); *Titres de la maison ducale de Bourbon*, I, no. 107, p. 25 (1224); de la Mure, *Histoire des ducs de Bourbon*, p. 128; and, for William of Beaujeu, Barber, *New knighthood*, pp. 169–70, and Demurger, *Last Templar*, passim.

[25] *Chart Roais*, no. 103, pp. 61–2 (1137), no. 104, pp. 62–3 (1137), no. 112, pp. 69–70 (1139), no. 110, p. 68 (1148), no. 115, pp. 71–3 (1141), no. 118, pp. 74–5 (1153), no. 159, pp. 164–5 (1158), no. 165, pp. 110–12 (1176); *Cart Rich*, no. 60, pp. 60–3 (1147), no. 92, p. 93 (1157), no. 98, pp. 97–9 (1169), no. 190, pp. 169–70 (1161), no. 201, pp. 178–9 (1174), no. 207, pp. 184–5 (1169). See also Durbec, *Templiers et hospitaliers*, pp. 76–7; Selwood, *Knights of the cloister*, p. 86; and Carraz, *L'ordre du Temple*, pp. 137–8.

the increase after 1139, although they became fewer again as the thirteenth century progressed. More and more often these benefactions included gifts of churches, cemeteries and oratories, which the Templars used as additional sources of revenue but which they also needed to meet an increasing demand for *cura animarum* – the cure of souls. Some churches they converted into new commanderies. Simon of Vermandois, bishop of Noyon, gave a church to the Templars, as did Archbishop Henry of Reims, whose gift of La Trinité enabled the Templars to establish a major commandery in Reims.[26] The bishop of Langres from 1139 to 1163, Godfrey of La Roche-Vanneau, donated churches at Leuglay and Voulaines to Templar Bure;[27] his successor, Walter of Burgundy (1163–79), leased the Templars of La Romagne a 50-per cent share in the church of St-Maurice-sur-Vingeanne and gave them a serf for the relief of his soul and the souls of his kindred.[28] In 1202, the bishop of Cahors, William of La Cras, made donations that enabled the Templars to establish a commandery at La Cras, and fifty-three years later his successor Bartholomew le Roux endowed La Cras with the church of St-Foy.[29] The bishop and chapter of Béziers granted the churches of St-Pierre of Cazouls and St-Véran of Usclas to Templar Pézenas in 1203, and twenty-nine years later their successor granted them St-André-de-Sesquier and St-Clément with their tithes and first fruits valuing them at an annual rent of two measures of grain and two measures of barley.[30]

Among the bishops who supported the Templars after 1139 those who adhered to new ideas of religious reform, and bishops with experience in (or a family history of) crusading, proved particularly influential. It could even be argued that support of religious reform and enthusiasm for crusading were characteristics of Templar-supporting bishops and prelates. Bishop Godfrey of La Roche-Vanneau of Langres, himself a Cistercian, and his successor Walter of Burgundy, both implemented reform ideas in their diocese and eventually retired into reform communities: Godfrey, who was related to Bernard of Clairvaux and to the Templar Andrew of Montbard, went on the Second Crusade and, in 1163, retired to Clairvaux; Walter entered the Chartreuse at Lugny,

[26] H. de Curzon, *La maison du Temple de Paris* (Paris, 1888), p. 12; Prutz, *Die geistlichen Ritterorden*, p. 374; P. Demouy, 'L'église de Reims et la croisade aux XIe–XIIe siècles', in Y. Bellenger and D. Quéruel (eds.), *Les champenois et la croisade. Actes des quatrièmes journées rémoises, 27–28 novembre 1987* (Paris, 1989), 31; *ObReims*, 330.

[27] ADCO 111 H 1166 (1163).

[28] ADCO 115 H 1242, liasse St-Maurice, no. 2 (1163) and BN, n.a.l., 53, fol. 249rv (1167×1168).

[29] J. Juillet, *Templiers et hospitaliers en Quercy: Commanderies et prieurés sur le chemin de Notre Dame de Rocamadour* (St-Yriex-la-Perche, 1975), p. 93.

[30] *HGL*, IV, p. 265; V, no. 114, col. 1436, 1232.

which, as a bishop, he had helped found.[31] Raymond of Montredon, who held the archbishopric of Arles from 1142 until 1160 and was a generous supporter of the Templars in the 1150s (his help was crucial for the establishment of the Order at Arles), was another influential reform bishop. He was, in the words of Carraz, 'the archetype of this new generation of prelates': a man from outside the local aristocratic circle with a good canonical training.[32] Simon of Vermandois, bishop of Noyon, gave the church of Tracy le Val to the Templars in 1146 and in the same year assisted in the foundation of Cistercian Ourscamp (where he was eventually buried). He took the cross and went on the Second Crusade to the Holy Land, where he died, at Seleucia, in 1148.[33] And Raymond of Posquières, bishop of Uzès, who over the course of thirty-odd years endowed the Templars with churches in the diocese of Rodez, at Trévils and at Berrias, came from a family of crusaders with close ties to the Templars.[34]

All these bishops were renowned reformers and if we leave aside considerations about the plight of pilgrims and concern for the holy places it seems that the Templars were seen as additional forces that could be used in the reformation of their dioceses. Moreover, their willingness to embrace the Temple seems to have been preconditioned by a positive stance towards crusading as a penitential act suitable even for secular ecclesiastics.

The logic that crusading and involvement with a military order shared the same religious values was not lost on the noble (and doubtless many non-noble) families, who, as we shall see, often invested heavily in orders of monastic reform as well as in the crusading movement and in military orders like the Order of the Temple. And it is to these families that many of the bishops who also patronised the Templars can be linked.

Bishops and church officials from Templar families

Many of the bishops whom we have seen supporting the Templars had relatives who were members of the Order or were in other ways associated

[31] *HdB*, v, p. 394; J.-V. Jourd'heuil, 'Sanctuaires, inhumations et sépultures des évêques de Langres des origines au XVI siècle', in V. Tabbagh (ed.), *Les clercs, les fidèles et les saints en Bourgogne médiévale* (Dijon, 2005), 40–1. On Godfrey of La Roche-Vanneau see also A. H. Bredero, *Bernard of Clairvaux. Between cult and history* (Grand Rapids, Mich., 1996), pp. 36, 50. For donations to the Templars see, e.g., ADCO III H 1166 (1163); BN, n.a.l., 53, fol. 249rv (1167×1168), 250rv (1169×1170).

[32] Carraz, *L'ordre du Temple*, p. 152.

[33] O. Guyotjeannin, *Episcopus et comes. Affirmation et déclin de la seigneurie épiscopale au nord du royaume de France Beauvais-Noyon, X^{e}–début XIIIe siècle* (Geneva, 1987), pp. 178–9.

[34] See generally Carraz, *L'ordre du Temple*, p. 551.

with it. This should not surprise us, considering that many twelfth- and thirteenth-century bishops and canons shared the social and regional background of the knights and nobles who also populated the military orders. It has been established, for example, that as many as two-thirds of the twelfth-century Burgundian bishops whose origin is known came from castellan, petty noble and knightly families;[35] in other words, they came from precisely that stratum of society from which the Templars are known to have recruited most heavily.

Bishops played important roles in the early administration of the Order's ecclesiastical possessions and the recruitment of Templar brothers and personnel. Even after 1139, when the Temple had gained the privileges to administer its own churches, they remained indispensable as intermediaries in disputes with local families and other religious houses. Moreover, most bishops were powerful lords in their own right and their benevolence and friendship gained the Templars many riches.[36] The Templars would not have benefited from an attempt to alienate the families of their members and supporters from local cathedral chapters. Instead it should be stressed that because the Templars recruited from the same families as did the cathedral chapters (the houses of Saulx, Grancey, Tilchâtel and Bricon, for example, supported the Templars and produced canons at the cathedral chapter of Langres)[37] it was easier for them to gain the favourable attention of powerful prelates.[38] These relationships were as common in the twelfth century as they were in the thirteenth and early fourteenth, and they help explain why, as Selwood has argued for Languedoc and Nicholson has postulated in general, so many bishops seem in fact to have taken a keen and generally friendly interest in the military orders.[39]

But family interest does not hold the key to all the answers. For it is also true that, as adherents of religious reform, many bishops avoided being

[35] Bouchard, *Sword, miter, and cloister*, p. 76. Even a high-born twelfth-century bishop like Walter of Langres may have been driven by family interests when he involved himself in Templar affairs. In 1175 he gave notice that his nephew Hugh the duke of Burgundy, 'for the salvation of his soul and those of his relatives', had confirmed a donation made by his vassal Simon of Bricon to the Templars at Voulaines. See J.-M. Roger, 'Les Morhiers champenois', *Bulletin philologique et historique du comité des travaux historiques et scientifiques français* (1980), no. 6, 108–9 (1175).

[36] On the power of bishops as feudal lords see O. Guyotjeannin, 'La seigneurie épiscopale dans le royaume de France (x^e–xiiie siècles)', *Chiesa e mondo feudale nei secoli x–xii. Atti della dodicesima Settimana internazionale di studio Mendola, 24–28 agosto 1992*, Miscellanea del Centro di studi medioevali, 14 (Milan, 1995), 151–88.

[37] *Cart Lan*, passim.

[38] This is in spite of the fact that, as Guyotjeannin ('La seigneurie épiscopale', p. 166) has observed, from the twelfth century bishops were more and more often elected from outside the cathedral chapters.

[39] Selwood, *Knights of the cloister*, pp. 80–1; Nicholson, *The Knights Templar: a brief history*, p. 173.

occupied with family politics.[40] Moreover, they could still have been attracted to the Templars for example for financial reasons.[41] Another reason why reform bishops embraced Templar communities was that they regarded them as potentially useful instruments to fulfil their reformist ambitions. Carraz has shown that bishops in Provence who were brought up between 1060 and 1130 as regular canons or reformed monks (he refers to them as the 'new generation' of bishops) became involved with the military orders and created 'un contexte particulièrement favorable à l'enracinement des frères [of the Temple and the Hospital] dans la région'.[42] What he implies, and what can be postulated *pro toto*, is that for these bishops, a commitment to religious reform was the driving force behind their decision to engage with the new military orders. This, and the fact that many of the reform bishops were Cistercian monks or supported Cistercian communities,[43] hardens the suspicion that it was religious reformers like them who helped create the spiritual context that allowed the Templars to operate in the religious landscape of medieval Europe. How closely the Templars could be linked to other reform communities, and notably to those of Cistercian provenance, needs to be examined next.

TEMPLAR FAMILIES AND CÎTEAUX

On 19 June 1202, the Master of the Temple, Philip of Plessis, wrote a letter to Arnold, abbot of Cîteaux, informing him about the new threats faced by Latin settlers in the Levant. The Aiyubid ruler of Syria and Egypt, Saif-ad-Din, had gathered his army at a time when most of the Latin defences had been destroyed by an earthquake, which had also caused havoc among the population. It is a harrowing account, not least because the master's blunt and unadorned words do not attempt to hide his despair and resignation. To encourage divine assistance in their suffering, he was counting on the prayers of the monks of Cîteaux. After all, was it not they who had brought his order to life in the first place?

> We need your prayers, in which we have faith in the Lord, to lift us out of the aforesaid calamitous tribulations we are suffering. And since our house had its origins in your house and your predecessors, it seems to us that we are bound by a special affection to you and you to us.[44]

[40] Parisse, 'Les évêques et la noblesse', p. 77; Y. Sassier, *Recherches sur le pouvoir comtal en Auxerrois du xᵉ au début du xɪɪɪᵉ siècle* (Auxerre, 1980), pp. 186–9.

[41] As demonstrated by Selwood, bishops could earn small fortunes from conducting arbitrations between the military orders and other parties. Selwood, *Knights of the cloister*, p. 81.

[42] Carraz, 'Les ordres militaires et la ville', 281.

[43] See generally Newman, *Boundaries of charity*, pp. 141–70.

[44] Bulst-Thiele, *Sacrae domus militiae*, App. 1, no. 2, pp. 360–1, translated in *TSS*, no. 20, pp. 99–100.

Philip of Plessis's remark that the Temple had its origin in Cîteaux is somewhat disconcerting, for contemporary writers such as William of Tyre, Bernard 'the Treasurer' and James of Vitry maintained that the Order had been founded in Jerusalem, by knights who had attached themselves as lay religious to, and adapted to the customs of, the reformed Augustinian chapter of the Holy Sepulchre, which had been established in 1114.[45] Had the master forgotten all about these old ties? Or was he deliberately ignoring them to the benefit of a new foundation myth that was now gaining prominence in the Order? Although the first question may never be answered, a close reading of the sources suggests that the second is touching on something very close to the truth. As far as I can tell no evidence exists that the Templars commemorated their early association with the Augustinian canons living at the Holy Sepulchre in Jerusalem, nor do they seem to have made any efforts to produce an official hagiography or institutional history that would manifest, once and for all, the Order's origin, spiritual valour and purpose.

One possible and commonly voiced explanation for the Templars' apparent reluctance, or failure, to produce an institutional history is that few brothers would have been prepared for the task of recording their history and ideals in writing. However, since the other two important military orders recruited the bulk of their brothers from the same clientele as the Templars but still managed to produce important hagiographical and historiographical works, and since the Templars, like the Hospitallers and Teutonic Knights, also employed priests and scribes with sufficient education to conduct and supervise modest literary projects, the argument that the Templars were incapable of conducting at least moderately elaborate literary tasks does not seem to carry much weight. Of course, one must allow for the possibility that oral histories existed, which were bound to be short-lived and would have been generally ill received (and thus forgotten) after the Order's fall from grace in 1312. With the transfer of much of the Templar property to the Order of St John some of these legends may have been revived in the context (and to the benefit) of Hospitaller spirituality, but so far none have been found.

The Cistercian legacy in the Temple

It would seem that with so little written information about their foundation to fall back on many Templars in the late thirteenth and early fourteenth centuries could not but believe the rumours circulating in the

45 C. Morris, *The sepulchre of Christ and the medieval west. From the beginning to 1600* (Oxford, 2007), p. 216.

Order that they had always been closely linked to Cîteaux, an assertion that may well have sounded plausible to those who had experienced these links in their own families. At the time of the Templars' arrest, at the instigation of King Philip IV of France, in 1307, only few brothers recalled the Order's Augustinian legacy or remembered its foundation by Hugh of Payns;[46] many more were convinced, as Philip of Plessis had been, that their order's origin was in Cîteaux and that St Bernard had played an important role in its establishment. Had he not instructed them to wear the cord (*cordula*) or girdle (*cingulus*) over their habit?[47] The Templar knight Gerard Beraud from Limousin for one was convinced, as he told the inquisitors after his arrest in 1307, 'that he wore the girdle over his shirt in honour of Blessed Bernard, who was the founder of this Order'.[48]

Confessions like Gerard's feed into a new narrative that linked the Temple with Cîteaux. Gerard, and other Templar prisoners like him, had good reasons to put their trust in that association. After all, Bernard and other Cistercian abbots had been involved in the drafting of the Order's primitive Rule at Troyes.[49] These included the Cistercian abbots of Cîteaux, Pontigny, Trois-Fontaines and Clairvaux. The secular host of the council of Troyes, Count Thibauld II of Champagne, was renowned for his piety and was a generous supporter of Cîteaux, as was his seneschal Andrew of Baudement, who was also present at the council and whose son Galeran had entered Clairvaux two years earlier.[50] William II, count of Auxerre, Nevers and Tonnerre, who also participated actively in the council, was strongly inspired by religious reform and later retired to La Grande Chartreuse.[51] Moreover, the Order of the Temple and the Order of

[46] Some Templars linked a head relic in the Order's commandery in Paris to Hugh of Payns. See Finke, *Papsttum und Untergang*, II, no. 155, p. 335.

[47] *PT*, I, pp. 603, 613, 615–16; II, pp. 223, 228, 232. See also J. S. C. Riley-Smith, *Templars and Hospitallers as professed religious in the Holy Land* (Notre Dame, Ind., 2010), p. 13.

[48] Schottmüller, *Untergang*, II, p. 67.

[49] *Templerregel*, pp. 131–2. See also J. Flori, *Chevaliers et chevalerie au Moyen âge* (Paris, 1998), p. 199; M. L. Bulst, 'Noch einmal das *Itinerarium Peregrinorum*', *DAEM*, 21 (1965), 598.

[50] On Galeran (Waleran) see Godfrey of Auxerre, *S. Bernardi vita et fragmenta*, ed. J. Mabillon, *PL*, CLXXXV, cols. 327 and 529–30. See also L. Veyssière, 'Le personnel de l'abbaye de Clairvaux au XIIe siècle', *Cîteaux*, 51 (2000), 50 and P. Aubé, *Saint Bernard de Clairvaux* (Paris, 2003), p. 186.

[51] Robert of St Marian, *Chronicon*, ed. O. Holder-Egger, *MGH SS*, XXVI (Hanover, 1882), pp. 233, 236; *Cartulaire du prieuré de La Charité-sur-Loire*, ed. R. de Lespinasse (Nevers, 1887), no. 55, pp. 134–6; Bernard of Clairvaux, *S. Bernardi opera*, ed. J. Leclercq and H.-M. Rochais, 8 vols. (Rome, 1957–77), VIII, pp. 453, 474; *Annales Nivernenses*, ed. G. Waitz, *MGH SS*, XIII (Hanover, 1881), p. 91.

Cîteaux were undeniably similar as regarded the social background of their fully professed brothers, their religious conduct and their outward appearance. In spite of the Augustinian elements which were mainly the remnants of the traditions and customs followed by the Templars as associates of the regular canons of the church of the Holy Sepulchre, the primitive Rule of the Templars was fundamentally Benedictine in character and put great emphasis on the inner development of its adherents.[52]

The clauses that constituted the primitive Rule ratified at Troyes provided the Templars with a Cistercian angle on some key issues concerning recruitment and the integration of lay associates.[53] These included a hesitant stand against child oblation and insistence on the novitiate. As Martha Newman has shown, as a result of the Cistercians' insistence on adult conversion many Cistercian postulants – Bernard of Fontaines lès Dijon and his band of friends are prominent examples – were unmarried *iuvenes* from knightly families who were otherwise prepared to live in the world as knights or, if they had received an education, as scholars. The Cistercians' reliance on these men and the necessity to communicate Cistercian values to them, which the same knights then annotated using the same knightly references once they had converted, were crucial factors for the development of a distinctive Cistercian culture that attributed great significance to military language, symbols and imagery, which were regarded as essential instruments for the transformation of knights into monks.[54] But there were further similarities. Both orders encouraged the involvement of non-professed laymen in the running of their houses and, in the case of the Templars, on the battlefield, with the role of the Templar sergeants originally being modelled on that of Cistercian *fratres conversi*.[55] Both orders also

[52] S. Cerrini, *Une expérience neuve au sein de la spiritualité médiévale: l'ordre du Temple (1120–1314). Étude et édition des règles latine et française*, 2 vols. (unpublished Ph.D. thesis, Paris: Université de Paris – Sorbonne (Paris IV), 1997), esp. II, p. 550. Dr Cerrini's thesis is expected to be published soon. I am very grateful to her for providing me with a copy. See also K. Toomaspoeg, 'I cavalieri templari e i giovanniti', in C. Andenna and G. Melville (eds.), *Regulae – Consuetudines – Statuta. Studi sulle fonti normative degli ordini religiosi nei secoli centrali del Medioevo*, Vita Regularis, 25 (Münster, 2005), esp. pp. 395–8; L. Garcia-Guijarro Ramos, *Papado, cruzadas, órdenes militares. Siglos XI–XIII* (Madrid, 1995), pp. 78–9; Demurger, *Les templiers*, pp. 96–7; J. M. Brodman, 'Rule and identity: the case of the military orders', *CHR*, 88 (2001), 397.

[53] The Cistercian influence in the Temple has been argued by A. Linage Conde, 'Tipología de vida monástica en los órdenes militares', *Yermo*, 12 (1974), 73–115. Evelyn Lord, *The knights Templar in Britain* (Harlow, 2002), p. 9 even went so far as to argue that 'the organisation of the Templars mirrored that of the Cistercians'.

[54] Newman, *Boundaries of charity*, pp. 23–37.

[55] K. Elm, *Umbilicus Mundi: Beiträge zur Geschichte Jerusalems, der Kreuzzüge, des Kapitels vom Hlg. Grab in Jerusalem unter den Ritterorden* (Sint-Kruis, 1998), pp. 498–506; C. Vogel, *Das Recht der Templer. Ausgewählte Aspekte des Templerrechts unter besonderer Berücksichtigung der Statutenhandschriften aus Paris, Rom, Baltimore und Barcelona*, Vita Regularis, 33 (Berlin, 2007), pp. 229–33.

shared a number of core values, first among them humility and obedience, which the Cistercians regarded as prerequisites for *caritas*.[56] They propagated an ascetic lifestyle and the ideal of poverty and established an early presence in Champagne and Burgundy. Their professed members were recruited from noble and knightly families (as, of course, were those of every other religious institution at that time), and in both orders full members were clad in a white habit (if they were of knightly stock, in the case of the Templars). Like the Cistercians the Templars were associated with the Virgin Mary;[57] and like them they were eventually exempt from episcopal jurisdiction.[58]

These similarities, superficial as they often were, should not detract from the fact that the Order of the Temple and the Order of Cîteaux were, in more fundamental ways of structure and organisation, very different from one another. Whereas the Cistercian Order consisted of independent religious houses with their own abbots, connected to each other by ties of filiation, the Templar Order, like the Order of St John, grew around a central convent in Jerusalem from where all power continued to radiate (at least in theory and more or less effectively). In terms of structure and organisation the Temple did not resemble Cîteaux at all and, as Karl Borchardt has argued very convincingly, the Temple and the Order of St John should therefore first and foremost be valued and examined as pioneers of organisational developments in the history of religious orders which became widespread in medieval Europe as the twelfth century progressed.[59]

Nor do these similarities serve as proof that Bernard of Clairvaux had personally masterminded the Rule's composition or that the Templar order had been designed in the spirit of Cîteaux. In 1908 the German scholar Prutz was already arguing that the alleged attribution of the composition of the Rule to Bernard was in fact evidence for the Templars' retrospective attempt to honour and explain their institutional ties with Cîteaux – ties which one scholar was even tempted to interpret as

[56] Newman, *Boundaries of charity*, pp. 55–9.

[57] Bulst-Thiele, 'Die Anfänge des Templer-Ordens', 315. The commonly held view that the Temple was dedicated to the Virgin Mary from the beginning is now being challenged in T. Licence, 'The Templars and the Hospitallers, Christ and the saints', *Crusades*, 4 (2005), 39–57.

[58] Innocent II, *Epistolae et privilegia*, *PL*, CLXXIX (1855), cols. 122–3 (1132); *PTJ I*, no. 3, pp. 204–10 (1139) and generally *PTJ II*, pp. 67–102.

[59] The thesis of the pioneering role of the military orders, which he also labelled as 'schools of administrators', was put forward by Borchardt in his keynote address (*Politics and power: some new thoughts on the origins of the crusades and the military orders*) at the Fifth International Military Orders Conference, held by the Cardiff Centre for the Crusades, Cardiff University, 3rd – 6th September 2009, the proceedings of which remain as yet unpublished.

a confraternity bond between the two orders.[60] As it stands, the question of Bernard's influence in the Rule remains the subject of hot scholarly debate, although there seems to be little doubt that he played an important role in the Rule's redrafting.[61]

That ties between the orders existed, however, is not only suggested by the Templars themselves, as we have seen; it is also supported by factual (if sometimes circumstantial) evidence, such as the similar patterns of early expansion of the Temple and of Cîteaux in England,[62] or the fact that Templars were habitually included in Cistercian commemoration lists.[63] And the charter evidence from both orders shows that it was not uncommon for donations to one order to be made in the house or into the hands of a member of the other. When the Burgundian knight Aimo of Marmagne decided to take the Cistercian habit at Fontenay, for instance, the donation that accompanied his entry was made into the hand of Ralph, who was a knight of the Temple;[64] and when William of Montpezat gave money to the Templars of Montsaunès, he did so in the nearby Cistercian abbey of Bonnefont (perhaps because Bonnefont was in possession of a scribe whereas Montsaunès was not).[65]

The possibility exists that the Templars had exaggerated their bonds with the Cistercians in an attempt to create, and then propagate, a Cistercian heritage for their order. But they were not the only ones who claimed the reality of these bonds and it now seems that there may have been a kernel of truth in their claim. As early as *c.* 1145 the deacon and convent of Notre

[60] Prutz, *Die geistlichen Ritterorden*, pp. 25–6, and more recently R. Hiestand, 'Kardinalbischof Matthäus von Albano, das Konzil von Troyes und die Entstehung des Templerordens', *Zeitschrift für Kirchengeschichte*, 99 (1988), 299–300. See also D. Selwood, '*Quidam autem dubitaverunt.* The saint, the sinner, the Temple and a possible chronology', in M. Balard (ed.), *Autour de la Première Croisade* (Paris, 1996), 228–9. A confraternity between the two orders is suggested in Bulst, 'Noch einmal das *Itinerarium Peregrinorum*', 598fn.

[61] Purkis, *Crusading spirituality*, p. 108.

[62] M. Gervers, 'Donations to the Hospitallers in England in the wake of the Second Crusade', in M. Gervers (ed.), *The Second Crusade and the Cistercians* (New York, 1992), 158–9. Close relations between the Templars and the Cistercians were also argued in K. Borchardt, 'The Templars in Central Europe', in Z. Hunyadi and J. Laszlovsky (eds.), *The crusades and the military orders. Expanding the frontiers of medieval Latin Christianity* (Budapest, 2001), 234.

[63] A. Manrique, *Annales Cistercienses*, 4 vols. (Lyon, 1613–59), I, p. 187:4. The Cistercian commemoration lists which Joachim Wollasch has subjected to closer scrutiny give the impression that the Temple and Cîteaux had since very early on been connected by a special spiritual bond. Of the 173 religious communities which were commemorated in the fourteen Cistercian commemoration lists investigated by Wollasch, for example, only nineteen were mentioned in all lists. One of them was the Temple. See J. Wollasch, 'Neue Quellen zur Geschichte der Cistercienser', *Zeitschrift für Kirchengeschichte*, 84 (1973), 188–232.

[64] P.-F. Chifflet, *Sancti Bernardi Clarevallensis abbatis genus illustre assertum*, ed. J.-P. Migne, *PL*, CLXXXV, no. C, 1462. On the knights of Marmagne and Fontenay see Bouchard, *Sword, miter, and cloister*, pp. 134–7.

[65] *Cart Mont*, no. 7, p. 229 (1167).

Dame in Paris acknowledged, in Bernard of Clairvaux's presence, Bernard's role as 'patron' (*patronus*) of the Templars and 'father' (*pater*) of their 'holy religion'; and in one general chapter the Cistercians themselves described their relationship with the Templars on one occasion as that of 'parents and children'. On another occasion they maintained that the Templars who had been killed at Jacob's Ford (*Vadum Jacobum*) in August 1179 should rightly be regarded as 'martyrs from the Cistercian family' (*familiae Cisterciensis subiungani Templi martyres*) and 'sons of Bernard' (*Bernardi filios*).[66] And if one is to trust Bernardo de Brito's transcription of the *forma iuramenti*, sworn by the Templar grandmaster on the occasion of his inauguration, which was discovered in the seventeenth century in a manuscript from Alcobaça in Portugal, the designated master's oath included the solemn promise to be always obedient 'according to the statues of Bernard our blessed father' (*secundum statuta beati patris nostri Bernardi*).[67]

Moreover, one can hardly overestimate the importance of Bernard's *De laude novae militiae* for the inner development of the Order of the Temple. Written before the council of Troyes and at a time when the religious orientation of the Templar community was still clouded by ambivalence, it provided the Templars with the spiritual identity that many had found lacking and which allowed them to be active warriors while remaining firmly rooted in the monastic tradition.[68] By juxtaposing the blessed status

[66] *Cartulaire général de Paris ou Recueil de documents relatifs à l'histoire et à la topographie de Paris, vol. I (328–1180)*, ed. R. de Lasteyrie (Paris, 1887), no. 321, pp. 297–8 (*c.* 1145); Manrique, *Annales Cistercienses*, II, pp. 185:4 and 309:10 (1158: at that time Everard of Barres, who had left the Temple for Cîteaux in 1152, was still living in Clairvaux, which may explain the particularly cordial relationship between the orders). At the very least, these comments should be regarded as evidence for the great impact that Bernard's *De laude novae militiae* and his alleged involvement in the redaction of the Templar rule had made on the collective memory of Templars and Cistercians alike. This development, as Francesco Tommasi argued, would also have been in the interest of the Order's founder Hugh of Payns. Tommasi believes that the attempt to camouflage the true origin of the Order by drawing it into the orbit of Cîteaux can be dated back to Hugh of Payns, who persuaded Bernard of Clairvaux to become the Order's *specialis patronus, commendator* and *adiutor*. See F. M. Tommasi, '"Pauperes commilitones Christi". Aspetti e problemi delle origini gerosolimitane', *'Militia Christi' e crociata nei secoli XI–XIII. Atti della undecima Settimana internazionale di studio. Mendola, 28 agosto – 1 settembre 1989*, Miscellanea del Centro di studi medioevali, 13 (Milan, 1995), 471–3. For the epithets *specialis patronus, commendator* and *adiutor* see Godfrey of Auxerre, *S. Bernardi vita et fragmenta*, cols. 320, 323.

[67] The *forma iuramenti* transcribed by Bernardo de Brito in the sixteenth century was disovered by Angel Manrique in a manuscript from Alcobaça in the seventeenth century. See Manrique, *Annales Cistercienses*, I, p. 187:4 and G. Schnürer, 'Zur ersten Organisation der Templer', *Historisches Jahrbuch*, 32 (1911), 512. For the Alcobaça MS see Bernardo de Brito, *Primeyra parte da Chronica de Cister: onde se contam as cousas principais desta religiam com muytas antiguidades, assi do Reyno de Portugal como de outros muytos da christandade* (Lisbon, 1602), and, as an introduction to the 'Fundo Alcobaça', J. Black and T. L. Amos, *The 'Fundo Alcobaça' of the Biblioteca Nacional, Lisbon, vol. III: Manuscripts 302–456* (Collegeville, Minn., 1990) (no. 288). As a caveat that this account may be fraudulent, see P. M. Cocheril, 'Saint Bernard et le Portugal. A propos d'une lettre apocryphe', *Revue d'histoire ecclésiastique*, 54 (1959), 429–30.

[68] See the discussion of *De laude* in S. Cerrini, *La révolution des templiers. Une histoire perdue du XII siècle* (Paris, 2007), pp. 94–9.

of the new knight in Christ to the inherently sinful state of the *miles* of the world and by invoking the powerful image of the new *miles Christi*, who, fighting Christianity's enemies with the twofold sword of spiritual and material coercion, gained glory in the eyes of the Lord, Bernard succeeded in providing a theologically refined concept of the Templars' mission and *raison d'être* that allowed them to quell internal criticism and focus on external expansion.[69] As a formative text for Templar identity the treatise *De laude novae militiae* was widely distributed among the brethren and in many cases attached to a copy of the Templar Rule.[70] One can easily imagine how its widespread popularity helped shape the Templars' image of St Bernard as their *pater* and *specialis patronus*, to use the terms adopted by the Templars in 1138 when they urged him to present their community in Rome with a tunic *pro eximia benedictione*.[71]

As 'special patron' of the Order Bernard would have achieved a high status in the Order, though in reality it remained ambiguous. For one thing, his veneration has left only sporadic traces in the Templars' liturgies,[72] and the little evidence that we have suggests that the liturgical celebration of St Bernard in a Templar community largely depended on the popularity and influence of the Cistercians in the diocese. In Palma de Majorca, for example, where the Cistercians of Poblet exercised great influence because of their involvement in the conquest of the island, the liturgy of the Temple in the late thirteenth century seems to have focused strongly on St Bernard.[73] The same was probably true for Acre, where by the mid thirteenth century the Templars celebrated the feast of St Bernard with a nine-lesson office.[74]

In spite of the similarities between the two orders, and despite the spiritual bonds to which both orders confessed, there was also an understanding between their members that if their professions were similar, they

[69] Y. Katzir, 'The Second Crusade and the redefinition of *ecclesia, christianitas* and papal coercive power', in M. Gervers (ed.), *The Second Crusade and the Cistercians* (New York, 1992), 8.

[70] Forey, 'Military orders', 195, and generally Cerrini, *La révolution des templiers*.

[71] Godfrey of Auxerre, *S. Bernardi vita et fragmenta*, col. 323.

[72] I agree with Sebastian Salvadó, who, referring back to Cristina Dondi's recent research, argued that it is better to speak of Templar liturgies. The liturgical practices of the Templars varied greatly from one diocese to the next and did not necessarily follow the example of the church of the Holy Sepulchre. See S. Salvadó, 'Interpreting the altarpiece of Saint Bernard: Templar liturgy and conquest in 13th century Majorca', *Iconographica*, 5 (2006), 52, with reference to C. Dondi, 'Manoscritti liturgici dei templari e degli ospitalieri: le nuove prospettive aperte dal sacramentario templare di Modena', in S. Cerrini (ed.), *I Templari, la guerra e la santità* (Rimini, 2000), pp. 85–131, and Dondi, *The liturgy of the canons regular*, p. 41.

[73] Salvadó, 'Interpreting the altarpiece of Saint Bernard'.

[74] This is evident from the Templar Breviary of Acre (Paris, BN, Fonds Latin, ms. 10478) as introduced and transcribed by Dondi, *The liturgy of the canons regular*, pp. 224–9 (227).

made different demands. The Cistercian monk Gaucher, whose letter to a Templar friend – of which more below – illustrates very uniquely the monk's longing for the sensual satisfaction of spiritual desires that Templar life in the East could offer, was nonetheless sceptical that the *magnum chaos* that now existed between them because of their respective dedication to the *disciplina militum et militiae Christi* and the *poenitentia pauperum Christi* could ever be calmed and a reconciliation between them effected.[75] Templar life, as the abbot of Bonnevaux once explained to Amadeus of Hauterive, was less strenuous than life in Cîteaux.[76] This was confirmed by the Templar Rule, which allowed brothers longing for a stricter order to leave the community of the Templars for Cîteaux once papal permission had been obtained.[77] Evidence for such transfers exists. The third grandmaster of the Temple, Everard of Barres, became a famous champion of Cîteaux after he resigned from the grandmastership in 1152 to spend his remaining years as a monk of Cîteaux.[78] The Cistercian general chapter reported another, attempted, transfer from the Temple to Cîteaux in 1151, which caused anxiety among the monks who believed that in this case permission to transfer had not been granted.[79] William of Cobrieux made a promise to transfer to Cîteaux or another stricter religious order while he was serving as a *miles ad terminum* in the Temple but later had second thoughts, which prompted Pope Alexander III to put the archbishop of Reims on his case.[80] The Templar Artaud, whom the Cistercians held in high regard for his effort in carrying sackfuls of relics to Clairvaux, also eventually joined the Cistercian Order.[81] And in 1307 the Templar knight Hugh of Calmont allegedly considered leaving the Temple for the Cistercian monastery in which his father, mother and brothers had been buried.[82]

Cases like that of Hugh of Calmont are good examples of how prominently the Cistercians featured in the lives of individual Templars. Especially in Burgundy and Champagne, where both orders peaked very

75 Vogel, *Das Recht der Templer*, p. 59.

76 *Vita Venerabilis Amedaei Altae Ripae*, ed. A. Dimier, *Studia Monastica*, 5 (1963), 282.

77 Bulst, 'Noch einmal das *Itinerarium Peregrinorum*', 595.

78 Barber, *New knighthood*, p. 71. A whole chapter is dedicated to his memory in the *Exordium magnum* of Cîteaux. See *Exordium magnum Cisterciense: sive narratio de initio cisterciensis ordinis auctore Conrado monacho Clarevallensi postea ad Eberbacensi ibidem abate ad codicum fidem recensuit*, ed. B. Griesser, *CCCM*, 138 (Turnhout, 1997), ch. 32, pp. 293–5. See also A. Dimier, 'Éberhard ou Évrard des Barres, grand-maître de l'ordre du Temple, moine de Clairvaux', *Cîteaux*, 27 (1976), 133–4.

79 *Statuta capitulorum generalium ordinis cisterciensis ab anno 1116 ad annum 1786, vol. I: 1116–1220*, ed. J. M. Canivez (Louvain, 1933), p. 42 and also Manrique, *Annales Cistercienses*, II, p. 185:4.

80 Alexander III, *Epistolae et privilegia*, *PL*, CC, no. 162, cols. 228–9 (1163).

81 Demurger, *Les templiers*, p. 179.

82 Since he made this statement while under arrest, however, Hugh's claims have to be treated with caution. *PT*, I, p. 405.

early, entire kin-groups engaged with them simultaneously. Their actions and transactions are recorded in charters and it is to these documents that one must turn if one wishes to disclose the religious predisposition of individual Templar and Cistercian postulants, and thus some of the elements that must have contributed to the decision to join either order. Examples of how patronage of one order was followed by profession into the other abound. Like Count Hugh of Champagne in the early twelfth century and the Occitan knights Berenguer of Auriac and his son Berenguer in the late twelfth century, numerous knights and noblemen had made donations to Cîteaux before associating with the Temple as brothers or *confratres*.[83] Andrew of Baudement, whose son was a Templar knight, assisted in the ratification of the Templar Rule but eventually entered the Cistercian order, as did Simon of Bricon, John of Possesse and Godfrey of Mousson, who also supported Templar communities and who entered Cîteaux, Clairvaux and Trois-Fontaines respectively.[84]

The ties between the Temple and Cîteaux that were created when different members of one family entered communities of both orders spread neither evenly nor simultaneously over France and their density varied greatly from one region to the next. In Champagne and Burgundy both orders became very popular very early, not least because of the strong presence of Bernard of Clairvaux, whose ties with the Temple were particularly close.[85] In Languedoc, the presence of the Templars preceded that of the Cistercians, who furthermore, as vocal opponents of popular heresies, alienated considerable parts of the landed gentry. The two regions – Champagne and Burgundy on the one hand and Languedoc on the other – must thus be examined separately at first; only then should a comparative conclusion be drawn.

[83] Count Hugh of Champagne gave money to Cîteaux before he entered the Order of the Temple in 1125. See Newman, *Boundaries of charity*, p. 173. Berenguer of Auriac and his son Berenguer both made donations to the Cistercian nunnery of Nonenque in 1173 and to Silvanès, Nonenque's sister-abbey, in 1175, but gave 'their bodies and souls', and thus themselves in confraternity, to the Templar commandery of Ste-Eulalie in 1178. One (presumably the elder Berenguer) later took full Templar vows. In a charter, which Brunel dated to *c.* 1178, he was recorded among the Templar brothers of Ste-Eulalie. See *PAC*, I, no. 165, pp. 153–4 (*c.* 1178); II, no. 423, pp. 62–3 (1178).

[84] *Feud Soc*, no. 47, p. 65 (*c.* 1205); *Diocèse ancien de Châlons-sur-Marne*, I, p. 234 (1165); *'Littere baronum'. The earliest cartulary of the counts of Champagne*, ed. T. Evergates (Toronto, 2003), no. 82, pp. 117–18 (1177); *Chartes des cisterciens de Saint-Benoît-en-Woevre des origines à 1300*, ed. J. Denaix (Verdun, 1959), p. 209. See also Evergates, *Aristocracy*, p. 217.

[85] For the argument that the Cistercian development in Burgundy was exceptional see C. H. Berman, *The Cistercian evolution: the invention of a religious order in twelfth-century Europe* (Philadelphia, Pa., 2000), p. xii; Marie, *Templiers de Langres*, p. 75.

Templar families and the Cistercians in Burgundy and Champagne

In 1994 Demurger published a short article illustrating the involvement of Lower Burgundy's lay aristocracy in the military orders in the twelfth century.[86] It contained a list of religious communities to which the comparatively small number of Templar and Hospitaller families from the region could also be linked. We thus know that noble families like the lords of Ancy-le-Franc, Noyers, Montréal, Chastellux, Mello and St-Vérain distinguished themselves not only as benefactors of the Templars and Hospitallers; they were generous patrons of great monasteries of international reputation (for example Cîteaux, Pontigny, Fontenay, Molesme and St-Germain of Auxerre), convents of local significance (for example Reigny, Crisenon, Jully-les-Nonnains), and small family foundations (for example Vausse or Marcilly-les-Avallon). Moreover, Demurger showed that Templar commanderies were often established in areas already crowded with religious communities. To cite just one example, the Templar house of St-Marc (or St-Medard) in the Tonnerrois stood in close vicinity to Molesmes, Pontigny, Fontenay, Saint-Michel of Tonnerre, Molosmes, Jully-les-Nonnains, Lézinnes, Quincy, Rougemont, Argenteuil and Ancy-le-Franc. And it was with most, if not all, of these houses that the Templars of St-Marc shared their patrons.[87] Relying on such overwhelming evidence, Demurger argued a strong case for the spiritual awareness of Templar families with multiple ties to religious houses.[88] It seems indeed unlikely that members of these families who became Templars had no preconceived concept of the Order of the Temple's religious conduct and spiritual value in mind when they joined it. To gain a superficial notion of the religiosity of the order they were about to join, all that was necessary was to compare their experience of the local Templar community to that of other religious communities with whom they were familiar.

Most monasteries listed by Demurger as being frequently visited and supported by Templar benefactors and relatives in Lower Burgundy were of Cistercian provenance or, like Molesme and Jully, renowned for a reformist outlook (the first two prioresses of Jully were Bernard's sister-in-law Elisabeth and her daughter Hombeline).[89] This is an important observation. Not only does it draw our attention once more to the often very personal relationships between Templar and Cistercian or other religious reform communities; it also suggests that these relationships were closely tied to the fact that these communities shared a

[86] Demurger, 'L'aristocrazia laica e gli ordini militari'. [87] Ibid., 63. [88] Ibid., 63–6.
[89] Bur, 'Le monachisme', 632.

common patronage with the Templars and that houses of both orders were often founded by members of the same kin-group, or indeed by the same person.[90]

A look at the extant Templar and Cistercian charters from Burgundy and Champagne confirms that of the families whose personal engagement and material support were largely responsible for the Cistercian expansion in Champagne and Burgundy many eventually extended their patronage to include the Templars, and vice versa. To some extent this can be explained by the fact that the founder of the Order, Hugh of Payns, was a Champenois nobleman with an established social network in the region, and that Count Hugh of Champagne, who seems to have been well acquainted with Hugh of Payns, had already joined the Templars in 1125.[91] One other reason why the Order was instantly successful in Burgundy and Champagne was that from the outset it attracted the attention of families with close ties to one of the most vocal proponents of religious reform: Bernard of Clairvaux. It was by means of this personal link with Cîteaux, created by common patronage, that the Templars, at an early stage, became associated with a religious order whose spiritual value at the time was undisputed.

The Bernardine network

As a member of the Burgundian knightly class Bernard of Fontaines-les-Dijon, first abbot of Clairvaux, had instant access to the wide aristocratic network that connected the medieval duchy of Burgundy with the county of Champagne. The son of a castle knight in the service of the lords of Châtillon, Bernard was personally related, by ties of blood or marriage, to a number of important households in both regions.[92] The

[90] Demurger, however, merely concludes that 'the secular aristocracy completely integrated the military orders in its strategy of conquering the afterlife: Templars, Cistercians, Mendicants – they are all efficient intermediaries between man and God' 'l'aristocrazia laica integra totalmente gli ordini militari nella sua strategia di conquista dell'aldilà: Templari, Cistercensi, Mendicanti, tutti sono degli intermediari efficienti tra l'uomo e Dio': 'L'aristocrazia laica e gli ordini militari', 66.

[91] Barber, *New knighthood*, p. 11. For Hugh of Payns's family network in Champagne see T. Leroy, 'Hugues, seigneur de Payns, premier maître de l'ordre du Temple', in D. Guéniot (ed.), *Mémoire de Champagne* (Langres, 2000), 181–91. His relationship with the comital family is also discussed in M. Bur, 'Les comtes de Champagne et les templiers', in M. Bur, *La Champagne médiévale: recueil d'articles* (Langres, 2005), 635–42.

[92] For Bernard's family ties see Godfrey of Auxerre, *S. Bernardi vita et fragmenta*, cols. 89–90; William of St-Thierry, *Vita prima Sancti Bernardi*, ed. J. Mabillon, *PL*, CLXXXV, cols. 225–68. Both Godfrey of Auxerre and William of St-Thierry mention a (not defined) relationship *secundum carnem* between Bernard and the viscount of Dijon, Josbert le Roux of Châtillon, which is ignored by Bouchard (*Sword, miter, and cloister*, pp. 237–8) and turned into a close family relationship between Bernard and the noble house of Châtillon by Jobin (*Saint Bernard et sa famille* (Paris, 1891)), J. Richard ('Le milieu familial', in *Bernard de Clairvaux*, Commission d'histoire de l'Ordre de

lords of Montbard counted as his relatives, as did, perhaps, the lords of La Ferté (whose exact involvement in the establishment of Clairvaux is still debated)[93] and the lords of Baudement – to name only a few families that also feature in the Templar records. Families which by the mid thirteenth century had married into Bernard's kindred network, and therefore could, at one time or another, lay claim to a relationship with him, included the lords of La Roche-Vanneau, Montréal, Sombernon and Arcy-sur-Cure; they too make frequent appearances in the Templar records. The lords of Grancey claimed St Bernard as one of their own in the sixteenth century.[94] As for the founding master of the Order of the Temple, Hugh of Payns, he was at the very least well acquainted with Bernard.[95]

All of the families just mentioned supported Templar communities as benefactors, members or lay associates. They also maintained close relationships with the Cistercian Order, and in particular with Clairvaux, where they appear in the charters among the benefactors, guarantors (*fideiussores*) and witnesses.[96] The documents show, for example, that the lords of La Roche-Vanneau played an important role in the foundation of the Cistercian abbey of Auberive and that they had been among the earliest benefactors of Cistercian Longué.[97] Agnes of La Roche-Vanneau, sister of Bishop Godfrey of Langres, became the first abbess of the reformed Benedictine house of Puits-d'Orbe, which had been founded with the help of the family of her sister-in-law Aanold's first husband Rainard of Montbard.[98] The lords of Sombernon co-founded La Bussière, a monastery to which they remained very close, and also made endowments to Cîteaux.[99] The lords of Montréal made donations to the Cistercian abbeys

Clairvaux, 3 (Paris, 1953), 3–15) and Maurice Chaume ('Les origines familiales de Saint Bernard', in *Recherches d'histoire chrétienne et médiévale. Mélanges publiés à la mémoire de l'historien avec une biographie* (Dijon, 1947), 110–40). See also Newman, *Boundaries of charity*, pp. 266–7fn.

93 Although the family of Josbert of La Ferté, whose relationship with Bernard is not entirely clear, certainly did make donations to Clairvaux, their involvement in the early development of the abbey seems to have been overrated. See Bouchard, *Sword, miter, and cloister*, pp. 237–8, and, for a brief summary of the debate, Newman, *Boundaries of charity*, p. 325fn.

94 *La roue de fortune ou chronique de Grancey. Roman généalogique écrit au commencement du XIVe siècle*, trans. É. Jolibois (Chaumont, 1872), p. 21. See p. 146 fn. 99 for a new dating of the chronicle.

95 S. Cerrini, 'Le fondateur de l'ordre du Temple à ses frères: Hugues de Payns et le *Sermo Christi militibus*', in M. Balard, B. Z. Kedar and J. S. C. Riley-Smith (eds.), *Dei gesta per Francos. Études sur les croisades dédiées à Jean Richard* (Aldershot, 2001), 99–110.

96 Newman, *Boundaries of charity*, pp. 173–4) has stated that Clairvaux and some of its affiliates maintained strong connections to the families of their monks, of which many were interrelated.

97 *HdB*, II, no. 245, pp. 213–15 (1126×1135). Founded in 1102 as a convent of canons, Longué was converted into a Cistercian monastery in *c.* 1150. See E. Collot, *Chronique de l'abbaye de Notre-Dame de Longuay (diocèse de Langres)* (Paris, 1868), pp. 49–53.

98 *Cart Mol*, I, no. 263, p. 244. For the foundation of Puits d'Orbe see Bouchard, *Sword, miter, and cloister*, p. 134.

99 For the family's association with La Bussière see Chifflet, *Sancti Bernardi*, no. xxiii, 1421D–2A; no. xxv, 1422C–D; no. xxviii, 1123D–4A; no. xxix, 1424B–C; no. xxx, 1424C–D; no. xxxv, 1427A–C;

of Reigny, Cîteaux, Mores and Pontigny;[100] the families of Broyes and Châteauvillain supported the Cistercian nunnery of Vauxbons;[101] the lords of Arcy were benefactors of Reigny;[102] and the Baudements assisted in the foundation of Cistercian Chaalis.[103] The lords of Grancey and Saulx, although not directly related to Bernard, were also involved in the foundation of Auberive.[104]

The religious association of the family of Bernard of Clairvaux's uncle Andrew of Montbard with the Temple and Cîteaux in particular is suggestive of how intertwined the social connections of the two orders sometimes were and how acutely aware Templars with Andrew's background must have been of the religious alternatives available to them. In fact, the case of the Montbards raises the question whether some Templars, along with their families, had consciously measured the spiritual value of the Temple against that of Cîteaux before deciding in favour of the former. When Andrew joined the Order of the Temple his brother Milo was already living as a lay brother in Cîteaux (only in 1188 were nobles formally prohibited from becoming lay brothers),[105] and his brother Rainard with his wife had already assisted in the foundation of Fontenay.[106] A third brother, Gaudry, lord of Touillon, had entered Cîteaux in 1113 following the example of his nephew Bernard, before transferring to Fontenay in 1119.[107] Later generations of Montbards and

Bouchard, *Sword, miter, and cloister*, pp. 123, 131, 133, 365; J. Marion, 'Notice sur l'abbaye de la Bussière', *BEC*, 4 (1842–3), 551, 554, 556; for transactions with Cîteaux see *HdB*, II, no. 411, p. 299 (1164) and *HdB*, III, no. 818, p. 293 (1189).

100 For Reigny see *CG(Yonne)*, I, no. 278, p. 429 (1147), no. 282, pp. 435–6 (1147, papal confirmation), and generally M. Helias-Baron, 'Reigny, Actes diplomatiques du XIIe siècle', *Bulletin du centre d'études médiévales d'Auxerre. Collection CBMA. Les cartulaires, Notices* (2008). For Mores see *Chart Mor*, no. 28, p. 61 (1186). For Cîteaux see *HdB*, III, no. 755, p. 269 (1186), no. 809, pp. 290–1 (1189, confirmation). For Pontigny see *Cart Pon*, no. 42, pp. 115–16 (1145×1146), no. 48, pp. 121–2 (1180), no. 49, p. 122 (1151), no. 214, pp. 254–5 (1235), no. 355, pp. 351–2 (1186×1187), no. 356, pp. 352–3 (1209), and Bouchard, *Holy entrepreneurs*, p. 104.

101 *Vauxbons. Abbaye cistercienne au diocèse de Langres (... 1175–1394 ...). Étude historique et édition du chartrier*, ed. B. Chauvin (Devecey, 2005), no. 4, pp. 69–71 (1198); no. 16, p. 80 (1236); no. 26, pp. 90–1 (1253); no. 27, p. 92 (1257); no. 30, p. 95 (1261); no. 39, pp. 103–4 (1277).

102 *CG(Yonne)*, I, no. 279, p. 430 (1147) and *Inventaire Chastellux*, no. 9, pp. 127–8 (*c.* 1150, but refers to the same donation as above) and no. 66, p. 140 (1241).

103 See pp. 100–1.

104 For example, the monk John of Grancey was witness when, in 1192, the wife of Henry of Saulx donated her rights at Praslay to Auberive. See Roussel, *Diocèse de Langres*, I, no. 144, p. 215 and also Bouchard, *Holy entrepreneurs*, p. 15.

105 *Statuta*, ed. Canivez, I, no. 8, p. 108 (1188) and Chifflet, *Sancti Bernardi*, no. xcix, cols. 1461C–2A for Milo as *conversus*.

106 Richard, 'Milieu familial', p. 14; P. Cousin, 'Les débuts de l'ordre des templiers et Saint Bernard', in *Mélanges de Saint Bernard. XXIVe congrès de l'association bourguignonne des sociétés savantes* (Dijon, 1953), 50; Bouchard, *Sword, miter, and cloister*, p. 134.

107 Gaudry died in *c.* 1130 and was buried at Clairvaux. See Veyssière, 'Le personnel', 51; Jobin, *Saint Bernard et sa famille*, no. 62, pp. 641–2.

their relatives continued to support Cîteaux. Andrew's nephew Robert of Châtillon joined Clairvaux and – after a time of doubts and second thoughts during which he escaped to Cluny – eventually succeeded to the abbacy of Cistercian Noirlac, in the diocese of Bourges.[108] A great-nephew of Andrew with the name of Rainer joined the Cistercian community of Fontenay,[109] the same community that another great-nephew, also called Andrew, supported with further endowments for which he received donations.[110] His wife Elvidis of Montréal became a benefactor of the Cistercians of Fontenay on her deathbed.[111]

Support of the Temple in the context of enthusiasm for Cîteaux was not limited to the lords of Montbard family, who were related to St Bernard by blood. Simon of Broyes, who made donations to the Templars some time between 1129 and 1132, is recorded alongside his father, mother and wife among the founding benefactors of the Cistercian abbey of Boulancourt.[112] The lords of Vergy, who supported Templar communities in the late twelfth century,[113] were patrons of at least five Cistercian houses: Auberive, Tart, Maizières, Cîteaux and La Bussière.[114] The counts of Joigny, who made donations to the Templars from 1192 at the latest, supported Pontigny,[115] as did the viscounts of Joigny and the lords of Noyers, who also made donations to the Templars in the late twelfth century and supported the Cistercian houses of Mores and Reigny, the latter of which they had helped found.[116] The lords of Bricon and Morhier were distantly related to Bernard of Clairvaux[117]

[108] Richard, 'Milieu familial', p. 14. For Noirlac see *Twelfth-century statutes from the Cistercian general chapter. Latin text with English notes and commentary*, ed. and trans. C. Waddel (Brecht, 2002), index I, p. 779.

[109] Chifflet, *Sancti Bernardi*, no. cvi, 1465.

[110] See e.g. ibid., no. cix, 1466–7, no. cx, 1467; *HdB*, II, no. 383, pp. 282–3 (1162).

[111] Chifflet, *Sancti Bernardi*, no. cxxv, 1476. [112] *Cart Boul*, p. 21.

[113] For Gerard (Wiard) of Vergy see *HdB*, III, no. 1432, p. 476 (1183). For Guy of Vergy's donation to the Templars during the siege of Acre see ibid., no. 867, pp. 314–15 (1191) and Richard, 'Les templiers et les hospitaliers', 235.

[114] See H. E. J. Cowdrey, 'Peter, monk of Molesme and prior of Jully', in M. Goodich, S. Menache and S. Schein (eds.), *Cross cultural convergences in the crusader period. Essays presented to Aryeh Grabois on his sixty-fifth birthday* (New York, 1995), 66–7; Bouchard, *Sword, miter, and cloister*, pp. 123, 185, 377; Bouchard, *Holy entrepreneurs*, pp. 38, 82; J. Richard, *Les ducs de Bourgogne et la formation du duché du XIe au XIVe siècle* (Paris, 1954), p. 431.

[115] *Cart Pon*, no. 124, p. 188 (1189×1190); no. 274, p. 299 (1180×1181).

[116] *CG(Yonne)*, I, no. 282, pp. 435–6 (1147); *Chart Mor*, no. 25, p. 59 (1180); *Chart St-Marc/Jully*, pp. 761–2 (*c.* 1186); *Cart Pon*, no. 55, pp. 127–8 (1189×1190). See also Helias-Baron, 'Reigny, Actes diplomatiques du XIIe siècle', in particular pp. 13–14 (foundation charter of Reigny, 1104). For the donation to Pontigny by the viscounts of Joigny see *Cart Pon*, no. 125, pp. 188–9 (1157×1158).

[117] The lords of Bricon were a collateral line of the family of La Ferté; in 1176 Baldwin of Bricon married the daughter of Walter of Nully, a relative of Bernard of Clairvaux. See Isenburg *et al.*, *Stammtafeln*, XIII/58; Roger, 'Les Morhiers', 79 and 82; Bouchard, *Sword, miter, and cloister*, p. 418.

and made donations to the Templars from perhaps as early as 1129 onwards.[118] In 1175 they gave the entire lordship of Voulaines to the Order, thus instigating the foundation of a new commandery.[119] From then until 1306 they were involved in a number of transactions with the Temple,[120] while remaining closely associated with the Cistercian communities of Longué, Auberive, Clairvaux, La Crête and Mores.[121]

The Templars produced by these families could hardly have been unaware of their relatives' relations with Cîteaux. They also would have been able to distinguish between the two orders' religious values and ways of life. On the same note, it does not seem plausible that those who had made up their minds about leaving the secular for the religious world would have entered Templar communities if they had considered their spirituality less efficacious than that of the Cistercians or of other religious houses with which they also had ties. Considering, moreover, that entry into a religious community was no private matter but one usually preceded by long discussions with friends and family, and that it ultimately required the approval of the latter, one must assume that in cases where friends and family were already engaged with the Cistercians, the decision to give oneself to another order would have been meticulously assessed.

In the light of these considerations the decision of individuals with ties to Cîteaux to enter a Templar community is noteworthy. As has been seen, two of Andrew of Montbard's brothers were already Cistercian monks by the time he joined the Temple. Similarly, two of William of Baudement's brothers joined Cîteaux at around the same time that he became a Templar. One, Galeran, entered Clairvaux in 1127 and became the first Cistercian abbot of Ourscamp in 1129; the second, Andrew, entered Pontigny and was the first Cistercian monk to hold the abbacy

[118] *CG*, no. 28, pp. 20–3 (1129×1143). Related by marriage to the lords of Bricon were the lords of Rochefort, who, in the thirteenth century, made at least one donation to the Templar community of St-Marc and one donation to Clairvaux. *Chart St-Marc/Jully*, p. 763 and BN, n.a.l., 54, fol. 43r (1234×1235); Roger, 'Les Morhiers', 101 (1275).

[119] Ibid., no. 6, 108–9 (1175).

[120] *HdB*, II, no. 638, pp. 399–400 (1178). Roger, 'Les Morhiers', 94, 99, no. 31, 126–7 (1289), no. 32, 127–9 and no. 33, 129–30 (1301); *Diocèse ancien de Châlons-sur-Marne*, I, no. 151, p. 436 (1306).

[121] Roger, 'Les Morhiers', 80, 84–7, 91–2 and no. 1, 104 (1138×1162), no. 3, 105–6, no. 4, 106 (1138×1158), no. 5, 107–8 (1164), no. 10, 112 (1182), no. 13, 114 (1196), no. 16, 116 (1198), no. 17, 116–17 (1198), no. 19, 118 (1202), no. 20, 118–20 (1205), no. 21, 119–20 (1205), no. 23, 121–2 (1218), no. 25, 123 (1218), no. 26, 123 (1223), no. 27, 124 (1224, 1227), no. 30, 125–6 (1253); *Chart Clairv*, no. 4, p. 13 (1135), no. 26, pp. 53–4 (1147), no. 285, pp. 354–6 (1190), no. 393, p. 504 (1199); *HdB*, II, no. 1595, p. 179 (1219). For quarrels which were peacefully resolved, see Roger, 'Les Morhiers', no. 2, 105 (1138×1158), no. 7, 109–10 (1176), no. 9, 111–12 (1178) no. 12, 112–13 (1194), no. 22, 120–1 (1214), no. 24, 122 (1218). They also conducted at least one property exchange with Auberive. See ibid., 95. At least two family members joined the Cistercian Order. One eventually became abbot of Longué, whereas the other entered and remained in Auberive. See ibid., 91, 98 and no. 27, 124 (1223), and Bouchard, *Sword, miter, and cloister*, p. 418.

of Chaalis.[122] And, such being the policy of decision-making, one has to assume that the choice of Andrew of Montbard and William of Baudement to join the Temple (a decision which usually required the provision of entry-gifts), and thus the arguments that supported it, had been assessed, accepted and supported by the same network of relatives and friends that in other cases had shown (or would show) so much dedication to the Cistercian cause. It is not very likely that either Andrew or William entered the Temple against the will of their families. The documentary evidence certainly suggests otherwise. In 1133 William's father, Andrew of Baudement, made an important donation to the Templars of Provins 'for his soul and for the souls of all his ancestors, and most of all for his son named William, who was then a knight of God and the Temple of Solomon', thus giving vocal expression to his affection and concern for his son.[123] The same can be said of Bernard of Clairvaux's letter to his uncle Andrew of Montbard, possibly written in 1153, which also indicates a friendly, even loving, relationship between the two in spite of their choice of different religious professions.[124]

The success of the Templars in Champagne and Burgundy therefore cannot be separated from the popularity of Bernard of Clairvaux in these regions, the persuasive power of his personality and, finally, his personal contacts. In the relationship between the Temple and Cîteaux he was the single most important unifying factor. His treatise *De laude novae militiae*, as already mentioned, provided the Templar community with a spiritual boost,[125] whereas in his letters he dealt personally with the concerns of individual Templar officials.[126] His wide-ranging network of relatives, friends and admirers guaranteed personal prosperity for both orders. And the resulting personal relationships between Templar and Cistercian communities would have facilitated the exchange of spiritual ideas and concepts of religious practice between them.

As has been seen, it was not uncommon for families to have relatives in both orders; nor was it uncommon for individual Templars and

[122] On Galeran see Godfrey of Auxerre, *S. Bernardi vita et fragmenta*, cols. 523–30; Veyssière, 'Le personnel', 50; Aubé, *Saint Bernard*, p. 186. For Andrew as the abbot of Chaalis see M. Bur, 'Braine', *LexMA*, II, 545.

[123] The donation consisted of all of Andrew's male and female serfs (*servi et ancillae*) in the domain of Baudement, all arable and waste lands, waters, meadows and bridges (meaning the bridge toll) and all revenues of the castle of Baudement. See *Cart Prov*, no. 81, pp. 102–3 (1133).

[124] Bernard of Clairvaux, *Epistolae*, *PL*, CLXXII, no. 288, cols. 493–4. See also Godfrey of Auxerre, *S. Bernardi vita et fragmenta*, col. 351 and Bulst-Thiele, *Sacrae domus militiae*, p. 58.

[125] See pp. 91–2 above.

[126] See Bernard's letter to Andrew of Montbard (referred to in fn.124, above), as well as Bernard of Clairvaux, *Epistolae*, no. 307, cols. 510–12 (concerning Geoffrey Fulchier) and no. 380, cols. 583–4 (concerning Everard of Barres).

Cistercians to be well acquainted with one another. That friendships persisted beyond the walls of the monastery is demonstrated by the example of the monk Gaucher from Clairvaux, whose letter to a close friend in the Temple has survived in the collection of Nicholas of Clairvaux. In the letter, which he sent to his friend along with two hides from Clairvaux, and which illustrates beautifully the mental preoccupation of a Cistercian monk with the spiritual and sensual experience of Holy Land crusading, Gaucher bemoaned bitterly the separation from his friend, who had entered the Order of the Temple because of his 'love for the sea' and who, as the letter implies, was garrisoned in the East. The letter leaves no doubt that Gaucher was fully aware that he would probably never lay eyes on his friend again; not, that is, until the day of the last judgement, in heaven, 'when we will see you, Oh Lord Jesus, sitting in splendour to the right of your father'. Meanwhile, Gaucher promised, he would be praying for his friend 'to the one who has never scorned nor looked down upon the prayers of the poor'. In spite of all the anguish which he felt about the lost friend and all his concerns for their friendship, which he expressed in the first half of his letter, however, Gaucher could not but envy his friend the opportunity to see the holy places and thereby literally to step into the footsteps of Christ; nor could he resist the opportunity to recommend his nephew to his friend, whom he expected to function as his guide overseas. 'Lucky are the eyes which see what you see', he wrote to his friend. After all,

> you worship in the places where His feet stood, you see where He was born, where He was tormented, where He conjured miracles, where He died . . . And finally, you see the tomb in which the body of Jesus was buried, where the chaste flower has seasoned the linen of Mary with its fragrances. It was from this place that this first and greatest flower that ever was in our world was resurrected. There, do not forget your Gaucher; but pray to the King of Glory that He who gave you eyes to see all this may implant what you see also in my senses and that He will not withdraw your prayers and His compassion from me. And behold! My nephew Gaucher comes your way and he shall represent me in name and blood. When you see him, you will see me. Whatever you do to him, will be done to me. He will put to the test how much love you have for me, my dearest, most beloved brother.[127]

These lines, written in the close confinement of the cloister, betray the longing of the monk for the sensual experience of Christ's holiness that only physical presence in the Holy Land could fulfil. Underlying them is a confidence, born from the intimacy of a close friendship, that the desires

[127] Nicholas of Clairvaux, *Epistolae*, *PL*, CXCVI, no. 18, cols. 1616–17.

were understood, even shared by the friend, and that the spiritual value of physical presence in the Holy Land was not lost to him. They betray, in short, a sense of shared spiritual values and expectations closely connected with the Holy Land, which, along with their friendship, was the common bond still connecting the writer of the letter with its addressee.

It is difficult to reconstruct in any detail whether, and to what extent, Templar spirituality was influenced by the Cistercians, but it seems increasingly likely that personal bonds between Templars and Cistercians were vital in the creation of institutional bonds. It has already been stated that knights responded positively to the religious culture of Cîteaux because its military language, symbols and imagery appealed to their knightly values, which in turn allowed the Cistercians to incorporate 'a knightly aggression' into their monastic life that could be 'redirected . . . toward spiritual, rather than material, ends'.[128]

Embedded as it was in a highly militarised monastic culture that emphasised the individual monk's ongoing spiritual battle for his own salvation and the necessity of extending *caritas* to others (it is this active charity, described by Newman as 'love shown through action', that encouraged so many Cistercians to involve themselves so passionately in crusading),[129] Cistercian theology provided an important allegorical perspective on the roles of crusaders and on the activity of crusading that was understood and adopted by the Cistercians' lay donor base. Anne E. Lester has convincingly shown just how intensely crusading families from Champagne identified the penitential piety of the Cistercians with the penitential sacrifices of the crusaders and that particularly from 1215 onwards an increasing number of female relatives of crusaders entered family-founded Cistercian nunneries (or female religious communities that were subsequently transformed into Cistercian nunneries) in an attempt 'to support, enhance and even mirror – in spiritual terms – male actions in the East'.[130] In fact, as the thirteenth century progressed and aspects of *imitatio Christi* in the crusading movement became more prominent, 'both endeavours – crusading and the active piety of Cistercian nuns who cared for the poor and sick – were seen as two sides of the same coin'.[131] The correlation between crusading and support for Cîteaux is an important and meaningful one that also affected the attitude of these families towards military orders like the Temple, as will be discussed in

[128] Newman, *Boundaries of charity*, p. 29 (for the quotation) and pp. 29–37 for further illustration on this point.

[129] Ibid., pp. 64–5.

[130] A. E. Lester, 'A shared imitation: Cistercian convents and crusader families in thirteenth-century Champagne', *JMH*, 35 (2009), 356.

[131] Ibid.

Chapter 5. What can be said is that many of the families who seem to have founded, and populated, Cistercian nunneries as a way of expressing their spiritual understanding of the penitential and charitable value of crusading also, and often at the same time, founded and supported Templar communities and that therefore the motivations for supporting each Order in the wider context of crusading must have been very similar.

Recent scholarship has produced convincing evidence that the spiritual relationship between the two orders could indeed be very close. Simonetta Cerrini's examination of the manuscript tradition of the Order of the Temple's normative texts shows clearly the Cistercians' conscious effort to include the Templars in the same category of religious men as themselves, the Cluniacs and the Carthusians by combining copies of the Templar Rule and St Bernard's *De laude novae militiae* into manuscripts with texts reflecting on other forms of reform monasticism. This can be seen, for example, in such a compilation of texts probably produced at Clairvaux in *c.* 1160×1180 but copied in the Cistercian abbey of Dunes and now kept in the Stedelijke Openbare Bibliotheck in Bruges (MS 131).[132]

Giving some consideration to the relationship between St Bernard and the Templars William J. Purkis argued that there can today be little doubt that 'Bernard [of Clairvaux] understood the spirituality of the Templars to be quite distinct from that of the crusaders' and that he valued them for their application of a very literal form of Christo-mimesis, given that their vows were not temporary (like the vows of crusaders) but for life.[133] Their burden of the Cross was permanent, as was their renunciation of the world. The brothers had sworn themselves to religious poverty and to a religious life of action and contemplation that was – as *Hugo Peccator* explained in his letter to his brethren and as Bernard of Clairvaux acknowledged – modelled on Christ. In the spirit of John 15:31 the Templar willingly expected to 'lay down his life for the lives of his friends', thus imitating Christ in his death. Equally important however, and central to St Bernard's presentation of the Templars, was the fact that, as contemplative religious, the Templars, like the Cistercians, were able to transcend the merely physical imitation of the human Christ and to understand him 'beyond the flesh'.[134]

Templar families and the Cistercians in Languedoc

Unlike in Burgundy and Champagne, where the development of the Templar order was closely associated with that of the Cistercian movement

[132] Cerrini, *La révolution des templiers*, pp. 90–119. [133] Purkis, *Crusading spirituality*, p. 101.
[134] Ibid., pp. 101–11; Riley-Smith, *Templars and Hospitallers as professed religious in the Holy Land*, p. 13.

and benefited greatly from the influence and personality of Bernard of Clairvaux, Templar communities in the south of France had some twenty years to prosper on their own before the Cistercians formally established their presence. What the 'Cistercians' actually consisted of in the first half of the twelfth century is still vigorously debated, not least because of Constance Hoffman Berman's forceful (and strongly contested) argument against the traditional understanding of the early development of the Cistercian Order as a rapid expansion by means of 'apostolic gestation', which, she believes, was founded on a misdating of the Order's 'primitive documents', the *Exordium parvum*, the *Summa cartae caritatis* and the *Exordium cistercii*.[135] Despite the contoversy her thesis has caused, its underlying argument, that for some time the Cistercian Order consisted of a congregation of autonomous reform houses which until the mid to late 1130s rarely extended in organisational terms beyond Burgundy, remains to be refuted. In southern France the Cistercian Order, once established, gained a strong presence by incorporating eremitic communities (which were key elements in the expansion of monastic estates),[136] as well as monastic congregations which had adopted Cistercian customs some time earlier, but which, nonetheless, had been founded independently of Cîteaux.[137]

The fact that the Templars arrived in southern France before the Cistercians – in Provence the Templars received donations as early as 1124 and expanded rapidly after 1136 [138] – by no means implies that the religious landscape of that region was by then not already affected by religious reform. On the contrary: a growing discontent and debates on how spiritual value could be gained and should be expressed made the south of France a hotbed of religious dissent in which charismatic laymen like the penitent brigand-turned-hermit Pons of Léras (founder of Silvanès), and wandering priests such as Gerald of Salles (founder of Dalon in the Limousin, Cadouin in Périgord and Grandselve north-west of Toulouse) roved the countryside, gathering crowds of followers

[135] Berman, *Cistercian evolution*, pp. 1–92.

[136] This holds true also for other parts of Europe. For example, T. Licence, 'The Benedictines, the Cistercians and the acquisition of a hermitage in twelfth-century Durham', *JMH*, 29 (2003), 315–29.

[137] Berman's terminology aptly describes the different stages of monastic association with, and incorporation into, the 'umbrella organisation' of Cîteaux: 'Pre-Cistercian' communities were religious houses, often hermitages, which were founded in the spirit of reform but were not yet in any way affiliated with the Cistercian congregation. 'Proto-Cistercian' communities had adopted Cistercian customs and regulation but were not – yet – incorporated into the Cistercian network. Cistercian communities were monastic communities that were bound to one another by ties of affiliation that converged on Cîteaux. See in particular Berman, *Cistercian evolution*, pp. 99–142.

[138] Carraz, *L'ordre du Temple*, pp. 87–97, 106.

wherever they went.[139] Their religious fervour and longing for a return to the simple lifestyle of the early Church was manifested in the foundation of new religious houses and numerous hermitages, which materialised in the most isolated places and which often became nuclei of new monastic communities. In terms of ideals and spirituality these communities had much in common with the Cistercian movement that manifested itself at the same time in Burgundy and Champagne, and it was for this reason that many of them, like so many eremitical foundations in Burgundy (among them Morimond, Pontigny and Reigny), eventually adopted Cistercian customs and were absorbed into the Cistercian network.

But before the arrival of the Cistercians in southern France the region's reformers were still lacking a common voice. It would be a logical fallacy, therefore, to argue that southern French men and women who supported the Templars in the 1130s and 1140s necessarily followed the example of so many of their contemporaries in Burgundy and Champagne and did so in the context of supporting Cîteaux. This is not to say that the Templars were not considered as reformers in spirit. They had abandoned earthly riches for a life in poverty as the 'poor knights of Christ',[140] and this achievement did not go unnoticed. Açalaidis from Roussillon presented the Templars in 1133 with allodial land and her own body and soul,

> because my Lord deigned to be a pauper for me; just as He was a pauper for me, so I wish to be a pauper for Him; that He might cause me to come to true repentance and true confession and make me arrive at His holy paradise . . .[141]

Here the Templars were seen as facilitators in the process of achieving poverty as a way to salvation. The Templars' own commitment to monastic poverty on the other hand resounded positively with Raymond of

[139] Pons of Léras was the 'successful director of a popular religious movement' and the founder of a congregation of hermits who settled in 1132 at Mas-Théron, on land belonging to Arnold of Pont, but later moved to a new site in the valley of Silvanès. It was here that the Cistercian community of Silvanès was formally established in 1138. However, for some time before they affiliated with Cîteaux, the monks of Silvanès had considered adopting the austere Carthusian way of life. But, as is convincingly argued by D. Baker, 'Popular piety in the Lodève in the early twelfth century: the case of Pons of Léras', in D. Baker (ed.), *Religious motivation: bibliographical and sociological problems for the Church historian* (Oxford, 1978), 40–3, the prior of the Grande Chartreuse, Guy, very probably refused to accept responsibility for a religious community as remote as the one founded and led by the layman Pons of Léras, who did not even have formal clerical training. See M. Mousnier, 'L'abbaye cistercienne de Grandselve du XIIe au début du XIVe siècle', *Cîteaux*, 34 (1983), 53–76 and 221–44, for Grandselve, and for related information B. Bligny, 'L'érémitisme et les chartreux', in *L'eremitismo in occidente nei secoli XI e XII. Atti della seconda Settimana internazionale di studio Mendola, 30 agosto – 6 settembre*, Miscellanea del Centro di studi medioevali, 4 (Milan, 1965), 252.

[140] Riley-Smith, 'The origin of the commandery', 12–13. See also Demurger, *Les templiers*, p. 148 and Barber, *New knighthood*, pp. 20–3.

[141] *CG*, no. 68, pp. 51–2 (1133). Translation taken from Barber, *New Knighthood*, p. 53.

Luzençon who, seven years after Açalaidis, declared upon entering the Temple:

I, renouncing secular life and its pomp, relinquishing everything, give myself to the Lord God and to the knighthood of the Temple of Solomon of Jerusalem, that, as long as I shall live, in accordance with my strength, I shall serve there as a complete pauper for God.[142]

These are revealing statements. The Templars' commitment to poor relief was inscribed in their Rule and regulated in their statutes, but it does not seem to have differed much from that of other monastic communities.[143] The association of the Templars with apostolic poverty put them in spiritual proximity to the communities of 'new hermits' that were founded in great number in southern France at that time and would often become very popular with future Templar supporters, among them many women like Açalaidis.[144] The *paupertas Christi*, which put charity at the centre of religion, was intrinsic to the spirit of *imitatio Christi* that, as Purkis has demonstrated, found its most spectacular expression in the First Crusade and that, as Tom Licence has shown, was also at the core of Templar spirituality.[145] The poverty of the Templars is frequently alluded to in the Order's early charters (*pauperes commilitones Christi* and *pauperes Christi* are but two references) and occasionally its significance as the *via Christi* is amplified by the allusion to Matthew 16:24 (*tunc Iesus dixit discipulis suis si quis vult post me venire abneget semet ipsum et tollat crucem suam et sequatur me*),[146] which the scribe responsible for the compilation of the cartulary of Richerenches for one assumed to have been generally so well known that it could be abbreviated.[147]

In a very literal form, Christ's poverty was imitated by each pilgrim or crusader who left his or her earthly belongings behind and embarked on the arduous journey to Jerusalem. In its anagogical sense it became synonymous with the endurance and selfless love of the monk as understood, for example, by St Bernard, who saw the monastic life, as offered by Cîteaux, the heavenly Jerusalem, as a more than adequate substitute for the physical journey to the earthly Jerusalem.[148] The Templars were

[142] *CG*, no. 207, p. 144 (1140). [143] For the statutes see Vogel, *Das Recht der Templer*, pp. 45–6.

[144] On these new foundations see H. Leyser, *Hermits and the new monasticism: a study of religious communities in Western Europe 1000–1150* (London, 1984), in particular pp. 18–28. For the popularity of these new eremitic communities among lay women see ibid., pp. 49–51.

[145] Purkis, *Crusading spirituality*, pp. 30–58; T. Licence, 'Military orders as monastic orders', *Crusades*, 5 (2006), 39–53.

[146] *CG*, no. 371, p. 237 (1145); *Cart Rich*, no. 3, p. 5 (1145).

[147] Ibid., no. 33, pp. 36–7 (n.d.), no. 146, pp. 133–4 (1157), and for the broader discussion Purkis, *Crusading spirituality*, pp. 104–6.

[148] Ibid., p. 99.

doubly fortunate in that they not only followed Christ in their poverty. They also carried his cross visibly in red cloth on their tunics, 'as a sign', as the Templar knight Berengard of Coll from Mas Deu expressed in his deposition, 'that they are ready to shed their blood against the Saracen enemies of Christ overseas and against the enemies of the Christian faith', thus illustrating their desire to imitate Christ, 'who has shed his blood for us'.[149]

Attitudes like that of Açalaidis or Raymond of Luzençon were perhaps commonly voiced; but they were seldom recorded in charters, which rather give the impression that more than anything else it was the Templars' military prowess and crusading background that inspired laymen in southern France to make benefactions to the Order.[150] If the conventional reasons for donations to religious communities (the remission of sins and the salvation of one's parents or other kin) that feature prominently in most Templar charters are anything to go by, then there can be little doubt that donors recognised the religious seriousness of the Templar vocation. But since it was as 'knights of the Temple', often with further allusions to Jerusalem, that the Templars were most commonly addressed in the charters, there is also good reason to believe that at least in the early decades of the Order's existence knights and noblemen, but also lesser lay men and women, flocked to it for its military prowess and association with the holy places.[151]

Moreover, the Templars offered noblemen a religious alternative to the monastic way of life that suited their knightly training. In southern France, this made them attractive even to knights from families with little interest in the movement of religious reform in the region, and at the same time to families like the Barbairas, who would eventually overstep the mark of what was permitted as reform within the Church and sympathise with heretics.[152] Unlike their contemporaries in Burgundy and Champagne, the Templars of southern France seem initially to have failed to create early personal ties with Cîteaux, which would have allowed them to

[149] Vinas, 'Le destin des Templiers', 194.

[150] Carraz, *L'ordre du Temple*, pp. 180–1. This seems to have been different in the Order of St John, where commitment to the poor remained a powerful motivation for joining the Order even in a military capacity. See Bronstein, 'Caring for the sick or dying for the Cross?', 41–2.

[151] Tommasi, 'Pauperes commilitones Christi', 447–53.

[152] For information on Chabert of Barbaira, a notorious heretic (in the eyes of Cistercian chroniclers) and enemy of the French in Languedoc, and his family see the many references in G. Langlois, *Olivier de Termes. Le cathare et le croisé (vers 1200–1274)* (Toulouse, 2001). Gregory Pegg has argued convincingly that the terms 'Cathars' and 'Albigensians' are in fact two misnomers that create a false sense of unity between diverse groups of heretics. See M. G. Pegg, 'On Cathars, Albigenses, and good men of Languedoc', *JMH*, 27 (2001), 192–3 and Pegg, *A most holy war: the Albigensian crusade and the battle for Christendom* (Oxford, 2008).

position themselves firmly in the reformist camp. But their spiritual value was not lost on a society that had already deeply invested in new forms of Christo-mimetic exercises associated with Christ's passion and Jerusalem. The rise of the Templars and other military orders therefore did not prevent the Cistercian and other monastic reform orders from prospering in these regions, as Édouard Baratier had once postulated for Provence; rather, as Mazel shows, although the military orders spread more rapidly and widely in Provence than the Cistercians, they shared many of their powerful patrons with reform monastic communities.[153]

The new Templar clientele

The Templars' military lifestyle within a familiar regular-religious framework and their link to Jerusalem initially guaranteed them enough recruits to establish a small number of commanderies in Provence and Languedoc. The situation changed after three papal bulls, issued between 1139 and 1145, recognised the Temple as an order of the Church and provided it with privileges and rights that enabled its members to engage in parish duties and the business of the *cura animarum*.[154] It was around that time that a wealth of new knightly and noble families began to consider associating with the Temple.

It is impossible to tell whether men and women who associated with the Templars after 1139 had regarded the Order and its peculiar concept of twofold warfare by prayer and sword with scepticism before 1139 or whether they had always been in favour of the 'new knighthood' but been reluctant to show their support until they were assured that the new community had gained papal approval.[155] What the sources do reveal is that the families of some Templar brothers and benefactors continued their association with the Temple for many years after their names were first recorded in the Templar documents, although for some of these families the evidence for involvement in the Order is sporadic at best. The evidence also supports the argument that most southern French knights who entered or gave to Templar houses during or after the period

[153] E. Baratier, *Enquêtes sur les droits et revenus de Charles Ier d'Anjou en Provence 1252 et 1278. Avec une étude sur le domaine comtal et les seigneuries de Provence au 13e siècle* (Paris, 1969), p. 175; Mazel, *Noblesse et l'église*, pp. 337–76.

[154] *PTJ I*, no. 3, pp. 204–10 (*Omne datum optimum*), no. 8, pp. 214–15 (*Milites Templi*), no. 10, pp. 216–17 (*Militia Dei*).

[155] Mazel for one concluded that 'generally speaking, it seems that new orders really attracted the interest of powerful laymen only once their spiritual standards and their integration into the ecclesiastical structure had been assured' ('d'une manière générale, il semble que les nouveaux ordres n'aient vraiment suscité l'intérêt des grands laïcs qu'une fois leur normalisation spirituelle et leur intégration aux structures ecclésiales assurée'): Mazel, *Noblesse et l'église*, p. 340.

from 1139 to 1145 were well attuned to the ideas of religious reformers and that they often came from families which supported, or would support, 'proto-Cistercian' monasteries like Silvanès.[156]

The foundation and early history of Silvanès is in many ways exemplary for the history and early development of numerous similar eremitical and monastic communities at the time.[157] In 1133, a nobleman from Rouergue, Arnold, castellan of Pont-de-Camarès, endowed a group of mendicant hermits led by the charismatic Pons of Léras with land on which to build a hermitage, which, originally situated at Mas-Théron, eventually became the nucleus of the Cistercian abbey of Silvanès in Rodez. Apart from Arnold of Pont-de-Camarès and his family, its patrons included the lords of Combret, who had married into the family of Pont by 1173, the lords of Luzençon and the lords of Cornus, all of whom would eventually produce benefactors, knights or lay associates of the Temple.[158] Silvanès was not the only Cistercian abbey with ties to Templar families. The counts of Comminges supported Cistercian Bonnefont and were connected to the foundation of Cistercian Les Feuillans and Cistercian Rieux.[159] The lords and knights of Albas, often mentioned in the charters of Templar Douzens, favoured Cistercian Fontfroide.[160] The families of Montpezat and Espaon,[161] the

[156] See also ibid., pp. 337–76.

[157] For Silvanès see G. Bourgeois and A. Douzou, *Une aventure spirituelle dans le Rouergue méridional au moyen âge. Ermites et cisterciens à Silvanès, 1120–1477* (Paris, 1999).

[158] *Cart Sil*, no. 25, p. 22 (1140), no. 28, p. 24 (1135), no. 35, pp. 28–9 (1133), no. 56, pp. 44–5 (1151), no. 95, p. 78 (1158), no. 131, pp. 103–4 (1167), no. 138, p. 109 (1159), no. 141, pp. 111–12 (1161), no. 160, pp. 132–3 (n.d.), no. 199, pp. 161–2 (1158), no. 244, pp. 196–7 (1167), no. 259, p. 209 (1146), no. 284, p. 228 (1163), no. 314, pp. 249–50 (1165), no. 357, pp. 281–2 (1138), no. 361, pp. 283–4 (1144), no. 369, pp. 289–90 (1165), no. 408, p. 321 (1146), no. 431, p. 338 (1147), no. 443, p. 347 (n.d.); *PAC*, II, no. 453, pp. 88–9 (1181); M. Mousnier, 'Impact social des abbayes cisterciennes dans la société méridionale aux XIIe et XIIIe siècles', *Cîteaux*, 50 (1999), 78. For relations with the Templars see, for Combret, *Cart LaS*, pp. 28, 75, no. 18, p. 134 (*c.* 1180), no. 24, pp. 137–8 (*c.* 1180), no. 61, p. 162 (*c.* 1180), no. 104, p. 190 (*c.* 1185), no. P20, pp. 289–90 (1237); Léonard, *Introduction*, p. 58; *CadC*, I, p. 335 (1290); for Luzençon *CG*, no. 207, p. 144 (1140) and no. 538, p. 331 (*c.* 1148); *Cart Douz*, pp. xxxviii, xxxix; A: no. 16, pp. 28–9 (1156), no. 17, pp. 29–30 (1153), no. 32, pp. 43–4 (1156), no. 48, p. 57–8 (1154), no. 50, p. 59 (1152), no. 134, p. 124 (1155), no. 146, p. 134 (1144), no. 152, pp. 138–9 (1156), D: no. 4, pp. 275–7 (1147); *PAC*, I, no. 58, pp. 62–3 (1150), no. 61, pp. 64–5 (*c.* 1150); ibid., II, no. 425, p. 64 (1178), no. 507, pp. 145–6 (1191); for Cornus *PAC*, II, no. 422, pp. 61–2 (1178), no. 424, pp. 63–4 (1178), no. 437, p. 74 (1179), no. 439, pp. 75–6 (1179), no. 450, pp. 85–6 (*c.* 1180), no. 477, pp. 112–13 (1185), no. 498, pp. 134–5 (1189); BN, n.a.l., 15, fols. 75r–7r (1199×1200), 323r–8r (1184).

[159] H. Castillon d'Aspet, *Histoire des populations pyrénéennes du Nébouzan et du pays de Comminges depuis les temps les plus anciens jusqu'à la révolution de 89*, 2 vols. (Toulouse, Paris, 1842), I, p. 216.

[160] See Auvenche, Bernard, Berenguer, Berenguer Avenche, Étienne, Giraud, Guilhem, Guilhem Raimaro, Guilhelm de la Rive, Jean, Pierre, Raymond, and Roger of Albas in *Chart Font.*

[161] *Act Bonne*, pp. 19–20, no. 6, p. 54 (1143), no. 30, pp. 60–1 (1155×1156), no. 69, pp. 69–70 (1162×1163), no. 90, p. 76 (n.d.), no. 102, p. 78 (1172), no. 169, p. 96 (1189), no. 184, p. 102 (1193), no. 202, p. 107 (1198), no. 212, p. 110 (1203), no. 232, p. 116 (1210), no. 245, p. 119 (1216), no. 258, p. 124 (1222), no. 261, p. 124 (1224×1225), no. 268, p. 126 (1227), no. 277, p. 127

Cardailhacs[162] and Aspets,[163] who all also eventually associated with Templar houses, favoured the Cistercian communities of Bonnefont, Berdoues and Gimont.[164] The lords of Combret had additional ties to the Cistercian communities of Ardorel,[165] Valmagne,[166] Bonnecombe[167] and Nonenque,[168] while the lords of Montpezat also made endowments to the Cistercians of Grandselve.[169] Other Montpezats established personal ties with the Cistercian nunnery of Fonts-lès-Alais, where Agnes of Montpezat had become the abbess by 1309.[170] Together with the Espaon branch of the Montpezats from Gers, men and women called 'of Montpezat' conducted at least thirteen transactions with the

(1230), no. 283, p. 129 (1231), no. 295, p. 134 (1234), no. 411, pp. 178–9 (1267), no. 424, p. 183 (1272), no. 446, pp. 188–9 (1283), no. 477, p. 201 (1308); *Cart Gim*, II, no. 11, pp. 95–7 (1162), no. 13, pp. 97–8 (1160), no. 42, p. 112 (1174), no. 43, pp. 112–13 (1162), no. 48, p. 115 (1162), no. 66, p. 125 (1187), no. 67, pp. 125–6 (1188), no. 137, p. 160 (n.d.), no. 177, p. 180 (1183), no. 206, pp. 195–6 (1215); V, no. 9, pp. 308–9 (1174); *Cart Léz*, I, no. 260, pp. 203–4 (1210).

162 *Cart Berd*, no. 650, pp. 442–3 (1159); *Act Bonne*, no. 55, p. 66 (1159), no. 68, p. 69 (1161×1163), no. 127, pp. 85–6 (1177×1178), no. 128, p. 86 (1178), no. 143, p. 89 (1184), no. 149, p. 90 (1185), no. 261, p. 124 (1224×1225), no. 302, p. 138 (1235×1236), no. 335, pp. 147–8 (1245), no. 343, p. 151 (1247), no. 385, pp. 167–71 (1256), no. 406, p. 177 (1264), no. 424, p. 183 (1272), no. 443, p. 188 (1281), no. 444, p. 188 (1281), no. 461, pp. 195–6 (1291); *Cart Bonnecombe*, no. 147, pp. 281–6 (1304).

163 *Act Bonne*, no. 55, p. 66 (1159).

164 Ibid., pp. 19–20, no. 6, p. 54 (1143), no. 19, p. 57 (1149×1150), no. 30, pp. 60–1 (1155×1156), no. 55, p. 66 (1159), no. 68, p. 69 (1161×1163), no. 69, pp. 69–70 (1162×1163), no. 90, p. 76 (n.d.), no. 102, p. 78 (1172), no. 127, pp. 85–6 (1177×1178), no. 128, p. 86 (1178), no. 143, p. 89 (1184), no. 149, p. 90 (1185), no. 169, p. 96 (1189), no. 178, p. 101 (1192), no. 184, p. 102 (1193), no. 202, p. 107 (1198), no. 212, p. 110 (1203), no. 232, p. 116 (1210), no. 245, p. 119 (1216), no. 253, p. 123 (1219), no. 258, p. 124 (1222), no. 261, p. 124 (1224×1225), no. 268, p. 126 (1227), no. 277, p. 127 (1230), no. 283, p. 129 (1231), no. 295, p. 134 (1234), no. 302, p. 138 (1235×1236), no. 334, pp. 146–7 (1245), no. 335, pp. 147–8 (1245), no. 343, p. 151 (1247), no. 372, p. 163 (1251), no. 385, pp. 167–71 (1256), no. 398, p. 174 (1259), no. 406, p. 177 (1264), no. 411, pp. 178–9 (1267), no. 424, p. 183 (1272), no. 432, p. 185 (1278), no. 443, p. 188 (1281), no. 444, p. 188 (1281), no. 446, pp. 188–9 (1283), no. 461, pp. 195–6 (1291), no. 477, p. 201 (1308); *Cart Gim*, II, no. 11, pp. 95–7 (1162), no. 13, pp. 97–8 (1160), no. 42, p. 112 (1174), no. 43, p. 115 (1162), no. 48, p. 115 (1162), no. 66, p. 125 (1187), no. 67, pp. 125–6 (1188), no. 137, p. 160 (n.d.), no. 177, p. 180 (1183), no. 206, pp. 195–6 (1215); V, no. 9, pp. 308–9 (1174); *Cart Léz*, I, no. 260, pp. 203–4 (1210); *Cart Berd*, no. 650, pp. 442–3 (1159); *Cart Bonnecombe*, no. 147, pp. 281–6 (1304). For relations with the Templars see, for Cardailhac, *Cart LaS*, p. 75, no. 4, p. 125 (*c.* 1180), no. 98, p. 186 (*c.* 1200), no. 109, p. 193 (*c.* 1210), no. 172, pp. 239–40 (*c.* 1170); Léonard, *Introduction*, pp. 66, 67; *PT*, I, p. 105; II, pp. 256–8; *GP(Toulouse)*, p. 335. For Aspet see ibid., p. 142 (1156); *PAC*, I, no. 97, p. 94 (*c.* 1160); *Cart Mont*, no. 40, p. 247 (n.d.); Léonard, *Introduction*, p. 80; *GP (Toulouse)*, p. 25.

165 *GC*, I, col. 80 (1139).

166 Ibid. Valmagne, which is located approximately 30 kilometres east of Béziers, had adopted Cistercian customs by the third quarter of the twelfth century. See Berman, *Cistercian evolution*, pp. 125–6 and 196–220. For the links of the lords of Combret with Valmagne see *Nécrologe de Sainte Marie de Cassan*, 16, 27.

167 *Cart Bonnecombe*, no. 204, p. 378 (1227).

168 *Cart Non*, no. 111, p. 183 (1303), no. 114, p. 200 (1305), no. 131, pp. 257–61 (1324), no. 150, pp. 302–3 (1337).

169 *DhT-G*, I, p. 185 (1187).

170 *HGL*, IV, p. 720.

Temple and twenty-nine transactions with 'Cistercian' houses between 1136 and 1203.[171] William of Cardailhac, in his function as bishop of Cahors, founded the Cistercian nunnery of Leyme in 1220.[172] And at least one female member of the seigniorial house of Luzençon entered Nonenque in the late thirteenth or early fourteenth century.[173]

These families, it appears, had not only associated with the Templars but also spent a considerable amount of time and material wealth on the patronage of Cistercian or 'proto-Cistercian' communities, where the ideas of reform and in particular the ideal of the *pauper Christi* were practised, as the reformers were often hermits. Like most families recorded here, their gifts to the monks and hermits who were eventually absorbed into the Cistercian Order seem to have preceded those to the Templars. Since such precedence cannot always be conclusively established, however, it seems safer to conclude generally that families that supported the Templars in the south of France after 1139 were also prone to endorse the movement of religious reform, in particular as represented by hermit communities and monasteries which eventually adopted Cistercian customs, although in some areas the two orders seem to have attracted different social groups: for example in the Rouergue, where the Cistercians seem to have been favoured by the noble elite (the *ric'hommes*) and the Templars of La Selve by knights and lesser noblemen.[174]

What exactly the spiritual influence of the Cistercians on the Templars amounted to is still difficult to ascertain, however. It is a curious coincidence that the Templars, who were initially devoted only to Christ,[175] began to associate with the Virgin Mary at the time when the Cistercians established their presence in southern France. Thirty of the ninety-eight charters dating to different years between 1156 and 1193 (although most charters cannot be precisely dated) which are collected in the cartulary of

[171] By 1167 Bernard Alegre of Montpezat was married to Sybille of Espaon, sister of Peter of Espaon. *Cart Gim*, II, no. 39, p. 111 (1167).

[172] P. R. Gaussin, 'Les communautés féminines dans l'espace languedocien de la fin du XIe à la fin du XIVe siècle', in *La femme dans la vie religieuse du Languedoc*, CdF, XXIII (Toulouse, 1988), 311.

[173] *Cart Non*, no. 111, p. 183 (1303) and no. 114, p. 200 (1305).

[174] *Cart LaS*, pp. 76–7. It is not easy to find explanations for this (admittedly very vague) social division. The prominence of the non-noble element in the Order in general was probably one reason why members from local high noble families were reluctant to join it; perhaps another was the particular political significance of association with the Cistercians in southern France from the late twelfth century onwards, which was felt more strongly by magnates who needed Cistercian allies if they wanted to stay in possession of their lands than by their dependent vassals. This was not a universal phenomenon, however. According to Jochen Burgtorf, for example, the military orders' higher ranks 'featured all shades of European nobility, from knightly houses to royal families'. See Burgtorf, *Central convent*, pp. 378–85 (p. 382 for the quotation).

[175] Licence, 'The Templars and the Hospitallers', passim.

Montsaunès contain Marian references. Seven of them were issued between 1161 and 1171, nine between 1172 and 1182, and fourteen between 1183 and 1193. Of the eighty Marian charters in the Vaour cartulary (which contains 119 documents in total, dating from 1143 until 1247×1248), forty-seven were issued between 1172 and 1182, twenty-seven between 1183 and 1193, and six between 1194 and 1204.

The increasing importance of Mary in the Templar charters coincides with what Miri Rubin has recently described as the 'creeping "marianization" of religious culture' during that time.[176] Licence, however, saw also very particular (and pragmatic) influences at work. He explains the growing importance of Mary in the Temple by the Order's increasingly successful efforts to gain possession of local churches, of which many were dedicated to Our Lady. The example of La Selve illustrates how important the incorporation of these churches was for the association of the Order with a new patron saint. Of the 204 charters in the La Selve cartulary (which date from 1160 until 1215), 194 were dedicated or contain reference to the Virgin Mary. Of these, 102 were issued before 1175, when the Templars were for the first time explicitly mentioned as being associated with La Selve. They were incorporated into the cartulary of the commandery without reference to their non-Templar status, indicating that by the time the cartulary was compiled, the Marian legacy of the church of La Selve had become part of the identity of the Templars of the commandery, which developed into a centre of Marian devotion *in qua fiunt multa miracula*, one of many Marian centres along the way to Santiago de Compostela.[177] The simplest explanation seems to be that by dedicating churches to the Virgin Mary the Templars followed a trend spearheaded by the Cistercians which they had witnessed and experienced time and again when personal ties or institutional business brought them in contact with their religious neighbours, as the Templar master of Rouergue, Helias of Montbrun, did in 1151 when attending the laying of the foundation stone of Silvanès's first church at the monastery's new site.[178]

The incorporation of local churches is a useful explanation for the growing importance of Mary in the Temple and may help explain why, as Francesco Tommasi has observed, many charters in the Albon cartulary refer to single Templar houses as *Sancta Maria de Templo*, whereas the Order as an institution

[176] M. Rubin, *Mother of God: a history of the Virgin Mary* (London, 2009), p. 177.

[177] J. Fuguet Sans, 'Maisons templières des chemins ibériques de Saint-Jacques', in *Les ordres religieux militaires dans le Midi (XIIe–XIVe siècle)*, CdF, XLI (Toulouse, 2006), 265–94.

[178] For the laying of the foundation stone of Silvanès's new church see *Cart Sil*, no. 61 and Bourgeois and Douzou, *Une aventure spirituelle*, p. 107.

is rarely associated with her.[179] The fact that at the time when the Templars in southern France were increasingly associated with Mary they were infiltrated by a new clientele of families with close ties to Cistercian or 'proto-Cistercian' communities suggests that the one phenomenon was linked to, or determined by, the other and that the spirituality of the Cistercians may have played a dominant role in the religious development of Templar families and thus, very likely, of Templar religious practice.

TEMPLAR FAMILIES AND THE CHURCH: INVOLVEMENT BEYOND CÎTEAUX

The relationship between families and the Temple has to be assessed in a broad religious context that takes into account the families' ties to and relations with communities other than Cîteaux or her affiliates and imitators. By the time the Templars came to Europe the landscapes of Burgundy, Champagne and southern France were scattered with churches and regular and secular religious convents following contemplative or apostolic observances. These churches and monasteries were important components of a social and economic network that included noble families. Most of all, they were places of remembrance, cornerstones of family identity and powerful spiritual intercessors.[180] Neither region was therefore short of religious communities with which pious laymen could associate themselves. They included Cluniac Benedictine houses such as, apart from Cluny herself, St-Bénigne in Dijon, Lézat in Ariège and Moissac in Tarn-et-Garonne; convents of Augustinian canons, like St-Étienne in Dijon or St-Sernin in Toulouse; Carthusian monasteries like Lugny in the Châtillonnais; and Premonstratensian communities such as St-Yved-de-Braine in Picardy. Since the maintenance and survival of these houses depended almost entirely on the charity and benevolence of neighbouring families, the very number of them gives testimony to the general willingness of knights and nobles to lend support to a religious cause. That among these families many also supported the Temple was to be expected, considering the rapid development of the Order in these regions. This however begs the question how selective Templar families actually were in their choice of spiritual associates. Did they continue to support traditional monastic communities after they had discovered the Temple and Cîteaux, or does their involvement in these

[179] Tommasi, 'Pauperes commilitones Christi', p. 447.

[180] See generally P. Geary, *Phantoms of remembrance: memory and oblivion at the end of the first millennium* (Princeton, N.J., 1994), and M. Lawers, *La mémoire des ancêtres, le souci des morts. Morts, rites et société au Moyen Âge (diocèse de Liège, XIe–XIIIe)* (Paris, 1997).

two orders constitute (and represent) a radical shift in their religious behaviour? And is it possible to discern from the multitude of charters documenting religious life from the eleventh to the fourteenth century particular patterns of patronage that predestined certain families to become involved with the Cistercians and eventually with the Templars? These questions will be given particular consideration on the following pages.

THE RELIGIOUS ASSOCIATIONS OF TEMPLAR FAMILIES: VARIETY AND PREFERENCE

As already noted, in a recent article Demurger was able to demonstrate how religiously active Templar families in Burgundy had been.[181] Following his lead it is indeed possible to trace the family names of known Templars or Templar benefactors in the surviving charters of religious institutions that were not associated with, and were often older than, Cîteaux. Among them Molesme and its dependent nunnery of Jully, which were both closely associated with the reform movement, feature prominently.[182] Families who gave to these and other traditional Benedictine communities in Burgundy and Champagne before and while they were establishing ties with the Temple and Cîteaux included the seigniorial families of Noyers, Montbard, Sombernon, Baudement, Grancey and Saulx (who extended their charity as far as Conques in the Rouergue).[183] In Languedoc, old Benedictine communities like the ones of Lézat, Moissac, Aniane, Gellone and Conques had attracted the spiritual attention of lay men and women for centuries, among them the lords

[181] Demurger, 'L'aristocrazia laica e gli ordini militari', passim.

[182] Bur, 'Le monachisme', 627–33.

[183] *Cart Jul*, pp. 26 (1186), 28 (1192×1193), 47 (1251); *Cart Mol*, II.1, no. 6, pp. 12–13 (1076×1077, 1081×1084), no. 11, p. 19 (1076×1077, 1081×1084), no. 70, pp. 77–8 (1085×1110), no. 218, 200–2 (1112×1116); ibid., II.2, no. 10, p. 541 (1174×1175), no. 80, p. 289 (1244), no. 98, p. 297 (1224×1225), no. 117, p. 302 (1234×1235); *Chronique de Saint-Pierre-le-Vif de Sens, dite de Clarius*, ed. R.-H. Bautier and M. Gilles (Paris, 1979), p. 170 (1113); *Vita Sancti Petri prioris juliacensis puellarum monasterii, et monachi molismensis*, ed. J. Mabillon, *PL*, CLXXXV, col. 1263 (1146); Albanès and Chevalier, *Gallia christiana novissima, vol. V: Toulon*, p. 47; *GC*, IV, Instrumenta, no. 38, col. 161 (1112×1115); *HdB*, III, no. 881, pp. 321–3 (1197), no. 912, pp. 332–3 (1194), no. 947, p. 347 (1196), no. 1015, p. 375 (1200); IV, no. 1616, p. 183 (1220); Chifflet, *Sancti Bernardi*, no. xi, 1418 (before 1143), no. xxi, 1419–20 (before 1185), no. xxvi, 1423 (n.d.); Bur, 'Braine', 545; M. Bur, 'Épernay', *LexMA*, III, 2047; Richard, *Ducs de Bourgogne*, p. 75; Bouchard, *Sword, miter, and cloister*, pp. 78, 134, 180. The lords of Grancey and one of their collateral families, the lords of Frolois, were also closely allied with the old Benedictine abbey of Flavigny. Raynald I was a vassal of Flavigny. See Richard, *Ducs de Bourgogne*, p. 75; *HdB*, IV, no. 340, pp. 259–60 (1154), and Isenburg *et al.*, *Stammtafeln*, XV/96. For the relationship of Saulx with Ste-Foy at Conques see *Cart Con*, no. 445, p. 325 (1086), no. 446, pp. 325–6 (*c.* 1086), no. 458, p. 331 (*c.* 1086), no. 488, pp. 354–5 (1110), no. 539, pp. 381–2 (1163×1179).

and knights of Cornus, Abeilhan, Cornone, Combret and Garrigue, who all also became involved with the Templars.[184]

There is, of course, nothing surprising about the fact that families which became involved with military orders like the Temple and reform monastic communities like Cîteaux had a history of giving to other religious houses. It is commonly acknowledged that lay men and women of the twelfth and later centuries distributed their charity among several institutions, thus enhancing their chances of spiritual security. The anonymous author of the 'Treatise on the various orders and professions that exist in the Church' (*Libellus de diversis ordinibus et professionibus qui sunt in aecclesia*), written in *c.* 1140, expressed in a few words the thoughts of many when he wrote that 'I desire prayers from each of those whom I know to be at one in the unity of the faith, for I am not eager to blame anyone for his order, but I desire to show that, though they live differently, they aspire from one beginning to the one end which is Christ.'[185]

The charter evidence for Templar family involvement in other orders than the Temple is too scattered, uneven and in many cases too scanty to allow any meaningful statistic to be drawn from them. But it nonetheless shows a trend of religious involvement that favoured the Cistercians and left old Benedictine communities and Augustinian houses trailing behind, although, for reasons that are explained below, the margin between Cîteaux and the orders is unlikely to have been as wide as the – necessarily selective – sample of charters and cartularies implies. Relying on the charters consulted for this study, about 45 per cent of the transactions of Templar families (or of groups of persons from a limited geographical area sharing a toponym who produced Templar brothers) in Languedoc were conducted with Templar communities, about 35 per cent with Cistercian or 'proto-Cistercian' monasteries, about 9 per cent with traditional Benedictine monasteries such as Aniane, Gellone, Lézat or Lagrasse (the cartularies of all of which have survived), about 8 per cent with Augustinian communities (many of them with St-Sernin in Toulouse, for which the

[184] *Cart Con*, no. 350, pp. 270–1 (*c.* 1065), no. 399, p. 295 (1060×1065), no. 462, pp. 334–5 (1061×1108), no. 463, p. 335 (1087×1108), no. 546, pp. 385–6 (after 1107); *Cart Léz*, II, no. 1027, pp. 25–8 (1245), no. 1028, p. 28 (1232), no. 1032, p. 30 (1238), no. 1033, pp. 30–1 (1245), no. 1035, pp. 32–3 (1247), no. 1036, pp. 33–4 (1247), no. 1037, p. 34 (1245), no. 1038, p. 35 (*c.* 1150); *Cart An*, no. 32, p. 169 (1151), no. 33, pp. 170–1 (1158), no. 34, pp. 171–2, no. 35, pp. 172–3 and no. 36, pp. 173–5 (all 1169×1170), no. 46, p. 166 (1175), no. 52, pp. 192–3 (1150), no. 82, pp. 220–1 (1183), no. 88, pp. 225–7 (1208), no. 107, pp. 249–50 (1213), no. 178, pp. 314–15 (1181), no. 182, pp. 318–21 (1202), no. 255, pp. 380–1 (1216), no. 256, pp. 381–3 (1216), no. 257, pp. 383–4 (1215×1216), no. 258, pp. 384–5 (1207), no. 301, p. 423 (1114); *Cart Vab*, no. 30, p. 101 (1067×1094).

[185] *Libellus de diversis ordinibus et professionibus qui sunt in aecclesia*, ed. and trans. G. Constable and B. S. Smith (rev. edn, Oxford, 2003), p. 27.

cartulary also has survived) and about 5 per cent with other communities. In Burgundy and Champagne 44 per cent of the transactions were conducted with Cistercian communities, 27 per cent with Templar houses, 16 per cent with traditional Benedictine houses (among which Molesme and the nunnery of Jully feature prominently), 6 per cent with Augustinian houses and 7 per cent with other religious institutions, among them Carthusian and Premonstratensian communities.

To give an even more focused account of the strong charitable emphasis of Templar families on Cistercian communities, the fifty-two transactions conducted between the lords of Bricon and their relatives the lords of Rochefort and religious communities in Burgundy and Champagne between 1125 and 1306 can be placed into different categories relating to their nature and their religious recipients. Most of them (thirty-five, or 67 per cent) concern donations to, resolved disputes or business transactions with Cistercian houses. Nine charters (17 per cent) concern donations to, disputes or business transactions with the Temple, which is still more than the family's transactions with the church of Langres (three, or 6 per cent), the Carthusian community of Lugny (three, or 6 per cent),[186] or with other religious communities.

The argument that kin-groups like that of Bricon-Rochefort were deeply involved with the Cistercians as well as being engaged in transactions with the Templars is therefore well supported. Moreover, the two broader surveys indicate that the religious outlook of many of the families who came to support reform communities like those of Cîteaux as well as the Temple must have been influenced by their longstanding support for old Benedictine communities, which sometimes survived but sometimes seems to have preceded their involvement with the new orders. In short, it was the families with a tradition of supporting traditional Benedictine houses and a new but strong affinity with the ideas of religious reform as promoted and represented by the Cistercians who, so the evidence would suggest, constituted the bulk of the Temple's supporters.

As indicated, however, the results displayed in the figures given above, for the south of France as well as for Burgundy–Champagne, require some further explanation. First, many Templar families from Burgundy were acquainted with Bernard of Clairvaux, as we have seen, and were thus under considerable pressure to give to Cistercian communities. Second, as a result of the diametrical imbalance of published Templar and Cistercian

[186] Lugny was also popular with the lords of Grancey. See J. Legendre, *La Chartreuse de Lugny des origines au début du 14ᵉ siècle 1172–1332* (Salzburg, 1975), p. 79 and p. 183 (donation to Lugny by Odo of Grancey and approval by his wife Nova, sons Raynald, Milo, Pons, and daughters Rovelina, Nigella, Margaret and Ayna (Agnes), *c.* 1172).

sources, Templar families from Burgundy and Champagne (a region for which little Templar material but much Cistercian has been published) tend to have well-documented Cistercian and haphazardly reconstructed Templar associations, whereas many of their contemporaries from Languedoc or Provence (from where comparatively more Templar cartularies have been published) also left a coherent track in the available Templar records. Third, the survival rate and accessibility of religious charters is generally biased in favour of Benedictine (including Cistercian) houses.[187] The predominance of Cîteaux over other religious orders or institutions results partly from the fact that a great proportion of the cartularies and charter collections investigated for these surveys were compiled in Cistercian scriptoria, although, in Champagne at least, few seem to have been written before 1150.[188] It is likely that a thorough examination of the many religious charters which remain unpublished but are nonetheless accessible in the departmental archives will do much to change these figures.

In particular, a thorough investigation of the involvement of Templar families with Augustinian canons – including the Premonstratensians, who resembled the Cistercians in many aspects – would be a worthwhile undertaking that would produce valuable insight into the spiritual awareness of Templar families in urban settings. After all, the Order of the Temple had an intrinsic apostolic element to it. Although the idea of combining a religious lifestyle with the profession of the knight may have appeared grotesque to some, the concept of submitting to a regular life while engaging in the alleviation of the plight of others was not beyond the comprehension of people who were acquainted with the canonist doctrine of 'teaching by word and by example'.[189] The Augustinian Rule, which has been described as 'a very generic code' that 'could be developed . . . in a variety of ways', was perfectly capable of supporting a military-religious construct, as the examples of the military-religious orders of St John and Santiago illustrate.[190] The Order of the Temple

[187] B. Delmaire, 'Cartulaires et inventaires de chartes dans le nord de la France', in Olivier Guyotjeannin, Laurent Morelle and Michel Parisse (eds.), *Les cartulaires. Actes de la table ronde organisée par l'École nationale des chartes et le G.D.R. 121 du C.N.R.S., Paris, 5–7 décembre 1991* (Paris, 1993), 306. The documents have not survived evenly or in equal numbers, however. In Champagne, Old Benedictine communities are represented by only a few documents and until the mid twelfth century the Cistercians are not much better off. Evergates, *Aristocracy*, p. 12.

[188] Ibid.

[189] On the spirituality of the canons see C. Walker Bynum, *Docere verbo et exemplo: an aspect of twelfth-century spirituality* (Missoula, Mont., 1979), in particular pp. 1–5 and 181–97. See also Brodman, 'Rule and identity', 385.

[190] C. H. Lawrence, *Medieval monasticism: forms of religious life in western Europe in the middle ages* (3rd edn, Harlow, 2001), p. 167.

itself had been founded by knights who had associated themselves to the Augustinian chapter of the church of the Holy Sepulchre and who, according to William of Tyre, aspired 'to live perpetually in the manner of regular canons'.[191] Examples of former Templars who entered, for example, the Order of Prémontré exist,[192] as do examples of Augustinian chapters which, like the convent of St-Vaast at Arras in the 1140s, aligned themselves spiritually with the Templars.[193]

I am aware of a number of Templar families which supported Augustinian communities either materially or personally and it can be suspected that in particular in cities like Toulouse, where Augustinian and other religious houses and Templar commanderies existed in close proximity to each another, personal relations between Augustinians and Templars through common patronage were commonplace.[194] Raymond Gaucelm of Lunel, for example, founded the Augustinian priory of Our Lady of Arboras and, in March 1214, chose to be buried on Templar ground.[195] The last Templar preceptor of Gardeny in Aragon, Arnold of Banyuls from Roussillon, had an Augustinian canon as brother, who stole possessions from Gardeny after Arnold had abandoned the commandery.[196] The lords of Beaujeu helped reform the local church of Our Lady of Beaujeu, which they had founded in the late tenth century, into an Augustinian community in the eleventh century. And Humbert of Beaujeu, who had become associated with the Temple in about 1142, while on crusade, founded the Augustinian house of Belleville in 1158.[197] Andrew of Baudement and his wife Agnes of Braine were the key instigators behind the conversion of the collegiate church of St-Yved of Braine into a Premonstratensian abbey, some time between 1130 and 1135,[198] and were patrons of the Augustinian abbey of St-Loup of Troyes.[199] The lords of Vergy also retained good relations with St-Loup.[200] And together with the lords and knights of Grancey they

191 William of Tyre, *Chronique*, p. 553.

192 The Levantine nobleman Julian of Sidon, for example, first joined the Templars, then the Hospitallers and finally the Premonstratensians. See Prutz, *Die geistlichen Ritterorden*, p. 59.

193 *CG*, no. 226, p. 153 (1141×1147).

194 See Oberste, *Zwischen Heiligkeit und Häresie* for a study of the complex religious entanglements of urban elites in Toulouse.

195 See *HGL*, VI, p. 457 and Prutz, *Die geistlichen Ritterorden*, p. 362.

196 A.J. Forey, *The fall of the Templars in the Crown of Aragon* (Aldershot, 2001), p. 13.

197 *Cartulaire Lyonnais. Documents inédits pour servir à l'histoire des anciennes provinces de Lyonnais, Forez, Beaujolais, Dombes, Bresse et Bugey, vol. I: Documents antérieurs à l'année 1255*, ed. M.-C. Guigue (Lyon, 1885), no. 39, pp. 53–8 (1158–79).

198 N. Backmund, 'St-Yved de Braine', *LexMA*, II, 545.

199 *Cart St-L*, no. 6, p. 19 (1136).

200 Hugh of Vergy, whose father acted as benefactor to the Templars in 1191, transferred his rights over a female serf from Montagnon to the Augustinian canons of St-Loup of Troyes. See ibid., no. 102, p. 141 (1189).

provided from the mid twelfth to the early thirteenth century four consecutive abbots to the Augustinian monastery of St-Étienne in Dijon.[201] These examples indicate that perhaps the support of the Templars in the twelfth century should be set more squarely into the context of lay enthusiasm for religious reform in general, with emphasis on Cistercian communities in particular. As it stands, however, the involvement of Templar families with Augustinian communities does not compare with their involvement in Benedictine reform communities like Cîteaux, to which the Templars seem to have regarded themselves as closely associated.

The same observation applies to the pattern of personal involvement of members of Templar families in religious communities including the Temple and Cîteaux, which, likewise, was marked by diversity with a heavy bias towards Cistercian monasteries. The families of Combret, Pont, Cornus and Luzençon not only provided Silvanès with six monks or *confratres* and the Temple with six knights or associates between 1138 and 1179. They also sent five relatives to join the old Benedictine abbey of Vabres, which had joined the congregation of St-Victor of Marseille in 1064. During the next century and a half they produced at least five more Cistercian monks and nuns and two Templar brothers or associates, but also one monk of Auterive, which was traditional Benedictine, and one canon. Among all the southern French families and wider kin groups which I have scrutinised in the course of my research, about 50 per cent of their religious offspring were Templar brothers or *confratres/consorores* (which is hardly surprising, given the focus of my research), about 20 per cent Cistercian, or 'proto-Cistercian', monks and nuns, about 20 per cent members or associates of traditional Benedictine communities, and about 5 per cent Augustinian canons. The Templar families or households of knights and nobles from Burgundy and Champagne which can be closely linked to the Temple distributed their personal involvement in religious orders and institutions in a similar pattern, although only about 30 per cent associated themselves with, or joined, Templar communities. About 20 per cent entered or associated with Cistercian communities, about 10 per cent entered traditional Benedictine communities, 3 per cent a Premonstratensian or Carthusian community, and about 30 per cent an Augustinian chapter. The rest were bishops and could have professed in

[201] Until his death in 1162 Gilbert of Grancey was the abbot of the Augustinian monastery of St-Étienne of Dijon. Harvey of Favernay, son of Humbert and Elisabeth of Vergy, was elected abbot of St-Étienne in 1162. Harvey, in turn, was succeeded by Milo of Grancey. He was followed by Stephen of Vergy, who held the abbacy of St-Étienne in 1203. See *GC*, IV, col. 756. For Milo of Grancey and Stephen of Vergy see ibid., col. 757 and also Bouchard, *Sword, miter, and cloister*, p. 378.

any of these orders. It would therefore seem that of the Templars' relatives in other religious communities or institutions approximately two-thirds had associated themselves with reform religious communities, including houses of Augustinian canons regular, which, again, underlines the strong personal ties between Templar communities and the religious reform movement.

It is difficult to find evidence that families consciously broke with their old religious alliances after the emergence of the Templars and Cistercians as a specific result of their involvement with the new orders. Most families continued to be sporadically involved with old Benedictine communities or other 'traditional' religious houses even after they had begun supporting Templar and other reform communities. There are, after all, good reasons why families should have been reluctant to break their old alliances with established religious communities, in particular those which they or their ancestors had founded or restored to regular life. The lords of Sombernon had helped found the Benedictine nunnery of Prâlon, and it was there that Agnes of Sombernon retired in 1220.[202] A brother of the Templar Andrew of Montbard had assisted in the foundation of the nunnery of Puits-d'Orbe[203] and it was very likely here that two of Andrew's nieces took the veil.[204] These abbeys and nunneries, as well as the houses of canons regular and collegiate churches which these families also frequented, were powerful prayer communities. As is now well known, families on the lookout for effective intercessors went to considerable lengths to maintain a personal presence in a small selection of monasteries which they regarded as spiritually sound.[205]

In particular the old reformers of the tenth and eleventh centuries, whose propagation of the monastic life as the *vita angelica* had secured them a steady following in the past, still attracted the association of some Templar families in the twelfth and thirteenth. Traditional Benedictine monasticism had not declined because of the Templars. In fact, the number of Benedictine foundations in all of France continued to grow

[202] Chifflet, *Sancti Bernardi*, no. xi, col. 1409A–C, and J. de la Croix Bouton, 'Saint Bernard et les moinales', in *Mélanges de Saint Bernard. XXIVe congrès de l'association bourguignonne des sociétés savantes* (Dijon, 1953), p. 230 for the foundation of Prâlon; and Chifflet, *Sancti Bernardi*, no. xxix, 1424 for Agnes's entry into the monastery.

[203] Bouchard, *Sword, miter, and cloister*, p. 134.

[204] *Cart Mol*, II.1, no. 218, pp. 200–2 (1112×1116).

[205] M. McLaughlin, *Consorting with saints: prayer for the dead in early medieval France* (Ithaca, N.Y., London, 1994), pp. 128–9. On the importance of family members in the monastery as providers of efficacious prayers see Bouchard, *Sword, miter, and cloister*, p. 63.

steadily until the middle of the twelfth century.[206] What cannot be disputed, however, is that the Templars gained followers among the lay supporters of religious reform communities and in particular among families with ties to Cîteaux and similar communities following her lead.

Neither before nor after 1139 were the Templars in a position to challenge the traditional monastic orders on intellectual grounds. On the whole Templar houses were badly equipped with liturgical books, and even copies of their own Rule seem to have been sparse.[207] Their recruits were predominantly men of the sword or labourers, not clergymen or trained theologians. The knights came from local families of low noble stock and, for the most part, they had little learning. This is illustrated by the fact that, as in La Selve in Rouergue, entire Templar cartularies were sometimes compiled in the local tongue and not in Latin, which made them easier for the Templars to consult.[208] Once these laymen had entered the Order, they underwent a religious training that was pragmatic, to say the least, and generally conducted on a need-to-know basis.[209]

For southern France it can be stated that rather than opposing the religious establishment, the Templars attempted successfully to assimilate into the existing network of lay-religious alliances, and thus into a society that displayed a remarkable tolerance for new religious trends. Here as in Burgundy and Champagne, it was only the combination of Templar support with enthusiasm for the Cistercian movement that threatened the established alignments of families with traditional Benedictine communities. Although families refused to make absolute choices between the Church and the monastery, or between traditional or new Benedictines (the distinctions between different orders were not always recognisable to outsiders),[210] Cîteaux's dominant presence in the religious life and background of Templar families can hardly be ignored.

In Burgundy and Champagne the personal interests of influential noble families in Cîteaux and the Temple were intrinsically linked from the start. Here transactions with both orders often followed in swift succession,

[206] G. Constable, *The reformation of the twelfth century* (Cambridge, 1996), p. 28; J. Van Engen, 'The "crisis of cenobitism" reconsidered: Benedictine monasticism in the years 1050–1150', *Speculum*, 61 (1986), 277, 302.

[207] Bulst, 'Noch einmal das *Itinerarium Peregrinorum*', 599.

[208] See *Cart LaS*, passim.

[209] Riley-Smith, 'The origin of the commandery', 13; Forey, 'Novitiate and instruction', 1–17.

[210] Constable, *Reformation*, pp. 47–58. See also K. Bosl, 'Das Verhältnis von Augustinerchorherren (Regularkanoniker), Seelsorge und Gesellschaftsbewegung in Europa im 12. Jahrhundert', in *Istituzioni monastiche e istituzioni canonicali in Occidente (1123–1215). Atti della dodicesima Settimana internazionale di studio Mendola, 28 agosto – 3 settembre 1977*, Pubblicazioni della Università Cattolica del Sacro Cuore. Scienze storiche, 9 (Milan, 1980), 451–2.

peaking at moments of crisis, such as the loss of Jerusalem in 1187, which resulted in the Third Crusade.[211] In Languedoc and other parts of southern France the Templars were immediately accepted as a body of communities that would support military causes in the Holy Land and on the Iberian peninsula. As religious men, the Templars may have been put into the same category as the hermits and monks who settled in independent communities and hermitages to celebrate the *paupertas Christi*, but it was only after 1139 that they gained widespread popularity. Within a few decades the Order had established numerous dependencies in southern France which were infiltrated by families who had supported the eremitical movement as represented by so-called 'proto-Cistercian' communities, and who had shown, or were soon about to show, great sympathy for Cîteaux.

Looked upon from a distance, the importance of the Order of the Temple for, and the support that it received from, families which can be linked to it often seems marginal; the Temple was never the sole focus of a family's attention or charity. Seen from a different angle, however, one notices that charity towards the Temple, meagre as it sometimes was, was firmly embedded in the tradition of making pious donations to religious communities. Certainly those early Templars who came from families with strong affiliations to other religious houses regarded a military religious order like the Temple as something different from, but not necessarily inferior to, the various other ecclesiastical and monastic institutions which they had been free to join if they so desired.[212] The men and women who engaged with the Templars were well accustomed to dealing with monastic communities and would have had very precise expectations about the spiritual rewards that they could expect in return for their financial and personal efforts to provide for the sustenance of religious houses.

The noble houses to which Bernard of Clairvaux was related, for example, were well known to one another and often bound together by marriage. All engaged themselves actively and personally in the life of the Church, and in particular with Benedictine communities, old and new. Members of these families who had joined the Temple between the 1130s and 1220s all had relatives or friends who were living in other religious

[211] On the same note, the military orders in England, in particular the Templars, began to flourish in the aftermath of the Second Crusade. See Gervers, 'Donations to the Hospitallers in England', 159.

[212] Anselm of Havelberg, *Dialogi*, *PL*, CLXXXVIII, col. 1156C, reports that at the council of Troyes it was established that the merit of the Templars 'was not inferior to that of the monks and the canons who lead a communal life'.

orders or were holding offices in the Church. In other words, they all had access to more traditional religious careers, should they have wanted to embark on them. One element that could tip the scale in favour of one order or another was the endorsement of new forms of religious life by the local clergy.

Early support from the ecclesiastics and the rapid spread of the popularity of particular religious communities in lay society were intrinsically linked. And bearing in mind the close personal connections between monasteries and Templar houses, we can assume that if not necessarily favouring charity towards the Temple, monks or other ecclesiastics were reluctant to discourage laymen from making endowments to, or joining, a Templar commandery in which they themselves had family. The most general conclusions that one might draw from the evidence are that rural Templar houses in Burgundy, Champagne and Languedoc were populated and frequented by individuals from families with a strong preference for Benedictine communities, traditional and reformed, and that support for Cîteaux and for a military order like the Temple complemented each other.[213] Such an argument suggests that the Temple too may have been perceived as reformist in character. But the pattern of involvement and the chronology of endowments of Templar families indicate more than this. It implies that the success of the Temple was intrinsically linked to that of Cîteaux.[214]

As a result, by the end of the thirteenth century the Templars, who had no collective memory or historiography to speak of, had forgotten their Augustinian origins and were instead attributing their origin to Bernard of Clairvaux and Cîteaux.[215] In Burgundy and Champagne, and later also in Languedoc, men and women interacted with the Templars in a thoroughly Cistercian context and the most efficacious Templar benefactors were those who were most deeply involved with Cistercian or 'proto-Cistercian' communities. The continuous involvement of families of Cistercian benefactors in the Order of the Temple is particularly revealing

[213] This does not only apply to the Templars. As shown by Mazel, *Noblesse et l'église*, pp. 341–57, the family of Baux in Provence was heavily involved in the Cistercian Order and in the Order of St John.

[214] In this context, it is interesting to note that the orders of Cîteaux, the Temple and the Hospital not only were introduced in England at the same time – in 1128, it seems – but that both Cîteaux and the Temple were instantaneously successful, whereas the Hospital initially lagged behind (a situation that changed in the middle of the twelfth century). See Gervers, 'Donations to the Hospitallers in England', 158–9.

[215] Tommasi, 'Pauperes commilitones Christi', 471–3. See also J. Sarnowsky, 'Das historische Selbstverständnis der geistlichen Ritterorden', *Zeitschrift für Kirchengeschichte*, 110 (1999), 322 and, for an example, *PT*, I, p. 121.

if one considers that, as Bouchard has shown for Burgundy, families who could afford to patronise only a few houses usually chose very similar ones.[216] Their expectations, and perception, of the Temple must have been similar to that of Cîteaux (or any other similar community they supported). For these families, support of the *novum monasterium* and the *nova militia*, be it material or personal, went hand in hand.

[216] Bouchard, *Sword, miter, and cloister*, pp. 138–42.

Chapter 3

TEMPLARS AND FAMILIES

The arrival of the first Templar master with five of his fellow brothers in France in 1127 was preceded by rumours about the new brotherhood's existence and mission. These rumours were spread by returning pilgrims and crusaders and also, presumably, by the Templars themselves. It has been disputed but is now again believed that perhaps as early as 1120 the Templar brothers Godfrey of St-Omer and Andrew of Montbard had travelled from Jerusalem to Clairvaux with a letter from King Baldwin of Jerusalem asking Abbot Bernard of Clairvaux to embrace and promote the young Templar community.[1] Bernard's influence reached far beyond the borders of Champagne and Burgundy and deep into the fabric of aristocratic and religious society. His support would have guaranteed the Templars a warm welcome in many dioceses. The ever-increasing number of returning pilgrims and crusaders would also have contributed to a heightened popular awareness of the practical value of the Templars' proclaimed aims and mission. Already in *c.* 1125 a charter from Flanders commented on the magnitude of the love and decency (*charitatis eminentia et laudabilis honestatis gratia*) which Templars had displayed to pilgrims en route to the holy places.[2] Coincidentally (or perhaps not), it was also around this time that William Clito, count of Flanders, made his first recorded endowments to the Templars, granting them liberties which were soon confirmed by Thierry of Flanders, and that Count Hugh of Troyes decided to join them in Jerusalem.[3]

[1] *CG*, no. 1, p. 1 (1119×1126). Prutz, *Die geistlichen Ritterorden*, p. 28, and later Gustav Schnürer ('Zur ersten Organisation', 512–20), have dated the letter to 1130×1131. The authenticity of the letter has been disputed – see e.g. *Cart Prov*, p. xxv and M. Melville, *La vie des templiers* (2nd edn, Paris, 1974), p. 23fn. – but Demurger (*Les templiers*, p. 52) now believes that the letter is genuine and was written in 1120. His authority is Pierre-Vincent Claverie's doctoral thesis, which, however, in its published form cautiously dates the letter 'before 15 October 1126', thus again leaving wide open the question of its precise dating. See P.-V. Claverie, *L'ordre du Temple en Terre Sainte et à Chypre au XIIIe siècle*, 3 vols. (Nicosia, 2005), III, no. 422, p. 353.

[2] *CG*, no. 4, pp. 2–3 (*c.* 1125).

[3] Ibid., no. 5, p. 3 (*c.* 1125×1130), no. 7, p. 5 (1127×1178); T. Leroy, *Hugues de Payns. Chevalier champenois. Fondateur de l'ordre des templiers* (Troyes, 2001) p. 76.

It was not until 1127, however, the year of the Templars' arrival in France, that the new Templar brotherhood attracted support on a larger scale. The arrival of Hugh of Payns and his companions once more set the machinery of kinship and feudal influences in motion that was already fuelling so many other religious communities with men and material. One of the Templars who came to France with Hugh of Payns was, again, Godfrey of St-Omer. Together the two men were able to cover large parts of northern France with personal requests for support. Whereas Hugh of Payns was able to call upon his ties to Hugh of Troyes and Count Thibaud when drumming up support for his brotherhood in Champagne, Godfrey's ties to the comital house of Flanders secured the Templars support in Flanders and Picardy.[4]

The personal networks of these two Templars thus provided the Templar community with a potential donor base to finance and support the establishment of the first commanderies. The castellans of St-Omer, to whom Godfrey was connected, soon became keen supporters of the Templars, endowing them, for example, with the fief of Bas-Warneton in Hainaut in 1128 and the churches of Slijpe and Leffinge in 1137.[5] They were part of a far-flung and close-knit kinship network that dominated politics in Picardy and that was distinctive for its involvement in the crusades and in affairs in the Holy Land.[6] Hugh of Payns, whose family held land near Troyes and the lordship of Montigny-Lagesse, once belonged to the peripatetic court of Hugh of Troyes.[7] A scion of one of the old landed families of Champagne, he was rooted in the social fabric of the county and thus able to call upon old ties of kinship, friendship and vassalage when recruiting for his new foundation. As we have seen, his former lord Hugh of Troyes had joined the Temple in 1125 in the Holy Land and it did not take long for Hugh of Troyes's nephew and successor Thibaud of Blois to issue the first of many concessions to the Templars in Champagne, which inspired numerous of his barons and other vassals to follow his lead.[8]

[4] Demurger, *Les templiers*, p. 51 does not believe that Godfrey belonged to the family of castellans of St-Omer. J. Hosten, *De tempeliers: de tempelorde tijdens de kruistochten en in de Lage Landen* (Amsterdam, 2006), pp. 237–43, however, argues otherwise.

[5] *CG*, no. 17, pp. 11–12 (1128); Prutz, *Die geistlichen Ritterorden*, p. 356.

[6] Apart from the castellans of St-Omer, Ardres and Fiennes, this group included the counts of Flanders, Boulogne and Guines, and the lords of Fauquembergues. See R. Fossier, *La terre et les hommes en Picardie jusqu'à la fin du XIIIe siècle*, 2 vols. (Paris, Louvain, 1968), II, pp. 542–6.

[7] Evergates, *Aristocracy*, p. 8; Demurger, *Les templiers*, p. 24; Leroy, *Hugues de Payns. Chevalier champenois*, pp. 43–62.

[8] *CG*, no. 9, p. 6. For the involvement of the counts of Champagne with the Templars (which, however, became more restricted over the years) see Bur, 'Les comtes de Champagne et les templiers'.

One young nobleman who had perhaps followed the example of Hugh of Troyes, or even that of Hugh of Payns himself, and had joined the Templar brotherhood before 1127 was William of Baudement, son of Andrew of Baudement, seneschal of Thibaud II. Thibaud II's leadership has been described as 'collegial', meaning that the barons of the county were involved in the count's decision-making and that the count relied on their advice and counsel.[9] As seneschal Andrew of Baudement was one of Thibaud's closest companions and bearing in mind Thibaud's 'collegial' policy-making it thus seems likely that after his son had joined the Templars Andrew would have encouraged any decision by the count, whose own uncle was by then a Templar, to support the nascent Templar community. He seems, in any case, to have participated in discussions about the conduct of the Templars and best possible rule for them, thus aiding the members of the council of Troyes to treat the topic 'in such a manner that by perfect, studious care they sought out that which was fine and disapproved [sic] that which did not seem right'.[10]

Over time, relationships between families and Templar commanderies could become very complex. Donations and business transactions sometimes followed each other in swift succession or were conducted simultaneously, and periods of intense involvement were followed by times of disputes and disagreement. Some generations produced multiple Templar associates, others none. Some families became heavily involved in the Temple during a short period of time and then disappeared from the charters; others gave to the Temple modestly, but over many generations. The charters in which the interactions between families and the Order have been transmitted to us are snapshots of how relationships between individuals and local Templar communities were acted out at particular times and under particular circumstances. If contextualised they reveal consistencies and changes in the way individuals and families interacted with the Order. Some hint at the intimate relationship that Templar communities could develop with the families of their benefactors. All of them contribute to the understanding of the intensity and social consequences of family involvement in the Order.

To assess how far families were united in their efforts to assist the Temple it is necessary to establish how long and to what extent they can be associated with it and to assess the social significance and consequences of their transactions. I mention this, because the act of making a donation to the Temple usually involved, and affected, more people than just the

[9] Evergates, *Aristocracy*, pp. 7, 10.

[10] *Templerregel*, p. 131 and *The Rule of the Templars: the French text of the Rule of the Order of the Knights Templar*, trans. J. M. Upton-Ward (Woodbridge, 1992), p. 21.

donor. It often had long-term repercussions within the donor's family; and it also forced bystanders to engage in negotiations with the Order.

THE INTENSITY OF FAMILY INVOLVEMENT

As was generally the case with the patronage of religious houses, families that became involved with the Order usually focused their charity on the nearest Templar community.[11] From this it does not necessarily follow that they all considered themselves to be closely attached to the Order. Judging from the surviving charter evidence, some noble families gave much in a short space of time, whereas others gave little over many years. Furthermore, the fact that families usually favoured nearby commanderies does not mean that they supported them exclusively.

The castellans of Auriac, a *castrum* situated about 28 kilometres south-west of Douzens on a mountain ridge overlooking the river Orbieu, supported the Templars of Douzens in the early 1140s,[12] but the members of the family and their household who joined the Order were all recorded at Pézenas, approximately 90 kilometres to the south-east of Douzens.[13] They should not be confused with the knights of Auriac who were recorded acting as donors to the Templar communities of La Selve and Ste-Eulalie and who probably hailed from Auriac-Lagast, which is situated about 5 kilometres north of La Selve and about 50 kilometres west of Ste-Eulalie.[14] By 1178 one family from Auriac-Lagast had provided Ste-Eulalie with possessions near the commandery, including the church of Le Gal, farms, weapons and horses, whereas by 1172 two generations of Williams and Berenguers of Auriac had entered the confraternity of La Selve.[15] One Berenguer and one William of Auriac took full Templar vows[16] and in *c.* 1180 Pons of Auriac, his son W[illiam] and daughter Gaillarda made further donations to La Selve.[17] A few years later another Berenguer of Auriac confirmed earlier concessions made by his

[11] That noble families in Burgundy favoured nearby reform monastic communities over more distant monasteries is demonstrated in Bouchard, *Sword, miter, and cloister*, pp. 138–42.

[12] *Cart Douz*, A: no. 42, pp. 52–3 (1142), no. 61, p. 67 (1141), no. 70, pp. 72–3 (1142).

[13] By 1146 Peter and Bartholomew of Auriac were recorded among the Templars of Pézenas. See *CG*, no. 400, pp. 251–2 (1146), no. 401, p. 252 (1146), no. 442, p. 277 (1147). Lawrence of Auriac was in June 1235 recorded acting as scribe for the Templars in the dependency of Pézenas at Cazouls. See BN, n.a.l., 17, fols. 351r–2 (1235).

[14] The two families may have been related, as both made extensive use of the names William, Peter and Berenguer, which (see Duhamel-Amado, *Genèse*, I, pp. 265–8), however, were very popular names in Languedoc at the time.

[15] *PAC*, I, no. 59, pp. 63–4 (1150), no. 135, pp. 126–7 (1172); ibid., II, no. 360, pp. 9–10 (1155), no. 455, pp. 90–2 (1165); *Cart LaS*, no. R17, p. 262 (*c.* 1160).

[16] *PAC*, I, no. 165, pp. 153–4 (*c.* 1178).

[17] *Cart LaS*, no. P9, pp. 280–1 (*c.* 1180).

father.[18] And by 1211 his brother William was recorded as a professed knight of the Temple.[19] Both families of Auriac were thus familiar with at least two Templar communities, and at least one of them had been patron of two Templar houses.

There are numerous possible explanations as to why families sometimes supported commanderies that were a long distance away from each other (in the case of Ste-Eulalie and La Selve the distance was more than 50 kilometres). The desire to support relatives who moved between different commanderies is one of them; marriage, as I will show, another.

The Order of the Temple was able to expand because knightly and noble families were willing to invest their lives and family fortunes in ideas of religious reform. The periods over which some families involved themselves in the Order seem to have been very short but intense. Particularly, this was the case where family piety expressed itself not only in an abundance of religious endowments but also in the transference of entire generations of family members into religious orders. This phenomenon, which one scholar has described as 'dynastic suicide', is not unknown among Templar families, although it did not necessarily manifest itself in the involvement of these families with the Temple, and I am not aware of any family that ceased to exist because too many male heirs had entered the Temple.[20] But involvement in the Temple could be part of the enthusiasm that caused some family branches to die out, as is revealed, for example, by a closer examination of the religious dealings of the lords of Baudement.

The religious charters of Burgundy and Champagne show that when William of Baudement entered the Order of the Temple some time before 1133, he was participating in what can be described as a fully-fledged exodus of family members into reformed religious communities. His brother Galeran had entered Clairvaux by 1127 and was the abbot of Ourscamp in 1129;[21] his father Andrew and mother Agnes entered Clairvaux and Prémontré respectively; his brother Andrew was a Cistercian monk of Pontigny and became the first Cistercian abbot of Chaalis. Another brother, Thibaud, became a canon of Prémontré and two of his sisters entered Jully, a house of Benedictine nuns under the governance of Molesme.[22] Before William's father Andrew entered

[18] *PAC*, II, no. 492, p. 127 (1187). [19] Carcenac, *Les templiers du Larzac*, p. 170.

[20] The term 'monastic suicide' is explained in A. Murray, *Reason and society in the middle ages* (Oxford, 1978), pp. 346–7.

[21] Godfrey of Auxerre, *S. Bernardi vita et fragmenta*, cols. 523–30; Veyssière, 'Le personnel', 50; M. Bur, *La formation du comté de Champagne* (Nancy, 1977), p. 432; Aubé, *Saint Bernard*, p. 186.

[22] A. Luchaire, *Louis VI le Gros, annales de sa vie et de son règne* (Paris, 1890), no. 563, p. 256, edited in M. H. d'Arbois de Jubainville and L. Pigeotte, *Histoire des ducs et des comtes de Champagne*, 7 vols.

Clairvaux in 1137, he and Lethericus of Baudement[23] endowed the Templars with the village of Dolgast, a fief between Baudement and Chantemerle, and a female serf in the village of Aulnoy (or Launay), for which the sons of Lethericus were reimbursed with the village of Dolgast, as well as with the serfs, lands, waters and meadows that Andrew possessed in the lordship of Baudement and the bridge-toll and revenues that Andrew received in the family castle. Only the castle of Baudement itself, one servant and the fiefs of his knights remained in Andrew's possession.[24] As part of the dowry of Andrew's remaining daughters and, later, of his great-granddaughter Elisabeth, the castle of Baudement passed into the hands of the counts of Dreux, and eventually into the possession of the Countess Blanche of Troyes, who purchased it from Elisabeth of Dreux in 1211.[25]

In the case of the lords of Baudement, after a few decades of extensive commitment to the Order of the Temple property that could be given to the Temple and male heirs who could join it were in short supply. In the case of the lords of Possesse in Champagne, the family line that had made endowments to the Order since 1142 was brought to an end by the desire of three brothers to enter the religious life or to go to the Holy Land.[26] Guy III of Possesse mortgaged his castle to Count Henry of Champagne before disappearing on what seems to have been a crusade or a pilgrimage to the Holy Land in the early 1160s.[27] In 1165 his brother John, who had succeeded him as lord of Possesse (without the castle), made endowments to five Cistercian houses, founded one hospital in Possesse and gave his possessions in the village of Maucourt to the Templars before taking the

(Paris, 1859–69), II, p. 378. See also *Le chartrier de l'abbaye prémontrée de Saint-Yved de Braine (1134–1250)*, ed. O. Guyotjeannin (Paris, 2000), p. 18fn. Agnes was the granddaughter of Andrew of Baudement, seneschal of Champagne, and Agnes of Braine, daughter of Guy of Dampierre. Her father was Guy of Baudement, count of Braine and the Templar William of Baudement was her uncle. She is not to be confused with her grandmother, as has happened. See R. L. Poole and A. L. Poole, *Studies in chronology and history* (Oxford, 1934), p. 265. Godefroy, 'La Maison d'Aulnoy-les-Minimes', 33–5, believed that she was the daughter of Andrew, but A. W. Lewis, 'Fourteen charters of Robert I of Dreux (1152–1188)', *Traditio*, 41 (1985), 158 and nos. 50, 51 (see also Peter of Celle, *The letters of Peter of Celle*, pp. xxix–xxx) proves that she was not.

23 In all likelihood he was the same Lethericus, lord of Aulnoy, who was the father of the Cluniac monk Peter of Celle and a relative of Agnes of Baudement. Peter made a career in the Church. He became bishop of Chartes, and was a friend of Bernard of Clairvaux and Thomas Becket. See Peter of Celle, *The letters of Peter of Celle*, ed. and trans. J. Haseldine, Oxford Medieval Texts (Oxford, 2001) pp. xxviii–xxxiii, and J. Godefroy, 'La Maison d'Aulnoy-les-Minimes, souche de Pierre de Celle', *Revue Mabillon*, 41 (1951), 33–5.

24 AN S 4968, dossier 24, no. 6, and *Cart Prov*, no. 81, pp. 102–3 (1133). See also Evergates, *Aristocracy*, p. 10.

25 Ibid., pp. 39, 124–5; *'Littere baronum'*, no. 21, pp. 63–4 (1211).

26 The lords of Possesse had made endowments to the Order from at least as early as 1142: see *Diocèse ancien de Châlons-sur-Marne*, I, p. 234.

27 For what follows see *Feud Soc*, no. 91, pp. 113–14 (1166) and T. Evergates, 'Nobles and knights in twelfth-century France', in T. N. Bisson (ed.), *Cultures of power. Lordship, status, and process in twelfth-century Europe* (Philadelphia, Pa., 1995), 21–4.

habit at Clairvaux, where he was still living in 1198.[28] The lordship went to the youngest of the three brothers, Hugh, who in the same year abandoned it to go to the Holy Land. He never reached the shores of the Levant but settled in Calabria instead. After an unsuccessful attempt to secure Hugh's return to Champagne, Possesse was eventually handed over to his cousin Guy of Garlande.[29]

The impact of heresy and the Albigensian crusades

The answer as to why a certain family disappeared from the Templar charters after a short period of intensive involvement in the Order does not always present itself as readily as in the case of the lords of Baudement or Possesse, but, particularly in southern France, political circumstance is certainly another factor that has to be taken into account. In Languedoc and Provence, many knights and lords had lost their property in the course of the Albigensian crusades and were reluctant or unable to continue their endowments to religious institutions. This may have been the case for the lords of Roquefort in Haute-Garonne who between 1160 and 1205 provided the Templar community of Montsaunès with men and material, but whose names fail to appear in charters recorded after 1205.[30]

The Albigensian crusades polarised southern French society as much as they tested existing alliances between families and religious institutions. Among the knights and nobles who supported the Order of the Temple in the regions affected by the crusades were many whose relatives took up arms against the invaders from the north. Pons of Montlaur, whose relatives included Templar knights and benefactors, for example, was, in the words of the Cistercian chronicler Peter of Les Vaux-de-Cernay, himself 'doing everything in his power to hinder the Church and the bishops and the promotion of peace in the area' before he was forced to submit himself and his possessions to the leader of the crusades army, Simon of Montfort.[31] The family of the two Templar associates William

[28] *Diocèse ancien de Châlons-sur-Marne*, I, p. 234 and no. 19, pp. 402–3 (1165), no. 37, p. 409 (1192, confirmation); *CG(Hosp)*, I, no. 342, p. 239 (1165); *Chart Clairv*, no. 376, pp. 480–1 (1198).

[29] Evergates, *Aristocracy*, p. 22. As lords of Possesse the Garlandes maintained their own relations with the Temple. See, e.g., Archives départementales de la Marne, Fonds 53H 90, no. 3 (as recorded in *Les plus anciens documents linguistiques de la France. Les chartes de la Marne (ChMa)*, ed. M.-D. Gleßgen and D. Chihaï [http://www.mediaevistik.uzh.ch/docling/data/c555580016.php]), which records the end of litigation between Anselm of Garlande, lord of Possesse, and the Templars of Neuville over the forests of Abelin.

[30] See pp. 169–70, below.

[31] Peter of Les Vaux-de-Cernay, *Historia Albigensium et Sacri Belli in eos anno 1209 suscepti, duce et principe Simone de Monteforti*, *PL*, CCXIII, col. 679A. The involvement of different families 'of Montlaur' is discussed in Chapter 5.

and Johanna Porcelet also opposed the Albigensian crusaders from very early on, as did members of the family of Barbaira and the castellans of Capendu, whose twelfth-century ancestors had been close associates of Templar Douzens.[32]

The Barbairas and Capendus were vassals of the viscounts of Béziers. And as the distance between the two *castra* was only 4 kilometres, the two families were probably well acquainted with each another.[33] Both families were among the most prolific supporters of Douzens during the first twenty years of the commandery's existence. Not only had the Barbairas given the Templars a large share in the lordship and *castrum* of Douzens, and thus the opportunity to establish what was perhaps the Order's first fortified commandery in Languedoc; they had also provided them with much of their patrimony in and near Douzens, including the church of Saint-Jean of Carrières, and, by 1153, with three fully professed brothers and three *confratres*.[34] Over the next twenty-five years, the two main branches of the noble family of Barbaira continued to donate land, rents, serfs and tenements to Douzens.[35] They witnessed a number of transactions at Pézenas, a fortified village with a castle about 25 kilometres northeast of Béziers, and inland from Agde, where the Templars maintained another commandery.[36] And in the years that followed they contributed more recruits, among them Raymond of Barbaira, who was recorded as a Templar at Richerenches in 1156 and 1157, and Peter Raymond of Barbaira, who was recorded at Douzens in 1158.[37] In the extant Templar records the Barbairas are mentioned for almost the last time in 1176, surfacing (perhaps) again only briefly in 1271 when a certain Berenguer of Barbaira was recorded among the Templar brothers of Mas Deu.[38]

In the meantime, individual members of the Barbaira family clan appeared sporadically in the charters of Cistercian Fontfroide (so for

[32] William Porcelet himself was possibly a close relative of the assassin of the papal legate Peter of Castelnau whose death in January 1208 triggered the crusade. Mazel, *Noblesse et l'église*, pp. 388, 390, 396.

[33] Both Raymond Ermengau of Barbaira and Bernard Raymond of Capendu were recorded at an assembly of Viscount Roger II's vassals at Sauzens in 1191. See *CadC*, I, pp. 66–7 and 310 for transactions involving the viscounts of Carcassonne and members of the family of Capendu.

[34] See Demurger, *Les templiers*, pp. 279–82 and Barber, 'The Templar preceptory of Douzens', in particular pp. 39 and 45.

[35] *Cart Douz*, A: no. 90, pp. 87–8 (1169), no. 91, pp. 88–9 (1169), no. 154, p. 140 (1169).

[36] BN, n.a.l., 15, fols. 261r–2r (1173×1174).

[37] *Cart Rich*, no. 76, p. 78 (1156), no. 77, pp. 78–9 (1156), no. 129, pp. 123–4 (1156), no. 146, pp. 134–5 (1157), no. 151, pp. 136–7 (1156), no. 152, p. 137 (1156), no. 154, p. 139 (1156), no. 158, pp. 141–2 (1156); *Cart Douz*, A: no. 63, pp. 68–9 (1158). Another Templar named Raymond de Barba vaira, who was possibly identical with the earlier-mentioned Raymond of Barbaira, was recorded at Montpellier in 1176. See BN, n.a.l., 15, fols. 31r–3r (1176).

[38] Vinas, *L'ordre du Temple*, p. 112.

example the brothers Aimeric, Isarn and Raymond Bernard in 1190, when they sold the monks a fief near Gaussan, or Arnold in 1216, when he witnessed at castle Durban the confirmation of donations to Fontfroide),[39] whereas others acquired reputations as 'heretics'. The knight Chabert of Barbaira, for example, was seen in the company of heretics[40] and in around 1248 described as a 'sentenced heretic and enemy of the king and Church' (*hereticus sententiatus et inimicus D[omini] Regis et ecclesiae*).[41] According to a letter addressed to the seneschal of Carcassonne he had raised his banner in the *castrum* of Montlaur (which, conquered by Simon of Montfort in 1214, had been returned to Lagrasse in 1215)[42] and was now waging a petty war against the village of Lagrasse, the king and the Church. With him was Aimeric of Montlaur, who was from another family with Templar ties but had put up fierce resistance to Simon of Montfort and the bishops – Pons of Montlaur's defiance is described above by Peter of Les Vaux-de-Cernay – and also displayed a strong and personal commitment to the heretical beliefs.[43]

The lords and knights of the *castrum* of Capendu, just east of Carcassonne, appear less often in the charters of Douzens than their neighbours the lords of Barbaira. Isarn of Capendu, sometimes referred to as Isarn of Molières, had entered the Temple at Douzens by 1157 and was recorded among the brothers (and for the last two years as preceptor) of that commandery until 1184.[44] As was customary, Isarn bequeathed landed possessions to the Order when he joined it, although some of these were reclaimed by his cousin Peter of Capendu, who quarrelled for a while with the Templars over the rent pertaining to them.[45] Peter relented eventually and since his brother Pons was already making new endowments to the Templars in 1163 it does not seem as if the brief quarrel between Peter and the Templars had caused any long-term rupture in the relations between the Order and his family.[46] Records of involvement with the Templars on the part of the lords and knights of

[39] *Chart Font*, no. 690, p. 319 (1190); no. 1198, pp. 550–1 (1216).

[40] Bernard of Caux, *Confessiones de V° libro lauraguesii fratris Bernardi de Cautio transcripto in hoc libro usque ad* CLXVIII *F° – Item a dicto folio deinceps de quarto libro dicti fratris Bernardi, Bibliothèque municipale de Toulouse, ms. 609*, ed. J. Duvernoy [http://jean.duvernoy.free.fr/text/listetexte.htm#sinquisit], fol. 126a.

[41] *CadC*, II, pp. 555–6 (*c.* 1248).

[42] The monks of Lagrasse had been in possession of Montlaur since 1172. See *La Grasse (II)*, p. xlvi.

[43] Peter of Les Vaux-de-Cernay, *Historia Albigensium*, col. 679A (and also col. 582D for the first uprising at Montlaur). Raymond Ermengau of Montlaur and his brother were known Cathar *faidits* (a colloquial term describing a rebel and patron of heretics). See also *Petri Vallium Sarnaii monachi Hystoria albigensis*, ed. P. Guébin and E. Lyon, I (Paris, 1926), no. 1, p. 147.

[44] *GP(Toulouse)*, p. 590; *Cart Douz*, A: no. 161, pp. 144–5 (1182), B: no. 46, p. 225 (1160), no. 47, pp. 225–6, no. 73, pp. 245–6 (1172).

[45] Ibid.: no. 46, p. 225 (1160). [46] *Cart Douz*, A: no. 65, pp. 69–70 (1163).

Capendu become increasingly spasmodic in the second half of the twelfth century, although they still appear occasionally as witnesses and benefactors and by 1194 had produced in Raymond William of Capendu, preceptor for Carcassès and Razès, at least one more Templar knight.[47] The reasons for the long period of silence that followed are not altogether clear, but it seems likely that they were connected to the events that led to the Capendu lords' loss of their *castrum* by 1209 (the lordship of Capendu was subsequently granted to the counts of Bar from Lorraine),[48] which in turn were caused by their loyalty to the viscounts of Carcassonne, whose vassals they were, and their role in the resistance to Simon of Montfort.

Their fall from power in the thirteenth century does not explain why the Capendus had disappeared from the charters as early as 1174; and with so little information available it seems futile to look for definite answers. According to the, admittedly very biased, account of the Cistercian chronicler Peter of Les Vaux-de-Cernay, relatives of Isarn seem to have developed a keen interest in heretical ideas by the beginning of the thirteenth century, which culminated in Bernard Raymond of Capendu's decision to become a 'Cathar' *faidit* in 1209, after he had been dispossessed of his castle, and in the marriage of his sister Alis to a well-known heretic, William of Peyrepertuse.[49]

It does not need to be pointed out that not all lords and knights who opposed the crusaders were necessarily heretics (these claims, if at all founded in reality, were customarily exaggerated by the chroniclers); many would have described their actions as acts of resistance to external oppression.[50] Nor were all families of 'heretics' necessarily lost to the Catholic Church, although some, like the lords of Capendu, may have turned their back on the Templars for good. Bernard Raymond of Capendu's son, Pons, still invested the bishop of Béziers with the *castrum* of Cazouls in 1230 and throughout the following decades Raymond of Capendu and a number of his relatives acted as proctors of the Benedictine abbey of Lagrasse. They also became heavily involved with the Benedictines of Montolieu and created ties to the church of Carcassonne. These engagements eventually paid off. In 1265 Bernard of Capendu was

47 BN, n.a.l., 15, fols. 204r–5r (1180); ibid., 18, fols. 387r–8r (1174). For Raymond William see ibid., fols. 494r–7r (1194).

48 See *CadC*, I, p. 309. References to the counts of Bar as castellans of Capendu are given in ibid., p. 311.

49 Peter of Les Vaux-de-Cernay, *Hystoria albigensis*, I, no. 4, pp. 146–7. Peter of Les Vaux-de-Cernay and the other chroniclers of the Albigensian crusade are discussed in Graham-Leigh, *Southern French nobility*, pp. 10–41.

50 Ibid., p. 27. For a critical reading of the chronicles of the Albigensian crusades see Pegg, *A most holy war*, passim.

elected bishop of Carcassonne and thirty years later Peter of Capendu became abbot of Montolieu.[51]

But the number of knights and nobles with ties to the Temple who fought the French crusaders and sympathised with heretical beliefs was not small either. In the urban context at least, as Jörg Oberste has shown, support for heretical 'good men' and 'good women' and engagement in Catholic institutions, including Templar communities, frequently occurred within the same families.[52] It is also plausible that some lay men and women engaged with the Temple as a way of avoiding accusations of heresy and in order to guard themselves against excommunication and the interdict, in much the same manner as some of their contemporaries suddenly involved themselves with Cîteaux.[53]

At the very least, the examples of the lords of Barbaira and Capendu testify to the disruption caused by the Albigensian crusades among the Templars' clientele in Languedoc. Moreover, the examples are illustrative of how in Languedoc the Albigensian crusades broke up the social infrastructure of the aristocracy but did not eliminate 'heresy'. The fact that families which had supported the Order materially and personally in the twelfth century disappeared or were disappearing from the Templar sources at the same time as they became associated with 'heretics' also weakens the argument, propagated, for example, by Prutz, that the Order of the Temple was generally regarded as a safe haven for heretics or that the Templars in Occitania had themselves adopted a form of 'Catharism'.[54] There is in any case little to suggest that the Order of the Temple was particularly welcoming to convicted or suspected heretics; it is more likely that Templar communities dissociated themselves from suspected supporters and their families.

It is also likely that families detached themselves from Templar communities which they suspected were collaborating with the crusaders from the north (which did not prevent the knight Raymond of Capendu from making donations to the Hospitallers of Béziers, however).[55] The example of the castellan family of Montredon near Carcassonne is a good case in

[51] *HGL*, IV, pp. 332, 458, 459, 738; V, col. 1669.

[52] Oberste, *Zwischen Heiligkeit und Häresie*, pp. 186–207. See also Oberste, 'Donaten', 21–4.

[53] Delaruelle, 'Templiers et hospitaliers en Languedoc', 328–9; Demurger, *Les templiers*, pp. 387–8; Graham-Leigh, *Southern French nobility*, pp. 84–6. On the same note, Constance Berman has argued that after 1200 the primary reason for the Trencavels to support the Cistercians may have been to avoid the accusation of heresy. See C. H. Berman, 'Origins of the filiation of Morimond in southern France. Redating foundation charters for Gimont, Villelongue, Berdoues, L'Escaledieu, and Bonnefont', *Cîteaux*, 41 (1990), 262.

[54] H. Prutz, *Geheimstatuten und Geheimlehre des Tempelherren-Ordens. Eine kritische Untersuchung* (Berlin, 1879), pp. 98–9.

[55] *HGL*, V, col. 1449 (1247).

point. The castellans had been on amicable terms with the Templars since at least the end of the twelfth century, when William Amel I of Montredon with his wife Cerdana and sons Peter of La Tour and William endowed the Templars with landed property outside the *castrum* of Montredon.[56] Relatives of William Amel witnessed transactions with the Templars,[57] and one may have joined them.[58] As can be reconstructed from the charters, in the course of the Albigensian campaigns Simon of Montfort deprived the lords of Montredon of their lordship and passed it on to the Templars.[59] His actions had a profound impact on how the former lords of Montredon regarded the Templars henceforward, and in 1230 the Templars of Montredon had to face the anger of the relatives of their former benefactors when two sons of William Amel I of Montredon, William Amel II and Arnold Amel, and one of his grandsons entered the *castrum* of Montredon by force and violently expelled them.[60]

Evidence also exists, however, that some Templar communities retained their connections with families of suspected or convicted heretics – after all, the lands of the Trencavels were densely populated with alleged heresy sympathisers in the early thirteenth century – and that they admitted anti-royal partisans into their communities.[61] The commandery of Mas Deu in Roussillon, for example, remained on friendly terms with a number of families who in the thirteenth century were known for having 'heretics' or 'heresy sympathisers' in their midst.[62] That Mas Deu itself was rife with anti-royal sentiments was confirmed when the Templars turned to Rome for help after James II of Majorca had occupied the commandery; they promised that, if it were returned to them, they would man the commandery with reliable men from whom the French king had nothing to fear.[63]

It is possible that the twelfth-century Templar Peter of Montlaur (recorded at Millau in Aveyron and Douzens in Aude)[64] and the thirteenth-century Templar Bernard of Montlaur (recorded in Aragon

[56] BN, n.a.l., 18, fols. 489r–93r (n.d.). [57] Ibid., 16, fols. 45r–7r (1193)

[58] William (*En Guillem*) of Montredon joined the Temple some time before 1206 and was recorded at different commanderies on the Iberian peninsula. Between 1206 and 1217 he presided over the commanderies of Gardeny and Mas Deu, at the latter of which he also, from 1213 until 1217, acted as tutor to James I of Aragon. He could have been a Catalan from near Vich. See James of Aragon, *The chronicle of James I King of Aragon, surnamed the Conqueror (written by himself)*, trans. J. Forster (London, 1883), p. 19; Forey, *Aragón*, p. 430; Verdon, *La terre et les hommes*, p. 217; Vinas, *L'ordre du Temple*, p. 29.

[59] Prutz, *Die geistlichen Ritterorden*, p. 362. [60] BN, n.a.l., 19, fols. 54r–63r (1230).

[61] Graham-Leigh, *Southern French nobility*, pp. 61–2; Demurger, *Les templiers*, pp. 387–8.

[62] Oberste, 'Donaten', 130 and Vinas, 'Le destin des templiers', passim.

[63] Prutz, *Entwicklung und Untergang*, pp. 61–2.

[64] *CG*, no. 585, pp. 359–60 (1150×1151); *Cart Douz*, A: no. 59, p. 66 (1164), no. 88, pp. 84–5 (1153).

and Roussillon)[65] were relatives of Bertrand, Pons, and William Seguier of Montlaur, whom witnesses interrogated by the inquisitor of Toulouse, Bernard of Caux, in 1245 and 1246 remembered as having enjoyed the company of heretics twenty or more years earlier.[66] Likewise, the heresy sympathiser Arnold of Auriac, reported by one of the witnesses to have rescued known heretics from imprisonment in around 1234, was a member of the same castellan family of Auriac that had supported Douzens in the 1140s and had provided the Templar community of Pézenas with numerous knights.[67] A better-known example is the Provençal troubadour Guy of Cavaillon, who had sided with the counts of Toulouse in their fight against Simon of Montfort. He supported the Templar community at Cavaillon and by 1222 had become a *frater et donatus* of the Order. Eventually he professed, and by 1252 he was recorded as residing in the commandery of St-Gilles. Guy was not the first in his family to enter the Temple, nor does he seem to have been the last, as from 1260 until 1270 a knight by the name of William of Cavaillon presided over the Templar commanderies of Arles and, later, St-Gilles.[68]

Anti-royal sentiments and heretical beliefs are not the same thing, however, and the fact that some Templars remained loyal to friends and relatives who had digressed from the path of Catholic orthodoxy says little about their own religious beliefs. Nothing in the 1309 and 1310 Templar depositions suggests that the conduct in the commandery of Mas Deu had been anything but orthodox.[69] Rather, the critique that the Templars of Mas Deu were evidently facing – both from the Pope and his legates and from the French king – such that they were obliged to promise to be more loyal to the king gives us a glimpse of how deeply Templar commanderies were embedded in society and how limited the exchange of Templar brothers between provinces must have been. On the commandery level, the confinement of Templars to their provinces can be explained by the inability of the provincial master to appoint brothers from outside the boundaries of his province as preceptors of his commanderies without the consent of the grandmaster and the convent.[70] But it seems that provincial masters and preceptors were generally reluctant to send brothers of their houses to live permanently in Templar communities beyond the borders of the province, with the obvious exception of the convents in the East.

65 Forey, *Aragón*, p. 422; Léonard, *Introduction*, p. 90; Verdon, *La terre et les hommes*, p. 217.
66 Ibid., fols. 67a, 126a. 67 Bernard of Caux, *Confessiones*, fol. 67a.
68 Another possible relative of Guy, Raymond Fulk of Cavaillon, made extensive landed donations to the Order in 1286. Carraz, *L'ordre du Temple*, pp. 414–15.
69 Vinas, 'Le destin des templiers', passim.
70 J. Delaville Le Roulx (ed.), 'Un nouveau manuscrit de la règle du Temple', *Annuaire-Bulletin de la Société de l'histoire de France*, 26 (1889), § 18.

Evidence for early long-term involvement in Burgundy and Champagne

The situation was different in Burgundy and Champagne, where there was no crusade to cause havoc among the Templars' social networks. In both regions families often involved themselves in the Order over long periods of time, although the surviving evidence suggests that these engagements were usually spasmodic. The involvement of the lords of Tilchâtel with the Templars, for example, lasted for a century and a half, if not longer. It began, so it would seem, in 1129, when a knight of the house of Tilchâtel by the name of Guy Cornelly approached the abbot of St-Bénigne with an unusual proposal. His wife Rezvinde, with whom he had three daughters, had contracted leprosy at a young age and the time had come when she and the girls, who seem also to have contracted the disease, needed to be segregated from their relatives. Devastated by the prospect of losing his wife and children Guy Cornelly had taken vows to end his life in the service of the Order of the Temple in the Holy Land, but before he could go, care for his wife and daughters had to be organised. He therefore offered guardianship over Rezvinde and her daughters to St-Bénigne, with the donation of Rezvinde's dowry as an incentive to the monks to take on this burden. In return, he hoped that the monks would subsidise his journey to Jerusalem. The abbot agreed to the proposal in principle but insisted that before any promises were made – and in order to forestall future claims to the property that was to be given – all interested parties should give their approval. Thus, on the agreed date Bishop Guilenc of Langres, Duke Hugh of Burgundy and a host of noblemen gathered at St-Bénigne to witness Guy Cornelly repeating his proposal to the abbot and offering his wife and daughters to the monks, who also received the possessions which Rezvinde had brought into the marriage as well as Guy Cornelly's possessions at Tilchâtel, Is, Marcilly, Marsannay-le-Bois, Pichanges, Flacey, Messigny and Savigny-le-Sec. In return, the monks provided him with two horses and the sum of 1000 *sous*. The bishop, the duke, a number of senior ecclesiastics from St-Bénigne and St-Étienne, and the noblemen Odo (Eblo) of Saulx, Aimo II of Tilchâtel, Warner of Sombernon, Havin of Beire, Thierry of Favernay, and Josbert of Châtillon witnessed and approved the transaction on the spot; the approval of Rezvinde's closest male relatives, her brother Frierius and her uncle Frierius, followed soon afterwards at Châtillon.[71]

At what stage relations between the family of Aimo II of Tilchâtel and the Order of the Temple intensified can no longer be established but in 1178, under Guy of Tilchâtel, they had already resulted in the

[71] *CG*, no. 27, p. 19 (1129×1132); *HdB* II, no. 244, pp. 9–12 (here dated *c.* 1129).

establishment of a Templar community in the old hospice of Tilchâtel and in the foundation of another Templar community in the nearby village of Fontenotte. In his role as lord of Pichanges Guy of Tilchâtel was involved when Odo of Pichanges made endowments to the 'Templars living near Tilchâtel' (*fratres militie Templi apud Tilecastrum commorantes*) for his soul and that of his mother, whom the Templars had received as *soror* into their community.[72] On various occasions the branch of the Tilchâtel family that held the lordship of Coublanc (which had come into the family by Guy II of Tilchâtel's marriage with Wil(lel)ma, daughter of Guy of Bourbonne and Coublanc) became involved in the affairs of the commandery of La Romagne,[73] whereas for the main line of Tilchâtel, the Templar community of Fontenotte became a focal point for religious attention. Both Aimo (III) and Guy II of Tilchâtel made endowments to that community, which in 1265 were confirmed and enhanced by Guy II's son Stephen, lord of Pichanges, with the approval of Stephen's older brother John.[74] Stephen died in 1271 and was buried before the altar in the church of Fontenotte under a tombstone that read: 'C'est la sépulture de monsr Estienne de Trichastail arère, l'an de l'incarnation de Nostre Seigneur M et II cens et septante et I'.[75] In 1274 his brother John confirmed Stephen's contributions to Fontenotte and added his own gift, consisting of the forests of Brosse-Férent and Touttes and forest rights at Velours, followed by another donation six years later. In the meantime William II of Tilchâtel, lord of Bourbonne, had acted as benefactor to the Templar house of Genrupt.[76]

The seigniorial families of Sombernon, Charny in Brie, St-Vérain, Montigny, Vergy, Noyers, Mello and Joigny, which were part of the wider Tilchâtel network, demonstrated similar degrees of commitment to the Order. Between them, they were involved in the foundation of a Templar community at Choisy, responsible for the establishment, and sustenance, of a Templar commandery at Sauce-sur-Yonne,[77] and

[72] *HdB*, II, no. 622, pp. 393–4 (1178).

[73] Faget de Casteljau, 'Les sires de Til-Châtel', 146 (1981), 101.

[74] Ibid., 144 (1981), 37, 38.

[75] Ibid., 38.

[76] Ibid., 143 (1980), 153 and (1981), 37, 38, 42; *HdB*, IV, no. 4162, p. 224 (1274); no. 4290, p. 246 (1276); no. 4491, p. 286 (1280).

[77] Sombernon: *CG*, no. 540, pp. 331–2 (1148×1162); Lavirotte, 'Mémoire statistique', 239 (1147), 260 (1234); *HdB*, II, no. 566, pp. 367–9 (1174); III, no. 729, p. 261 (1185), no. 773, p. 276 (1187), no. 867, pp. 314–15 (1191), no. 929, pp. 339–40 (1196), no. 974, pp. 359–60 (1197); Charny (which must not be confused with the lordship of the same name which the lords of Mont-St-Jean held from the dukes of Burgundy south of Semur): AN S 5186/A, dossier 1, no. 2 (*c.* 1181); AN S 5186/B, dossier 10, nos. 1 (1170), 3 (1221), 6 (1224), 11 (1229), 25 (1247×1248), 34 (1254); AN S 5186/B, dossier 11, nos. 3 (1270), 4 (1271), 6 (1275), 7 (1275). See also *OdM*, I, pp. 182, 184, 185; *Inventaire Chastellux*, no. 33, p. 133 (1177×1194); St-Vérain: AN S 5150, dossier Saussay, no. 24 (before

provided Bure and La Romagne with a preceptor in the late 1260s.[78] How intimate the relationship between a family and a nearby Templar community could become is particularly well documented in the charters from the Templar commandery of Bure in Burgundy, of which the lords of the nearby castle of Grancey were important patrons. Judging by the charter evidence from Bure, the relationship of the house of Grancey and its collateral branches with the Order lasted for over 160 years. Throughout this time members of the Grancey family and their relations made donations to the Templars, sold them property, joined the Order or associated with it as *confratres*. They were buried with the Templars, arranged for commemoration services with them, or fought with them over property.

A Templar family: the lords of Grancey

In 1197 Lord Odo II of Grancey issued the following charter:

In the name of our Lord Jesus Christ. I, Odo, lord of Grancey, make it known to all present and in the future that it has been recognised in our presence and in the presence of many other men that Raynald, the father of my grandfather, brother Odo, from Bure, has freely given the tenements which the brothers of the Temple have acquired in the lordship of Grancey, and which he himself had given in alms to God and the house of the Temple. He also gave them what he had in the village that is called Montenaille and in its territory, except for the fiefs of the provost and of Enjordanus. The father of my grandfather, Raynald, and my grandfather, Odo, and his sons Rainard, who was my father, Milo, Pons and Hugh, who were knights, confirmed this charitable donation.

1270); AN S 5243, dossier 80, no. 1 (1190) (see also *OdM*, I, pp. 355, 366); AN S 5237, dossier 32, no. 7a and *CG(Yonne)*, III, no. 606, p. 295 (1262); AN S 5235, dossier 1, no. 1, fol. 11v (1255); AN S 5240, dossier 60, no. 33 (BN, n.a.l., 55, fols. 271r–2r) (1272); AN S 5240, dossier 57, no. 29 (BN, n.a.l., 55, fols. 400r–5r) (1292); Montigny: ADCO 115 H 1242, dossier St-Maurice, no. 1 (BN, n.a.l., 53, fols. 241r–3r) (1163×1173); ADCO H 1230, La Romagne (BN, n.a.l., 53, fol. 261rv; *HdB*, III, no. 1340, p. 455) (1215); ADCO H 1239, La Romagne (BN, n.a.l., 53, fol. 271r) (1228); ADCO 115 H 1242, La Romagne (BN, n.a.l., 53, fols. 282r–3v) (1240); ADCO 115 H 1242, dossier St-Maurice, no. 52 (BN, n.a.l., 53, fol. 304rv) (1269×1270); Vergy: BN, n.a.l., 53, pp. 248–9 (1241), 255–6 (and *HdB*, III, no. 867, pp. 314–15) (1191), 299–300 (1259), 301–2 (1260), 305–8 (1271), 322–3 (1213); Marie, *Templiers de Langres*, pp. 43, 49–50, 74; Richard, 'Les templiers et les hospitaliers', p. 235; Noyers: *Chart St-Marc/Jully*, pp. 761–2 (and BN, n.a.l., 55, p. 555) (1186×1187); *CG(Yonne)*, II, no. 406, pp. 412–13 (*c.* 1190); BN, n.a.l., 55, fols. 366r–9r (1284), 388r–91r (1287), 392r–5r (1256, 1287); AN S 5241, dossier 66, no. 4 (1284) and no. 5 (1287); Mello: AN S 5235, dossier 1, no. 1, fol. 1r (1216); AN S 5237, dossier 32, no. 2 (BN, n.a.l., 54, fols. 91r, 92r; Lavirotte, 'Mémoire statistique', 272; *Cart Pon*, no. 342, p. 344) (1216); AN S 5235, dossier 1, no. 1, fol. 1r (BN, n.a.l., 54, fol. 95r; *Inventaire Chastellux*, no. 50, p. 136) (1223); AN S 5239, dossier 51, no. 3 (BN, n.a.l., 55, fols. 351r–3r) (1281); AN S 5239, dossier 51, no. 4 (BN, n.a.l., 55, fols. 414r–17r) (1294); Joigny: AN S 5235, dossier 1, no. 1, fol. 1v–2r and 3r (1196, 1222, 1235, 1238, 1240); AN S 5236/B, dossier 19, nos. 1, 2 and 3 (1275).

[78] BN, n.a.l., 53, fol. 304rv (1269×1270)

Later, my grandfather Odo, who was then the lord of Grancey, with the approval of his four sons . . . gave the entire fief of Bonin, Pidot of Grancey with his descendants and entire tenement, Huy of Poinson and his brother Hohn with their entire tenement and descendants, Peter of St-Bénigne, and a certain woman with the name of Tecia with her entire tenement, to the said brothers of the Temple.

Hereafter a dispute arose between my grandfather Odo, who was then lord of Grancey, and the brothers of the Temple over a certain part of the territory of Poinson and over a place called 'Allo' . . . This and other things, which have been mentioned above, we have given to the above-mentioned brothers faithfully and freely to possess in perpetuity. . . . And I have confirmed it with my seal in the year of the Lord 1185.

I, Odo, lord of Grancey, like my ancestors before me, have approved and conceded that the Templars possess these charitable donations in perpetuity, and I have confirmed this with my seal . . . Written in the year of the Lord 1197.

Then my grandfather, brother Odo of Bure, died. Upon his death the mourning brothers [i.e. of the Temple] sent for me, Odo, lord of Grancey. I, who was myself in much sorrow about the demise of my grandfather, went to Bure with my uncles Peter, Pons and Hugh, and with many others. We remained there for as long as the ceremony of the holy offices lasted. After the celebration of the divine offices we proceeded to the tomb, and with great honour was the body of my grandfather buried. Afterwards, in accordance with old customs, we returned to the *monasterium*. Brother Guy Bordel, who was the preceptor of Bure, demanded silence and said: 'Listen to me and attend to the voice of the one who speaks! Our brother Odo, grandfather of this Odo here, has passed away. Know that he has made us many charitable donations of which we possess a charter, which shall be read out to all of you, if this is what you wish.' Everyone agreed. Abbot Peter, son of the late Odo, took up the charter and read it to me and to all other men who had assembled there. I, Odo, lord of Grancey, approved everything that was recorded in the charter. Afterwards, I, Odo, lord of Grancey, promised and swore that I . . . would protect all possessions of the Templars of the house of Bure, and that I, to the best of my abilities, would defend them against wrong-doers, if any damages should occur to the brothers through my or my children's actions. This came to pass in the year of the Lord 1197 . . .[79]

In the charter Odo II of Grancey summarised some of the key events that determined his family's good relations with the commandery of Bure, which is situated 12 kilometres northwest of modern-day Grancey-le-Château. It illustrates how intimate had become the relationship between Odo's family and the Templars by 1197, in particular after Odo's grandfather had joined the Order. Because the charter omitted some events that had led to the situation in which Odo found himself after the death of his

[79] ADCO 111 H 1161/1, dossier Montenaille (1197 and *vidimus* 1276, separate charter) and 111 H 1156, no. 1 (1276). *HdB*, III, no. 881, pp. 321–3 (1197).

grandfather, however, and because the Granceys were still recorded in connection with the Templars in 1299, it is worth assessing the scale of this family's involvement with the Order in more detail.

The house of Grancey seems to have consisted of three branches.[80] First, there were the counts (later lords, since the family sold the county in 1178) of Saulx. Second, there were the descendants of Raynald I of Grancey, who was probably Count Guy of Saulx's brother. Male descendants of his branch were usually named Raynald or Odo and they provided the dukes of Burgundy with a number of constables. Third, there were the descendants of Calo, castellan of Grancey, who at the end of the eleventh century had established himself as a powerful lord in his own right. His family line provided the dukes of Burgundy with a number of seneschals, and by 1187 his descendants were recorded among the principal barons of the duchy.[81] The lords of Saulx and the family of Calo of Grancey had stakes in the lordship of Lucenay, which could mean that Calo was another close relative of Raynald of Grancey and Guy of Saulx. Members of all three branches witnessed each other's charters and had particular names in common, such as William and Hugh. They were vassals of the dukes of Burgundy, supported monastic houses of religious reform and were prolific crusaders. And all were patrons of the Templar commandery of Bure.

Count Odo (Eblo) of Saulx is first mentioned in connection with the Temple in 1129 when he witnessed Guy Cornelly of Tilchâtel's visit to St-Bénigne, Dijon, before the latter's departure for Jerusalem to become a Templar, described above.[82] Raynald II of Grancey and his immediate family were recorded four years later when they supported Payen of Bure's entry into the Order. It was the donation accompanying Payen's entry that eventually enabled the Templars to establish a community at Bure. Also present on this occasion were Count Odo (Eblo) of Saulx with members of his family, including his brother William.[83]

Soon after he had witnessed Payen's entry into the Order Raynald II of Grancey conducted his own transactions with the Templars, which were

[80] I am following mainly the genealogies in *HdB*, VI, App., pp. 537–48, Isenburg *et al.*, *Stammtafeln*, XV/95, and Bouchard, *Sword, miter, and cloister*, of the Templars since 1127; Lavirotte ('Mémoire statistique', 235–6) has set the *datum post quem* impossibly early at 1120. Petit's early date results from a misreading of Odo of Grancey's account of his grandfather's funeral, which is recorded above. In his version of the account the second paragraph from below – Odo's confirmation of the endowments made by his ancestors – is dated 1127 (the *vidimus* of 1276 gives 1117 as the date), but a close examination of the earliest charters in the departmental archives of Côte d'Or recording the transaction (ADCO 111 H 1156, no. 5 and 111 H 1161/1, dossier Montenaille) clearly shows that the date in question must read 1197.

[81] *HdB*, III, no. 756, pp. 269 (1187). [82] Ibid., II, no. 244, pp. 209–12 (*c.* 1129).

[83] Ibid., no. 255, pp. 218–19 (1133).

eventually confirmed by his son Raynald, who succeeded him as lord of Grancey, and later by his grandson Peter.[84] The count of Saulx gave servants and possessions at Busserotte to the Templars in the late 1160s and 1170s,[85] while Rainard of Grancey endowed them with even more land at Peisso-lo-Franc and Bussières when he and his brother Milo were fighting at the siege of Acre, in October 1189.[86]

Rainard's father Odo of Grancey entered the Templar community of Bure before 1193 and it was on the occasion of his burial in 1197, as we have seen, that his closest male relatives gathered in the commandery to confirm his endowments to the Order and to renew their ties with it.[87] As it turned out, these ties would never be cut, and subsequent generations of lords of Grancey repeated, copied and confirmed the promise of Odo II of Grancey to defend the community of Bure against all evildoers, first recorded in the charter cited above.[88]

At around the same time that he witnessed his father's burial, and probably earlier, Hugh of Grancey entered the confraternity of Bure for which he promised to pay an annual rent of 5 *sous* for the memory of his soul, his ancestors' souls and *pro confraria*.[89] His nephew Odo II made further endowments in 1202 and in 1238 Odo III, lord of Grancey, and his brother Raynald were present when the Templars bought property from their vassals.[90] In March 1241×1242 Odo III, with the consent of his wife Elisabeth, sold the Templars half of the village (*villa*) of Poinson and made further gifts consisting of the fiscal revenues.[91] At around the same time he was also recorded for the first time as arbitrator in a dispute that had broken out between the Templars and some of his nephews, and this dispute seems to have disrupted that generation's amicable relations with the Order.[92] Further disputes between the lords of Grancey and the Templars of Bure concerning their possessions at Montenaille were arbitrated in December 1269 and it was not until 1273 that Lord William of Grancey sold his tithes in Recey to the Templars (most likely of Épailly), although in the meantime he and his predecessor had

[84] Raynald II's donation of fiefs in Grancey is alluded to in ibid., III, no. 881, pp. 321–3 (1197). This seems also to be the donation referred to in *CG*, no. 380, 240–1 (1145×1178).

[85] *HdB*, II, no. 490, pp. 335–6 (n.d., but probably *c.* 1169), no. 566, pp. 367–9 (1174).

[86] Ibid., III, no. 815, p. 293 (1189). See also *CG(Yonne)* II, no 405, pp. 411–12 (1189).

[87] *HdB*, III, no. 899, p. 329 (1193).

[88] The confirmation of the oath of 1197 was copied by Artandus, dean of the ducal chapel, in 1276 (ADCO, 111 H 1161/1, dossier Montenaille).

[89] ADCO 111 H 1156, no 5 (1197) (see also *HdB*, III, no. 958, p. 352).

[90] ADCO, 111 H 1161/1, dossier Poinson, no. 1 (1238); Lavirotte, 'Mémoire statistique', 236 (1202).

[91] ADCO, 111 H 1161/1, dossier Poinson, no. 2 (1241×1242).

[92] Ibid., 111 H 1156, no. 10 (1241).

witnessed, arbitrated and confirmed the dealings with Bure of some of their vassals.[93]

In 1280 William issued a charter announcing his purchase of the lands of Thil and of Nuilly from the Templars of Val de Thors. Fifteen years later it was he who was locked in a dispute with the Order, this time over the division of juridical rights in Grancey.[94] This dispute did not prevent other family members from making new endowments, however. It seems, in fact, that as the thirteenth century drew to a close the Granceys and their vassals prepared themselves for a renaissance of intensive engagement with the Templars.[95] Donations to the Order by Hugh of Grancey, in his will, in February 1299 were followed by Odo IV of Grancey's confirmation of his father William's transaction with Templar Bure involving the fief of 'Petit Poissons'. In 1299 Hugh followed this up with transactions of his own, including the donation to Bure of the fiefs of Bussières, Chaugey, Montenaille and Romprey. At around the same time William's widow Isabel gave her house and chapel at Courcelles to the Templars of Bure, on condition that the chapel would be maintained and the anniversaries of her and her husband's deaths be celebrated at Bure.[96]

In February 1301 Hugh of Grancey confirmed with his seal, and on the instigation of Guy of Villar Morhier, an agreement Guy had reached with the Templars of Bure over the mill of Colmier.[97] In 1304, Odo IV gave notice that the preceptor of Bure had returned a horse to him which had killed an infant in a freak accident; he was adamant that he did not wish any blame or prejudice to be heaped upon the Templars, a statement that seems to underscore once more the good relationship between the lords of Grancey and the Templars of Bure.[98]

The involvement of the noble houses of Grancey and Saulx with the Templars had lasted for almost the entire duration of the Templars'

[93] Ibid., 111 H 1161/1, dossier Montenaille, no 3 (1269); *HdB*, v, no. 3631, p. 292 (1268); no. 3678, p. 302 (1269); no. 3751, p. 315 (1270×1271); BN, n.a.l., 53, fol. 199 (1280).

[94] ADCO, 111 H 1156 (1280); ibid., 111 H 1156, no. 12 (1295), no. 13 (1296×1297) (BN, n.a.l., 56, fols. 139r–40v, 141r–2r).

[95] Bartholomew of Grancey, who seems to have been a well-off vassal of Grancey, endowed Bure with further rights and possessions at Busserotte. See Lavirotte, 'Mémoire statistique', 245 (1299).

[96] ADCO, 111 H 1161/1, dossier Poinson, nos. 2 and 3 (1299) (BN, n.a.l., 56, fols. 143r–5v, 146r–7r) and ADCO, 111 H 1156, no. 1 (BN, n.a.l., 56, fol. 148r) (1299). See also *HdB*, vi, no. 5425, p. 451, no. 5430, p. 452, no. 5431, p. 452 (all 1299); Lavirotte, 'Mémoire statistique', 236 (1299); Marie, *Templiers de Langres*, pp. 49, 71, 94fn. Isabel seems to have chosen her burial at Les Cordeliers at Beaune, where an epitaph commemorates a certain 'domina Isbellis de Granceyo domina de [Verduno]'. See *HdB*, v, no. 3890, p. 445 (n.d.).

[97] Roger, 'Les Morhiers', 94 and no. 32, 127–9 (1301).

[98] ADCO 111 H 1156, no. 16 (1304) (BN, n.a.l., 56, fol. 150r; *HdB*, vi, no. 5786, p. 511).

presence in Burgundy.[99] Such a long involvement may have been exceptional, but, as the previous examples suggest, it would hardly have been unique. Right from the start, in Burgundy and Champagne at least, and undoubtedly also elsewhere, the Templars could rely on a strong donor base that continued to support them throughout periods of crisis and often even up until the eve of the trial. These were the people who knew the Templars best. The fact that they visited Templar communities frequently, associated with them freely and continued their support for so long makes it very hard to believe the idea that the Templars with whom they had such close contact and in whom they were investing so much were practising the esoteric rites of which they were later accused. In the course of the involvement of the houses of Grancey and Saulx, with the Templars, the Templar commandery of Bure had become a focal point for family commemoration and thus an element of family identity. It is to these and other so-called 'social consequences' of different forms of transaction between individuals and the Templars, and ultimately between families and the Order, that I will turn next.

THE SOCIAL SIGNIFICANCE OF TRANSACTIONS

In the last twenty-five years, scholars interested in the social aspects and consequences of gift-giving in the middle ages have produced a vast amount of literature, of which the most influential contributions have been reviewed by Arnoud-Jan Bijsterveld.[100] In pioneering studies Penelope Johnson, Barbara Rosenwein, Bouchard, Stephen White and Megan McLaughlin[101] have demonstrated that the relationship between noble families and religious houses in the early and high middle ages was often very intimate and that gifts, even when they were symbolic, along with the very act of gift-giving, played an important role in creating, fostering and maintaining bonds between families and religious institutions on an economic, religious, juridical, moral, aesthetic, mythological

[99] A brief mention of Odo of Grancey's entry into the Temple at Bure in the preface aside, the Templar connection is absent from the family chronicle *La roue de fortune*, which, however, contrary to Jolibois's belief, was not composed in *c.* 1300. Instead, it has now been labelled as 'un roman généalogique forgé de toutes pièces, à l'époque de la Renaissance, par un faussaire ignorant'. See L. Delisle, 'Girard de Hautgué et Jean de Vesvres, prétendus auteurs de la Roue de Fortune', *Histoire littéraire de la France*, 33 (1906), 264–70 (p. 270 for the quotation).

[100] Bijsterveld, 'The medieval gift', passim.

[101] P. D. Johnson, *Prayer, patronage, and power: the Abbey of la Trinité, Vendôme, 1032–1187* (New York, 1981); B. H. Rosenwein, *Rhinoceros bound: the abbey of Cluny in the tenth century* (Philadelphia, Pa., 1982); Bouchard, *Sword, miter, and cloister*; White, *Custom, kinship, and gifts to saints*; B. H. Rosenwein, *To be the neighbor of Saint Peter: the social meaning of Cluny's property, 909–1049* (Ithaca, N.Y., 1989); Bouchard, *Holy entrepreneurs*; McLaughlin, *Consorting with saints.*

and socio-morphological level – to paraphrase White's characterisation of the gift.[102]

On the following pages I will try to illustrate some of the long-term social consequences of transactions with the Templars. The aim is to show how the men and women who were involved in the process of gift-giving, and those who were affected by it, often used their influence and acquaintance with the Templars to encourage and enable others to make endowments to the Order. Endowments, once they were made, were often repeatedly used by donors and their relatives to renew and confirm their association with the Order. This, as Rosenwein has shown, was common practice in the relationship between religious communities and their lay patrons, and one that had important social implications and consequences.[103] In particular, the social aspects of donations – the fact that they needed to be witnessed and confirmed – led to the creation of vassal and friendship networks (which often overlapped), the members of which influenced and helped each other in their support of Templar communities.

The laudatio

Apart from being a step on the ladder to salvation for those who made them, donations were important because they kept open the communication channels between Templar communities and local families and encouraged an ever-changing set of bystanders to engage with, or at least become familiar with, local Templar communities. People who were usually involved in donations included family members and 'friends' of the donor (who were often his vassals) and, if the property that was given were not part of the allodial possessions of the giver, his feudal lord. The responsibility of these men and women was to consent (*laudare*) to the donation if they had any claim in the property concerned, or to confirm it (*confirmare*) at a later date.[104] When Baldwin of Brochet gave his possessions at Planque to the Templars, he did so in the presence of his brothers (*fratres*), relatives (*cognates*) and 'friends' (*amici*), namely his brother Bernard Vacca with his sons Baldwin and Letard, his two other brothers Letard of Belmont and Anulf Brochet, Gunmerus of Chery and his son Oliver, Hugh of St-Albin with his brother Guarin, and Theoderic of

[102] White based his ideas largely on those developed by the French sociologist Marcel Mauss. White, *Custom, kinship, and gifts to saints*, p. 4. See also Bijsterveld, 'The medieval gift', 130.

[103] Rosenwein, *To be the neighbor of Saint Peter*, passim.

[104] White, *Custom, kinship, and gifts to saints*, passim; Bouchard, *Holy entrepreneurs*, pp. 79–87; Evergates, *Aristocracy*, pp. 91–3.

Courrières; also present was his wife Adeline. It was only after he had obtained the consent of these people that Baldwin of Brochet could alienate his property.[105] Pons of Dun joined the Order, and made endowments to it, with the consent of eleven relatives, namely his wife, four sons, three daughters, one daughter-in-law, and two grandsons.[106] When William of Vennes and his wife Alis of Barges gave part of the mills of Barges to La Romagne only members of her family were required to consent to it (a clear indication that the donation was drawn from Alis's inheritance or dowry), including her mother, brothers, sister Liegart and brother-in-law.[107] Count Guy of Saulx's transfer into the possession of the Templars of his man Bartholomew of Grancey with his family and possessions at Busserotte was confirmed by two of his sons, three of his brothers, as well as by William of Saulx and Odo of Grancey, to whose tenement Bartholomew was bound, and by his daughter-in-law Petronilla and her children.[108]

Like other religious recipients of charity, the Templars sometimes went to great length to ensure that the donations they received were approved by the requisite number of relatives as well as by the donor's feudal suzerain. Clarembaud of Chappes's donation of possessions in Ménois and of land near Sancey to the Templars in May 1213 is a good example. Consisting of his vassals' fiefs in the village of Ménois as well as all possessions which Clarembaud held by right of inheritance in the same village, which had been a cause for dispute with the Templars in the past, the donation was confirmed by Clarembaud's brother Guy, but not by his younger brother Walter, who was still under age and living under the tutelage of his mother at the time. Concerned that Walter's agreement to the gift could not be obtained the Templars asked Clarembaud to assure them that within a year and a day Walter too would confirm the transaction, which Clarembaud did. Still not satisfied, the Templars then approached Clarembaud's suzerain Blanche of Troyes to vouch for Clarembaud and to confirm his promise that Walter would agree to the donation once he had come of age. In a separate charter from the same year Blanche complied, thus soothing the Templars' obvious concern that the absence of Walter's consent would put the transaction into jeopardy.[109]

By obtaining the *laudatio* of a donor's relatives and 'friends' the Order, like any other religious community, hoped to forestall claims before they

[105] *CG*, no. 4, pp. 2–3 (*c.* 1125).

[106] AN, S 5038, dossier 101, no. 2 (BN, n.a.l., 51, fols. 9r–10r) (1192×1193).

[107] ADCO 115 H 1234, dossier Barge, no. 2 (BN, n.a.l., 53, fols. 280r–1v) (1241).

[108] *HdB*, II, no. 490, pp. 335–6 (n.d.).

[109] AN S 4956, dossier 17, nos. 1 and 2 (BN, n.a.l., 52, fols. 48r–9r) (1213).

arose. As Bouchard remarked when examining the Cistercian Order, however, to consider the *laudatio* only as an integral part of property transfer and as a means to avoid disputes would be neglecting its significance as a means of integrating the donor's family into the network of friendship which these transactions helped create.[110] To use a modern expression, donations worked as 'social glue'.[111] They brought about short-term economic changes, but they were also intended to create long-term bonds between people and religious communities.[112]

This applies to Burgundy and Champagne as well as to southern France. Many donation charters include formulations indicating that the transactions recorded in them not only benefited the donor, but also his kin and relatives. In his testament issued on 28 May 1175, Roger of Lespinassière (Spinaceira) gave his possessions in two villages and in the entire *patria* of Carcassonne (with the exception of the *albergue*, that is the right to receive support in victuals, for two knights that he was owed by the wife of Raymond Cornus) 'for the love of God, for the redemption of all my sins and those of all my relatives and for the sins of the deceased faithful'. This he did with the counsel and following the wish of his wife, 'so that God may forgive us our sins', an expression clearly indicating that his wife was expected to partake in the spiritual benefits deriving from the transaction.[113]

Transactions as 'social glue'

Donations

In order for donations to be effective, they needed to be remembered by the donor and his or her family. Charters helped to create and conserve this memory. But for most lay donors and their families these charters were not easily accessible. They were no replacement for personal interaction and the memory-enhancing power of rituals. The frequent allusion to disputes, quarrels and law suits in the charters shows how often and how easily concessions to the Order, or at least their implications, were forgotten, neglected or confused. To minimise confusion and neglect, the Templars, like other religious institutions, expected donors to produce witnesses who could be called upon in case of controversy. Moreover,

[110] Bouchard, *Holy entrepreneurs*, pp. 86–7. Generally on this topic White, *Custom, kinship, and gifts to saints*, pp. 40–85.

[111] Bijsterveld, 'The medieval gift', 131 and 151; Rosenwein, *To be the neighbor of Saint Peter*, p. 13.

[112] On the transcendental nature of religious donations see e.g. P. Geary, 'Exchange and interaction between the living and the dead in early medieval society', in P. Geary, *Living with the dead in the middle ages* (Ithaca, N.Y., London, 1994), 77–92, and McLaughlin, *Consorting with saints*.

[113] BN, n.a.l., 18, fols. 397r–8r (1175).

they expected donors and their families to confirm their endowments to the Order regularly. Often these confirmation ceremonies took place after claims to the possessions of the Templars had been raised and dismissed. In these cases their obvious goal was to prevent similar events from happening in the future. In November 1162, for example, Pons Roger of Villalier visited the commandery of Douzens to confirm a donation to the Order that he had made some time earlier. He agreed never to break the arrangements of the donation (which would suggest that he had done so in the past) and swore on the Gospels to remain henceforth and for the rest of his life a faithful defender and helper of the Order, a promise for which the Templars rewarded him with 2 sestiers of grain and 1 sestier of barley.[114]

The people who raised claims were sometimes the donors themselves, but were more often knights and nobles who had newly risen to a position of power and were trying to maximise their wealth and influence by revoking earlier donations of land and privileges. At the very least, the confirmation ceremony was a precaution against possible claims. When Henry of Vergy and his wife confirmed the testament of Henry's father, which also included endowments to the Templars of La Romagne, they acknowledged the right of the bishop of Langres 'to excommunicate us or our heirs if we should act or rebel against this [donation] which was made in alms'.[115] But confirmation ceremonies were more than the consequence of disputes or a precaution against them. They were also a means by which lay men and women secured themselves participation in the spiritual benefits earned by their ancestors. Moreover, these ceremonies confirmed to lay men and women that the memory of their ancestors was preserved and celebrated, and that, in time to come, so would theirs.

Some donations were not merely confirmed; they were re-enacted. This meant that the same piece of property was given to the Temple on multiple occasions and always in the guise of a proper donation.[116] The ritual of re-enactment shows that the very act of gift-giving could be a means to an end. It created a social contract between individuals and the Order of which the donation itself was the concrete expression and the charter the written proof. Material possessions had to change hands at some stage as compensation for the spiritual intercession that the religious were required to exercise for the donor and his or her kin. Once the

[114] *Cart Douz*, A: no. 143 p. 131 (1162). For similar examples see, e.g., *Cartulaire Lyonnais*, I, no. 444, pp. 559–60 (1250); *Doc Dur*, I, no. 62, pp. 45–6 (1269).
[115] BN, n.a.l., 53, fol. 291rv (1247).
[116] See also Rosenwein, *To be the neighbor of Saint Peter*, pp. 122–5.

donation had been made, however, and in particular if it was substantial, it was possible for donors and their heirs to re-enact it or to recall it if they wanted to have their relations with the Templars and their place on the commemoration list of the Order confirmed, or if they wished to renegotiate the terms of association. This is what Raymond and Arnold of Gaure seem to have done in the 1130s when they granted the Order possession of their *honor* in Gaure and Pomas over and over again.[117]

Likewise, in 1199, in the cemetery of Pézenas, Arzendis Dalmas made a donation to the Templars consisting of 'the alms and donation that our mother has made to this house for the redemption of her soul, namely the men within the boundaries of St-Vérain-de-Teslac with their tenements, possessions and posterity'. For this the Templars accepted her 'as participant and companion in all spiritual benefits that are going to be said and done in perpetuity in the house of the Temple'.[118] And in September 1231, a certain Josbert – most likely Josbert of Ancy(-le-Franc) – endowed the Templars of St-Marc with a rent in the mill of Ancy which his relative Lord Roncius of Ancy had already bequeathed to the Templars at an earlier date.[119] Some endowments were confirmed and re-enacted not once, but many times. The donation of the right of pasturage in the land of Spoy, which Guy II of Tilchâtel had made to the Templars of Fontenotte in 1216, for example, was re-enacted in 1265 and confirmed in 1271 and 1274.[120]

Business transactions

Business transactions, like donations, affected not only the men and women who conducted them but also their descendants, relatives and feudal and ecclesiastic relations. Possessions that were sold were lost to the heirs; a fief sold or pledged meant new feudal associations and arrangements for the person who owned it or for the person who held it. Debts which were incurred had to be redeemed, if not by the debtor, then by his or her heirs. Business transactions, in other words, rarely involved only one individual and the Temple, but created new channels of communication between Templar communities and local families which sometimes remained open for many generations and extended horizontally across families and kin-groups and vertically along feudal lines. After Bernard of Paulignac had sold his manse in St-Vincent of Carcassonne to the Templars of Douzens, for example, Lady Dias and her son William Calvet, Bernard's former lords, were confronted with the Order as a new

[117] *Cart Douz*, A: no. 174, pp. 156–7 (1136), no. 175, pp. 157–8 (1138), no. 181, pp. 160–1 (1137). See also below, pp. 163–4.

[118] BN, n.a.l., 17, fols. 331r–2r (1199). [119] Ibid., 55, fol. 576r (1231).

[120] Faget de Casteljau, 'Les sires de Til-Châtel', 144 (1981), 37, 38, 42.

tenant, who owed them 12 *deniers* p.a.[121] The count and countess of Bar and the count and countess of Nevers all issued charters of confirmation and clarification after Guy of Toucy's generous endowment of the Templars of Sauce-sur-Yonne with fiscal and rental revenues at Vincelles, Vincelottes and Escolive.[122] And lord Hugh of Beaumont was forced to engage with the Templars when Peter of Chacenay decided to sell them a piece of land which he held as fief from him, thus prompting Hugh, as lord of the land, to confirm the sale, which he and his wife did in return for a transfer fee of 100 *sous*.[123]

Such transfer fees aside, the lords of laymen who sold or otherwise transferred feudal possessions to Templar communities also acquired new responsibilities towards the Order, responsibilities that were intrinsic to the function of feudal lord. These included the obligation to advise and defend the Order in all matters relating to the fief. Thus, when Bernard Raymond of Capendu, in 1174, confirmed the donation of an entire *honor* that Roger of Cabriac and his brother Peter Roger had made to the Templars some time previously, he assured the Templars that henceforth he would act as their helper and defender in all matters concerning the *honor* which they now possessed.[124]

Disputes

Disputes were as much a feature of the long-term relationship between families and Templar communities as were donations, sales and acts of personal association.[125] They could arise for a variety of reasons. Some claimants were genuinely confused about the boundaries of the Order's property.[126] Others questioned the way in which the Order had come into the possession of certain property, often maintaining that their consent had not been obtained, or they were objecting to the Order's behaviour as landlord. Not everyone associated with the Order willingly or voluntarily. As a consequence of the generosity that landed families displayed towards the Templars many saw their possessions in jeopardy and themselves confronted with a new landlord who demanded homage and fealty. Peter Sachet, a petty landholder in Douzens, was outraged when the Templars moved into his village, tore down the walls of the castle and erected mills and weirs on the river Aude. He also claimed that the *honor* which the brothers Raymond and William Ermengau from

[121] *Cart Douz*, A: no. 150, pp. 137–8 (1159). [122] See p. 232, fn. 126.
[123] ADCO 115 H 1234, dossier Autrey, no. 5 (BN, n.a.l., 53, fol. 324rv) (1228).
[124] BN, n.a.l., 18, fols. 387r–8r (1174).
[125] See generally Rosenwein, *To be the neighbor of Saint Peter*, pp. 49–77.
[126] For a discussion of 'gifts and claims' in the context of family involvement with religious orders see Bouchard, *Sword, miter, and cloister*, pp. 209–17.

Douzens had passed to the Templars when they had given themselves to the Order, and which bordered on property belonging to Peter and his family, had in fact been snatched from him. The bottom line of his tirade was, however, that he refused to subject himself to the lordship of the Templars.[127]

Most commonly the claimants were relatives of the person who had alienated property. The rural tenement (*casal*) of La Bena, which Raymond Ato II of Aspet had given to the Templars of Montsaunès before he departed for Jerusalem, for example, was reclaimed by his son Roger in around 1160.[128] As noted earlier, new heirs of lordships often invested much time and energy during their first years in power trying to bring back into their domain old family rights and possessions which their ancestors had handed out to religious orders. In this respect they treated the Temple like any other religious community. The most favourable time for them to raise their claims was after the original donor had died. In May 1168 Bernard of Couts raised claims in the land of Couts, which his late father Raymond William had given to Montsaunès when he had joined the Order.[129] Raymond and Berenguer of Montesquieu unsuccessfully disputed their late father's last gift to the Templars of Pézenas in 1198.[130] After the death of William of Montpezat, Pons of Montpezat and his brother Pelegrin contested his donation of the *casal* of Pagesencs to the Templars. They were compensated with 25 *sous* and in return promised to abandon all claims in the *casal* now and forever.[131]

Some claimants had on earlier occasions made their own donations to the Order, while others would do so after a claim had been raised. According to a pancarte dating from 1174, the same Guy II of Sombernon who once had endowed the Templars with rights and possessions in Uncey and Avosne was at another time contesting the possessions which the Order held from his uncle (or brother) Harvey in the village of Sombernon. The dispute was brought before the bishop of Langres, who compelled Guy to abandon his claims and confirm the donation, which Guy did.[132] Ten years later Guy and the Templars were again quarrelling, this time over property near Avosne, which Guy claimed to be his, and over a *guageria* (a property given as pledge) which he held from Barnuin of Drée. The dispute was brought before the Church court and also resolved

[127] *Cart Douz*, A: no. 11, pp. 23–4 (1141). For Raymond and William Ermengau's donation of themselves and their *honor* see *Cart Douz*, A: no. 5, pp. 13–14 (1139).

[128] *PAC*, I, no. 97, p. 94 (*c.* 1160).

[129] *Cart Mont*, no. 62, pp. 259–60 (1168).

[130] BN, n.a.l., 16, fols. 109r–15r (1198).

[131] *Cart Mont*, no. 80, p. 269 (1176×1177).

[132] *HdB*, II, no. 566, pp. 367–9 (1174).

in favour of the Templars. The verdict was confirmed by Duke Hugh of Burgundy, but this did not put an end to Guy's claims. In 1185 the Templars asked the count and his court in Dijon to aid them in the dispute over the same issues that they were now conducting with Guy II of Sombernon and his son Walter.[133] It was not until 1187 that Walter and his brothers Guy and Warner, in the presence of the bishop of Langres, withdrew their claims in the property in Avosne, which their father, who seems to have been dead by then, and his uncle Harvey had given to the Order.[134] Ten years later, however, the wife and sister-in-law of Walter's brother Guy, who were both daughters of the knight John of Drée, were unsuccessfully employing the help of Guy to reclaim the possessions in Avosne which the Templars held from their father and grandfather.[135] Their claim too was dismissed. To ensure that henceforth the agreement between the Order and the family of Sombernon would be maintained, the court put Warner of Sombernon and Guy of Cohun under obligation, by threat of interdict, to keep the peace.[136]

The lords of Vergy were another family that engaged in multiple disputes during its almost ninety years of involvement with the Order. Hugh of Vergy, whose father Guy had made donations to the Temple on the Third Crusade, disputed his families' donations to the Order soon after he had succeeded to the lordship of Vergy.[137] In particular, he objected to

[133] Ibid., III, no. 729, p. 261 (1185), which also alludes to the previous conflict.

[134] Ibid., no. 773, p. 276 (1187).

[135] According to Marie (*Templiers de Langres*, p. 103), Warner of Sombernon's brother Guy was the husband of Mary of Drée. He was identical with Guy of Cohun, as is stated in the charter, and with Guy de Toreis, recorded alongside his brothers Walter of Sombernon and Warner of Montoillot in 1210 (Chifflet, *Sancti Bernardi*, no. xxvii, col. 1423c). Three observations suggest that by 1197 Warner of Sombernon (by 1210 also identified as 'of Montoillot') had married the mother of Mary and Jordana, which means that he had become his brother's father-in-law. First, John of Drée, the real father of Mary and Jordana (who is last mentioned in 1193), was certainly dead when his two daughters, with the support of Guy of Cohun, reclaimed his and his father's donations from the Temple. Second, Warner's wife Alix, who is first recorded in 1220, after Warner had died, bears the same first name as the mother of Mary and Jordana. Third, the charter from 1220 also records a John of Sombernon among the children of Warner and Alix. This name, which is the same as that of the father of Mary and Jordana, was until then not used in the family of Sombernon. It is likely that it had been chosen by Warner's wife Alix in memory of her first husband.

[136] *HdB*, III, no. 974, pp. 359–60 (1197).

[137] Hugh succeeded Guy before the latter went on crusade. See Bouchard, *Sword, miter, and cloister*, p. 378. Marie (*Templiers de Langres*, p. 105) argues that Hugh of Vergy had also gone on the Third Crusade because he too had made a donation to the Templars at Acre. If her Appendix v, which (allegedly) lists all the donations to the Temple made by crusaders from Burgundy collected in her database and in Petit's nine volumes on the history of the dukes of Burgundy, is anything to go by, however, it is clear that she confuses Hugh's donation with that of his father Guy. The only donation in her list that she attributes to Hugh dates to 1197. The donation of Guy of Vergy, who, according to the same list, died in 1189, on the other hand dates to 1191 (see her Appendix v, p. 161). There is, in other words, not much sense to be made of this list and for lack of better evidence I hold firm to the belief that Hugh of Vergy was not a Third Crusader.

the Order's possession of a tenement (*casamentum*) and of certain rights in the village of Avosne (this village seems to have caused the Templars real trouble). Only in 1197, and following the intercession of Duke Odo of Burgundy, was peace restored between the parties, whereupon Hugh agreed to withdraw his claims against the Order.[138] The thirteenth century saw at least two more disputes between the Order and the lords of Vergy. One, which was fought over undisclosed issues and involved William of Vergy and his wife, ended in August 1228;[139] the other had erupted by January 1292 and centred on Henry of Vergy's accusation that the Templars were misusing their power and privileges in Autrey, of which he, a cantor of Besançon, was the lord. He complained that they were unlawfully collecting plough taxes in his lordship, that they had erected a house on land that belonged partly to the people of Autrey, and that they had begun selling wine within the walls of their settlement, and thus within the ban of Autrey, without paying the customary due to the inhabitants of the village.[140]

Such quarrels, unpleasant as they were at the time, seldom alienated religious communities from their patrons or prevented relations between the parties from being re-forged at a later date. The resistance of Peter Sachet, who had so vocally expressed his objections when the Templars took over land that he claimed to be his own, was typical in that it was short-lived and ultimately unsuccessful. In December 1141, the same year that Peter's complaints were recorded, another charter was drafted in which he declared that his previous claims had been unjust and devoid of reason. He dropped all charges and accepted the Templars as his new lords, 'because I owe them homage and they can exercise their justice over me as they can over all men of Douzens, and because I hold the same *honor* from them that my father has held from those from whom they have acquired everything they have in Douzens'. By doing so he was following the counsel and wish of his mother Mary, his cousin Bernard of Caunes and his sister, and Bernard of Caunes's wife, Ricardis, who also confirmed the charter. As a man of the Temple Peter received a new fief which bordered on one side a garden that already belonged to him, and which he was allowed to hold for the rest of his life.[141]

Over the following years Peter Sachet and his brothers William and Gerald of Angles were frequent guests in the commandery of Douzens, where they witnessed charters for the brethren, made endowments to the Templars and sold them possessions including their mills on the river

[138] *HdB*, III, no. 963, p. 354 (1197). [139] BN, n.a.l., 53, fols. 326r–7v (1228, two charters).
[140] Ibid., fols. 343r–5v (1293). [141] *Cart Douz*, A: no. 11, pp. 23–4 (1141).

Aude.[142] Before he died, Peter made arrangements that the brothers of Douzens would receive two pieces of allodial land in the territory of Douzens, the fourth part (*quartus*) of the vineyards which he held from Raymond of Artiguas and a garden near Bouilhonnac 'for the love of God and the remission of my sins'.[143]

Peter Sachet, who seems to have recanted his accusations against the Temple entirely, was only a petty landowner. Many of the noblemen who troubled the Templars with claims after they had succeeded to their lordships were eventually reconciled with the Order on their own terms. Most of them recognised the value of powerful spiritual advocates and made efforts to re-establish their ties with the religious associates of their forefathers, often by repeating donations which they had previously recalled, or to gain new advocates, as we have seen. The lords of Vergy, who first quarrelled with the Templars in the twefth century, had by 1213 resumed their role as patrons of the Temple; this is illustrated by the fact that in this year Hugh's wife Gill and her son William of Vergy gave two of their serfs as alms to the commandery of La Romagne.[144] Even violent disputes or quarrels that had dragged on for many years, and which indicated a more serious disagreement between family members and the Order, were often resolved if not amicably then at least in a manner that allowed both parties to coexist peacefully and even to forge business or feudal relationships in the future. The lawsuit that followed the violent expulsion of the Templars from Montredon by members of the former castellan family in 1230, for example, ended with the entry of the two main protagonists of the raid, Arnold Amel of Montredon and his brother William Amel, into a vassal relationship with the Order.[145] It is possible, although not necessarily likely, given the ubiquity of the toponym Montredon (*Monte Rotundo*), that the Templars Berenguer of Montredon, who was the preceptor of Arles in 1285, and Hugh of Montredon, who joined the Order in the Holy Land some time before 1287, were relatives of these former enemies.[146] In Burgundy, the lords of

[142] Ibid. A, no. 2, pp. 6–8 (1152). For more transactions featuring Peter and his relatives see ibid., no. 7, pp. 16–17 (1169), no. 9, pp. 20–1 (1157), no. 14, pp. 26–7 (1161), no. 16, pp. 28–9 (1156), no. 17, pp. 29–30 (1153), no. 18, pp. 30–1 (1166), no. 19, pp. 31–2 (1166), no. 20, pp. 32–3 (1167), no. 25, pp. 37–8 (1146), no. 28, p. 40 (1171), no. 30, pp. 41–2 (1159), no. 33, pp. 44–5 (1157), no. 35, pp. 46–7 (1163), no. 39, p. 50 (1156), no. 44, p. 54 (1159), no. 49, pp. 58–9 (1145), no. 50, p. 59 (1152), no. 52, pp. 60–1 (1147), no. 55, p. 63 (1150), no. 67, p. 71 (1162), no. 75, p. 76 (1170), no. 76, pp. 76–7 (1152), no. 77, p. 77 (1157), no. 80, pp. 78–9 (1157), no. 81, p. 79 (1155).

[143] *Cart Douz*, A: no. 84, pp. 80–1 (1163×1164).

[144] *HdB*, III, no. 1288, p. 445 (1213). [145] BN, n.a.l., 19, fols. 54r–63r (1230).

[146] Léonard, *Introduction*, p. 36; *Le procès des templiers d'Auvergne, 1309–1311. Édition de l'interrogatoire de juin 1309*, ed. A.-M. Chagny-Sève and R. Sève (Paris, 1986), p. 271. Alternatively, Hugh and

Grancey quarrelled with the Templars for many years over the division of juridical rights in Bure – which constituted a valuable source of income. Even though the dispute was officially settled in 1295, it is obvious from the charters that the lords of Grancey were still contemplating the issue in 1314, by which time Bure had come into the possession of the Order of St-John.[147] As we have seen, however, this did not prevent them from making more endowments to the Temple after 1295.

The Templars as lords and neighbours

A significant long-term consequence of family donations to, and business transactions with, the Templars was that the Order established itself as lord and landowner in castles and villages, exposing itself to social communities which, for better or worse, could not avoid engaging with it. Albas in the Corbières, situated around 35 kilometres southeast of Douzens, was one castle in which the Templars gained at least partial lordship thanks to the generosity of a powerful ally. On 30 April 1196 Ermengard of Narbonne issued her testament, in which she made arrangements for her burial in the cemetery of Templar Mas Deu, and to secure her burial with the Templars she decreed that the Templars should be endowed with the castle, lands and rights of Albas.[148]

The castellans and knights of Albas had already established close relations with the Templars of Douzens by then. Raymond of Albas (*de Albariis*), who may have been destined for the religious life, functioned as a scribe for the Templars of Douzens on numerous occasions between 1152 and 1167 and for the Cistercians of Fontfroide on at least one occasion, in 1157.[149] On 5 March 1169 he issued his testament and gave to the commandery his body and soul, as well as his *honor* and landed

Berenguer, like William (*En Guillem*) of Montredon, master of the Temple in Aragon and Catalonia from 1213 until 1220 and tutor of James I of Aragon, may have been Catalan and from near Vich. See James of Aragon, *Chronicle*, p. 19. Today, localities by the name of Montredon can be found in the départements of Languedoc-Roussillon (3x), Midi-Pyrénées (4x) and Auvergne.

[147] ADCO, 111 H 1156, no. 12 (1295) (BN, n.a.l., 56, fols. 139r–40v); BN, n.a.l., 56, fol. 151r (1314); *Registres du trésor des chartes, vol. 1: Règne de Philippe le Bel. Inventaire analytique*, ed. J. Glénisson, J. Guerout and R. Fawtier (Paris, 1958), no. 1925, p. 392 (1314).

[148] The most recent edition of the testament is that provided in J. Caille, 'Ermengarde, vicomtesse de Narbonne (1127/29–1196/97). Une grande figure féminine du midi aristocratique', in *La femme dans l'histoire et la société méridionales (IXe–XIXe siècles). Actes du 66e congrès de la Fédération Historique du Languedoc Méditerranéen et du Roussillon, Narbonne, 15–16 octobre 1994* (Montpellier, 1995), pp. 43–6. See also F. L. Cheyette, *Ermengard of Narbonne and the world of the troubadours* (Ithaca, N.Y., London, 2001), pp. 341–2.

[149] *Cart Douz*, A: no. 17, pp. 29–30 (1153), no. 18, pp. 30–1 (1166), no. 20, pp. 32–3 (1167), no. 41, pp. 51–2 (1152), no. 44, p. 54 (1159), no. 76, pp. 76–7 (1152); D: no. 6, p. 278 (1153), no. 8, pp. 279–80 (1158), no. 10, pp. 281–3 (1166); *Chart Font*, no. 151, pp. 82–3 (1157).

possessions on the road to Douzens and near Cabriac.[150] Two years later, and with Bernard Raymond of Capendu and Peter Raymond of Alaric witnessing, his testament was confirmed by his sister Garsendis.[151] By then his nephew Hugh Inard had already transferred to the Order his rights in one of his subordinate families.[152] Good relations were further strengthened after the Templars had established their lordship over the castle. Arnold Rubeus of Albas (*de Albars*) was a Templar by 1215. Another likely family member, Raymond of Albas, held the office of preceptor of Mas Deu in Roussillon in 1225, 1226 and from 1235 until 1237.[153] It is likely that he was a relative of the Cistercian monk Raymond of Albas, who was recorded at Fontfroide in 1234.[154] After all, the lords of Albas had been involved with Fontfroide before. It is also possible that he was another relative of Raymond of Albas (*de Albaribus*), whose widow made endowments, among them rights in the castle of Carcassès, to the Templars of Laroque-de-Fa (*de Petrociis*) in Aude in 1270×1271. The house of Laroque was only about 14 kilometres from Albas near Durban. It is therefore likely that both Templar communities benefitted from the generosity of the same family.[155]

The fact that the Order received the lordship over a castle or village does not necessarily imply that it henceforth held the place in its totality, in particular not in Languedoc, where co-lordship has been described as 'one of the fundamental forms of social organization'.[156] Certainly in Languedoc the settlement of the Templars in a castle or village rather seems to have been the beginning of a long period of intense business activity between the Order and local families. For example, the Templars did not become the sole owners of Brucafel after Roger of Béziers, the most powerful feudal lord in the region, transferred his lordship over the village to them in 1133. There were the viscount's bailiffs, Bernard and William Miro, who exercised the right of guarde (*badlia*) and received the income of their office (*ministeralia*) in Brucafel, and who needed to be compensated for losing it. In 1138, five years after the 'hand-over' of Brucafel to the Templars, Roger therefore enfeoffed Bernard and William Miro with two manses in return for their promise to renounce, now and

150 *Cart Douz*, A: no. 8, pp. 18–19 (1169) and *TSS*, no. 38, pp. 164–6 for the translation.
151 BN, n.a.l., 18, fols. 335r–6r (1171).
152 *Cart Douz*, A: no. 27, p. 39 (1167), no. 69, p. 72 (1167).
153 Arnold Rubeus: BN, n.a.l., 19, fol. 22r (1215); Raymond: Léonard, *Introduction*, p. 90.
154 *Chart Font*, no. 1455, pp. 670–1 (1234).
155 *GP(Toulouse)*, p. 592 (1270); BN, n.a.l., 17, fols. 404r–6r (1271).
156 F. L. Cheyette, 'The "sale" of Carcassonne to the counts of Barcelona (1067–1070) and the rise of the Trencavels', *Speculum*, 63 (1988), 827.

forever, their offices.[157] A number of lords from the region of Carcassonne held possessions in Brucafel independently. These included the Montirats, whose main castle lay a little over 7 kilometres east of Brucafel. They possessed land in Brucafel which they sold piecemeal to the Templars of Douzens in the 1150s and 1160s.[158] Other families with possessions in or around Brucafel included the family of Peter Adalbert. In 1157 he, along with his wife and children, exchanged his *honor* in one of the Order's vineyards in Brucafel for arable land at a nearby place called Combelas, of which he agreed to pay the Templars a quarter of the yield.[159] Another landowner in Brucafel was Bernard of St-Julien, who in July 1167 sold to the Templars of Douzens, for 700 *sous* in money of Melgueil and a measure of grain, a manse with its tenants and their rights as well as the possessions which he held as fief from William of La Cauna in the village and within the boundaries of Brucafel. William of La Cauna, to whom the possessions lawfully belonged, confirmed the transaction and was compensated by the Templars with a lump sum of 100 *sous* in money of Melgueil and a measure of grain.[160]

When the Templars received ownership in villages and castles, therefore, this usually marked the beginning of a series of arrangements with other individuals and families who also had claims in these places. Even in the *castrum* of Douzens, which was the location of a major commandery of the Order, or in the *castrum* of Albas, the Templars could not rule without also considering the rights of others. The family of Capmont, for one, retained property in Albas and Douzens until at least 1215, as can be deduced from a charter issued in the Templar house of Narbonne in that year, in which Bernard of Capmont sold to the Order his *honor* in the village of Cabriac, in the *castrum* of Douzens and in the *castrum* of Albas.[161]

To assess the intensity and duration of a family's involvement with the Templars is often a difficult task. The scarcity and eclectic nature of the evidence make it impossible to establish conclusively the exact year when particular families began engaging with Templar communities and how long their engagements lasted. But even approximate dates illustrate clearly that time spans over which families and Templar communities retained relations, however sporadic, could be very long, sometimes

[157] *Cart Douz*, A: no. 124, pp. 116–17 (1138).

[158] Ibid., no 117, pp. 109–10 (1153); no. 119, pp. 112–13 (1163).

[159] Ibid., no. 126, pp. 118–19 (1157).

[160] Ibid., no. 116, pp. 108–9 (1167). Later in that year, William and Berenguer of Malemort, who seem to have had claims in the *honor*, also agreed to the transaction. See ibid., no. 137, p. 126 (1167).

[161] BN, n.a.l., 19, fols. 31r–7r (1215).

extending over more than three generations. Donations and other grants played a pivotal role in creating and maintaining these bonds, but equally important, as Rosenwein has also demonstrated for Cluny, were disputes and confirmations.[162]

Not only did all these transactions create actual links between families and commanderies through the property that was confirmed, given or otherwise transferred; they also forced and encouraged third parties to contact or engage with the Order. These encounters were not always peaceful. Not everyone was happy to have the Temple as a new lord or neighbour. And as has long been suspected, the Templars do indeed seem to have often misused and exaggerated their economic power and rights as landlords to the detriment of local landowners.[163] But even unfriendly, or violent, encounters could gain the Templars new allies. And although the bonds which evolved from disputes may in the individual case have only existed on parchment, they nonetheless ensured that the communication channels between families and the Order remained open. Within the kin-group of Templar benefactors or associates, transactions such as donations, which were re-enacted or re-confirmed with varying regularity, enforced and fostered a continuing dialogue with the Order. Outside these groups these transactions forced bystanders and their families – those, in other words, who witnessed and confirmed transactions, or were otherwise affected by them – to become acquainted with the Order. Examining the intensity and social significance of the acts that constituted a family's involvement therefore helps us understand how and why families with Templar ties became acquainted with and related to each other, thus creating networks between families with ties to the Order that sometimes even extended into the Holy Land.

FRIENDSHIP AND FEUDAL NETWORKS

The importance of relatives, 'friends' and feudal lords in the process of Templar benefactions is reflected in the emphasis that donors and medieval scribes put on the *concilium* that donors received from these people. When Payen of Bure gave the village and appurtenances of Bure as an entry gift to the Order in 1133, he was following the counsel (*concilium*) of Bishop Guilenc of Langres and that of his lords and friends (*amici*).[164] Only a few years earlier, before he left for the Holy Land to become a Templar, Guy Cornelly of Tilchâtel had rendered his leprous wife and daughters

[162] Rosenwein, *To be the neighbor of Saint Peter*, pp. 122–5.

[163] See e.g. Prutz, *Entwicklung und Untergang*, pp. 66–7.

[164] ADCO, 111 H 1156, no. 2 (1133) (*HdB*, II, no. 255, pp. 218–19).

into the care of the monks of St-Bénigne 'following the advice and counsel of his friends'.[165] In 1169 Bernard of Domneuve gave to the Templars of Douzens his body and soul and his entire possessions in the village and surroundings of Domneuve and within the boundaries of Aiglino and Villa Mania, having obtained the counsel and agreement of his daughter, son-in-law and brothers.[166]

The *amici* who gave advice are often to be found among the witnesses to the transactions. They were usually lords and knights from neighbouring castles and villages, who could be trusted vassals – in this case it would have been their duty to provide aid and counsel – and they were often, but not necessarily, related to the donor either by marriage or by blood. More than giving advice, they also acted as advocates of donors or as business associates. 'Friendship' (*amicitia*) in the middle ages had a more complex meaning than it has today. As Gerd Althoff describes it, friendship 'was not the expression of a subjective feeling or emotion, but rather a type of contract carrying with it an obligation of mutual help and support' and was 'intended as something permanent'.[167] As such it was closely tied to the concept of fealty and became a key component of what Althoff has called 'co-operative groups' (*Genossenschaften*): institutionalised groups of men of equal standing acting in their common interest.[168] The frequency with which 'friends' appear in each other's charters makes apparent the prominent role of networks that were based on these 'friendship' obligations of help and support in creating and developing bonds between families and local Templar communities.

Networks of friendship (with all its implications) could extend into the Templar commandery. In 1183 five Templar brothers were recorded as present when the countess of Burgundy, Empress Beatrix, approved (after initial resistance) the Order's possession of the village of Barges in the county of Burgundy.[169] Their names were Guy of Jonvelle (*Jociuilla*), Renier of Bourbonne (today Bourbonne-les-Bains), Humbert of Genrupt, William of La Ferté(-sur-Amance) and Gerard (Wiard) of Vergy.[170] Guy of Jonvelle came from a powerful and well-connected family in the county of Burgundy that was known in particular for its support of Cistercian Clairfontaine and shared its roots and coat of arms

[165] *CG*, no. 27, p. 19 (1129×1132); *HdB*, II, no. 244, pp. 9–12 (here dated *c.* 1129). See p. 139 above.

[166] *Cart Douz*, A: no. 104, pp. 98–9 (1169).

[167] Althoff, *Family, friends, and followers*, p. 66.

[168] For general discussion see ibid., pp. 65–101.

[169] M.-T. Allemand-Gay, *Le pouvoir des comtes de Bourgogne au XIIIe siècle* (Paris, 1988).

[170] ADCO H 1235, Fonds de la Romagne, liasse Barge, no. 1 (1185) (and also J.-Y. Mariotte, *Le comté de Bourgogne sous les Hohenstaufen (1156–1208)* (Paris, 1963), p. 204; *HdB*, III, no. 1432, p. 476).

with the better-known family of Joinville in Champagne.[171] Renier, Humbert and William held their names from castles that were located in close vicinity to each other and only a few kilometres to the west of Barge. It is possible, therefore, that these three Templars had known each other before they joined the Order. In 1163, before he entered the Temple, Renier had endowed the Order with landed possessions between Bourbonne and La Ferté, a strong suggestion that his lands bordered on those of William's family.[172] On the same occasion he also gave to the Templars a fief belonging to Hugh of Bourbonne. It was either the same Hugh of Bourbonne or a namesake of his who, at the siege of Acre, endowed the Templars with pasture rights at Genrupt, which proves that the lords of Bourbonne had a stake in Genrupt too. Among the witnesses to his donation was Arard of La Ferté-sur-Amance, perhaps a relative of William who had accompanied him on crusade.[173]

Friendship and feudal networks (which would often be one and the same) also manifested themselves in the members' mutual duty to provide one another with counsel and to function as witnesses and *laudatores* in each other's transactions. Within these networks, individual dealings, in particular if conducted by men of power, could have a 'domino effect' in that they provided bystanders with the incentive to engage in Templar activities of their own. In one of his memorable phrases Richard Southern drew attention to the 'sustained corporate effort' of barons and their vassals that was needed to bring monasteries into being and to maintain them.[174] Something similar can be said about the sustenance and maintenance of Templar communities. As the following three case studies will illustrate, it was usually the corporate effort of bands of nobles and knights connected to each other by ties of blood, marriage and feudal 'friendship' that allowed commanderies to develop.

The influence of the Trencavels

The viscounts of Béziers and Carcassonne, commonly known as the Trencavels, and their entourage provide an illustrative example of how a powerful family's interest in the Temple could have triggered similar interests in other families within the same social networks. On 1 April 1132 the brothers Roger of Béziers, Raymond Trencavel and Bernard

[171] J.-B. Coudriet and P. F. Chatelet, *Histoire de la seigneurie de Jonvelle et de ses environs* (Besançon, 1864). On the connection with Clairfontaine see also R. Locatelli, *Sur les chemins de la perfection. Moines et chanoines dans le diocèse de Besançon vers 1060–1220* (Saint Étienne, 1992), pp. 206–7.

[172] *HdB*, III, no. 1428, p. 475 (1163). [173] Ibid., no 866, pp. 313–14 (1191).

[174] R. W. Southern, *The making of the middle ages* (Cambridge, 1953), pp. 150–1.

Aton gained the approval of their mother and the consent of the barons to free a serf and his family from all services and to give him with his manse below the city walls of Carcassonne to the Templars, who were making their first bid for expansion in the region.[175] On the same day one year later, on 1 April 1133, Roger of Béziers further endowed the Templars with the village of Brucafel and land and possessions in the suburb of St-Michel of Carcassonne.[176] The donation was witnessed by his trusted advisor Bernard of Canet. As a core member of Roger's entourage Bernard would have been aware of his lord's feelings towards the new order, as would have been Aimeric of Barbaira, another member of the Trencavel court and frequent advisor to Roger,[177] whose influential status among the barons is illustrated by the fact that he and his brother William Chabert were present when Roger of Béziers issued his testament and requested burial with the Templars in 1150.[178]

Ten days after Roger had given Brucafel and possessions in St-Michel to the Templars, Bernard of Canet and his family as well as Aimeric and William Chabert of Barbaira and a great number of their relatives were recorded making their own first donations to the Order. Consisting of their possessions in the *castrum* of Douzens these donations enabled the Templars to found a new commandery.[179]

Once the Templars were provided with the opportunity to found a commandery of Douzens they also received donations further afield. In August 1134 Roger's mother Cecilia and her three sons Roger, Raymond and Bernard gave their allodial possessions in the village and land of Gaure in the Aude region, about 12 kilometres south of Carcassonne, to the Templars.[180] This donation seems to have initiated the interest in the Order of the castellan family of Gaure. In 1134 Raymond of Gaure offered the Templars his entire *honor* in the villages and lands of Gaure and Pomas if they agreed to redeem the pledges with which he had burdened these possessions. The Templars seem to have regarded this as a worthwhile investment. Raymond and his brother Arnold presented themselves as *confratres* to the community of Douzens; and acknowledging that the

[175] *Cart Douz*, A: no. 171, pp. 152–4 (1132). [176] Ibid., no. 115, pp. 106–8 (1133).

[177] Graham-Leigh, *Southern French nobility*, pp. 134–5; Débax, *Féodalité languedocienne*, pp. 252 and 316–17. For Bernard of Canet's status at the viscomital court see C. Duhamel-Amado, 'L'indispensable Bernard de Canet. L'ascension d'un chevalier aux cours des Trencavels (1110–1154)', in H. Débax (ed.), *Les sociétés méridionales à l'âge féodal: Espagne, Italie et sud de la France, x^e-xiiie s. Hommage à Pierre Bonnassie* (Toulouse, 1999), 355–64.

[178] *HGL*, v, no. 580, cols. 1118–20 (1150).

[179] *Cart Douz*, A: no. 1, pp. 3–5 (1133) and generally Barber, 'The Templar preceptory of Douzens', passim.

[180] *Cart Douz*, A: no. 172, p. 154 (1134).

Templars had indeed redeemed his pledges, Raymond and Arnold repeated and confirmed their donation on several occasions.[181]

The charters recording the Order's acquisition of property in Gaure show that after the viscounts of Carcassonne had introduced the Templars to Gaure, the castellans of Gaure continued to support the Order intensely for a short period. Raymond and Arnold of Gaure became lay associates of Douzens; and considering the many occasions on which Raymond was recorded acting on the Order's behalf, it is even likely that he had at some point taken full Templar vows.[182] Arnold and his sons made further endowments to Douzens in 1148. Another possible relative, Roger of Gaure, was recorded among the witnesses to Templar charters in 1150;[183] and in 1167 Arnold's son Raymond of Gaure once more confirmed the donations which his father and his uncle had made to the Order.[184] Within a brief period of time, it thus would seem, the sympathy of the viscounts for the Templars was taken up by members of their entourage who had either witnessed it or had been directly affected by it, and whose enthusiastic support assured the Templars a foothold in the region.

A lordship and friendship network in Burgundy

Similar influences between Templar supporters can be detected among landowning families in the diocese of Langres. These included the noble houses of Tilchâtel, Baudement, Grancey, Saulx, Sézanne and Sombernon in the duchy of Burgundy, most of which had ties to other Templar-supporting families in Burgundy, the county of Champagne and further afield. Among the knights and nobles mentioned in connection with Guy Cornelly of Tilchâtel's preparation to join the Templars in 1129, for example, and who seem to have included the *amici* referred to in the

[181] Ibid., no. 175, pp. 157–8 (1138). It is from this account that we know about the arrangements that Raymond and the Order had made four years earlier. Already in January 1136 Arnold of Gaure had issued a charter in which he acknowledged having exchanged property with his brother Raymond, who was acting on behalf of 'the holy knighthood of Jerusalem and all those who serve God in this knighthood now and in the future'. A year later, in October 1137, Arnold of Gaure had given himself as *confrater* and his entire *honor* in the village and territory of Gaure, except for the church of Gaure, which he held as fief from Peter of Pomas, to 'God and Blessed Mary and the knighthood of the Temple of Solomon in Jerusalem, and to you, Arnold of Bedos and Raymond of Gaure, and to all your other *confratres* who serve God in this knighthood now and in the future'. Ibid.: no. 174, pp. 156–7 (1136); no. 181, pp. 160–1 (1137).

[182] Ibid.: no. 23, pp. 35–6 (1139), no. 57, pp. 64–5 (1138), no. 73, p. 74 (1157), no. 83, p. 80 (1141×1150), no. 124, pp. 116–17 (1138), no. 175, pp. 157–8 (1138), no. 186, p. 164 (1136), no. 205, pp. 178–9 (1140); B: no. 1, pp. 185–6 (1136), no. 9, p. 195 (1138), no. 11, p. 197 (1139).

[183] Ibid., A: no. 177, pp. 158–9 (1150), no. 178, p. 178 (1150), no. 179, pp. 159–60 (1150), no. 180, p. 160 (1150). See also *HGL*, II, pp. 713–14 and V, no. 533, cols. 1020–1 (1136).

[184] *Cart Douz*, A: no. 182, pp. 161–2 (1167).

charter detailing the transfer of his wife and daughters to St-Bénigne, were William of Baudement and and another local knight, Payen of Bure. Both had accompanied Guy Cornelly on an earlier visit to St-Bénigne to arrange a date for the transfer of his wife and daughters into the care of the monks before he could set out for Jerusalem to join the Temple.[185] William of Baudement was already a Templar by then and his father Andrew soon made generous benefactions to the Order.[186] Payen of Bure joined the Order in 1133 and it is reasonable to assume that in his case too his aquaintance with William had influenced the decision to embrace the new order.

The actual transaction between Guy Cornelly and St-Bénigne was also witnessed by Duke Hugh of Burgundy, Count Odo (Eblo) of Saulx, and the noblemen Aimo II of Tilchâtel, Warner of Sombernon and Josbert of Châtillon, viscount of Dijon.[187] Three of these noblemen – Hugh of Burgundy, Aimo II of Tilchâtel and Odo of Saulx – also witnessed Payen of Bure's request for entry into the Order in 1133, which was accompanied by his donation of the village and appurtenances of Bure. Before his entry into the Order of the Temple Payen of Bure had frequently appeared as witness in the charters of the counts of Saulx, which suggests that he was one of their important vassals. We know that he held Bure from the lords of Grancey who in turn seem to have been related to the counts of Saulx, which explains why Raynald of Grancey was present with his wife and children to confirm Payen's donation of Bure to the Temple.

Also present on the day when Payen made his entry gift were the knights Guy and William of Fossée, who on the same occasion gave a meadow to the Templars, a donation to which Aimo II of Tilchâtel was the main witness.[188] They were vassals of Tilchâtel and may have known Payen of Bure well enough to be inspired by his decision to take up the Templar habit. They too joined the Order. And not long after their donation and entry had been recorded (and before 1137) William of Fossée was mentioned alongside Payen of Bure as a Templar witness when the bishop of Langres confirmed a donation of tithes to the nuns of Jully.[189]

Most witnesses to Guy Cornelly's transaction with St-Bénigne and Payen of Bure's entry gift to the Templars and their families eventually

[185] See above, p. 139.

[186] Evergates, *Aristocracy*, pp. 9–10; *Cart Prov*, no. 81, pp. 101–3 (1133). According to a pancarte dated 1129×1143, Roscelin of Sézanne and his uncle Aimeric le Roux had given the tithes of Barbonne and one meadow to the Templars, whereas Nicholas had endowed the Order with a market stall (*estal*) in Sézanne. See *CG*, no. 28, pp. 20–3 (1129×1143).

[187] *HdB*, II, p. 21 and no. 244, pp. 209–12 (1129).

[188] ADCO, 111 H 1156, no. 2 (1133) (see also *HdB*, II, no. 255, pp. 218–19).

[189] *Cart Jul*, p. 9.

established their own ties with the Temple. In about 1165, Guy of Tilchâtel, Odo of Grancey and Calo of Grancey were present when Guy of Saulx transferred a serf belonging to a tenement held by Odo of Grancey with his family into the possession of the Templars.[190] Odo of Grancey later joined the Temple and ended his life at Bure; Calo made his own endowments to the Templars of Bure by 1174 at the latest;[191] and members of all family branches of Grancey, including the counts (later lords) of Saulx, were still recorded among the patrons of Templar Bure at the end of the thirteenth century. The lords of Tilchâtel became important patrons of Templar Fontenotte, whereas the Sombernons, who probably shared their origin with the Tilchâtels, were actively engaged in the Temple, and made donations to the Hospital of St John, until at least 1234.[192] To the Templars they gave Uncey, which became home to a Templar community, and their share in the lordship of Avosne;[193] to the Hospitallers they gave the hospital (*domus Dei*) of Sombernon.[194] They also endowed the Templars with the rights of pasturage and forestage in their lands and with rights and property in the village of Sombernon, thus enabling the foundation of another Templar house in Sombernon in the mid or late thirteenth century.[195]

A lordship and friendship network in Comminges

Yet another network of Templar supporters centred on the counts of Comminges, in the foothills of the Pyrenees. Here the focus was the Templar commandery of Montsaunès, founded in 1156 on the site of an ancient settlement on a hill between the valleys of the Salat and Garonne. As Charles Higounet, the editor of the Montsaunès charters, has pointed out, at one time or another this network of supporters included almost every important family in the county, the comital family being the most prominent.[196] A Templar brother (*fray* in the local vernacular) by the

[190] See above, p. 144. [191] *HdB*, II, no. 566, pp. 367–9 (1174).

[192] Lavirotte, 'Mémoire statistique', 239 (1147), 260 (1234); *CG*, no. 540, pp. 331–2 (1148×1162); *HdB*, III, no. 773, p. 276 (1187), no. 867, pp. 314–15 (1191), no. 929, pp. 339–40 (1196). Their family relationship with Tilchâtel is suggested by Bouchard, *Sword, miter, and cloister*, p. 363.

[193] Lavirotte, 'Mémoire statistique', 239 (1147); *HdB*, II, no. 372, pp. 276–7 and *CG*, no. 540, pp. 331–2 (1148×1162).

[194] Chifflet, *Sancti Bernardi*, no. xxvii, col. 1423C (1210).

[195] *HdB*, II, no. 566, pp. 367–9 (1174); III, no. 929, pp. 339–40 (1196); Lavirotte, 'Mémoire statistique', 260 (1234). Both the gift of Avosne and that of possessions in Sombernon became the subject of legal disputes. It was not until 1187 that Walter of Sombernon and his brothers Guy and Warner, in the presence of Bishop Manasses of Langres, conceded and quit-claimed the possessions in Avosne which their father Guy and uncle Harvey had made to the Templars. See *HdB*, III, no. 729, p. 261 (1185), no. 773, p. 276 (1187).

[196] *Cart Mont*, p. 220.

name of Pey de Comenge is recorded at Montsaunès as early as June 1156, but he seems to have been a Knight from Comigne in the parish of Douzens and not a member of the comital family.[197]

Between 1161 and 1184 Count Bernard III of Comminges and his son Bernard IV, along with their closest relatives, endowed Montsaunès with rents, land, serfs and tax exemptions.[198] They arbitrated in conflicts between the Templars and local families and, as patrons, received donations for the Templars from vassals.[199]

In *c.* 1176, not long before his death, Bernard III of Comminges entered Montsaunès as a fully professed brother[200] and throughout the remaining twelfth and the entire thirteenth century the comital family of Comminges remained closely associated with the commandery. For his own and his father's salvation and for the benefit of his children Bernard IV, in around 1200, transferred to the Templars of Montsaunès all his rights in the land of Berald and his aunt Martha of St-Gaudens.[201] Bernard IV confirmed previous donations of two fiefs in 1254, added another fief in 1258 and transferred rights in the territory of Morcens to the Templars ten years later,[202] while the wife of his cousin Roger of Comminges, viscount of Couserans, acted on her concerns for the redemption of her soul and her kin and endowed Montsaunès with two *casales* and their men and appurtenances.[203]

Bernard III of Comminges's entry in particular would have enticed members of the comital court and their vassals to add Montsaunès to their list of charitable donations, although in many cases these ties already existed. Among the noble families whose members appear frequently alongside the counts in the early charters of Montsaunès were the families of Martres, Tersac, Montpezat, Roquefort and Couts.

Arnold William of Martres and Roger of Tersac were witnesses when Bernard III of Comminges entered the Order at Montsaunès in the spring of 1176, and at least Roger of Tersac was already acquainted with the Order by then.[204] He had received donations on behalf of the Order when Raymond William of Couts had become a Templar eight years earlier, and he had arbitrated in disputes that had arisen subsequently between Raymond William's heirs and Montsaunès.[205] Arnold William of Martres in turn was the grandson of the Templar Arnold of Martres,

[197] *GP(Toulouse)*, no. 37, pp. xxvi–xxvii (1156).
[198] *Cart Mont*, no. 1, pp. 223–6 (1176), no. 2, p. 226 (*c.* 1182), no. 3, p. 227 (before May 1176), no. 5, pp. 227–8 (1184), no. 24, pp. 238–9 (1178).
[199] Ibid., no. 11, pp. 231–2 (after 1180), no. 80, p. 269 (1176×1177).
[200] Ibid., no. 1, pp. 223–6 (1176). [201] *GP(Toulouse)*, no. 44, p. xxx (*c.* 1200).
[202] *Cart Mont*, p. 182. [203] Ibid., no. 46, p. xxx (1256). [204] Ibid., no. 1, pp. 223–6 (1176).
[205] Ibid., no. 62, pp. 259–60 (1168), no. 39, p. 246 (1171).

who resided at Montsaunès and its dependency at St-Sirac when Bernard III joined the Order.[206]

By 1178 the families of Tersac and Martres were tied to each other by marriage and Roger and Arnold William were brothers-in-law. Although it is impossible to establish with certainty that it was the marriage of Roger's brother Adhemar of Gensac to the granddaughter of the Templar Arnold of Martres that had prompted Roger and his brothers Adhemar and William Raymond to make endowments to Montsaunès, the chronology of donations as recorded in the extant charters points in that direction. What can be established is that in the 1180s the Tersac brothers made their first recorded donation to Montsaunès, consisting of the rights of *herbaitges* in all their land, for which they received a horse as countergift.[207] It was also in the 1180s that members of the family of Martres made their first recorded endowments to Montsaunès. One donation, made by Arnold William, Roger and their sister Martina with Count Bernard IV of Comminges acting as intercessor, consisted of a vineyard and was rewarded with a countergift of 200 *sous*; a second, issued in March 1188 by Arnold William, Roger and Martina, included another vineyard in return for 25 *sous*.[208]

The counts of Comminges and the castellans of Tersac and Martres make frequent appearances in charters recording the dealings of the three castle-holding families of Montpezat, Roquefort and Couts with the Templars.[209] The castles from which these families held their names were situated in close proximity to one another and to Montsaunès. The lords of Montpezat are recorded from 1161 until 1187 among the benefactors of Montsaunès. In little more than twenty-five years (some donations can only be dated approximately) two generations of family members endowed the Templars with 450 *sous* held as pledge from a vassal, three *casales*, five serfs, and one mill.[210] In the same period they also sold another *casal* for 240 *sous* and one field for a horse and 30 *sous* to Montsaunès. A certain William of Montpezat donated another serf to Mas Deu in Roussillon.[211] And by the end of the century a possible relative of William by the name of Fulk had joined the Order. Between 1199×1200 and 1234, and mainly in his function as master in Provence

206 Ibid., p. 204 and no. 80, p. 269 (1176).

207 Ibid., no. 9, pp. 230–1 (1180×1188). Rights of *herbaitges* were the same as *albergue*: the right to receive victuals to support a specified number of knights.

208 Ibid., no. 11, pp. 231–2 (after 1180); no. 63, p. 260 (1188).

209 See e.g. ibid. and no. 83, p. 271 (1161).

210 Ibid., no. 7, p. 239 (1167), no. 20, pp. 235–6 (n.d.), no. 73, p. 265 (after 1180), no. 80, p. 269 (before 1176×1177), no. 82, p. 270 (1182), no. 83, p. 271 (1161); *PAC*, II, no. 481, p. 116 (1186).

211 *Cart Mont*, no. 4, p. 227 (n.d.), no. 12, p. 232 (n.d.); Verdon, *La terre et les hommes*, p. 170.

and Spain, he was recorded visiting the commanderies of Montpellier, Jalez, Mas Deu, Le Puy and Pézenas.[212]

Little is known about the castellans of Roquefort(-sur-Garonne), who held their name from a castle belonging to the powerful Escafred family that was situated on a mountain ridge overlooking the Garonne and Salat rivers, opposite the castle of Montpezat, and in which the family of Aspet at one point also had a stake;[213] almost nothing is known about the lords of Couts, whose castle, situated on the same mountain ridge as that of Roquefort, has now disappeared. They seem to have been tied to the house of Aspet, as is suggested by the fact that in November 1279 Raymond Aton of Aspet gave to the Templars his possessions in the territory of Couts.[214] Members of the Roquefort and Couts families appear in the company of the lords of Martres, for example after 1180, when six men from Roquefort and Bertrand of Couts were recorded as witnesses when Arnold William of Martres, his brother Roger and his sister Martina endowed the Templars with a vineyard.[215]

Members of the Roquefort and Couts families were also frequently recorded alongside each other in the extant charters of Montsaunès and there is reason to believe that the two houses in fact constituted two branches of the same family. Both became very actively involved in the Order of the Temple, and in particular in Montsaunès: Gilbert of Couts, Bernard of Couts, Gilbert of Roquefort and Arnold William of Roquefort were all recorded as donors to Montsaunès in the 1160s,[216] and Gilbert of Roquefort had joined the Order by 1168. His brother Bonhomme and relatives, including his aunt Martha of St-Gaudens, provided the Templars with land and serfs, including, at one point, the *casal* of Sancho of Audressein, one of Bonhomme's knights.[217] In 1184 Gilbert's other brother Berald with his aunt Martha of St-Gaudens gave to Montsaunès possessions at St-Gaudens, and it was on this occasion

[212] Léonard, *Introduction*, pp. 21, 25, 47, 49, 53, 89; BN, n.a.l., 15, fols. 75r–7r (1199×1200); *Cart Puy*, p. xvi, no. 5, pp. 5–6 (1210), no. 6, pp. 6–7 (1210), no. 7, pp. 8–9 (1210×1216), no. 8, pp. 13–14 (1210×1215), no. 12, p. 16 (*c.* 1213), no. 15, pp. 19–21 (1215), no. 22, p. 26 (1218×1219), no. 24, pp. 27–8 (1218×1219). See also Verdon, *La terre et les hommes*, p. 21.

[213] See *HGL*, v, col. 1019 (1139) for Hugh Escafredi and the homage of his brothers Aimeric and Isarn to Roger of Béziers for the castle of Roquefort. On the family of Roquefort see Higounet, *Comté de Comminges*, I, pp. 265–7. In 1306 Raymond Aton of Aspet gave rights in the castle and *villa* of Roquefort in exchange to Montsaunès. See *GP(Toulouse)*, p. 183.

[214] Ibid., p. 192. [215] *Cart Mont*, no. 11, pp. 231–2 (after 1180).

[216] Ibid., no. 96, pp. 277–8 (n.d.), no. 97, p. 278 (1164).

[217] Ibid., no 8, p. 230 (1184), no. 10, p. 231 (n.d.), no. 40, p. 247 (after 1179), no. 71, p. 264 (after 1180).

that Berald also joined the Order.[218] In the same year and possibly on the same day (as the charter was also issued at St-Gaudens) Berald's feudal lord Bernard IV of Comminges granted the Templars rights in lands which Berald had hitherto held of him.[219] It is plausible that the two events, Berald's entry into and Bernard IV's donation to the Order, were linked. Berald of Roquefort is last mentioned in the extant Montsaunès charters in 1192.[220] Thirteen years later the third of the Roquefort brothers, Bonhomme, followed his brothers' example and took up the Templar habit.[221]

Bernard of Couts, who was recorded alongside Gilbert of Roquefort as donor to Montsaunès in 1168, was the son of another Templar, Raymond William of Couts. His relationship with Montsaunès had not always been easy, as illustrated by the claim he and his brothers made in May 1168 to possessions which their father had once given to the Templars as an entry gift. In the claim, brought before Roger of Tersac, who had supervised the original donation,[222] Bernard and at least two of his brothers, Hugh and Gerald, represented the family of Couts, while the Templar brothers Bernard Vilani and Gilbert of Roquefort were summoned by Roger of Tersac to represent the Templar community of Montsaunès. Roger eventually ended the dispute by dividing the land in question between the Order and Bernard of Couts and his brothers. Another family member, William of Couts, who was perhaps a son of Bernard of Couts, witnessed the proceedings.[223] He was again recorded in a charter in 1171 when he concluded his own dispute with the Templars over tithes. The case was once more brought before Roger of Tersac and again it was resolved by arbitration.[224] A few years later William of Couts pledged his rights in the tithes of the church of La Pujole to the Order for 130 *sous*.[225] By then his brother Bernard had joined the Order, which again illustrates how little effect these legal disputes usually had on the personal relations between religious communities and their patrons.[226] But unlike the lords of Roquefort, the lords of Couts disappear from the charters of Montsaunès after 1180.[227]

[218] The donation was concluded 'ante portal de manso Sancti Gaudenzii'. See *Cart Mont*, no. 8, p. 230 (1184). Martha was the daughter of Walter of St-Gaudens. See *Act Bonne*, no. 35, p. 62 (1153).

[219] *Cart Mont*, no. 5, pp. 227–8 (1184). [220] Ibid., no. 43, pp. 249–50 (1192).

[221] Higounet, *Comté de Comminges*, I, p. 266fn.

[222] *Cart Mont*, no. 9, pp. 230–1 (1180×1188), no. 39, p. 246 (1171), no. 62, pp. 259–60 (1168).

[223] *Cart Mont*, no. 62, pp. 259–60 (1168). [224] Ibid., no. 39, p. 246 (1171).

[225] Ibid., no. 42, p. 249 (*c.* 1179) [226] Ibid., no. 58, pp. 256–7 (1179).

[227] Nor are their names to be found in the charter collection of the nearby Cistercian monastery of Bonnefont that was so popular with other benefactors to the Temple, such as, for example, the families of Montpezat, Aspet, Cardailhac or Aure. See *Act Bonne*, p. 43.

Templars in the network

The *amici* who influenced the decisions of donors sometimes included relatives who were Templars, as seems to have been the case with the donations of the lords of Luzençon in 1140 and the lords of Barbaira in 1153 mentioned earlier; they could also include Templars who were from the same region as the donor and who had been born into families of similar standing and were therefore familiar with him. The Templar William of Baudement, for example, was present when John of Pleurs made endowments to the Order some time between 1129 and 1143.[228] As the castles of Pleurs and Baudement were located in close proximity to each other, it is almost certain that William of Baudement, whose father was the seneschal of Champagne, and John of Pleurs were acquainted. Similarly, in 1180 Raymond of Cazouls transferred his possessions in the village, territory and parish of Cazouls to the Templars of Pézenas in the presence of the Templar knight Peter Raymond of Cazouls, who hailed from the same village and may have been a relative of his.[229] And when Rixendis of Abeilhan issued her testament in April 1198 in which she made arrangements to be buried among the Templars of the nearby commandery of Pézenas, she did so in the presence of the former castellan of Abeilhan, Berenguer of Abeilhan, who had joined the Temple in 1177 and who was still resident at Pézenas at that time.[230]

On crusade, the presence of a countryman who was a Templar could influence the knights' decisions to endow particular communities at home. It is of course also feasible that crusaders who wanted to endow a particular community at home did so in the presence, and into the hands, of a Templar brother who was familiar with it and who could be expected to return to it or to a community nearby. In any case, the charters suggest that, not least for reasons of communication, regional identity played a role in deciding who of the Templars received or witnessed the donations of crusaders overseas. In one document, which is dated 1254 but records events from 1201 and 1205, the Templar marshal William of Arzillières and the preceptor of Acre, Robert of Camville, were the two Templar knights present at Acre when Vilain of Aulnay (*de Alneto*) gave his possessions in the village (*villa*) of Sancey with all their appurtenances, including mills, forests and pastures, to the Order.[231] The charter recording the transaction is a snapshot of a friendship and kindred network in action that included a member of the Order and

[228] AN S 4968/A, no. 1 (*CG*, no. 28, pp. 20–3) (1143). [229] BN, n.a.l., 17, fols. 312r–15r (1180).

[230] Ibid., fols. 324r–6r (1198). Berenguer's entry into the Order is recorded in ibid., 15, fols. 382r–90r (1177).

[231] According to the charter, which includes the donation and its confirmation by Vilain's brother Odarchus, marshal of Champagne, in 1205, and was sealed by the comital chancery in November

extended into the Holy Land. Vilain and William were knights from Champagne (Aulnay and Arzillières are located 21 kilometres apart) and they were almost certainly related to one another by blood.[232] According to Evergates, Robert of Camville too was from Champagne, but it is also possible that he came from Chanville near Metz in Lorraine, or from Normandy, as Claverie has suggested, or indeed from England, in which case he may have been a younger brother of the English knight Richard of Camville, who had died at Acre in 1191.[233] Perhaps he was identical with Robert of Aulnay (*Robertus de Alnetis*), a knight from the county of Troyes, whose donation of milling rights at Aulnay, and its confirmation by his son Peter and grandson Ralph, was confirmed by Count Thibaud in 1200.[234]

The witnesses to the donation included Ogier of St-Chéron, who in 1201 confirmed the charter with his seal, and his brother William, as well as Clarembaud IV of Chappes, Vilain's uncle Godfrey of Villehardouin, and Godfrey 'Putefin'. The first four witnesses were noblemen from Champagne. Villehardouin is located 12 kilometres north of Aulnay, Chappes 32 kilometres. The castle of St-Chéron is situated 22 kilometres northwest of Aulnay and only 2 kilometres north of Arzillières. William of Arzillières and Godfrey of Villehardouin were relatives, as were, it would seem, Godfrey of Villehardouin and Vilain of Aulnay.[235] As immediate neighbours William of Arzillières and Ogier and William of St-Chéron must have been acquainted. Eventually, Ogier's grandson William would marry into the Arzillières family. It would also seem that William of Arzillières and Guy and Clarembaud of Chappes knew each other before they went on crusade, for charter evidence exists to the effect that members of both families had witnessed donations to other religious houses together in the past.[236] William of Arzillières and Vilain of Aulnay were also almost certainly related, and thus William may have played an important role in convincing Vilain to give land in a region that they both called home to a Templar community which they both knew well.

The fact that Vilain had become interested in the Templars in the first place, and that he decided to make his donation at Acre, where the Order

1254, the donation was put in writing and sealed by Ogier of St-Chéron in 1201. Since the transaction took place in Acre, it probably predates the first charter and should be placed before 1197; AN S 4956, dossier 15, no. 3 (1201–54). See also *HdB*, III, no. 1455, pp. 482–3 and Burgtorf, *Central convent*, p. 671, who gives 1200×1204 as an approximate date, although the charter clearly reads *m° cc° j°* for the signing of the donation.

232 Evergates, *Aristocracy*, p. 263 (genealogy Villehardouin).

233 *Feud Soc*, no. 80, p. 102 (1201); Claverie, *L'ordre du Temple*, II, p. 338; Burgtorf, *Central convent*, pp. 645–6.

234 AN S 5176/B, dossier 18, no. 22 (1200).

235 The genealogy of the Villehardouin family provided in Evergates, *Aristocracy*, p. 263 suggests as much.

236 See e.g. *Cart Mol*, II.2, no. 436, p. 411 (1122×1145).

had established its new headquarters, also leads to the suggestion that he may have been a close relative of the former Templar seneschal Urs of Aulnay, who is believed to have died at the battle of Cresson in 1187 and who was probably still remembered by Templars residing in Acre.[237] Another underlying reason why Vilain gave to the Templars could have been the fact that the idea of crusading resonated so strongly with his relatives and wider social contacts of whom a great number – among them Henry of Arzillières, Ogier of St-Chéron, Vilain of Nully, Godfrey of Villehardouin and his nephew, Guy and Clarembaud of Chappes, and William of Aulnay – had taken the cross together and journeyed to Palestine in the entourage of Henry of Champagne, who died in 1197. After returning to Europe all of them joined the Champagne contingent on the Fourth Crusade (William of Aulnay after donating, together with Robert, lord of Aulnay, and a number of other persons, shares in the mills of Précy to the Templars).[238] And most of them, especially Godfrey of Villehardouin, subsequently spent many years in Greece.[239]

Ties of lordship and kinship with other Templar supporters but also geographical proximity to a Templar commandery obviously were important reasons why noblemen and their knights and relatives became involved in the affairs of Templar communities and with the Order at large. They help explain the chain reactions that caused different individuals to interact with Templar communities often in quick succession to one another, as seems to have been the case with the arrangements of Guy Cornelly of Tilchâtel to join the Order in the Holy Land. These were probably influenced by the earlier entry of his companion William of Baudement into the Order, which may in turn have influenced his other companion Payen of Bure in his decision to become a Templar four years later and, by way of Payen, Raynald of Grancey to become a patron of the Order.

The interrelationships between Templars and individual donors, and between the donors themselves, created channels of influence and mutual interests that could be transported across the sea and found wherever members of the same social networks and Templars with ties to these networks encountered one another. It is to the strongest of these networks, the one created by family ties, that I will now turn my attention.

[237] For Urs of Aulnay see Burgtorf, *Central convent*, p. 666.

[238] AN S 5188/A, dossier 25, no. 4 (1202×1203).

[239] *Joinville and Villehardouin: Chronicles of the crusades*, trans. C. Smith (New York, London, 2009), pp. 6–7, 31, and, generally, J. Longnon, *Les compagnons de Villehardouin: Recherches sur les croisés de la quatrième croisade* (Geneva, Paris, 1978).

Chapter 4

FAMILY NETWORKS

In its simplest form, a Templar family network consisted of two families related to each other by blood or marriage and which both supported the Temple. If the two families were neighbours, then the Templar community which both supported was very likely the same. The lords of Roquefort and Couts, who would seem to have been closely related, supported nearby Montsaunès; the lords of Barbaira and Canet, who also seem to have been related, supported Douzens. The lords of Cardailhac, who made donations to La Selve in the late twelfth century,[1] and who produced four, perhaps five, Templar brothers in the thirteenth century,[2] were by the late twelfth century related by marriage to the viscounts of Comborn, who eventually produced at least one Templar knight and who also supported La Selve.[3]

The lords and knights of Calmont in Aveyron, who, between *c.* 1180 and 1300, seem to have provided the Order in Languedoc with at least seven knights,[4] and who made at least one endowment to La Selve in

[1] *Cart LaS*, no. 4, p. 125 (*c.* 1180), no. 171, p. 239 (*c.* 1170).

[2] They were Guiral of Cardailhac, Bertrand of Cardailhac, two Williams of Cardailhac – of whom one became the preceptor of La Selve and the other was a sergeant – and Raymond of Cardailhac, who was the preceptor of Golfech in 1285 and 1286. See Léonard, *Introduction*, pp. 66 and 67; *PT*, I, p. 105 and II, pp. 256–8; *GP(Toulouse)*, p. 335. A family relationship of the sergeant William of Cardailhac with the other four Templars from Cardailhac, who all seem to have been knights, is questionable but not impossible.

[3] Bertrand of Cardailhac, who joined the Temple in *c.* 1200, was related by marriage to the viscounts of Comborn. See *GC*, I, col. 131. For the Templar connection see Léonard, *Introduction*, p. 169; *PT*, I, pp. 235, 617; II, pp. 86, 123, 127–8, 179, 222, 227, 303.

[4] A certain P. of Calmont was recorded at La Selve in *c.* 1180, Raymond of Calmont at La Selve in 1186. See *Cart LaS*, no. 63, pp. 164–5 and H. de Barrau, *Ordres équestres. Documents sur les ordres de Temple et de Saint-Jean-de-Jérusalem en Rouergue. Suivis d'une notice sur la Légion-d'Honneur et du tableau raisonné de ses membres dans la même pays* (Rodez, 1861), p. 14. Raynald of Calmont was recorded at Toulouse in 1281 and Vaour in 1286–97 (Schottmüller, *Untergang*, II, pp. 183, 215), Hugh of Calmont at Toulouse in 1295 (*PT*, I, pp. 82, 108, 377, 402–5) and John of Calmont at Cours from 1300 until 1306 (*GP(Toulouse)*, p. 406; Finke, *Papsttum und Untergang*, II, no. 152, p. 320; Léonard, *Introduction*, p. 87).

1292,[5] were related to the lords of Arpajon by ties of lordship and perhaps kinship. The Arpajons were powerful lords in the Gévaudan. The eponymous castle, however, once situated on the eastern slope of the wild Méjean plateau, has now disappeared from the map of France. What can be established is that by 1260 the Arpajons claimed a stake in the lordship of Calmont, which would suggest that the two families were by then closely connected, in particular if one considers that it was Hugh of Arpajon who knighted Hugh of Calmont on the day when the latter joined the Order of the Temple in Toulouse in 1294.[6]

The lords of Arpajon were ardent supporters of the Temple. By 1178 a member of the family or household was serving in the Templar commandery of Ste-Eulalie.[7] He was either identical with, or related to, the Templar knight Gerald of Arpajon who held the office of preceptor at Espalion in Aveyron in 1197[8] and who in turn seems to have been a close relative of another Gerald of Arpajon, who in 1198 witnessed a donation to the Templar commandery of La Cavalerie.[9] Another member of the Arpajon–Calmont clan, Arnold Arpajon of Calmont (who is often simply referred to as Arnold of Calmont), was for a period of thirty-five years (from 1267 until 1302) recorded as preceptor at various Templar communities in the south of France.[10] He may have been related to Raynald Arpajon of Calmont who was a Templar knight in the commanderies of Toulouse and Vaour from 1284 until 1287 and the preceptor of Vaour in 1286 and 1287.[11]

Two interrelated families that were part of the supporting network of Templar Pézenas were a family of *familiares* of the viscounts of Carcassonne and Béziers from Pézenas and the lords of Abeilhan.[12] Both

5 Doat, 41, fols. 140–5 (1292).

6 *PT*, I, p. 404. In 1183 William of Calmont witnessed a donation by Bernard of Arpajon to Bonnecombe. On 24 April 1260 a second Bernard of Arpajon paid homage and promised fealty to Count Alphonse of Toulouse for the castle of Calmont (*Cart Bonnecombe*, no. 170, p. 350; *Droits et possessions du comte de Toulouse dans l'Albigeois au milieu du XIIIe siècle. Documents publiés et annotés*, ed. E. Cabié (Paris, Toulouse, Albi, 1900), p. 118). The names Hugh and Guibert were in use in both families, which could – in theory – hint at a common ancestry. In 1192, Guibert of Calmont witnessed a donation to Bonnecombe, and in 1294 Guibert of Arpajon witnessed a donation to Nonenque. See *Cart Bonnecombe*, no. 2, pp. 2–3 (1192) and *Cart Non*, no. 100, pp. 153–4 (1294). However, because the names Hugh and Guibert were not uncommon among families in Languedoc in general, their use in the families of Calmont and Arpajon provides weak evidence to support a claim of common ancestry.

7 *PAC*, II, no. 425, p. 64 (1178). See also ibid., I, no. 201, pp. 188–9 (1182).

8 Doat, 140, fols. 107–8 (1197). 9 *PAC*, I, no. 321, pp. 319–20 (1198).

10 Léonard, *Introduction*, pp. 68, 72, 75, 77, 81. See also BN, n.a.l., 22, fols. 115r–18r (1270), 468r–71r (1267); ibid., 32, fols. 491r–2r (1290). See also Arch. Dép. de l'Aveyron, G 555 (1302), as cited in Miquel, *État des sources archivistiques*, p. 38.

11 Schottmüller, *Untergang*, II, pp. 183, 215.

12 See Duhamel-Amado, *Genèse*, I, pp. 235 (Abeilhan), 250 (Pézenas); II, pp. 355–7 (Pézenas).

the fact that the Templars were in possession of a major commandery at Pézenas and the fact that by 1140 Hugh of Pézenas had taken full Templar vows strongly suggest that some of the co-lords of Pézenas had established close links with the Order from very early on.[13] Like the lords of Barbaira and the lords of Canet, who supported Douzens, William Pons of Pézenas (1088–1117) and his son Peter (1117–52) were often found in the company of the Trencavel viscounts of Carcassonne and Béziers, to whose patrimony Pézenas belonged until 1209.[14]

In 1189 or 1199 Peter's daughter (or granddaughter) Ermengard (or Ermessendis) was recorded endowing the Templar community of Pézenas with a family of serfs and two fiefs 'for the love of God and for the redemption of her soul and the souls of her parents, brothers and all deceased faithful'– a formulation that is suggestive of how closely the memory of her family was linked to the commandery.[15] At around the same time, in 1193, Peter's grandson and namesake issued his testament and endowed the local Templar community with all his men, women and mill shares in the parish of the nearby church of Ste-Marie of Lézignan. He also proposed to endow the Templars with the mills of his brother Hugh, if they were willing to redeem them for 4,000 *sous*, which the brothers refused to do without further instructions from their master.[16] Soon afterwards two relatives of Peter, Peter Bernard of Pézenas and his wife Ermessendis, sold to the Order tithes in the boundaries of St-André of Sesquière.[17]

The lords of Pézenas were related by marriage to the lords of Abeilhan, whose castle was located only about 10 kilometres to the west of Pézenas. A certain Peter Ermengau of Pouzolles married the woman who seems to have been the heiress of Abeilhan some time before 1088 and three generations later the toponym Abeilhan was frequently applied to identify descendants of his grandson Pons of Pézenas, son of Peter Ermengaud's daughter and William Pons of Pézenas, and his wife Mary.[18] Rixendis of Abeilhan, who in April 1198 issued her testament and made arrangements to be buried among the Templars of Pézenas, may therefore have been a

[13] *CG*, no. 215, p. 148 (1140); no. 400, p. 251 (1146); no. 462, p. 277 (1147). A simple genealogy of the lords of Pézenas, which does not mention Hugh, is provided in Duhamel-Amado, *Genèse*, I, p. 250.

[14] See e.g. *HGL*, v, no. 422, cols. 794–6 (1105), no. 456.iv, col. 853 (1117). See also Duhamel-Amado, *Genèse*, I, pp. 206–7, 316; II, pp. 354–7.

[15] BN, n.a.l., 15, fols. 404r–8r (1189).

[16] Ibid., 16, fols. 45r–7r (1193). The donation was later disputed by Peter's sons Berenguer and Raymond of Montesquieu, who, however, withdrew their claims in 1198. Ibid., fols. 109–15 (1198).

[17] Ibid., fols. 60r–2r (1194).

[18] See Duhamel-Amado, *Genèse*, I, pp. 235 (Abeilhan) and 250 (Pézenas).

kinswoman of Peter of Pézenas's great-nephew William of Abeilhan.[19] By the end of the twelfth century the Templars had established a strong presence in Abeilhan, where they had received one third of the castle and lordship when William's co-lord Berenguer of Abeilhan entered into the Order in 1187. Their power over the lordship further expanded in 1208 when William sold them his possessions in the land of St-Pierre of Pézenas and after they had bought further land and rights in the suburbs of Ste-Marie of Lézignan and St-Pierre of Cazouls from William's nephew Peter Seguier.[20]

The lords of Pézenas and Abeilhan were neighbours and relatives and as such they shared a common heritage and probably political interests in the region. These were two of a kaleidoscope of reasons why families became involved with religious orders in general. As networks grew bigger and spread wider, however, geopolitical and even cultural boundaries were sometimes crossed and experiences were no longer easily shared among distant relations. But individual experiences still created memories, informed behaviour patterns and shaped identities which travelled across boundaries and between families in the minds of spouses and widows who would relate them to their husbands, children and relatives.

THE ROLE OF WOMEN

Marriage ties played an important role in the decision as to which Templar communities a family would frequent and endow. The dowries of noble women often included landed possessions, or entitlements to such, that were isolated from the patrimonies of the families of their spouses. Marriage ties may help explain, for example, why the lords of Auriac near Ste-Eulalie had come into the possession of the church of Le Gal, which was situated 50 or more kilometres away from their family castle. Detached as they often were from the possessions of the household into which the woman had married, these dowry lands were not always easily manageable, which could lead to the decision to dispose of them by means of sale, exchange, pledge, or donation.[21] Religious institutions, including Templar communities, were convenient business partners or recipients of charity because they usually had monetary assets at their disposal and could in any case offer spiritual services.

19 BN, n.a.l., 17, fols. 324r–6r (1198).

20 Ibid., 16, fols. 217r–25r (1208), 296r–307r (1214). Another (possible) relative who joined the Order was Rostaign of Avène, who may have been related to William of Abeilhan's brother-in-law (by his sister Belissendis) Dalmas of Avène. Rostaign had joined the Order by 1227. Ibid., 17, fols. 386r–91r (1202×1203) and Débax, *Féodalité languedocienne*, p. 191fn. for Dalmas.

21 For Champagne this is discussed in Evergates, *Aristocracy*, pp. 103–4.

Women were usually given a role in the transactions involving their dowries, and they did not always agree with their husbands' plans to dispose of the possessions which they, the wives, had brought with them into the marriage.[22] Lady Clemence of Fouvent, for example, did not object when her son Henry of Vergy, lord of Mirebeau, sold a family with their possessions at Valleroy and Fouvent to the Templars of La Romagne, but the charter makes clear that her consent was explicitly required as the property concerned was part of her inheritance.[23] Emeline of Broyes, on the other hand, seems to have threatened her husband Erard II of Chacenay with (or caused him to contemplate) divorce after she had caught him selling his stepdaughter's inheritance to the Templars;[24] and the widow of Robert of Sablonnières successfully reclaimed her dowry from the Templars after she discovered that it had been included in a donation made by Robert to the Templars during the Third Crusade along with the inheritance of Robert's sister, who also brought suit against the Templars and won.[25]

This is not to say that women could not have their own reasons to give to the Order. In northern France, notably in Champagne, married aristocratic women often had a wealth of possessions at their disposal and the argument that women featured less prominently in Templar charters than men fails to acknowledge that they could be the driving force behind donations.[26] As Bouchard has remarked, 'women . . . played an important role in deciding where a family would make its pious gifts. Their influence seems to have been wielded behind the scenes, but it was no less effective.'[27] Women did feature less prominently and less often in the Templar charters than men, but they were still frequently recorded alongside their husbands with whom they held possessions in conjugal community.[28] Some women, like Lauretta of Pignan, gave part of their inheritance to the Order;[29] others, like Ermessendis of Rovira in Catalonia, used their dowries.[30]

[22] For Champagne and Burgundy see ibid., pp. 103–18.

[23] *HdB*, v, no. 3140, pp. 180–1 (1259): 'We Clemence, lady of Fouvent, to whose inheritance this pertains, have given our approval and consent to this sale and pledge. And to witness this affair and have it confirmed and fixed, we have brought the present letters, sealed with our seals, before said *commandeur* and brothers' ('Nos Clemence, dame de Fouvenz, de cui heritaige ce muet, avons otroié et consanti bonsment ceste vandue et loée, et an tesmoignaige de ceste chose, et por ce que ce soit ferme chose et estauble, nos avons bailliees as devant diz commandeor et as Freres ces presahies letres saelees de nos saels').

[24] *Feud Soc*, no. 30, pp. 45–7 (1224); Evergates, *Aristocracy*, pp. 103, 116.

[25] *Cart Prov*, no. 87, p. 107 (1994); Evergates, *Aristocracy*, p. 114.

[26] Ibid., pp. 89–91.

[27] Bouchard, *Sword, miter, and cloister*, p. 142.

[28] For Champagne see Evergates, *Aristocracy*, pp. 91–3, 94–6.

[29] *Cart Douz*, A: no. 40, pp. 50–1 (1133×1134).

[30] *CG*, no. 341, p. 221 (1144).

Moreover, donations were regularly subjected to the approval and counsel of wives, widows and mothers, whose opinions would have influenced the decision as to what and how much husbands, sons and daughters were able to give away. Some women were genuinely attracted to Templar communities. In the obituary of the Templar church of La Trinité in Reims, for example, fifty-seven women are commemorated by name. Some are recorded alongside their husbands, others because their husbands or sons had made donations in their memory either to the Templars or to the Church's previous occupants. Most, however, seem to have been benefactors and business associates of the Order in their own right and to have made extensive endowments to secure the annual commemoration of their deaths.[31]

The appeal of La Trinité for women is well illustrated because the obituary of the church has survived, but it is not unique. As Carraz has shown, in commanderies in the Lower Rhône valley women appear on average in 38 per cent of the charters, sometimes alone (10.5 per cent) but more often along with their spouses (13.4 per cent).[32] Throughout the Order's existence women, some of them former spouses of Templar brothers, aspired to burial in the Temple, joined the Order's confraternities, associated themselves as donats (albeit only rarely), and volunteered to work in the Order's hospices and hospitals.[33] In 1160 a certain Ponsia Raina and her daughter gave themselves to Douzens;[34] the mother of Odo of Pichanges had become a sister (*soror*) of the Templar hospital at Tilchâtel by 1178;[35] in 1209 Helvis, who was the widow of Theoderic of St-Jean-de-Verrières, made arrangements to become a sister (*soror*) of the Templar community of Villers-lès-Verrières in Burgundy;[36] Mary Boverie was recorded as a *soror et donata* of the Templar community of Montpellier in October 1221;[37] the widow of John of Châtillon, Margaret, joined the confraternity of Saulce in July 1249;[38] Beatrix, widow of William of Fos, that of St-Maurice in Provence in 1262;[39] and the widow of Thomas of St-Germain, Cecilia of Joigny, entered the confraternity of the Templar community of Châlons-sur-Marne along with her two daughters Margaret and Isabel in 1284.[40]

[31] See *ObReims*, passim. [32] Carraz, 'Présences et dévotions féminines', especially p. 73 table 1.
[33] Ibid., pp. 81–6. [34] *Cart Douz*, A: no. 10, pp. 22–3 (1160).
[35] *HdB*, II, no. 622, pp. 393–4 (1178).
[36] A. Pétel, 'La maison de Villers-Lès-Verrières', *MSA Aube*, 69 (1905), 374.
[37] BN, n.a.l., 15, fols. 95r–6r (1221).
[38] AN S 5235, dossier 1, no. 1, fols. 3v–4r (1249) (BN, n.a.l., 15, 54, fols. 213r–14r).
[39] Durbec, *Templiers et hospitaliers*, p. 194.
[40] *Diocèse ancien de Châlons-sur-Marne*, I, no. 134, p. 431 (1284).

It is by now a firmly established fact that women in the middle ages played a crucial role in communicating religious and social ideas between families and kin-groups and also 'significantly aided the spread of church reform'.[41] They were targeted by crusade preachers for their ability to stir their husbands (who in any case required their wives' consent before they could submit to a crusade) and sons into taking the cross, thereby – as James of Vitry did not fail to point out when preaching the Fifth Crusade – becoming crusaders themselves.[42] Often marginalised in their families of origin, women became the centre of new family units once they had married. Their values, traditions and opinions had a profound impact on the education and development of their children, for whom they usually constituted the primary, and sometimes only, person of reference.[43] The number of widows who made endowments to the Templars for the soul of their deceased spouses and in the presence of their children shows how important they were in communicating family traditions to a younger generation, which is all the more significant if one considers how many of these women had sustained personal losses as a result of crusading.[44]

Women were often responsible for the continuation of family support for particular Templar houses. What is more, they could play an important role in directing the charity of new families – those into which they had married – towards Templar communities that were favoured by their own relatives or by the families of former spouses. The lords of St-Vérain, for example, had ties with the nearby Templar community of Villemoison and it was only after Hugh of St-Vérain had married Elisabeth of Noyers that his name appears among the benefactors of Sauce in the parish of Escolives, a commandery that was situated almost 60 kilometres away from St-Vérain but was closely linked to the family of Elisabeth's first husband William of Joigny, into which Elisabeth had married at the age of ten. So for example in June 1262, a charter records Hugh's and Elisabeth's substantial donation in alms to the Templars of Sauce, consisting of a

[41] Bouchard, *Sword, miter, and cloister*, p. 142 (and generally pp. 142–8). This applies in particular to the communication of crusade enthusiasm. See Riley-Smith, *First Crusaders*, pp. 5, 93–105 and J. S. C. Riley-Smith, 'Family traditions and participation in the Second Crusade', in M. Gervers (ed.), *The Second Crusade and the Cistercians* (New York, 1992), 103.

[42] James of Vitry, *Lettres de Jacques de Vitry (1160/1170–1240) évêque de Saint-Jean-d'Acre. Édition critique*, ed. R. B. C. Huygens (Leiden, 1960), no. 1, p. 77.

[43] One only has to read the autobiography of the Benedictine abbot Guibert of Nogent to realise just how much a mother's opinion and beliefs could influence the religious outlook of young men of knightly stock. See Guibert of Nogent, *Self and society in medieval France. The memoirs of Abbot Guibert of Nogent*, trans. J. F. Benton (Toronto, 1984); and N. R. Hodgson, *Women, crusading and the Holy Land in historical narrative* (Woodbridge, 2007), pp. 157–9 for general remarks.

[44] See Chapter 5, below, and Evergates, *Aristocracy*, p. 145 on the heavy toll that crusading took on Champenois families

motte near the commandery, their dependencies and lands adjoining those of the Templars, a piece of land situated within the Templars' territory, and lands and pastures near Courcelles, as well as all justicial rights that were not held by the lords of Champs and the lords of Vincelles.[45] These possessions were clearly tied to the authority of Elisabeth's first husband, William of Joigny. In a different charter, Elisabeth herself acknowledged that the property concerned came from her, and Count John of Joigny, her grandson, and that they were held in fief from him.[46] Already on 23 March 1271 the donations had been confirmed by John, who had swiftly followed up with his own donations consisting of his feudal rights in the fief.[47] All the donations were confirmed by Count Robert of Nevers and, eventually, by the count of Auxerre.[48]

Considering her young age when she married William, and even allowing for the possibility that this was merely the consent to marriage and that cohabitation had come later, it is likely that by the time of William's death she had adopted the religious associations and preferences of her in-laws, which would explain why she had promoted Sauce to her second husband and not St-Marc, the commandery her own father had once supported.[49]

Not least because of the extensive research on marriage patterns in Champagne undertaken by Evergates, we can now safely suggest that Elisabeth's case would have been neither singular nor uncommon, for it was customary that women married in their mid teens and took a second husband (or chose another form of 'second career') in their thirties and thus entered the households of at least two families other than their own.[50] In the light of this, marriage ties may also explain, for example, why the lords of Bricon had by 1201 come into possession of property near Grancey and why they, who had traditionally supported Templar Voulaines, emerged as benefactors of Templar Bure near Grancey in the

[45] AN S 5237, dossier 32, nos. 7a (1262), 7b (1262, *reprise*), 7c (1264, *vidimus*), and *CG(Yonne)*, III, no. 606, p. 295. For another transaction, between Peter of St-Vérain, his wife Benedicta and the Templars (but not specifically the commandery of Sauce), see AN S 5235, dossier 1, no. 1, fol. 11v (1255).

[46] Ibid., no. 36 (1275). [47] AN S 5237, dossier 32, no. 7d (1271).

[48] Ibid., no. 7e (1272); AN S 5235, dossier 1, no. 36 (1275). See also Demurger, 'La constitution d'un patrimoine foncier', 447–8.

[49] See BN, n.a.l., 55, fol. 555r (1186×1187) for her father's benefaction to St-Marc. It is possible that Elisabeth had also promoted Sauce to the household of her original family. This is suggested by the fact that in 1254 a certain Humbert of Noyers and his wife Ermenburgis had become involved in a business transaction with Sauce: see AN S 5235, dossier 1, no. 1, fol. 26r (1256) (BN, n.a.l., 54, fols. 392r–3r).

[50] Evergates, *Aristocracy*, pp. 140–52.

thirteenth century, a role that they continued to play until the early fourteenth century.[51] Likewise, one of the sisters of the Templar William of Baudement could have played a role in communicating her family's affinity for the Templar community of Provins to her second husband Guy of Dampierre and Moëlein, viscount of Troyes, who, if the few surviving sources are anything to go by, appeared as a donor in the Templar charters from Provins only after he had married her.[52]

In short, women from families with Templar associations were sometimes responsible for introducing the Order to relatives of their spouses. During the middle decades of the twelfth century, when the Templars had not yet established a strong presence in the dioceses of Burgundy, Champagne or Languedoc, the survival and growth of Templar communities must have relied strongly on this kind of word-of-mouth propaganda. In general, however, direct lines of influence are very difficult to establish and the fact that Guy of Dampierre, one of the earliest benefactors of Templar Provins, was recorded as benefactor shortly after his brother-in-law William of Baudement had made his first recorded endowment to the Temple, for example, may well have been coincidental. What can be said is that women regularly attended, witnessed and confirmed their husbands' transactions with the Order, often with their children, that they made their own donations and, as Carraz could show for Provence, that they personally added to the 'familial constraints' which pressured them and their offspring into continuing their ancestors' close relationships with the Temple and other military orders.[53]

A first-glance examination of the family networks connecting Templars and Templar supporters furthermore creates the impression that Templar families often chose to marry their offspring into other families with Templar ties. The aforementioned Elisabeth of Noyers, Hugh of St-Vérain, Odo of Lanty and Blanche of Bricon all had a history of Templar benefaction running in their families by the time they married. Although it is always difficult to establish who or what had instigated a family's involvement with the Templars, what can also be said is that the idea of supporting the Order circulated among families that were connected to one another either by blood or by marriage and that women played a part in spreading and keeping alive the support for the Temple in these connected families.

[51] The lords of Grancey supported Bure. By 1207 a nephew of the Templar Odo of Grancey, Odo of Lanty, was married to Blanche of Bricon and the couple had at least five children. For the support of the lords of Bricon for Voulaines see Roger, 'Les Morhiers', 86, 94 and no. 6, 168–9 (1175). See also *HdB*, II, no. 638, pp. 399–400 (1178); III, no. 1041, p. 382 (1201); Roger, 'Les Morhiers', 94, 99 and no. 31, 126–7 (1289), no. 32, 127–9 (1301), no. 33, 129–30 (1301).

[52] *CG*, no. 28, pp. 20–3 (1129×1143).

[53] Carraz, 'Présences et dévotions féminines', 86–7.

NETWORKS IN EXISTENCE

Placing Templar brothers and benefactors in a wider family context is not always easy as so many of them were of low noble or non-noble stock and are therefore seldom mentioned in the written sources of the time, and when they are, it is under varying surnames. In Languedoc the situation was complicated by the Albigensian crusades, which caused turmoil in social networks. Fortunately, however, the number of well-connected and well-documented families of knightly and noble stock with ties to the Order is not small either and charters in particular allow us to provide the families of some donors and Templar brothers with more than one marriage relationship. As can be shown, for example, by 1145 the castellans of Abeilhan not only had marriage ties with the lords of Pézenas but also with the Corneilhan family, which was an old aristocratic family from near Béziers whose members in the twelfth century were part of the Trencavel entourage.[54] They witnessed transactions with the Templars and provided them with personnel.[55]

We have seen that an extensive network of interrelated families with Templar ties can be associated with the counts of Comminges and that other networks can be centred on the lords of Tilchâtel and other noble households in Burgundy and Champagne. These 'networks' are artificial creations in so far as the families on which they are centred serve merely as starting points for the unfolding of webs of marriage and blood relationships that linked families with Templar ties. Neither the counts of Comminges nor the lords of Tilchâtel, in other words, had instigated enthusiasm for the Temple in the networks of which they were a part, nor were they necessarily the most prominent Templar supporters among the members of these groups; but as starting points they serve us well.

The case of the counts of Comminges not only illustrates how much a single commandery, in this case Montsaunès, profited from the ties of friendship and lordship created between its benefactors, which I have illustrated earlier, but also how networks of families can be constructed in which enthusiasm for an institutionalised form of crusading as exemplified by the military orders spread horizontally between branches and vertically through different generations. Within these networks differing

[54] By 1145 Raymond of Abeilhan had married Bernarda, sister of the episcopal seneschal of Béziers Pons of Corneilhan. A genealogy of Abeilhan is provided in Duhamel-Amado, *Genèse*, I, p. 235. See also Débax, *Féodalité languedocienne*, p. 278; Duhamel-Amado, *Genèse*, I, pp. 231, 232, and *HGL*, V, no. 506, cols. 960–2 (1130), no. 523:iii, cols. 1018–19 (1138) for membership in the Trencavel entourage. By the mid thirteenth century the lords of Corneilhan were vassals of the counts of Toulouse. See *Droits et possessions*, ed. Cabié, p. 15.

[55] *CG*, no. 65, p. 50 (1133), no. 128, pp. 89–90 (1136); *Cart Douz*, A:, no 8, pp. 18–19 (1169) and no. 38 p. 49 (1134×1135), no. 117, pp. 109–10 (1153).

types of association by members of varying social status were possible, and they were not necessarily mutually exclusive, as vassals could be blood relatives of their lords and it was not uncommon for lords and castellans to marry into the families of their knights.[56]

The networks centred on the lords of Tilchâtel and other noble houses in Burgundy and Champagne show how extensive such relationship networks could become and how far they could reach. As will become apparent, it is possible to link families with Templar ties in Burgundy with others from near Carcassonne by mapping the channels of communication and personal influence through which travelled ideas of crusading and enthusiasm for support of religious communities with military vocations like the Order of the Temple, thus connecting like-minded individuals and their kin.

The network of Comminges

I have already discussed the network of interrelated families in the county of Comminges that provided the Templar commandery of Montsaunès with personnel, land and material support in the twelfth century and in which the counts of Comminges played a central role.[57] These relations supplemented the web of marriage ties and family relationships that connected in particular the counts to other prominent Templar benefactors and these to each other.

In 1134 Bernard I of Comminges had already assisted the bishop of Toulouse in his donation of the church of Laramet to the Templars but only in the second half of the twelfth century did he, his relatives and his successors become more deeply involved in the affairs of the local commandery of Montsaunès. His son Dodon of Samertan (who became known as Bernard III) joined the Order in 1176; Arnold Roger, bishop of Comminges and Bernard I's brother, arbitrated in disputes between the Templars and relatives of other benefactors; and Bernard IV, Bernard III's grandson, conceded land and lordship rights to Montsaunès, accepted donations for the Templars living there and eventually requested burial at Montsaunès.[58]

The enthusiasm of the counts of Comminges in the main line for a military order like the Order of the Temple, of which their engagement in

[56] Bouchard, *Those of my blood*, pp. 30–6. [57] See above, pp. 166ff.

[58] Higounet, *Comté de Comminges*, I, pp. 42–3; *Cart Mont*, no. 1, pp. 223–6 (1176), no. 2, p. 226 (*c.* 1182), no. 3, p. 227 (*c.* 1176), no. 5, pp. 227–8 (1184), no. 11, pp. 231–2 (after 1180), no. 24, pp. 238–9 (1178), no. 80, p. 269 (1176×1177); *GP(Toulouse)*, no. 44, p. xxx (*c.* 1200). For Bernard IV's burial see Guillaume de Puylaurens, *Chronique, 1145–1275*, ed. and trans. J. Duvernoy (Paris, 1976; reprint: 1999), pp. 45, 123 (his burial at Montsaunès is recorded in the margin of the manuscript). See also Higounet, *Comté de Comminges*, I, p. 105fn.

Templar affairs at Montsaunès was an expression, was matched by that of the families into which the counts and their siblings married. Bernard IV's first wife Beatrix of Marsan, countess of Bigorre and daughter of Centulle of Marsan and Mabille of Baux, was the descendant of a powerful Provençal family with strong ties to the Order of St John – her brother William became a Hospitaller knight at Trinquetaille – and (albeit less so) to the Order of the Temple on her mother's side, and the daughter and granddaughter of the founding donors of the Templar commandery of Bordères on her father's side.[59] Their daughter Petronilla married as her first husband Viscount Gaston VI of Béarn from the powerful Catalan family of Montcada, which had strong ties with the Cistercian community at Santes Creus and with the Templars, with whom the lords of Montcada shared power in the city of Tortosa.[60] As early as 1134 Gaston VI's grandfather William Raymond, seneschal to Count Raymond Berenguer IV of Barcelona, and his brother Odo had promised the Templars their personal service as well as material support from their income from the frontier castle of Granyena.[61] Gaston VI made his own donations to Templar Bordères in 1205 and Petronilla hers in 1247.[62] Gaston's brother William Raymond lavishly endowed the Temple, the Hospital and other religious institutions before setting out on a pilgrimage to Rome in 1215 to reconcile himself with the Pope. These endowments were followed eight years later by further donations to the Templars, which were meant to compensate for William Raymond's failure to go on crusade.[63] Two members of the Montcada family were appointed as provincial masters of Aragon in the thirteenth century.[64]

From 1139 the counts of Comminges were also linked by marriage to the Trencaval family, which ruled over Béziers and Carcassonne, and from 1151 to the counts of Foix.[65] Both families had become involved with the Templars in the 1130s. Roger I of Béziers, who had married Bernarda,

[59] In 1148 Peter of Marsan, his wife Beatrix, countess of Bigorre, and their son Centulle, future husband of Mabille of Baux and father of Bernard IV's wife Beatrix, placed the *villa* of Bordères under the protection of the Templars, thus enabling the latter to establish a commandery there. See *GP (Toulouse)*, no. 62, pp. xliii–xliv (1148). For the involvement of the house of Baux in the Temple and Hospital see Mazel, *Noblesse et l'église*, pp. 353–6 and Carraz, *L'ordre du Temple*, pp. 349, 364.

[60] A good illustration of the longstanding ties between the barons of Montcada and the Templars, in particular in Tortosa, is provided in N. Jaspert, 'Bonds and tensions on the frontier: the Templars in twelfth-century western Catalonia', in J. Sarnowsky (ed.), *Mendicants, military orders, and regionalism in medieval Europe* (Aldershot, 1999), esp. pp. 30–1. For relations of the Montcadas with Santes Creus see J. C. Shideler, *A medieval Catalan noble family: the Montcadas, 1000–1230* (Berkeley, Calif., 1983), pp. 109–12.

[61] Ibid., p. 96. [62] *GP(Toulouse)*, no. 63, p. cliv (1205), no. 64, p. xliv (1247).

[63] Shideler, *A medieval Catalan noble family*, p. 140. [64] Ibid., p. 86.

[65] Bernard IV's brother Roger married a sister of Count Raymond Roger of Foix and his son Bernard V a niece of Roger's wife. See Isenburg *et al.*, *Stammtafeln*, III/146.

sister of Bernard III of Comminges, in 1139, supported Douzens and eventually requested burial with the Templars.[66] Sybille of Foix, the wife of Bernard IV's brother Roger of Couserans, was the daughter of Roger III of Foix, whose endowment of the Templars with land near La Nougarède in 1136 resulted in the foundation of the Templar commandery of Villedieu.[67] She was also the granddaughter of Raymond Trencavel, and therefore a niece of Roger I of Béziers.[68] The counts of Foix supported the Hospitallers at Capoulet and by the end of the thirteenth century at least one member of one of their cadet branches, Loup of Foix, had become a professed Hospitaller knight.[69] Moreover, by the middle of the thirteenth century the counts of Comminges were also connected by marriage to the family of the viscounts of Cardona in Catalonia, which had produced Templars and Templar benefactors since 1133 and would continue to do so until 1307.[70]

Guy and Fortanier of Comminges, a brother and son of Bernard III, married women from noble families of local significance who also had ties to the military orders. Guy married Bertranda of Aure in 1180, whose nephew (most likely) Sancho Garcia witnessed at least one donation to Montsaunès in 1184.[71] Later in life, he entered the Order of St John, in which the family of the viscounts of Aure had become heavily involved.[72] Another possible nephew of Bertranda by the name of William Garcia of Aure, who could also have been a younger son or grandson of her and Guy, entered the Order of the Temple in the thirteenth century and held the office of preceptor of Puyfortéguille in Gascony from 1237 until 1243.[73]

[66] *HGL*, v, no. 580, cols. 1118–21 (1150). [67] Ibid., no. 533, cols. 1020–1 (1136).

[68] I am referring here to the genealogy of the Trencavel family as provided in Débax, *Féodalité languedocienne*, p. 345.

[69] In 1274 Loup of Foix was recorded as preceptor of Hospitaller Aure and Poucharramet. See *GP (Toulouse)*, p. 211 and pp. 172–3 for donations to Capoulet.

[70] *CG*, no. 66, p. 50 (1133) and BN, n.a.l., 17, fols. 90r–3r (1246). Templars and Templar benefactors belonging to the Cardona family are recorded in J. Miret y Sans, *Les cases de templers y hospitalers a Catalunya. Aplec de noves i documents històrics* (Barcelona, 1910), p. 516. See also P. Bonneaud, *Le prieuré de Catalogne, le couvent de Rhodes et la couronne d'Aragon 1415–1447* (Millau, 2004), p. 353; Forey, *Aragón*, pp. 82, 312, 347, 430; J. Ballaró y Casas, *Historia de Cardona* (Barcelona, 1905) p. 57; N. Coureas, 'The role of the Templars and Hospitallers in the movement of commodities involving Cyprus', in P. Edbury and J. Phillips (eds.), *The experience of crusading, vol. II: Defining the crusader kingdom* (Cambridge, 2003), 261.

[71] *Cart Mont*, no. 77, p. 268 (1184).

[72] Four members of different branches of the Aure family were recorded as Hospitaller knights in the second half of the thirteenth century: Bertrand of Aure (1260, commander Hosp. Fronton 1251–2); Bernard of Aure (commander Hosp. Toulouse 1260–1265×1266; Renneville 1265–70; Thor-Boulbonne 1272); Raymond of Aure (vice prior Hosp. Toulouse; commander Hosp. Garidech 1275–6); Sancho of Aure (1266–94). See *GP(Toulouse)*, pp. 64, 65, 83, 115, 145, 216, 284, and pp. 23, 24, 199 for Sancho (Garcia) of Aure.

[73] *GP(Toulouse)*, p. 394; Léonard, *Introduction*, p. 85.

Fortanier married the granddaughter of a powerful Templar associate, Raymond Ato II of Aspet, who, on two separate occasions in the summer of 1156, gave the castle, village and church of Canens with all appertaining lands, people, rights and seigniorial powers and his rights in three little hamlets as well as himself to the Templar community of Montsaunès,[74] followed by a third endowment in preparation for his journey to Jerusalem some time before 1160.[75] He was the first in a long line of kinsmen of the wife of Bernard III of Comminges to make donations to or seek personal association with the Templars of Montsaunès. Raymond of Aspet entered the Temple in 1186 with two of his fiefs as entry gift. So did Bernard William of Aspet before 1245.[76] Arnold of Aspet gave another fief in the early spring of 1256×1257, by which time another likely kinsman, Ariol of Aspet, had already entered the Order (he was recorded as preceptor of Montsaunès from 1253 to 1260).[77] By 1277 Arnold of Aspet had taken the Templar habit and was serving the Order at Toulouse.[78] Fortanier's granddaughter Navarra married Arnold of Martres, whose family, as we have seen, acted as patrons to Montsaunès and who was a namesake of the twelfth-century Templar Arnold of Martres, the administrator of the small Templar house at St-Sirac in 1169.[79] As late as 1302×1303 the family collaborated with the Order in the foundation of a new *bastide* (the term describes a fortified building at the entrance to a town) at Plagne.[80] It was not until 1306 that the final transaction between a member of the house of Aspet and the Templars of Montsaunès was recorded.[81]

The counts of Comminges were therefore members (if not necessarily the centre) of a group of sometimes interrelated families who were bound to the counts (and sometimes to each other) by ties of marriage, in whose profiles support for the military orders was a persistent feature, and for whom – since Bernard III of Comminges may have died at Montsaunès, Bernard IV requested burial there, and Bernard V was buried in the Hospitaller commandery of Toulouse – Templar and Hospitaller commanderies were desired places for family commemoration.[82]

[74] *GP(Toulouse)*, pp. 142, 178, no. 37, pp. xxvi-xxvii (1156); *Cart Mont*, no. 41, pp. 247–8 (1156).

[75] *PAC*, I, no. 97, p. 94 (1160). Raymond Ato's other daughter would marry Pons of Francazal, who became another benefactor of Montsaunès. See e.g. *GP(Toulouse)*, p. 179.

[76] Ibid., pp. 25, 178–9, 385, 390, 394. References to members of the family of Aspet can also be found in Castillon d'Aspet, *Histoire*, I, passim.

[77] *GP(Toulouse)*, pp. 182, 200, 203. [78] Ibid., p. 83.

[79] *Cart Mont*, p. 218. See above, pp. 167-8, for the family of Arnold of Martres.

[80] C. Higounet, 'Une bastide de colonisation des templiers dans les Pré-Pyrénées', *Revue de Comminges*, 62 (1949), 81–97.

[81] *GP(Toulouse)*, p. 184.

[82] See ibid., p. 40 for the burial of Bertrand V of Comminges at Toulouse (1240).

Burgundian–Champenois networks

A number of potentially even more impressive networks of interrelated families with Templar connections can be constructed from charters from medieval Burgundy and Champagne. One such network centred, again, on the seigniorial family of Tilchâtel, whose involvement with the Templars dates back to 1129, when Aimo II of Tilchâtel witnessed the preparations of his knight Guy Cornelly to join the Order in the Holy Land.[83] By the end of the thirteenth century noble households which can be linked to the Tilchâtels included the house of Mont-St-Jean with its cadet branches of Ancy(-le-Franc) and Charny;[84] the lords of Bourbonne in the county of Burgundy; as well as the seigniorial households of Dampierre, Noyers, Arzillières, Chappes (to which the Order of the Temple's founding master Hugh of Payns may have been related by marriage), La Roche-Vanneau, and Grancey, which all provided Templar communities with professed brothers (in the case of Bourbonne, Arzillières, Grancey and perhaps Chappes), extensive landed property and lordship rights.[85]

Each of these families with their households brought into the network complex family relationships that were usually the results of inheritance patterns and marriage arrangements. The alliances within these groups of connected families could be multilateral and often overlapped, thus tightening the network even more closely. Even in the expanded network, however, patronage over Templar establishments (and support for other military orders) remained a prevailing feature.

[83] See p. 139 above.

[84] In *c.* 1196×1197 Stephen of Mont-St-Jean was referring to Hugh of Tilchâtel as his nephew. See *HdB*, III, no. 951, pp. 349–50.

[85] Some time after 1196 Guy II of Tilchâtel married Wil(lel)ma of Bourbonne and in September 1276 William II of Tilchâtel was explicitly recorded as holding the lordship of Bourbonne (Bouchard, *Sword, miter, and cloister*, pp. 283, 368–9; *HdB*, III, no. 951, pp. 349–50 (1196×1197); VI, no. 4290, p. 246 (1276)). Beatrix of Tilchâtel was by 1239 married to Raynald III of Dampierre and Hugh of Tilchâtel by 1246 to Philippa of Noyers, daughter of Milo of Noyers and Agnes of Brienne. John of Tilchâtel and Walter of Arzillières married each other's sisters in 1248 and by 1256 respectively (Evergates, *Aristocracy*, p. 105; *Chart LanFran*, no. 19, pp. 19–20). Margaret of Tilchâtel was married to Odo of Ray, son of Odo of La Roche, duke of Athens, and Isabel of Chappes, whose relative Pons of La Roche is recorded among the benefactors of Templar La Romagne. Isabel of Tilchâtel in turn married William of Grancey before 1282 and in 1300 her son Odo of Grancey inherited the lordship of Tilchâtel. See generally Faget de Casteljau, 'Les sires de Til-Châtel'. A marriage relationship between Hugh of Payns and the lords of Chappes (his wife would have been Elisabeth of Chappes) is proposed in Leroy, *Hugues de Payns. Chevalier champenois*, pp. 95–102. For donations see e.g. *Diocèse ancien de Châlons-sur-Marne*, I, no. 32, p. 407 (*c.* 1190), no. 41, p. 410 (1202×1203), no. 68, p. 414 (1234); *HdB*, III, no. 866, pp. 313–14 (1191), no. 1428, p. 475 (1163), no. 1432, p. 476 (1183), no. 1464, p. 484 (1209), no. 1466, p. 484 (1210); VI, no. 4290, p. 246 (1276); *Chart Mor*, no. 64, pp. 77–8 (1209); BN, n.a.l., 51, fols. 114r (1191×1202), 138r (1232); AN S 4956, dossier 17, nos. 1 and 2 (1213); BN, n.a.l., 53, fol. 252rv (1180×1193).

One person who seems to have been particularly useful in promoting the Templars among families connected to the lords of Noyers was Elisabeth of Noyers.[86] The daughter of Milo of Noyers and Agnes of Brienne, Elisabeth married her first husband William of Joigny at the tender age of ten, after which she spent most of her formative years in the fold of a family with ties to the Templar communities of La Madelaine at Joigny and Sauce-sur-Yonne, as I will illustrate in more detail below. The family of her second husband supported the commandery of Villemoison before they too directed their charity and business interests towards Sauce, a move for which Elisabeth may have been partly responsible.[87]

The lords of Tilchâtel were also linked to the lords of Mont-St-Jean. These in turn were connected to the lords of Noyers and perhaps also to the counts (later lords) of Saulx, who were patrons of Templar Bure. Certainly connected to them were the families and households of Saudon, Champlitte and Vergy, which all, at different times and with varying intensity, became involved in Templar affairs and acted as donors to local Templar communities.[88] The lords of Vergy, who married into the family of Mont-St-Jean before 1152 and later into that of Noyers, and whose relatives, the lords of Pierre-Perthuis, occasionally engaged with the Templar community of Saulce-d'Island in the thirteenth century, gave to the Templars from before 1183 until at least 1271, but were mentioned in the charters for even longer.[89] The son and grandson of William of Mont-St-Jean and his wife, the daughter of

[86] See above, pp. 180–1.

[87] See above, p. 180. Some time after 1255 Elisabeth married John III of Arcis-sur-Aube, son of Guy of Arcis-sur-Aube and Mathilde of Chacenay. See Evergates, *Aristocracy*, pp. 252 (genealogy Broyes), 253 (genealogy Chacenay). See also genealogy table 2 in *HdB*, v, App. x, p. 296.

[88] Hugh II of Mont-St-Jean married Elisabeth, daughter of Harvey of Vergy, and in 1196×1197 Stephen of Mont-St-Jean referred to Hugh of Vergy as his relative and shared the lordship of Vergy with him. At the same time Stephen of Mont-St-Jean is recorded as brother-in-law of the lord of Champlitte, who was in turn related to one of the earliest patrons of the Order, Hugh of Champagne. In the second half of the thirteenth century the lords of Champlitte were recorded among the business associates of Templar Bure. By 1202 Bertrand of Saudon was married to Elisabeth (or Isabel) of Mont-St-Jean, the sister of Stephen of Mont-St-Jean. Shortly afterwards, in 1205 and 1206, he was recorded as patron of the Templar community at Beaune. Stephen of Mont-St-Jean's brother Pons of Charny, who died in 1230, was the husband of Sybille of Noyers. See Bouchard, *Sword, miter, and cloister*, p. 377; *Documents inédits pour servir à l'histoire de Bourgogne*, ed. M. Canat de Chizy (Chalon-sur-Saône, 1863), I, pp. 64–5; *HdB*, III, no. 951, pp. 349–50 (*c.* 1196×1197), no. 1059, p. 387 (1202), no. 1108, p. 401 (1205), no. 1135, p. 407 (1206); Lavirotte, 'Mémoire statistique', 244 (1267)

[89] See Hugh of Poitiers, *Chronique de l'abbaye de Vézelay*, p. 552 for the relationship of the house of Vergy with the lords of Pierre-Perthuis and, for donations by members of the family of Pierre-Perthuis to Saulce, BN, n.a.l., 55, fols. 517r (1219; *vidimus* April 1263), 531r (1260; *vidimus* April 1263); *Recueil des pièces pour faire suite au cartulaire général de l'Yonne*, ed. M. Quantin (Paris, 1873), no. 609, p. 297 (1263).

Josbert of Ancy(-le-Franc), supported Templar St-Marc during the first half of the thirteenth century,[90] while the lords of Charny, who by the second decade of the thirteenth century had merged with the house of Mont-St-Jean, had been patrons of Templar Choisy since 1170 at the latest.[91]

In July 1231 Beatrix of Tilchâtel, daughter of Guy II of Tilchâtel and Wil(lel)ma of Bourbonne, lady of Coublanc, married Walter of Arzillières, nephew of the Templar marshal William of Arzillières. Radiating from his family were ties to the comital family of Joigny and to the seigniorial family of Montréal. These were the families into which William's brother Henry had tapped when he married first Agnes of Joigny, formerly the wife of Simon of Broyes, lord of Beaufort, and later Agnes of Montréal.

The counts of Joigny were patrons of the Hospitaller commandery of St-Thomas at Joigny by 1188 and made charitable concessions to the hospital of the Teutonic Order at Beauvoir in 1223.[92] From 1192 at the latest they also supported the Templar community of Sauce-sur-Yonne, near Auxerre, which was within the banal jurisdiction of the counts, and for which William of Joigny declared in 1235 that he cared deeply (*et habitatores eiusdem domus sincera in Domino diligimus caritate*).[93] Over a period of roughly eighty-five years, in fact, the counts and their relatives provided the commandery and its small dependency of La Madelaine at Joigny with serfs, meadows and farmland near Escolive and on the river Yonne, shares in the tolls of Joigny, vineyards, willow trees and meadows in the territory of Courcelles, shares in the rent-paying lands (*censiva*) of Lord Anseric of Barzarnes, rights in the lordship of Sauce, men, judicial rights, fiefs and rear-fiefs in Vaux, a house, willow grove (*saussaie*) and vineyards at Fontenelles in the Val-Constan, land near Tournan and Serein, and juridical rights in Vaux, Augy and Baulche.[94] By 1235 William of Joigny had founded a chapel at Sauce-sur-Yonne, as we know from a charter of that year in which he allowed the Templars to connect the path passing by their house with their mills and the river Yonne.[95] Three years later, in July 1238, he founded another

[90] See *HdB*, III, no. 951, pp. 349–50 (1196×1197). For transactions with Templar St-Marc see e.g. BN, n.a.l., 55, fols. 571r (1224), 572r (1226), 576r (1231), 585r–6r (1250; see also *Chart St-Marc/Jully*, pp. 765–6).

[91] See p. 140, fn. 77.

[92] *OdM*, I, p. 346 (1188); *Chartes de la commanderie de Beauvoir de l'ordre teutonique*, ed. C. Lalore, *Collection des principaux cartulaires du diocèse de Troyes*, III (Paris, Troyes, 1878), no. 22, p. 191 (1223).

[93] AN S 5235, dossier 1, no. 1, fol. 1r (1235).

[94] *Inventaire Chastellux*, no. 33, p. 133 (1192), no. 49, p. 136 (1221), no. 64, p. 139 (1240); *OdM*, I, p. 347 (1219); AN S 5235, dossier 1, no. 1, fol. 3r (BN, n.a.l., 54, fol. 154) (1240); AN S 5237/A, dossier 32, no. 7 (BN, n.a.l., 55, fols. 261–2 (1271, confirmation), 301–3 (1275), 304–6 (1276)). See also Demurger, 'Les templiers à Auxerre', 302.

[95] AN S 5237, dossier 30, no. 4 (1235). See also ibid., dossier 32, no. 5 and S 5235, dossier 1, no. 1, fol. 1v (BN, n.a.l., 54, fol. 135r) (1238); *Inventaire Chastellux*, no. 60, p. 138; *OdM*, I, p. 354.

chaplaincy (*capellania*) for the Templars at Sauce(-sur-Yonne).[96] And in October 1240, the year when William finally set out on crusade, his aunt Amicia endowed the commandery with more vineyards.[97] Since Andrew was a name that was already in use in the comital family of Joigny in 1192 it even seems likely that the Templar Andrew of Joigny, preceptor of Payns in 1263 and 1266, was related to the counts of Joigny.[98]

Relatives of Henry of Arzillières's second wife Agnes of Montréal engaged with the Templars sporadically during the first half of the thirteenth century.[99] The lords of Montréal shared their origin with the old aristocratic house of Chacenay in Champagne but had come to political power in the duchy of Burgundy, where the family had contracted alliances with the powerful houses of Montbard, Courtenay, Vergy and Thil. The mother-in-law of Henry's brother Vilain of Arzillières, Countess Mathilda of Rethel, was commemorated for her charity in the Templar obituary of La Trinité in Reims to which she had given '40 *livres* of Paris for the buying of rents for the annual celebration of her anniversary Mass'.[100] One daughter of Vilain married as her second husband Erard of Aulnay, whose family supported the Order from before 1176 until the early thirteenth century. The lords of Aulnay may have produced at least one Templar brother by the name of Urs of Aulnay.[101]

In about 1259 a great-nephew and namesake of the Templar William of Arzillières took Agnes of Plancy as his first wife (he would later marry Anne of Aulnay). Her family was part of the old aristocracy of Champagne and probably related to the powerful family of Chappes, from whom the Plancys held their castle.[102] By 1143 her ancestor Hugh of Plancy had

96 AN S 5237, dossier 30, no. 5 (1238).

97 AN S 5235, dossier 1, no. 1, fol. 3r (1240). Although the entry in the cartulary clearly reads 'Agnes, *relicta Galteri de Jovgniaco*', Walter of Joigny, who died in 1237, had been married to Amicia of Montfort.

98 For Andrew of Joigny as preceptor of Payns see Léonard, *Introduction*, p. 145 and *HdB*, v, no. 3297, p. 218 (1263).

99 Henry of Arzillières was the husband of Agnes of Montréal, daughter of Anseric IV of Montréal and Sybille of Burgundy. See Longnon, *Les compagnons de Villehardouin*, p. 22. For transactions between members of the seigniorial family of Montréal and the Temple see BN, n.a.l., 55, fol. 521r (1220; *vidimus* April 1263); *Chart St-Marc/Jully*, pp. 764–5 (1245) and also Lavirotte, 'Mémoire statistique', 269.

100 See *TSS*, no. 34, p. 150.

101 AN S 5188/A, dossier 29, no. 1 (*OdM*, 1, pp. 186–7) (1176). Urs of Aulnay, whose donations to the Order were confirmed by his lord Harvey of Donzy in *c*. 1190 (AN S 5244, dossier 5, no. 1) was first recorded as Templar seneschal in Acre in 1179×1181 (BN, n.a.l., 21, fols. 5, 25bis). See generally Burgtorf, *Central convent*, p. 666. For the relations between the lords of Arzillières and the lords of Aulnay see *Diocèse ancien de Châlons-sur-Marne*, 1, p. 288.

102 T. Evergates, *Feudal society in the bailliage of Troyes under the counts of Champagne, 1152–1284* (Baltimore, Md., 1975), pp. 102–13.

already given pasture rights and rent entitlements to the Templars and these donations were followed, in 1155, by Milo of Plancy providing the Templars with the house of Le Poncet, where a Templar community was soon established.[103]

This network of families with Templar ties centred on the lords of Tilchâtel overlapped with other similar networks, which the charters of Templar and other religious communities allow us to re-create. Almost every family that can be linked to a Templar community can serve as a starting point. For example, in May 1209 Count Milo IV of Bar-sur-Seine ratified the donation of land at Bissey-la-Côte made by his vassal Guy of Chappes. With the consent of his wife Helisent of Joigny and son Walter he made his own donation of possessions at Bissey-la-Côte and at Courban to the Templars a year later, followed by donations to the Templar community at Épailly in 1214 and a gift of 30 *livres*, to be drawn from the castle revenue of Bar-sur-Seine, to the grandmaster of the Order at the siege of Damietta in August 1219.[104] As we have seen, Helisent came from a family that supported, at different times, communities of three different military orders: the Order of the Temple, the Order of St John and the Teutonic Order.[105]

Guy of Chappes, lord of Jully, whose donation to the Templars Milo IV had ratified in 1209, was bound to the counts of Bar-sur-Seine by more than ties of vassalage. His wife Petronilla of Champlost, daughter of Thibaud of Bragelogne and Champlost and Margaret of Chacenay, was one of the nieces of Count Milo III of Bar-sur-Seine, which made Guy of Chappes the brother-in-law of Agnes, wife of Philip of Plancy.[106] It has been suggested that the lords of Chappes were related to the family of the founding master of the Order Hugh of Payns, either directly by marriage or when they married into the family of Vendeuvre, which, as Thierry Leroy believes, had tied itself to the family of the first Templar master when Laurent of Vendeuvre took Hugh of Payns's daughter Isabel as his wife. Apparently, Isabel and her first husband Guy Bordel of Payns had

[103] *CG*, no. 28, pp. 20–3 (for Hugh of Plancy see p. 22) (1129×1143); *OdM*, I, p. 202 (1155). William of Tyre states that Milo, who arrived in the Holy Land in 1160, came 'from Champagne, from the land of Count Henry of Troyes' (*de Campania ultramontana de terra Henrici comitis Trecensis*).

[104] ADCO, 111 H 1184 and 111 H 1187 (1210, 1214; see also *HdB*, III, no. 1121, p. 404, no. 1465 p. 484); BN, n.a.l., 53, fol. 86r (1219).

[105] Like his wife and son Walter, Milo IV of Bar-sur-Seine, too, supported the commandery of the Teutonic Order at St-Michel of Champs. *Chartes Beauvoir*, no. 10, p. 184 (1218), no. 26, pp. 194–5 (1225), no. 28, pp. 195–6 (1225).

[106] *HdB*, III, no. 1464, p. 484 (1209), no. 1465, p. 484 (1210), no. 1478, p. 404 (1214); BN, n.a.l., 53, fol. 86r (1219); AN S 5238, dossier 41, no. 5 (BN, n.a.l., 55, fols. 223r–4r) (1268). For marriage ties between the house of Chappes and the counts of Bar-sur-Seine see Longnon, *Les compagnons de Villehardouin*, pp. 50, 57.

once held fiefs from Clarembaud of Chappes and their son, also named Guy Bordel, joined the Temple. He was preceptor of Fontenotte in 1178 and of Bure from about 1185 at the latest until at least 1199.[107] As preceptor of Bure he presided over the burial of Odo of Grancey at Bure in 1197. Considering that his mother's second husband may have been Laurent of Vendeuvre, it is possible that Guy Bordel was acquainted with (and perhaps related to) his fellow Templar knight William of Vendeuvre (*Vendobre*), who was recorded at Tyre, in the Holy Land, in October 1187.[108]

Margaret, sister of Milo IV of Bar-sur-Seine, married Simon I of Rochefort, son of Simon of Bricon and Mathilda of Rochefort, and before 1250 Milo's own daughter Beatrix in turn married the eldest offspring of that union, her cousin Simon II of Rochefort. The counts of Bar-sur-Seine had thus become twice entangled with a family that boasted the Templar grandmaster William of Chartres (1210–19), a cousin of Simon I of Rochefort, among its relatives, and whose own history as patrons of the Templars, mainly through a sideline established by Wiard Morhier, lasted for over 160 years.[109] Through his grandmother Agnes of Baudement Milo IV of Bar-sur-Seine was also directly related to one of the key players in the ratification of the first Templar Rule at Troyes, Andrew of Baudement. He was therefore a blood relative of one of the earliest recorded Templars from Champagne, William of Baudement, who would have been one of Agnes's uncles. Even older was his family's relationship with the house of Chacenay, staunch supporters of Cîteaux and ardent crusaders with close family ties to the royal household of Jerusalem in the 1220s.[110] The Chacenays provide the basis for another Templar family network.

I have yet to find the evidence that would allow me to link any member of the old aristocratic family of Chacenay in Champagne to the Order of the Temple other than as relatively late and sporadic benefactors and business associates, but from the few charters that mention members of

[107] Leroy, *Hugues de Payns. Chevalier champenois*, pp. 97–114.

[108] *RRH*, I, no. 665, p. 177; *Documenti sulle relazioni delle città Toscane coll'Oriente Christiano e coi Turchi fino all'anno MDXXXI*, ed. G. Müller (Florence, 1879), no. 25, 30–1 (1187); V.-L. Bourrilly, 'Essai sur l'histoire politique de la commune de Marseille, des origines à la victoire de Charles d'Anjou (1264): Pièces justificatives', *Annales de la Faculté des Lettres d'Aix* (1921–2), 286 (1187).

[109] *CG*, no. 28, pp. 20–3 (1129×1143); Roger, 'Les Morhiers', 86, 94, 99 and no. 6, 108–9 (1175), no. 31, 126–7 (1289), no. 32, 127–9 (1301), no. 33, 129–30 (1301); *HdB*, II, no. 638, pp. 399–400 (1178); *HdB*, III, no. 1041, p. 382 (1201) and *Diocèse ancien de Châlons-sur-Marne*, I, no. 151, p. 436 (1306). For the relation with William of Chartres see Roger, 'Les Morhiers', 100fn.

[110] For the support of the lords of Chacenay of Molesme and the Cistercian houses of Larrivour, Mores, Longué and Clairvaux see *Les sires et barons de Chacenay*, ed. C. Lalore (Troyes, 1885), passim.

the family in connection with the Order it is obvious that one member in particular, Erard II of Chacenay, provided the Templars of the commandery of Épailly in 1218, and again in 1224, with important property when he sold them his wife Emeline's dowry in the village of Courban, much to Emeline's displeasure, as the property was originally intended to be inherited by her daughter from a previous marriage.[111] Also in 1218, and as part of his concentrated attempt to have his recent excommunication for opposing Blanche of Champagne revoked, his father's memory enhanced and himself prepared for crusade, Erard also made his first recorded donation to the Templars of Troyes.[112] Soon afterwards he left on the Fifth Crusade, only to be recorded again at the siege of Damietta, when he made donations to the Teutonic Order.[113]

As it turns out, Erard's engagement with the Templars may have been influenced by a marriage arrangement with the lords of Broyes and Châteauvillain.[114] Erard II's wife was Emeline of Broyes, whose previous husband Odo of Champlitte, a grandson of the Templar Count Hugh of Champagne, had died on the Fourth Crusade. Although she seems to have been genuinely upset by Erard's attempt to disinherit her daughter from her first marriage by selling her dowry to the Templars, her background suggests that she had also long been familiar with the Order. Some time between 1129 and his death in 1132 her grandfather had made a perpetual endowment to the Templars of 100 *sous* from his rents (*in censu suo*) collected at Sézanne, and in *c.* 1189×1190 her half-brother Godfrey of Joinville, who was preparing his departure to Jerusalem, began to engage

[111] ADCO 111 H 1184, no. 2 (1124). See now also J.-B. de Vaivre, *La commanderie d'Épailly et sa chapelle templière durant la période médiévale* (Paris, 2005), no. 12, pp. 169–70 (1224) and no. 13, p. 170 (1224).

[112] *Sires et barons de Chacenay*, no. 104, pp. 47–8 (1218). See also ibid., no. 142, pp. 65–6 (1232), no. 148, pp. 69–70 (1236); *Cart St-L*, no. 195, pp. 239–40 (1218); *Feud Soc*, no. 30, pp. 45–7 (1224); and Alanièce and Gilet, *Avaleur*, p. 63 for further transactions. In 1216 civil war had broken out between Blanche of Navarre, regent of Champagne since the death of her husband Count Thibaud III in 1201, on the one side, and Erard of Brienne on the other over the succession to the county of Champagne and Brie, which Blanche claimed for her son Thibaud IV and Erard for himself by merit of his marriage to Philippa, daughter of Count Henry II of Champagne. Most barons remained loyal to Blanche, who also enjoyed the support of the king of France and the Pope. Those who sided with Erard of Brienne, including Erard of Chacenay, were excommunicated as a result, and the rebellion soon collapsed. See Evergates, *Aristocracy*, pp. 39–42.

[113] *Chartes Beauvoir*, no. 14, pp. 185–6 (1219), and R. Röhricht, *Studien zur Geschichte des Fünften Kreuzzugs* (Innsbruck, 1891), p. 94.

[114] Simon of Broyes, the family's first donor to the Templars, held three castles in Champagne: Broyes, Châteauvillain and Beaufort. The first two went to his son Hugh, the third to his son Simon. As a result of Hugh of Broyes's second marriage to Elisabeth of Dreux, Châteauvillain was passed on to Elisabeth's son Simon (Emeline's brother), who adopted the toponym of that lordship. Under pressure from Count Thibaud III to become his liegeman, Simon severed his vassal ties with his half-brother Simon of Broyes-Commercy, making Châteauvillain an independent lordship. See Evergates, *Aristocracy*, pp. 180–1.

with the Templar commandery of Ruetz.[115] But the most significant connection of Emeline's family was with a hospital dedicated to the Virgin Mary at Mormant, which had been founded before 1121 at the instigation of Emeline's great-grandfather Hugh II 'Bardoul' of Broyes. Put under the ecclesiastical jurisdiction of the bishop of Langres, the hospital was initially administered by Augustinian canons but later transformed into an abbey. In 1302 it was given to the Templars in the hope that they would reform it.[116] The lords of Broyes and their cousins the lords of Châteauvillain remained attached to the community of Mormant, which they treated as a family foundation, and in 1270 Emeline's nephew John of Châteauvillain made donations to it to prepare for the annual commemoration of his mother Alix and sister Agnes, lady of Joigny.[117] Not surprisingly, it was at the Templar house of Mormant that John's son and namesake John of Châteauvillain joined the Order of the Temple in 1306 and where he was arrested a year later.[118]

Mathilda (or Mahaut Felicitas) of Donzy, mother of Erard II of Chacenay, came from a cadet branch of the counts of Chalon-sur-Saône. Of her four half-brothers one, William, was recorded making donations to the Templars of Villemoison while at the siege of Acre, while another, Harvey IV of Donzy, sometimes with and sometimes without his brother Raynald, leased them property and confirmed further donations made to them by his vassals Urs of Aulnay and Hugh or Arconid at around the same time at home in Burgundy.[119] In March 1216, a possible relative of Mathilde, Stephen, son of Haton of Donzy, and his wife Heremburga endowed the Templars of Sauce-sur-Yonne with their shares in the mills of Vincelles. The count of Joigny, their lord, and his wife confirmed the donation in the following month.[120]

The lords of Chacenay were connected in various ways to the other networks I have described above. Families into which Mathilda's ancestors married included the lords of Toucy, who produced an exceptionally high number of crusaders but who also, at least from the thirteenth century onwards, displayed an active (if not always benevolent) interest in the affairs of local Templar communities such as Villemoison and Sauce-sur-Yonne.[121]

[115] *CG*, no. 28, p. 21 (1129×1143); H.-F. Delaborde, *Jean de Joinville et les seigneurs de Joinville, suivi d'un catalogue de leurs actes* (Paris, 1894), no. 82, p. 260 (before 1190), no. 83, p. 260 (before 1190).

[116] Marie, *Templiers de Langres*, pp. 143–4.

[117] *HdB*, v, no. 3704, p. 307 (1270).

[118] *PT*, ii, p. 369.

[119] AN S 5242, dossier 75, no. 1 (1189), no. 2 (1190) and AN S 5244, dossier 5, no. 1 (*c.* 1190).

[120] AN S 5238, dossier 43, nos. 1 and 2 (1216×1217).

[121] AN S 5235, dossier 1, no. 1, fols. 1v (1233), 15v–16r (1231), 16r (1241); AN S 5237, dossier 33, nos. 5 (1233) and 6 (1242); AN S 5238, dossier 42, no. 4 (1226×1227); AN S 5237, dossier 33, no. 6 (1243) (BN, n.a.l., 54, fol. 160r); AN S 5235, dossier 1, no. 1, fol. 13r (1255) (BN, n.a.l., 54, fols.

The lords of Chacenay had other relations with Templar ties, including the lords of Grancey, who were deeply involved in the affairs of Templar Bure. From Grancey, ties can again be established to the lords of Tilchâtel, of Bricon (later lords of Villar Morhier), of Rougemont, whose members supported the Templar community of St-Marc in the mid thirteenth century, and of Ancy-le-Franc and Champlitte.[122]

The web of blood and marriage ties that can be spun around individual Templar donors, brothers and associates eventually included a large proportion of the Burgundian and Champenois aristocracy and covered many of the Order's major commanderies in those regions. Illustrating it in all its dimensions would be a fruitless task, considering the transient nature of these relations and the inevitable lacunae in our geneaologies. But already the closer examination of a single string helps demonstrate how tightly the web could be spun and what distances these relationships could cover. The string that tied together the seigniorial families of Tilchâtel and Noyers, for example, also connected members of the houses of Montbard, Chappes, Joigny, Brienne, St-Vérain and Arcis-sur-Aube – houses into which the lords of Noyers had married – to the Tilchâtel network, as well as the lords of Pierre-Perthuis, who were related to the lords of Noyers by blood.[123] All of these families had strong Templar ties.[124] Going further and concentrating on the relations of the counts of Joigny, the lords of Broyes and the lords of Mello (who were also related to the lords of Montbard and who helped found the commandery of Sauce-sur-Yonne) can also be added.[125] From the lords of Mello the string continues to Toucy, Frolois and via the house of Traînel to the

294–7); AN S 5238, dossier 41, nos. 2–5 (1268) (BN, n.a.l., 55, fols. 207r–8r, 209r–13r, 223r–4r, 225r); AN S 5242, dossier 75, no. 4 (1204) (BN, n.a.l., 55, fol. 500r). See also Demurger, 'La constitution d'un patrimoine foncier', 442.

[122] Isenburg *et al.*, *Stammtafeln*, XV/95, 96. For the lords of Rougemont as donors to St-Marc see BN, n.a.l., 55, fol. 584 (1246). For the Templar Hugh of Rougemont, who became the provincial master for Burgundy, see Léonard, *Introduction*, p. 155.

[123] Isenburg *et al.*, *Stammtafeln*, III/681; VII/14; XV/126; Hugh of Poitiers, *Chronique de l'abbaye de Vézelay*, p. 552; Bouchard, *Sword, miter, and cloister*, pp. 390–1; Richard, 'Milieu familial', 14.

[124] The counts of Brienne, for example, were necessarily involved in the affairs of Templar Bonlieu, which had been founded on their lands (AN S 4958, dossier 36, throughout), but the stronger allegiance was with the nearby Hospitaller commandery of L'Orient, where John of Brienne had founded a chapel in his memory (see the confirmation by his brother Hugh in 1270: AN S 4958, dossier 35, no. 7) and to which his ancestors had made landed endowments (see, e.g., AN S 4958, dossier 35, no. 1 for 1235).

[125] Dreux V of Mello was the husband of Helvis of Époisses, daughter of Andrew III of Montbard, lord of Époisses. See *HdB*, IV, p. 462. For relations with the Templars see *OdM*, I, p. 354 (1206); *Cart Pon*, no. 342, p. 344 (1216); AN S 5235, dossier 1, no. 1, fol. 1r (3x) and AN S 5237, dossier 32, no. 2 (BN, n.a.l., 54, fols. 91r, 92r and 95r; Lavirotte, 'Mémoire statistique', 272) (1216, 1223 n.st.); AN S 5236/B, dossier 19, no. 2 (BN, n.a.l., 55, fols. 301r–3r) (1276); AN S 5239, dossier 51, no. 3 (BN, n.a.l., 55, fols. 351r–3r) (1281); AN S 5240, dossier 57, no. 29 (BN, n.a.l., 55, fols. 400r–5r) (1292); AN S 5239, dossier 51, no. 4 (BN, n.a.l., 55, fols. 414r–17r) (1294).

viscounts of Polignac in Auvergne, who had assisted the Templars in establishing a commandery at Le Puy(-en-Velay).

Pons V of Polignac, lord of Montlaur, who in October 1223 married Alix of Traînel, was the eldest of three sons of the viscount-turned-Cistercian monk Pons IV of Polignac and his wife Alis of Montlaur. Both his parents came from families with strong ties to the Order. Pons's grandfather Pons III of Polignac had been one of the first noblemen to support the newly founded Templar community at Le Puy(-en-Velay),[126] which was soon also patronised by his mother's parental families of Montlaur and Posquières.[127] Two members of the powerful Posquières clan (which had its main possessions in Provence and was related by marriages to the Trencavels) seem to have joined the Order in the twelfth century and two in the thirteenth: Hugh of Posquières (*Hugo Poscherius*) and Raymond of Posquières (*Raimundus de Poscheriis*) were both recorded among the Templars (although neither specifically as a *frater*) in the witness list of a transaction issued for the Templar community of St-Gilles in June 1188;[128] from 1259 until 1289 another Raymond of Posquières was recorded as Templar preceptor in commanderies in the Tarn and Aveyron regions of Languedoc and, without reference to a particular office, as present in the company of the preceptor of Le Puy(-en-Velay) during a transaction in the archiepiscopal palace in Arles.[129] Another likely family member, a certain G. of Posquières, joined the Temple before the arrest of the Templars in 1307.[130]

For the Montlaur family it can be established that Heraclius of Montlaur, uncle of Pons V of Polignac, exchanged property with the Templars of Le Puy(-en-Velay) in 1236,[131] but it seems that his family had been more closely involved with the Templars than that, in spite of the

[126] *Cart Puy*, no. 1, pp. 1–2 (*c.* 1170). See also P. Vial, 'Les templiers en Velay aux XIIème et XIIIème siècles', in *Forez et Velay, questions d'histoire et de philologie, Actes du 98ème Congrès national des sociétés savantes, section d'archéologie (Saint-Étienne, 1973)* (Paris, 1975), 82–3.

[127] J. B. de Courcelles, *Histoire généalogique et héraldique des pairs de France, des grands dignitaires de la couronne, des principales familles nobles du royaume, et des maisons princières de l'Europe, précédée de la généalogie de la maison de France, vol. VIII: De Polignac* (Paris, 1827), pp. 10–12.

[128] Andrew is the only witness to be identified as *frater*. As the heading under which the names of Andrew, Raymond and Hugh are listed speaks of Templars in the plural (*templarii*), however, it seems safe to suggest that Hugh and Raymond, too, were in one way or another associated with the Order (and very likely had taken Templar vows). For the charter see *Chart St-Gilles*, no. 174, pp. 536–7 (1188).

[129] *HGL*, IV, p. 673 (1259); *Chart St-Gilles*, no. 478, pp. 670–1 (1263×1264); *GP(Toulouse)*, p. 562 (1264–80), p. 582 (1289); Barrau, *Ordres équestres*, p. 15 (1274).

[130] He was a member of the Order when it was disbanded, although it is not known whether he was arrested. What can be said is that by 1338 he and another former Templar (and likely relative), Raymond of Orange, had returned to Provence, where they were living in the commandery of Ruou, which had by then become Hospitaller. See P.-A. Sigal, 'Une seigneurie ecclésiastique en Provence orientale au moyen âge: La commanderie de Ruou', *Provence historique*, 15 (1965), 127.

[131] *Cart Puy*, no. 26, pp. 32–5 (1236).

important caveat that not all Templar brothers, benefactors and associates identified by the Montlaur toponym were necessarily related to one another. Peter of Montlaur, who had joined the Temple before 1147, may have been a relative of Heraclius and of Pons of Montlaur, who, with his wife, was recorded making donations to the Templar house of St-Gilles in 1162;[132] another relative was perhaps Hugh of Montlaur, who joined the Order after 1218, held the office of master of Provence from 1236 until 1238, and died during the battle of La Forbie in 1244 as marshal of the Order.[133] The Montlaurs of Le Puy(-en-Velay) were recorded as landlords in the dioceses of Le Puy, Mende, Viviers and Nîmes and, according to Augustin Chassaign's estimate, their lordship comprised up to 900 fiefs.[134] Another family by the name of Montlaur can be traced in the Aude region, where it held the castle of Montlaur almost half-way between Carcassonne and Narbonne.[135] Members of this second family were recorded in a prominent position among witnesses in important documents from Languedoc, which illustrates their high social standing. Pons of Montlaur, for example, witnessed the conflict settlement (*concordia*) between Bernard Aton of Béziers and Countess Philippa of Poitiers in 1114 and the marriage contract between Count Bernard IV of Melgueil and Willelma of Montpellier in 1120,[136] and he was present when Count Bernard IV of Melgueil gave himself as donat to the abbey of St-Théofrède in 1132.[137] Montlaurs also appear in Templar charters from Aveyron and Aude. A certain Peter of Montlaur professed into the Order in or before 1151,[138] a namesake of his testified transactions at Templar Douzens in June 1153 and December 1164,[139] and a Bernard of Montlaur (*Montelauro, Monlor*) was recorded as Templar preceptor in Aiguaviva in Aragon in 1249 and 1252, as preceptor of Mas Deu in Roussillon in 1258 and 1259, and as *comendator* of Castellote in 1260.[140]

[132] See *CG*, no. 425, p. 206 (1147), no. 462, p. 277 (1147), no. 585, pp. 359–60 (1150×1151) for Heraclius, and Boutiot, 'Les templiers', no. 21, 485 (1162) for Pons of Montlaur and Willelma.

[133] Burgtorf, *Central convent*, pp. 564–6. [134] *Cart Puy*, p. xxxii fn.

[135] The ties between the Montlaurs from Auvergne, to whom the Montlaurs from Aude may have been related, and the viscounts of Carcassonne would have been further strengthened by the marriage of Pons of Montlaur with Agnes of Posquières, who, as a descendant of Viscount Bernard Aton of Carcassonne, Razès and Béziers was related to the Trencavels. For the marriage of Rostaign of Posquières to Bernard Ato's daughter Ermessendis in 1121 see *HGL*, v, no. 475, cols. 894–6.

[136] Ibid., no. 451, col. 845 (1114), no. 472, cols. 886–8 (1120).

[137] Ibid., no. 520, col. 983 (1132).

[138] He seems to have been living in the Templar community of Millau. See *CG*, no. 585, pp. 359–60 (1150×1151).

[139] *Cart Douz*, A: no. 59, p. 66 (1164), no. 88, pp. 84–5 (1153).

[140] Forey, *Aragón*, p. 422; Léonard, *Introduction*, p. 90; Verdon, *La terre et les hommes*, p. 217; *Cart Cast*, no. 84, pp. 171–3, no. 85, p. 173, no. 90, pp. 178–9.

The network that by the end of the thirteenth century connected the lords of Tilchâtel in Burgundy with the Montlaurs of Le Puy(-en-Velay) (and perhaps Carcassonne) is impressive. Many of its members had, at one time or another, given to, joined or otherwise engaged with the Order. The more the web of interrelated families expanded chronologically and spacially, however, the less likely it was that members were aware of each other. For most families it was not easy to keep track of their own history and lineage; and it is therefore questionable whether they were always well informed about the relationships of the families into which they would marry.[141] This is not to say that knowledge about one's family was impossible to obtain; it was in fact vital that noblemen and women retain a general idea of who their cousins were and how they were related to them. This was necessary to avoid marriages within the forbidden degrees of kinship, although it is well known that knowledge of their relationship did not always prevent cousins from marrying each other.[142]

It has been argued that in some regions of Europe (Italy being the most notable exception) to impose a rule that prohibited people from intermarrying with relatives within four degrees of kinship, as a measure to force families to create new bonds of friendship, would have been a step too far, as in most families family-awareness did not even extend to third cousins.[143] Valid as it is, this statement should not be regarded as an absolute. It is well known that in England, for example, most people were hardly aware of their more distant relatives' whereabouts, but that some were able to trace their ancestry and relations a long way back when it came to asserting their claim over property.[144] Surviving medieval genealogies and family histories dating from the eleventh century onwards are also tangible proof that even families of low or modest stock sometimes had considerable knowledge about their ancestors and living relatives, although it still holds true that this knowledge seldom extended beyond the fourth degree of kinship or the fourth generation. In the second half of the twelfth century, for example, Lambert of Wattrelos, who came from a knightly family in Flanders, composed a short genealogy of his ancestors, in which he recalled no fewer than seventy-three relatives within four generations.[145]

[141] Bouchard, *Those of my blood*, pp. 32–5.

[142] On the forbidden degrees of marriage see Bouchard, *Those of my blood*, pp. 40–4.

[143] D. d'Avray, 'Lay kinship solidarity and papal law', in p. Stafford, J. L. Nelson and J. Martindale (eds.), *Law, laity and solidarities. Essays in honour of Susan Reynolds* (Manchester, 2001), 198.

[144] P. A. Brand, 'Family and inheritance, women and children', in C. Given-Wilson (ed.), *An illustrated history of late medieval England* (Manchester, 1996), 59.

[145] It is telling, however, if by no means unexpected, that Lambert's memory obviously grew hazier the further removed in time his relatives were from him: he remembered only thirty-five of his relations by name, of whom seventeen were of his parents' generation, seven of his grandparents' and one a

Even if the number of medieval families with an awareness of more than three generations of ancestors was higher than one would assume, awareness of one's ancestry did not necessarily prevent distant relatives from marrying if by doing so they could strengthen old social bonds or secure political influence. Networks with multilateral relations between members like the one that I have centred on the family of Tilchâtel only support the view that whereas marriages between close relatives may have been very rare in the central middle ages, those between more distant cousins were not uncommon.[146]

Within any medieval kin-group, identification with a famous ancestor (alleged or factual), collegiate commemoration of common relatives and association with religious institutions were important factors determining identity. But whereas holy men or crusaders could inspire descendants to create genealogies around them, Templar membership or association do not seem to have been eulogised. Sometimes they were quietly accepted as part of a kin-group's collective memory.[147] At other times, and in other families, however, Templar relatives were explicitly incorporated into the memorial fabric of tombs, buildings or objects. The tomb of Mary of Dreux at St-Yved of Braine, now lost, seems to have been an exceptionally illustrative example of (selective) family identity and consciousness put into stone. The Premonstratensian abbey of St-Yved had been the chosen burial place of the counts of Dreux ever since Robert, the fifth son of King Louis VI, and Agnes of Braine had married in 1152. And although none of the monuments has survived the vandalism of the French Revolution, detailed drawings of some of them from the end of the sixteenth century have allowed historians to study them carefully.[148] The drawings of the

fourth-generation relative. See Lambert of Wattrelos, *Annales Camaracenses*, ed. G. H. Pertz, *MGH SS*, XVI, 511–12. See also G. Duby, 'Structures de parenté et noblesse dans la France du nord aux XIe et XIIe siècles', in *La société chevaleresque. Hommes et structures du moyen âge (I)* (Paris, 1988), 145–57 and F. Vercauteren, 'Une parentèle dans la France du nord aux XIe et XIIe siècles', *Le moyen âge*, 69 (1963), 223–45.

[146] Bouchard, *Those of my blood*, p. 43. The Church's regulations on kinship marriage were in any case a product of 'instrumental rationality', understood by David d'Avray 'as the calculation of practical and logical consequences', rather than of 'value rationality', which draws its strength from world-views and conviction. See D. d'Avray, 'Lay kinship solidarity and papal law', in particular pp. 21–3, 193–4.

[147] Even within the Order the sort of hagiographical history that would have inspired the relatives of Templar brothers to celebrate the memory of their family members in the Order never seems to have been given much encouragement. See Licence, 'The Templars and the Hospitallers', 53; Demurger, *Les templiers*, p. 181.

[148] S. Prioux, *Monographie de l'ancienne abbaye royale de Saint-Yved de Braine, avec la description des tombes royales et seigneuriales renfermées dans cette église. 27 planches dont 12 sur acier, 6 en chromo-lithographie et 9 en lithographie tirées en bistre* (Paris, 1859). See also M. Bur, 'Une célébration sélective de la parentèle. Le tombeau de Marie de Dreux à Saint-Yved de Braine, XIIIe siècle', *Comptes-rendus de l'Académie des Inscriptions et Belles-lettres*, 135 (1991), 301–18. For the history of the drawings see H. Bouchot, *Inventaire des dessins exécutés pour Roger de Gaignières et conservés aux départements des*

tomb of Mary of Dreux († 1274), daughter of Archambaud of Bourbon (not to be confused with the lords of Bourbonne) and Beatrix of Montluçon, and widow of the crusader John, count of Dreux and Braine, have received particular attention for their depiction of a relief with thirty-six figurines adorning the base of the tomb and featuring the names of a selected number of close and distant relations of the princess. These include her father, mother and brother-in-law Thibaud IV of Champagne on the right of the head base of the tomb, and her brother Archambaud with his wife Yolanda of Châtillon on the left. Lined up along the base on the right side of the tomb were thirteen figures depicting her sister Margaret and her relations through Margaret's marriage with Thibaud IV, as well as her brother William. On the left side stood twelve figures of her brother's relatives through his marriage with Yolanda, including the counts and countesses of Nevers and king and queen of Sicily. Last in this line, facing east, was her husband John of Dreux, whose body was buried in Nicosia but whose heart rested at St-Yved. He was flanked, at the short end of the tomb, by his daughter-in-law Beatrix of Montfort, followed by his son Robert, daughter Yolanda, son-in-law John of Trie, count of Dammartin, and the Templar John of Dreux, son of Mary and John I, who disappears from the sources in the same year as his mother.[149] As Michel Bur has pointed out, the reliefs reflect a highly selective (and therefore highly political) accounting of Mary's family relations that puts clear emphasis on three distinctively illustrious pedigrees commencing with Mary's father, while ignoring older generations of relatives and collateral families, including even the counts of Flanders. Under-age children were ignored, only married couples were honoured with inclusion into this narrative, with only three celibate members of her family given an exemption: the princes Peter and William of Navarra, and the Templar John of Dreux, whose important role in the constructed family narrative was thus amplified.[150]

Where family members were buried did matter to relatives. Commemoration of the dead remained a serious concern and donations to the Templars were frequently made for that reason, which clearly indicates that the Order of the Temple was treated just like any other religious institution. The burial of the Templar Odo of Grancey at Bure, the commemoration of William and Isabel of Grancey at Bure, the burial of Stephen of Tilchâtel at Fontenotte, the burial and commemoration of William and Johanna Porcelet at St-Gilles – these were events that

estampes et des manuscrits, I (Paris, 1891), and E. A. R. Brown, *The Oxford collection of the drawings of Roger de Gaignières and the royal tombs of Saint-Denis*, Transactions of the American Philosophical Society, 78:5 (Philadelphia, Pa., 1988), in particular pp. 40–1.

149 Bur, 'Une célébration sélective de la parentèle', 306, 309.

150 Ibid., 309, 311.

guaranteed that until its dissolution the Order was given a place in the identities of noble and knightly families. And it seems that this aspect of their identity was something that Templar families responded to if they found it in others.

Under close scrutiny, however, it is clear that enthusiasm for the Temple among the members of networks varied greatly from one family to the next. Whereas some families produced Templar knights or lay associates of the Order, others apparently did not. Moreover, compared to the enthusiasm that they displayed for other religious institutions, the support of most of these families for the Temple was only marginal. This and the fact that Templar associates often married their offspring into families which would only eventually, and sometimes only sporadically, support the Order of the Temple (or another military order) suggests that the actual link with the Order may have been less important than the mindset of which it was an expression. What shaped this mindset was the experience of these families not only with the ideology of religious reformers, as discussed in Chapter 2, but also with crusading. An idea of how much the common link with the Holy Land in particular contributed to the creation of family networks in which support for the Temple could prosper can be gained from a closer examination of the crusading legacies in the families involved.

Chapter 5

CRUSADING AND ITS LEGACY IN TEMPLAR FAMILIES

With the capture of Jerusalem by the First Crusaders on 15 July 1099 a city had come into Christian hands that had always occupied the minds of European Christians as the place where Christ had suffered and the prophecies of the Old Testament would be fulfilled.[1] Pilgrims, who had been making the arduous journey from Europe to Jerusalem for centuries, now arrived in the Holy Land in greater numbers than ever.[2] They were joined by crusaders, who, following the call of churchmen and secular rulers to come to the military aid of the newly established Latin Kingdom, descended upon the Holy Land in the hope of spiritual rewards. The pilgrims and crusaders who returned from these journeys played an important role in keeping the public informed about the situation in the Holy Land and the crusading memory alive. Their experiences entered the popular domain by various means. Those who had money sometimes hired artists to decorate the hall of a castle or a church with scenes from Jerusalem or crusading episodes.[3] Some named new settlements after places they had visited. Such topological references to the Holy Land are particularly plentiful, for example, in the lands of the counts of Nevers, who were ardent crusaders. Here we find Bethlehem as a suburb of Clamécy. Other examples are Jérusalem, Jericho and Jordan as place

[1] See generally H. Möhring, *Der Weltkaiser der Endzeit: Entstehung, Wandel und Wirkung einer tausendjährigen Weissagung* (Stuttgart, 2000).

[2] Morris, *The sepulchre of Christ*, in particular pp. 200–5. On pilgrimages to the Holy Land in the aftermath of the First Crusade see B. Hamilton, 'The impact of Jerusalem on western Christendom', *CHR*, 80 (1994), in particular pp. 704–5. For pilgrims to Jerusalem from Burgundy in the eleventh century see in particular J. Richard, 'Départs de pèlerins et de croisés bourguignons au XIe siècle: à propos d'une charte de Cluny', *AB*, 60 (1988), 139–43.

[3] C. Morris, 'Picturing the crusades: the uses of visual propaganda, c. 1095–1250', in J. France and W. G. Zajac (eds.), *The crusades and their sources. Essays presented to Bernard Hamilton* (Aldershot, 1998), 199. See generally Morris, *The sepulchre of Christ*, pp. 219–53, and J. Sureda i Pons, 'Schönheit und Bedeutung von Bildern im Zeitalter der Kreuzzüge', in R. Cassanelli (ed.), *Die Zeit der Kreuzzüge. Geschichte und Kunst* (Stuttgart, 2000), 457–85.

names in the lordship of St-Vérain, which was held by another family with a strong crusading background and ties to the Templars.[4]

A considerable number of crusaders returned with relics with which they endowed local churches or monasteries.[5] Particularly sought after were objects associated with Christ's passion and first and foremost among them were pieces of the Holy Cross.[6] The Templars played a part in the transfer of relics from the East to Europe and thus in keeping the memory of Jerusalem and the holy places alive in the West, although this role is not well documented.[7] Count Guige of Nevers and Forez, who died on crusade in 1241, received a piece of the True Cross from the master of the Temple, which he passed on to his son.[8] In 1272 the Templars were involved in the transfer from the Holy Land to England of a piece of the True Cross, relics of Saints Philip, Helena, Stephen, Lawrence, Euphemia and Barbara, and of a fragment of the *mensa Domini*.[9] They also brought a vial of the Sacred Blood to England and another piece of the Holy Cross to Paris.[10] One particular Templar, known only as Artaud, carried sackfuls of relics to Clairvaux before he transferred into the Cistercian Order.[11] And the town of Trapani in Sicily ended up with a holy statue of the Virgin Mary, which the Templars had brought from one of their houses in Syria and which had originally been destined for Pisa.[12]

[4] P. Murat, 'La croisade en Nivernais: transfer de propriété et lutte d'influence', in *Le concile de Clermont de 1095 et l'appel à la croisade. Actes du colloque universitaire international de Clermont-Ferrand (23–25 juin 1995) organisé et publié avec le concours du conseil régional d'Auvergne* (Clermont-Ferrand, 1995), 295; A. Longnon, *Les noms de lieu de la France: leur origine, leur signification, leurs transformations* (Paris, 1920; reprint: 1973), pp. 375–6. In the lordship of Puisaye, between the Yonne and Loire rivers, new settlements from the time of the crusades included Jerusalem, Jericho, Nazareth and Bethphage. See M. Bloch, *Les caractères de l'histoire rurale française* (Paris, 1931), p. 11 and M. W. Beresford, *New towns of the middle ages: town plantation in England, Wales and Gascony* (2nd edn, Gloucester, 1988), p. 384fn.

[5] Riley-Smith, *First Crusaders*, pp. 150–2.

[6] Ibid. See also Purkis, *Crusading spirituality*, pp. 64–5; Rubin, *Mother of God*, pp. 169–76.

[7] The best study is still F. Tommasi, 'I templari e il culto delle reliquie', in G. Minnucci and F. Sardi (eds.), *I templari: mito e storia* (Siena, 1989), 191–210.

[8] *Titres de la maison ducale de Bourbon*, no. 221, pp. 46–7 (1241); *Chartes du Forez antérieures au XIVe siècle*, ed. G. Guichard *et al.*, 18 vols. (Mâcon, 1933–80), XI, p. 3.

[9] Bulst-Thiele, *Sacrae domus militiae*, no. 87, p. 254.

[10] See Matthew Paris, *Chronica majora*, IV, pp. 640–1 and, for Paris, the *Breviario Parisiensis* (1778), p. 359, as recorded in P. Riant (ed.), *Exuviae sacrae Constantinopolitanae*, 2 vols. (Geneva, 1878–9), II, p. 24.

[11] These relics, which were recorded in Clairvaux's inventory in 1504, included pieces of the True Cross, the head of St Barnabas, fragments of the heads of St Minas, St Cyprian the Martyr and St Mark the Evangelist, one arm each of St Thomas the Apostle and St Lawrence, the *scapulae* of Saints Blaise, Philemon and Theodore the Martyr, and relics of St John the Baptist. They may also have included relics of Saints Malachy, Stephen Protomartyr, Nicholas, Agatha the Virgin, George, Thaddaeus, and the mysterious Domister the Martyr (*Sancti Domistri martiris*), whom I was not able to identify. See Riant (ed.), *Exuviae sacrae Constantinopolitanae*, II, pp. 193–7.

[12] Tommasi, 'I templari e il culto delle reliquie', 202.

In particular the many pieces of the True Cross which the Templars imported into Europe served as mnemonic devices to canvass support for the land in which Christ had suffered and spilled his blood, and which was now again in peril of being lost to unbelievers. One monastery that benefited greatly from the generosity of pilgrims or crusaders was that of Cassan in Languedoc, which, besides a collection of other relics, was by October 1115 in possession of a piece of the True Cross.[13] Another piece of the Cross could be found in the abbey of St-Guilhem at Gellone. Here, and even before the First Crusade, a confraternity of the True Cross had been established in which the veneration of Christ and Jerusalem took centre stage and which attracted families that eventually also produced crusaders, Templar brothers and Templar benefactors, among them the lords of Pézenas and Montagnac.[14] Many more pieces of the Cross were locked away in Templar churches and commanderies, for example Peniscola in Catalonia, Corbins in Catalonia, and Grasse and Limaye in Provence.[15]

An increased traffic in relics, new developments in the fields of art, architecture and liturgy, as well as an increased general interest in pilgrimage and crusading ensured that Jerusalem was a place to which many lay men and women in Christian Europe could relate spiritually and personally. For those who had gained personal experience of the Holy Land, and of the strenuous journey to it, or who had pilgrims to Jerusalem and crusaders among their relatives, the proximity of the Templars to the holy places may well have been a tangible measure of their religious value; their dedication to Jerusalem, 'the City of God', was pointed out in the works of medieval chroniclers such as Anselm of Havelberg, Otto of Freising and Ernoul and his continuator.[16] As Tommasi has shown, the association of the Templars with Jerusalem is also echoed in the writings of ordinary scribes, who routinely adorned the Templars with epithets emphasising their link with the holy city and the Temple of Solomon, thereby

[13] *HGL*, v, no. 455, cols. 850–1 (1115).

[14] Pons of Pézenas, whose family eventually provided the Templar commandery of Pézenas with a number of knights and benefactors, entered the confraternity of Gellone some time between 1088 and 1117. Another member of the confraternity was the First Crusader Peter Bernard of Montagnac, whose relative William of Montagnac joined the Temple in the thirteenth century. See Duhamel-Amado, *Genèse*, I, p. 316 for Peter Bernard. For William, at Acre, see *Documents concernant les templiers extraits des archives de Malte*, ed. J. Delaville Le Roulx (Paris, 1882), no. 21, pp. 31–5 (1262), no. 23, p. 36 (1262) and *RRH*, I, no. 1318, p. 344 (1262).

[15] J. Rubió *et al.* (eds.), 'Inventaris inèdits de l'ordre del Temple a Catalunya', *Anuari*, I (1907), no. 4, 393–6; J. Miret y Sans, 'Inventaris de les cases del Temple de la corona d'Aragó en 1289', *Boletín de la real academia de buenas letras de Barcelona*, 42 (1911), 70; J.-A. Durbec, *Les templiers dans les Alpes-Maritimes. Notice historique sur les maisons et possessions du Temple dans les diocèses de Antibes-Grasse, Nice, Vence et Glandèves* (Nice, 1938), p. 263; Schottmüller, *Untergang*, II, p. 430.

[16] Anselm of Havelberg, *Dialogi*, col. 1156B; Otto of Freising, *Chronicon*, ed. R. Wilmans, *MGH SS*, XX, pp. 252–3; *Chronique d'Ernoul et de Bernard le trésorier*, ed. L. de Mas Latrie (Paris, 1871), pp. 7–8.

illustrating that in popular perception the Templars remained closely associated with the place of their origin and the location of their second headquarters.[17]

From the evidence cited by Tommasi and other historians it would seem that it was because of their association with Jerusalem and the Holy Land that the Templars gained much, if not most, of their support. This chapter will examine how the military concept of the Temple was communicated to the laity in the West and to what extent the experience of crusaders from Burgundy, Champagne and Languedoc determined support for the Temple in their homelands.

COMMUNICATING THE IDEAL: POPULAR PERCEPTION OF THE TEMPLE AS A CRUSADING INSTITUTION

As has been seen, news from the Latin East reached Europe in various ways, most commonly by letters or word of mouth. Returning pilgrims and crusaders played an important role in keeping the public informed about the situation in the Holy Land and the crusading memory alive. Monastic and other religious communities were generally also reliable transmitters of news from the East. They were recipients of letters and wills from crusaders who were in need of spiritual assistance. Some corresponded with the Templars personally,[18] and more than a few engaged with crusading ideology visually (and sometimes critically) in

[17] The charters can be very explicit in this respect. In 1132, for example, Bishop Elbert of Châlons-sur-Marne made his endowments to 'the knights of the Temple of the holy city of Jerusalem'. Other twelfth-century donations were addressed to 'the knights of Jerusalem who live in one spirit in the Temple of Solomon', to 'God the Lord and the Holy Sepulchre and to the knighthood of the Temple of Solomon', or to 'God and the holy knighthood of the Temple of Solomon in Jerusalem'. See *Diocèse ancien de Châlons-sur-Marne*, I, no. 1, pp. 394–5 (1132); *Cart Douz*, A: no. 40, pp. 50–1 (1133×1134), C: no. 4, p. 264 (1133×1134); BN, n.a.l., 18, fols. 440r–5r (1180). See also Tommasi, 'Pauperes commilitones Christi', 450–1. As Tommasi shows, 140 of the first 200 charters in the Albon cartulary were addressed to the 'knights of the Temple of Solomon', the 'knights of the Temple', the 'knights of the Temple in Jerusalem' or the 'knights of the Temple of Solomon in Jerusalem'. Only about twenty charters associated the Templars with Christ. See ibid., in particular pp. 452–3. Examination of other Templar cartularies provides similar results. Only one charter in the Templar cartulary of La Selve refers to Christ; 129 charters, on the other hand, mention Jerusalem. The cartulary of Vaour contains one charter with reference to Christ, one with reference to the Temple of Solomon and seventy-nine charters with reference to Jerusalem. The charters of Montsaunès contain no reference to Christ, but mention Jerusalem six times and the Temple of Solomon five times. And of the few Templar charters from Neuville in Champagne which Barthélemy has abstracted rather than transcribed into his collection of documents from the diocese of Châlons-sur-Marne, three mention Jerusalem, two the Temple of Solomon and one Christ.

[18] See e.g. the letters written by the master of the Temple to the bishop of Ely in 1220 and 1221, which are copied in Roger of Wendover, *Chronica, sive flores historiarum*, ed. H. O. Coxe, 5 vols. (London, 1841–4), IV, pp. 72, 79 and Matthew Paris, *Chronica majora*, III, pp. 64 and 68.

mural paintings and sculptural programmes.[19] Moreover, religious communities, who had a natural interest in the whereabouts and physical condition of local knights and nobles who had pledged or otherwise made available possessions to them in order to finance their journeys, were frequented by returning crusaders who came to redeem their pledges, show their gratitude or mourn their dead.[20] Occasionally, crusaders entered religious orders after their return from the East, thus carrying the stories of their crusading adventures into the monastery.

In short, many religious communities were well attuned to changes and developments in the Latin states overseas. They had far-reaching social networks at their disposal by which news and pleas from lay associates on crusade could be communicated. They had the means to communicate their version of events in writing or from the pulpit. And they had the ears of noblemen and women who had often already proved their eagerness to gain spiritual salvation by material means and through personal sacrifice. Religious communities were therefore particularly well equipped to promote the Templar cause at home. As is well known, no churchman was more beneficial to the Templar cause when the Order was in its infancy than the Cistercian abbot Bernard of Clairvaux, to whom I must now, again, return.

The influence of Bernard of Clairvaux

Some time before 1126, King Baldwin II of Jerusalem dispatched a letter to Bernard of Clairvaux urging him to use his influence to assist 'the brothers Templar whom the Lord has called forth to defend this province and whom He has miraculously kept from harm' in obtaining apostolic confirmation of their order and a rule of life. He justified his plea: 'The customs of the Templars are such that they do not recoil from the noise and turmoil of battle and are thus of much use to the Christian princes.'[21] By 1129 Bernard had delivered what the king had asked of him. At the council of Troyes the community of the Temple gained the approval of leading churchmen, among them the papal legate Matthew of Albano, and received a Rule that confirmed their role as fighters 'for the defence of

[19] See e.g. E. Lapina, 'The mural paintings of Berzé-la-Ville in the context of the First Crusade and the Reconquista', *JMH*, 31 (2005), 309–26.

[20] For monasteries as important financiers of crusaders see Riley-Smith, *First Crusaders*, pp. 109–29; S. D. Lloyd, 'The crusading movement, 1096–1274', in J. S. C. Riley-Smith (ed.), *The Oxford illustrated history of the crusades* (London, 1995), 56 and the examples provided in Murat, 'La croisade en Nivernais', passim.

[21] See p. 126 fn. 1 above.

the Holy Church'.[22] But Bernard went further in his assistance. Re-dating one of the Order's most important normative texts, Cerrini has argued that even before the council Bernard had succumbed to the pleas of the first master of the Temple, Hugh of Payns, and composed an exhortation on behalf of the Templars, known as *De laude novae militiae*, in which he celebrated their uniqueness and, with the use of Scripture, legitimised their vocation as the 'true knights of Christ' and the 'defenders of Christians'.[23]

Copies of *De laude* can today be traced in forty-one manuscripts from different religious libraries, which has prompted Cerrini to conclude that the treatise 'soon enjoyed a certain editorial success, especially in the most innovative monastic and canonical circles'.[24] This seems to be an understatement, as in fact Bernard's assessment of the Templars as defenders of the Christian faith had wide repercussions in secular and ecclesiastical circles. Echoes of it can be found in the *Dialogues* of Bishop Anselm of Havelberg, which, written in 1145, were addressed to Pope Eugenius III, and in Bishop Otto of Freising's *Chronicon*, also written in the 1140s.[25] In 1130×1131, during a chapter meeting in the cathedral of Noyon, at which were also present Bernard of Clairvaux and two other Cistercian abbots[26] who were familiar with the Templars, Bishop Simon of Noyon expressed his personal as well as his chapter's support for 'Hugh, master of the knighthood of the Temple, and [for] all who fight under him as religious', to whom he granted a share in the annual revenues of the prebends of each canon on his leaving the chapter. After all, it was the will of God the Father and his son Jesus Christ that the original order of the *defensores* should be restored where the Church had first blossomed, in the holy city of Jerusalem.[27]

Describing the Order of the Temple as a divine attempt to restore the role of armsbearers in the Church by linking them to Jerusalem provided the Templars with a powerful justification for their existence. In 1199 the

[22] The most erudite study to date of the rule's genesis is Cerrini, *Une expérience neuve*. See also A. J. Forey, 'The emergence of the military orders in the twelfth century', *Journal of Ecclesiastical History*, 36 (1985), 175–95, here p. 185.

[23] Cerrini, *La révolution des templiers*, pp. 94–9. D. R. Carlson, 'The practical theology of Saint Bernard and the date of the *De laude novae militiae*', in J. R. Sommerfeldt (ed.), *Erudition at God's service*, Studies in medieval Cistercian history, Cistercian Studies Series, 98 (1987), 143–5, has suggested autumn 1131 as the most likely date for the composition of the *De laude*.

[24] Cerrini, *La révolution des templiers*, p. 95.

[25] Anselm of Havelberg, *Dialogi*, col. 1156; Otto of Freising, *Chronicon*, pp. 252–3.

[26] The two abbots were Guy, abbot of Troisfontaines, who had participated in the council of Troyes, and Galeran of Baudement, abbot of Ourscamp, who was the brother of one of the first known Templars from Burgundy, William of Baudement.

[27] *CG*, no. 31, pp. 23–4 (1130×1131).

Templar preceptor of France, Andrew of Colours, took up a line of argument similar to that put forward by Simon of Noyon to defend the Order's position in a dispute between the Templars and the canons of Péronne over the prebends of the church of Péronne. He reasoned that his order should have access to the prebends since 'God the Father and Our Lord Jesus Christ, Son of the Lord of Lords, in compassion for His Church, by filling our hearts with the holy spirit, has deemed the ruined order [of armsbearers] worthy of restoration in the holy city where the Church had first blossomed'.[28]

Bernard's influence resounds loudly in these speeches. It can also be traced in the decision reached at the council at Reims in October 1131, where he was also present and where, as the archbishop of Reims informed the bishop of Thérouanne afterwards, it was agreed that every year during the three Rogation days and the five days thereafter the knights of the Temple in Jerusalem were to receive the oblations which were made to the chapel of Ypres at Obstal.[29] Outside the closed circle of prelates with direct access to Bernard and long after Bernard's death, his message was taken on and contemplated upon by knights, noblemen and bishops, who referred back to it when justifying acts of personal transfer into the Order – like Bishop Raynald of Chartres, who explained the entry into the Temple of the knight Giselbert of Crechis with the fact that Giselbert, 'because he thought little of the worldly knighthood and chose the gift of celestial knighthood, ... has turned himself into a knight of Christ. He has therefore become a knight of the Temple and a faithful companion of the Templars.'[30]

Papal and episcopal promotion

The definition of the Order of the Temple as a new and effective instrument by which 'Jerusalem could be cleansed of the infidels', as Bernard of Clairvaux had formulated it in his *De laude*, was also distributed by the papal curia and from there transmitted to the bishops. In his bull *Omne datum optimum* of 1139, Pope Innocent II addressed the Templars as the 'true Israelites' and the 'most disciplined fighters of the divine battle'. The Lord had appointed the Templars, who, in accordance with the Gospel, 'had no fear to lay down their lives for their brothers and to defend them against the pagans' and were the 'defenders of the Catholic Church' and 'attackers of the enemies of Christ'. It was

[28] *PTJ II*, no. 123, pp. 325–6 (1199).

[29] *CG*, no. 41, p. 31 (1131). For details on the council of Reims see Aubé, *Saint Bernard*, pp. 251–8.

[30] AN S 4999/A, dossier 6, no. 3 (1197×1198) (BN, n.a.l., 45, fols. 35r–6r).

their duty, in the name of God, to save the Holy Land from the tyranny of the pagans.[31]

In the preamble (*arenga*) of another bull Innocent praised the Order of the Temple as 'the venerable knighthood which has assembled for the honour of God and for the defence of the holy Church', whose members went to great lengths in their efforts to fight the enemies of Christendom and defend the faithful.[32] In 1144 Celestine II promoted the Templars to the archbishops, bishops, abbots and other prelates as

> the Knights of the Temple at Jerusalem, new Maccabees in this time of Grace, denying worldly desires and abandoning personal possessions, [who] have taken up Christ's cross and followed Him. It is through them that God has freed the eastern church from the filth of the pagans and defeated the enemies of the Christian faith. They do not fear to lay down their lives for their brothers and protect pilgrims from the attacks of the pagans as they go on their journeys to and from the holy places.[33]

His successor Eugenius III reminded a similar audience in 1151 that the Templars were needed 'for the defence of the eastern church and the repression of the wickedness of the pagans';[34] while three years later Anastasius IV ordered them to prevent alms being stolen from the Templars who defended the Church in the East against the enemies of Christ and who were coming to the aid of all those pilgrims who wanted to visit the holy places.[35] Alexander III, in a bull issued on 11 June 1170, reminded the faithful that the Templars were 'fighting against the enemies of Christendom',[36] while in another bull he emphasised once again their constant exposure to danger when 'defending Christendom against the pagans'.[37]

The terminology of defensive violence which Bernard of Clairvaux, the papacy (and perhaps the early Templars themselves) repeatedly employed to explain and promote the Order of the Temple was also picked up and further elaborated on by the bishops.[38] One participant of the council of Troyes, Bishop Elbert of Châlons-sur-Marne, in 1131 praised the 'knights of the Temple of the holy city of Jerusalem', who, 'having professed a knighthood of the most high and pacific king, furnish so great a relief and so much safety to the needy, pilgrims, poor and all

[31] *PTJ I*, no. 3, pp. 204–10 and *II*, pp. 96–103 (1139). A translation of the bull is provided in *TSS*, no. 7, pp. 59–64.

[32] *PTJ I*, no. 6, pp. 212–13 (1139×1143).

[33] Ibid., no. 8, pp. 214–15 (1144) and *TSS*, no. 8, pp. 64–5 for the translation.

[34] *PTJ I*, no. 15, pp. 221–2 (1151). [35] Ibid., no. 21, p. 225 (1154).

[36] Ibid., no. 59, p. 259 (1170). [37] Ibid., no. 77, p. 271 (1160×1176).

[38] Forey ('The emergence of the military orders', 185) confirms that the 'terminology of defence' of the Templar rule had 'many parallels in papal bulls and royal and princely charters'.

wishing to go to the Sepulchre of the Lord, [that] we do not believe it should be unrecognised in the charity of the faithful'.[39]

Bishop Ulger of Angers, striking a more belligerent note, promoted visiting Templars to the clergy in his bishopric some time between 1144 and 1149 as

> the ambassadors, officers and fellow knights of those who fight for Christ, in the very holy Temple of the Lord in Jerusalem. Their military service is certainly genuine and most pleasing to God, for they have abandoned the desires of the world, that is the joys of marriage and all manner of pleasures, renounced ownership of personal property, have professed an arduous monastic life to earn eternal happiness. They have chosen to fight against the enemies of God, who attack the Holy City of Jerusalem and other cities in the East, and do not hesitate to give their lives and shed their blood to destroy and drive out the impious gentiles from those most sacred places that the Lord chose for His nativity, passion and life.[40]

Bishop Ulger's promotion of the Templars, composed soon after the fall of Edessa and with preparations for another crusade either under way or already concluded, was intended to motivate the clergy of his bishopric to encourage lay support for a community to which the comital family of Anjou was already personally linked. The image of the Templars put forward by Ulger balanced their arduous way of life with their military motivation. Some inside knowledge obtained from Fulk of Anjou, who had associated himself with the Temple in Jerusalem in 1120, or from someone who had accompanied Fulk to the East may have been at work here.[41]

Popular awareness of the military role of the Temple

Only a few charters provide explicit evidence that the Order's donors were aware of the extraordinary logistical tasks and military nature of the religious community they were about to endow. One example is a charter which the Marquis d'Albon has dated to about 1125 but which may have been written some time later. It recalls the donation made by the knight Baldwin Brochet to the Templars, whose acquaintance he seems to have made during his time in the Holy Land, as either a pilgrim or a crusader. The wording of the charter suggests that the encounter had made a lasting

[39] *Diocèse ancien de Châlons-sur-Marne*, I, no. 1, pp. 394–5 (1132). The translation of this passage is provided in M. Barber, 'The social context of the Templars', *Transactions of the Royal Historical Society*, 5 (1984), 40. The parenthetical insertion is mine.

[40] *CG*, no. 21, pp. 15–16. The date 1144×1149 (as opposed to 1128×1149, given by Albon) is suggested in *TSS*, no. 31, p. 131.

[41] Orderic Vitalis, *Historia aecclesiastica*, VI, pp. 308–10.

impression on Baldwin and, as the following words from the donation charter indicate, also on others:

Those who frequently visit holy Jerusalem and the tomb of the Lord, travelling through hostile waters and difficult territories, guided by pious devotion, will knowingly testify to the great charity and the gift of praiseworthy honesty with which the knights of the Temple of Jerusalem seem to be overflowing. And that in order that pilgrims may more securely journey to the holy places, which have been consecrated by the presence of the incarnate Jesus Christ, our Lord, the said knights are ready to take them there and bring them back, those knights whose fame is glorious and has clearly spread throughout the countries and has become known to many and has inspired many to offer them beneficial donations in abundance.[42]

Another early example can be dated to about 1133, when Lauretta of Pignan made her donation to the Templars. She too was full of praise for the knights, those

soldiers from Jerusalem who live as one in the Temple of Solomon and who fight the Saracens eager to bring about the destruction of the law of God and His faithful servants, and who, following the words of the Gospel, battle daily and courageously, faithful and without deceit, against these most impious of people.[43]

At around the same time, on 1 April 1133, Roger of Béziers made endowments to the Templars who, he claimed, were fighting 'for the protection and defence of the holy city of Jerusalem and the God of holy Christendom'. Similar statements were made on both sides of the Pyrenees in, for example, 1134, 1146 and 1156.[44] By the end of the twelfth century knowledge of the Templars' role and deeds in the Holy Land had spread widely and penetrated deeply into western society, as is testified by their increasingly frequent appearance in chronicles, chansons and *gesta*.[45] Godfrey of Arcy-sur-Cure associated himself with the Order of the Temple some time before 1180, thereby 'devoting himself to the defence of the religion of Christ'.[46] In January 1190, at a time of heightened crusade frenzy (although the date in the manuscript is difficult to read), William Amel and his wife Cerdana gave land, a house (which the Templars had already erected), as well as further building rights and rights

[42] *CG*, no. 4, pp. 2–3 (*c.* 1125). [43] *Cart Douz*, A: no. 40, pp. 50–1 (1133).

[44] Ibid., no. 115, pp. 106–8 (1133); *CG*, no. 87, p. 66 (1134); *CTGard*, no. 1, pp. 408–9 (1146); *Col·lecció diplomàtica de la casa del Temple de Gardeny (1070–1200)*, ed. R. Sarobe i Huesca, XII (Barcelona, 1998), no. 69 (1156).

[45] See H. J. Nicholson, *Love, war, and the Grail* (Leiden, Boston, 2001), passim.

[46] AN S 5235, dossier 1, no. 1, fol. 4r–v (*c.* 1180). Godfrey's brother Gerard of Arcy-sur-Cure, abbot of Vézelay (1171–98), was a cousin of the bishop of Auxerre (1167–81), William of Toucy. See Bouchard, *Sword, miter, and cloister*, p. 431.

of way outside their castle of Montredon, near Carcassonne, to 'God Omnipotent, his mother Virgin Mary, the venerable knighthood of the Temple of Solomon and all brothers fighting for God'. This they did 'for the remission of our sins' and the 'redemption of our souls and the souls of all our forefathers and of all faithful dead', but also 'for the protection of Christianity' by the Templars, 'in Judaea and in all regions bordering the pagans and in all the world'.[47] When Raymond Sicredi associated himself with the Templars of Douzens as a donat and *confrater* in 1265, he gave orders that after his death his heirs should pay the Templars the sum of 20 *sous* to provide for weapons and other items that were needed for the defence of the Christian possessions in the Levant.[48]

These and similar accounts of transactions with the Temple are important in so far as they make allusion to some form of public acknowledgement in the West of the Templars' role as providers of military aid and security in the Holy Land.[49] As has been seen, churchmen in these parts of France, and notably in the county of Champagne (where aristocrats had been extremely responsive to all calls for crusades), were aware of the Templars' military functions and focus on Jerusalem.[50] It was not least due to the preaching of these prelates that the Templars' military message was communicated even to laymen who had no crusade experience of their own, at a time when the Temple had not yet established itself as a permanent feature of the religious landscape in the West or as a

[47] BN, n.a.l., 18, fols. 489r–93r (1190?). [48] Ibid., 19, fol. 200r (1265).

[49] In June 1233 Anseric of Toucy, lord of Bazarnes, made a donation to the Templars of Sauce, near Auxerre, for the remission of his sins and 'for the benefit of the Holy Land' (AN S 5237, dossier 33, no. 5; AN S 5235, dossier 1, no. 1, fol. 1v, copied in BN, n.a.l., 54, fol. 113r and *Inventaire Chastellux*, no. 56, p. 137). In March 1212 Peter Bertrand of Villeneuve made endowments to the Templars of Pézenas 'for the defence of the land of Jerusalem' (BN, n.a.l., 16, fols. 282r–3r). Thomas Strabo from Champagne gave to the church of La Trinité at Reims (which Archbishop Henry of Reims had given to the Templars in the 1160s) 18 *sous* in rent and 3 marks of gold for the assistance of the land of Jerusalem (for which he was commemorated in *ObReims*, 323; Archbishop Henry of Reims is commemorated ibid., 330). Henry of la Porte de Mars (whose parents seem to have been benefactors to the Temple, for they were buried in the cemetery of St-Nicholas of the Templar church of La Trinité in Reims) gave to the brothers of the commandery of Reims half of his house at the Porte de Mars, to be sold. The rents resulting from the proceedings of this sale were to be divided into quarters, one of which should be used to help the Holy Land (ibid., 326).

[50] The relentless commitment of the counts and aristocracy of Champagne to the cause of the crusades is illustrated in A.-É. Prévost, 'Les champenois aux croisades', *MSA Aube*, 85 (1921), 109–86; D. E. Queller *et al.*, 'The Fourth Crusade: the neglected majority', *Speculum*, 49 (1974), 441–65; Longnon, *Les compagnons de Villehardouin*; Y. Bellenger and D. Quéruel (eds.), *Les champenois et la croisade. Actes des quatrièmes journées rémoises 27–28 novembre 1987* (Paris, 1989); T. Evergates, 'The origin of the lords of Karytaina in the Frankish Morea', *Medieval Prosopography*, 15 (1994), 81–113; P. Lock, *The Franks in the Aegean 1204–1500* (New York, 1995); D. Quéruel (ed.), *Jean de Joinville. De la Champagne aux royaumes d'outre-mer* (Langres, 1998); M. Lower, *The Barons' Crusade: a call to arms and its consequences* (Philadelphia, Pa., 2005); C. Smith, *Crusading in the age of Joinville* (Aldershot, 2006).

permanent fighting force in the East. During these years this kind of ecclesiastical endorsement was vital to secure the survival of Templar communities in Europe. The patronage of bishops and other ecclesiastical dignitaries therefore played an important role in promoting the Templar cause in regions which were remote from any crusading theatre and among families which might hitherto have proved resistant to crusade enthusiasm.

In short, accounts like those of Godfrey of Arcy-sur-Cure and Raymond Sicredi indicate how many men and women in the West were aware of the functions of the Templars other than as religious and approved of them – an approval that is nowhere better demonstrated than by the fact that by 1225 a special crusader confraternity had already been established in the Templar church of Paris.[51] By the mid thirteenth century, however, the situation had become different. Now, after papal decrees had enabled the Templars to get involved in the preaching and preparation of crusades, even laymen with no crusading experience had ample reason to associate them with the continuing struggle for the Christian cause overseas.[52]

But the grass-roots support for the crusading cause and thus for a military order like the Temple was not only the result of ecclesiastical propaganda. It grew, perhaps primarily, from the personal experiences of returning pilgrims and crusaders and from the emotional relationship with the Holy Land which these men, and women, instilled in their families. Unfortunately, this process is not readily revealed by the sources. The scribes of Templar charters restricted themselves to producing short and often formulaic narratives which usually followed standard patterns of charter writing. They tell us little about a donor's underlying intentions, merely reflecting what the scribe considered to be necessary to determine the legal status of the transaction. In order to determine the influence of crusading on people's decisions to support, or associate with, the Order of the Temple it is therefore necessary to examine thoroughly the personal records and social backgrounds of individual Templar donors or associates. What will be apparent is that many knights and ecclesiastics who engaged with the Templars had either been personally involved in crusading or pilgrimage, or were closely related to someone who had. Having assessed the magnitude of their involvement, it will become obvious just how much the survival of the crusader states depended on the ties with the West which these Templar networks provided.

[51] Curzon, *La maison du Temple de Paris*, p. 67.

[52] For the argument that in the thirteenth century the Templars were involved in the collecting of crusading taxes see e.g. Powell, *Anatomy*, pp. 92–3.

THE CRUSADING CONTEXT OF TEMPLAR SUPPORT

Information on the crusading background of individuals provided in the Templar charters is often sparse; very rarely the addition *Jerosolimam profecturus* to a name indicates that a particular donation or transaction was made or conducted in preparation for a crusade or pilgrimage. It is only with the help of additional material – chronicles, necrologies, obituaries, letters, passenger lists and non-Templar charters – that the crusading legacies of particular Templar brothers, associates or benefactors and their close relatives come to light. From this material it can be concluded that three motives in particular – a concern for spiritual and material security, financial need, and the wish to fulfil their ambition to reach and fight in the Holy Land – compelled laymen to turn to the Templars before a crusading campaign. The sources also give insight into why crusaders supported, even joined, the Templars on campaign and why they started, took up or intensified their support for, or involvement in, the Order once they had safely returned.

Preparing for the Journey

In 1190 Robert of Milly from Champagne knew that he was going on crusade. With no children to call his own and concerned, as he was, about the spiritual wellbeing of his soul and of the souls of those whom he would leave behind, Robert was determined to put his earthly possessions to good use by making a donation to the Temple. Contemplating his death on crusade without children he arranged that his arable land at Trilbardou, 10 arpents of meadowland and one serf with his family should be given to the Templars of Moisy. In return, the Templars made Robert a *confrater* of the Order. They also promised to commemorate his mother at Moisy and to let his sister Amelia and brother-in-law Manasses participate in the Order's spiritual benefits.[53]

Robert's is not an isolated case. Like him a great number of prospective crusaders and pilgrims to Jerusalem (the charters rarely make a clear distinction between the two) made arrangements with the Templars before they set out on journeys from which many doubted they would ever return. For them, donating to the Templars or selling them rights and property was part of the preparation for going on a crusade or pilgrimage. Their motives varied, but two that would have been more powerful than many others were the desire to secure the spiritual and physical protection

[53] AN S 5009, dossier 40, no. 1 (1190).

of a military order while on crusade or a pilgrimage and the need to meet the financial demands of the journey.

Security

The arrangements made by crusaders to secure the spiritual and financial backing of religious houses that would set them on their journeys with bolstered spirits and a filled purse has been thoroughly researched.[54] So suffice to say that in this respect prospective crusaders treated Templar communities no differently. In December 1142, for example, Ralph William *de Trossito* made a donation to the Templars at Arles 'when he travelled to Jerusalem to visit the tomb of the Lord';[55] and eight months later Pons Chalveria, 'wishing to travel to Jerusalem to visit the tomb of the Lord', made donations to the commandery of Roaix so that 'God Omnipotent may forgive me all my sins and let me return to my possessions happily'.[56]

These arrangements intensified after the fall of Edessa, when, enticed by the preaching for another crusade, knights flocked to Templar houses to express their eagerness to support them. Among them were Hugh IV of Beaumont, from Burgundy, and his son Hugh V, who made endowments to the Templars at La Romagne in 1144,[57] not long before Hugh V and his uncle Josbert of La Ferté, viscount of Dijon, went on the Second Crusade.[58] In November 1146, with preparations for the Second Crusade well under way, the southern French nobleman Pons of Meynes, whose family held lordships in the county of Tripoli became a brother of the Temple by offering himself 'to God Omnipotent and the knighthood of the Temple of Solomon in Jerusalem, promising to serve and to fight for God under the obedience of the master for the rest of the days of my life'.[59] In the same year, the Provençal knight Bertrand of Bourbouton joined the recently founded Templar community at Richerenches, offering his body and soul 'to the service and defence of the Christian faith in the society of the *confratres* of the Temple of Solomon, so that God and our Lord Jesus Christ may grant me and my kin indulgence for our sins and

[54] See e.g. Bull, *Knightly piety* and Riley-Smith, *First Crusaders*.

[55] *CG*, no. 281, pp. 183–6 (1142).

[56] Ibid., no. 307, p. 200 and *Cart Rich*, App. I, no. 6, p. 233 (1143).

[57] *HdB*, II, no. 284, pp. 233–5 (1144).

[58] *Feud Soc*, no. 86, p. 109 (1146). For Hugh V of Beaumont on crusade see *Chronique de l'abbaye de Saint-Bénigne de Dijon, suivie de la chronique de Saint-Pierre de Bèze*, ed. É. Bougard and J. Garnier (Dijon, 1875), pp. 492–3. But see also *HdB*, II, p. 95, where it is maintained that Hugh IV and not Hugh V went on crusade.

[59] *CG*, no. 411, pp. 258–9 (1146). Pons of Meynes was lord of Nefin in the county of Tripoli. See *RRH*, I, no. 78, p. 18, and J. Richard, 'Les Saint-Gilles et le comté de Tripoli', in *Islam et chrétiens du Midi (XIIe-XIVe siècles)*, CdF, XVIII (Toulouse, 1983), 73.

offences, and make us coheirs of the heavenly fatherland'.[60] On 19 August 1147 Roger of Béziers, who was on his way to Jerusalem, met with the Templars in the port of Tourette, near Agde, to confirm his donation of the village of Campagne and other possessions.[61] Perhaps at around the same time, Virgil of Vézin, a knight from Rouergue, gave to the Templars his manse of Frontinet and the rights in Azinières when he wanted to go to Jerusalem (*quant volo anar in Iherusalem*) [sic].[62] In September 1148 the brothers Raymond, William and Gerald of La Baume made donations to Richerenches to prepare for Raymond and William's journey to Jerusalem, for which they hoped to be rewarded with an indulgence for all their sins.[63]

Subsequent crusades gave rise to similar waves of enthusiasm. Raymond Isarn of Cabriac gave himself and his son Raymond to Templar Douzens in June 1188, when news of the loss of Jerusalem had reached Europe and crusade preachers were again starting to attract large crowds.[64] Hagan of Ervy, from Champagne, made donations before he went on the Third Crusade in around 1190,[65] as did Guy II of Tilchâtel in 1216 when he must have already been toying with the idea of taking part in what would become the Fifth Crusade.[66] William II of Joigny's endowment to the Templars coincided with his signing up for the Barons' Crusade in 1235 and he made further donations and founded the chapel of the Templar commandery of Saulce in 1238, the year before he actually set out on crusade with the duke of Burgundy.[67]

Support for the Templars in anticipation of a long journey or military campaign was of course not restricted to periods of intense crusade preaching such as the years preceding the Second, Third or Fifth Crusades. For many crusaders and pilgrims to the Holy Land the idea of gaining and confirming the support of a powerful ally with possessions and

[60] *Cart Rich*, no. 59, pp. 59–60 (1146); Selwood, *Knights of the cloister*, pp. 134–5.

[61] *Cart Douz*, D: no. 4, pp. 275–7 (1147) (the day was a Tuesday and not, as the charter has it, a Monday).

[62] *CG*, no. 537, pp. 330–1 (*c.* 1148). See also *PAC*, 1, no. 85, pp. 84–5 (which gives *c.* 1160 as the approximate date of the transaction).

[63] *Cart Rich*, no. 43, pp. 45–6 (1148).

[64] Having agreed to the transfer of her husband and son into the Order, Raymond Isarn's wife decided to join the monastery. See BN, n.a.l., 18, fols. 486r–8r (1188).

[65] *Feud Soc*, no. 51, p. 69 (*c.* 1190).

[66] Faget de Casteljau, 'Les sires de Til-Châtel', 144 (1981), 37.

[67] AN S 5237, dossier 30, no. 5 (1238). See also AN S 5237, dossier 32, no. 5; AN S 5235, dossier 1, no. 1, fol. 1v (BN, n.a.l., 54, p. 135) (1238) and *Inventaire Chastellux*, no. 57, pp. 137–8 (1235), no. 60, p. 138. For William on crusade see 'The Rothelin continuation of William of Tyre', in J. Shirley (ed.), *Crusader Syria in the thirteenth century* (Aldershot, 1999), ch. 20, p. 38 and Lower, *Barons' Crusade*, p. 43. He died in Palestine in 1255. See Quantin, 'Les croisés de la Basse-Bourgogne', 311, 313.

influence in the crusader states and along the major travelling routes would simply have made good sense. Raymond of Cassagne, who made donations to the Templars 'when he went across the sea' (*quant anet oltra mar*), Raymond Ato of Aspet, who 'was planning to go to Jerusalem', William of Pons and his wife Stephanie, who gave landed property to Templar Gardeny before setting out for Jerusalem, and Peter of Cadenet and Bartholomew, son of Tecelina of Chevillon, who embarked on their respective journeys to the Holy Land, also seem to have been occupied with crusade or pilgrimage arrangements and would have regarded their involvement with the Temple as part of their preparations.[68]

Not every transaction which noblemen conducted with the Templars before they went on crusade or pilgrimage was a donation, of course. On the day of his departure to Jerusalem William Gerald of Visan, from Provence, summoned his mother, brothers, cousins, nephews and friends to the Templar commandery of Richerenches where he had them confirm and consent on the Gospels to every donation that his parents or brothers had ever made to the Templars of this house. This was considered a precautionary measure 'so that the peace may remain forever firm'.[69] On other occasions, prospective crusaders or pilgrims approached the Templars with business proposals to finance their journeys or to ensure that their lands would not fall into disarray during their absence – precautions that are replicated in countless charters from other religious houses.

Financial demands of the journey

Financial concerns were another powerful driving force behind arrangements between prospective crusaders and the Templars. The charters recording the involvement of prospective crusaders or pilgrims with the Temple include numerous references to sales, leases and pledges, which is of little surprise as crusading in particular was an extremely costly undertaking that required great amounts of liquid cash.[70] The crusaders and their families seem to have raised most of this money by selling or pledging parts of their possessions to religious communities including houses of the military orders. In June 1160 Pons Lautier of Colonzelle pledged land to

[68] *PAC*, I, no. 75, pp. 75–6 (1155), no. 97, p. 94 (*c.* 1160); Durbec, *Templiers et hospitaliers*, p. 100 (1185); *Col·lecció diplomàtica Gardeny*, no. 69 (1156); BN, n.a.l., 51, fols. 235r–6r (1200).

[69] *Cart Rich*, no. 84, pp. 84–5 (1159).

[70] See generally G. Constable, 'The financing of the crusades in the twelfth century', in B. Z. Kedar, H. E. Mayer and R. C. Smail (eds.), *Outremer: studies in the history of the crusading kingdom of Jerusalem presented to Joshua Prawer* (Jerusalem, 1982), 64–88, and J. S. C. Riley-Smith, 'Early crusaders to the east and the costs of crusading, 1095–1130', in M. Goodich, S. Menache and S. Schein (eds.), *Cross cultural convergences in the crusading period. Essays presented to Aryeh Grabois on his sixty-fifth birthday* (New York, 1995), 237–57.

the Templars of Richerenches, which they were to have and to hold while he was in the Holy Land. If he should fail to return after fifteen years, he agreed that the land should come into the permanent possession of the Templars to compensate them for their help in preparing his journey to Jerusalem.[71] The nobleman Godfrey of St-Vérain, from the diocese of Auxerre in Burgundy, vifgaged the so-called 'bishop's mills' to the Templars for an annual rent of three measures of oats and one measure of grain before he went on the Third Crusade.[72] Similarily, before he went on the Third Crusade, as we know from a charter which he issued at Acre in 1191, Guy of Vergy granted the Templars of Autrey the right to hold and use his lands, woods and pastures for three years, by which time he expected to have returned from Jerusalem.[73] Another nobleman with ambitions to reach Jerusalem, Stephen of Bussières, pledged his possessions to the Templars of Avaleur in Champagne and the Cistercians of Mores in Champagne in 1196 to finance his journey.[74] Presumably guided by similar motives, Milo IV (or V) of Noyers sold possessions to the Templars in June 1238 shortly before his departure on crusade.[75]

These transactions, with which crusaders financed their journeys, were not always conducted prior to departure. For a variety of reasons the liquid assets which knights and nobles brought with them on crusade were often exhausted before the campaign had ended. In particular, sieges, which were usually accompanied by inflation in prices of victuals, caused the monetary assets of crusaders to dry up rapidly. It was on these occasions that the Templars and their banking network, which enabled them to conduct business transactions over long distances, proved particularly useful. As is revealed in numerous charters from France, and as will be discussed in greater detail below, the Templars of Champagne and Burgundy benefited greatly from the benevolence and the financial needs of their countrymen at the siege of Acre during the Third Crusade.

Once they had established credit with a Templar house at home, crusaders and pilgrims could approach other Templar dependencies on

[71] *Cart Rich*, no. 163, pp. 145–6 (1160) and *TSS*, no. 28, pp. 126–7 for the translation. See also M. Barber, 'Supplying the crusader states: the role of the Templars', in B. Z. Kedar (ed.), *The Horns of Hattin* (Jerusalem, 1992), 320.

[72] AN S 5243, dossier 80, no. 1 (1190).

[73] ADCO, 115 H 1234, dossier 19, Autrey, no. 1 (1191) (BN, n.a.l., 53, fols. 255rv; *HdB*, III, no. 867, pp. 314–15). See also Richard, 'Les templiers et les hospitaliers', 235 and Marie, *Templiers de Langres*, p. 43.

[74] After his death in around 1200, the monks of Mores and the Templars of Avaleur disregarded the seigneurial rights of his son Thomas and divided among themselves the high, middle and low justice of Bussières, as well as the revenues of the lordship. Alanièce and Gilet, *Avaleur*, p. 58.

[75] ADCO, 111 H 1184, Courban, no. 7 (as listed in Marie, *Templiers de Langres*, App. V, p. 162).

the way for money. The Burgundian nobleman John of Nuilly vifgaged property to a local Templar commandery before he left his home to go overseas (probably to fight in the Fifth Crusade) but he did not take with him the money which he had borrowed, 50 *livres* in the currency of Provins. Instead, he made arrangements with the Templars that the money would wait for him at Marseille, from where he planned to continue his journey by sea. Upon his arrival at Marseille John, for unknown reasons, decided not to board ship after all. But he still approached the local Templars for the money in question, which he duly received. It was at Marseille that he sealed the charter in which the context of his arrangements with the Order was recorded. As the charter itself has survived in one of the charter collections from Burgundy, however (at least this is where Albon collected it), it is likely that some time after the events recorded in them the charters documenting John's transactions with the Order, or copies thereof, were transferred back to the place where the initial arrangements for the loan had been made.[76]

Another way of using the Templars to help satisfy a personal crusading desire (or obligation) was to provide them with the financial and material means to support a substitute if the person embarking on the journey were unable to complete it. A dying knight from Morvan, Odo of Roussillon, attempted to arrange for just that when he asked one of his peers to complete his journey to the Holy Land, for which he gave him 100 pounds and a knight's armour. Should the other knight fail to board ship in the next general passage (Latin *passagium generale*, which describes a crusade in the ordinary sense), however, it was arranged that the money and equipment would go to the Templars, whose task it then was to equip another knight for fighting in the service of God in the donor's stead.[77] Others, like William Raymond of Montcada, viscount of Béarn, had failed to live up to their crusading promises and thus supported the Temple *in recompensationem peregrinationis* by providing it with the material means to muster a contingent of men-at-arms on their behalf (which in William Raymond's case would have amounted to payment for 200 knights and 30 footsoldiers and archers).[78]

Not all of these arrangements were conducted between the Templars and prospective pilgrims to Jerusalem or crusaders to the Levant, of course,

[76] BN, n.a.l., 53, fol. 84r (1218).

[77] J.-G. Bulliot, *Essai historique sur l'Abbaye de Saint-Martin d'Autun de l'Ordre de Saint-Benoît* (Autun, 1849), pp. 263–4; J.-F. Baudiau, *Le Morvand, ou essai géographique, topographique et historique sur cette contrée*, 2 vols. (Nevers, 1854), II, pp. 335–6.

[78] *GP(Toulouse)*, no. 58, at p. xxxviii (1223). To aid his reconciliation with the church and to end his excommunication, William Raymond had in 1215 agreed to go on crusade for five years taking with him 200 knights, thirty footsoldiers and archers. See Shideler, *A medieval Catalan noble family*, p. 140.

although it seems that crusaders to the Holy Land constituted the majority of Templar benefactors with travelling ambitions. Other donors went to Iberia, either on pilgrimage or to take part in the reconquest of the peninsula, and some set out on other military campaigns.[79] Duke Odo III of Burgundy made substantial endowments to the Templars the year before he embarked on the Albigensian crusade in 1209. Most importantly, he donated to them the lordship over the castle of Île-d'Ouche and the village of Crimolois 'for the defence of the catholic faith', a comment that betrays his belief that the Albigensian crusaders and the Templars were ultimately serving a common cause.[80] The knight Bernard of Turre is another example. In August 1229 he became a *confrater* of the Temple and gave his body, horse, and iron and wooden weapons to the commandery of Mas Deu in Roussillon before leaving for Majorca in the crusading army of James of Aragon.[81]

Desire for the Holy Land

The prospect of fighting overseas, as well as the prospect of being able to use the Templar network and infrastructure, which undoubtedly made it easier for men with crusading ambitions to reach their destinations, drew a constant stream of fighters into the Order, of whom some, those who professed, stayed permanently, while others remained for a limited period of time, as we have seen.[82] Some may have felt pressured by relatives to join the Order to go on crusade. A Templar knight from Hautmesnil (*G. de Alto Maynillo*), for example, confessed in his deposition that he had not dared to leave the Order for fear of his parents, 'who were convinced that the Order was holy and good, and who had made great financial sacrifices to equip him for the journey across the sea' (*fecerant magnas expensas pro parando ipsum ad eundum ultra mare*), and that, if things had been different, he would have declined to go overseas since his heart was not in it.[83]

But others made no secret of their ambition to go fighting in the Holy Land and of their support for those who associated with the Order for the same reason. A rich landowner from Provence by the name of Jauma Baston, for example, approached the Templars with the request,

[79] When William Stephen wanted to go to Spain (*volens ire in Hispaniam*), for example, he drew up his testament in which he made donations to a number of religious communities, among them the Temple (*Cart An*, no. 138, pp. 280–1, n.d.). In September 1157 Herman of Bordels granted the Templars of Richerenches pasture rights in all his lands before he set out on (or continued) his pilgrimage to Compostela (*Cart Rich*, no. 92, p. 93).

[80] *HdB*, III, no. 1168, p. 416 (1208). Another donation made by the duke to the Templars in the same year is recorded in ibid., no. 1169, p. 416 (1208).

[81] Doat, 40, fols. 232–5 (1229). [82] See above, pp. 70ff. [83] *PT*, II, p. 360.

accompanied by a generous donation, that they should make her bailiff Helisard a knight, equip him with a horse, weapons and the appropriate knightly apparel (*apparatus*), and lead him overseas (*ultra mare*); they should also accept him as a *frater* should he wish to join the Temple.[84] It is not known whether Helisard ever became a Templar, but the charter recording Jauma's request shows clearly that she approached the Order in its function as a crusader institution with sufficient means and manpower to enable prospective crusaders like her bailiff to reach their desired destinations.

That knights and noblemen joined the Order of the Temple or otherwise engaged with it can, therefore, also be explained as a consequence of their attitude towards crusading, as well as of the longing which many of them displayed for Jerusalem. We will remember the case of Godfrey of Arcy-sur-Cure, who associated himself with the Temple in around 1180, expecting that by doing so he would participate in the spiritual benefit of those 'who battle for Christ' and secure for himself the spiritual advocacy of powerful intercessors in the afterlife.[85] Other sources reveal that Godfrey was busy preparing his journey to Jerusalem at that time; and it seems plausible that the two events – his association with the Temple and his departure to the East – were linked and that both resulted from the belief that crusading and association with a military order were complementary actions.[86]

His is not a solitary example. The biographies of other knights show similar connections between Templar association and crusading. By 1133 Payen of Bure had already joined the Order and given it his possession at Bure to support 'the *expeditio* of the Temple of the Lord and of the knights who fight in it', which suggests that he too was busying himself with crusading plans when he joined the Order.[87] Pons of Meynes, from Provence, joined the Order of the Temple in 1146, and thus at a time of intense crusade preparations in Europe, promising 'to serve and soldier for God under the command of the master of the Temple for the rest of [his] life'.[88] The knight Stephen Raynald from Languedoc was at least toying with the idea of joining the Temple when he made preparations to visit the Holy Sepulchre at an unknown date; before he left he made arrangements in case he should die on the journey or 'remain a brother of the house of the knighthood of the Temple'. The Templars would receive

[84] *Act Porc*, no. 312. [85] See above, pp. 71–2, 76–8, 212–14.

[86] For Godfrey preparing a crusade or pilgrimage to Jerusalem see *HdB*, IV, no. 2958, p. 467 (1180); *CG(Yonne)*, II, no. 293, p. 312 (*c.* 1180), no. 304, pp. 324–5 (1180). See also Murat, 'La croisade en Nivernais', 295, who comments in similar terms on the relationship between the counts of Nevers and the Teutonic knights and Hospitallers.

[87] ADCO, 111 H 1156, no. 2 (1133) (see also *HdB*, II, no. 255, pp. 218–19).

[88] See e.g. *CTGard*, no. 1, pp. 408–9 (1146).

all his allods, 'wherever they are', which they were to possess 'as long as I am a brother of this house of the knighthood of the Temple and when I will have been made a brother of this house'. This formulation indicates that he intended to associate himself with the Order as a *miles ad terminum*, and thus as a temporary brother, initially, with the option of full profession at a later date. Should he decide not to remain in the Order he arranged for the allods in question to be re-transferred into his possession.[89] Stephen Raynald seems to have associated himself with the Templars with the prospect of combining his pilgrimage to Jerusalem with a more active role in defending the cause of Christendom overseas. Another nobleman who, at a later date, joined the Order with the explicit wish to partake in the military fight for the Christian cause overseas was William of Chartres. In 1192×1193 his brother Robert (himself no stranger to the Templars) recalled of him that he had joined the Order 'when he wanted to fight overseas for the highest creator'.[90]

That these sentiments were still relevant in the late thirteenth century can be concluded from the Templar knight Adhemar of Sparres's confession after his arrest in 1307 that he had entered the Order out of a desire to come to the aid of the Holy Land.[91]

On crusade

Entering a religious order was a serious commitment to a new way of life in every circumstance. Entering a military order in the East during a fully-fledged crusade, and thus in the face of the unembellished reality of the full scope and nature of the Templar vocation, however, also indicates, on the one hand, a real personal commitment to the crusading cause, and on the other how deeply the perils they had overcome had affected some crusaders. Even though the bulk of the documentary evidence of the Templars' endowments and possessions in the Latin East – the material collected in the central archive of the Order in Jerusalem and later in Acre – has been lost, and with it the traces of many westerners who had associated themselves with, or had given to, the Templars in the face of crusading reality, a few of the remaining charters allow us to reconstruct some of the scenarios in which noblemen associated with the Order in the East.

[89] See above, p. 73.

[90] See Bulst-Thiele, *Sacrae domus militiae*, pp. 162–3fn. In *c.* 1198 Robert of Chartres was recorded as arbitrator in a dispute concerning the Templars' possessions in the villa of 'Rosetum'. See AN S 4999/A, dossier 6, no. 4 (1197×1198) (BN, n.a.l., 45, fols. 40r–1r).

[91] Schottmüller, *Untergang*, II, p. 31.

Joining the Templars in the East

In 1148 Humbert III of Beaujeu joined the Order in Palestine. He had arrived there as a participant in the Second Crusade after a frightful encounter with the ghost of one of his vassals, who had died unabsolved in Humbert's 'godforsaken' (as the Cluniac abbot Peter the Venerable described it) war against Amadeus of Savoy and now suffered in purgatory for his sins. Here, as the ghost informed Humbert, he had encountered Humbert's father, who was also in dire need of prayers and deeds of charity. Disturbed by this news, Humbert had instigated charitable acts and, concerned about his own sinful past, so Peter the Venerable would have us believe, had decided to go to Jerusalem.[92] Humbert was a Templar only for a short while (he withdrew from the Order on his way home). Yet his may be seen as an example of the mindset of many pilgrims when faced with the opportunity of attaching themselves to Jerusalem by joining a religious community whose purpose was to safeguard the very places they so dearly longed to visit and whose military activity was pleasing to God.

Unlike most of their brothers in western commanderies (with the exception of the Iberian peninsula), the Templars in the East spent much of their time engaged in military missions, on patrol duty or on the march. Their primary task was the protection of pilgrim routes, which made them particularly attractive to veteran pilgrims like Count Hugh of Troyes, who, having already been to the Holy Land from 1104 until 1108, again went on pilgrimage to Jerusalem in 1114 and became a brother of the Temple in Jerusalem in 1125.[93] News of the Templars' existence had not yet spread very far by 1125 and it is therefore likely that Count Hugh had made up his mind to join the Order only after encountering it in the Holy Land. Things were different after Hugh of Payns had begun promoting his fraternity and a new crusade on his tour through northern France in the months leading up to the council of Troyes. Soon knights and nobles made plans to join the Order once they were in the Holy Land and evidence exists that some had even journeyed to Jerusalem to precisely that end, thus turning the whole process of profession into a pilgrimage-like experience.

Guy Cornelly of Tilchâtel, whom we have already encountered, was one of these. In *c.* 1129 he left his leprous wife and three daughters in the

[92] Peter the Venerable, *De miraculis libri duo*, ed. D. Bouthillier, *CCCM*, 83 (Turnhout, 1988), pp. 82–7. For Humbert in the Holy Land see also *RRH*, 1, no. 260, p. 66 (1150).

[93] J. S. C. Riley-Smith, 'Families, crusades and settlement in the Latin East 1102–1131', in H. E. Mayer (ed.), *Die Kreuzfahrerstaaten als multikulturelle Gesellschaft* (Munich, 1997), 4. In 1130, in Jerusalem, he is recorded as *Hugo, comes Trecensis* among the witnesses of a charter, after the seneschal (*dapifer*) of the Temple, William. *RRH*, 1, no. 133, p. 33 (1130).

care of the Cluniacs of St-Bénigne of Dijon so that he could travel to Jerusalem, where he wished to pursue a career in the Temple 'as a knight in the service of God to the end of his life'.[94] Other knights had come to the East as crusaders, and thus with military intentions. The knight Bertrand of Sartiges from Auvergne, for example, who entered the Order in Tortosa in *c.* 1279, seems to have been a crusader as his father once had been.[95] As such he would already have gained a very precise picture of, and taken an active interest in, the situation in the Latin states overseas by the time he became personally involved with the Order. As the Templar main archives are now lost, however, it is no longer possible to establish how many crusaders and pilgrims dedicated their lives to the protection of the holy places once they had seen them with own eyes; nor, in fact, can we say with certainty that Bertrand of Sartiges was one of them. That going on crusade could lead into entry in the Temple is illustrated in the example of the Angevin nobleman Robert of Sablé. He went on the Third Crusade as a layman, joined the Order in 1191, and became the grandmaster almost immediately afterwards. He would almost certainly have been familiar with the Order through his kinship with the second grandmaster of the Temple, Robert Burgundio, although it seems likely that his entry into the Order and subsequent election to the grandmastership was the result of intensive lobbying by his feudal lord King Richard of England.[96]

With few exceptions, only Templar brothers of high noble birth or with important offices and functions in the Order have, like Robert of Sablé, left sufficient traces in the charters and narrative sources to enable historians to reconstruct their careers and to come to conclusions about their motivation for joining.[97] Even so, we know from other archives that crusaders joined military orders, and even founded them (as Edward I of England had done with the Order of St Edward at Acre), as a means of prolonging their military involvement in the Holy Land, and there is no reason to doubt that this included the Temple.[98]

[94] *CG*, no. 27, p. 19 (1129×1132); *HdB* II, no. 244, pp. 9–12 (here dated *c.* 1129).

[95] Walter of Sartiges had crusaded in 1248. See J.-B. Bouillet, *Nobiliaire d'Auvergne*, 8 vols. (Clermont-Ferrand, 1846–57), VI, pp. 141–2, and *PT*, ii, p. 153 for Bertrand's reception in Tortosa.

[96] Bulst-Thiele, *Sacrae domus militiae*, pp. 123–34; Barber, *New knighthood*, p. 123. For insight into Robert's family background see W. S. Jessee, 'The family of Robert the Burgundian and the creation of the Angevin march of Sablé and Craon', *Medieval Prosopography*, 16 (1995), 31–67.

[97] Burgtorf, *Central convent*, pp. 7–8. A catalogue of surviving documents relating to the Order of the Temple in the East is provided in Claverie, *L'ordre du Temple*, II, pp. 411–50 and III, pp. 39–620.

[98] N. E. Morton, *The Teutonic knights in the Holy Land 1190–1291* (Woodbridge, 2009), p. 22. Information on the Order of St Edward is provided in M. Prestwich, *Edward I* (2nd edn, New Haven, Conn., 1997), p. 79.

Supporting the Temple on crusade

It is not difficult to imagine that of the crusaders who had benefited from the Order's prowess on the battlefield, or had simply witnessed it, some responded by making on-the-spot endowments to the Templars while they were still overseas; the same would apply to pilgrims who had benefited from the Templars on their journeys. As already discussed, evidence of the generosity of crusaders to the Templars in the Holy Land is sparse, although some information can be drawn from western charter collections. From what these sources tell us, crusaders and pilgrims were most generous when they were most vulnerable. At no time did this become clearer than during the siege of Acre, which lasted from 1189 to 1191, and which constituted the most dramatic, and traumatic, event of the Third Crusade.

The siege of Acre provided crusaders with a multitude of reasons to engage with the Temple. Their blood-toll was high, as was the amount of money they had to raise to save themselves from starvation. Ultimately, however, they succeeded in taking, and holding, a well-fortified city in the face of an immediate danger posed by a Muslim relief force.

Confronted with the prospect of death on the battlefield or from disease, and in the face of financial disaster, numerous crusaders turned to the Templars for spiritual intercession and monetary assistance.[99] These personal needs aside, their generosity may also have been a response to the enormous losses in manpower which the Order had suffered in the defeat of the Latin army at the Horns of Hattin on 3 July 1187 (on which Pope Gregory VIII had put particular emphasis in his crusading bull) and during a more recent battle on 4 October 1189 at Acre.[100] On that second date the crusaders conducted a daring attack on Saladin's camp outside the city, and would have been trapped between Saladin's forces and the garrison of the city, had not the Templars covered their retreat. The grandmaster of

[99] That the Third Crusade was particularly popular with noblemen from the diocese of Langres (or that it was at least exceptionally well documented in the charters from that diocese) is obvious from Marie's list of noblemen from this diocese who were crusaders and appeared in Templar charters as either donors or as witnesses. Of the forty-nine entries in her list, thirty-nine refer to Third Crusaders. Marie, *Templiers de Langres*, App. v, pp. 161–2. The participation of Burgundian knights and nobles in the Third Crusade is also recorded and documented in *HdB*, iii, pp. 37–72.

[100] On the battle of Hattin see *De expugnatione Terrae Sanctae per Saladinum libellus*, in Ralph of Coggeshall, *Chronicon anglicanum*, ed. J. Stevenson, Rerum britannicarum medii aevi scriptores, 66 (London, 1875), pp. 218–26; *Chronique d'Ernoul*, pp. 157–70; *L'estoire de Eracles empereur et la conqueste de la terre d'outremer; la continuation de l'estoire de Guillaume arcevesque de Sur*, Recueil des Historiens des Croisades, Historiens occidentaux, ii (Paris, 1859), pp. 48–64. See also *RRH*, ii, no. 664, pp. 45–6 and *OFWT*, §§ 76–7 for Saladin's order to kill all Templars captured at Hattin and §§ 82–6 for the death of the Templar grandmaster at Acre in 1189.

the Order, Gerard of Ridefort, was captured and killed by the enemy during the attempt to guide the crusaders back to defensible territory.[101] As a consequence of the Order's losses at Acre Pope Clement III issued a bull on 11 January 1190 in which he called upon the barons not to prevent the Templars from obtaining the equipment necessary for their survival through sales of property or otherwise;[102] and perhaps some of the charity displayed towards the Order at Acre should be regarded as a response to the Pope's pleading.

King Philip II of France was the most important French crusader to make concessions to the Templars during the siege.[103] He was joined by a number of knights and nobles, many of them his vassals. In particular, the crusaders from Champagne and Burgundy provided the Templars with numerous endowments. Most of them would have sailed with Henry II of Champagne, who disembarked at Acre in late July 1190,[104] but some had already arrived earlier and thus obtained a fairly precise picture of the development of the siege and the role the Templars had played. As early as 20 October 1189, at Acre, the Burgundian nobleman Rainard of Grancey had therefore decreed in writing that certain of his possessions should be transferred to the Templars.[105] Clarembaud of Noyers, who arrived at the siege in October 1189 and thus at around the time of the death of Gerard of Ridefort,[106] granted the Templars a monetary rent of 60 *sous* 'for the salvation of his soul'. He combined his donation with an attempt to direct the attention of those fellow crusaders who still had possessions towards the 'honesty and praiseworthy zeal that the house of the Temple displays in its service for Christ'. The Templars, he announced to his fellow crusaders, went to great lengths to support their brothers who were 'effectively, actively and devotedly serving God and the Cross there [at Acre]' as well as the noblemen who were 'in great need of resources'. All the Order's efforts would be meaningless however, if they were not maintained and their expenses not met 'with the help of good men'.[107]

In 1191, and also at Acre, the crusader Hugh of Bourbonne, who was concerned about the salvation of his soul and those of his kin, donated to

101 *OFWT*, §§ 82–6.

102 *PTJ I*, no. 217, pp. 392–3. See also ibid., no. 222, pp. 396–9 (30 August 1190), in which Clement III ordered the archbishops, bishops and prelates to use ecclesiastical punishment against everyone who had physically attacked a Templar.

103 *Catalogue des actes de Philippe-Auguste. Avec une introduction sur les caractères et l'importance historiques de ces documents*, ed. L. Delisle (Paris, 1856; reprint: Geneva, 1975), no. 339, pp. 81–2 (1191) and Prutz, *Entwicklung und Untergang*, App. III, no. 1, p. 296 (1191).

104 J. Richard, *The crusades c. 1071–c. 1291* (Cambridge, 1999), p. 222.

105 *HdB*, III, no. 815, p. 293 (1189). See also *CG(Yonne)*, II, no. 405, pp. 411–12 (1189).

106 He had come to Acre in October 1189.

107 *CG(Yonne)*, II, no. 406, pp. 412–13 (*c.* 1190).

the Templars of Genrupt the pasture rights which he had vifgaged to them to finance his journey before his departure to the East.[108] In the same year, Count Henry II of Champagne announced that for the salvation of his soul and the souls of his kin and ancestors he would confirm all his grandfather's endowments to the Temple and take the possessions of the Order under his protection. He also provided them with privileges which allowed them to acquire further possessions in his lands.[109] The brothers Guy and Odo of Choili promised to pay the Templars an annual rent of 60 *sous* in silver from Épernay for the salvation of their souls and the souls of their kin and ancestors.[110] Guy of Vergy abandoned in perpetuity to the Templars the piece of land which he had rented out to them, for an envisaged period of three years, before he had set out on crusade.[111] Henry of Arzillières, evidently in an attempt to raise more money, sold them his revenues in Sartrouville near Paris.[112] And Henry of Mousson, count of Bar, granted them the right to receive annually 15 *livres*' worth of the customary dues and payments that were levied on the passage to Bar (*consuetudinem et usagium XV librarum de passagio Barri annuatim*), which, he decreed, they should use to finance one knight 'in the parts of Jerusalem, for the defence of the land'.[113]

Supporting Templar relatives

Some crusaders carried the burden of knowing a family member or friend fighting among the brothers of the Order; or they had relatives in the Temple who were still resident at home but who could be transferred to the East as soon as the political situation required it. It is not difficult to imagine that crusaders who had experienced the blood-toll of the Templars on the battlefield would have gained a fairly good picture of the fate that could await a Templar relative or friend when he was shipped to the Levant as reinforcement. Clarembaud of Noyers, whose donation to the Templars at Acre has been mentioned, for example, was the brother of Guy of Noyers, who may have entered the Order prior to the Third

[108] *HdB*, III, no. 1432, p. 476 (1183). See also Richard, 'Les templiers et les hospitaliers', 235.

[109] BN, n.a.l., 52, fol. 15r (1191) (d'Arbois de Jubainville and Pigeotte, *Histoire des ducs et des comtes de Champagne*, III, no. 160, p. 477). See also Barber, *New knighthood*, p. 263.

[110] BN, n.a.l., 51, fol. 103r (1190×1191).

[111] Ibid., 53, fol. 255r–v (1191) (*HdB*, III, no. 867, pp. 314–15).

[112] H. E. Mayer, *Die Kanzlei der lateinischen Könige von Jerusalem*, 2 vols. (Hanover, 1996), II, Exkurse, no. 14, pp. 911–14 (1190×1191).

[113] The donation was later confirmed by his brother Thibaud. See BN, n.a.l., 51, fol. 221r (1189×1197).

Crusade and was present among the Templars fighting at the siege.[114] With this in mind Clarembaud's donation to the Templars and the plea to his fellow crusaders to come to the help of the Order becomes even more pressing. It was perhaps in response to similar concerns that the knight William of Chartres made a donation to the Order of the Temple in 1219, during the Damietta campaign.[115] He was the nephew and namesake of the grandmaster William of Chartres, who had died on 26 August 1219 from wounds received in a Muslim attack on the Christian camp at Damietta.[116] Although the exact date of the donation can no longer be established, the possibility exists that the death of a Templar relative on the Egyptian campaign encouraged William, who may have had a second relative fighting as a Templar in the crusade, to act as donor.[117]

RETURNING FROM CRUSADE

Spiritual awareness

Going on crusade was, like making a pilgrimage, a profound spiritual experience that left hardly anyone untouched. Once the task of reaching the Holy City had been completed some pilgrims and crusaders decided not to return to their homelands but to stay and die in Jerusalem. Those who went home often made pious endowments to religious houses or entered monastic communities, as did Peter and Pons of Montlaur from Languedoc after their return from the First Crusade.[118] Their names re-appear in local charters during the first half of the twelfth century, but it seems that neither Pons nor Peter ended his life in the manner he had lived before becoming a crusader. Pons of Montlaur joined the Order of St John some time before 1120, whereas Peter of Montlaur took monastic vows and went into Benedictine seclusion. By 1140 he was the prior of the monastery of Lapeyre; and in 1159 a monk by his name was recorded living in the abbey of Vabres.[119]

[114] For Guy of Noyers's enrolment in the Temple before his departure to the East (where he perished) see *HdB*, iii, pp. 43, 61. Quantin ('Les croisés de la Basse-Bourgogne', 296 and 303) holds the opinion that Clarembaud of Noyers too had been a Templar. This, however, seems very unlikely, considering that Clarembaud was able to give away family possessions during the siege, which he would not have been allowed to possess as a Templar. Perhaps he had once joined the confraternity of the Order.

[115] Bulst-Thiele, *Sacrae domus militiae*, pp. 162–3fn. [116] Barber, *New knighthood*, pp. 121–2.

[117] He was probably also related to the Templar Goherus Garini, who may have taken part in the crusade. Bulst-Thiele, *Sacrae domus militiae*, pp. 162–3fn.

[118] *Documens historiques et généalogiques sur les familles et les hommes remarquables du Rouergue dans les temps anciens et modernes*, ed. H. de Barrau, 4 vols. (Rodez, 1853–60), I, p. 117; *HGL*, iii, p. 482.

[119] For Pons of Montlaur see *CG(Hosp.)*, i, no 42, p. 36 (1118×1120), no. 56, pp. 46–7 (1126). He must have joined the Order in or after 1114, when he was recorded among the witnesses of William V of Montpellier's testament. See *HGL*, v, no. 450, cols. 841–5 (1114). For Peter of Montlaur see *Cart Sil*, no. 18, p. 18 (1149), no. 133, p. 105 (1159), no. 312, pp. 248–9 (1162).

Their careers exemplify well that the act of crusading was a moving and spiritual experience which could ultimately lead to radical changes in the way crusaders perceived and assessed their lives and ways of conduct. It is possible that the experiences of the First Crusade inspired Pons and Peter, once they had returned to their homeland and settled their mundane affairs, to submit to religious rules which they hoped would cater for their spiritual needs. As a Benedictine monk, Peter would have become once more a *miles Christi*, this time fighting the enemies of Christ within with means of prayer. Pons, on the other hand, dedicated his life to a community that saw Christ in the suffering of the poor and that served God in the world with love and charity. It is reasonable to suppose that these crusaders' spiritual awareness was influenced by what they experienced on crusade.

Peter and Pons of Montlaur satisfied their spiritual desires with contemplation and charitable deeds. But other crusade veterans experienced needs, not necessarily less spiritually profound, which required remedies only a religious order dedicated to the military defence of the holy places could provide. All practical motivations, such as the desire for social recognition, aside, their decision to join the Order of the Temple rather than any other religious community should be seen as a conscious attempt at perpetuating, prolonging, or replicating a previous crusade experience. Knights who joined the Order of the Temple on or after a crusading campaign, some of whom have already been mentioned, include William of Arzillières from Champagne, who participated in the Third Crusade as a layman but in 1204 (and probably from 1200) resided as marshal of the Temple in Acre;[120] Hugh of Berzé, who joined the Order some time after he returned from the Second Crusade; Bernard III of Comminges, who became a Templar sixteen years after going to the Holy Land; and possibly Peter of Lespinasse. The latter embarked from Marseille on the Fifth Crusade in 1218 and may have been identical with the Templar preceptor of Celles in 1246 known as Peter of Lespinasse from St-Beauzire in Auvergne.[121]

[120] It was at William's instigation that his brother Henry sold the Templars his revenues in Sartrouville during the siege of Acre. Mayer, *Kanzlei*, II, Exkurse, no. 14, pp. 911–14, argues that this might indicate William's familiarity (and perhaps association) with the Templars. This familiarity would explain why William joined the Order during, or soon after, the siege of Acre. See R. Röhricht, *Geschichte des Königreichs Jerusalem 1100–1291* (Innsbruck, 1898), p. 523 for Walter of Arzillières and Burgtorf, *Central convent*, p. 671 and also *RRH*, II, no. 797a, p. 52, for William's career; and also ibid. for William's mention as marshal of the Temple in Acre.

[121] *PAC*, I, no. 97, p. 94 (*c.* 1160); Röhricht, *Studien*, Epist. no. 7, pp. 46–8 (1218); J. Phillips, *The Second Crusade. Extending the frontiers of Christendom* (New Haven, Conn., 2007), p. 104. For Peter the crusader, see Röhricht, *Studien*, Epist. no. 7, pp. 46–8 (1218). For Peter of Lespinasse as Templar see Léonard, *Introduction*, p. 171 and H. Bouffet, *Les templiers et les hospitaliers de Saint-Jean en Haute-Auvergne* (Marseille, 1976), p. 98.

Gratitude

Crusaders who resumed their ordinary lives after returning from crusade were no less affected by their experiences and often turned to Templar communities to express their gratitude for the aid and support the Templars had given them during their journey or while abroad. Thus, when Henry of Troyes, count of Champagne, in 1152×1153 made endowments to the Templars for the soul of his father and 'as remuneration for the service and respect that you have shown me and my men in the land of Jerusalem' he was evidently expressing his gratitude to the Templars on behalf of many of the Champenois knights and nobles who had accompanied him on the Second Crusade. Among other things, they had witnessed and experienced first-hand how the Templars had successfully taken command of the crusader army in January 1148, when continuous harassment by the Turks on a particularly perilous stretch of the journey through Anatolia had brought discipline and morale to a new low-point.[122] Dreux IV of Mello, lord of St-Bris in the county of Auxerre, left for Jerusalem in 1190 and after his return made endowments to the Templars to 'benefit his soul and support the holy land in Outremer' and for the express purpose of compensating them for the help and friendship he had received overseas.[123] Similarly, when the Fifth Crusader Henry I of Rodez lay seriously ill in the hospital of the Order of St John at Acre in October 1222 he ordered additions to be made to his testament, which he had drafted before his departure for the East. These included substantial endowments to the Hospital of St John, but also to the Order of the Temple, which, so the testament informs us, had done him 'much service in these parts'.[124] And when Anseric of Toucy donated the mills of Sauce to the Templars of Sauce (the date given in the cartulary of Auxerre is June 1233), he did so for the benefit of his soul and the souls of his ancestors, as well as *pro terre sancte utilitate* – for the use of the Holy Land.[125]

Other accounts are less specific but suggest similar contexts. Guy of Toucy in March 1267×1268 endowed the Templars of Sauce(-sur-Yonne) with one third of his revenues in Vincelles and Vincellottes as compensation for 'the good deeds and services which I and my predecessors have in the past received from the brothers of the knighthood of the Temple', for which he demanded in return that the anniversary of his death would be commemorated in the commandery church; he followed up his donation

[122] BN, n.a.l., 51, fols. 2r–3r (1152×1153). For events in Anatolia see Odo of Deuil, *De profectione*, pp. 124–7 and Phillips, *Second Crusade*, pp. 201–2.

[123] *Cart Pon*, no. 342, p. 344 (1190); AN S 5239, dossier 51, no. 3 (BN, n.a.l., 55, fols. 351r–3r) (1281, copy).

[124] *CG(Hosp)*, II, no. 1760, pp. 308–9 (1222). [125] AN S 5235, no. 1, fol. 1v (1233).

one month later with the sale and donation of fiscal revenues at Vincelles, Vincelottes and Escolives, again for the benefit of his and his ancestors' souls and to secure the commemoration of his anniversary 'in the house or chapel' of the Templar commandery of Sauce(-sur-Yonne).[126] In 1284 Milo IV of Noyers and his wife Mary of Crécy,

> considering and addressing all the great selfless and charitable acts performed daily by the brothers of the knighthood of the Temple both this side and beyond the sea, never fearing to spill their blood against the enemies of the Faith to avenge the shame (*la honte*) of Jesus Christ, and especially the courteous and honourable deeds which the above-mentioned brothers have performed for our predecessors and for us, and which they still perform, have performed, and perform often.

gave to the Templars of France the village and lordship of Vermenton for the benefit of their and their ancestors' souls and because of the 'great devotion and affection that we have, always have had, and again will have for the Order of the Temple'.[127] In 1287, on the feast of Saints Peter and Paul (29 June), Milo and his wife Mary of Crécy repeated the donation, again putting emphasis on their 'devotion and affection for the preceptor and brothers of the house of the knighthood of the Temple in France' and on their desire to compensate the said preceptor and his brothers 'for the good deeds and the courtesies which they have shown us'.[128]

Memory and obligations

Another obvious motivation for involvement with a military order after the return from a journey to the Holy Land was the desire of former pilgrims and crusaders to maintain a connection with Jerusalem, a motivation also exemplified by the previous Holy Land experience of many crusaders. Andrew of Baudement, for example, had been on pilgrimage to Jerusalem twice before he attended the council of Troyes that provided the Templars with a Rule in 1129 and, in 1133, became a patron of the

[126] AN S 5238, dossier 41, nos. 2 and 3 (BN, n.a.l., 55, fols. 207r–8r, 209r–13r) (1268). In March 1267, Guy's fiscal and rental endowments at Vincelles and Vincelottes were confirmed by his brother Raynald and by Count Thibaud of Bar and his wife Johanna, who guaranteed the Templars' possession of the rights and properties *in perpetua et pacifica in manum mortuam*. This was followed, in May 1270, by the count of Nevers's amortisation of the rental and fiscal revenues and the amortisation by the count of Auxerre in 1275. See AN S 5238, dossier 41, nos. 4, 5 (1267×1268), and 6 (1270) and AN S 5235, dossier 1, no. 36 (1275).

[127] Ibid. 5241, dossier 66, no. 4 (1284 and *vidimus*).

[128] Ibid., no. 5 (and BN, n.a.l., 55, fols. 388r–91r) (1287). Possibly Milo was the son of Milo of Noyers who had crusaded in 1239. See for him ADCO, 111 H 1184, Courban, no. 7 (as listed in Marie, *Templiers de Langres*, App. v, p. 162).

Order.[129] Bishop Pons of St-Paul-Trois-Châteaux, one of the more prolific and powerful early patrons of Templar Richerenches, was a veteran of the First Crusade.[130] Bernard of Durfort, from Languedoc, was a veteran of the Third Crusade. His family has left no trace as Templar patrons in the family cartulary which predates his departure to the East. Only after his return from crusade do the lords of Durfort seem to have involved themselves with the Order, and very likely the involvement had been instigated by Bernard himself. He and his brother Bernard Peter first made endowments to the Templars of Golfech in 1207, and in 1211 they sold them landed property. A time of sporadic donations and business transactions followed until in February 1268 Raymond of Durfort endowed the Templars of Golfech with his rights and *honor* in the parish of Golfech, in return for which the brothers were required to celebrate solemn high mass for his memory and that of his family; this was followed by a final donation in 1269.[131]

The charters also suggest that a number of crusaders and pilgrims who had already established relations with the Temple before their departure to the East, either personally or through relatives, were inspired to intensify these contacts after their successful return. Walter of Sombernon, whose family had been involved with the Order in the past, renewed this involvement a few years after his return from the Third Crusade with donations which enabled the Order to build a new house at Avosne.[132] Robert of Milly, who, as has already been noted, had entered the confraternity of the Templars before he left for Jerusalem on the Third Crusade, also returned from the campaign safely.[133] He fathered two daughters, which meant that his earlier donation to the Templars, issued prior to his crusade departure and on the condition that he die without

[129] *RRH*, I, no. 52, pp. 10–11 (1108), no. 80, pp. 18–19 (1115); *Chartes de la terre sainte provenant de l'abbaye de Notre-Dame de Josaphat*, ed. H.-F. Delaborde (Paris, 1880), no. 6, pp. 29–32 (1115). See also Riley-Smith, *First Crusaders*, p. 168. For his first recorded donation to the Templars in 1133, see *Cart Prov*, no. 81, pp. 102–3 (1133).

[130] See *Cart Rich*, p. cxlvii and, e.g., *CG*, no. 120, p. 84 (1136), no. 121, pp. 84–5 (1136×1139), no. 122, p. 85 (1136×1139) for Pons's role in the foundation and development of Richerenches. For Pons as crusader see Riley-Smith, *First Crusaders*, p. 218.

[131] For Bernard of Durfort see Macé, *Comtes de Toulouse*, p. 274. The transactions are recorded in *DhT-G*, II, pp. 53 (1211), 55 (1268); BN, n.a.l., 15, fol. 139r (1267); *Doc Dur*, I, no. 18, pp. 13–14 (1207), no. 19, p. 14 (1211), no. 20, pp. 14–15 (1211), no. 31, pp. 22–3 (1242), no. 33, pp. 24–5 (1242), no. 62, pp. 45–6 (1269).

[132] *HdB*, III, no. 929, p. 339 (1196); Bouchard, *Sword, miter, and cloister*, p. 365.

[133] He was one of the veterans of the Third Crusade who were questioned in 1213 about the marriage of Henry of Champagne to Isabel, widow of Conrad of Montferrat, whose marital status with Humphrey IV of Toron, her first husband, was a matter of dispute. See *RRH*, I, no. 867, p. 233 (1213). That he was in 1203 the father of two daughters is recorded in the *Cartulaire de l'abbaye de Paraclet*, ed. C. Lalore (Paris, Troyes, 1878), no. 123, p. 139 (1203). Robert was the chamberlain of Champagne from 1167 to probably 1222. He is recorded in the entourage of the count on several

heirs, became null and void. The fact that the Templars eventually established a house at Trilbardou, and thus on the land that Robert had initially granted to them, indicates, however, that at some point after his return Robert had renewed his donation to the Order.[134] He even seems to have multiplied his efforts to assist in the Order's territorial expansion. A confirmation charter issued by Thibault of Champagne in 1198 indicates that he had leased to the Templars of Coulommiers the field of Orgeval, cultivated land outside Coulommiers, and meadows and land below a vineyard belonging to the Order for an annual rent of 10 measures of grain from one of their granges.[135] He also endowed the Templars with the mills of Montceaux, thus laying the foundations of a long dispute between the Templars and the monks of Montier-la-Celle, which dragged on until 1216.[136] More concessions to the Temple followed in 1227, when Robert exempted the Order from paying rent for their grange of Champfleury, near Montceaux, for the lump sum of 40 *sous*.[137]

Of course, not every Templar benefactor was a crusade veteran or pilgrim. And it is impossible to tell with certainty whether families whose earliest recorded transactions with the Templars postdate a crusade or pilgrimage of one or more of their members had established their ties with the Order as a consequence of these events. The written evidence is usually too random to allow such a conclusion; at least, that is, unless the family in question had produced pilgrims before 1120 or First Crusaders, in which case the chronological sequence of exposure to the Holy Land and to the Temple is clear. The charters generally say little about the motivation behind individual transactions other than that by giving to the Order the donor hoped to gain spiritual benefits. And one also needs to take into account that even families which had produced early pilgrims or First Crusaders made endowments to the new military religious communities for reasons that had nothing to do with the donor's obvious association with the crusading movement or Jerusalem.

THE CRUSADING LEGACY IN TEMPLAR FAMILIES

In spite of the caveats just mentioned, the fact that a great number of knights and noblemen who gave to, or joined, the Temple after they had

occasions, as e.g. in *Littere baronum*, no. 22, pp. 64–5 (1205) and App. I, pp. 159–60 (1198). He retired from the office of chamberlain in 1222 but was still alive in 1238. *Feud Soc*, no. 60, p. 79 (1238).

134 For the Templar settlement at Trilbardou see AN S 5009, dossier 40, and *OdM*, I, pp. 248–9.

135 AN S 5176A, dossier 1, no. 2 (1198). 136 *Cart Mon*, no. 161, p. 165 (1216).

137 AN S 5179A, dossier 1, no. 6 (1227).

returned from crusade or a pilgrimage came from families which do not seem to have appeared as donors and associates in earlier surviving Templar documents strongly suggests that Templar support and crusading occurring in the same families was not entirely coincidental. Instead it seems that if they had not already done so while in the East, scores of pilgrims and crusaders, high- and low-born, made attempts to associate with the Temple once they had returned to their homelands.[138] Many of the Order's other benefactors were sons, brothers, nephews, wives, daughters or even more distant relatives of crusaders, who responded to a desire nourished in their families to support military campaigns in defence of the Holy Land and for whom the Templars were the ideal proxies to express that desire.

The monetary donation of 100 *sous* made by Simon of Broyes to the Templars some time between 1129 and 1132, for example, thus could also be interpreted as a response to the crusade experiences of his father Hugh II 'Bardoul', his uncle Raynald and his grandfather Milo of Bray, all three of whom had participated in the First Crusade,[139] or of other relatives, since on his mother's side Simon was a descendant of the Montlhéry clan of crusaders.[140] A similar influence can be assumed for Tiburge of Orange's donation to the Templars of Richerenches and Orange in 1136, as she was the daughter of a First Crusader who never returned from the Holy Land and the wife and sister-in-law of two more crusaders.[141] But only a closer examination of how long the interest in crusading and the Temple persisted in the families of those individuals who had been exposed to both will help us to understand the extent to which the crusades, and crusading ideology, influenced the attitude of whole kin-groups towards the Temple.

How returning crusaders communicated their experiences to friends and relatives is difficult to establish in individual cases and an even more difficult topic about which to generalise. What can be said is that the stories of relatives or friends who had been on crusade seem to have helped families like the different houses of 'Montlaurs' to create a real and personal link with Jerusalem and the Holy Land which prepared them to respond favourably to new attempts to come to the aid of

[138] It has already been stated by Carraz, 'Les Ordres militaires et la ville', 280, that; because of their familiarity with the Order's work in the East, a later association with the Temple was particularly desirable for returning crusaders and their families.

[139] *CG*, no. 28, pp. 20–3 [21] (1129×1143). See also Riley-Smith, *First Crusaders*, pp. 211, 215, 218. For Raynald, who had followed the call of Peter the Hermit, see esp. Albert of Aachen, *Historia Hierosolymitana*, ed. and trans. S. B. Edgington (Oxford, 2007), pp. 14–15, 24–7, 38–9, 40–1.

[140] His mother was Emmeline of Montlhéry. See *Cart Boul*, p. 21.

[141] *Cart Rich*, p. cxlvii and no. 10, pp. 13–14 (1136).

Christianity.[142] Relying on name-similarities alone, we can conclude that for over a century different individuals from Languedoc identified as being from Montlaur (which applies to several locations) engaged themselves in crusading and associated closely with the Temple, although it is not possible to connect any of them with certainty to the two First Crusaders Peter and Pons, mentioned above. By 1147, and thus in the wake of the Second Crusade, a Peter of Montlaur had joined the Temple.[143] A certain Hugh of Montlaur entered the Order some time after 1218; he was recorded as the master of Provence from 1234 until 1238, later as the marshal of the Order in the East, and died at La Forbie in 1244.[144] He could have been related to P. of Montlaur, who accompanied Count Alphonse of Toulouse on crusade in 1252,[145] and who, in turn, was perhaps identical with Pons of Montlaur. In June 1248, before his departure on crusade, this Pons made considerable donations to the Templars of St-Gilles, consisting of the *castrum* of Générac and Aigues-Vives with all rights and appurtenances.[146] From the *castrum* of Montlaur in the Aude region came another crusader, Arbert of Montlaur. He was in the Holy Land perhaps as early as 1132 and certainly by 1142.[147] A likely relative of his, Bernard of Montlaur, was recorded as a Templar from 1249 until 1259, when he was serving in commanderies on the Iberian peninsula, in Majorca and in Roussillon.[148]

142 The role of the legacy of the First Crusade in the build-up to the Second Crusade is explained, for example, in Phillips, *Second Crusade*, pp. 17–36. Examples of First Crusaders and their relatives who also participated in the Second Crusade are provided in Riley-Smith, 'Family traditions', passim. See also Riley-Smith, *First Crusaders*, pp. 169–88 for the importance of crusading in the Monthléry family network.

143 *CG*, no. 425, p. 266 (1147), no. 462, p. 277 (1147), no. 585, pp. 359–60 (1150×1151). See also *Cart Douz*, A: no. 59, p. 66 (1164), no. 88, pp. 84–5 (1153), which mention Peter but do not identify him as a Templar *frater*.

144 Selwood, *Knights of the cloister*, p. 146; Forey, *Aragón*, p. 420. For Hugh's career in the Temple see *Cart Puy*, pp. xxxi, xxxii, no. 2, pp. 2–3fn.; Prutz, *Entwicklung und Untergang*, App. VII, p. 365; *La règle*, §§ 585, 592 and 615. See also Bulst-Thiele, *Sacrae domus militiae*, p. 209.

145 *HGL*, VIII, no. 432, cols. 1314–16 (1252). 146 Carraz, *L'ordre du Temple*, p. 402.

147 Wolfgang Antweiler (*Das Bistum Tripolis im 12. und 13. Jahrhundert* (Düsseldorf, 1991), p. 44) and Reinhold Röhricht (*RRH*, I, no. 211, p. 53 and ibid., II, no. 142a, p. 11) before him assumed that the person called Arbert who received Tortosa and other possessions as fiefs from Pons of Tripoli in 1132 may have been identical with Arbert of Montlaur who, ten years later, witnessed charters in the Holy Land alongside Peter of Puylaurens, lord of Gibelacar, whose family castle was situated near Castres in Languedoc. For Peter of Puylaurens see J. Richard, *Le comté de Tripoli sous la dynastie toulousaine (1102–1187)* (Paris, 1945), p. 75.

148 Burgtorf, *Central convent*, pp. 564–5; Léonard, *Introduction*, p. 90; Forey, *Aragón*, pp. 222, 433, 434; Verdon, *La terre et les hommes*, p. 217. Bearers of the name Bernard/Bertrand among the Montlaurs were usually destined for the religious life. for example, a Hospitaller knight with the name of Bernard of Montlaur is recorded in the commandery of Prugnes in 1154. See *Cart Sil*, no. 170, pp. 138–40, no. 174, pp. 143–5. B(ernard) of Montlaur was the abbot of Candeil in 1222, Bertrand of Montlaur was the abbot of Ardorel in 1294 and Magna of Montlaur was the abbess of Ste-Marie-des-Olieux in 1300. See *GC*, I, cols. 57–8 (for B), 81 (for Bertrand) and *HGL*, IV, p. 687 (for Magna).

As stated before, the exact relationships between various Templars and crusaders by the name of Montlaur and their relationships with the earlier-mentioned First Crusaders Peter and Pons of Montlaur are far from clear. But even if these knights held their names from different locations, which seems likely, the cumulative evidence suggests strongly that at least two groups, one from the Aude region near Carcassonne, the other connected to Le Puy in Haute-Loire, had participated in the crusades and welcomed the Templars with open arms.

Their attitude was shared by a great number of families with similar backgrounds. In fact, most Templars with previous crusading experience who have already been mentioned had close relatives who were crusaders. Hugh of Berzé was the son of a crusader or pilgrim to Jerusalem, and seems to have conveyed his enthusiasm to his relative and namesake Hugh 'the Poet'. The latter was a great admirer of the Templars and, convinced as he was that his generation should emulate the crusading spirit of their forefathers, he may have gone on the Third Crusade and certainly went on the Fourth.[149] The Templar William of Arzillières was the brother of crusaders and had relatives who took part in the Fourth Crusade and in the Albigensian campaign of 1226.[150] The father of Templar Bertrand of Sartiges accompanied Louis IX on crusade in 1248.[151] And Pons of Meynes, who joined the Temple at Montfrin in Provence in 1146, when preparations for the Second Crusade were in full swing, came from a family of crusaders with possessions in the county of Tripoli.[152] His situation seems to have been similar to that of the Templar Odo of Avallon from Burgundy, whose family had ties to the courts of Champagne and Burgundy and landed interests in the crusader states that over the years also produced a number of crusaders.[153]

[149] Hugh of Berzé's father Rollan Bressan was recorded in the East in 1120. See *Necrologium ecclesiae Sancti Petri Matisconensis*, ed. M.-C. Guigue (Bourg-en-Bresse, 1874), p. 89 (1120). For Hugh 'the Poet', see Smith, *Crusading in the age of Joinville*, pp. 89–90.

[150] *Feud Soc*, no. 80, pp. 102–3 (1201); *Chart Chem*, p. 72 (1202); d'Arbois de Jubainville and Pigeotte, *Histoire des ducs et des comtes de Champagne*, V, pp. 82, 100 and A. de Barthélemy, 'Pèlerins champenois en Palestine', *Revue d'Orient Latin*, I (1893), no. 37, 366–7 (1202); Mayer, *Kanzlei*, II, Exkurse, no. 14, pp. 913–14 (1190 × 1191); *Itinerarium peregrinorum et gesta regis Ricardi*, ed. W. Stubbs, *Rerum Britannicarum Medii Aevi Scriptores* (London, 1864), p. 93(1190); *Diocèse ancien de Châlons-sur-Marne*, I, p. 288.

[151] Bouillet, *Nobiliaire d'Auvergne*, VI, pp. 141–2; *PT*, II, p. 153.

[152] *CG*, no. 411, pp. 258–9 (1146). For Pons of Meynes in Lebanon see *RRH*, I, no. 78, p. 18 (1115). See generally Carraz, *L'ordre du Temple*, pp. 74, 79, 124, 178.

[153] Some time before 1147 his likely relative Chalo of Avallon had married Agnes of Beirut. That Chalo came from Burgundy is indicated by the fact that his and Agnes's donation to the Hospitallers at Acre received confirmation from Laura of Avallon in Burgundy. Long after Odo had died, a certain Peter of Avallon became constable (*constabularius*) of Tiberias and lord of Adelon. He is recorded in the East in 1250, 1253, 1254 and 1256. And a certain Peter of Avallon from Champagne is recorded in Louis IX's crusading army in 1249. See *RRH*, I, no. 364, p. 95 (*c.* 1160), no. 1205, p. 317 (1253), no. 1217, p. 321 (1254), no. 1247, p. 328 (1256); *Feud Soc*, no. 3, p. 4 (1201); Quantin, 'Les croisés de la Basse-Bourgogne', 294–5, 314; Petit, *Avallon et l'Avallonnais*, p. 148.

The family of the Templar Andrew of Joinville, which had ties with the commanderies of Thors and Ruetz, produced a long list of crusaders, among them Andrew's father, who perished at Acre in August 1190, and his older brother Godfrey, who went on the Third Crusade with his father. Godfrey later went on the Fourth Crusade but refused to take part in the siege of Constantinople. Instead he completed his journey to the Holy Land, where he died in 1204 in the Hospitaller castle of Crac des Chevaliers.[154] As Caroline Smith has pointed out, between 1147 and 1248 'every major crusade campaign to the Levant or north Africa included a member of the [Joinville] family'.[155] Less prominent was the case of Raynald of Ulmeto, another knight from Burgundy, who joined the Temple some time between 1162 and 1180 and whose uncle had died overseas.[156]

Similar links between association with the Order of the Temple, crusade experience or aspiration, and a family legacy of crusading can be traced in the biographies of many of the Order's lay associates. John I of Chalon-sur-Saône, who took the cross in 1235, a year after entering the confraternity of the Temple, is one example.[157] Among his ancestors were at least one eleventh-century pilgrim to Jerusalem, two First Crusaders and at least one participant in the Third Crusade.[158] Another example is Raymond Ato of Aspet from Comminges. He associated himself with the Temple on 28 July 1156 and in 1160 went on crusade to Jerusalem in the company of the future Templar Bernard III of Comminges, although in his case no connection can be securely established between his decision to associate with the Templars and previous involvement of family members in crusading.[159]

THE CORRELATION BETWEEN CRUSADING AND TEMPLAR SUPPORT

The examples that I have given so far already indicate that in many families with Templar ties, clustered in the previous chapter into networks, crusading was a common activity. It sometimes affected the Order's benefactors and potential recruits indirectly if crusaders were among

[154] Smith, *Crusading in the age of Joinville*, p. 172; Delaborde, *Jean de Joinville et les seigneurs de Joinville*, pp. 37, 44–5 and no. 26, p. 247 (1137), no. 82, p. 260 (before 1190), no. 83, p. 260 (before 1190), no. 92, p. 263 (1193), no. 108, p. 266 (1199), no. 135, p. 273 (1205), no. 154, p. 277 (1210), no. 243, p. 297 (1225), no. 300, p. 310 (1240), no. 396bis, p. 331 (1261), no. 423, p. 336 (1264), no. 494, p. 353 (1272), no. 502ter, p. 355 (1273), no. 508bis, p. 357 (1275), no. 517bis, p. 359 (1277), no. 520, p. 360 (1277), no. 524bis, p. 361 (1278), no. 530, p. 363 (1279), no. 533, p. 363 (1279), no. 631, p. 385 (1297) for the ties with Ruetz and, less extensively, Thors.

[155] Smith, *Crusading in the age of Joinville*, p. 172. [156] BN, n.a.l., 53, fols. 4r–6r (1162×1180).

[157] Lavirotte, 'Mémoire statistique', 264 (1234); Lower, *Barons' Crusade*, p. 42.

[158] Riley-Smith, *First Crusaders*, pp. 95, 202; *HdB*, III, no. 799, pp. 286–7 (1189); Alberic of Trois-Fontaines, *Chronica a monacho novi monasterii Hoiensis interpolata*, ed. P. Scheffer-Boichorst, *MGH SS*, XXIII (Hanover, 1874), pp. 674–950, here p. 864.

[159] *Cart Mont*, no. 41, pp. 247–8 (1156); *PAC*, I, no. 97, p. 94 (*c.* 1160).

their relatives, but at other times could have an immediate impact on their lives. Where it existed, the influence of crusading on the decisions and religious activities of individuals in affected families would have varied according to the amount of time that lapsed between the actual crusade involvement and the first recorded donation to the Order. Pons of Polignac, for example, who counted at least three First Crusaders among his close relatives, may have been less affected by their experiences when he made his family's first recorded endowments to the Templars of Le Puy in around 1170 than were Bernard Ato Trencavel and Raymond Trencavel by theirs during the First and Second Crusades when they made early donations to Douzens.[160] Very likely, he was also less affected than were the lords of Possesse, multi-castle barons from Champagne and regular benefactors of the Templars since at least 1142, whose crusading legacy dated back to the First Crusade and gained momentum in the 1160s and thus coincided with their involvement with the Temple.[161]

The overall impression is that crusade enthusiasm and interest in the Temple were mutually influential but that it was the sustained effort of crusaders and their families on which the prosperity of the Order of the Temple, and its military success in the crusader states, relied most heavily. The correlation between crusading and Templar support is particularly evident in the (extended) noble families of Aspet in Comminges, Grancey in Burgundy, Joigny in Champagne, Chastellux, Noyers and Montbard in Burgundy; a second, closer look at them will help to illustrate this point.

The crusading legacy: six examples

Raymond Ato of Aspet, who joined the confraternity of Montsaunès in 1156 and crusaded with Bernard III of Comminges in 1160, and the Templar Odo of Grancey both had sons who supported the Order and went on the Third Crusade.[162] Fighting alongside Odo's sons at Acre were Hugh of Grancey, who was a Templar benefactor in his own right,

[160] *Cart Puy*, no. 1, pp. 1–2 (*c.* 1170). For Bernard Ato and Raymond Trencavel as crusaders see *La Grasse (I)*, no. 166, pp. 226–7 (1101); *Cart Gell*, no. 299, pp. 248–9 (1101); *HGL*, III, p. 754. For Bernard Ato and the crusader relatives of Pons of Polignac see also Riley-Smith, *First Crusaders*, pp. 94, 119, 166, 201.

[161] Simple but useful genealogies of the Possesse family are provided in Evergates, *Aristocracy*, p. 255 and Evergates, 'Nobles and knights', 22. See also William of Tyre, *Chronique*, pp. 138–9, 201, 203; *Diocèse ancien de Châlons-sur-Marne*, I, pp. 234, 401–2; *Feud Soc*, no. 91, pp. 113–14 (1166).

[162] Arnold Raymond of Aspet went, and very likely perished, on the Third Crusade. His brother Gaucerand continued the family's tradition of making endowments to Montsaunès. See *HGL*, VI, p. 134; Higounet, *Comté de Comminges*, I, pp. 249–50; *Cart Mont*, no. 40, p. 247 (n.d.).

Calo of Grancey, and their brother-in-law Amadeus of Arceaux.[163] The crusading engagement of the lords of Aspet cannot be traced further than the sons of Raymond Ato. In the case of the lords of Grancey, however, relatives of Odo who did go, or may have gone, on crusading campaigns after 1190 included another Hugh of Grancey, who may have gone on the Fifth Crusade, Pons of Grancey from the cadet branch of Frolois (he was also known as Pons of Frolois), who certainly participated in the Fifth Crusade,[164] Odo's grandson Hugh of Arceaux, who signed up for the Barons' Crusade in 1235,[165] and William of Saulx, whose family would seem to have been related to the house of Grancey, as has been seen.[166] William was in the Holy Land in October 1251, when a letter written by him to Louis IX reveals that he was staying at Château Pèlerin. As illustrated in Chapter 3, throughout this time members of the house of Grancey and its related branches remained closely involved with the Templars in Burgundy, and notably with the commandery of Bure.[167]

The legacy of crusading was also prominent in the family of the lords of Chacenay, which produced a number of crusaders, among them Jacob and Anseric of Chacenay, who went on the Second Crusade; Erard I of Chacenay, who departed on crusade for the first time in 1179 and who died at Acre twelve years later;[168] and Erard II of Chacenay, who went on the Fourth and Fifth Crusades.[169] Freshly returned from the Fourth Crusade, Erard II of Chacenay married the young widow Emeline of Broyes, whose first husband, the war hero Odo 'the Champenois' of Champlitte, had died in Constantinople the previous year.[170] Her family had been deeply affected by the call to the East. Three of her direct ancestors had fought in the First Crusade and at least one, her great-uncle Raynald of Broyes, had died at Nicaea in 1096.[171] Her uncle Robert II of Dreux had been a key figure in the Third Crusade, in which he had participated with his brother the bishop of Beauvais. Soon both would also involve themselves in the Albigensian campaigns,[172] as did two

[163] *HdB*, III, no. 815, p. 293 (1189).

[164] For Hugh of Grancey as a possible Fifth Crusader see *HdB*, III, no. 1217, p. 465 (1217).

[165] Lower, *Barons' Crusade*, p. 42. [166] See pp. 141–6 above.

[167] See pp. 141ff. above, but also Röhricht, *Studien*, p. 113; Claverie, *L'ordre du Temple*, II, no. 10, pp. 422–3 (1251).

[168] *Chart Clairv*, no. 34, p. 61 (1147×1158); Barthélemy, 'Pèlerins champenois', 358.

[169] *Feud Soc*, no. 30, pp. 45–7 (1224), no. 76, p. 94 (1218); Powell, *Anatomy*, App. II, p. 219.

[170] Odo's death in Constantinople and burial in the church of the Holy Apostles are recorded in *Joinville and Villehardouin: Chronicles of the crusades*, p. 71 [§ 114]. For his and his brother William's role in the crusades see also Longnon, *Les compagnons de Villehardouin*, pp. 209–12; Mayer, *Kanzlei*, II, p. 727; Powell, *Anatomy*, App. II, p. 225.

[171] Albert of Aachen, *Historia Hierosolymitana*, pp. 14–15, 24–7, 38–9, 40–1.

[172] Röhricht, *Königreich Jerusalem*, pp. 503, 524, 586fn., 587, 589; Peter of Les Vaux-de-Cernay, *Historia Albigensium*, cols. 592, 595–6; Pegg, *A most holy war*, pp. 106–7.

relatives of Erard II of Chacenay, his uncle Harvey IV of Donzy, count of Nevers, and his cousin Milo IV, count of Bar-sur-Seine.[173] Among the relatives who, a decade later, were recorded alongside Erard at the siege of Damietta were again his uncle Harvey and his cousin Milo, but also his cousin John of Brienne and Milo's son Walter. Present were furthermore the Templar grandmaster William of Chartres, who may have been related to Milo,[174] and at least one nephew of William.[175] By that time both Erard and Harvey had become Templar benefactors (in each case before they set out on crusade),[176] whereas Milo IV of Bar-sur-Seine made donations to the Templars on his deathbed at Damietta. Later generations of family members produced further crusaders, among them Hugh V of Broyes, who began preparations to take the cross in 1230 and eventually joined the Barons' Crusade,[177] and Emeline's son Erard III of Chacenay, who in 1249 entrusted his land to the care of Raynald of Grancey, lord of Larrey, to go and fight in the East.[178]

In comparison with the Granceys and Chacenays the involvement of the lords of Chastellux in crusading seems to have been short-lived, but also far more intense. Six members of the nuclear family of Chastellux, lord Artaud with five sons, participated in the Second Crusade, and at least one of them, Obert of Chastellux, also made substantial donations to the Order of the Temple consisting of the village and land of Busserotte, which his son confirmed in 1219.[179] Through the marriage of another of Artaud's crusading sons, Artaud II of Chastellux, to the ex-wife of the Second Crusader William of Marrigny the lords of Chastellux became connected to another family with emotional links to the Holy Land. That

173 Peter of Les Vaux-de-Cernay, *Historia Albigensium*, cols. 565A/B, 612C/D.

174 The quotation in Oliver of Paderborn, *Historia Damiatina* in *Die Schriften des Kölner Domscholasters, späteren Bischofs von Paderborn und Kardinal-Bischofs von S. Sabina, Oliverus*, ed. H. Hoogeweg (Tübingen, 1894), pp. 187–8, to the effect that the crusader casualties at Damietta included 'comes Barri et filius eius, frater Willehelmus de Carnoto, magister militie Templi, Herveus de Wirsone, Iterius de Tecce' has been interpreted as evidence that William of Chartres was the son of Count Milo of Bar, while others have maintained that he was the count's brother. J. L. La Monte, 'The Lords of Le Puiset on the crusades', *Speculum*, 17 (1942), 111, points out, however, that the names of Milo (with reference to his son) and William occur in a longer list of crusaders who perished on campaign and are not grouped together because of a family connection. Neither the first nor the second claim is therefore substantiated by evidence.

175 Bulst-Thiele, *Sacrae domus militiae*, pp. 162–3fn.; Barber, *New knighthood*, pp. 121–2.

176 *OdM*, I, pp. 336, 366; AN S 5241, dossier 75, no. 2 (BN, n.a.l., 55, fols. 496r–7r) (1190).

177 Barthélemy, 'Pèlerins champenois', no. 66, 374 (1239) and *Cartulaire de l'abbaye de Saint-Pierre d'Oyes (canton de Sézanne), suivi d'une note sur les anciens seigneurs de Broyes*, ed. É. de Barthélemy (Châlons-sur-Marne, 1882), pp. 8–9 (although the chronology cannot be trusted; instead I follow Evergates, *Aristocracy*, App. E, Genealogies, p. 252: Broyes–Beaufort–Châteauvillain); Lower, *Barons' Crusade*, pp. 42, 48.

178 Barthélemy, 'Pèlerins champenois', no. 87, 378 (1249).

179 Petit, *Avallon et l'Avallonnais*, p. 144; *HdB*, ii, p. 97.

Artaud's descendants remained responsive to the needs of the Holy Land is demonstrated by the fact that his grandson or great-nephew Artaud III went on the crusade of Louis IX and that another, likely, relative by the name of John of Chastellux joined the Temple in the thirteenth century and became preceptor of Laumusse.[180] By that time Artaud III's daughter Eglantine was already married to Harvey of Pierre-Perthuis, whose family's engagement in crusading and the Temple will be mentioned further below.

The example of Count William II of Joigny resembles that of Obert of Chastellux in that he, too, was a Templar benefactor with a strong crusading background and pedigree; it is different only insofar as, with a high degree of probability, his donation can be linked directly to his crusading endeavour. Following the example of his suzerain Thibaud of Champagne he took the cross in 1235, but did not set out on crusade until 1240, after founding the Templar chapel of Sauce, near Auxerre.[181] His ancestors and closest relatives included Guy and Raynald of Joigny, who went on the Second Crusade, William I of Joigny, who went on the Third Crusade, and Walter of Joigny, lord of Châteaurenard, who in 1209 accompanied Duke Odo III of Burgundy on the Albigensian campaign.[182] A family bond with Andrew of Joigny, the Templar master of Payns in Champagne in the March 1263, is likely but cannot be established with certainty.[183]

In the case of the lords of Noyers, crusaders and Templar benefactors included Clarembaud of Noyers, whose substantial endowments to the Templars of St-Marc in 1186×1187 were followed by deathbed donations

[180] William of Marrigny made concessions to Clairvaux before his departure on crusade in 1147, which are recorded in *Chartes et documents concernant l'abbaye de Cîteaux 1098–1182*, ed. J. Marilier (Rome, 1961), no. 130, p. 114. Obert's donation to the Temple has also survived in the confirmation charter of his son Artaud II from 1219. See *HdB*, IV, no. 2975, p. 470 (1210) and Petit, *Avallon et l'Avallonnais*, p. 471 (1219). For Obert's father and grandson or great-nephew, Artaud I and Artaud III, on crusade see Quantin, 'Les croisés de la Basse-Bourgogne', 294, 297 (Artaud I) and 313 (Artaud III). John the Templar was recorded as a *miles* of the Order, which indicates his noble origin, and held the office of preceptor at Laumusse during the final two decades of the Order's existence. See Léonard, *Introduction*, p. 156 (1281–99) and Lavirotte, 'Mémoire statistique', 283 (1299–1311).

[181] AN S 5237, dossier 30, no. 5 (1238); Rothelin, 'Continuation', ch. 20, p. 38 (1239); Lower, *Barons' Crusade*, p. 43.

[182] For Raynald and Guy see H. Bouvier, *Histoire de l'église et de l'ancien archidiocèse de Sens*, 3 vols. (Amiens, 1906–11), II, p. 47. For William see *CG(Yonne)*, II, no. 407, pp. 413–14 (1190). For Walter see *HdB*, III, p. 165; Peter of Les Vaux-de-Cernay, *Historia Albigensium*, col. 565B.

[183] For Andrew of Joigny, preceptor of the *baillie* of Payns in 1263 and 1266, see AN S 4968, dossier 30, no. 4 (1263) and Léonard, *Introduction*, p. 145. It is possible that Andrew was a scion of the family of the viscounts of Joigny who, as Bouchard (*Those of my blood*, p. 160) has shown, were not related to the counts. But even in this case Andrew would have a crusader pedigree. See Quantin, 'Les croisés de la Basse-Bourgogne', 301 and 304.

at Acre in around 1190.[184] As already mentioned, he also had a brother who was a Templar and fought at Acre. On his father's side Clarembaud's family was tied to the lords of Pierre-Perthuis, and it was from this branch that two more Third Crusaders, Stephen and Guy of Pierre-Perthuis, emerged.[185] On his mother's side at least one relative, Walter of Chappes, had been on the First Crusade. Two more, Guy and Clarembaud of Chappes, had gone on the Third Crusade and at least one, Clarembaud, had also supported the Temple.[186]

The lords of Noyers continued to appear in Templar charters after the Third Crusade and supported the Temple throughout much of the thirteenth century.[187] The lords of Pierre-Perthuis made gifts to the Order on at least two occasions after the Third Crusade, once in 1219, when preparations for the Fifth Crusade were under way, and a second time in 1260.[188] And in 1204 Guy and Clarembaud of Chappes were already en route to another crusade. Clarembaud died during the campaign and the death of another brother, Warner, on the same crusade seems at least plausible.[189] In the meantime, a relative of Guy of Chappes, Clarembaud of Broyes, had been appointed to the archbishopric of Tyre,

[184] BN, n.a.l., 55, fol. 555r (1186×1187); *CG(Yonne)*, II, no. 406, pp. 412–13 (*c.* 1190). Clarembaud of Noyers arrived at Acre in October 1189. See Richard, *The crusades*, p. 222.

[185] Guy of Noyers's participation in the events of the Third Crusade can be concluded from a charter dating *c.* 1190, which recalls the donations which he had made to Reigny 'before his departure to Jerusalem'. See *Inventaire Chastellux*, no. 29, p. 133. Stephen of Pierre-Perthuis was Clarembaud's paternal cousin. See *CG(Hosp)*, I, no. 900, p. 571 and *CG(Yonne)*, II, no. 406, pp. 412–13 (*c.* 1190). Guy of Pierre-Perthuis was either Stephen's brother or his uncle. For his testament at Acre, which included donations to the Templars, see *CG(Yonne)*, II, no. 429, pp. 433–4 (1191).

[186] Walter of Chappes may have been identical with Walter, son of Ansculf of Chappes, whose name is recorded in a pancarte from Clairvaux dating from 1147 but recalling earlier donations to the abbey (*Chart Clairv*, no. 15, pp. 29–33 [31]). For Walter (Walker) as crusader see Albert of Aachen, *Historia Hierosolymitana*, p. 98 and Riley-Smith, *First Crusaders*, p. 223. Clarembaud of Chappes made donations to Montiéramey in 1189, before 'leaving for Jerusalem' (*Cart Montier*, no. 83, p. 114). His brother Guy was another of the veterans of the Third Crusade who were later questioned about the circumstances leading to the marriage of Henry of Champagne with Isabel of Toron in 1192 (p. 233 fn. 133 above). See *The Conquest of Jerusalem and the Third Crusade*, ed. and trans. P. Edbury (Aldershot, 1998), Selected Sources, no. 6e, pp. 172–4 (1213). For the donation see *OdM*, I, p. 303 (1171).

[187] BN, n.a.l., 55, fol. 568 (1217); AN S 5235, dossier 1, no. 1, fol. 26r (BN, n.a.l., 54, fols. 392r–3r) (1256); AN S 5235, dossier 1, no. 1, fol. 65v and AN S 5240, dossier 60, no. 13 (BN, n.a.l., 54, fols. 406r–7v) (1256); AN S 5241, dossier 66, nos. 4 (1284) and 4bis (1284, *vidimus*), nos. 5 and 6 (1287) (BN, n.a.l., 55, fols. 366r–9r, 388r–91r, 392r–5r).

[188] BN, n.a.l., 55, fols. 517r (1219, *vidimus* April 1263) and 531r (1260; *vidimus* April 1263).

[189] J. Dufournet, 'Villehardouin et les champenois dans la quatrième croisade', in Y. Bellenger and D. Quéruel (eds.), *Les champenois et la croisade. Actes des quatrièmes journées rémoises 27–28 novembre 1987* (Paris, 1989), 56. That Clarembaud went on crusade (or at least overseas) is obvious from *HdB*, III, no. 1069, p. 390 (1203). That he never returned from the campaign can be concluded from *Cart Montier*, no. 222, pp. 228–9 (1205) and no. 223, p. 229 (1206). However, the obituary of St-Pierre, Troyes, insists that Clarembaud died while on pilgrimage to Compostela. See *Collection des documents inédits relatifs à la ville de Troyes et à la Champagne méridionale*, ed. Sociéte

an act that would have given his relations in Champagne a new incentive to interest themselves in the affairs of the Kingdom of Jerusalem.[190] Guy of Chappes made donations of land to the Temple in May 1210 and in May 1213 and before his death in 1246 his nephew Clarembaud, whose father had died on crusade, made further endowments including the lordship of Ménois.[191] Six years later the knight Peter de Capis was killed at Damietta. Peter hailed from Cyprus but his family was rooted in Champagne, which could make him a distant cousin of Guy and Clarembaud of Chappes. If, and how, he was also distantly related to a Templar preceptor of the same name who presided over the Templar community of Dijon in 1275 is debatable.[192]

The lords of Montbard, finally, had been involved with the Templars since Andrew of Montbard had joined the Order in the 1120s and become its grandmaster. And like most of the other families, the lords of Montbard and their closest relatives continued to produce not only Templar benefactors but also numerous crusaders. Therefore, by the time Bernard III of Montbard, lord of Époisses, made his donation to the Order of the Temple in 1210, he could look back on a long line of crusaders in his family that included his grandfather Anseric III of Montréal and his uncle Anseric IV of Montréal, who had fought on the Second and Third Crusades respectively, his uncle John I of Arcis-sur-Aube, who had fought on the Third Crusade (on which he and Anseric III of Montréal had died), as well as two distant relatives, Godfrey of La Roche-Vanneau, bishop of Langres (1139–63) and his brother Rainer, who had also gone on the Second Crusade.[193] Following Bernard's donation, his cousin John II of

académique de l'Aube, 5 vols. (Troyes, 1878–93), II, pp. 196–7. Warner of Chappes was the chancellor of the count of Champagne and recorded as dead in 1206. See *Cart S-P*, no. 116, pp. 117–18 (1206).

[190] For archbishop Clarembaud see Comte Chandon de Briailles, 'Bulle de Clérembaut de Broyes, archevêque de Tyr', *Syria*, 21 (1940), 82–9, and Mayer, *Kanzlei*, I, pp. 300–1. Like so many other members of the family of Chappes, Clarembaud was commemorated at St-Étienne of Troyes. See *Collection Troyes et Champagne*, II, no. 210, p. 232.

[191] *HdB*, III, no. 1466, p. 484 (1210); AN S 4956, dossier 17, no. 1 (BN, n.a.l., 52, fols. 48r–9r) (1213, copy). See also A. Pétel, 'La maison de Serre-lès-Monceaux', *MSA Aube*, 70 (1906), 259, and Longnon, *Les compagnons de Villehardouin*, p. 60 for the year of Clarembaud's death.

[192] Peter de Capis is cited in a charter issued by King Hugh I of Cyprus in 1210 and recorded among the witnesses of a donation to the Order of St John at Nicosia, Cyprus, in 1217. At Damietta, he can be found in the company of Philip of Navarra, count of Champagne, and of Raoul of Tabarie. By 1230 his widow and one of his daughters had married the brothers Anceau and John II of Brie, two members of another family of knights from Cyprus with links to Champagne. See E.-M. Rey (ed.), *Les familles d'outre-mer de Du Cange* (Paris, 1869), p. 604; *RRH*, I, no. 896, p. 240 (1217). That there existed a family of knights with the name Chappes on Cyprus can also be deduced from *Les gestes des Chiprois*, ed. G. Paris and L. de Mas Latrie, *Recueil des historiens des croisades. Documents arméniens*, II (Paris, 1906), p. 862. On Peter of Chappes as Templar see Léonard, *Introduction*, p. 151.

[193] *HdB*, II, p. 95; III, no. 809, pp. 290–1 (1189); IV, p. 459 and no. 2981, p. 470 (1219); BN, n.a.l., 53, fol. 86r (1219); Röhricht, *Studien*, Epist. no. 33, p. 66 (1219); Odo of Deuil, *De profectione*, p. 69;

Arcis-sur-Aube went on the Fifth Crusade, as did his own son Andrew (who was also the son-in-law of John II of Arcis-sur-Aube), who died at the siege of Damietta.[194] Of Bernard's maternal relations, his cousin Agnes of Montréal married Henry of Arzillières, whose brother William was a Templar and who went on crusade twice. The marriage between Bernard's granddaughter Helvis and Dreux V of Mello eventually tied the Montbards to another family of ardent crusaders and Templar supporters. These included Dreux's grandfather, who was a veteran of two crusades and who had been instrumental in the foundation of the commandery of Sauce-sur-Yonne, as well as his father, who had fought in the Third Crusade and was a Templar benefactor by 1223, and his uncle Raynald, who had been in the Holy Land as either a pilgrim or crusader.[195]

In summary, what the evidence tells us is that crusading and Templar support were activities that were often acted out simultaneously and by succeeding generations within the same family groups.

TEMPLAR AND CRUSADER NETWORKS

The examples show clearly that the men and women from these families who became involved with the Order at home generally were aware of its military purpose and that many would have had ample reason for supporting it. From very early on the Order was promoted as a military institution by the papal curia and by influential church figures such as Bernard of Clairvaux, Peter the Venerable and Suger of St-Denis.[196] The knights and nobles who engaged with the Templars in the context of later crusades, when the Order was well established, may of course have been guided by the simple rationale that such an undertaking needed financing and that the Temple was an institution with money at its disposal and with wide representation throughout Europe and the Holy Land, which enabled crusaders to raise money on the way and whilst abroad.

In general the knights and nobles who approached the Templars for financial assistance did not rely on them alone in their pursuit of monetary

Alberic of Trois-Fontaines, *Chronica*, pp. 864, 908; *CG(Yonne)*, I, no. 278, p. 429 (1147); Bouchard, *Sword, miter, and cloister*, pp. 198fn. and 340; Richard, *The crusades*, p. 222; Richard, *Ducs de Bourgogne*, p. 408; Quantin, 'Les croisés de la Basse-Bourgogne', 306; Powell, *Anatomy*, App. II, p. 231; P. Van Kerrebrouck, *Les capétiens, 987–1328*, 2 vols. (Villeneuve d'Ascq, 2000), pp. 565–6.

[194] *Chartes Beauvoir*, no. 16, p. 187 (1219). His death is recorded in James of Vitry, *Lettres de la cinquième croisade*, V:282, VI:220 and VII:537.

[195] *HdB*, III, p. 47; *OdM*, I, p. 354; *Cart Pon*, no. 342, p. 344 (1190); AN S 5235, dossier 1, no. 1, fol. 1r (BN, n.a.l., 54, fol. 95) (1223); Chérest, 'Vézelay', 22 (1868), 155; Röhricht, *Studien*, p. 112.

[196] Demurger, *Les templiers*, p. 202; Bulst-Thiele, *Sacrae domus militiae*, pp. 47–51.

assets but engaged in transactions with a number of religious houses. But for some crusaders, as well as pilgrims, the motives for association with the Temple went beyond such mundane concerns. Before Godfrey of Arcy-sur-Cure set out on his journey to Jerusalem, he secured himself money from Vézelay, blessings from Crisenon and the association of the Templars.[197] He also hoped that associating himself with the Templars – and providing them with a house and oratory – would earn him spiritual rewards as well as the opportunity to join in the physical battle against the enemies of Christ. Like him, numerous other knights gave to, or associated with, the Temple with the intention not only of participating in, or financing the pursuits of, a military Order in a crusading campaign but also of committing themselves to a military exercise that was spiritually rewarding. At the very least they had agreed to a formulation of their wills and transactions by the scribes that included what could be described as the 'crusading element'.

It would be impossible to tell how many of the knights and nobles who gave to or joined the Temple had been inspired by the stories of crusader relatives who had witnessed the human, military and financial efforts of the Order in the Latin states in the East, but for many this must have been the case; some may even have witnessed these sacrifices with their own eyes. Driven by the memory of what they had experienced, in admiration of the Templars' commitment to the crusading cause, or simply grateful for the help they had received while in the East, they decided to establish relations with the Templars either whilst still in the Holy Land or after their return home. In other words, for many knights and noblemen with a crusading background support of the Temple, and doubtless of other military orders, became an obligation born out of wartime experience.[198]

As an integral element of individuals' crusading experience support for the Temple thus became part of the crusading tradition of families and eventually an aspect of it. This development was sometimes consciously promoted by the crusaders themselves. When Henry I of Rodez was dying at Acre, he drew up his testament in which he ordered his relatives and descendants 'to uphold, defend, protect and guard the said Order of

[197] AN S 5235, no. 1, fol. 4r–v (*c.* 1180); *CG(Yonne)*, II, no. 293, p. 312 (1180), no. 304, p. 324 (1180).

[198] Some families did support more than one military order. The counts of Brienne constitute one example. In July 1269 Hugh of Brienne issued extensive endowments to Templar Bonlieu, whereas less than a year later, in April 1270, he confirmed his deceased brother John's endowment to the Order of St John of a chapel dedicated to Our Lady at Orient, hoping thereby to participate in the donation's spiritual rewards. See AN S 4958, no. 6 (1269) and dossier 35, no. 7 (1270).

the Temple as much as they can'.[199] It would seem, however, that in general the relatives of crusaders did not need written instructions to establish or maintain ties with the Templars. They did so as a way of expressing their own traditions. But throughout the twelfth and thirteenth centuries they also gave to the Order because for many of them crusading was a reality that still affected their families and friends. It is striking how many Templars and Templar supporters were close relatives or direct descendants of crusaders who had fought, and too often had died, in the Levant. In the families of many of them an attitude seems to have prevailed for decades, and sometimes centuries, that led members to take the cross.

For some families participation in crusading became a matter of pride, prestige and tradition; and there are plenty of examples which show that from very early on particular kin-groups provided not one but many crusaders who usually travelled together and of whom some participated in more than one crusading campaign.[200] Riley-Smith coined the term 'crusading ethos' that existed within particular families of First Crusaders and resulted from the 'collective memory of some cousinhoods' in which pride in the crusading experiences was 'locked deeply'.[201] Martin Erbstösser attempted to explain the participation of different members of the same families in multiple crusades with the 'tradition consciousness' (*Traditionsbewußtsein*) of these crusaders.[202]

To what extent families with a serious commitment to crusading and a demonstrable interest in their crusading legacy also commemorated the deeds of Templar relatives is a difficult question to answer. Charters, which were seldom used for eulogies, are usually silent about the fate of relatives in religious orders. What can hardly be disputed, however, is the fact that large numbers of families of crusaders often supported the Order of the Temple materially as well as personally. And it seems that in doing so, consciously or unconsciously, they were led by their ethos or sense of

[199] *CG(Hosp)*, II, no. 1760, pp. 308–9 (1222). See also Barrau, *Ordres équestres*, p. 2 and, for the English translation of the charter, L. and J. Riley-Smith, *The crusades, idea and reality, 1095–1274* (London, 1981), no. 47.2, pp. 175–6.

[200] Two formidable examples of families with long-lasting crusading ambitions are the Montlhérys and the family of the counts of Nevers. See Riley-Smith, *First Crusaders*, pp. 169–88 for Montlhéry and Murat, 'La croisade en Nivernais', passim, for the counts of Nevers and their relatives. The frequent occurrence of family ties among crusaders has also been noted by Powell, *Anatomy*, pp. 82–4, and Lloyd, 'The crusading movement', 52.

[201] Riley-Smith, *First Crusaders*, pp. 21 and 102–3. That a crusading ancestry did not necessarily lead to a positive response to upcoming crusade appeals is argued in J. Phillips, 'The murder of Charles the Good and the Second Crusade: household, nobility, and traditions of crusading in medieval Flanders', *Medieval Prosopography*, 19 (1998), 55–75.

[202] Martin Erbstösser, *Die Kreuzzüge. Eine Kulturgeschichte* (Bergisch Gladbach, 1998), pp. 180–1.

tradition to regard support for a military order like the Temple as a further means of expressing their attachment to crusading. It was this ethos which also seems to have been the defining criterion of Templar family networks. If the networks are reconsidered with these findings in mind, new conclusions present themselves.

Looking at Templar family networks with the knowledge of their members' crusading legacy, it has become increasingly obvious that in these networks the experience of crusading and, often associated with it, the existence of ties to the Holy Land, played at least as important a role as relations with the Templars. Considering the esteem in which crusaders were generally held by their families and taking into account that some of these families supported the Temple only sporadically and many other religious communities at the same time (and often more intensely), it seems in fact more likely that the driving force behind Templar family networks was the desire of families with experience in crusading to connect with other crusader families. Of the three families into which Elisabeth of Noyers had married, for example, two can be connected to the Templars, as I have shown, but all three had produced crusaders. The family of her first husband William of Joigny, whose great-uncle William IV of Nevers died at Acre, contracted alliances with the houses of Courtenay, Brienne and Nevers, all three of which were formidable crusading families. Her second husband, Hugh of St-Vérain, was on his mother's side also related to the Courtenays and on his father's side to the lords of Toucy, who were patrons of Sauce-sur-Yonne and had provided crusaders since 1096.[203] Her third husband John III of Arcis-sur-Aube was the grandson and nephew of crusaders. Elisabeth herself could count at least five Third Crusaders among her relatives.[204]

What therefore emerges are not so much networks that centred on common support for the Temple as networks that were established by and among the families of crusaders whose spiritual outlook was largely conditioned by the reality of crusading, but also by their proximity to proponents of religious reform, and for whom support of military institutions like the Order of the Temple had become a default action. The fact that so many of the families that produced crusaders also took up supporting the Temple only illustrates how intrinsically they continued to associate the Order with crusading. Of the brothers whom the Templars recruited from these families some, like Odo of Grancey, who had joined

[203] Murat, 'La croisade en Nivernais', 299–300.

[204] In 1189 her grandfather Clarembaud of Noyers had embarked on crusade, as had his brother Guy (allegedly a Templar), his cousins Guy and Stephen of Pierre-Perthuis and his nephew Geoffrey of Argenteuil. See *HdB*, III, p. 43 and also *CG(Yonne)*, II, no. 406, pp. 412–13 (*c.* 1190).

the Order in old age, may have been content with the prospect of ending their lives peacefully in one of the Order's communities in the West. Many more, however, may have been inspired by a strong sense of mission and purpose when they joined the Order or made endowments to it – a sentiment that had been instilled into them by their own families, the families to which they were related, and often by their friends.

CONCLUSION

On 13 October 1307 officials of King Philip arrested the Templar knight John of Châteauvillain at the Templar house of Mormant in the diocese of Langres. John was then twenty-nine or thirty years old and had spent four years in the Order, which he had joined at the same place as he was captured, at Mormant, as was only befitting considering that the house was a family foundation. The site had originally been occupied by Augustinian canons and the Templars had only recently, and possibly with the help of John's family, gained possession of it.[1] Very likely John had been among the first professed Templar brothers to occupy Mormant. Little did he know that his profession was to mark both the pinnacle and the end of his family's dedication to the Order, a dedication that we can now trace back four generations to the time of Simon I of Broyes and that was also shared by members of collateral families, including John's great-uncle Erard II of Chacenay, his aunt and uncle Amicia (or Agnes) and Walter of Joigny, and his remote cousins the lords of Joinville, all of whom we have encountered in the previous chapters.

In this book I have examined the religious and social features that one could describe as characteristic of kin-groups which, like John of Châteauvillain's extended family, produced Templar brothers, associates and benefactors. I have attempted to show the religious and social circumstances that influenced families in their decision to become involved in the Temple, the forms in which this involvement manifested itself, and how these families were interconnected. In doing so I have diverted attention away from the microstudy of social networks of individual Templar communities, which are clogged with names of knights and lesser free men of indistinguishable heritage whose engagement in the commandery and relationship to one another are often impossible to disentangle over

[1] Marie, *Templiers de Langres*, 143–4. John's deposition is recorded in *PT*, II, p. 369.

the *longue durée*. Instead I have shifted the focus to the religious and social background of those families and individuals whose frequent occurrence in religious documents including those of the Temple marked them as socially and religiously very active. Admittedly, this approach only helps to account for some of the motives of (usually well-to-do) families with comparatively strong Templar records but largely ignores the majority of (usually less affluent) individuals whose transactions are less frequently recorded, or less easily traceable, in the documents. These less-well-known supporters included servants and serfs of more prominent Templar donors, but also castellans and castle knights with their families, who are, in the written documents, not always easily distinguishable from their lords. In the few cases where these families have left traces in documents other than Templar charters, the familiar pattern of involvement with the Temple (or other military orders) and in crusading characteristic of better-recorded Templar families is usually easily established.[2]

Support for the Order of the Temple came in many shapes and forms. Grants were an obvious means by which sympathy for the Order was expressed and transmitted. But even sales and pledges created opportunities for long-term relations between families and commanderies. And the evidence has shown that some lords and knights went to great lengths to help the Templars create or maintain dependencies in nearby places,[3] thus allowing the Order to become a constant feature in the feudal landscape of the regions. Families were bound to the brothers of local Templar houses either by law or by contract and these bonds were regularly confirmed or re-enacted. At the very least the ties were reconfirmed once a year when the Templars or their bailiffs collected the Order's rightful share of the revenues. Donations and business transactions thus provided communication channels which enabled kin-groups and Templar communities to establish and maintain formal relationships, while acts of lay association allowed individuals to express their affinity for the Temple and their identification with it in a personal way.

[2] For example, Calo, castellan of Grancey, about whom little else is known, is mentioned as donor to the Temple in a pancarte dating from 1173. His son witnessed donations to the Templars at Acre in 1191 (*HdB*, III, no. 867, pp. 314–15) and was recorded as benefactor to the Templar hospital at Tilchâtel in 1193. His grandson, Hugh li Chanjons, quarrelled with the Cistercians of Auberive (which his ancestors had supported), which resulted in his excommunication and subsequent embarkment on crusade (ibid., no. 1414, p. 472). Before leaving, he, with the consent of his wife and son Bartholomew, made donations to the Hospitallers (ibid., no. 1482, p. 486).

[3] Roger I of Béziers, Roger III of Foix, Godfrey of Arcy-sur-Cure and William of Faugères, for example, all gave land and privileges to the Order for the explicit purpose that it should establish a settlement, house or chapel in the vicinity. *Cart Douz*, A: no. 115, pp. 106–8 (1133); *HGL*, V, no. 533, cols. 1020–1 (1136); *CG(Yonne)*, II, no. 291, pp. 310–11 (1180); BN, n.a.l., 15, fols. 332r–4r (1184).

As *confratres* and *consorores* or *donati* and *donatae* they committed themselves to a greater or lesser degree to individual Templar communities. Some lived among the Templars semi-religiously, others remained in the world. All of them created personal bonds between individual Templar houses and their families, which were recognised and often maintained by their relatives and descendants.

One reason why the families most easily traceable in the documents began supporting Templar communities – often instigating their foundation – was that they associated the Order closely with Cistercian ideals as propagated, first and foremost, by Bernard of Clairvaux, although it appears that in Languedoc this association with Cîteaux took place some years later than in Burgundy and Champagne and gained momentum only after the Order had become exempt from episcopal jurisdiction. The first core argument of this book is, therefore, that landowning families in France who began supporting the Order of the Temple in the twelfth century very often did so in the context of supporting other religious reform communities – notably Cistercian houses – and that this context, in turn, was indicative of the spiritual and religious demands that guided their actions. It is no coincidence that the region with the greatest density of Templar commanderies, along the border region in the diocese of Langres separating the county of Champagne and the duchy of Burgundy, was also home to the first Cistercian monastic foundations.[4] Indeed, the very fact that, as economic enterprises, Cistercian and Templar houses were often at loggerheads over properties they held in close proximity to one another, or in which they each claimed to have rights, confirms that both orders were served by the same benefactors and, as is suggested by the swift succession of donations to both orders, often in the same spirit.[5]

It can be argued that in the development of the Temple as a religious institution the year 1139 was, in its own way, as significant as 1129, the year of the council of Troyes. While the first Rule provided the Templars with an inner structure and a sense of identity, the Bull *Omne datum optimum* of 1139 gave them religious credibility and caused a major change in the way the Order was perceived by the pious laity. Before 1139 the Templars would have been badly equipped to ease the everyday anxieties of the lay pious, for it was only then that they obtained the exemptions, privileges and official authority to offer help to lay men and women in search of spiritual guidance and protection. Until 1139 the Templars in Burgundy and Champagne would have been able to rely on the spiritual

[4] The relevant literature on Cistercian foundations in the border region of Burgundy and Champagne is cited in Lester, 'A shared imitation', in particular p. 358.

[5] Christian Vogel (*Das Recht der Templer*, p. 58) reaches a similar conclusion.

advocacy of the Cistercians, to whom they were often personally connected. The religious charters from Burgundy and Champagne leave no doubt that until the end of the twelfth century at least (and often well into the thirteenth) Cistercian and Templar communities maintained close personal ties, with kin-groups often setting up and supporting houses of both orders in quick succession. Newman has shown that in the early decades of the twelfth century it was not uncommon for large groups of friends and relatives (usually *iuvenes* of knightly stock) to enter Cistercian monasteries together.[6] And examples such as that of Andrew of Montbard, who became a Templar shortly after a group of his male relatives had entered Cîteaux, now suggest that profession into the Temple could be part of that mass movement. As a result, during the Order of the Temple's formative years Templars and Cistercians from knightly families not only were aware of each other; they often shared familial bonds. Andrew of Montbard had two brothers and two nephews (and a few more distant relatives, like Godfrey of La Roche-Vanneau) who were Cistercians and he maintained contact with at least one of them, his famous nephew Bernard. As has been seen, the same may have been true of the Templar William of Baudement, whose relations among the Cistercians included two of his brothers and, eventually, his father. The Cistercian monk Gaucher, whose letter to a Templar friend (discussed in Chapter 2) has survived in the collection of Nicholas of Clairvaux, had not forgotten his old friendship with a Templar knight whose physical proximity to the holy places he envied and whom he expected to look after his nephew in Jerusalem.[7] Better than any charter, Gaucher's letter illustrates the old ties of family and friendship that could – and often did – bind together Cistercians, Templars and crusaders, or pilgrims to the Holy Land, and that allowed ideas about *imitatio Christi* and the redemptive and penitential value of armed pilgrimage to flow freely between the outside world, the Cistercian monastery and the Templar community.

Where they existed, these personal relationships influenced the spiritualities of Templars as well as Cistercians, and they would have been one reason why, as Michael Casey has pointed out, Cistercian communities were spiritually far more heterogenous than the Order's normative texts would have us believe.[8] Not all Cistercians embraced the concept of a military order, however, and some, Abbot Isaac of l'Étoile being one

[6] Newman, *Boundaries of charity*, pp. 24–9, 50–3. [7] See p. 102 fn. 127 above.

[8] M. Casey, '*In communi vita fratrum*. St. Bernard's teaching on cenobitic solitude', *Analecta Cisterciensia*, 46 (1990), 245. See also W. Knoch, 'Gebets- und Lebensgemeinschaften in Freundschaft – Bernhardinische Reformimpulse', in G. Krieger (ed.), *Verwandtschaft, Freundschaft, Bruderschaft. Soziale Lebens- und Kommunikationsformen im Mittelalter* (Berlin, 2009), 125.

example, viewed the Templars' active involvement in warfare and their insistence on martyrdom with suspicion or even outright hostility (Isaac referred to the Order of the Temple as both a *nova militia* and a *monstrum novum*).[9] But their outcries did not prevent influential reformers – Bernard of Clairvaux and Guigo of La Grande Chartreuse first among them – from embracing the Templars for the penitential nature of their service.[10] And in the end, even the Cistercian General Convent willingly attested to the spiritual bonds between the orders.

All things considered, one wonders if an exchange of ideas and spiritual aspirations between friends and relatives who had taken different habits did not occur more frequently than is implied by the few surviving letters of Bernard of Clairvaux to his Templar relative Andrew of Montbard or Gaucher's single surviving letter to his Templar friend.[11] So far, historians have paid much attention to Bernard's impact on the Templars. But little thought has been given to the possibility that the association of so many of the Cistercians' friends, patrons and relatives with the Order of the Temple may have influenced the Cistercians' own communal life and their understanding, and expression, of *caritas* and self-dedication to Christ as defined in the Order's normative documents. After all, in their primitive form these multi-authored and often revised documents were only slightly younger than the Temple or Bernard of Clairvaux's correspondence with Hugh of Payns, and more material was added to them over time.[12]

If the Templars of Champagne and Burgundy were closely tied to the Cistercians, the situation was different in southern France, where the early development of the Order of the Temple lacked the underpinning of Cistercian support. Here, the spiritual experience of the early Templars must have been distinct from that of their contemporaries in the north, in particular as it is very unlikely that the laymen who became Templars in the period immediately following the council of Troyes had received the necessary theological training to formulate a religious agenda that could convincingly argue the case for the Order's twofold military and religious nature. For this reason alone it seems likely that the Templars' initial message to the laity in regions with no strong Cistercian presence would have been primarily military and Crusading, a suggestion that is supported

[9] Isaac of L'Étoile, *Sermons*, ed. A. Hoste and G. Raciti, 3 vols. (Paris, 1967–8), III, pp. 158–60.

[10] Riley-Smith, *Templars and Hospitallers as professed religious in the Holy Land*, pp. 12–13.

[11] See p. 102 above.

[12] According to Newman (*Boundaries of charity*, p. 15), 'the primitive kernels of both the *Exordium parvum* and the *Carta caritatis* were written between 1116 and 1119; the *Exordium cistercii* was composed in 1123 or 1124, probably at Clairvaux; and the statutes contained in the *Summa cartae caritatis* describe decisions of the Chapter General made before 1124'. For a later dating of the documents see Berman, *Cistercian evolution*, pp. 1–92.

by the early donation of castles to the Templars on the Iberian peninsula. In 1128 and 1130 the Order of the Temple received important castles in Portugal and in the county of Barcelona. Although the brothers initially refused to garrison them, the donations had to be regarded as a serious attempt to draw the infant order into the Christian reconquest of the peninsula. They constitute some of the earliest acknowledgements of the Order's military role by western magnates.[13] On a smaller scale, knights and noblemen paid heed to the Temple's crusading mission by making donations for military purposes and by endowing it with their arms and horses when they entered the Templar community, or by making clear allusions to its role as protector of pilgrims and defender of the Holy Land.

Once recognised as an order of the Church and equipped with a variety of privileges, the Templars in all three regions, while still focusing on their military mission overseas, became actively engaged in parish duties and the *cura animarum*, the cure of souls, of their parishioners, thus evoking the interest and support of a wider audience of laymen, including those seeking spiritual guidance, and priests.[14] They were encouraged in this endeavour by a number of influential bishops, who often – the Cistercian bishops of Langres Godfrey of La Roche-Vanneau (1139–63) and Warner of Rochefort (1193–1200) are two examples from Burgundy – shared close social bonds with the Templars and their lay supporters.[15] With its exemption in 1139, the Order of the Temple thus became an acknowledged and accepted proponent of religious reform. This was the case in Champagne and Burgundy as well as in the south of France, where those who entered Templar communities or made donations to them after 1139 were the same men and women who had initiated and supported the eremitical movement and new monastic communities which celebrated the ideal of the *pauper Christi* and which were eventually incorporated into the Cistercian community. Like their peers in the north, the families of these new supporters could become deeply involved with the Templars, often establishing relations with commanderies that, albeit often sporadically, lasted for many generations. Judging from the charter evidence, the lords of Roquefort in Comminges engaged with the Order for almost

[13] *CG*, no. 10, p. 7 (1128), no. 33, p. 24 (1133); Barber, *New knighthood*, p. 32; Selwood, *Knights of the cloister*, pp. 35, 136.

[14] The priest Itier of Barbonne, for example, not only gave vineyards and pastures to the Templars, but also his breviary and missal, for which he clearly thought the Templars would find some use. He further promised them his house and entire manse after his death or all his possessions if he should take up a religious habit. See *CG*, no. 29, p. 23 (1129×1145) and no. 28, pp. 20–3, where Itier is clearly identified as *presbiter*.

[15] Godfrey of La Roche-Vanneau was related to the fifth grandmaster of the Temple (Andrew of Montbard), and Warner of Rochefort was a nephew of the crusader and Templar benefactor Simon of Rochefort.

forty years (1164–1205), the lords and knights of Pézenas for more than seventy years (from before 1140 to 1214). In Burgundy and Champagne, the counts of Joigny engaged with the Order for more than eighty years years (1192–1276), the lords of Mello and the lords of Sombernon for almost eighty years (from before 1216 to 1292, 1147–1234), the lords of St-Vérain for almost 100 years (1190 until before 1292), the lords of Noyers for at least 100 years (1187–1287), the lords of St-Maurice for 110 years or more (from before 1144 to 1252) and the lords of Tilchâtel for almost 180 years (1129–1280).

It is necessary at this point to say something about changes in the Order of the Temple's social profile, since the social networks of individual commanderies should not be confused with the social networks of Templar families scrutinised in this book. Because this book has focused, largely, on the Templar ties of well-connected families and has put little emphasis on the social complexities within individual commanderies, a few qualifications to the picture that has emerged from the investigation need to be made. The first is that not only in southern France, where decades of warfare caused the social networks of many religious houses to collapse and where, as a consequence of the war, the question of religious patronage had become radically politicised, but also in Burgundy and Champagne the supporter base of Templar houses was far from homogeneous and changed, often considerably, over time. Exceptions aside – many of them feature in this study – Templars in the late thirteenth and early fourteenth centuries seldom came from families that had founded Templar houses throughout the twelfth and early thirteenth centuries. One reason for this was the top-down influence, or 'domino effect', of patronage. As has been seen, aristocratic donations often triggered responses from vassals, friends, family members and other 'bystanders', whose names – and the names of whose relatives and descendants – subsequently appeared in the charters and cartularies as witnesses, donors, associates or brothers.[16] Many of these new lineages infiltrated, or were eventually absorbed by, older families, who, as a result, fragmented their inheritances into ever-smaller parcels and ceased their material support of Templar houses.

But social mobility and the fragmentation of economic resources are not sufficient to explain demographic changes in the Order's membership that seem to have occurred as the Order developed, despite its best efforts to distinguish and privilege its knightly members.[17] Knights were the core

[16] See above, pp. 160ff.

[17] Riley-Smith, *Templars and Hospitallers as professed religious in the Holy Land*, pp. 38–40; Vogel, *Das Recht der Templer*, pp. 171–5.

of the Templar fighting convent and had exclusive access to the most important offices in the Order, but they were outnumbered – in the Order of the Temple more so than in the Order of St John – by sergeants-at-arms and sergeants-at-service.[18] The data collected by Carraz reveals that in Provence the number of sergeants was double that of knights and that in Auvergne there were five times as many, which makes the Temple in Provence remarkably more 'aristocratic' than in Auvergne.[19] The numbers of knights and sergeants seem to have diverged as the Order's responsibility and obligations in the crusader states grew, to the extent that by the late thirteenth century many of the Order's western commanderies were almost entirely run by brothers of non-noble stock. This development was not unusual (socio-demographic changes have also been observed in Cistercian houses) and can be partly explained by the unceasing demand for knights in the Order's Levantine commanderies.[20] The constant drain of knights undoubtedly affected the social composition of Templar communities in the West. Perhaps more significantly, however, the reason for this demographic change was linked to the dominant role that sergeants were allowed to play in the Order. Non-noble sergeants could have remarkable careers and it is now known that many successful sergeants created their own influential social networks and successfully recruited friends and relatives, thereby contributing to the Order's changing social profile.[21]

The social composition of religious communities says little about their appeal to the outside world or the social standing of the individuals who supported them. Yet it was inevitable that as the number of non-nobles entering Templar communities increased, the influence of non-noble

[18] Riley-Smith, *Templars and Hospitallers as professed religious in the Holy Land*, p. 38.

[19] Carraz, *L'ordre du Temple*, p. 297.

[20] In the German Cistercian case from the late middle ages these changes in social composition and distribution of responsibilities have been interpreted as indicators that reform was successful. See K. Schreiner, *Mönchsein in der Adelsgesellschaft des hohen und späten Mittelalters. Klösterliche Gemeinschaftbildung zwischen spiritueller Selbstbehauptung und sozialer Anpassung* (Munich, 1989), p. 60, and, for a critical analysis of different strands of developments underlying social and economic changes within Austrian and German Cistercian monasteries, K. Schreiner, 'Zisterziensisches Mönchstum und soziale Umwelt. Wirtschaftlicher und sozialer Strukturwandel in Hoch- und Spätmittelalterlichen Zisterzienserkonventen', in K. Elm and P. Joerißen (eds.), *Die Zisterzienser. Ordensleben zwischen Ideal und Wirklichkeit. Ergänzungsband*, Schriften des Rheinischen Museumsamtes, 18 (Cologne, 1982), passim. See also, more recently, C. Kleinjung, 'Nonnen und Personal, Familien und Stifter: Zisterzienserinnenkonvente und ihre soziale Umwelt', in F. J. Felten and W. Rösener (eds.), *Norm und Realität. Kontinuität und Wandel der Zisterzienser im Mittelalter*, Vita Regularis, 42 (Münster, 2009), in particular pp. 237, 254–5. In the thirteenth century new Templar recruits were often posted to the Levant immediately after being received into the order. See, most recently, Riley-Smith, *Templars and Hospitallers as professed religious in the Holy Land*, p. 27.

[21] Schenk, 'Aspects of non-noble family involvement', passim.

relatives who constituted their support network grew stronger, which made it increasingly difficult for the established aristocratic clientele to identify with the community. This, of course, only renders all the more noteworthy the long-term involvement of certain noble and knightly families and kin-groups with the Order and the dedication of individual members of these families – like Raynald Blondel of Charny, who joined the confraternity of the Temple at Choisy in, or shortly before, June 1275.[22]

If association with reform monasticism was the reason why families began supporting Templar communities, the connection of the Order with Jerusalem and crusading was the reason why so many of them continued their support. It is the second core argument of this book that families with ties to Cistercian (and other) reform communities primarily associated with the new military orders in the context of crusading. How prevalent the impulse to go on crusade could be among Templar patrons is exemplified in the charters and letters pertaining to, or dealing with, the relatives of Dreux IV of Mello, constable of France, who was himself a patron of the strict reform community of Grandmont.[23] Not only did Dreux IV of Mello co-found the Templar commandery of Sauce-sur-Yonne,[24] but after his return from the Third Crusade, during which he had at one point been granted joint custody of Acre,[25] he made donations to the Templars to reward them for their help and friendship during his crusade. The donations are recorded in a copy charter dating from 1281, which cites 'les grans bontis et les cortoisies que li Temple nous a faites on tans passé' and the wish to benefit his soul and support the Holy Land in Outremer as motivation for his continuing patronage.[26] Dreux IV's donations to Sauce-sur-Yonne were confirmed by his sons William and Dreux in 1216.[27] At the same time their father was preparing another journey to Jerusalem, which also seems to have entailed further involvement in the affairs of the Cistercians of Pontigny and

[22] For Raynald Blondel see AN S 5186/B, dossier 11, no. 7 (1275).

[23] *CG(Yonne)*, II, no. 226, pp. 242–3 (1172).

[24] AN S 5235, dossier 1, fol. 1r (confirmation, 1216). Demurger, 'La constitution d'un patrimoine foncier', 441, showed that the donation to the Templars of a building and its appurtenances at Sauce must have occurred between 1210 and 1216.

[25] Ralph de Diceto, *Radulfi de Diceto decani lundoniensis opera historica. The historical works of master Ralph de Diceto, dean of London*, ed. W. Stubbs, Rolls Series 68, 2 vols. (London, 1876), II, p. 79; Benedict of Peterborough, *Gesta regis Henrici secundi Benedicti abbatis. The Chronicle of the reigns of Henry II and Richard I, AD 1169–1192*, ed. W. Stubbs, 2 vols. (London, 1867), II, pp. 179–80; Roger of Howden, *Chronica*, ed. W. Stubbs, 4 vols. (London, 1868), III, p. 122. See also D. Power, *The Norman frontier in the twelfth and early thirteenth centuries* (Cambridge, 2004), p. 358.

[26] See *Cart Pon*, no. 342, p. 344 (1190) for his crusade preparations and AN S 5239, dossier 51, no. 3 (BN, n.a.l., 55, fols. 351r–3r) (1281) for his donation.

[27] AN S 5235, dossier 1, fol. 1r and dossier 32, no. 2 (1216) (BN, n.a.l., 54, fols. 91r, 92r; Lavirotte, 'Mémoire statistique', 272).

other religious houses.[28] Both sons were ardent crusaders in their own right. William, lord of St-Bris, had fought with his father at Acre and, along with his son Dreux V, went on fighting in the Albigensian crusade.[29] In 1216 he made his own endowments to the Cistercians of Reigny, by 1222 he was a Templar benefactor, and in later years he involved himself as arbitrator and guarantor in the affairs of his father's Templar foundation at Sauce-sur-Yonne.[30] His son Dreux V of Mello married into the family of the Templar master Andrew of Montbard and joined the Barons' Crusade of 1239.[31] His son William accompanied King Louis on the Seventh Crusade and died in Cyprus, as did his nephew Archambaud of Bourbon (son of William I of Mello's half-brother Guy of Dampierre and Mathilda of Bourbon) and Archambaud's brother-in-law John, count of Dreux, father of the Templar knight John of Bourbon.[32] As late as 1294 the lords of St-Bris are still recorded exchanging possessions with the Templar commandery of Sauce-sur-Yonne.[33] As shown in Chapter 5, the collective biography of the lords of Mello was not unique. Like them, throughout the twelfth and thirteenth centuries, numerous knightly and noble families produced Cistercian monks, crusaders, and Templar brothers and benefactors.

The evidence therefore points to the conclusion that along with a positive attitude towards (Cistercian) reform ideas, commitment to crusading must be regarded as another, and arguably the most important, defining feature of Templar families, and that participation in the crusade movement and support of the Temple at home and abroad were two commitments instigated and maintained by the same impulse: to help support the Christian cause in the Holy Land and to promote the penitential nature of *imitatio Christi* as inspired by Cistercian theology and expressed by the Templars. This observation – that involvement in the

[28] *CG(Yonne)*, III, no. 155 (1215), no. 177 (1216). His participation in the crusade is stated in Röhricht, *Studien*, p. 112.

[29] *Cart Pon*, no. 342, p. 344 (1190); William of Tudela and an anonymous successor, *The song of the Cathar wars. A history of the Albigensian crusade*, trans. J. Shirley (Aldershot, 1996), laisse 196, p. 151 and laisse 200, p. 160.

[30] *CG(Yonne)*, III, no. 176 (1216); AN S 5235, dossier 1, fols. 1r (1223) and 6v (1236) (BN, n.a.l., 54, fols. 95r and 128r).

[31] Alongside Thibaud, king of Navarra, the count of Nevers and Forez, and Raynald of Courtenay, he was one of five intended recipients of a letter drafted in *c.* 1239 by the barons and bishops of the Latin Kingdom and the masters of the Temple and the Hospital guiding them to the Holy Land. See E. Martène and U. Durand, *Thesaurus novus anecdotorum*, 5 vols. (Paris, 1717), I, col. 1012 (*c.* 1239).

[32] Vincent de Beauvais, *Speculum historiale*, ed. J. Meutelin (Strasbourg, 1473), pp. xxxii, 89–98, as cited in *The Seventh Crusade, 1244–1254: Sources and documents*, trans. P. Jackson (Aldershot, 2009), no. 72, p. 120. John, count of Dreux, died and was buried in Nicosia in 1248. See Bur, 'Une célébration sélective de la parentèle', 310.

[33] AN S 5239, dossier 51, no. 4 (1294) (BN, n.a.l., 55, fols. 414r–17r).

Temple and in crusading complemented each other, and that both activities were connected to religious reform – is in line with the recent trend in crusade scholarship to define the crusades as a religious movement and crusading as a religious activity that became habitual in certain families and influenced patronage decisions.[34] Studies by Riley-Smith, Christoph Maier, Penny Cole and others have made abundantly clear that by the end of the twelfth century crusading was firmly established as a penitential exercise set within a broadly defined notion of religious reform that demanded the spiritual involvement of all Christians, including women, a message that popes and preachers did not fail to disseminate widely among the Christian faithful.[35] Crusade preachers, among them many Cistercians, addressed their sermons to large audiences and encouraged those among their listeners who could not, or would not, fight to sponsor substitutes or make financial contributions to the pious cause. This advice led to an increase in the number of donations to Cistercian and Templar foundations, demonstrating what Lester has described as 'the expansion of the crusades as a movement that incorporated the home front in a specific institutionalised form'.[36] As the same historian has convincingly

[34] See generally Riley-Smith, *First Crusaders*, and Bull, *Knightly piety*. Among the more focused studies examining the patronage patterns of individual crusader families see A. de Barthélemy, 'Chartes de départ et de retour des comtes de Dampierre-en-Astenois (IVe et V[e] croisades)', *Archives de l'Orient latin*, 2 (1883), 1–24; E. Siberry, 'The crusading counts of Nevers', *Nottingham Medieval Studies*, 34 (1990), 64–70; J.-N. Mathieu, 'Nouvelles recherches concernant le lignage de Joinville', *Les cahiers haut-marnais*, 190 (1992), 1–25; J.-N. Mathieu, 'À propos des châtelains de Châtillon-sur-Marne', *Société d'agriculture, commerce, sciences et arts de la Marne*, 107 (1992), 7–27; Evergates, 'The origin of the lords of Karytaina'.

[35] J. S. C. Riley-Smith, *Crusades, Christianity, and Islam* (New York, 2008), pp. 29–44; C. T. Maier, 'Crisis, liturgy and the crusades in the twelfth and thirteenth centuries', *Journal of Ecclesiastical History*, 48 (1997), 628–57; C. T. Maier, *Preaching the crusades. Mendicant friars and the cross in the thirteenth century* (Cambridge, 1994); P. J. Cole, *The preaching of the crusades to the Holy Land, 1095–1270* (Cambridge, Mass., 1991). See also Lester, 'A shared imitation', 353–6; C. M. Rousseau, 'Home front and battlefield: the gendering of papal crusading policy (1095–1221)', in S. B. Edgington and S. Lambert (eds.), *Gendering the crusades* (New York, 2001), in particular pp. 31–5; J. Bird, 'Innocent III, Peter the Chanter's circle and the crusade indulgence: theory, implementation and aftermath', in A. Sommerlechner (ed.), *Innocenzo III: urbs et orbis. Atti del congresso internazionale Roma, 9–15 settembre 1998* (Rome, 2003), 503–24; J. Bird, 'Reform or crusade? Anti-usury and crusade preaching during the pontificate of Innocent III', in J. C. Moore (ed.), *Pope Innocent III and his world* (Aldershot, 1999), 265–85; M. Markowski, 'Peter of Blois and the conception of the Third Crusade', in B. Z. Kedar (ed.), *The Horns of Hattin. Proceedings of the second conference of the Society for the Study of the Crusades and the Latin East* (Jerusalem, 1992), 261–9; Powell, *Anatomy*, pp. 20–1, 51–65; and N. Housley, *Contesting the crusades* (Oxford, 2006), pp. 48–60 for a closer discussion.

[36] Lester, 'A shared imitation', 358. One such substitute was the knight Raynald II of Dampierre, whom Thibaud of Champagne chose as his replacement when it became clear that his illness would prevent him taking part in the Fourth Crusade. Raynald had made donations to the Templars on at least one occasion (BN, n.a.l., 55, fol. 133r). True to his word that he would aid Jerusalem, Raynald did not join the crusader force in Venice but sailed straight to the Holy Land, where he was captured by Muslims and imprisoned for thirty years. His eventual release was aided by the

demonstrated, albeit in more general terms and only with regard to crusader families from Champagne, the correlation of involvement in (Cistercian) reform monasticism with involvement in crusading went beyond the duration of individual crusade preparations and also affected the religious associations of crusaders' female relatives, who often entered Cistercian nunneries as a means to participate spiritually in the crusade movement.[37] Not surprisingly, it was the same concern with religious reform and self-dedication to Christ that made the Templars attractive to these families.

The Order of the Temple has been called an 'institutionalised crusade'.[38] Although this is a rather sweeping claim, the often synchronic evidence of Templar and Cistercian support suggests that, apart from the obvious benefits that would-be crusaders gained by associating with the Temple and its support network, relatives of crusaders and crusader veterans were attracted to the Order because, like Cistercian and other reform communities, it provided them with the opportunity to replicate, to some extent, the penitential experience of crusading. The extended family of John of Châteauvillain, mentioned at the beginning of this Conclusion is exemplary in this respect. His father had been a crusader with King Louis and before him his cousin Hugh V of Broyes and ancestors Milo of Bray, Raynald and Hugh II 'Bardoul' of Broyes, and Robert II of Dreux had taken the cross. By way of the Broyes family line John was descended from the founding patrons of the Cistercian abbey of Reclus, near Épernay, and counted among his relatives donors to the reformed Benedictine nunnery of Jully, the nuns of Andecy, and the Cistercian abbey of Auberive. His line of the family had always maintained a good relationship with the reformed cathedral chapter of Langres.[39] In the context of these diverse influences the Châteauvillains and lords of Broyes had also supported the Temple.

The evidence is too fragmentary and scattered to allow us always to discern the precise circumstances that triggered the interest of a family in the affairs of the Holy Land; nor is it always possible to establish whether the interest of individuals in the crusades was the consequence of a previous association with the Temple at home or its cause. But the charters clearly show that many crusaders were married landowners and that crusading featured strongly in those Templar families which were part of wider networks. In fact, they supported the Order to such an extent

Hospitallers to whom he showed his gratitude after his return to Champagne. See Alberic of Trois-Fontaines, *Chronica*, pp. 878, 930; D. E. Queller and T. F. Madden, *The Fourth Crusade: The conquest of Constantinople* (2nd edn, Philadelphia, Pa., 2007), pp. 15, 23, 47–8.

[37] Lester, 'A shared imitation', in particular 368–70. [38] Vogel, *Das Recht der Templer*, p. 44.

[39] *Cart Lan*, passim; Bur, *La formation du comté de Champagne*, p. 319fn.; Roger, 'Les Morhiers', 86; M. Le Grand, 'Le chapitre cathédral de Langres. De la fin du XIIe siècle au concordat de 1516', *Revue d'histoire de l'Église de France*, 16 (1930), 527; *Chart St-Marc/Jully*, p. 12.

that it now seems that Templar family networks were by-products of the enthusiasm (inspired by spiritual anxiety, as well as worldly demands or family obligation) for the crusading cause that welded together kin-groups from different regions. The centre points of these networks are difficult to trace. But it is clear that strong-minded individuals (women among them), famous and influential ancestors (like Bernard of Clairvaux) or feudal demands played an important role in their creation. Regarded as a whole, networks such as the ones that I have centred on the counts of Comminges or the lords of Tilchâtel first of all manifested a mindset that dominated the actions of a great number of families in the twelfth, thirteenth and fourteenth centuries. They show how much society was affected by the crusades and how deeply the notion that Christianity could be helped by the sword had penetrated general religious and social conduct.

None of the above is to say that support for the Temple at the 'home front' was always guided by altruistic motives or religiously inspired. Although the formulaic language of the charters tends to render the motives for charitable deeds extremely uniform, in reality the motives for such deeds often changed considerably over time. First-time donors to Templar communities, and early-twelfth-century donors to the Templars more generally, often (but not always) responded to different pressures, demands and expectations from those confronting later family members, whose transactions with the Templars helped them to continue or renew existing ties.[40] The admiration for the Order's ideals that is often detected in early association or donation charters is largely absent in charters from the mid thirteenth century onwards. Baldwin Brochet's eloquent allusion to the hardship of the Templars' abundance of charity, Lauretta of Pignan's admiration for their courageous daily battle in the name of the Gospel, Roger of Béziers's appreciation of their role as defenders and protectors of God's will and the holy city of Jerusalem, Clarembaud of Noyers's respect for the Templars' 'honesty and praiseworthy zeal in the service of God' and their 'zealous and devout work for God and the Salutary Cross', and Dreux IV of Mello's gratitude for the Order's generous and honourable support for him on crusade[41] – comments like these

[40] However, the fact that by the middle of the thirteenth century business transactions outnumbered donations does not necessarily imply that donations were in steady decline. In fact, in the Auxerrois – home of important Templar families like the lords of Mello, the lords of St-Vérain and the counts of Joigny – the number of donations to the Temple reached an all-time peak during the decades from 1250 and 1260. See Demurger, 'La constitution d'un patrimoine foncier', 440, 450 (table).

[41] *CG*, no. 4, pp. 2–3 (*c.* 1125); *Cart Douz*, A:. no 40, pp. 50–1 (1133); ibid.: no. 115, pp. 106–8 (1133); *CG(Yonne)*, II, no. 156, pp. 412–13 and no. 406, pp. 412–13 (*c.* 1190); AN S 5239, dossier 51, no. 3 (and also BN, n.a.l., 55, fols. 351r–3r) (1281).

are seldom found in later documents. Instead, idealist expectations have given way to worldly motivations, including the wish to secure political, economic or military allies, and the desire for safe havens, transport facilities and financial assistance on a planned journey. This shift in emphasis from the spiritual to the mundane, which was never absolute, is, first of all, attested in the charter collections and cartularies, which are evidence that business transactions far outnumbered donations by the middle of the thirteenth century. This, however, was nothing unusual and also occurred, at different times, at Cluny and Cîteaux.[42] Nor was it necessarily always a sure indicator that relations with donors were deteriorating. Rather, a religious community's ability to barter for specific assets (although neither side would have described the transaction in these terms) and thereby to enhance or concentrate its patrimony in a meaningful way was in itself proof of success.

The significance of the observation that families engaged with the Order in a variety of ways and for a variety of motives other than religious fervour rather lies in the conclusion that even family members who engaged with the Order for outwardly mundane – even opportunistic – reasons still acted within the same preconditioned frameworks as their more religiously inspired relatives. They engaged in Templar commanderies in similar contexts, and used a similar language, thereby contributing to the collective memory of a meaningful relationship between family and Order. Apart from the reasons outlined in Chapter 3, if analysed as a development within the narrower context of family–Templar relations, the changes in the nature of transactions between families and the Order not only indicate that by a certain time the Templars had secured themselves a firm position in the religious landscape of France; they also show that the Order had become a permanent fixture on the mental maps that conditioned new generations of knights and nobles to support Templar communities within traditional patterns, even if to them their decisions seemed primarily functional. A concomitant reason why spiritual ideals and expectations receded into the background was that for later-generation crusaders who came from families with vested interests in the crusader principalities, crusading itself had become in many respects more mundane an activity (if not necessarily a secular experience) than it had been for their ancestors. Although many armed pilgrims returned from their journeys considerably poorer and weaker than when they had set out, only to have a relative take up the cross again and repeat the

[42] Newman, *Boundaries of charity*, p. 286fn.; Rosenwein, *To be the neighbor of Saint Peter*, pp. 202–5; White, *Custom, kinship, and gifts to saints*, pp. 191–2; McLaughlin, *Consorting with saints*, pp. 255–6.

experience, it was also true that as the crusader principalities in the Latin East developed, the number of families who sent representatives across the sea to look after their possessions, and who therefore had self-interested reasons to respond to calls for crusades and to support the military orders' tasks overseas, also increased.

This necessary caveat has little bearing on the arguments of this book, since religious and self-serving motives could, and often did, go hand in hand and in any case did not generally disqualify actors from altruistic behaviour. The fact that members of landowning families went to the East for business purposes or political reasons does not necessarily imply that the spiritual significance and penitential value of the Templars' work, or, for that matter, of crusading, was irrelevant to them. Both the Templar life and the life of the crusader encapsulated integral elements of *imitatio Christi* – self-sacrifice, charitable compassion – to which lay people in the thirteenth century responded enthusiastically and *en masse*, even if other motivations also guided their actions.[43] As an example, the powerful family of Porcelet from Arles had substantial possessions in the county of Tripoli and the family's male members are frequently recorded in the East.[44] When in 1174 William and Johanna Porcelet gave their possessions to the Templars of St-Gilles they were therefore, in a very direct way, contributing to the protection of their overseas holdings. However, this motivation alone does not explain why they also wished henceforth to be regarded as members of the Order, why if one of them should die the other would live with the Templars, and why both wanted to be buried in the Order's cemetery at St-Gilles.[45]

Nor do the above-mentioned qualifications diminish the significance of the fact that the Order had fixed itself permanently in the collective memory of a large number of families and kin-groups who associated closely with Jerusalem and the Holy Land crusades. The combination of support for the Order with a strong and active commitment to crusading was undoubtedly the most striking feature of Templar families, bearing in mind that only a fraction of the knights and nobles of France joined the Order of the Temple and only a minority ever went

[43] On the concept of *imitatio Christi* in the context of the crusades see Purkis, *Crusading spirituality*; W.J. Purkis, 'Elite and popular perceptions of *imitatio Christi* in twelfth-century crusade spirituality', in K. Cooper and J. Gregory (eds.), *Elite and popular religion*, Studies in Church History, 42 (Woodbridge, 2006), 54–64; and generally G. Constable, *Three studies in medieval religious and social thought. The interpretation of Mary and Martha, the ideal of the imitation of Christ, the orders of society* (Cambridge, 1995), pp. 198–228.

[44] On the Porcelet family's involvement in crusading see Aurell i Cardona, *Une famille de la noblesse*, pp. 147–54; Richard, 'Le comté de Tripoli dans les chartes', passim; Carraz, *L'ordre du Temple*, pp. 74, 76, 79.

[45] Prutz, *Entwicklung und Untergang*, p. 20 and Prutz, *Die geistlichen Ritterorden*, p. 362.

on crusade.[46] The number of Templars who had in their former lives been crusaders or who were relatives of men who had fought on crusading campaigns suggests that many already felt strongly associated with the movement when they joined the Order. Furthermore, although financial support of, or a business engagement with, the Temple can never be compared with the act of actually setting out on a crusade, in the case of many of the individuals mentioned in this book the motivation for both actions seems to stem, at least partially, from the same sources: an awareness of the situation in the Holy Land, a sense of family tradition, and therefore a feeling of obligation towards one's family to aid in the defence and recapture of the holy places, and particularly Jerusalem.[47] More than that, the networks and the particular involvement of each of its member families in the Order of the Temple show clearly that in Burgundy, Champagne and Languedoc the Order had in place a strong support network of knightly and noble families, in spite of the changes in its donor base and its internal failings and mismanagement.[48] They were connected by links that stretched horizontally, between various branches of a family and their associates, and vertically along feudal lines, and were willing to invest in its ideals sometimes for many generations. As has been seen, these families were uniquely identifiable by their interest in rigorous monastic observance (and in particular in the Cistercians) and their active involvement in crusading. They were spiritually connected to the Templars, whom they endowed with landed possessions, churches and oratories in return for votive masses, the guarantee of a burial place and other forms of *memoria*. Whether these networks existed also in other parts of France and Europe is a question that only further research can answer. But Bishop Peter of Lérida's lament, mentioned at the beginning of this book, suggests that the patterns of family involvement in the Order of the Temple in Burgundy, Champagne and vast regions of southern France were not unique.

[46] R. Hiestand, 'Some reflections on the impact of the papacy on the crusader states and the military orders in the twelfth and thirteenth centuries', in Z. Hunyadi and J. Laszlovsky (eds.), *The crusades and the military orders. Expanding the frontiers of medieval Latin Christianity* (Budapest, 2001), 17, estimated the numerical strength of the military orders in East and West at 1,000–1,500 knights maximum even at the height of the orders' power. That crusaders (although never constituting the majority of knights and nobles) were nonetheless numerous is shown, for example, in J. France, 'Patronage and the appeal of the First Crusade', in J. Phillips (ed.), *The First Crusade: origins and impact* (Manchester, 1997), 6.

[47] Petit argues such a case for the relatives of the Templar Odo of Grancey. See *HdB*, III, pp. 39–40.

[48] The Order's internal failings and mismanagement included a lack of supervision and obvious negligence in keeping its normative texts sufficiently updated. See Riley-Smith, 'Structures', and Riley-Smith, 'Were the Templars guilty?', passim.

BIBLIOGRAPHY

ARCHIVAL SOURCES

Dijon, Archives départementales de la Côte-d'Or (ADCO)
111 H 1156 (Fonds de Bure), 111 H 1161/1 (Fonds de Bure), 111 H 1184 (Fonds Épailly), 111 H 1186 (Fonds Épailly), 115 H 1234 (Fonds La Romagne), 115 H 1232 (Fonds La Romagne)
Paris, Archives Nationales de France (AN)
S 4956, 4957, 4958, 4959, 4967, 4968/A, 4968/B, 5008/A, 5008/B, 5150, 5178, 5179/A, 5186, 5188/A, 5188/B, 5235, 5236, 5237/A, 5237/B, 5238, 5241, 5242, 5243, 5244/A, 5249, 5250/B, 5252
Paris, Bibliothèque nationale de France (BN)
Collection Doat, 40, 41, 124, 140
Cartulaire manuscrit d'Albon, n.a.l. 7, 15, 16, 17, 18, 19, 20, 21, 22, 32, 51, 52, 53, 54, 55, 56, 57

PRINTED SOURCES

Les actes de la famille Porcelet d'Arles. Texte (972–1320), ed. Martin Aurell, *Collection de documents inédits sur l'histoire de France* (Paris, 2001).

Albanès, Joseph Hyacinthe and Cyr Ulysse Joseph Chevalier, *Gallia christiana novissima. Histoire des archevêchés, évêques et abbayes de France d'après les documents authentiques recueillis dans les registres du Vatican et les archives locales, vol. v: Toulon* (Valence, 1911).

Alberic of Trois-Fontaines, *Chronica a monacho novi monasterii Hoiensis interpolata*, ed. Paul Scheffer-Boichorst, *MGH SS*, XXIII (Hanover, 1874), 674–950.

Albert of Aachen, *Historia Hierosolymitana*, ed. and trans. Susan B. Edgington (Oxford, 2007).

Alexander III, *Epistolae et privilegia, PL*, CC, cols. 69–1320C.

Annales Nivernenses, ed. Georg Waitz, *MGH SS*, XIII (Hanover, 1881), 88–92.

Anselm of Havelberg, *Dialogi, PL*, CLXXXVIII, cols. 1139–1248B.

Benedict of Peterborough, *Gesta regis Henrici secundi Benedicti abbatis. The Chronicle of the reigns of Henry II and Richard I, AD 1169–1192*, ed. William Stubbs, 2 vols. (London, 1867).

Bernard of Caux, *Confessiones de V libro lauraguesii fratris Bernardi de Cautio transcripto in hoc libro usque ad CLXVIII F°. – Item a dicto folio deinceps de quarto libro dicti fratris Bernardi,*

Bibliothèque municipale de Toulouse, ms. 609, ed. Jean Duvernoy [http://jean.duvernoy.free.fr/text/listetexte.htm#sinquisit].
Bernard of Clairvaux, *Epistolae, PL*, CLXXII, cols. 67–662.
S. Bernardi opera, ed. Jean Leclercq and Henri-Maria Rochais, 8 vols. (Rome, 1957–77).
Liber ad milites Templi de laude novae militiae, ed. Jean Leclercq, Henri-Maria Rochais and Charles Holwell Talbot, *S. Bernardi Opera*, 8 vols. (Rome, 1957–77), III, 205–39.
Bernardo de Brito, *Primeyra parte da Chronica de Cister: onde se contam as cousas principais d'esta religiam, commuytas antiguidades, assi do reyno de Portugal como de outros muytos da christandade* (Lisbon, 1602).
La 'Bible' au seigneur de Berzé, ed. Félix Lecoy (Paris, 1938).
Cartulaire de l'abbaye de Berdoues, ed. Jean-Marie Cazauran (The Hague, 1905).
Cartulaire de l'abbaye de Bonnecombe, ed. Pierre-Aloïs Verlaguet (Rodez, 1918–25).
Cartulaire de l'abbaye de Boulancourt: de l'ancien diocèse de Troyes, aujourd'hui du département de la Haute-Marne, ed. Charles Lalore (Troyes, 1869).
Cartulaire de l'abbaye de Conques en Rouergue, ed. Gustave Desjardins (Paris, 1879).
Cartulaire de l'abbaye de Gimont, ed. Adrien Clergeac (Paris, 1905).
Cartulaire de l'abbaye de Lézat, ed. Anne-Marie Magnou and Paul Ourliac, 2 vols. (Paris, 1984–7).
Cartulaire de l'abbaye de Montiéramey, ed. Charles Lalore, *Collection des principaux cartulaires du diocèse de Troyes*, VII (Paris, Troyes, 1890).
Cartulaire de l'abbaye de Paraclet, ed. Charles Lalore (Paris, Troyes, 1878).
Cartulaire de l'abbaye de Saint-Loup de Troyes, ed. Charles Lalore, *Collection des principaux cartulaires du diocèse de Troyes*, I (Paris, Troyes, 1875).
Cartulaire de l'abbaye de Saint-Pierre d'Oyes (canton de Sézanne), suivi d'une note sur les anciens seigneurs de Broyes, ed. Édouard de Barthélemy (Châlons-sur-Marne, 1882).
Cartulaire de l'abbaye de Silvanès, ed. Pierre-Aloïs Verlaguet (Rodez, 1910).
Cartulaire de l'abbaye de Vabres au diocèse de Rodez. Essai de reconstruction d'un manuscrit disparu, ed. Étienne Fournial (Rodez, Saint Étienne, 1989).
Cartulaire de Béziers (Livre Noir), ed. Julien Rouquette (Paris, Montpellier, 1918).
Cartulaire de la cathédrale de Dax. Liber Rubeus *(XIe–XIIe siècles)*, ed. and trans. Georges Pon and Jean Cabanot (Dax, 2004).
Cartulaire de la commanderie de Richerenches de l'Ordre du Temple (1136–1214), ed. Marquis de Ripert-Monclar (Avignon, Paris, 1907; reprint: 1978).
Le cartulaire de La Selve. La terre, les hommes et le pouvoir en Rouergue au XIIe siècle, ed. Paul Ourliac (Paris, 1985).
Cartulaire de Montier-la-Celle, ed. Charles Lalore, *Collection des principaux cartulaires du diocèse de Troyes*, VI (Paris, Troyes, 1882).
Cartulaire de Saint-Pierre de Troyes, ed. Charles Lalore (Paris, Troyes, 1880).
Cartulaire des templiers de Montsaunès, ed. Charles Higounet, *Bulletin philologique et historique du comité des travaux historiques et scientifiques* (1957), 211–94.
Cartulaire des templiers de Vaour (Tarn), ed. Charles Portal and Edmond Cabié (Toulouse, Albi, 1894).
Cartulaire des templiers du Puy-en-Velay, ed. Augustin Chassaing, *Annales de la Société d'agriculture, sciences, arts et commerce de Puy*, 33 (Paris, 1882), 139–263.

Cartulaire du chapitre cathédral de Langres, ed. Hubert Flammarion (Turnhout, 2004).
Cartulaire du prieuré de La Charité-sur-Loire, ed. René de Lespinasse (Nevers, 1887).
Cartulaire du prieuré de Jully-les-Nonnains, ed. Ernest Petit, *BuSoScYonne*, 38 (Auxerre, 1884), 249–301.
Cartulaire et archives des communes et l'ancien diocèse et de l'arrondissement administratif de Carcassonne, ed. Alphonse J. Mahul, 6 vols. (Paris, 1857–71).
Cartulaire et documents de l'abbaye de Nonenque, ed. Camille Couderc and Jean-Louis Rigal, *Archives historiques du Rouergue*, 18 (Rodez, 1950).
Cartulaire général de l'ordre des hospitaliers de St-Jean de Jérusalem (1100–1310), ed. Joseph Delaville Le Roulx, 4 vols. (Paris, 1894–1906).
Cartulaire général de l'ordre du Temple, ed. Alexis Marie Joseph André Marquis d'Albon (Paris, 1913).
Cartulaire général de l'Yonne, ed. Maximilien Quantin, 2 vols. (Auxerre, 1854–60).
Cartulaire général de Paris ou Recueil de documents relatifs à l'histoire et à la topographie de Paris, vol. I (328–1180), ed. Robert de Lasteyrie (Paris, 1887).
Cartulaire Lyonnais. Documents inédits pour servir à l'histoire des anciennes provinces de Lyonnais, Forez, Beaujolais, Dombes, Bresse et Bugey, vol. I: Documents antérieurs à l'année 1255, ed. Marie-Claude Guigue (Lyon, 1885).
Cartulaires de l'abbaye de Molesme. Ancien diocèse de Langres 916–1250. Recueil de documents sur le nord de la Bourgogne et le Midi de la Champagne, ed. Jacques Laurent, 2 vols. (Paris, 1907–11).
Cartulaires des abbayes d'Aniane et de Gellone, vol. I: Cartulaire de Gellone, ed. Paul Alaus, Léon Cassan and Edmond Meynial (Montpellier, 1898).
Cartulaires des abbayes d'Aniane et de Gellone, vol. II: Cartulaire d'Aniane, ed. Léon Cassan and Edmond Meynial (Montpellier, 1900–10).
Cartulaires des templiers de Douzens, ed. Pierre Gérard and Élisabeth Magnou, *Collection des documents inédits sur l'histoire de France*, III (Paris, 1965).
El cartulario de la encomienda templaria de Castellote (Teruel), 1184–1283, ed. Sandra de la Torre Gonzalo (Zaragoza, 2009).
Catalogue des actes de Philippe-Auguste. Avec une introduction sur les caractères et l'importance historiques de ces documents, ed. Léopold Delisle (Paris, 1856; reprint: Geneva, 1975).
Catalogue des actes des comtes de Bar, 1022 à 1239, ed. Marcel Grosdidier de Matons (Bar-le-Duc, 1922).
Chartes de l'abbaye de Mores, ed. Charles Lalore, *MSA Aube*, 37 (1873), 5–107.
Chartes de la commanderie de Beauvoir de l'ordre teutonique, ed. Charles Lalore, *Collection des principaux cartulaires du diocèse de Troyes*, III (Paris, Troyes, 1878), 177–328.
Chartes de la terre sainte provenant de l'abbaye de Notre-Dame de Josaphat, ed. Henri-François Delaborde (Paris, 1880).
Chartes des Cisterciens de Saint-Benoît-en-Woevre des origines à 1300, ed. Jean Denaix (Verdun, 1959).
Chartes des maisons de Montfrin et du Gard rhodanien, ed. Joseph Hyacinthe Albanès and Cyr Ulysse Joseph Chevalier, *Gallia christiana novissima. Histoire des archevêchés, évêques et abbayes de France d'après les documents authentiques recueillis dans les registres du Vatican et les archives locales, vol. V: Toulon* (Valence, 1911).
Chartes des maisons du Temple d'Arles, Tarascon, Avignon, Montfrin et du Gard rhodanien, St-Gilles, in Damien Carraz, *Ordres militaires, croisades et sociétés méridionales.*

L'ordre du temple dans la basse vallée du Rhône (1124–1312), vol. III: Sources (Ph.D. thesis, Lyon: Université de Lyon 2, 2003).

Chartes du Forez antérieures au XIVᵉ siècle, ed. Georges Guichard, Édouard Perroy, Marguerite Gonon and Étienne Fournial, 18 vols. (Mâcon, 1933–80).

Chartes en langue française antérieures à 1271 conservées dans le département de la Haute-Marne, ed. Jean-Gabriel Gigot (Paris, 1974).

Chartes et documents concernant l'abbaye de Cîteaux 1098–1182, ed. Jean Marilier (Rome, 1961).

Chartes originales provenant de la commanderie des templiers de Saint Marc à Nuits-sur-Amançon et du prieuré de Jully-les-Nonnains, ed. Ernest Petit, *Bulletin philologique et historique* (1897), 759–89.

Le chartrier de l'abbaye cistercienne de Fontfroide (894–1260), ed. Véronique de Becdelièvre, 2 vols. (Paris, 2009).

Le chartrier de l'abbaye prémontrée de Saint-Yved de Braine (1134–1250), ed. Oliver Guyotjeannin (Paris, 2000).

Chartularium domus Templi Hierosolymitani de Roais diocesis Vasionensis, ed. Joseph Hyacinthe Albanès, Cyr Ulysse Joseph Chevalier, in *Cartulaires des hospitaliers et des templiers en Dauphiné*, III (Vienne, 1975), 61–136.

Chifflet, Pierre-François, *Sancti Bernardi Clarevallensis abbatis genus illustre assertum*, ed. Jacques-Pierre Migne, *PL*, CLXXXV (Dijon, 1660; reprint: 1885), cols. 1383–2018.

The chronicle of the Third Crusade. A translation of the 'Itinerarium Peregrinorum et Regesta Regis Ricardi', trans. Helen J. Nicholson (Aldershot, 1997).

Chronique d'Ernoul et de Bernard le trésorier, ed. Louis de Mas Latrie (Paris, 1871).

Chronique de l'abbaye de Saint-Bénigne de Dijon, suivie de la chronique de Saint-Pierre de Bèze, ed. Émile Bougard and Joseph Garnier (Dijon, 1875).

Chronique de Saint-Pierre-le-Vif de Sens, dite de Clarius, ed. Robert-Henri Bautier and Monique Gilles (Paris, 1979).

Col·lecció diplomàtica de la casa del Temple de Gardeny (1070–1200), ed. Ramon Sarobe i Huesca, 2 vols, XII (Barcelona, 1998).

Collection des documents inédits relatifs à la ville de Troyes et à la Champagne méridionale, ed. Sociéte académique de l'Aube, 5 vols. (Troyes, 1878–93).

Conciliorum oecumenicorum decreta, ed. Giuseppe Alberigo (3rd edn, Bologna, 1973).

The Conquest of Jerusalem and the Third Crusade, ed. and trans. Peter Edbury (Aldershot, 1998).

Cronaca del Templare di Tiro (1243–1314). La caduta degli stati crociati nel racconto di un testimone oculare, ed. Laura Minervini (Naples, 2000).

De expugnatione Terrae Sanctae per Saladinum libellus, in Ralph of Coggeshall, *Chronicon anglicanum*, ed. Joseph Stevenson, Rerum britannicarum medii aevi scriptores, 66 (London, 1875).

Delaville Le Roulx, Joseph (ed.), 'Un nouveau manuscrit de la règle du Temple', *Annuaire-Bulletin de la Société de l'histoire de France*, 26 (1889), 185–214.

Diocèse ancien de Châlons-sur-Marne, histoire et monuments. Suivi des cartulaires inédits de la commanderie de la Neuville-au-Temple, des abbayes de Toussaints, de Monstiers et du prieuré de Vinetz, ed. Édouard de Barthélemy, 2 vols. (Paris, Chaumont, Châlons-sur-Marne, 1861).

Documens historiques et généalogiques sur les familles et les hommes remarquables du Rouergue dans les temps anciens et modernes, ed. Hippolyte de Barrau, 4 vols. (Rodez, 1853–60).

Documenti sulle relazioni delle città Toscane coll'Oriente Christiano e coi Turchi fino all'anno MDXXXI, ed. Giuseppe Müller (Florence, 1879).

Documents concernant les templiers extraits des archives de Malte, ed. Joseph Delaville Le Roulx (Paris, 1882).

Documents historiques sur le Tarn-et-Garonne, ed. François Moulenq, 4 vols. (Montauban, 1879–94).

Documents inédits pour servir à l'histoire de Bourgogne, ed. Marcel Canat de Chizy (Chalon-sur-Saône, 1863), vol. I.

Documents sur la maison de Durfort (XIe–XVe siècle), ed. Nicole de Peña, 2 vols. (Bordeaux, 1977).

Droits et possessions du comte de Toulouse dans l'Albigeois au milieu du XIIIe siècle. Documents publiés et annotés, ed. Edmond Cabié (Paris, Toulouse, Albi, 1900).

L'estoire de Eracles empereur et la conqueste de la terre d'outremer; la continuation de l'estoire de Guillaume arcevesque de Sur, Recueil des historiens des croisades, Historiens occidentaux, II (Paris, 1859), 1–481.

Exordium magnum Cisterciense: sive narratio de initio cisterciensis ordinis auctore Conrado monacho Clarevallensi postea ad Eberbacensi ibidem abate ad codicum fidem, ed. Bruno Griesser, *CCCM*, 138 (Turnhout, 1997).

Feudal society in medieval France. Documents from the county of Champagne, trans. Theodore Evergates (Philadelphia, Pa., 1993).

Gallia christiana in provincias ecclesiasticas distributa, ed. Paul Piolin, 13 vols. (Paris, 1870–8).

Gesta pontificum Autissiodorensium, in L.-M. Duru (ed.), *Bibliothèque historique de l'Yonne ou collection de légendes, chroniques et documents divers pour servir à l'histoire des différentes contrées qui forment aujourd'hui ce département*, 2 vols. (Auxerre, 1850–63), vol. I.

Les gestes des Chiprois, ed. Gaston Paris and Louis de Mas Latrie, Recueil des historiens des croisades. Documents arméniens, II (Paris, 1906), 643–872.

Godfrey of Auxerre, *S. Bernardi vita et fragmenta*, ed. Jean Mabillon, *PL*, CLXXXV, cols. 301–68, 523–30.

Guibert of Nogent, *Self and society in medieval France. The memoirs of Abbot Guibert of Nogent*, trans. John F. Benton (Toronto, 1984).

Guillaume de Puylaurens, *Chronique, 1145–1275*, ed. and trans. Jean Duvernoy (Paris, 1976; reprint: 1999).

Henry of Huntingdon, *Historia Anglorum*, ed. Thomas Arnold (London, 1879).

Histoire et cartulaire des templiers de Provins. Avec une introduction sur les débuts du Temple en France, ed. Victor Carrière (Paris, 1919; reprint: Marseille, 1978).

Hugh of Poitiers, *Chronique de l'abbaye de Vézelay*, ed. Robert Burchard Constantijn Huygens, *CCCM*, 42 (Turnhout, 1976), 395–607.

Innocent II, *Epistolae et privilegia*, *PL*, CLXXIX (1855), cols. 53–658.

Inventaire de la collection de Chastellux, ed. Charles Porée, *BuSoScYonne*, 57 (1903), 117–292; 58 (1904), 35–144, 229–318; 59 (1905), 227–98.

Isaac of L'Étoile, *Sermons*, ed. Anselme Hoste and Gaetano Raciti, 3 vols. (Paris, 1967–8).

Itinerarium peregrinorum et gesta regis Ricardi, ed. William Stubbs, Britannicarum Medii Aevi Scriptores (London, 1864).

James of Aragon, *The chronicle of James I King of Aragon, surnamed the Conqueror (written by himself)*, trans. John Forster (London, 1883).

James of Vitry, *Lettres de Jacques de Vitry (1160/1170–1240) évêque de Saint-Jean-d'Acre. Édition critique*, ed. Robert Burchard Constantijn Huygens (Leiden, 1960).

Lettres de la cinquième croisade, ed. Robert Burchard Constantijn Huygens, trans. Gaston Duchet-Suchaux (Turnhout, 1998).

Joinville and Villehardouin: Chronicles of the crusades, trans. Caroline Smith (New York, London, 2009).

Lambert of Wattrelos, *Annales Carmaracenses*, ed. Georg Heinrich Pertz, *MGH SS*, XVI (Hanover, 1859), 509–54.

Libellus de diversis ordinibus et professionibus qui sunt in aecclesia, ed. and trans. Giles Constable and B. S. Smith (revised edn, Oxford, 2003).

'Littere baronum'. The earliest cartulary of the counts of Champagne, ed. Theodore Evergates (Toronto, 2003).

Manrique, Angel, *Annales Cistercienses*, 4 vols. (Lyon, 1613–59).

Martène, Edmond and Ursin Durand, *Thesaurus novus anecdotorum*, 5 vols. (Paris, 1717).

Matthew Paris, *Chronica majora*, ed. Henry Richards Luard, Rolls Series, 57, 7 vols. (London, 1872–83).

Nécrologe de Sainte-Marie de Cassan, ed. Henri Barthés, *Les documents nécrologiques du diocèse de Béziers. Nécrologes et obituaires du XIe au XVIIe siècles* (St-Geniès-de-Fontedit, 1988), 7–62.

Necrologium ecclesiae Sancti Petri Matisconensis, ed. Marie-Claude Guigue (Bourg-en-Bresse, 1874).

Nicholas of Clairvaux, *Epistolae, PL*, CXCVI, cols. 1590–1654.

Obituaire de la commanderie du Temple de Reims, ed. Édouard de Barthélemy, *Mélanges historiques. Collection des documents inédits*, IV (Paris, 1882), 313–32.

Odo of Deuil, *De profectione Ludovici VII in Orientem*, ed. and trans. Virginia Gingerick Berry (New York, 1948).

The old French continuation of William of Tyre, ed. Peter Edbury, *The conquest of Jerusalem and the Third Crusade* (Aldershot, 1998), 11–145.

Orderic Vitalis, *Historia aecclesiastica*, ed. and trans. Marjorie Chibnall, 6 vols. (Oxford, 1969–80).

Otto of Freising, *Chronicon*, ed. Roger Wilmans, *MGH SS*, XX (Hanover, 1868), pp. 83–301.

Peter of Celle, *The letters of Peter of Celle*, ed. and trans. Julian Haseldine, Oxford Medieval Texts (Oxford, 2001).

Peter of Les Vaux-de-Cernay, *Historia Albigensium et sacri belli in eos anno 1209 suscepti, duce et principe Simone de Monteforti, PL*, CCXIII, cols. 543–711.

Petri Vallium Sarnaii monachi Hystoria albigensis, ed. Pascal Guébin and Ernest Lyon, I (Paris, 1926).

Peter the Venerable, *De miraculis libri duo*, ed. Denise Bouthillier, *CCCM*, 83 (Turnhout, 1988).

Les plus anciennes chartes en langue provençale, ed. Claude Brunel, 2 vols. (Paris, 1926–52).

Les plus anciens documents linguistiques de la France. Les chartes de la Haute-Marne (ChHM), ed. Martin-D. Gleßgen, Jean-Gabriel Gigot, Dumitru Chihaï and Benoît-M. Tock [http://www.mediaevistik.uzh.ch/docling/corpus.php].

Les plus anciens documents linguistiques de la France. Les chartes de la Marne (ChMa), ed. Martin-D. Gleßgen and Dumitru Chihaï [http://www.mediaevistik.uzh.ch/docling/corpus.php].

Le premier cartulaire de l'abbaye cistercienne de Pontigny (XIIe–XIIIe siècles), ed. Martine Garrigues (Paris, 1981).

Le procès des templiers, ed. Jules Michelet, 2 vols. (Paris, 1841; reprint: 1987).

Le procès des templiers d'Auvergne, 1309–1311. Édition de l'interrogatoire de juin 1309, ed. Anne-Marie Chagny-Sève and Roger Sève (Paris, 1986).

Ralph de Diceto, *Radulfi de Diceto decani lundoniensis opera historica. The historical works of master Ralph de Diceto, dean of London*, ed. William Stubbs, Rolls Series 68, 2 vols. (London, 1876).

Recueil des actes de l'abbaye cistercienne de Bonnefont en Comminges, ed. Charles Samaran and Charles Higounet (Paris, 1970).

Recueil des chartes de l'abbaye de Clairvaux au XIIe siècle, ed. Jean Waquet (Paris, 2004).

Recueil des chartes de l'abbaye de La Grasse, vol. I: 779–1119, ed. Élisabeth Magnou-Nortier and Anne-Marie Magnou (Paris, 1996).

Recueil des chartes de l'abbaye de La Grasse, vol. II: 1117–1279, ed. Claudine Pailhès (Paris, 2000).

Recueil des chartes de l'abbaye de Notre-Dame de Cheminon, ed. Édouard de Barthélemy (Paris, 1983).

Recueil des pièces pour faire suite au cartulaire général de l'Yonne, ed. Maximilien Quantin (Paris, 1873).

Regesta regni Hierosolymitani 1097–1291, ed. Reinhold Röhricht, 2 vols. (Innsbruck, 1893–1904).

Registres du trésor des chartes, vol. I: Règne de Philippe le Bel. Inventaire analytique, ed. Jean Glénisson, Jean Guerout and Robert Fawtier (Paris, 1958).

La règle du Temple, ed. Henri de Curzon (Paris, 1888).

Robert of St Marian, *Chronicon*, ed. Oswald Holder-Egger, *MGH SS*, XXVI (Hanover, 1882), 226–87.

Robert of Thorigny, *Chronique et opuscules religieux*, ed. Léopold Delisle, 2 vols. (Rouen, 1872–3).

Roger of Howden, *Chronica*, ed. William Stubbs, 4 vols. (London, 1868).

Roger of Wendover, *Chronica, sive flores historiarum*, ed. Henry O. Coxe, 5 vols. (London, 1841–4).

'The Rothelin continuation of William of Tyre', in Janet Shirley (ed.), *Crusader Syria in the thirteenth century* (Aldershot, 1999).

La roue de fortune ou chronique de Grancey. Roman généalogique écrit au commencement du XIVe siècle, trans. Émile Jolibois (Chaumont, 1872).

The Rule of the Templars: the French text of the Rule of the Order of the Knights Templar, trans. Judi M. Upton-Ward (Woodbridge, 1992).

Die Schriften des Kölner Domscholasters, späteren Bischofs von Paderborn und Kardinal-Bischofs von S. Sabina, Oliverus, ed. Hermann Hoogeweg (Tübingen, 1894).

The Seventh Crusade, 1244–1254: Sources and documents, trans. Peter Jackson (Aldershot, 2009).

Les sires et barons de Chacenay, ed. Charles Lalore (Troyes, 1885).
Statuta capitulorum generalium ordinis cisterciensis ab anno 1116 ad annum 1786, vol. I: 1116–1220, ed. Joseph Marie Canivez (Louvain, 1933).
The Templars. Selected sources, trans. Malcolm Barber and Keith Bate (Manchester, New York, 2002).
Titres de la maison ducale de Bourbon, ed. Albert Lecoy de la Marche and Jean-Louis-Alphonse Huillard-Bréholles, 2 vols. (Paris, 1867–74).
Twelfth-century statutes from the Cistercian general chapter. Latin text with English notes and commentary, ed. and trans. Chrysogonus Waddel (Brecht, 2002).
Die ursprüngliche Templerregel, ed. Gustav Schnürer (Freiburg im Breisgau, 1903).
Vauxbons. Abbaye cistercienne au diocèse de Langres (... 1175–1394 ...). Étude historique et édition du chartrier, ed. Benoît Chauvin (Devecey, 2005).
Vincent de Beauvais, *Speculum historiale*, ed. Johann Meutelin (Strasbourg, 1473).
Vita Sancti Petri prioris juliacensis puellarum monasterii, et monachi molismensis, ed. Jean Mabillon, *PL*, CLXXXV, cols. 1257–70.
Vita Venerabilis Amedaei Altae Ripae, ed. Anselme Dimier, *Studia Monastica*, 5 (1963), 265–302.
William of Saint-Thierry, *Vita prima Sancti Bernardi*, ed. Jean Mabillon, *PL*, CLXXXV, cols. 225–68.
William of Tudela and an anonymous successor, *The song of the Cathar wars. A history of the Albigensian Crusade*, trans. Janet Shirley (Aldershot, 1996).
William of Tyre, *Chronique*, ed. Robert Burchard Constantijn Huygens, *CCCM*, 63, 63A (Turnhout, 1986).

SECONDARY LITERATURE

Alanièce, Valérie and François Gilet, *Les templiers et leurs commanderies: l'exemple d'Avaleur en Champagne* (Langres, 1995).
Allard, Jean-Marie, 'Le contrôle des paroisses, un enjeu entre les ordres militaires et l'épiscopat: le cas aquitain', in *Les ordres religieux militaires dans le Midi (XIIe–XIVe siècle)*, CdF, LI (Toulouse, 2006), 21–52.
Allemand-Gay, Marie-Thérèse, *Le pouvoir des comtes de Bourgogne au XIIIe siècle* (Paris, 1988).
Althoff, Gerd, *Family, friends and followers: political and social bonds in medieval Europe*, trans. Christopher Carroll (Cambridge, 2004).
Angenendt, Arnold, Thomas Braucks, Rolf Busch and Hubertus Lutterbach, 'Counting piety in the early and high middle ages', in Bernhard Jussen (ed.), *Ordering medieval society. Perspectives on intellectual and practical modes of shaping social relations* (Philadelphia, Pa., 2001), 15–54.
Antweiler, Wolfgang, *Das Bistum Tripolis im 12. und 13. Jahrhundert* (Düsseldorf, 1991).
Aubarbier, Jean-Luc and Michel Binet, *Les sites templiers de France* (Rennes, 1997).
Aubé, Pierre, *Saint Bernard de Clairvaux* (Paris, 2003).
Aurell i Cardona, Martin, 'Les cisterciennes et leurs protecteurs en Provence rhodanienne', in *Les cisterciens de Languedoc (13e–14e s.), CdF*, XXI (Toulouse, 1986), 235–67.
Une famille de la noblesse provençale au Moyen Âge: Les Porcelets (Aubanel, 1986).

Averkorn, Raphaela, 'Die Cistercienserabteien Berdoues und Gimont in ihren Beziehungen zum laikalen Umfeld. Gebetsgedenken, Konversion und Begräbnis', in Franz Neiske, Dietrich W. Poeck and Mechthild Sandmann (eds.), *Vinculum societatis. Joachim Wollasch zum 60. Geburtstag* (Sigmaringendorf, 1991), 1–35.

Backmund, Norbert, 'St-Yved de Braine', *LexMA*, II (Munich, 2002), 545.

Baker, Derek, 'Popular piety in the Lodève in the early twelfth century: the case of Pons of Léras', in Derek Baker (ed.), *Religious motivation: bibliographical and sociological problems for the Church historian* (Oxford, 1978), 39–47.

Balları́ y Casas, José, *Historia de Cardona* (Barcelona, 1905).

Baratier, Édouard, *Enquêtes sur les droits et revenus de Charles Ier d'Anjou en Provence 1252 et 1278. Avec une étude sur le domaine comtal et les seigneuries de Provence au 13e siècle* (Paris, 1969).

Barber, Malcolm, 'The social context of the Templars', *Transactions of the Royal Historical Society*, 5 (1984), 27–46.

'Supplying the crusader states: the role of the Templars', in Benjamin Z. Kedar (ed.), *The Horns of Hattin. Proceedings of the second conference of the Society for the Study of the Crusades and the Latin East* (Jerusalem, 1992), 314–26.

The new knighthood: a history of the Order of the Temple (Cambridge, 1994).

'The Templar preceptory of Douzens (Aude) in the twelfth century', in Catherine Léglu and Marcus Bull (eds.), *The world of Eleanor of Aquitaine* (Woodbridge, 2005), 37–55.

Barbero, Alessandro, 'Motivazioni religiosi e motivazioni utilitarie nel reclutamento negli ordini monastico-cavallereschi', in *'Militia Christi' e crociata nei secoli XI–XIII. Atti della undecima settimana internazionale di studio, 28 agosto – 1 settembre*, Miscellanea del Centro di studi medioevali, 13 (Milan, 1992), 717–29.

Barrau, Hippolyte de, *Ordres équestres. Documents sur les ordres de Temple et de Saint-Jean-de-Jérusalem en Rouergue. Suivis d'une notice sur la Légion-d'Honneur et du tableau raisonné de ses membres dans la même pays* (Rodez, 1861).

Barthélemy, Anatole de, 'Chartes de départ et de retour des comtes de Dampierre-en-Astenois (IVe et Ve croisades)', *Archives de l'Orient Latin*, 2 (1883), 1–24.

'Pèlerins champenois en Palestine', *Revue d'Orient Latin*, 1 (1893), 355–78.

Baudiau, Jean-François, *Le Morvand, ou essai géographique, topographique et historique sur cette contrée*, 2 vols. (Nevers, 1854).

Beech, George T., Review of Jonathan Riley-Smith, *First Crusaders* (Cambridge, 1997), in *Medieval Prosopography*, 19 (1998), 77–80.

Beech, George T., Monique Bourin and Pascal Chareille (eds.), *Personal name studies of medieval Europe. Social identity and family structures* (Kalamazoo, Mich., 2002).

Bellenger, Yvonne and Danielle Quéruel (eds.), *Les champenois et la croisade. Actes des quatrièmes journées rémoises 27–28 novembre 1987* (Paris, 1989).

Beresford, Maurice Warwick, *New towns of the middle ages: town plantation in England, Wales and Gascony* (2nd edn, Gloucester, 1988).

Berman, Constance H., 'Origins of the filiation of Morimond in southern France. Redating foundation charters for Gimont, Villelongue, Berdoues, L'Escaledieu, and Bonnefont', *Cîteaux*, 41 (1990), 256–77.

The Cistercian evolution: the invention of a religious order in twelfth-century Europe (Philadelphia, Pa., 2000).

Bijsterveld, Arnoud-Jan A., 'The medieval gift as agent of social bonding and political power: a comparative approach', in Esther Cohen and Mayke B. de Jong (eds.), *Medieval transformations. Texts, power, and gifts in context* (Leiden, Boston, Mass., Cologne, 2001), 123–56.

Bird, Jessalynn, 'Reform or crusade? Anti-usury and crusade preaching during the pontificate of Innocent III', in John Clare Moore (ed.), *Pope Innocent III and his world* (Aldershot, 1999), 265–85.

'Innocent III, Peter the Chanter's circle and the crusade indulgence: theory, implementation and aftermath', in Andrea Sommerlechner (ed.), *Innocenzo III: urbs et orbis. Atti del congresso internazionale Roma, 9–15 settembre 1998* (Rome, 2003), 503–24.

Black, Jonathan and Thomas L. Amos, *The 'Fundo Alcobaça' of the Biblioteca Nacional, Lisbon, vol. III: Manuscripts 302–456* (Collegeville, Minn., 1990).

Blévec, Daniel le, 'Les templiers en Vivarais. Les archives de la commanderie de Jalèz et l'implantation de l'ordre du Temple en Cévennas', *Revue du Vivarais*, 84 (1980), 36–49.

Blévec, Daniel Le and Alain Venturini, 'Cartulaires des ordres militaires, XIIe–XIIIe siècles (Provence occidentale – Basse vallée du Rhône)', in Olivier Guyotjeannin, Laurent Morelle and Michel Parisse (eds.), *Les cartulaires. Actes de la table ronde organisée par l'École nationale des chartes et le G.D.R. 121 du C.N. R.S., Paris, 5–7 décembre 1991*, Mémoires et documents de l'École des Chartes, 39 (Paris, 1993), 451–65.

Bligny, Bernard, 'L'érémitisme et les chartreux', in *L'eremitismo in occidente nei secoli XI e XII. Atti della seconda Settimana internazionale di studio Mendola, 30 agosto – 6 settembre*, Miscellanea del Centro di studi medioevali, 4 (Milan, 1965), 248–70.

Bloch, Marc, *Les caractères de l'histoire rurale française* (Paris, 1931).

Bonneaud, Pierre, *Le prieuré de Catalogne, le couvent de Rhodes et la couronne d'Aragon 1415–1447* (Millau, 2004).

Borchardt, Karl, 'The Templars in Central Europe', in Zsolt Hunyadi and Jósef Laszlovsky (eds.), *The crusades and the military orders. Expanding the frontiers of medieval Latin Christianity* (Budapest, 2001), 233–44.

Bosl, Karl, 'Das Verhältnis von Augustinerchorherren (Regularkanoniker), Seelsorge und Gesellschaftsbewegung in Europa im 12. Jahrhundert', in *Istituzioni monastiche e istituzioni canonicali in Occidente (1123–1215). Atti della dodicesima Settimana internazionale di studio Mendola, 28 agosto – 3 settembre 1977*, Pubblicazioni della Università Cattolica del Sacro Cuore. Scienze storiche, 9 (Milan, 1980), 419–549.

Bouchard, Constance Brittain, *Sword, miter, and cloister: nobility and the Church in Burgundy, 980–1198* (Ithaca, N.Y., 1987).

Holy entrepreneurs: Cistercians, knights, and economic exchange in twelfth-century Burgundy (Ithaca, N.Y., 1991).

Strong of body, brave and noble: chivalry and society in medieval France (Ithaca, N.Y., London, 1998).

Those of my blood: constructing noble families in medieval Francia (Philadelphia, Pa., 2001).

Bouchot, Henri, *Inventaire des dessins exécutés pour Roger de Gaignières et conservés aux départements des estampes et des manuscrits*, I (Paris, 1891).

Bouffet, Hippolyte, *Les templiers et les hospitaliers de Saint-Jean en Haute-Auvergne* (Marseille, 1976).

Bouillet, Jean-Baptiste, *Nobiliaire d'Auvergne*, 8 vols. (Clermont-Ferrand, 1846–57).

Bourg, Antoine du, *Ordre de Malte. Histoire du grand prieuré de Toulouse et des diverses possessions de l'Ordre de Saint-Jean de Jérusalem dans le sud-ouest de la France* (Toulouse, 1888).

Bourgeois, Ginette and Alain Douzou, *Une aventure spirituelle dans le Rouergue méridional au moyen âge. Ermites et cisterciens à Silvanès, 1120–1477* (Paris, 1999).

Bourquelot, Félix, 'Notice sur le cartulaire des templiers de Provins', *BEC* 4th ser., 4 (1858), 171–90.

Bourrilly, Victor-Louis, 'Essai sur l'histoire politique de la commune de Marseille, des origines à la victoire de Charles d'Anjou (1264): Pièces justificatives', *Annales de la Faculté des Lettres d'Aix* (1921–2), 23–308.

Boutiot, Théophile, 'Les templiers et leurs établissements dans la Champagne méridionale', *Annuaire administratif de l'Aube*, 41 (1866), 27–56.

Bouvier, Henri, *Histoire de l'église et de l'ancien archidiocèse de Sens*, 3 vols. (Amiens, 1906–11).

Brand, Paul A., 'Family and inheritance, women and children', in Christopher Given-Wilson (ed.), *An illustrated history of late medieval England* (Manchester, 1996), 58–81.

Bredero, Adrian Hendrik, *Bernard of Clairvaux. Between cult and history* (Grand Rapids, Mich., 1996).

Brodman, James M., 'Rule and identity: the case of the military orders', *CHR*, 88 (2001), 383–400.

Bronstein, Judith, 'Caring for the sick or dying for the Cross? The granting of crusader indulgences to the Hospitallers', in Karl Borchardt, Nikolas Jaspert and Helen J. Nicholson (eds.), *The Hospitallers, the Mediterranean and Europe. Festschrift for Anthony Luttrell* (Aldershot, 2007), 39–46.

Brown, Elizabeth A. R., *The Oxford collection of the drawings of Roger de Gaignières and the royal tombs of Saint-Denis*, Transactions of the American Philosophical Society, 78:5 (Philadelphia, Pa., 1988).

Brundage, James A., *The medieval origins of the legal profession: canonists, civilians, and courts* (Chicago, Ill., London, 2008).

Bull, Marcus, *Knightly piety and the lay response to the First Crusade: the Limousin and Gascony, c.970–c.1130* (Oxford, 1993).

Bulliot, Jacques-Gabriel, *Essai historique sur l'Abbaye de Saint-Martin d'Autun de l'Ordre de Saint-Benoît* (Autun, 1849).

Bulst, Marie Luise, 'Noch einmal das *Itinerarium Peregrinorum*', *DAEM*, 21 (1965), 593–606.

Bulst-Thiele, Marie Luise, *Sacrae domus militiae Templi Hierosolymitani magistri. Untersuchungen zur Geschichte des Templerordens 1118/19–1314*, Abhandlungen der Akademie der Wissenschaften in Göttingen. Philologisch-Historische Klasse, 86 (Göttingen, 1974).

'Die Anfänge des Templer-Ordens. Bernard von Clairvaux. Citeaux', *Zeitschrift für Kirchengeschichte*, 104 (4th series 42) (1993), 312–27.

Bur, Michel, *La formation du comté de Champagne* (Nancy, 1977).

'Une célébration sélective de la parentèle. Le tombeau de Marie de Dreux à Saint-Yved de Braine, XIIIe siècle', *Comptes-rendus de l'Académie des Inscriptions et Belles-lettres*, 135 (1991), 301–18.

'Braine', *LexMA*, II (Munich, 2002), 545

'Épernay', *LexMA*, III (Munich, 2002), 2047

'Le monachisme en Champagne méridionale et dans le nord du diocèse de Langres à l'arrivée de saint Bernard à Clairvaux en 1115', in Michel Bur, *La Champagne médiévale* (Langres, 2005), 617–34.

'Les comtes de Champagne et les templiers', in Michel Bur, *La Champagne médiévale: recueil d'articles* (Langres, 2005), 635–42.

Burgtorf, Jochen, *The central convent of Hospitallers and Templars: history, organization, and personnel (1099/1120–1310)* (Leiden, 2008).

Bynum, Caroline Walker, *Docere verbo et exemplo: an aspect of twelfth-century spirituality* (Missoula, Mont., 1979).

Caille, Jacqueline, 'Ermengarde, vicomtesse de Narbonne (1127/29–1196/97). Une grande figure féminine du midi aristocratique', in *La femme dans l'histoire et la société méridionales (IXe–XIXe siècles). Actes du 66e congrès de la Fédération Historique du Languedoc Méditerranéen et du Roussillon, Narbonne, 15–16 octobre 1994* (Montpellier, 1995), 9–50.

Carcenac, Antoine-Régis, *Les templiers du Larzac. La commanderie du Temple de Sainte-Eulalie de Larzac* (Nîmes, 1994).

Carlson, David Richard, 'The practical theology of Saint Bernard and the date of the *De laude novae militiae*', in John Robert Sommerfeldt (ed.), *Erudition at God's service*, Studies in medieval Cistercian history, Cistercian Studies Series, 98 (1987), 133–47.

Carraz, Damien, 'Les ordres militaires et la ville (XIIe–début du XIVe siècle): L'exemple des commanderies urbaines de la Basse Vallée du Rhône', *AdM*, 114 (2002), 275–92.

Ordres militaires, croisades et sociétés méridionales. L'ordre du Temple dans la basse vallée du Rhône (1124–1312), 3 vols. (Ph.D. thesis, Lyon: Université de Lyon 2, 2003).

L'ordre du Templedans la basse vallée du Rhône (1124–1312). Ordres militaires, croisades et sociétés méridionales (Lyon, 2005).

'Présences et dévotions féminines autour des commanderies du Bas-Rhône (XIIe–XIIIe siècle)', in *Les ordres religieux militaires dans le Midi (XIIe–XIVe siècle)*, CdF, LI (Toulouse, 2006), 71–99.

'Mémoire lignagère et archives monastiques: les Bourbouton et la commanderie de Richerenches', in Martin Aurell (ed.), *Convaincre et persuader: communication et propagande aux XIIe et XIIIe siècles*, Civilisation Médiévale, 17 (Poitiers, 2007), 465–502.

'Les ordres militaires et le fait urbain en France méridionale (XIIe–XIIIe siècle)', *CdF*, XLIV (Toulouse, 2009), 127–65.

Casey, Michael, '*In communi vita fratrum*. St. Bernard's teaching on cenobitic solitude', *Analecta Cisterciensia*, 46 (1990), 243–61.

Castillon d'Aspet, H., *Histoire des populations pyrénéennes du Nébouzan et du pays de Comminges depuis les temps les plus anciens jusqu'à la révolution de 89*, 2 vols. (Toulouse, Paris, 1842).

Cerrini, Simonetta, *Une expérience neuve au sein de la spiritualité médiévale: l'ordre du Temple (1120–1314). Étude et édition des règles latine et française*, 2 vols. (unpublished Ph.D. thesis, Paris: Université de Paris – Sorbonne (Paris IV), 1997).

'Le fondateur de l'ordre du Temple à ses frères: Hugues de Payns et le *Sermo Christi militibus*', in Michel Balard, Benjamin Z. Kedar and Jonathan S. C. Riley-Smith (eds.), *Dei gesta per Francos. Études sur les croisades dédiées à Jean Richard* (Aldershot, 2001), 99–110.

La révolution des templiers. Une histoire perdue du XII siècle (Paris, 2007).

Chandon de Briailles, Comte, 'Bulle de Clérembaut de Broyes, archevêque de Tyr', *Syria*, 21 (1940), 82–9.

Charmasse, Anatole de, 'État des possessions des templiers et des hospitaliers en Mâconnais, Charollais, Lyonnais et Forez', *Mémoires de la Société Éduenne* (1879), 105–47.

Chastang, Pierre, *Lire, écrire, transcrire: le travail des rédacteurs de cartulaires en Bas-Languedoc, XIe–XIIIe siècles* (Paris, 2001).

Chaume, Maurice, 'Les origines familiales de Saint Bernard', in *Recherches d'histoire chrétienne et médiévale. Mélanges publiés à la mémoire de l'historien avec une biographie* (Dijon, 1947), 110–40.

Chérest, A.-A., 'Vézelay. Étude historique', *BuSoScYonne*, 16, 22 (1862, 1868), 209–525, 5–631.

Cheyette, Frederic L., 'The "sale" of Carcassonne to the counts of Barcelona (1067–1070) and the rise of the Trencavels', *Speculum*, 63 (1988), 826–64.

Ermengard of Narbonne and the world of the troubadours (Ithaca, N.Y., London, 2001).

Claverie, Pierre-Vincent, *L'ordre du Temple en Terre Sainte et à Chypre au XIIIe siècle*, 3 vols. (Nicosia, 2005).

Cocheril, Maur, 'Saint Bernard et le Portugal. A propos d'une lettre apocryphe', *Revue d'histoire ecclésiastique*, 54 (1959), 426-77.

Cole, Penny J., *The preaching of the crusades to the Holy Land, 1095–1270* (Cambridge, Mass., 1991).

Collot, E., *Chronique de l'abbaye de Notre-Dame de Longuay (diocèse de Langres)* (Paris, 1868).

Constable, Giles, 'The financing of the crusades in the twelfth century', in Benjamin Z. Kedar, Hans Eberhard Mayer and Raimund Charles Smail (eds.), *Outremer: studies in the history of the crusading kingdom of Jerusalem presented to Joshua Prawer* (Jerusalem, 1982), 64–88.

Three studies in medieval religious and social thought. The interpretation of Mary and Martha, the ideal of the imitation of Christ, the orders of society (Cambridge, 1995).

The reformation of the twelfth century (Cambridge, 1996).

Coudriet, Jean-Baptiste and Pierre François Chatelet, *Histoire de la seigneurie de Jonvelle et de ses environs* (Besançon, 1864).

Courcelles, Jean B. de, *Histoire généalogique et héraldique des pairs de France, des grands dignitaires de la couronne, des principales familles nobles du royaume, et des maisons princières de l'Europe, précédée de la généalogie de la maison de France, vol. VIII: De Polignac* (Paris, 1827).

Coureas, Nicholas, 'The role of the Templars and Hospitallers in the movement of commodities involving Cyprus', in Peter Edbury and Jonathan Phillips (eds.),

The experience of crusading, vol. II: Defining the crusader kingdom (Cambridge, 2003), 257–74.

Cousin, Patrice, 'Les débuts de l'ordre des templiers et Saint Bernard', in *Mélanges de Saint Bernard. XXIVe congrès de l'association bourguignonne des sociétés savantes* (Dijon, 1953), 41–52.

Cowdrey, Herbert Edward John, 'Peter, monk of Molesme and prior of Jully', in Michael Goodich, Sophia Menache and Sylvia Schein (eds.), *Cross cultural convergences in the crusader period. Essays presented to Aryeh Grabois on his sixty-fifth birthday* (New York, 1995), 59–73.

Croix Bouton, Jean de la, 'Saint Bernard et les moinales', in *Mélanges de Saint Bernard. XXIVe congrès de l'association bourguignonne des sociétés savantes* (Dijon, 1953), 225–47.

Curzon, Henri de, *La maison du Temple de Paris* (Paris, 1888).

d'Arbois de Jubainville, Marie Henri and L. Pigeotte, *Histoire des ducs et des comtes de Champagne*, 7 vols. (Paris, 1859–69).

d'Avray, David, 'Lay kinship solidarity and papal law', in Pauline Stafford, Janet Loughland Nelson and Jane Martindale (eds.), *Law, laity and solidarities. Essays in honour of Susan Reynolds* (Manchester, 2001), 188–99.

Débax, Hélène, *La féodalité languedocienne aux XIe–XIIe siècles. Serments, hommages et fiefs dans le Languedoc des Trencavel* (Toulouse, 2003).

Delaborde, Henri-François, *Jean de Joinville et les seigneurs de Joinville, suivi d'un catalogue de leurs actes* (Paris, 1894).

Delaruelle, Étienne, 'Templiers et hospitaliers en Languedoc pendant la croisade des Albigeois', in *Paix de Dieu et guerre sainte en Languedoc au XIIIe siècle*, CdF, IV (Toulouse, 1969), 315–34.

Delisle, Léopold, 'Girard de Hautgué et Jean de Vesvres, prétendus auteurs de la Roue de Fortune', *Histoire littéraire de la France*, 33 (1906), 264–70.

Delmaire, Bernard, 'Cartulaires et inventaires de chartes dans le nord de la France', in Olivier Guyotjeannin, Laurent Morelle and Michel Parisse (eds.), *Les cartulaires. Actes de la table ronde organisée par l'École nationale des chartes et le G.D.R. 121 du C.N.R.S., Paris, 5–7 décembre 1991*, Mémoires et documents de l'École des Chartes, 39 (Paris, 1993), 301–22.

Delmas, Jean, 'L'inventaire des biens de la commanderie de Sainte-Eulalie du Larzac en 1308', in Anthony Luttrell and Léon Pressouyre (eds.), *La commanderie, institution des ordres militaires dans l'Occident médiéval* (Paris, 2002), 319–27.

Demouy, Patrick, 'L'église de Reims et la croisade aux XIe–XIIe siècles', in Yvonne Bellenger and Danielle Quéruel (eds.), *Les champenois et la croisade. Actes des quatrièmes journées rémoises, 27–28 novembre 1987* (Paris, 1989), 19–38.

Demurger, Alain, *Vie et mort de l'ordre du Temple, 1118–1314* (Paris, 1985).

'L'aristocrazia laica e gli ordini militari in Francia nel duecento: l'esempio della Bassa Borgogna', in Enzo Coli, Maria de Marco and Francesco Tommasi (eds.), *Militia Sacra. Gli ordini militari tra Europa e Terrasanta* (Perugia, 1994), 55–84.

'Les templiers à Auxerre (XIIe–XIIIe siècles)', in Patrick Boucheron and Jacques Chiffoleau (eds.), *Religion et société urbaine au moyen âge. Études offertes à Jean-Louis Biget* (Paris, 2000), 301–11.

The last Templar. The tragedy of Jacques de Molay, last grand master of the Temple, trans. A. Nevill (London, 2004).

'La constitution d'un patrimoine foncier: les templiers dans le comté d'Auxerre (XIIIe s.)', in Isabel Cristina F. Fernandes (ed.), *As ordens militares e as ordens de cavalaria na construção do mundo ocidental – Actas do VI encontro sobre ordens militares* (Lisbon, 2005), 439–50.

Les templiers. Une chevalerie chrétienne au moyen âge (Paris, 2005).

Dimier, Anselme, 'Éberhard ou Évrard des Barres, grand-maître de l'ordre du Temple, moine de Clairvaux', *Cîteaux*, 27 (1976), 133–4.

Dondi, Cristina, 'Manoscritti liturgici dei templari e degli ospitalieri: le nuove prospettive aperte dal sacramentario templare di Modena', in Simonetta Cerrini (ed.), *I templari, la guerra e la santità* (Rimini, 2000), 85–131.

The liturgy of the canons regular of the Holy Sepulchre of Jerusalem: a study and a catalogue of the manuscript sources (Turnhout, 2004).

Duby, Georges, *La societé aux XIe et XIIe siècles dans la région mâconnaise* (Paris, 1971).

Medieval marriage: two models from twelfth-century France, trans. E. Forster (Baltimore, Md., London, 1978).

'Structures de parenté et noblesse dans la France du nord aux XIe et XIIe siècles', in *La société chevaleresque. Hommes et structures du moyen âge (I)* (Paris, 1988), 143–66.

Rural economy and country life in the medieval West, trans. C. Postan (Philadelphia, Pa., 1998).

Dufournet, Jean, 'Villehardouin et les champenois dans la quatrième croisade', in Yvonne Bellenger and Danielle Quéruel (eds.), *Les champenois et la croisade. Actes des quatrièmes journées rémoises 27–28 novembre 1987* (Paris, 1989), 55–69.

Duhamel-Amado, Claudie, 'L'indispensable Bernard de Canet. L'ascension d'un chevalier aux cours des Trencavels (1110–1154)', in Hélène Débax (ed.), *Les sociétés méridionales à l'âge féodal: Espagne, Italie et sud de la France, X^e^–XIIIe s. Hommage à Pierre Bonnassie* (Toulouse, 1999), 355–64.

Genèse des lignages méridionaux, vol. I: L'aristocratie languedocienne du Xe au XIIe siècle (Toulouse, 2001).

Genèse des lignages méridionaux, vol. II: Portraits de familles (Toulouse, 2007).

Dunbabin, Jean, 'From clerk to knight: changing orders', in Christopher Harper-Bill and Ruth E. Harvey (eds.), *The ideas and practices of medieval knighthood II* (Woodbridge, 1988), 26–39.

Durbec, Joseph-Antoine, *Les templiers dans les Alpes-Maritimes. Notice historiques sur les maisons et possessions du Temple dans les diocèses de Antibes-Grasse, Nice, Vence et Glandèves* (Nice, 1938).

Templiers et hospitaliers en Provence et dans les Alpes-Maritimes, intro. Jacques Juillet (Grenoble, 2001).

Elm, Kaspar, *Umbilicus Mundi: Beiträge zur Geschichte Jerusalems, der Kreuzzüge, des Kapitels vom Hlg. Grab in Jerusalem unter den Ritterorden* (Sint-Kruis, 1998).

Erbstösser, Martin, *Die Kreuzzüge. Eine Kulturgeschichte* (Bergisch Gladbach, 1998).

Evergates, Theodore, *Feudal society in the bailliage of Troyes under the counts of Champagne, 1152–1284* (Baltimore, Md., 1975).

'The origin of the lords of Karytaina in the Frankish Morea', *Medieval Prosopography*, 15 (1994), 81–113.

'Nobles and knights in twelfth-century France', in Thomas N. Bisson (ed.), *Cultures of power. Lordship, status, and process in twelfth-century Europe* (Philadelphia, Pa., 1995), 11–35.
The aristocracy in the county of Champagne, 1100–1300 (Philadelphia, Pa., 2007).
Faget de Casteljau, Henri de, 'Les sires de Til-Châtel féaux de Langres aux marches des deux Bourgognes, x–xv siècles', *Cahiers Haut-Marnais*, 143(1980), 145–59; 144(1981), 36–48; 146 (1981), 101–12.
Favreau, Robert and Jean Michaud (eds.), *Corpus des inscriptions de la France médiévale, vol. xxi: Yonne* (Paris, 2000).
Finke, Heinrich, *Papsttum und Untergang des Templerordens*, 2 vols. (Münster, 1907).
Flori, Jean, *Chevaliers et chevalerie au moyen âge* (Paris, 1998).
Forey, Alan John, *The Templars in the Corona of Aragón* (London, 1973).
'The emergence of the military orders in the twelfth century', *Journal of Ecclesiastical History*, 36 (1985), 175–95.
'Novitiate and instruction in the military orders in the twelfth and thirteenth centuries', *Speculum*, 61 (1986), 1–17.
'Recruitment to the military orders (twelfth to mid-fourteenth centuries)', *Viator*, 17 (1986), 139–73.
'Towards a profile of the Templars in the early fourteenth century', in Malcolm Barber (ed.), *The military orders, vol. 1: Fighting for the faith and caring for the sick* (Aldershot, 1994), 196–204.
'The military orders, 1120–1312', in Jonathan S. C. Riley-Smith (ed.), *The Oxford illustrated history of the crusades* (London, 1995), 184–216.
The fall of the Templars in the Crown of Aragon (Aldershot, 2001).
'The charitable activities of the Templars', *Viator*, 34 (2003), 109–41.
Fossier, Robert, *La terre et les hommes en Picardie jusqu'à la fin du xiiie siècle*, 2 vols. (Paris, Louvain, 1968).
France, John, 'Patronage and the appeal of the First Crusade', in Jonathan Phillips (ed.), *The First Crusade: origins and impact* (Manchester, 1997), 5–20.
Frizot, Julien, *Les grands sites templiers en France* (Rennes, 2005).
Fuguet Sans, Joan, 'Maisons templières des chemins ibériques de Saint-Jacques', in *Les ordres religieux militaires dans le Midi (xiie–xive siècle)*, CdF, xli (Toulouse, 2006), 265–94.
García-Guijarro Ramos, Luis, *Papado, cruzadas, órdenes militares. Siglos xi–xiii* (Madrid, 1995).
Gaussin, Pierre Roger, 'Les communautés féminines dans l'espace languedocien de la fin du xie à la fin du xive siècle', in *La femme dans la vie religieuse du Languedoc*, CdF, xxiii (Toulouse, 1988), 299–332.
Geary, Patrick, 'Exchange and interaction between the living and the dead in early medieval society', in Patrick Geary, *Living with the dead in the middle ages* (Ithaca, N.Y., London, 1994), 77–92.
Phantoms of remembrance: memory and oblivion at the end of the first millennium (Princeton, N.J., 1994).
Gervers, Michael, 'Donations to the Hospitallers in England in the wake of the Second Crusade', in Michael Gervers (ed.), *The Second Crusade and the Cistercians* (New York, 1992), 155–61.

Gervers, Michael and Nicole Hamonic, 'Scribes and notaries in twelfth- and thirteenth-century Hospitaller charters from England', in Karl Borchardt, Nikolas Jaspert and Helen J. Nicholson (eds.), *The Hospitallers, the Mediterranean and Europe. Festschrift for Anthony Luttrell* (Aldershot, 2007), 181–92.

Godefroy, J., 'La Maison d'Aulnoy-les-Minimes, souche de Pierre de Celle', *Revue Mabillon*, 41 (1951), 33–5.

Goody, Jack, *The development of the family and marriage in Europe* (Cambridge, New York, 1983).

Graham-Leigh, Elaine, *The southern French nobility and the Albigensian crusade* (Woodbridge, 2005).

Guyotjeannin, Olivier, *Episcopus et comes. Affirmation et déclin de la seigneurie épiscopale au nord du royaume de France Beauvais-Noyon, x^{e}–début XIIIe siècle* (Geneva, 1987).

'La seigneurie épiscopale dans le royaume de France (x^{e}–XIIIe siècles)', *Chiesa e mondo feudale nei secoli X–XII. Atti della dodicesima Settimana internazionale di studio Mendola, 24–28 agosto 1992*, Miscellanea del Centro di studi medioevali, 14 (Milan, 1995), 151–88.

Hamilton, Bernard, 'The impact of Jerusalem on western Christendom', *CHR*, 80 (1994), 695–713.

Harper-Bill, Christopher, 'The piety of the Anglo-Norman knightly class', *Anglo-Norman Studies*, 2 (1979), 63–77.

Helias-Baron, Marlène, 'Reigny, Actes diplomatiques du XIIe siècle', *Bulletin du centre d'études médiévales d'Auxerre. Collection CBMA. Les cartulaires, Notices* (2008) [http://cem.revenues.org/index5652.html].

Herlihy, David, *Medieval households* (Cambridge, Mass., 1985).

Hiestand, Rudolf, *Papsturkunden für Templer und Johanniter: Archivberichte und Texte*, Abhandlungen der Akademie der Wissenschaften in Göttingen. Philologisch-Historische Klasse, 77. Vorarbeiten zum Oriens pontificius, 1 (Göttingen, 1972).

Papsturkunden für Templer und Johanniter: neue Folge, Abhandlungen der Akademie der Wissenschaften in Göttingen, Philologisch-Historische Klasse 3. Folge, Nr. 135. Vorarbeiten zum Oriens pontificius, 2 (Göttingen, 1984).

'Kardinalbischof Matthäus von Albano, das Konzil von Troyes und die Entstehung des Templerordens', *Zeitschrift für Kirchengeschichte*, 99 (1988), 295–323.

'Some reflections on the impact of the papacy on the crusader states and the military orders in the twelfth and thirteenth centuries', in Zsolt Hunyadi and Jósef Laszlovsky (eds.), *The crusades and the military orders. Expanding the frontiers of medieval Latin Christianity* (Budapest, 2001), 3–20.

Higounet, Charles, *Le comté de Comminges de ses origines à son annexion à la couronne*, 2 vols. (Toulouse, 1949).

'Une bastide de colonisation des templiers dans les Pré-Pyrénées', *Revue de Comminges*, 62 (1949), 81–97.

Hodgson, Natasha R., *Women, crusading and the Holy Land in historical narrative* (Woodbridge, 2007).

Hosten, Jan, *De tempeliers: de tempelorde tijdens de kruistochten en in de Lage Landen* (Amsterdam, 2006).

Housley, Norman, *Contesting the crusades* (Oxford, 2006).

Howe, John, 'The nobility's reform of the medieval Church', *American Historical Review*, 93 (1988), 317–39.

Isenburg, Wilhelm Karl, Frank Freytag von Loringhoven and Detlev Schwennicke, *Europäische Stammtafeln: Stammtafeln zur Geschichte der europäischen Staaten* (Berlin, Marburg, 1936–78).

Jaspert, Nikolas, 'Bonds and tensions on the frontier: the Templars in twelfth-century western Catalonia', in Jürgen Sarnowsky (ed.), *Mendicants, military orders, and regionalism in medieval Europe* (Aldershot, 1999), 19–45.

Jaurgain, Jean de, *La Vasconie: étude historique et critique sur les origines du royaume de Navarre, du duché de Gascogne, des comtés de Comminges, d'Aragon, de Foix, de Bigorre, d'Alava et de Biscayne, de la vicomté de Béarn et des grands fiefs du duché de Gascogne*, 2 vols. (Pau, 1898–1902).

Jessee, Winfield Scott, 'The family of Robert the Burgundian and the creation of the Angevin march of Sablé and Craon', *Medieval Prosopography*, 16 (1995), 31–67.

Jobin, Jean-Baptiste, *Saint Bernard et sa famille* (Paris, 1891).

Johnson, Penelope D., *Prayer, patronage, and power: the Abbey of la Trinité, Vendôme, 1032–1187* (New York, 1981).

Jourd'heuil, Jean-Vincent, 'Sanctuaires, inhumations et sépultures des évêques de Langres des origines au XVI siècle', in Vincent Tabbagh (ed.), *Les clercs, les fidèles et les saints en Bourgogne médiévale* (Dijon, 2005), 27–55.

Juillet, Jacques, *Templiers et hospitaliers en Quercy: Commanderies et prieurés sur le chemin de Notre Dame de Rocamadour* (St-Yriex-la-Perche, 1975).

Katzir, Yael, 'The Second Crusade and the redefinition of *ecclesia, christianitas* and papal coercive power', in Michael Gervers (ed.), *The Second Crusade and the Cistercians* (New York, 1992), 3–11.

Kerrebrouck, Patrick van, *Les capétiens, 987–1328*, 2 vols. (Villeneuve d'Ascq, 2000).

Klapisch-Zuber, Christiane, *L'ombre des ancêtres: essai sur l'imaginaire médiéval de la parenté* (Paris, 2000).

Kleinjung, Christine, 'Nonnen und Personal, Familien und Stifter: Zisterzienserinnenkonvente und ihre soziale Umwelt', in Franz J. Felten and Werner Rösener (eds.), *Norm und Realität. Kontinuität und Wandel der Zisterzienser im Mittelalter*, Vita Regularis, 42 (Münster, 2009), 225–63.

Knoch, Wendelin, 'Gebets- und Lebensgemeinschaften in Freundschaft – Bernhardinische Reformimpulse', in Gerhard Krieger (ed.), *Verwandtschaft, Freundschaft, Bruderschaft. Soziale Lebens- und Kommunikationsformen im Mittelalter* (Berlin, 2009), 118–26.

Lacordaire, A., *Les seigneurie et féavltez de Bovrbonne ensemble les déduictz et desnombrements d'icelles. Étude historique d'après les documents existant aux archives, 612–1780* (Arcis-sur-Aube, 1883).

La Monte, John Life, 'The lords of Le Puiset on the crusades', *Speculum*, 17 (1942), 100–18.

Langlois, Gauthier, *Olivier de Termes. Le cathare et le croisé (vers 1200–1274)* (Toulouse, 2001).

Lapina, Elizabeth, 'The mural paintings of Berzé-la-Ville in the context of the First Crusade and the Reconquista', *JMH*, 31 (2005), 309–26.

Laurent, Jacques and Ferdinand Claudon (eds.), *Abbayes et prieurés de l'ancienne France, vol.* XII*: Province ecclésiastique de Lyon, part* III*: Diocèses de Langres et de Dijon* (Ligugé, 1941).

Lavirotte, César, 'Mémoire statistique sur les établissements des templiers et des hospitaliers de Saint-Jean de Jérusalem en Bourgogne', *Congrès archéologique de France*, 19 (1853), 224–91.

Lawers, Michel, *La mémoire des ancêtres, le souci des morts. Morts, rites et société au Moyen Âge (diocèse de Liège,* XI*ᵉ–*XIII*ᵉ)* (Paris, 1997).

Lawrence, Clifford Hugh, *Medieval monasticism: forms of religious life in western Europe in the middle ages* (3rd edn, Harlow, 2001).

Legendre, Jacqueline, *La Chartreuse de Lugny des origines au début du 14ᵉ siècle 1172–1332* (Salzburg, 1975).

Le Grand, Michel, 'Le chapitre cathédral de Langres. De la fin du XIIᵉ siècle au concordat de 1516', *Revue d'histoire de l'Église de France*, 16 (1930), 501–32.

Léonard, Émile-G., *Introduction au cartulaire manuscrit du Temple (1150–1317), constitué par le marquis d'Albon et conservé à la Bibliothèque nationale, suivie d'un tableau des maisons françaises du Temple et de leurs précepteurs* (Paris, 1930).

Leroy, Thierry, 'Hugues, seigneur de Payns, premier maître de l'ordre du Temple', in Dominique Guéniot (ed.), *Mémoire de Champagne* (Langres, 2000), 181–91.

Hugues de Payns. Chevalier champenois. Fondateur de l'ordre des templiers (Troyes, 2001).

Lester, Anne E., 'A shared imitation: Cistercian convents and crusader families in thirteenth-century Champagne', *JMH*, 35 (2009), 353–70.

Lewis, Andrew W., 'Fourteen charters of Robert I of Dreux (1152–1188)', *Traditio*, 41 (1985), 145–79.

Leyser, Henrietta, *Hermits and the new monasticism: a study of religious communities in Western Europe 1000–1150* (London, 1984).

L'Hermite-Leclercq, Paulette, 'Reclus et recluses dans le sud-ouest de la France', in *La femme dans la vie religieuse du Languedoc (13ᵉ – 14ᵉ s.)*, CdF, XXIII (Toulouse, 1988), 281–98.

Licence, Tom, 'The Benedictines, the Cistercians and the acquisition of a hermitage in twelfth-century Durham', *JMH*, 29 (2003), 315–29.

'The Templars and the Hospitallers, Christ and the saints', *Crusades*, 4 (2005), 39–57.

'Military orders as monastic orders', *Crusades*, 5 (2006), 39–53.

Ligato, Giuseppe, 'Fra ordini cavallereschi e crociata: "milites ad terminum" e "confraternitates" armate', in *'Militia Christi' e crociata nei secoli* XI–XIII*. Atti della undecima Settimana internazionale di studio, 28 agosto – 1 settembre*, Miscellanea del Centro di studi medioevali, 13 (Milan, 1992), 645–97.

Linage Conde, Antonio, 'Tipología de vida monástica en los órdenes militares', *Yermo*, 12 (1974), 73–115.

Livingstone, Amy F., 'Noblewomen's control of property in early twelfth-century Blois–Chartres', *Medieval Prosopography*, 18 (1997), 55–71.

Lloyd, Simon D., 'The crusading movement, 1096–1274', in Jonathan S.C. Riley-Smith (ed.), *The Oxford illustrated history of the crusades* (London, 1995), 34–65.

Locatelli, René, *Sur les chemins de la perfection. Moines et chanoines dans le diocèse de Besançon vers 1060–1220* (Saint Étienne, 1992).

Lock, Peter, *The Franks in the Aegean 1204–1500* (New York, 1995).

Longnon, Auguste, *Les noms de lieu de la France: leur origine, leur signification, leurs transformations* (Paris, 1920; reprint: 1973).

Longnon, Jean, *Les compagnons de Villehardouin: Recherches sur les croisés de la quatrième croisade* (Geneva, Paris, 1978).

Lord, Evelyn, *The knights Templar in Britain* (Harlow, 2002).

Lower, Michael, *The Barons' Crusade: a call to arms and its consequences* (Philadelphia, Pa., 2005).

Luchaire, Achille, *Louis VI le Gros, annales de sa vie et de son règne* (Paris, 1890).

Luttrell, Anthony, 'The earliest Templars', in Michel Balard (ed.), *Autour de la première croisade. Actes du colloque de la Society for the Study of the Crusades and the Latin East, Clermont-Ferrand, 22–25 juin 1995* (Paris, 1995), 193–202.

Macé, Laurent, 'L'utilisation des ressources hydrauliques par les templiers de la commanderie de Douzens, XIIe siècle (Aude)', *Archéologie du Midi Médiéval*, 12 (1994), 99–113.

Les comtes de Toulouse et leur entourage. Rivalités, alliances et jeux de pouvoir XIIe–XIIIe siècles (Toulouse, 2003).

Magnou, Élisabeth, 'Oblature, classe chevaleresque et servage dans les maisons méridionales du Temple au XIIème siècle', *AdM*, 73 (1961), 377–97.

Maier, Christoph T., *Preaching the crusades. Mendicant friars and the cross in the thirteenth century* (Cambridge, 1994).

'Crisis, liturgy and the crusades in the twelfth and thirteenth centuries', *Journal of Ecclesiastical History*, 48 (1997), 628–57.

Mannier, Eugène, *Ordre de Malte. Les commanderies du Grand-prieuré de France, d'après les documents inédits conservés aux Archives nationales à Paris*, 2 vols. (Paris, 1872; reprint: 1998).

Marie, Delphine, *Les templiers dans le diocèse de Langres. Des moines entrepreneurs aux XIIe et XIIIe siècles* (Langres, 2004).

Marion, Jules, 'Notice sur l'abbaye de la Bussière', *BEC*, 4 (1842–3), 549–63.

Mariotte, Jean-Yves, *Le comté de Bourgogne sous les Hohenstaufen (1156–1208)* (Paris, 1963).

Markowski, Michael, 'Peter of Blois and the conception of the Third Crusade', in Benjamin Z. Kedar (ed.), *The Horns of Hattin. Proceedings of the second conference of the Society for the Study of the Crusades and the Latin East* (Jerusalem, 1992), 261–9.

Mathieu, Jean-Noël, 'À propos des châtelains de Châtillon-sur-Marne', *Société d'agriculture, commerce, sciences et arts de la Marne*, 107 (1992), 7–27.

'Nouvelles recherches concernant le lignage de Joinville', *Les cahiers haut-marnais* 190 (1992), 1–25.

Mayer, Hans Eberhard, *Die Kanzlei der lateinischen Könige von Jerusalem*, 2 vols. (Hanover, 1996).

Mazel, Florian, *La noblesse et l'église en Provence, fin X^{e}–début XIVe siècle. L'exemple des familles d'Agoult-Simiane, de Baux et de Marseille* (Paris, 2002).

McLaughlin, Megan, *Consorting with saints: prayer for the dead in early medieval France* (Ithaca, N.Y, London, 1994).

Melville, Marion, *La vie des templiers*(2nd edn, Paris, 1974).

Menache, Sophia, 'The Templar order: a failed idea?', *Catholic Historical Review*, 79 (1993), 1–21.

'Rewriting the history of the Templars according to Matthew Paris', in Michael Goodich, Sophia Menache and Sylvia Schein (eds.), *Cross cultural convergences in the crusader period. Essays presented to Aryeh Grabois on his sixty-fifth birthday* (New York, 1995), 183–214.

Mignard, M., 'Statistique de la milice du Temple en Bourgogne et importance du Grand Prieuré de Champagne qui avait son siège à Voulaine (Côte-d'Or)', *Congrès Archéologique de France*, 19 (1852–3), 205–16.

Miquel, Jacques, *État des sources archivistiques et bibliographie des commanderies templières et hospitalières du Rouergue du XIIème au XVIIIème siècle* (Unpublished document available from Conservatoire Larzac Templier et Hospitalier).

Miramon, Charles de, *Les donnés au moyen âge. Une forme de vie religieuse laïque v.1180–v.1500* (Paris, 1999).

Miret y Sans, Joaquim, *Les cases de templers y hospitalers a Catalunya. Aplec de noves i documents històrics* (Barcelona, 1910).

'Inventaris de les cases del Temple de la corona d'Aragó en 1289', *Boletín de la real academia de buenas letras de Barcelona*, 6 (1911), 61–75.

Möhring, Hannes, *Der Weltkaiser der Endzeit: Entstehung, Wandel und Wirkung einer tausendjährigen Weissagung* (Stuttgart, 2000).

Morelle, Laurent, 'De l'original à la copie: remarques sur l'évaluation des transcriptions dans les cartulaires médiévaux', in Olivier Guyotjeannin, Laurent Morelle and Michel Parisse (eds.), *Les cartulaires. Actes de la table ronde organisée par l'École nationale des chartes et le G.D.R. 121 du C.N.R.S., Paris, 5–7 décembre 1991*, Mémoires et documents de l'École des Chartes, 39 (Paris, 1993), 90–104.

Morris, Colin, 'Picturing the crusades: the uses of visual propaganda, *c.* 1095–1250', in John France and William G. Zajac (eds.), *The crusades and their sources. Essays presented to Bernard Hamilton* (Aldershot, 1998), 195–216.

The sepulchre of Christ and the medieval west. From the beginning to 1600 (Oxford, 2007).

Morton, Nicholas Edward, *The Teutonic knights in the Holy Land 1190–1291* (Woodbridge, 2009).

Mouillebouche, Hervé, *Les maisons fortes en Bourgogne du nord du XIIIe au XVIe s.* (Dijon, 2002).

Mousnier, Mireille, 'L'abbaye cistercienne de Grandselve du XIIe au début du XIVe siècle', *Cîteaux*, 34 (1983), 53–76, 221–44.

'Impact social des abbayes cisterciennes dans la société méridionale aux XIIe et XIIIe siècles', *Cîteaux*, 50 (1999), 67–83.

Murat, Philippe, 'La croisade en Nivernais: transfer de propriété et lutte d'influence', in *Le concile de Clermont de 1095 et l'appel à la croisade. Actes du colloque universitaire international de Clermont-Ferrand (23–25 juin 1995) organisé et publié avec le concours du conseil régional d'Auvergne* (Clermont-Ferrand, 1995), 295–312.

Mure, Jean-Marie de la, *Histoire des ducs de Bourbon et des comtes de Forez*, I (Paris, 1809).

Murray, Alexander, *Reason and society in the middle ages* (Oxford, 1978).

Newman, Martha G., *The boundaries of charity: Cistercian culture and ecclesiastical reform, 1098–1180* (Stanford, Calif., 1996).

Nicholas, David, *The evolution of the medieval world: society, government and thought in Europe, 312–1500* (London, 1992).

Nicholson, Helen J., *Templars, Hospitallers, and Teutonic knights: images of the military orders, 1128–1291* (Leicester, 1993).
Love, war, and the Grail (Leiden, Boston, 2001).
The Knights Templar: a new history (Stroud, 2001).
The Knights Templar: a brief history of the warrior order (updated edn, Philadelphia, Pa., London, 2010).
Oberste, Jörg, 'Donaten zwischen Kloster und Welt. Das Donatenwesen der religiösen Ritterorden in Südfrankreich und die Entwicklung der städtischen Frömmigkeitspraxis im 13. Jahrhundert', *Zeitschrift für Historische Forschung*, 29 (2002), 1–37.
Zwischen Heiligkeit und Häresie. Religiosität und sozialer Aufstieg in der Stadt des hohen Mittelalters, vol. II: Städtische Eliten in Toulouse (Cologne, Weimar, Vienna, 2003).
Orlandis Rovira, José, '*Traditio corporis et animae*. La *familiaritas* en las iglesias y monasterios españoles de la alta Edad Media', *Anuario de historia del derecho español*, 24 (1954), 95–279.
Parisse, Michel, 'Les évêques et la noblesse: continuité et retournement (XIe–XIIe siècles)', *Chiesa e mondo feudale nei secoli X–XII. Atti della dodicesima Settimana internazionale di studio Mendola, 24–28 agosto 1992*, Miscellanea del Centro di studi medioevali, 14 (Milan, 1995), 61–85.
Paterson, Linda M., *The world of the troubadours: medieval Occitan society, c. 1100–c. 1300* (Cambridge, 1993).
Pegg, Marc Gregory, 'On Cathars, Albigenses, and good men of Languedoc', *JMH*, 27 (2001), 181–95.
A most holy war: the Albigensian crusade and the battle for Christendom (Oxford, 2008).
Pétel, Auguste, 'La maison de Villers-Lès-Verrières', *MSA Aube*, 69 (1905), 373–478.
'La maison de Serre-lès-Monceaux', *MSA Aube*, 70 (1906), 254–318.
'Le Temple de Bonlieu', *MSA Aube*, 74 (1910), 1–300.
Petit, Ernest, *Avallon et l'Avallonnais* (Auxerre, 1867).
Histoire des ducs de Bourgogne de la race capétienne, 9 vols. (Paris, 1885–1905).
Phillips, Jonathan, 'Hugh of Payns and the 1129 Damascus crusade', in Malcolm Barber (ed.), *The military orders, vol. I: Fighting for the faith and caring for the sick* (Aldershot, 1994), 141–7.
'The murder of Charles the Good and the Second Crusade: household, nobility, and traditions of crusading in medieval Flanders', *Medieval Prosopography*, 19 (1998), 55–75.
'Odo of Deuil's *De profectione Ludovici VII in Orientem* as a source for the Second Crusade', in Marcus Bull and Norman Housley (eds.), *The experience of crusading, vol. I: Western approaches* (Cambridge, 2003), 80–95.
The Second Crusade. Extending the frontiers of Christendom (New Haven, Conn., 2007).
Picó, Fernando, 'Non-aristocratic bishops in the reign of Louis IX', *Medieval Prosopography*, 2 (1981), 41–54.
Poole, Reginald Lane and Austin Lane Poole, *Studies in chronology and history* (Oxford, 1934).
Postles, Davis, 'Small gifts, but big rewards: the symbolism of some gifts to the religious', *JMH*, 27 (2001), 23–42.

Powell, James M., *Anatomy of a crusade, 1213–1221* (Philadelphia, Pa., 1986).
Power, Daniel, *The Norman frontier in the twelfth and early thirteenth centuries* (Cambridge, 2004).
Prestwich, Michael, *Edward I* (2nd edn, New Haven, Conn., 1997).
Prévost, Arthur-Émile, 'Les champenois aux croisades', *MSA Aube*, 85 (1921), 109–86.
Prioux, Stéphane, *Monographie de l'ancienne abbaye royale de Saint-Yved de Braine, avec la description des tombes royales et seigneuriales renfermées dans cette église. 27 planches dont 12 sur acier, 6 en chromo-lithographie et 9 en lithographie tirées en bistre* (Paris, 1859).
Prutz, Hans, *Geheimstatuten und Geheimlehre des Tempelherren-Ordens. Eine kritische Untersuchung* (Berlin, 1879).
Kulturgeschichte der Kreuzzüge (Berlin, 1883).
Entwicklung und Untergang des Tempelherrenordens (Berlin, 1888).
Die geistlichen Ritterorden, ihre Stellung zur kirchlichen, politischen, gesellschaftlichen und wirtschaftlichen Entwicklung des Mittelalters (Berlin, 1908).
Purkis, William J., 'Elite and popular perceptions of *imitatio Christi* in twelfth-century crusade spirituality', in Kate Cooper and Jeremy Gregory (eds.), *Elite and popular religion*, Studies in Church History, 42 (Woodbridge, 2006), 54–64.
Crusading spirituality in the Holy Land and Iberia, c. 1095–c. 1187 (Woodbridge, 2008).
Quantin, Maximilien, 'Les croisés de la Basse-Bourgogne en Terre Sainte', *Mémoires de la société de l'Yonne* (1893), 287–317.
Queller, Donald Edward, Thomas K. Compton and Donald A. Campbell, 'The Fourth Crusade: the neglected majority', *Speculum*, 49 (1974), 441–65.
Queller, Donald Edward and Thomas F. Madden, *The Fourth Crusade: The conquest of Constantinople* (2nd edn, Philadelphia, Pa., 2007).
Quéruel, Danielle (ed.), *Jean de Joinville. De la Champagne aux royaumes d'outre-mer* (Langres, 1998).
Rey, Emmanuel-Guillaume (ed.), *Les familles d'outre-mer de Du Cange* (Paris, 1869).
Riant, Paul (ed.), *Exuviae sacrae Constantinopolitanae*, 2 vols. (Geneva, 1878–9).
Richard, Jean, *Le comté de Tripoli sous la dynastie toulousaine (1102–1187)* (Paris, 1945).
'Le milieu familial', in *Bernard de Clairvaux*, Commission d'histoire de l'Ordre de Clairvaux, 3 (Paris, 1953), 3–15.
Les ducs de Bourgogne et la formation du duché du XIe au XIVe siècle (Paris, 1954).
'Le comté de Tripoli dans les chartes du fonds des Porcelets', *BEC*, 130 (1972), 339–82.
'Les templiers et les hospitaliers en Bourgogne et en Champagne méridionale (XIIe–XIIIe siècles)', in Josef Fleckenstein and Manfred Hellmann (eds.), *Die geistlichen Ritterorden Europas*, Vorträge und Forschungen, 30 (Sigmaringen, 1980), 231–42.
'Les Saint-Gilles et le comté de Tripoli', in *Islam et chrétiens du Midi (XIIe–XIVe siècles)*, CdF, xviii (Toulouse, 1983), 65–75.
'Départs de pèlerins et de croisés bourguignons au XIe siècle: à propos d'une charte de Cluny', *AB*, 60 (1988), 139–43.
The crusades c. 1071–c. 1291 (Cambridge, 1999).
'Vézelay', *LexMA*, VIII (Munich, 2002), cols. 1609–10.

Riley-Smith, Jonathan S.C., *The Knights of St John in Jerusalem and Cyprus* (London, 1967).
'Family traditions and participation in the Second Crusade', in Michael Gervers (ed.), *The Second Crusade and the Cistercians* (New York, 1992), 101–8.
What were the crusades? (2nd edn, Houndsmills, 1992).
'Early crusaders to the east and the costs of crusading, 1095–1130', in Michael Goodich, Sophia Menache and Sylvia Schein (eds.), *Crosscultural convergences in the crusading period. Essays presented to Aryeh Grabois on his sixty-fifth birthday* (New York, 1995), 237–57.
'Families, crusades and settlement in the Latin East 1102–1131', in Hans Eberhard Mayer (ed.), *Die Kreuzfahrerstaaten als multikulturelle Gesellschaft* (Munich, 1997), 1–12.
The First Crusaders, 1095–1131 (Cambridge, 1997).
'The origin of the commandery in the Temple and the Hospital', in Anthony Luttrell and Léon Pressouyre (eds.), *La commanderie, institution des ordres militaires dans l'Occident médiéval* (Paris, 2002), 9–18.
'The structures of the Orders of the Temple and the Hospital in c.1291', in Susan J. Ridyard (ed.), *Medieval crusade* (Woodbridge, 2004), 125–43.
'Were the Templars guilty?', in Susan J. Ridyard (ed.), *Medieval crusade* (Woodbridge, 2004), 107–24.
The crusades. A history (2nd edn, London, 2005).
Crusades, Christianity, and Islam (New York, 2008).
Templars and Hospitallers as professed religious in the Holy Land (Notre Dame, Ind., 2010).
Riley-Smith, Louise and Jonathan Riley-Smith, *The crusades, idea and reality, 1095–1274* (London, 1981).
Roger, Jean-Marc, 'Les Morhiers champenois', *Bulletin philologique et historique du comité des travaux historiques et scientifiques français* (1980), 77–130.
Röhricht, Reinhold, *Studien zur Geschichte des Fünften Kreuzzugs* (Innsbruck, 1891).
Geschichte des Königreichs Jerusalem 1100–1291 (Innsbruck, 1898).
Rosenwein, Barbara H., *Rhinoceros bound: the abbey of Cluny in the tenth century* (Philadelphia, Pa., 1982).
To be the neighbor of Saint Peter: the social meaning of Cluny's property, 909–1049 (Ithaca, N.Y., 1989).
Roserot, Alphonse, *Dictionnaire historique de la Champagne méridionale (Aube) des origines à 1790*, 4 vols. (Angers, 1942–8).
Roure, A. du, *Notice historique sur une branche de la famille de Sabran* (Marseille, 1888).
Rousseau, Constance M., 'Home front and battlefield: the gendering of papal crusading policy (1095–1221)', in Susan B. Edgington and Sarah Lambert (eds.), *Gendering the crusades* (New York, 2001), 31–44.
Roussel, Charles-François, *Le diocèse de Langres. Histoire et statistique*, 4 vols. (Langres, 1873–9).
'Les templiers dans le diocèse de Langres à l'époque de leur suppression', *Revue de Champagne et de Brie*, 16 (1884), 401–13.
Rubin, Miri, *Mother of God: a history of the Virgin Mary* (London, 2009).
Rubió, Jordi, Ramón d'Alós and Francisco Martorell (eds.), 'Inventaris inèdits de l'ordre del Temple a Catalunya', *Anuari 1* (1907), 385–407.

Salvadó, Sebastian, 'Interpreting the altarpiece of Saint Bernard: Templar liturgy and conquest in 13th century Majorca', *Iconographica*, 5 (2006), 48–63.

Sarnowsky, Jürgen, 'Das historische Selbstversändnis der geistlichen Ritterorden', *Zeitschrift für Kirchengeschichte*, 110 (1999), 315–30.

Sassier, Yves, *Recherches sur le pouvoir comtal en Auxerrois du xe au début du XIIIe siècle* (Auxerre, 1980).

Schenk, Jochen Georg, 'Aspects of non-noble family involvement in the Order of the Temple', in Judi M. Upton-Ward (ed.), *The military orders, vol. IV: On land and by sea* (Aldershot, 2008), 155–62.

'Forms of lay association with the Order of the Temple', *JMH*, 34 (2008), 79–103.

Schnürer, Gustav, 'Zur ersten Organisation der Templer', *Historisches Jahrbuch*, 32 (1911), 298–316, 511–46.

Schottmüller, Karl, *Der Untergang des Templerordens mit urkundlichen und kritischen Beiträgen*, 2 vols. (Berlin, 1887).

Schreiner, Klaus, 'Zisterziensisches Mönchstum und soziale Umwelt. Wirtschaftlicher und sozialer Strukturwandel in Hoch- und Spätmittelalterlichen Zisterzienserkonventen', in Kaspar Elm and Peter Joerißen (eds.), *Die Zisterzienser. Ordensleben zwischen Ideal und Wirklichkeit. Ergänzungsband*, Schriften des Rheinischen Museumsamtes, 18 (Cologne, 1982), 79–135.

Mönchsein in der Adelsgesellschaft des hohen und späten Mittelalters. Klösterliche Gemeinschaftbildung zwischen spiritueller Selbstbehauptung und sozialer Anpassung (Munich, 1989).

Selwood, Dominic, '*Quidam autem dubitaverunt.* The saint, the sinner, the Temple and a possible chronology', in Michel Balard (ed.), *Autour de la Première Croisade* (Paris, 1996), 221–30.

Knights of the cloister. Templars and Hospitallers in central-southern Occitania 1100–1300 (Woodbridge, 1999).

Shideler, John Clement, *A medieval Catalan noble family: the Montcadas, 1000–1230* (Berkeley, Calif., 1983).

Siberry, Elizabeth, *Criticism of crusading: 1095–1274* (Oxford, 1985).

'The crusading counts of Nevers', *Nottingham Medieval Studies*, 34 (1990), 64–70.

Sigal, Pierre-André, 'Une seigneurie ecclésiastique en Provence orientale au moyen âge: La commanderie de Ruou', *Provence historique*, 15 (1965), 126–46.

Smail, Raimund Charles, *Crusading warfare, 1097–1193* (2nd edn, Cambridge, 1956).

Smith, Caroline, *Crusading in the age of Joinville* (Aldershot, 2006).

Southern, Richard W., *The making of the middle ages* (Cambridge, 1953).

Sureda i Pons, Joan, 'Schönheit und Bedeutung von Bildern im Zeitalter der Kreuzzüge', in Roberto Cassanelli (ed.), *Die Zeit der Kreuzzüge. Geschichte und Kunst* (Stuttgart, 2000), 257–85.

Thompson, Kathleen Hapgood, 'Family tradition and the crusading impulse', *Medieval Prosopography*, 19 (1998), 1–33.

Tommasi, Francesco, 'I templari e il culto delle reliquie', in Giovanni Minnucci and Franca Sardi (eds.), *I templari: mito e storia* (Siena, 1989), 191–210.

'"Pauperes commilitones Christi". Aspetti e problemi delle origini gerosolimitane', *'Militia Christi' e crociata nei secoli XI–XIII. Atti della undecima Settimana internazionale di studio. Mendola, 28 agosto – 1 settembre 1989*, Miscellanea del Centro di studi medioevali, 13 (Milan, 1992), 443–75.

Toomaspoeg, Kristjan, 'I cavalieri templari e i giovanniti', in Christina Andenna and Gert Melville (eds.), *Regulae – Consuetudines – Statuta. Studi sulle fonti normative degli ordini religiosi nei secoli centrali del Medioevo*, Vita Regularis, 25 (Münster, 2005), 387–401.

Torre Muñoz de Morales, Ignacio de la, *Los templarios y el origen de la banca* (Madrid, 2004).

Ubieto Arteta, Augustín, 'Cofrades aragoneses y navarros de la milicia del temple (siglo XII). Aspectos socio-económicos', *Aragón en la edad media*, 3 (1980), 29–93.

Vaissète, Joseph, Claude Devic and Édouard Dulaurier, *Histoire générale de Languedoc*, 16 vols. (Toulouse, 1872–1904).

Vaivre, Jean-Bernard de, *La commanderie d'Épailly et sa chapelle templière durant la période médiévale* (Paris, 2005).

Van Engen, John, 'The "crisis of cenobitism" reconsidered: Benedictine monasticism in the years 1050–1150', *Speculum*, 61 (1986), 269–304.

Vauchez, André, *The laity in the middle ages: religious beliefs and devotional practices*, trans. Margery J. Schneider (Notre Dame, Ind., 1993).

Vercauteren, Fernand, 'Une parentèle dans la France du nord aux XIe et XIIe siècles', *Le moyen âge*, 69 (1963), 223–45.

Verdon, Laure, 'Les revenus de la commanderie templière du Mas Déu (Roussillon) d'après le terrier de 1264', *AdM*, 210 (1995), 167–93.

'La seigneurie templière à Perpignan au XIIIe siècle', in Noël Coulet and Oliver Guyotjeannin (eds.), *La ville au moyen âge, vol. II: Sociétés et pouvoirs dans la ville* (Paris, 1998), 221–8.

La terre et les hommes en Roussillon aux XIIe et XIIIe siècles. Structures seigneuriales, rente et société d'après les sources templières (Aix-en-Provence, 2001).

Veyssière, Laurent, 'Le personnel de l'abbaye de Clairvaux au XIIe siècle', *Cîteaux*, 51 (2000), 17–89.

Vial, Pierre, 'Les templiers en Velay aux XIIème et XIIIème siècles', in *Forez et Velay, questions d'histoire et de philologie, Actes du 98ème Congrès national des sociétés savantes, section d'archéologie (Saint-Étienne, 1973)* (Paris, 1975), 81–94.

Vinas, Robert, *L'ordre du Temple en Roussillon* (Canet, 2001).

'Le destin des templiers du Roussillon, 1276–1330', in *Les ordres religieux militaires dans le Midi (XIIe–XIVe siècle)*, CdF, LI (Toulouse, 2006), 187–210.

Vogel, Christian, *Das Recht der Templer. Ausgewählte Aspekte des Templerrechts unter besonderer Berücksichtigung der Statutenhandschriften aus Paris, Rom, Baltimore und Barcelona*, Vita Regularis, 33 (Berlin, 2007).

Walker, David, 'The organisation of material in medieval cartularies', in Donald Auberon Bullough and Robin Lindsay Storey (eds.), *The study of medieval records: essays in honour of Kathleen Major* (Oxford, 1971), 132–50.

Weinberger, Stephen, 'Donations-ventes ou ventes-donations? Confusion ou système dans la Provence du XIe siècle', *Le moyen âge*, 105 (1999), 667–80.

White, Stephen D., *Custom, kinship, and gifts to saints: The laudatio parentum in western France, 1050–1150* (Chapel Hill, N.C., 1988).

Wollasch, Joachim, 'Neue Quellen zur Geschichte der Cistercienser', *Zeitschrift für Kirchengeschichte*, 84 (1973), 188–232.

Wood, Susan, *The proprietary church in the medieval West* (Oxford, 2006).

Appendix

GENEALOGIES

Name	Person / family involved with the Order of the Temple
Name (underlined)	Person / family involved in crusading
Name	Separate Genealogy
archbf.	archbishop
bf.	bishop
ct.	count
cts.	countess
d.	died
ld.	lord/lady
m.	married
O.Ben.	Benedictine Order
O.Cart	Carthusian Order
O.Cist.	Order of Cîteaux
O.Clun.	Order of Cluny
O.Font.	Order of Fontevrault
O.Hosp.	Order of the Hospital of St John
O.Prem.	Order of Prémontré
O.Temp.	Order of the Temple
O.S.A.	*Ordo Sancti Augustini* (Augustinian Order)
rel.	religious
sec.	secular
vct.	viscount
vcts.	viscountess

Geneaologies

(a) Burgundy and Champagne
- 1 Baudement and Dreux
- 2 Broyes–Châteauvillain–Rethel
- 3 Chacenay–Arcis-sur-Aube–Bar-sur-Seine
- 4 Grancey
- 5 Mello
- 6 Mont-Saint-Jean
- 7 Noyers
- 8 Tilchâtel

(b) Languedoc
- 1 Aspet
- 2 Aure
- 3 Comminges
- 4 Martres and Tersac

Baudement and Dreux

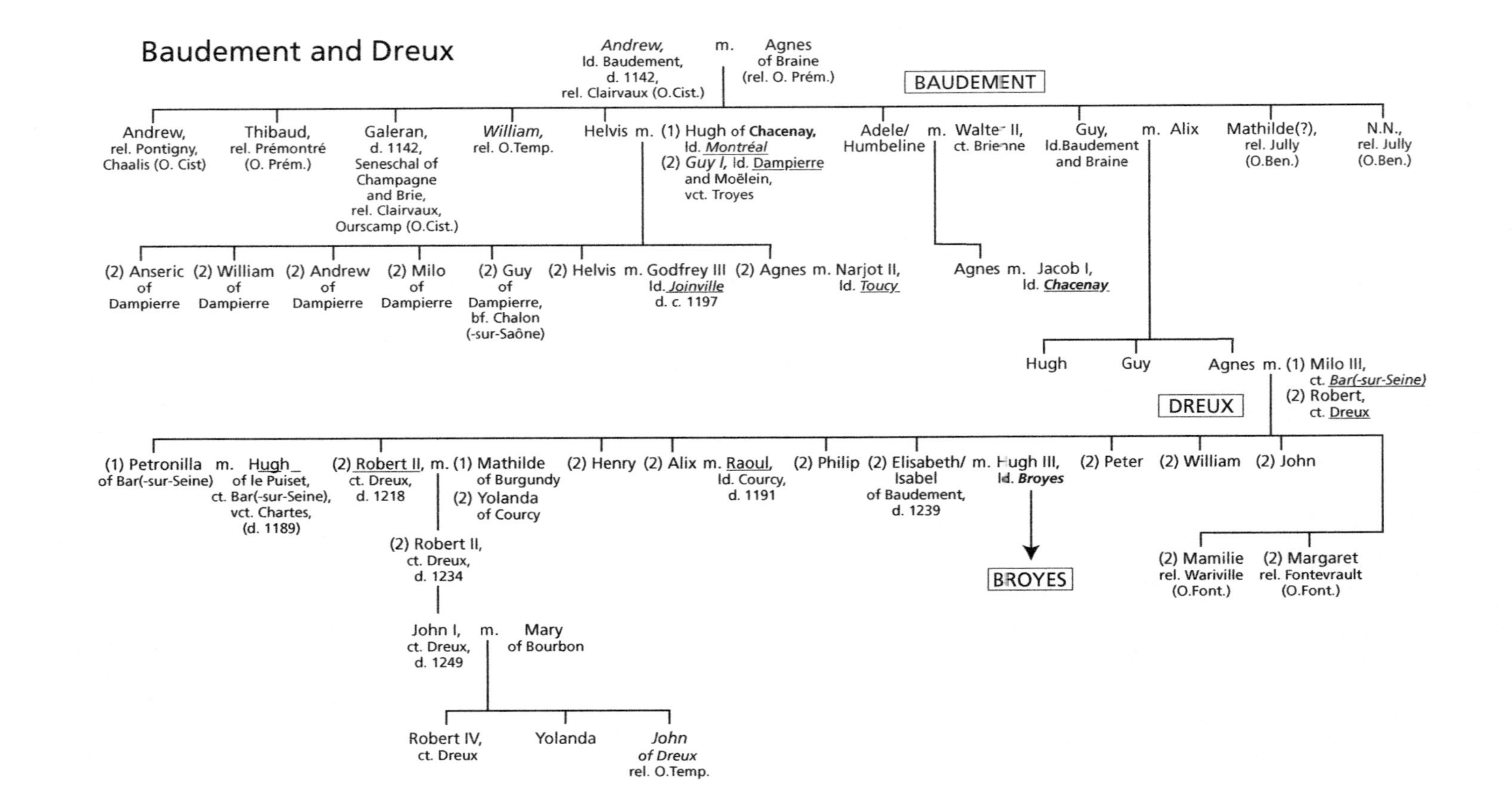

Broyes–Châteauvillain–Rethel

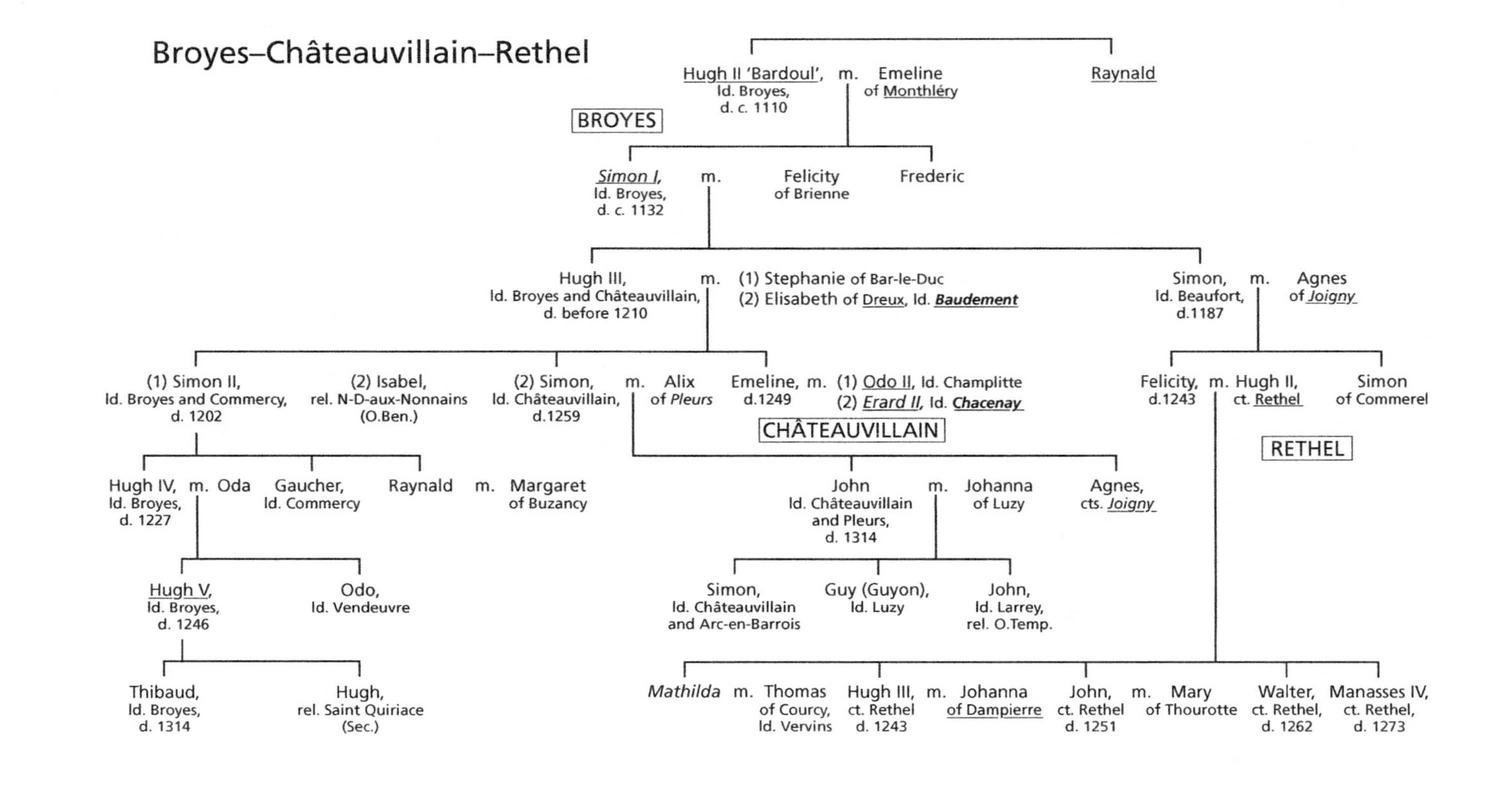

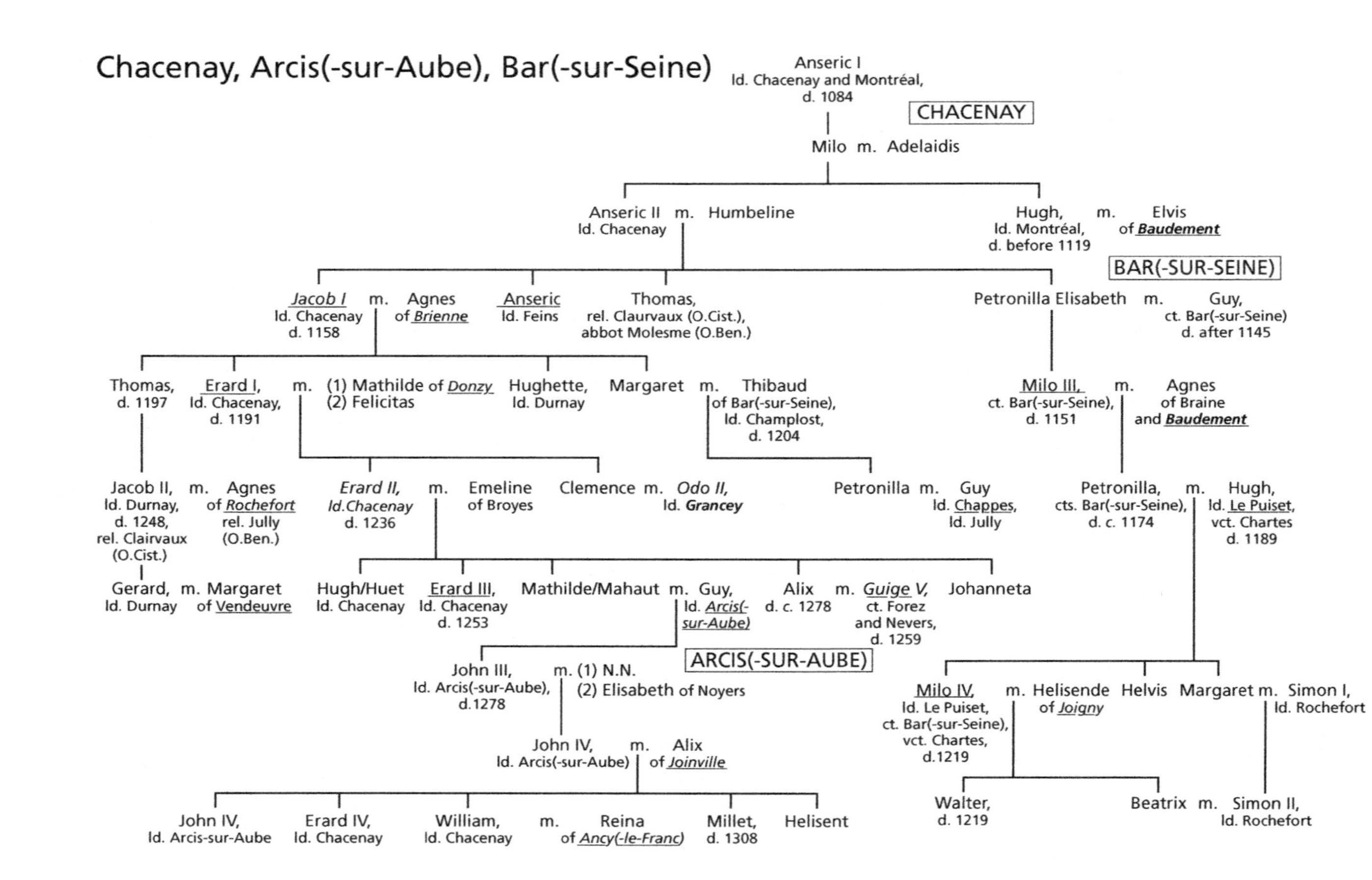
Chacenay, Arcis(-sur-Aube), Bar(-sur-Seine)
Anseric I
ld. Chacenay and Montréal,
d. 1084
CHACENAY
Milo m. Adelaidis
Anseric II m. Humbeline
ld. Chacenay
Hugh, m. Elvis
ld. Montréal, of Baudement
d. before 1119
BAR(-SUR-SEINE)
Jacob I m. Agnes
ld. Chacenay of Brienne
d. 1158
Anseric
ld. Feins
Thomas,
rel. Claurvaux (O.Cist.),
abbot Molesme (O.Ben.)
Petronilla Elisabeth m. Guy,
ct. Bar(-sur-Seine)
d. after 1145
Thomas,
d. 1197
Erard I,
ld. Chacenay,
d. 1191
m. (1) Mathilde of Donzy
(2) Felicitas
Hughette,
ld. Durnay
Margaret m. Thibaud
of Bar(-sur-Seine),
ld. Champlost,
d. 1204
Milo III, m. Agnes
ct. Bar(-sur-Seine), of Braine
d. 1151 and Baudement
Jacob II, m. Agnes
ld. Durnay, of Rochefort
d. 1248, rel. Jully
rel. Clairvaux (O.Ben.)
(O.Cist.)
Erard II, m. Emeline
ld.Chacenay of Broyes
d. 1236
Clemence m. Odo II,
ld. Grancey
Petronilla m. Guy
ld. Chappes,
ld. Jully
Petronilla, m. Hugh,
cts. Bar(-sur-Seine), ld. Le Puiset,
d. c. 1174 vct. Chartes
d. 1189
Gerard, m. Margaret
ld. Durnay of Vendeuvre
Hugh/Huet
ld. Chacenay
Erard III,
ld. Chacenay
d. 1253
Mathilde/Mahaut m. Guy,
ld. Arcis(-sur-Aube)
Alix m. Guige V,
d. c. 1278 ct. Forez
and Nevers,
d. 1259
Johanneta
ARCIS(-SUR-AUBE)
John III, m. (1) N.N.
ld. Arcis(-sur-Aube), (2) Elisabeth of Noyers
d.1278
John IV, m. Alix
ld. Arcis(-sur-Aube) of Joinville
John IV,
ld. Arcis-sur-Aube
Erard IV,
ld. Chacenay
William, m. Reina
ld. Chacenay of Ancy(-le-Franc)
Millet,
d. 1308
Helisent
Milo IV, m. Helisende
ld. Le Puiset, of Joigny
ct. Bar(-sur-Seine),
vct. Chartes,
d.1219
Helvis
Margaret m. Simon I,
ld. Rochefort
Walter,
d. 1219
Beatrix m. Simon II,
ld. Rochefort

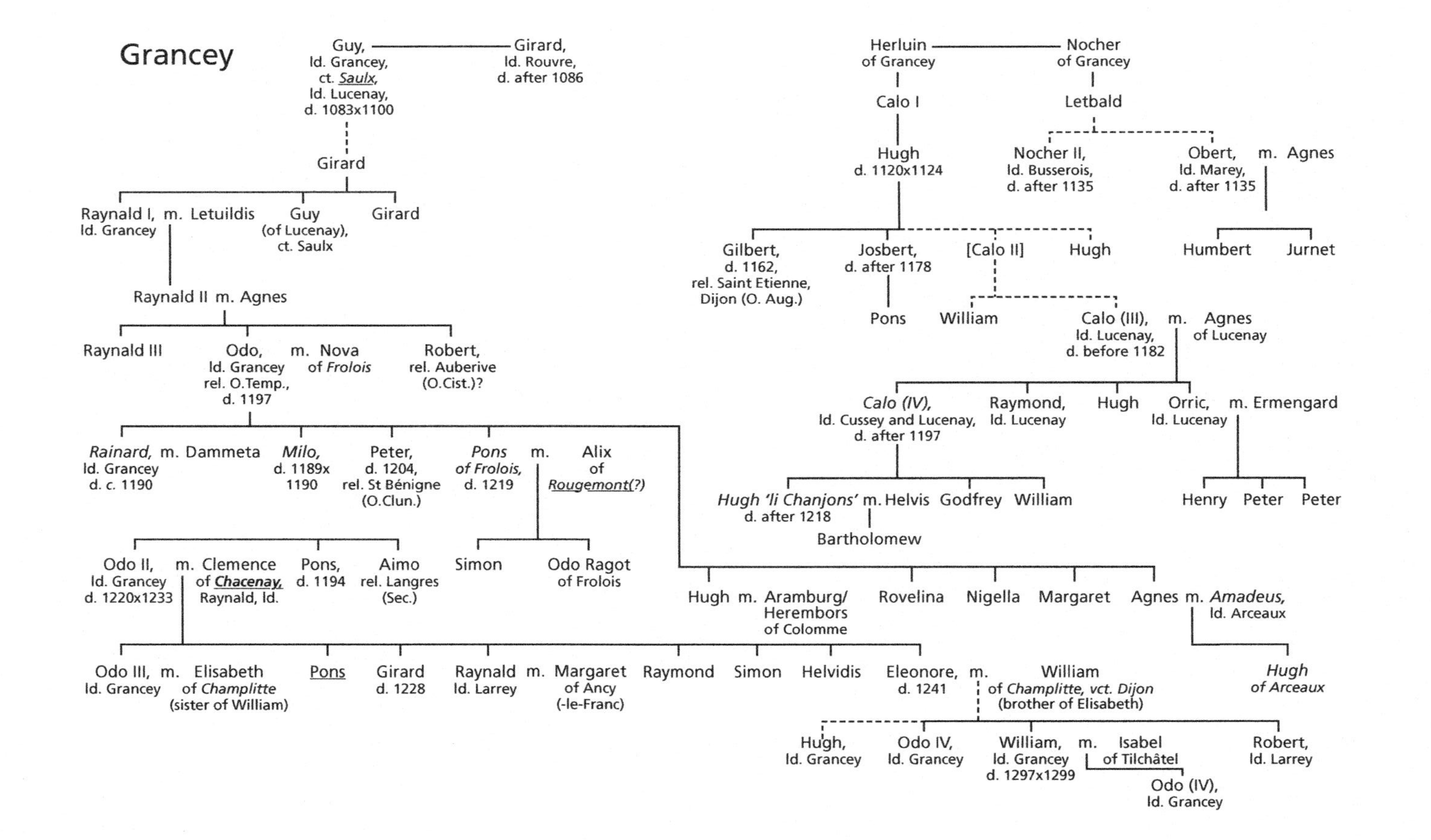
Grancey
Guy, Id. Grancey, ct. Saulx, Id. Lucenay, d. 1083x1100
Girard, Id. Rouvre, d. after 1086
Girard
Raynald I, Id. Grancey m. Letuildis
Guy (of Lucenay), ct. Saulx
Girard
Raynald II m. Agnes
Raynald III
Odo, Id. Grancey rel. O.Temp., d. 1197 m. Nova of Frolois
Robert, rel. Auberive (O.Cist.)?
Rainard, Id. Grancey d. c. 1190 m. Dammeta
Milo, d. 1189x 1190
Peter, d. 1204, rel. St Bénigne (O.Clun.)
Pons of Frolois, d. 1219 m. Alix of Rougemont(?)
Odo II, Id. Grancey d. 1220x1233 m. Clemence of Chacenay, Raynald, Id.
Pons, d. 1194
Aimo rel. Langres (Sec.)
Simon
Odo Ragot of Frolois
Hugh m. Aramburg/ Herembors of Colomme
Rovelina
Nigella
Margaret
Agnes m. Amadeus, Id. Arceaux
Odo III, Id. Grancey m. Elisabeth of Champlitte (sister of William)
Pons
Girard d. 1228
Raynald Id. Larrey m. Margaret of Ancy (-le-Franc)
Raymond
Simon
Helvidis
Eleonore, d. 1241 m. William of Champlitte, vct. Dijon (brother of Elisabeth)
Hugh of Arceaux
Hugh, Id. Grancey
Odo IV, Id. Grancey
William, Id. Grancey d. 1297x1299 m. Isabel of Tilchâtel
Robert, Id. Larrey
Odo (IV), Id. Grancey
Herluin of Grancey
Nocher of Grancey
Calo I
Letbald
Hugh d. 1120x1124
Nocher II, Id. Busserois, d. after 1135
Obert, Id. Marey, d. after 1135 m. Agnes
Gilbert, d. 1162, rel. Saint Etienne, Dijon (O. Aug.)
Josbert, d. after 1178
[Calo II]
Hugh
Humbert
Jurnet
Pons
William
Calo (III), Id. Lucenay, d. before 1182 m. Agnes of Lucenay
Calo (IV), Id. Cussey and Lucenay, d. after 1197
Raymond, Id. Lucenay
Hugh
Orric, Id. Lucenay m. Ermengard
Hugh 'li Chanjons' d. after 1218 m. Helvis
Godfrey
William
Henry
Peter
Peter
Bartholomew

Mello

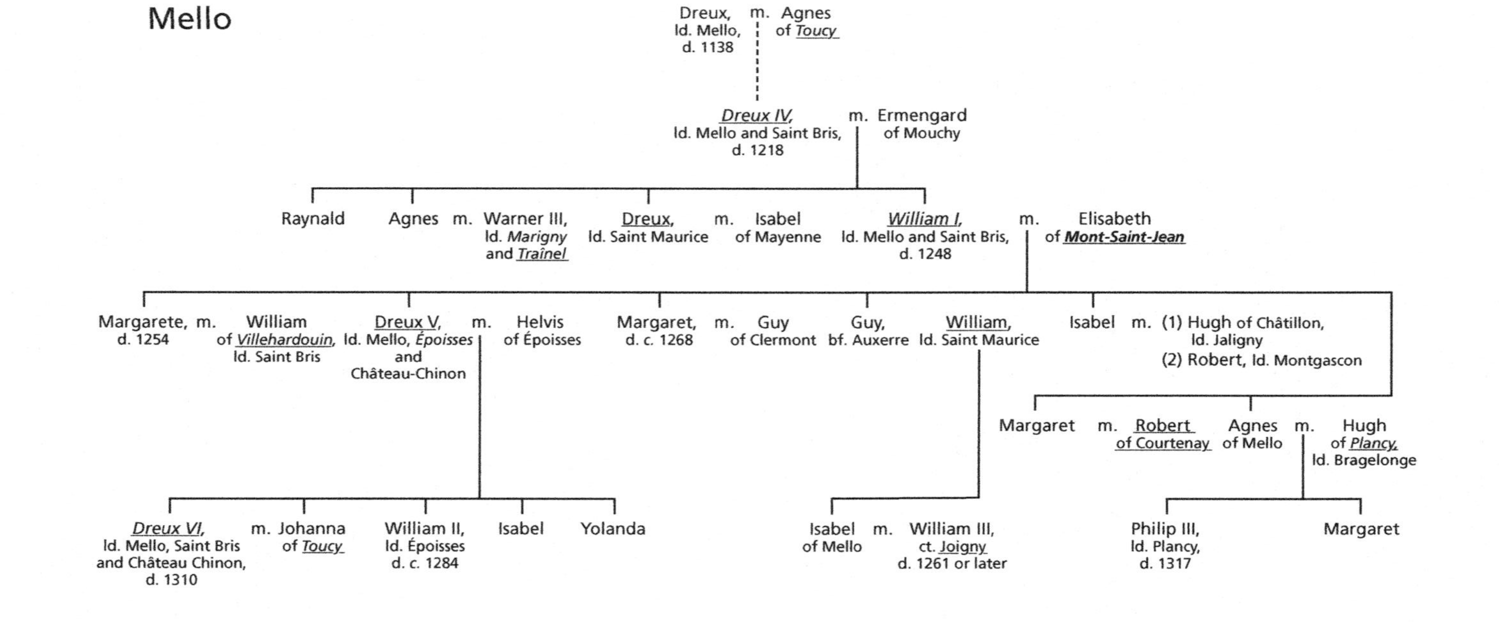

Dreux, Id. Mello, d. 1138 m. Agnes of Toucy
Dreux IV, Id. Mello and Saint Bris, d. 1218 m. Ermengard of Mouchy
Raynald
Agnes m. Warner III, Id. Marigny and Traînel
Dreux, Id. Saint Maurice m. Isabel of Mayenne
William I, Id. Mello and Saint Bris, d. 1248 m. Elisabeth of Mont-Saint-Jean
Margarete, d. 1254 m. William of Villehardouin, Id. Saint Bris
Dreux V, Id. Mello, Époisses and Château-Chinon m. Helvis of Époisses
Margaret, d. c. 1268 m. Guy of Clermont
Guy, bf. Auxerre
William, Id. Saint Maurice
Isabel m. (1) Hugh of Châtillon, Id. Jaligny (2) Robert, Id. Montgascon
Margaret m. Robert of Courtenay
Agnes of Mello m. Hugh of Plancy, Id. Bragelonge
Dreux VI, Id. Mello, Saint Bris and Château Chinon, d. 1310 m. Johanna of Toucy
William II, Id. Époisses d. c. 1284
Isabel
Yolanda
Isabel of Mello m. William III, ct. Joigny d. 1261 or later
Philip III, Id. Plancy, d. 1317
Margaret

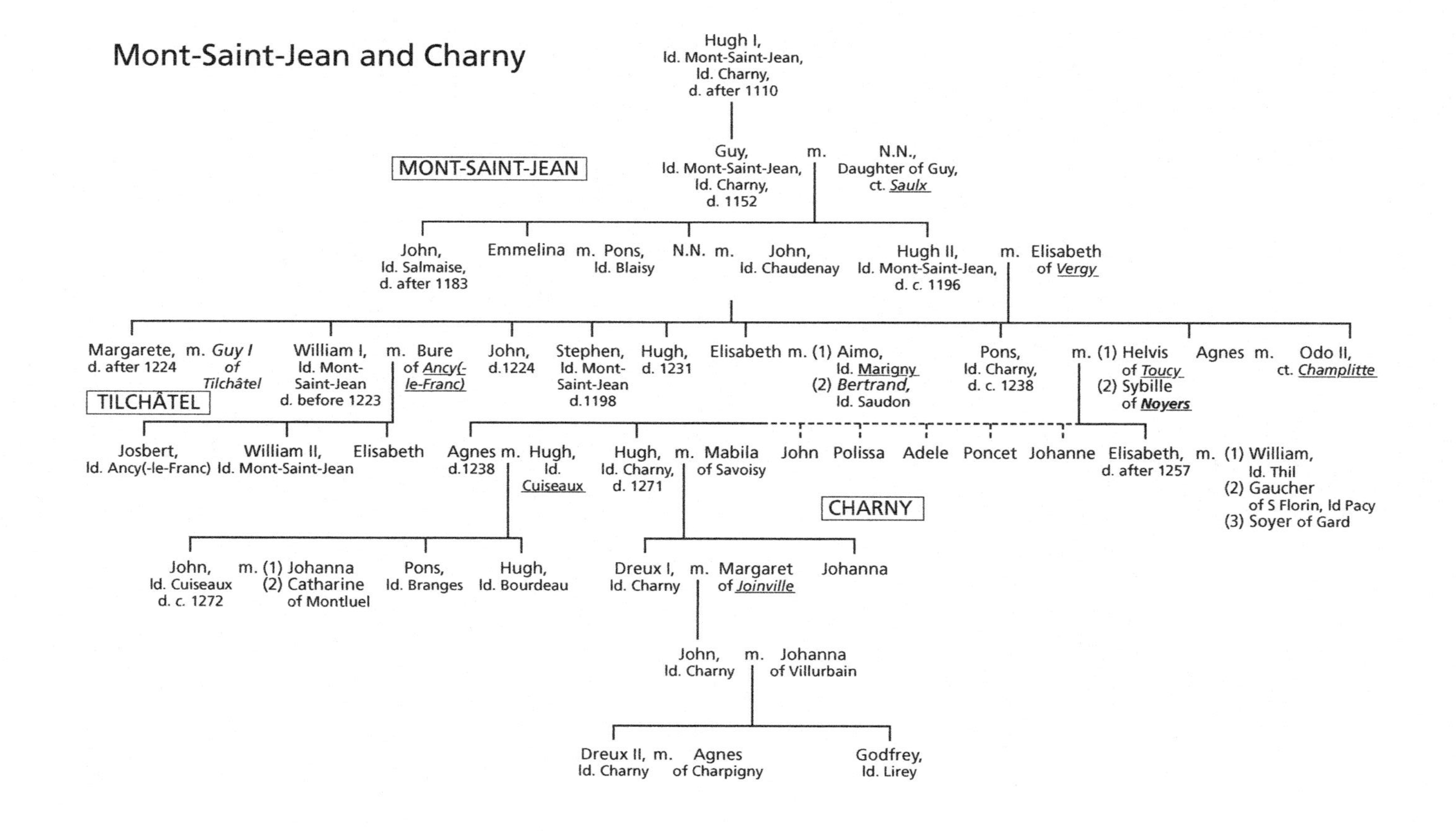
Mont-Saint-Jean and Charny
Hugh I, ld. Mont-Saint-Jean, ld. Charny, d. after 1110
MONT-SAINT-JEAN
Guy, ld. Mont-Saint-Jean, ld. Charny, d. 1152 m. N.N., Daughter of Guy, ct. Saulx
John, ld. Salmaise, d. after 1183
Emmelina m. Pons, ld. Blaisy
N.N. m. John, ld. Chaudenay
Hugh II, ld. Mont-Saint-Jean, d. c. 1196 m. Elisabeth of Vergy
Margarete, d. after 1224 m. Guy I of Tilchâtel
TILCHÂTEL
William I, ld. Mont-Saint-Jean d. before 1223 m. Bure of Ancy(-le-Franc)
John, d.1224
Stephen, ld. Mont-Saint-Jean d.1198
Hugh, d. 1231
Elisabeth m. (1) Aimo, ld. Marigny (2) Bertrand, ld. Saudon
Pons, ld. Charny, d. c. 1238 m. (1) Helvis of Toucy (2) Sybille of Noyers
Agnes m. Odo II, ct. Champlitte
Josbert, ld. Ancy(-le-Franc)
William II, ld. Mont-Saint-Jean
Elisabeth
Agnes d.1238 m. Hugh, ld. Cuiseaux
Hugh, ld. Charny, d. 1271 m. Mabila of Savoisy
John
Polissa
Adele
Poncet
Johanne
Elisabeth, d. after 1257 m. (1) William, ld. Thil (2) Gaucher of S Florin, ld Pacy (3) Soyer of Gard
CHARNY
John, ld. Cuiseaux d. c. 1272 m. (1) Johanna (2) Catharine of Montluel
Pons, ld. Branges
Hugh, ld. Bourdeau
Dreux I, ld. Charny m. Margaret of Joinville
Johanna
John, ld. Charny m. Johanna of Villurbain
Dreux II, ld. Charny m. Agnes of Charpigny
Godfrey, ld. Lirey

Noyers, Pierre-Perthuis, Bar(-sur-Seine)

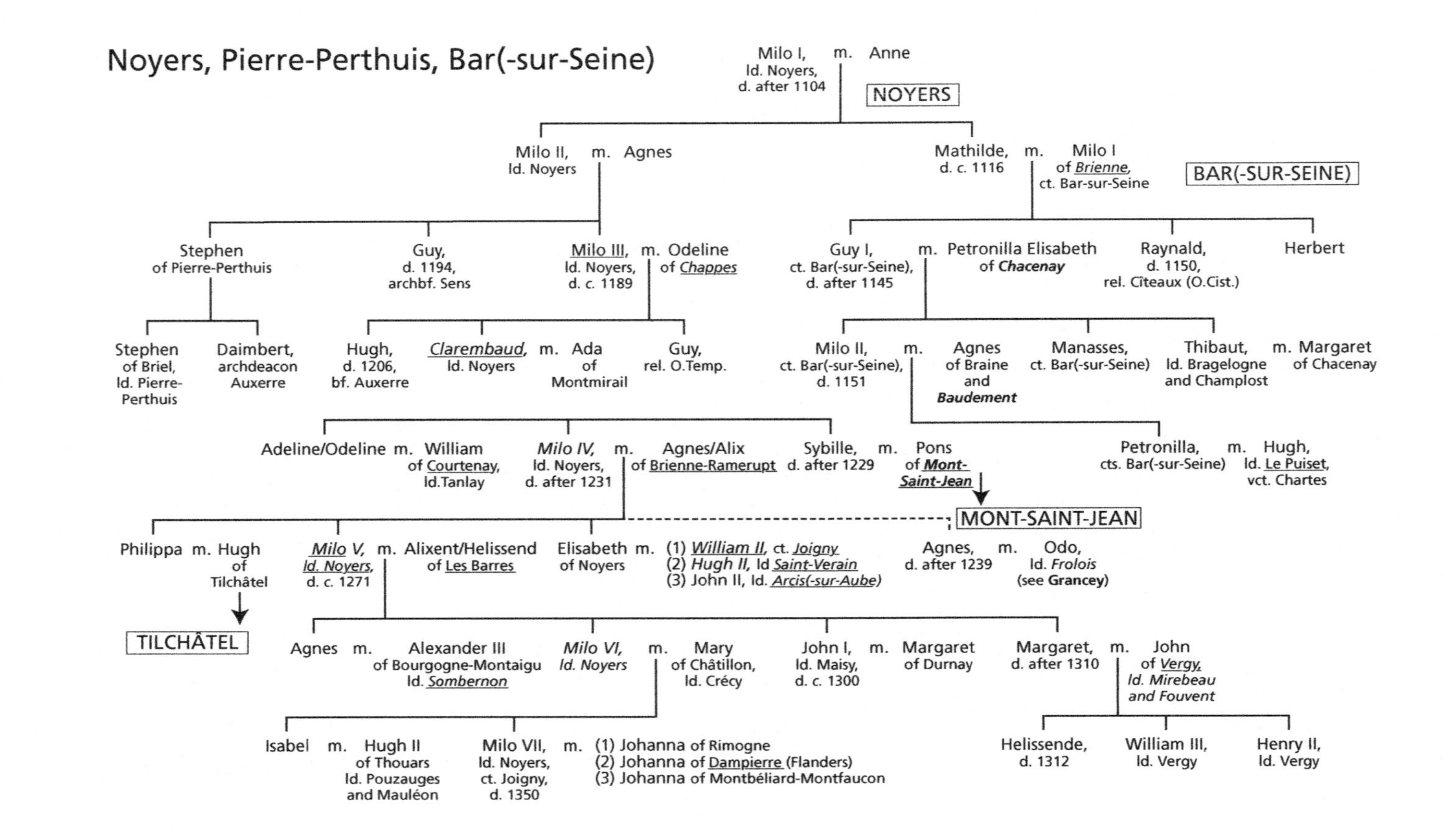

Tilchâtel

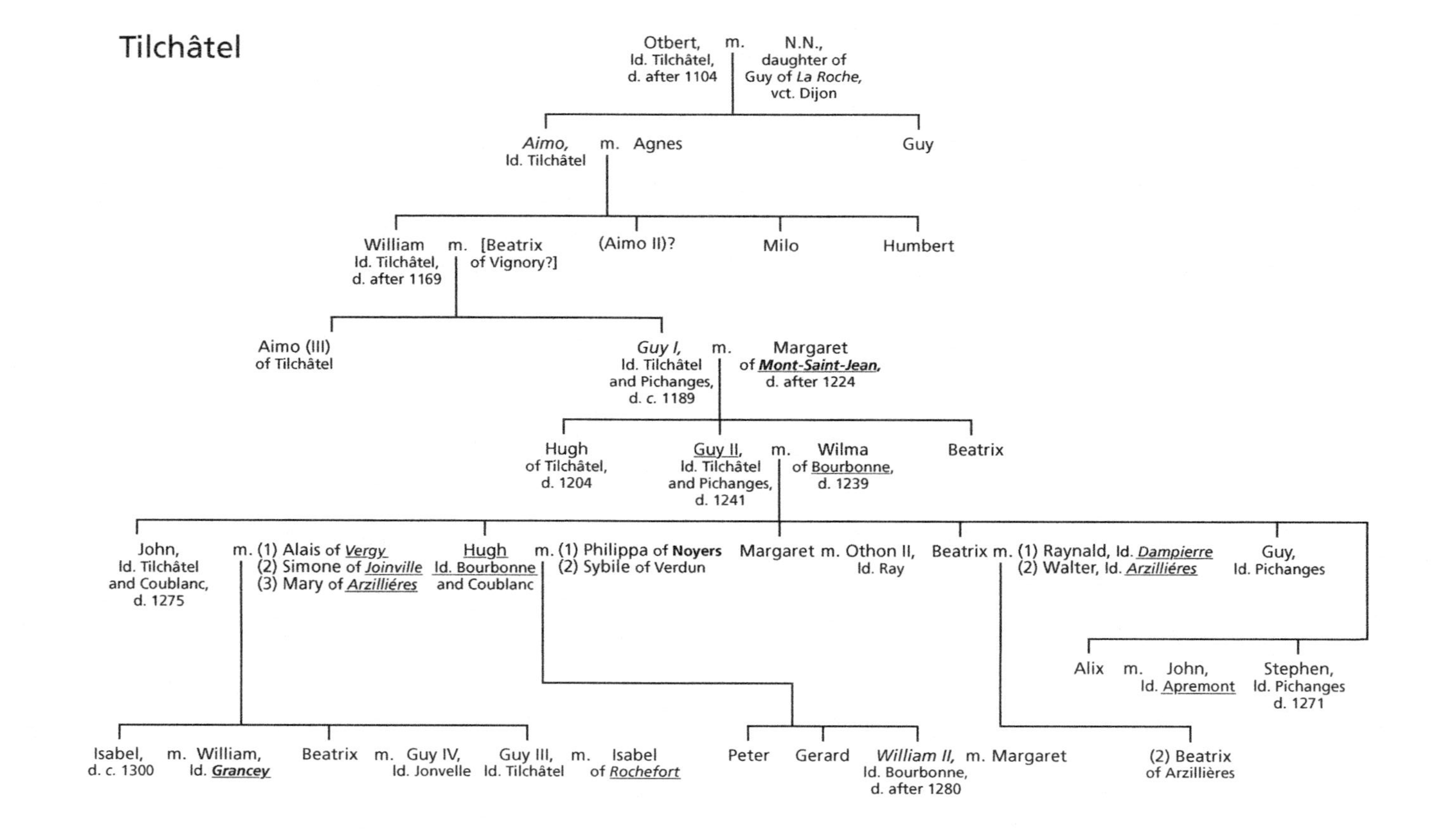

Otbert, m. N.N.,
ld. Tilchâtel, d. after 1104
daughter of Guy of La Roche, vct. Dijon
Aimo, ld. Tilchâtel m. Agnes
Guy
William ld. Tilchâtel, d. after 1169 m. [Beatrix of Vignory?]
(Aimo II)?
Milo
Humbert
Aimo (III) of Tilchâtel
Guy I, ld. Tilchâtel and Pichanges, d. c. 1189 m. Margaret of Mont-Saint-Jean, d. after 1224
Hugh of Tilchâtel, d. 1204
Guy II, ld. Tilchâtel and Pichanges, d. 1241 m. Wilma of Bourbonne, d. 1239
Beatrix
John, ld. Tilchâtel and Coublanc, d. 1275 m. (1) Alais of Vergy (2) Simone of Joinville (3) Mary of Arzilliéres
Hugh ld. Bourbonne and Coublanc m. (1) Philippa of Noyers (2) Sybile of Verdun
Margaret m. Othon II, ld. Ray
Beatrix m. (1) Raynald, ld. Dampierre (2) Walter, ld. Arzilliéres
Guy, ld. Pichanges
Alix m. John, ld. Apremont
Stephen, ld. Pichanges d. 1271
Isabel, d. c. 1300 m. William, ld. Grancey
Beatrix m. Guy IV, ld. Jonvelle
Guy III, ld. Tilchâtel m. Isabel of Rochefort
Peter
Gerard
William II, ld. Bourbonne, d. after 1280 m. Margaret
(2) Beatrix of Arzillières

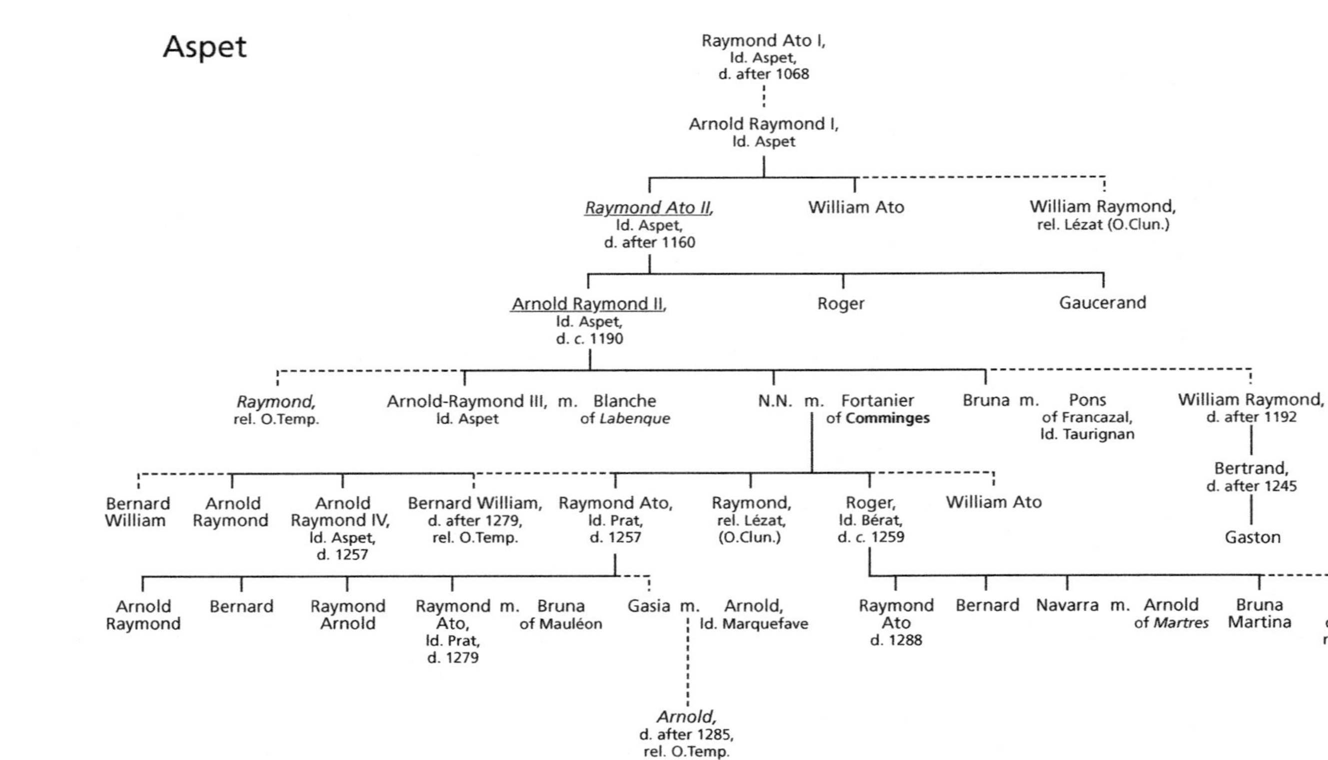
Aspet
Raymond Ato I, ld. Aspet, d. after 1068
Arnold Raymond I, ld. Aspet
Raymond Ato II, ld. Aspet, d. after 1160
William Ato
William Raymond, rel. Lézat (O.Clun.)
Arnold Raymond II, ld. Aspet, d. c. 1190
Roger
Gaucerand
Raymond, rel. O.Temp.
Arnold-Raymond III, ld. Aspet
m.
Blanche of Labenque
N.N.
m.
Fortanier of Comminges
Bruna
m.
Pons of Francazal, ld. Taurignan
William Raymond, d. after 1192
Bertrand, d. after 1245
Gaston
Bernard William
Arnold Raymond
Arnold Raymond IV, ld. Aspet, d. 1257
Bernard William, d. after 1279, rel. O.Temp.
Raymond Ato, ld. Prat, d. 1257
Raymond, rel. Lézat, (O.Clun.)
Roger, ld. Bérat, d. c. 1259
William Ato
Arnold Raymond
Bernard
Raymond Arnold
Raymond Ato, ld. Prat, d. 1279
m.
Bruna of Mauléon
Gasia
m.
Arnold, ld. Marquefave
Arnold, d. after 1285, rel. O.Temp.
Raymond Ato d. 1288
Bernard
Navarra
m.
Arnold of Martres
Bruna Martina
Roger, d. after 1267, rel. Bonnefort (O.Cist.)

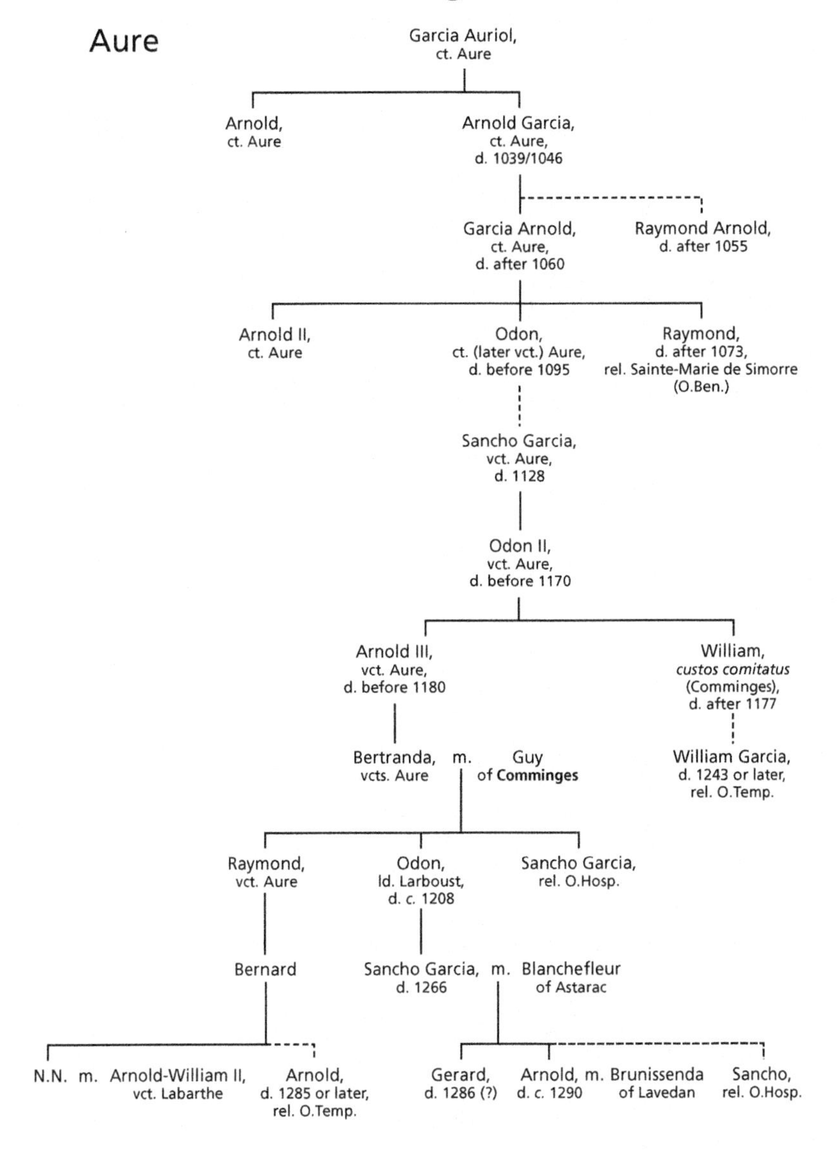
Aure
Garcia Auriol,
ct. Aure
Arnold,
ct. Aure
Arnold Garcia,
ct. Aure,
d. 1039/1046
Garcia Arnold,
ct. Aure,
d. after 1060
Raymond Arnold,
d. after 1055
Arnold II,
ct. Aure
Odon,
ct. (later vct.) Aure,
d. before 1095
Raymond,
d. after 1073,
rel. Sainte-Marie de Simorre
(O.Ben.)
Sancho Garcia,
vct. Aure,
d. 1128
Odon II,
vct. Aure,
d. before 1170
Arnold III,
vct. Aure,
d. before 1180
William,
custos comitatus
(Comminges),
d. after 1177
Bertranda, m. Guy
vcts. Aure
of Comminges
William Garcia,
d. 1243 or later,
rel. O.Temp.
Raymond,
vct. Aure
Odon,
ld. Larboust,
d. c. 1208
Sancho Garcia,
rel. O.Hosp.
Bernard
Sancho Garcia, m. Blanchefleur
d. 1266
of Astarac
N.N. m. Arnold-William II,
vct. Labarthe
Arnold,
d. 1285 or later,
rel. O.Temp.
Gerard,
d. 1286 (?)
Arnold, m. Brunissenda
d. c. 1290
of Lavedan
Sancho,
rel. O.Hosp.

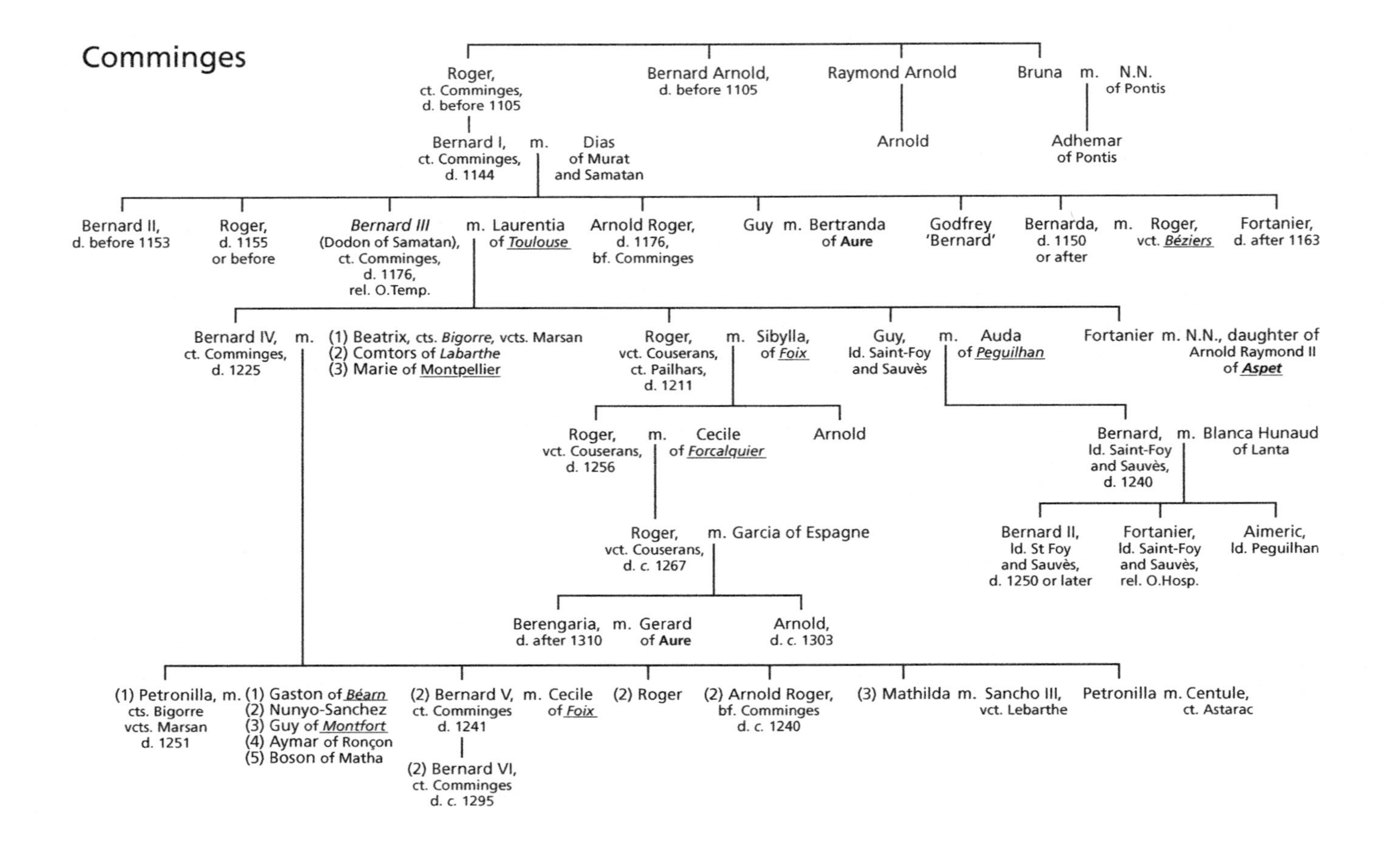
Comminges
Roger, ct. Comminges, d. before 1105
Bernard Arnold, d. before 1105
Raymond Arnold
Bruna m. N.N. of Pontis
Arnold
Adhemar of Pontis
Bernard I, ct. Comminges, d. 1144 m. Dias of Murat and Samatan
Bernard II, d. before 1153
Roger, d. 1155 or before
Bernard III (Dodon of Samatan), ct. Comminges, d. 1176, rel. O.Temp. m. Laurentia of Toulouse
Arnold Roger, d. 1176, bf. Comminges
Guy m. Bertranda of Aure
Godfrey 'Bernard'
Bernarda, d. 1150 or after m. Roger, vct. Béziers
Fortanier, d. after 1163
Bernard IV, ct. Comminges, d. 1225 m. (1) Beatrix, cts. Bigorre, vcts. Marsan (2) Comtors of Labarthe (3) Marie of Montpellier
Roger, vct. Couserans, ct. Pailhars, d. 1211 m. Sibylla, of Foix
Guy, ld. Saint-Foy and Sauvès m. Auda of Peguilhan
Fortanier m. N.N., daughter of Arnold Raymond II of Aspet
Roger, vct. Couserans, d. 1256 m. Cecile of Forcalquier
Arnold
Bernard, ld. Saint-Foy and Sauvès, d. 1240 m. Blanca Hunaud of Lanta
Roger, vct. Couserans, d. c. 1267 m. Garcia of Espagne
Bernard II, ld. St Foy and Sauvès, d. 1250 or later
Fortanier, ld. Saint-Foy and Sauvès, rel. O.Hosp.
Aimeric, ld. Peguilhan
Berengaria, d. after 1310 m. Gerard of Aure
Arnold, d. c. 1303
(1) Petronilla, cts. Bigorre vcts. Marsan d. 1251 m. (1) Gaston of Béarn (2) Nunyo-Sanchez (3) Guy of Montfort (4) Aymar of Ronçon (5) Boson of Matha
(2) Bernard V, ct. Comminges d. 1241 m. Cecile of Foix
(2) Bernard VI, ct. Comminges d. c. 1295
(2) Roger
(2) Arnold Roger, bf. Comminges d. c. 1240
(3) Mathilda m. Sancho III, vct. Lebarthe
Petronilla m. Centule, ct. Astarac

Martres and Tersac

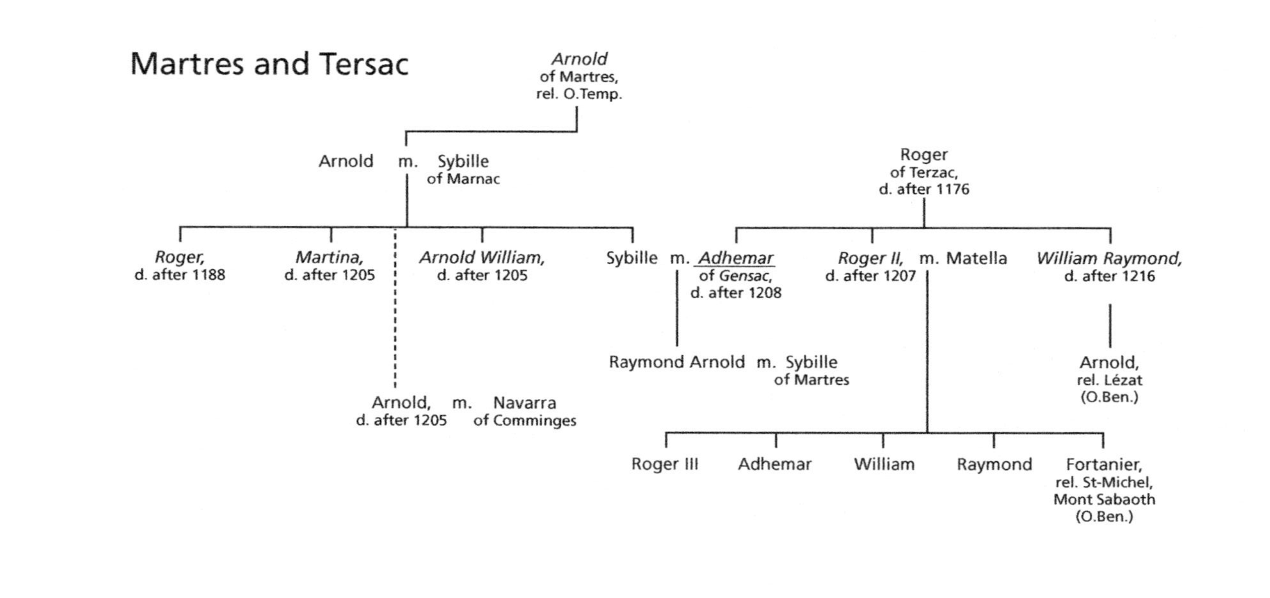

INDEX

Cross-referencing convention

In cross-references to names of lords, bishops, preceptors etc. 'territorial' names, as given in the appropriate index entries, are implicit. Thus under 'Arzillières: lords of', the cross-reference to 'Henry' implies, but does not state, 'of Arzillières'.

Notes on the order of entries

'and', 'of', 'de/des' (excluding the '*De*' in Bernard of Clairvaux' *De laude novae militiae*) and 'the' are ignored for the purposes of alphabetisation. Thus the sub-entry 'and the imitation of Christ' falls between sub-entries 'family and social network of' and 'influence on T rule', 'Bernard of Capmont' is listed before 'Bernard Carrella', and 'Peter the Hermit' before 'Peter Itier'.

Roman numerals are ignored for the purposes of alphabetisation, though they are presented sequentially following alphabetical sorting of other elements. Thus 'Roger II of Martres' is listed after 'Roger of Lespinassière', and 'Archambaud VIII of Bourbon' is listed before 'Archambaud IX of Bourbon'.

'St(e)' is alphabetised as if it were written in full, and the 'e' of 'Ste' is ignored. Thus 'Bernard of St-Julien' is listed before 'Bernard Sesmon of Bézu', and 'Ste-Eulalie' is listed before 'St Euphemia'.

A word preceding a comma in an entry is listed before a word preceding a space. Thus 'Bernard IV, count of Melgueil' is listed before 'Bernard Alegre of Montpezat'. Hyphens are treated as if they were spaces. Thus 'St-André of Sesquière' is listed between 'St Agathe the Virgin' and 'St Barbara', and 'Mont-St-Jean' before 'Montagnac'.

Parentheses and inverted commas are ignored for the purposes of alphabetisation. Thus the entry 'Gerard (Viard) of Vergy (T)' is treated as if it were 'Gerard of Vergy', and 'Hugh II "Bardoul" of Broyes' is listed amongst the Hughs of Broyes and not between 'Hugh of Arpajon' and 'Hugh III of Baux'.

Abbreviations

arr. = *arrondisement* (France, Belgium)
com. = *comunidad autónoma* (Spain)
cant. = *canton* (France)
dist. = *distrito* (Portugal); district (Israel; Lebanon)
H = Hospitaller/Hospital
mod. = modern
prov. = *province* (Belgium); *provincia* (Spain)
reg. = *région* (France); *regione* (Italy); *bölge* (Turkey)
T = Templar/Temple
TO = Teutonic Order

Index

Index

Index

Index